THE SPIDER AND THE ANT

"RENEE IMAGINES the beast before him. He senses an animal, a large white pillow of fur softly bordered by rainbow spots that fade into a deep blue.

A claw comes down towards Renee's face.

For a moment, Renee lets it overcome him. The blank white comfort of slumber draws him closer. But he worries that if he sleeps now, he will never awake. For a moment, that does not seem so bad. But the bear's weight shifts violently, jerking Renee from his thoughts. Renee finds he is completely unable to move. The bear feels Renee's weakness and his growls rise in excitement in anticipation of his meal, meager as it may be. Finally, the claw comes rushing down toward our prince's face."

For thinkers and pure adventurers alike, join Renee and Dewey in the final battle of reason versus experience. This is about the human experience of every day, and this may change the way you look at things forever.

This is something you won't want to miss.

www.jrbecker.com

ISBN 978-0-615-45112-1

Published in the United States by Imaginarium Press LLC, a New York Limited Liability Company.

Cover art by Harriet R. Goren Design, Goren.com

Photo by Michael Chiert, Michaelchiert.com

Printed in the United States of America on acid-free paper.

Visit jrbecker.com
2010

First Edition

THE SPIDER AND THE ANT

J. R. Becker

PURIFICATION POOLS
KAHN
HOUSE OF WAX
republic of KALLIPOLIS
MT. KORA
CAVES
AXIOS RIVER
CHERAVA WOODS
N

Agostino
CARRARIAN QUARRIES
MARINA DE CARRARA
LAKE TIRRENO
RENNA
SPRING 2
AXIOS RIVER
LAKE OHRID
Nicomachus
MACEDON
LAKE PRESPA
sensor
checkpoint
sensor
checkpoint
Lyceum
PLAZA
FARMS
checkpoints
HIGH COURT
Brittany
LIBRARY OF THE SENSORS
J.R.B.

J. R. Becker

INTRODUCTION, ACKNOWLEDGMENTS, & THINGS OFTEN LEFT UNSAID

The only people for me are the mad ones, the ones who are mad to live, mad to talk, mad to be saved, desirous of everything at the same time, the ones who never yawn or say a commonplace thing, but burn, burn, burn, like fabulous yellow roman candles exploding like spiders across the stars and in the middle you see the blue centerlight pop and everybody goes "Awww!"
Jack Kerouac

I first conceived of the idea for my story while studying philosophy and literature in college. I owe much gratitude to Professor David Johnson who taught me much of the philosophy I understand today, and much of the philosophy I don't. (Though he never did quite succeed in fitting Aristotelian Logic in my head, as his logic course was truly, as he most accurately describes it, "much like being in a burning building, with no doors, windows, nor exits." But I thank him for helping me find an exit, even if it did involve the bar exam.) I thank Professor David Hoffman for keeping me after literature class one day to urge me in the strongest yet kindest terms to always keep writing, no matter what else I do. It was during this time that I became greatly inspired with the works of writers like Jonathan Swift, Salmon Rushdie, and Kurt Vonnegut. I was amazed at the possibilities of it all, how literary genres such as satire and magical realism can completely change our world merely by creating their own. I was as impressed by the way Ayn Rand or George Orwell describes an entire society just as Virginia Woolf describes the quest to purchase a pencil. After venturing into the dystopias and utopias of countless other writers, I began to conceive of my own, most of which did not make it on paper.

But one idea kept coming back to me; it would not let me be. It turned and turned in my head, forming itself into a story. First came the characters, then nations, governments, wars, love, conflicts, resolutions, and thus, a novel. It mostly grew when my mind sat still and my imagination was free to roam. It grew during bus and train rides, while I was emptying the day's trivial tasks from my mind in the shower, and it stirred me from sleep at night, when my other senses had no distractions so that my mind filled with blank space in which my imagination was able to wander. It grew inside my head until it became too great, too heavy, and too promising not to be written down. But at that time I was studying law at Emory University Law School. I thought I had no time. But it was Celeste Katz and Professor Timothy Terrell who made sure I was given the time and the resources to begin writing my novel (which, at the time, was entitled *Of Orange Peels and a Ball of Wax.*) If this book ever would have been completed without them (as I doubt it would have), it would not have been for a very, very long time.

At that time it never even entered my mind that one day I may publish my story. That was no concern of mine; I was content merely getting it on paper. It was more of an unloading process, and it felt good. Indeed, it was only when I was halfway through that I considered publication (which probably explains why the second half of this book is twice as entertaining and suspenseful as the first part). But I never knew that it would last four years. If I did, I probably never would have begun. But there are many who kept me going throughout that time, and I owe them all much gratitude. Seth Jacobson spent much time reading portions of my manuscript and sending me back insightful feedback, while Avromi and Michal Sommers did the same (all the way from Israel). I would like to give a special thanks to Natan Davidovics who read the manuscript in its entirety and offered thorough feedback over a significant amount of time. I feel truly honored to have such good and perceptive friends. This book would not have been the same without them.

Thank you to my editor Sarah Jolly for doing such a tremendous and thorough job. You are truly a 'kickass editor' as your domain name reflects. I also wish to thank Harriet for professionally and seamlessly designing such a beautiful book cover, but more for her never-ending patience with my wandering artistic imagination and apparent inability to grasp the mechanics of good book-formatting. But we got through it in the end, right?

I'd like to thank Starbucks Coffee locations in Manhattan for giving me a place to write when my tiny apartment became too much. I hope I didn't take up too much room. Besides, I even bought a drink once in a while.

Though it may be uncharacteristic of this section to list the musical artists who helped inspire me while writing, not one word of this book has been written while I was not under the trance of one of their works. Thus I feel to say nothing of them would be a terrible omission. I simply could not have written this novel without music. Thank you to Sigur Ros, The Album Leaf, Explosions in the Sky, Andrew Bird, Sufjan Stevens, Bon Iver, Bright Eyes, Radiohead, and so many others, and to the jazz of Brad Mehldau, Jim Hall, Miles Davis, John Coltrane, Thelonious Monk, and countless others. Your music was the vehicle of my typing fingers just as my mind and heart.

I would like to thank my parents for always fostering my abilities and offering the most important thing a child could have: room to be themselves. Thank you for understanding that it is not good enough to treat someone the way you would want to be treated, but you must treat them the way they want to be treated themselves, whether you understand it or not.

I want to thank my wife Leah for constantly shining her light into my life, our home, and my heart. I am confident that some of her light made its way onto these pages as it does in everything else that I do and am.

THIS BOOK is dedicated to the wanderers. To the thinkers, the artists brave enough to sail from the harbor of conformance, routine, and uniformity to ride and crash upon the tumultuous waves of human emotion where only few will go. It is no surprise that this most noble venture is also the most difficult. As they trudge through the human experience, it often sticks to them, weighing them down into misery as it becomes too much to bear. But some stay afloat with the thought of their true purpose burning in their mind, despite the chance that they will not succeed. And what would success mean? They do this for one reason only: to bring back that something, that one gem of human emotion so accurately captured in a canvas, a melody, a block of stone so honestly exposed to the world for people to share and reflect and consider and suffer and grow from, and in turn to create their own expressions to continue this important cycle. These creations fill our world like mobile banks of the most precious of all human currency—emotion—for some to make withdrawals whenever they like, and for others, the most noble of us, to make deposits. While others spend their time studying how we live, creating medicines, building bridges, roads, computers, and elevators so that we may live more efficiently for longer periods of time, it is our thinkers, our artists who tell us *why* we live. It need not be said that I am only talking about those who constantly ensure that their success and reputation are the mere effects of their works, never their cause. It is they who quietly remind us why we are here, to stir human emotion to love, to cry, to build, to share, to inspire and conceive. And it is they who tell us that it is not those that wander who are lost, but more often, it is those who have never wandered at all.

I present this book as a wish to stand among them, and in doing so, I hope that my story will inspire readers to sail out of their own personal harbor, if for a day.

TABLE OF CONTENTS

J. R. Becker

REKHA: CREATOR OF WORLDS

(A PROLOGUE)

PROLOGUE

And God said to her: 'Two nations are in your womb; two regimes from your insides shall be separated; the might shall pass from one regime to the other, and the elder shall serve the younger.'
Genesis (25:19)

The tall green grass suffers the bare feet of an old woman who has walked the same path year after year, week after week, day after day. Every morning she rises with the sun and leaves her hut on the banks of the boggy brown river to walk along the river's edge. Sometimes, when she gets close enough to the current beside her, she can feel the river's moisture in the soil under her feet. Her steps make a loud squishing sound in the muck. Her footprints fill with water, forming lakes of their own behind her as if secretly compensating for the haste in which she leaves them deserted, naked, and dry. She does not look back to see the long string of small lakes her footsteps have made. But if she did, she might pretend the lakes are as large as oceans, her footsteps as deep as canyons, and the nearby shrubbery as dense as forest. Such a sight would only tickle her excitement, perhaps even forcing a chuckle from her already jovial demeanor.

But most often she remains a few feet from the riverbank, close to the trail under the roof of leaves looking down upon her in amusement from above. She strolls south, between the trees on her right and the tall shrubs at the riverbank to her left. Her small feet are stained yellow from years of crumbling grass and the dead li'l critters that give their life for her monotonous walk. The brown bugs jump around, and many times under, her feet, as if eager to lose their life to cushion her walk. The worn path reflects the years of aging apparent in her small dark eyes, the way her cheekbones protrude handsomely, lightly adorning her warm face.

Today, her small feet put the grass in its place. At first, the grass had tried to reach out to her and resist, standing tall and earnest like a diminutive band of sentinels with their spears raised high, making their last valiant effort against the strength of this giant's steps. But it did not take long until they began scrambling between her toes and writhing beneath her heels. Now they submit with minimal protest, much like the soft river blanket to her left surrenders to its path, tearing itself apart over the obtrusive granite below.

Her name is Rekha, and she makes this trek with a terra-cotta jug held over one shoulder and harmony upon her sun-tinged face. Her big brown eyes open like two large doorways to a deep cool cave, an escape of calm from the rest of her old body's sorrows. Her small feet earnestly support her short frame that lies comfortably in her maroon robe, corpulent though delicate as it makes its way south, further down the path. Her golden brown lips only part occasionally, both small and thin like the path upon which they ride. Today, her steps are quick and rapid, but soft as flour. Her light brown hair is long and thin; enjoying their ride, the hairs sit back with their arms up, proudly exhibiting their slow moon dance, then altering their signature on the wind to a more rapid, exuberant hop, and finally lying back, they close their eyes and allow themselves to just drift slowly, disintegrating into the breeze.

While she has lost count of her years long ago, Rekha still remembers her sixty-fourth birthday, for that was the day her husband Ariston left her. Frustrated with her inability to have children *what's wrong with you, woman* he had left in huff.

That was over ten years ago today.

Indeed, ten years of walking had settled her footsteps into the trail, staining the grass like speckles of splashed wine on a newly white cloth. Before Ariston left her, Rekha walked this same trail to deliver water to him from the distant spring. She would often bring some to her friend Perictione too.

But now they are gone.

Yet she continues to draw water from the spring. She does not know why. Sure, her camels need to drink, as any do. But she cannot fool herself. She knows what those humps are for. A camel does not need fresh water every day. Perhaps Rekha is lost in the present, and this is her way of holding onto her past. This march is her plank to grasp onto in a torrent sea of memories. Her constant. In the end, it is one thing she still knows how to do.

But today, her walk is different. She had felt it would be—when she first opened her eyes from sleep. *After fifty years, I've finally done it,* she thinks, *after fifty years of marriage.* As always, her walk began after the sun had fully risen. As always, she walked down the riverside, red jug in hand, her dark maroon robe flowing behind her beneath her light brown hair. As always, Rekha made her way south as she has so many times before. But this is the moment that everything changes.

This is when she feels the first kicks.

The first kick or two are nothing jarring, though she knows exactly where they have come from, for a mother always knows when her children misbehave. *After fifty years of infertility, here we go!* Surely she knew this was coming, for her tummy began to swell many weeks previous. But it does not really hit her until now. You must understand, dear reader, that when a woman remains barren through fifty years of marriage, mere weight gain is explainable by many other causes, *pregnant at this age??!* especially at the age Rekha has managed to reach *impossible!* Further, she cannot remember the last time she was with a man, so she assumes it has been a while *impossible! I am an old widow. It would defy the laws of nature! A miracle? It cannot be!*

Often the human mind will go to great lengths to avoid the obvious, even when it is most fortunate, *especially* when it is most fortunate; of course, there is a perfectly reasonable scientific explanation for everything, and this masterpiece one would call Universe was just another accident—BANG! There it is—an enormous accident, a mere incident—almost as functional as it is meaningless! The text of this page is the result of an erroneous ink spill—there is no author, no right or wrong. A stomach swells? Sure, that can all be explained. After fifty years of marriage, BANG! Could it be? Could there be a creator who was known as Rekha?

The first kicks come as she veers near the hum of the closest village, just a mile away. Its sounds and smells float over Rekha's path before melting into the sunlight above. But they trigger short, rapid jabs in Rekha's belly that become sharper as the minutes pass. Another set of kicks occur at every passing of a sound or whiff of baked goods from the adjacent village. The tequila arrives from men's tongues as rapidly as the money clanging through their fingers. As old jewelry exchanges hands, fresh pastries glide in and out of hot ovens, and neglected flowers get crushed on the dirt beneath busy children's feet, wave after wave of sounds and smells make their way over the trees, into Rekha's nose, ears, and apparently, her womb.

The smell of hot cherries catches her attention. Kick! Rekha hears a child scream for her mother. Kick! The sounds of a ukulele flutter past. Kick! Kick! *Now you decide to finally show up. Fifty years of marriage, of prayer, of rubbing ointments, and now this.* The kicks continue for weeks, but only in response to each sensation. *And now this.*

But just as Rekha learns when to expect the kicks, their nature changes in the most peculiar way. They begin to visit her in the deep silence of night. This time they are of a completely different species. They begin with a slow rubbing of her insides, an almost meditative rubbing and pushing like that of a cat slowly toying with an injured mouse, gauging its strength slowly, prodding its boundaries. These motions translate into slow kicks, long and hard, like she has never felt before.

But most peculiar is that these kicks do not respond to the sensations of the village. No, these new kicks first arise as she passes an abandoned schoolyard of a once famous school that stood in a beautiful garden called Academia. These new kicks occur in silence, when the trail and the soft river are the only things around. They occur as Rekha passes an abandoned church, castle ruins, a library. They occur when Rekha passes a cave, a pond, a place of study. But mostly, they occur when Rekha passes nothing at all.

She does not understand because they seem like such opposites. First, her creation had longed for sensory experience, for the market, the noise, the smells, *and now this,* now her child longs for the peace of the intellect, of study, of silence.

Now, her baby has decided to kick both while wide awake and in the dead of night, both while experiencing the world and merely venturing through stillness, both through the hum of the market and through houses of study, through tequila smells and chambers of thought, and through outer experience and inner reason.

ΩΨΩ

We all know what happens next, where the story goes from here. Months pass. Rekha continues her daily stroll, never allowing her newfound company to impede her pace nor burden her spirit. Her stride may be more trying, but it has by no means lost the continuity and flow it has enjoyed through the years. She tries to fathom a child with such contradictory impulses that would lead to such a peculiar pattern of kicks. She knows they are not random, since every small impact feels so determined and thought out, as if each punch was carefully mapped out and considered by its author. She feels her child's passion, that it is trying to tell her something, that every punch and kick has a meaning and a message. Of this she is sure.

The solitude of her walk has become routine through the years, and she has lost the sense of urgency that her situation has brought to her: isolated and alone, she is not surrounded by any other adult who can help her in case there is a need. So while the life inside her is changing, she merely looks on down the path, walking without concern. She drifts on, picking her brain regarding her child's nature, as if she has all the time in the world.

Or so she thinks.

The contractions arrive, shocking her muscles into spasms every three minutes or so. The contractions first strike her during her walk, when she is just an hour from the spring.

She falls to the ground.

Lying on her back in the dirt, she grasps her belly, waiting for the spasms to pass. Her shouts and moans are there, though no one is around to hear them. If a tree falls in the forest, of course it makes a sound. The presence of an audience, or an open ear, is of no consequence at all. Rekha's cries are there, all right. She is there, but she can't testify to it herself. No, she is not listening to her bellows and her cries. Rather, her mind is distracted, stricken by surprising hesitations. A wave of doubts overwhelms her. *I can't do this. After fifty years. At this age.* Rekha does not trust her fragile body. She does not trust the kicks inside her. But most of all, she does not trust in the kind of child she will bear.

*What kind of monster is inside me...*She scolds herself for thinking so. Is this how a mother should react? She struggles to amend her thoughts. *What kind of creation could send such contradictory messages, and then just expect me to bear it? What if I don't want to go through with this? What about me?* She feels forced, controlled. *What kind of creation could just...use my body, my nutrients, and then just leave whenever it sees fit?*

Minutes later, Rekha's moans and breathy shouts begin to subdue with the contractions, fading into mere sighs. She rubs her belly and slowly opens her eyes, regaining her surroundings.

Lying in the dirt path, Rekha discovers that her jug has fallen before her body, shattering itself into many pieces that now lie beneath her. She spots the rock upon which it split. *Better the jug than my head.* The rock bears a red stain from the impact, and Rekha is stained with red sand. She picks up her arm and feels a sharp pain. She discovers a wet stain of blood on the spindly green grass where her arm lay. *And now this.* The stain seems black, and the grass is soaking it up as if refreshed by the wet contact of something other than Rekha's parched feet. The back of her arm is badly cut, from her right shoulder almost to her elbow. She brushes out whatever jug shards she can, the red terra-cotta sand staining her robe, her skin. She sits a few more minutes, just rubbing her body and taking in the past event, still astonished at the thoughts her maternal mind has managed to conjure.

Finally, she begins to crawl.

She rolls over onto her stomach, but cannot bring herself to her feet. Her legs refuse to respond. She does not know why. So she jerks herself up on her elbows, and begins her army-crawl to the spring, as if determined to finish this stroll, even if it may be her last.

Now, Rekha may want to make it to fresh water since she may need it for giving birth, perhaps to cool and clean her and the infant. She may want to find help, an aid to take care of her child, for her body is old and worthless, already bleeding as if it only stood previously in order to create another life. Now that it will fulfill its purpose, it can soon crumble, melting into the path, the river, the dirt from whence it came. Or maybe Rekha is trying to reach the spring so desperately for her own selfish reasons, to clean herself, heal, and rest, even if her baby might die. Her stroll was always important to her; perhaps her creation *what kind of monster* is not. Her intent is not clear to her. She is in shock, and she does not know.

Nevertheless, on she goes.

Rekha crawls on for what seems like hours, stopping every now and then to absorb the convulsions and spasms her belly suffers every few minutes, but never to recover or rest. She winces as pebbles and tree-roots unmercifully dig their teeth into her arms. But she crawls on quietly, always looking ahead, though sometimes gazing into the woods with the occasional cry for help. She knows no one will come and does not expect it, but no one ever likes to cast a small net.

She is not aware that her body has lost a significant amount of blood. Further, she has not eaten that day, arising as usual to venture down her path. A few gulps of water had been enough for breakfast; there was no time for anything more. She crawls on with her last reserves of strength. Since she does not expect any help, she is surprised by the sight she encounters as she nears the spring.

A brown child in white clothing stands in her way. He studies her plainly, curiously cocking his head to the side like a bird on a rooftop waiting for something to happen. He stands above her, not moving, looking down at her as if she is the child. He looks about six years of age, a handsome child, arms at his sides, cleanly cut hair upon his head. His clothes are neatly tailored, Rekha notices, his thin black suspenders knit in such a way that only a skilled set of hands could have achieved. But her thoughts are interrupted as the boy frowns.

It seems to her that he can read her thoughts. *What kind of monster...no, I would never think that!* The brown child's eyebrows furrow in concentration. *Who, me? I love my child!* Rekha desperately wishes the boy would do *say* something. She looks around desperately to see if anyone else is present. She cannot see anyone or anything. Even the river seems to stop in its tracks. The village no longer exists, and the trees have vanished too. There is only Rekha, lying in her own blood, belly hanging out of her ripped robe, and the boy, *that boy,* standing over her like some neo-God, reading her every thought. Finally, there is nothing, and for Rekha, all is suddenly black.

ΩΨΩ

Nicomachus sits in his favorite rocking chair on his porch, watching it get dark outside as he has so many times before. He is a tall black man, suited in long brown slacks, a white shirt, and his favorite vest with yellow stripes across the sides. He smokes a pipe. 'A pipe and some Cab Calloway,' he would often say, 'that's all a sunset really needs. Maybe some Armstrong, some Goodman, uh, Thelonious Monk, and when the mood is really fine, just maybe, some Miles.' His long white sleeves cover a wiry body, skinny and long, though he is not without muscle strength if it is ever needed. His gray eyes hide behind thick bifocals that rest on the end of his large, protruding nose as if they are in constant danger of falling off. He crosses his legs and brings his pipe to his lips quietly, as if not to disrupt the dusk from conducting its business.

As a tall, civilized man who always seems to be deep in thought, Nicomachus is almost as smart as he looks. In his prior life, he had been the top physician in Macedon, serving in the village, the market, and the neighboring cities. In his position there, he thought he had seen it all. However, nothing could have prepared him for the sight he was about to behold, nor for the importance of the deed he has been chosen to fulfill.

His eight-year-old son scampers out of the woods before him. He is a handsome boy no doubt, though his face is stricken by a terror, a sense of urgency that makes Nicomachus's heart sink.

"Papa! Papa! There's a woman in the forest," the boy begins.

Nicomachus throws down his pipe and rises from his chair. He runs off the porch and down the hill towards his youngest child, who continues to speak.

"Near the river—there's a woman, a woman—"

"Hush, child, tell me what happened." Nicomachus tries to maintain a façade of calm.

"A woman, by the river banks, she, she fell," he barely manages to say between breaths, "I was just playing—I, I didn't see what happened. I was just—"

"You were *where?* But didn't I tell you not to go near the riv—"

"I didn't mean to! My ball had gotten lost. It was kicked too far away. I had to look for it! I had to—" The boy collapses, his eyes filling with tears. Nicomachus reaches out to catch him.

"Now, now son, it's going to be okay. Maybe you should come inside the house." But then ole Nico remembers the oath he himself had made the day he became a physician. He sighs.

"Where is this woman you speak of?" he asks quickly. Suddenly, the boy picks his head up, and grabbing his father's hand, he begins to pull him back into the woods. Nicomachus pulls back, interrupting.

"You just let me go. You go inside the house. How far?" he asks.

"What?"

"*How far is she?*"

"Oh, how far?" The boy shakes his head, as if he was interrupted from deeper thoughts, "I, I should show you, it's hidden, near the spring. Say, about an hour's run from here," the boy replies, "We, uh, you, could go and bring her back. But you must make sure they don't see."

"Okay," Nicomachus stops. He looks back up the hill into the front windows of his house, squares of white light illuminating the warm, sticky dark of night. None of the women have looked outside yet, and Nicomachus is not about to wait until they do. Deep in thought, he seems to be evaluating the situation. "Okay, you get the wheel cart, and we will bring her back to the tent. I will get my medicines."

"Yay! I could come? Wow! I—"

"Now!"

The two venture off to get what they need, a man and his boy. Nicomachus does not need to tell his son not go into the house or tell his mother, for both know that Phaestis would start spewing verbal rubbish all over the kitchen like a monkey throwing his excrement at a dancing ghost only he himself sees, making a mound out of a molehill as women of her type often do. *You cannot go*, she would say, *this woman, we don't even know who she is, and what about our family? Your family? It's dark out! I just made dinner, and you're going off on your doctor-adventures. You wanna play hero? Well you can do that just fine right here at the dinner table, here you go, and I'll tell you one thing...*she would not stop. Sometimes the only way to get things done is just to do it yourself. Nicomachus knows even better than his son not to even consider such disclosures as the two wander off into the vast and distant gloom.

ΩΨΩ

Rekha wakes to see a large white fabric ceiling above her supported by thin but lofty wooden spires towering upwards like slender willows, still and strong. Their sleek towering bodies extend high above her, making the faces that come into focus below seem all the more closer. As her eyes regain focus in the dark of the night, she notices the two black faces peering at her through the dark. Their features dance rapidly in the wavering yellow light emanating from a torch in a corner of the tent.

The faces seem kind. First there is the face of a man that seems fraught with concern, though such concern is keenly concealed under the guise of calm and focused concentration only a physician could display. Such composure contrasts sharply with the waves of disorder in the eyes of the boy standing at her feet. *That boy.* That boy, yes, he is the one who saved her, who could read her thoughts after she had fallen on the path, after she had cut herself. Rekha does not need to lift her arm to look, for she already feels the bandage hugging it, and realizes most of her body seems to be bandaged or stitched up neatly, like the boy's suspenders.

Suddenly, she remembers. Quickly, she lifts her head up and looks at her belly and reaches out to feel it. But her neck hurts and she moans in pain. A man's hand settles itself on her forehead, urging her head back down.

"The baby is fine. It is still there," he says.

Rekha notices threads dangling from rips in Nicomachus's sleeve. The rips look fresh, as if Nicomachus had just ripped into his shirt a few minutes ago. The threads hang in disarray and stand out from the order and quality of the rest of his shirt. But the rips look oddly straight, as if they were pulled open with a composed hand even in a hasty situation. She looks back at his face.

"How long—" she begins, but is interrupted by a violent cough.

"Don't speak," Nicomachus replies, "Just...don't speak." He continues, "You were badly bruised and cut all over your legs, arms, hands, and face, but they have been treated and you are going to be just fine," he lies. He does not tell her that she has lost a significant amount of blood, is white in the face, and is in dire need of a blood transfusion that he is unable to give.

But Rekha sees the concern behind the older man's eyes, her hope dripping down from his forehead in small illuminated beads of sweat. She looks to the child for hope but he has already stepped back. She wants to call out to him, to make him her own. She wants to win him back, to have him at her side. *A monster? Who would ever think such thoughts? Surely not a mother, surely not...A mother, I am full of love, you will see. I am not scared, I am not scared, I am not scared...*As contractions re-ignite her body into motion, she hears Nicomachus tell his son to stay back. She opens her legs, submitting to the labor of pregnancy that has already begun.

Drifting in and out of sleep, from soft moans to bitter, strained yells of pain, she feels cold waterfalls of rivers being poured, passing over her face. Closing her eyes, she inhales the cool white snow blanket resting upon her forehead, the spring of wet hydration slipping its way through her desert parched lips, snaking its way down her throat into her stomach to wrestle with the small hot flame still writhing its way out. The excess liquid does not make it through her lips, forming its own stream down her pale soft chin, over the beautifully aged ripples of her fragile porcelain throat, finally settling between the hills of her chest. Her soft breasts direct the stream, assisting it to form its own pond before stopping beneath her Everest of a belly, still rising and falling with the sounds from her throat.

Her body convulses violently, sometimes actually lifting completely off the bed, throwing blankets onto the ground. Now her eyes remain open as she hears repeated orders to push. *I can do this, I am not scared. I am not scared. I am—*

She begins to push.

As the efforts begin, her strained cries briefly turn to determined groans of exertion. But nothing comes, and the pain rises in her sides. Nicomachus turns to his son and returns to Rekha with a malleable ball of wax. She feels the clear white wad being pushed into her right hand. She begins to squeeze. It is a soft, clean, pasty substance, known in the region as Plado. It comforts her, reassuring her palm through its resilient inviting nature (and vague honey scent). Sure, she remembers. Plado was sold in the market, for all types of purposes. People would clog it in their ears at night to muffle the violent snores of their lovers. Others would stuff it in their children's mouths when their language was bad, and still others, the most peculiar of the region, would place it in their tea after a night spent in their ears, since it was said the salty taste would bring much good fortune.

However, as Rekha wrings it through her fingers, the Plado begins to change shape entirely. After some time, it is not what it was before, but a completely different product indeed. The heat of her palm has caused its honey flavor to fade. Its absorption of her sweat and blood has tarnished its clarity. Its scent is vanishing and its color is changing. Its density is thinning and its shape is lost. Rekha feels the complete transformation passing through her hand. She feels wax hiding in her palm, but then she feels a heart, the back of a horse, the brick of a house. She feels the water jug her palm knew so well. The wax confuses her, but she tries to hold onto it, not knowing when she will need it most.

The head of the sun begins to peak out from the tops of distant hills, announcing that several hours have passed. Rekha has gone in and out of contractions, and is doing better than expected. It is clear her years of independent walking, carrying, and longing have strengthened her body, her mind, to deal with such pangs of strain. She is drinking water regularly now, and even has begun to engage the boy in friendly conversation. As Nicomachus sits quietly by the door of the tent, he knows she is far from done, and as the sun continues to rise, Rekha's body begins to speak again. *And now this.*

Another contraction propels her lower body in the air, and she screams in pain. The doc returns to the bedside, but there is little he can do. Rekha's right hand grasps the Plado tightly, for she really depends on it for the first time. But now, the Plado has been writhed, pushed, and pulled to the point where its strength has been depleted. It crumbles easily in her hand, offering no support. Now that she really depends on it, she feels cheated. *Was that the real "you" before?* She begins to wonder. Though she knows it is mere wax, she wonders which of the many guises it has adopted accurately displays its true essence. Simply, which wax is the real wax? *Was that the real you before, or was the honey flavor just a trick? Just a mask, to make me believe you would help, to dangle false hope in front of my face?* As the contractions get more intense, the pain grows unbearable.

She fears she will not make it; she knows the Plado is deceitful; it alone will not do.

Nicomachus turns from her bedside and begins rummaging through his bag. He returns to place a bigger, stiffer ball in her other, left hand. She squeezes hard as the contractions come, but this solid ball does not relent. It gives just a little, just enough to let Rekha know she is squeezing, while inherently retaining its true form. Unlike the Plado, the ball is refreshing in its consistency. The ball seems to speak to Rekha. *I am what I am, and that I will always be.* Merely acknowledging her strength, the ball becomes her lifeline, her aid. The ball rides the erratic waves of the scene in the tent, but always remains the same. It swims and bounces through the cries and tears, allowing Rekha to moan, to kick, to grip, and to clench. Rekha collects the strength to look at the ball in her hand for one moment, she does not know why. The ball is bright orange, perfectly round, appearing the same from every angle, in every shadow, by every motion. It is simple. It is round. It does not change. It is her sphere of strength, an oasis of stability in the midst of such chaotic motion that surrounds.

As both of her hands squeeze their contents, Rekha lets out a most shrilling scream. Her belly rises and falls showing new motions inside. A crow flies away from a nearby branch. Suddenly, the head of a baby begins to emerge from her womb. Nicomachus turns to get a blanket, ordering his boy back in his place. *What kind of monster...I am not scared.* Rekha's head jolts backward, her chest in the air, fists clenching their contents like a lifeline in a drowning man's hands. *I am not scared.* The infant slips out quite smoothly, until all is revealed but its feet. The baby's torso emerges into our world, the world of the tent, the village, the path.

It is a baby boy.

As the baby's cries join that of its mother's, Rekha's left hand opens and drops the orange ball across the tent floor.

The baby's lungs suddenly pump into action like a broken engine regaining its function. Put-put-put-pt-pt-hmmmMMM. It seems shocked by the machinery inside itself. As its cries grow louder, Nicomachus moves forward to pull the baby out.

It does not budge.

It seems the womb of Rekha, or something inside, does not wish to give up the infant so easily. Something is holding onto the infant's feet, pulling the baby back inside the womb. The child's eyes flutter and his cries increase. The eight-year-old boy begins to jump with excitement, and Nicomachus shouts for his exit. The boy leaves the tent at once, though remaining right outside the entrance so as to hear anything that may occur.

Nicomachus prepares for a second attempt when he looks down and sees why the baby will not lift. Old Nico was the top physician in Macedon; he had served all citizens from the poorest of the poor, to the royalty right under King Amyntas the Third. But he has never seen anything quite like this.

A hand is grasping the infant's heel, trying to pull it back into the womb. Indeed, a new infant's hand has emerged from the womb of Rekha to grab his brother's heel, a hand that still wants his first-born rights.

But Nicomachus pulls the first child out, and the second one follows, grasping his brother's heel. Rekha's cries return as the second infant starts to emerge. It holds fast to his brother's heel, still trying to assert his right to be born first.

It is now that Rekha understands the nature of the kicks that she had felt while pregnant. *What kind of creature could send such contradictory messages?* Sure, now it all makes sense. There were two children, two opposites. Now Rekha understands how her belly could feel kicks both for the experience of the village and for the stillness of the night, how one child must have kicked for sensory experience and the other, for silent study and prayer.

What kind of monster? One child had been enough. And now this. As the contractions regain control of Rekha's body, the swirling of her mind does not cease. Doubts set in. *After fifty years of marriage, an old woman, I'm just an old woman and two lives are too much. Who can carry such a load? The younger one tries to restrain the older, and I am just an observer. Helpless, I can do nothing but watch. An old woman, I can do nothing...I am not scared.*

Rekha's head jolts back again, her chin reaching up towards the closed peak of the tent. Her chest rises, stomach pumping like a locomotive machine, her arms writhing wildly then straightening out tight, left hand squeezing, palm pierced by clenching fingernails digging deep into her leather skin. Her right hand opens, dropping the Plado to the ground as the second child finally emerges completely, just managing to fit its large body through the doorway of this life. It too, seems to be a boy.

A boy much larger than his older twin brother.

Nicomachus has managed to free the little one from his younger brother's grasp, briefly turning him this way and that, attempting to pat the fluid from his lungs. The umbilical cord is severed. The boy is crying incessantly as Nico hands him to his son who is waiting nearby with a blanket. Then both sets of eyes turn to the younger boy, the large one who has just emerged.

Unlike his brother, this infant is silent. His eyes remain closed, sausage arms sprouting out of large, broad shoulders that seem to make his head look almost too small for such a body. He squints and grimaces uncomfortably at the new world around him as if trying to shut it out. While the older one cries with eyes wide open, this one just keeps murmuring to himself as if disappointed about the loss of his first born rights. Rekha's eyes go wide as she just watches the child in amazement; deep in thought, the close-eyed baby seems to comprehend all that surrounds him without opening his eyes, possessing inside knowledge he is content with keeping to himself.

Rekha's arms reach out to hold the younger child and he is accepted into her arms. The boy seems to look at her through his eyelids, as if their eyes meet for one second. The infant's face begins to change. *Did he just wince? Smirk at me?* Rekha bursts into tears. *I am not scared. I am not scared. Iamnotscared.* This is her baby, her youngest, and she feels he will be a great man whose lips will only part for the sweetest of words. She hugs the large child in her right arm.

In the wild sea of commotion surrounding, no one notices a baby bee fly into the tent through a gap in the linen wall. The bee circles around above everybody's head, surveying the scene with curiosity as if it does not know its reason for being there. It swings around the womb of the tent uncomfortably, awkwardly looking where to go, like a backstage actor caught behind a curtain raised prematurely. Finally, the bee's orbit begins to narrow to the area above the larger child quiet in Rekha's arms. None see the bee, none but the eight-year-old child who opens his mouth to speak, but the fear of his father's rebuke keeps him silent.

The bee settles on the younger infant's lips and just sits there in front of Rekha's eyes. The infant's eyes flutter open for the first time, and they meet those of his mother. But Rekha's eyes turn to the bee on the child's lip in horror, and she cannot find the strength to react. Genuinely puzzled, she knows bees do not come out now, in early dawn. Her thoughts quickly return to the situation before her, but she feels helplessly frozen in the spotlight of her child's eyes. They seem to speak to her. *Please mother, please help me, save me from this bee. I love you, but why can't you help, move, do something,* they seem to plea. But before Rekha can move or speak, the bee begins to walk across the child's lower lip leaving a trail of wet behind it, a balancing act with the most attentive audience such a show has ever enjoyed. Everyone is silent; even the older infant has stopped crying to join in this controlling event. The bee peacefully arrives at the end of its journey, to the side of the child's delicate mouth. Now, it peacefully flutters its wings, that being the only sound in the tent. The bee slowly rises, looking in one direction only, not acknowledging anyone else's presence. With all eyes following its every move, the bee rises and rises, finally leaving the tent, its inhabitants new and old. As they follow the bee's direction, no one notices the smile slowly forming at the edge of the younger infant's lips.

ΩΨΩ

Nicomachus places the other child in Rekha's right arm. Rekha puts her head back and lets her children suckle in peace for the first time. Nicomachus stands back, stretching out for the first time in hours, studying the two lives he and Rekha had brought into this world through their joint effort, their concerted action. However, Rekha is stuck in another world, the world of the bee. In fact, she is drifting through many worlds, and with a child in each arm, she begins to fade.

Two infants complete their travels through the doors of death and birth as Rekha just hardly prepares to begin hers. *Pack your bags, it's time to go.* However, this may cause one to ask where these two new lives have just come from. But that is a story to be told on another day. For now, it should be enough to know, dear reader, that Rekha passes away some time afterward. Having few friends, she is buried by her neighbors in a nearby cave under Mt. Korab and this is seen as some sort of an embarrassment in the times in which she lives. No one is present at the ceremony, save her neighbors, Old Nico and son, a few friends, and her two new children.

Now, this all took place many centuries ago, and its telling has increased in time. Many have grown to deny its probity, accuracy, some going so far as to say that it may not have happened at all. However, none of this is the point. Simply, it is a story that can be told, celebrated, and mourned. It is a story that can be listened to and learned from. Its premises make sense, and its conclusions admirable. Whether fable or history, flavor or fact, this is no matter for us to decide. The events recorded give way to a very important story, and Rekha could never have known that to be true.

Of course Rekha could not have known what her two sons would become, or how they would be worshipped by great nations for hundreds and hundreds of years. She could not have known that their descendants would form great empires that would rise just as quickly as they would fall from their own contentions. She only acted on what she knew at the time, and, shortly before her death, she wished her young children farewell. She named her firstborn El Totsira, and her second creation would go on to acquire the title O'Talp for himself.

While these two lives erect themselves, one destructs. But destructs only for a moment...to be born again, in a different scene entirely. But of course, that is another story for a different place, a different time.

I

THE CHILDHOOD KINGS

1

Our truest life is when we are in dreams awake.
Henry David Thoreau

The beginning of any good story usually opens with a description of the times, an introduction of the characters, or a tour of the place in which they dwell. A tale often begins with the birth of a child, the death of an old man, the Once Upon a Time in a land far, far away...yet why it must be so far away always boggles the mind, let alone the author's unexplained knowledge of the reader's present location. But of course, that is no matter, for we are not here to tell anyone else's story.

We are here to celebrate our own.

ΩΨΩ

When Renee was born, he was empty.

The problem was that he seemed to stay that way all the time. Months after his twin brother Dewey had learned to crawl, exploring the palace grounds, feeding his head from the spout of life, filling himself with new experiences, behaviors, and desires, Renee remained in his blanket, his body white and still like a small loaf of bread. The people of Lyceum waited for him to become one of them, but no color grew inside their prince. While Dewey blossomed with all the other Posteriorian children, not even the faint glow of youth came from Renee.

But Katherine would hold her Renee like a mother bear would hold her cub, protectively, feeding him her creamy white rations in harmony with her body's slow sways rocking from side to side like an abandoned swing in a soft wind. 'Renee,' she would call him, 'Renee Don Cartez, drink up, drink up, for the cows are not a comin...' as Renee lay still, his eyes closed as if deep in thought, his lips cold and still, his throat bobbing in and out just enough to take the sustenance he needed for another day alone wrapped deep in his blanket cave.

But Dewey soon pulled Renee into the sunlight of the outdoors. It was at this time that Katherine died of tuberculosis. The boys were just one year of age. Left to themselves, the boys enjoyed their own indulgences, having the chance to live in their fabricated environments of dragon fire, dungeons, and true love, without having the credits roll down on their show prematurely, obtruding their view, interrupting their fun. For years they would scramble through the animated labyrinths of precious stones, Persian rugs, hidden doors, secret rooms, and the whole system of hallways and corridors that fill the palace like complex tunnels and dark ominous passageways running through the body of a large whale. They would slip through the veins, and hide behind the lungs. They would hang from the rib cage ceiling rafters of their room, jumping up and down on the large fluffy tongue beds with smiles stuck on their faces. They would march like kings, flags held high over their heads. Through the heavens they would soar, through intestines they would crawl, until their little bellies hurt with laughter, their minds overcome with exhaustion, and their little feet could take no more.

Somewhere in their young minds, they knew that mother was gone. They did not know how long their imaginations would last. But they did not care. As long as they were swimming through their imaginary oceans of treasure, nothing else seemed to matter.

But it did not take long for Renee to withdraw. It was then that the boys noticed their mother was missing. Renee never remembered her being sick. It was as if she was there one moment, and in another she was gone. Renee wanted to ask others what really happened, but no one seemed to want to talk about it. Sometimes Renee missed his mother, but he could never decide if it was Katherine he missed, or just a mother at all. Dewey never seemed bothered by her absence, though he used to keep this a secret. There are times when he pretends to miss Katherine, but all he really misses is someone to play with.

"But what about father?" Dewey asks Renee one day. His words are lost as he scrambles away from Renee and runs down the yard, chasing a hoop with a stick. The hoop rolls towards the edge of the city on the northern tip of the palace grounds. Renee looks up for a moment. He squints and the sun hurts his eyes. But for an instant he can see the sun bounce off Dewey's long golden hair like white fire, illuminating each thread so that it seems that his head is the sun itself, swimming across the grass, a fluffy mop of light bouncing up and down with Dewey's jumps over his various toys sprawled across the field.

Renee sits cross-legged on the ground a few feet away. He does not answer. He has been sitting for the better part of an hour, inspecting something in the dirt. Even as infants, Dewey remembers, Dewey would excitedly jump from toy to toy while Renee would deeply inspect a pebble or speck of dirt like a farmer would a piece of fruit.

"Renee!" Dewey comes bumbling back, breathing heavily.

"Oh," Renee looks up startled, "I am sorry. Did you say something?"

"What about father? Why can't he play with me?"

"You know that father does not play hoop—"

"I'm not playing hoop anymore! Look!" Dewey holds up the toy in his hands, "Now I have another game!"

"Father does not play games."

"Then why won't you play with me? Please? Just this once?"

"I am just not in the mood. I am working on something," Renee looks down at the grass, a look of undisturbed focus on his face.

Dewey looks at his brother and wonders how they could have come from the same mother. He sees Renee's small ears and wonders if they have ever grown since he was born, still two white flaps pressed too closely against his head as if gravitating toward his mind, scared to be free. As unfitting for a Posteriorian as this trait is, such a thing may be hidden in the streets of Lyceum. But in the palace where they live everything is public. It always has been. The people know their royalty and they like it that way. Of course, Renee's soft white face, brown eyes, and spindly black hair have done nothing to help.

"Well if you won't come play with me," Dewey says, "and father does not play games, who should I play with?"

"Father Joachim plays games," the voice of a woman says, "They are just games of a different kind."

The boys look up to see their father's lover, Helene, a smile of amusement on her face. Both boys smile back; it is hard not to. Nearly thirty-five years of age, Helene's yellow blonde hair hangs from her head like a river, a golden waterfall in suspension above her white linen robes always adorned with bright orange, green, and blue depictions of flutes, horns, animals, and flowers. A pink moon sails across her lower breast while blue stars dance all down her back above and below the large cows and unicorns dancing in between. Her legs are long and her smile kind. Her skin is golden and her stride certain. But most alluring is the maternal love in her eyes, the love that has carried her through her adoption into the castle, the love that brought envy to all that saw her, the love that gave her the strength to raise the children as if they were her own.

"Like grown-up games?" Dewey asks.

"Like grown-up games," Helene says.

"Well why can't he play kid games? With me. Because, I, I am just a kid."

"Your father knows that, Dewey. But he has great responsibility. He is the great judge in the High Court at Brittany and the people need him. Sometimes even more than you do."

Since arriving in Lyceum, Helene has wished Joachim could spend more time with her and the children, but she understands that the nature of the legal system requires his continued presence. Though trials proceed extremely quickly, some taking less than one hour indeed, criminals are most always tried again at least fifteen times. Simply, Posteriorian litigants are able to appeal again and again, since no sentence is completely binding as more evidence keeps pouring in. The Posteriorians deeply consider every piece of evidence discovered, thus often putting a man deemed innocent years ago to a new trial founded upon damning evidence just discovered. Likewise, many men are set free upon revealing evidence that comes to surface after years and years of involuntary servitude, lashes, or solitary confinement (the latter of which is considered worse than death). No, there is no rule 403 bar, and even if such evidence is more prejudicial than probative, the Posteriorians take joy in the task of separating the two, sifting through all evidence available, seeking out the good seeds from the bad, filtering out the needles in the hay, sieving the gems from obscurity, no matter how long it might take.

This makes Joachim a very busy man. Also, since the Posteriorians have no fundamental, 'natural,' law (there are no statutes), all law is case law coming from precedent, and as such is always changing, being reshaped, modified, cropped and primed to adjust accordingly to the situation at hand. But while reliance on case precedent is of the utmost priority, stare decises is extremely weak and thus consistency in sentencing almost completely nonexistent, owing to the Posteriorian's nature of swaying this way and that. No case ever lasts a month before being blatantly overruled so that the prior case law in that area of human conduct has to be erased completely and drafted all over again, from the ground up. Everything changes in Lyceum, and the law is no exception.

But this arduous task is celebrated by the Posteriorians. (Indeed, the courtrooms still show an ambience of celebration, filled with all types of flower bouquets, adorning trinkets, the walls lined with bright multi-colored terra-cotta moldings, stones, and ornaments celebrating the worthy tasks of the living law.) The men continue their work with smiles on their hearts and harmony in their focused minds, never resting in the sea of experience, never neglecting anything before them, but always, gathering, yes, gathering and scrutinizing all that can possibly land on the table before them.

All trials are decided by a jury of hundreds of excited Posteriorians. But this hardly lightens Joachim's load of maintaining order in such a large court with so many jurors that desperately need instruction. Jurors are asked to bring all their past experiences into the courtroom to help them decide the matter; voire dires are generally never conducted, except in the gravest of circumstances when a juror's thoughts are completely impaired and as such, just cannot behave at all.

Joachim's submission to the long hours that repeated trials, analysis of extensive evidence, and colossal juries require probably lends itself to the cause of his solemn nature during the few hours he spends at home. While a man of life and veracity on the bench, he comes home a man who has been holding a burden too heavy for too long. The color, animation, and glowing energy emanating from him in the High Court is left at the courtroom's doors like an abandoned sack of luggage as he exits to return home. His soul looks weary dragging his seven-foot frame slowly around the castle. His step bears a weight with every pace he takes; his face wears a crease for every case he's tried. His long black hair, always pulled back tightly in a bun, is finally beginning to gray. But the strain his body suffers hides under his bright colored robes finely wrought with designs expected to be shown on a judge of any high Posteriorian court. Like Helene's, his robes depict forms and images of Gods, angels, moons, trumpets, animals, people, stars, and cherubs. His robe seems to follow him in his step, its long white fringes trailing fast behind. But for his children, he just has nothing left.

"But you should know all of this by now, boys," Helene says.

But to all present it seems she is talking to Dewey since he is the only one paying attention. Helene often says 'boys' just to try to include Renee. He hates when she does that.

Renee returns his gaze down to the grass before him. He inspects the blades for just the right one. He does not see the servants at Helene's side. As Helene continues to speak to Dewey, one of the servants looks at Renee, then looks away, then looks back at him, troubled at something foreign.

Renee also hates that.

"But guess what Dewey? *I* will play with you!" Helene's words come out in a laugh. Dewey has secretly tried to imitate her jovial way of speaking, but he can never quite pull it off like she.

Helene smiles and winks at Renee as she kicks off her shoes and runs past him, stealing a ball from Dewey's thick and greedy fingers. She runs away with it, down the grassy hill.

"Hey!" Dewey's face turns red with frustration, but then he smiles and charges after her, his arms outstretched. Renee looks up, a mild satisfaction in his eyes. He sees the two red silhouettes *woman and boy* bleeding into the burnt orange Lyceum afternoon haze. Minutes pass. Helene enjoys the view, taking a deep breath of the rich warm air. Dewey walks over to Renee and kneels in front of him.

"Maybe you can show me what you...what you are doing," he says, catching his breath "That way, we can do something together."

"I am trying to make a whistle."

"What?"

"I have been inspecting the surface of this blade of grass," Renee holds up a tiny blade of dark green, "and I see that it has ridges."

"So?"

"If you let me explain. See, I think that if I can hold this blade of grass real, real tight between two of my fingers, allowing just a bit of space on either side of it, it will create a passageway through which I could blow. And as the air passes through the grass, it will whistle—"

"C'mon, you're talking too long already!" Dewey smacks the blade of grass from Renee's hands and laughs. "Stupid grass. Boring, if you ask me! Besides, that won't ever work," he says.

"Why not?"

"Silly, grass is one of the most quietest things in the world! Have, have you ever heard a grass whistle? You could be so silly sometimes, like that...that fool we saw at the circus with his face painted white and red who thought that—that—his gun would shoot water, but all that came out was a sign that said bang or, or boom—"

"A clown."

"What?"

"He was a clown."

"Yeah. That."

A moment of silence passes as a breeze blows by, ruffling Dewey's hair.

Renee looks down, but says, "Why do you always trip over your words?"

"What? I don't know," Dewey blushes with a smile, "I, I guess I get, uhm, excited sometimes."

Renee closes his eyes and cocks his head the way he sometimes does when deep in thought. His hands brush through the grass, looking for the special blade he had before. He finds it, and carefully wedging it between his two thin thumbs, he brings it to his mouth for another try.

But a group of girls pass by on the closest street, and even from a distance, they can see Dewey the prince, his cheeks still in a blush. They giggle at him and he giggles back, turning towards them with excitement. One of them makes a funny face at him and he makes one back and they all break out in laughter. As the girls depart, their laughter continues with that of Dewey's, and no one can hear the thin sound of a whistle pierce through the air.

No one, that is, except the sensors standing behind Renee. There is no sound their large ears can miss. Indeed, the sensors are able to pick up each sight, smell, sound, or sensation floating though the air like feathers, chasing each other through the soft liquid blue.

"Don't look at them," Helene says.

Renee does not hear her, but he does not need to be reminded. Helene continues anyway. "You know you are not allowed to look at the sensors," she says, "They have their job, and you have yours."

Who are the sensors, you ask? I must apologize to the curious reader for not explaining sooner. Though Helene speaks to Renee about them right now, I feel the need to explain because I have been in Lyceum longer than Helene, far longer than some of the oldest Posteriorians in the nation. I have studied their way of life, their customs, their dress, and the aesthetics with which they so carefully choose to surround themselves. As such, I must welcome the curious reader with a short but detailed description of the manner of the Posteriorians through which the twin brothers thread their adventures of fairies, dances, and jokes.

ΩΨΩ

The Posteriorians, one must understand, are obsessed with recording everything that goes on in the great empire, both inside the palace walls and out. Indeed, hills and hills of buildings have been set aside in Lyceum to be libraries filled with vast recordings and catalogues; these great libraries are the heart of the people, cataloguing the recordings of the sensors. While the purpose of such efforts need not concern us now, it should gratify the reader that this is the only way Posteriorians can learn from their mistakes; as a nation, their achievements have been built upon their history, through the trial and error of time. Such precise recording requirements have gotten them through a lot. As such, the law remains clear: everything experienced by anyone in the nation, from a frown to an orgasm, must be recognized, identified, analyzed, recorded, and documented with the greatest precision and detail so as not to miss something valuable, something that the empire could learn from perhaps centuries in the future.

One need not engage in deep thought to realize the great burden of fulfilling such an arduous task. Realize, while one woman cries in the east, a man enjoys a breeze in the west. A baby is born in the north while a child scrapes his knee in the south. Every second, in every place, people are teeming with sensations that emerge from the way they experience their bodies, other people, the weather, the entire world around them. Every smile, every groan, every sigh or wince of pain, this must be recorded to the fullest extent of the law. No experience is too big or small, from the slow bite of a piece of chocolate cake to the love that warms one's heart. However, such a resourceful and prudent people have not come to this task fully unprepared. Indeed, the government has employed and bred such sensors over the years, a people little in stature, though numbering in the hundreds of thousands, enough for eight or nine sensors to be assigned to each household in the kingdom, usually enough for two or three per person. It is upon the shoulders of this small ambitious people that such a burden has been placed.

Since most sensors stand no more than three feet from the ground, the tallest reaching four feet, there have been stories of sensors getting stuck in chimneys or crevices inherent in any house. Indeed, many have been lost through the years. It is ironic that this has been a small matter to their masters because the job of the sensors is seen as the highest calling of Lyceum: to record the experiences of the nation. Still, sensors are held naturally inferior to man, much like slaves (though they are carefully distinguished from women, whom also are considered naturally inferior to man due to their naturally inferior intelligence). Lyceum has lost many sensors eaten by their masters' dog, while others have been left drowning while recording in the baths of their masters who would hardly notice the rising bubbles behind them as they scrub themselves playfully, sometimes with their children, their lovers, or more sadly, all by themselves. Often they would stare at themselves with utter amazement for many moments, before wandering off to other mental worlds or playing with themselves with glee, completely preoccupied with themselves while a different, smaller life expires just behind them.

Sensors are not allowed to speak. But they would never want to, for any noise or attention they would make would have to be recorded, and they have enough to record as it is. Thus, all sensors go to great lengths to conduct themselves so as not to be noticed and their plainly ordinary facial features surely aid them in this regard. They are the only ones in the entire nation who do not dress in bright colors; they look extremely ordinary (besides their enormously large ears and eyes that have evolved over generations to trap and receive most any sound or sight) and would always remain unnamed, anonymous, so as not to arouse any sensations or disruptions in the minds of others. They have no identity, no names, no ages. They are anonymous; Lyceum's citizens must not notice them. As such, they dart around quietly, moving slowly in between their fast sprints that sometimes become necessary to keep up with their subjects, always leaving their trail of parchment sliding quietly behind them.

This small resolute group of servants had to go where their subjects would go, eat where their subjects would eat, sleep where their subjects would sleep. At night, they would sit quietly behind their subject's bed, for days if necessary, their left hands moving rapidly down the pages they held to write out every experience without ever making a sound. They would follow their master to the toilet, the bath, or they would run out after his kids who played in the forest out back. They hardly ever needed to eat, drink, sleep, or piss, though the ability of their nature is most peculiar and most Posteriorians are smart enough to avoid its inquiry for fear of impinging on the gifts of the necromancers of the nation. See, sensors had these gifts of stamina given to them by the necromancers and magicians of the empire so that most Posteriorians were scared to inquire as they may upset a magician and be turned into a sensor themselves (as a good number were) and others knew it beyond them to even bother. This was not difficult; it is not in the nature of Posteriorians to question that which works.

The citizens of Lyceum also know of the sensors' prohibitions, namely, that the sensors are never to cross the line of their silent mechanical duty. They are never to interact with the world, to make a noise, a smell, an action that would disrupt the natural order of things they are required to record. Even if they were to witness a murder, a rape, they are to stand there quietly recording the events at hand as they have for generations and generations. Their records enter the great libraries of the sensors as pure recordings of the unadulterated world.

"Even though they may be pretty astounding," Helene explains, "most Posteriorians have no trouble taking them for granted, my Renee. And you should be no different."

Helene takes a deep breath and looks at Renee. He has not looked up from the ground once, she notices. She sometimes wonders why she talks to him at all.

"This is stupid!" Dewey's whines pierce the silent air behind Helene. She turns around. "All we ever get to play in is the palace grounds. Why can't we ever go out to town?"

"You want to chase those girls, don't you, my boy? Your time will come, Dewey, your time—"

"What does that even mean? And who made you the boss?"

Helene does not have to answer; they both know that these are Joachim's rules. Joachim has always thought he has enough to worry about without his boys scrambling through the heart of a wild Posteriorian circus.

"Well, what do you want to do?" Helene asks, "Where exactly do you want to go?"

"Oh!" Dewey looks up at the clouds as if entering a dream, "Oh, how I wish I could just taste the Posteriorian buffet that we are famous for—the one I only get to hear about from within these palace walls! Oh, how, how great it would be to attend one of our team sporting events. I hear they are wildly entertaining," Dewey stands tall and his face lights up as he begins to talk with his hands flying wildly with his words, "as the players ride horses, dancing wildly through large hoops of fire and noise. Butterflies just…hovering around them, filling the scene with the most amiable colors, alluring aromas, creating one of the most cordial sights, men just…coming together and falling apart in, in perfect unison, with each note in its place, each, each soul supplying its perfect function, its absolute goal, painting the perfect picture one can never imagine: a perfectly bubbling harmony that will rapidly fill the lower arena floor with hot fervor, rising up to be hungrily absorbed by the dreaming fans' eyes, ears, and noses, all…all gaping wide open to receive their meal of synchronized experience, never ever closing for even a second of rest as they suck their eye candy dry till they are so so full that their brain stings with pain, forcing them to pause for just a moment. Then they search for more, and there in Lyceum, there is always more to be found."

Dewey's hands fall to his sides, "And, and all this time, Renee and I are locked up in our own song and dance from the comfort of the enclosed stone palace walls. But it is getting quite boring with a brother who would rather stay in his room."

"Well, well," Helene smiles, nodding her head in approval, "You sure expressed yourself there." It is rare Helene allows Dewey to continue one of his detailed rants. Her eyes twinkle as they do only when she has a secret.

"What is it?" Dewey says. Renee looks up.

"Tomorrow, there is an art contest in the land," Helene says slowly, savoring each word, "and we are going to be the royal guests!"

Dewey jumps as high as his short legs can take him, pumping his thick fist high into the air. He trips over himself, his belly jiggling as he falls on the grass with a hearty laugh. Renee smiles and stands up, carefully brushing the grass off his lap. Helene looks at the boys with love in her eyes.

"Come on," she puts her hands on the boys' backs, "It is getting cold. It is time to go in."

With the monstrous haze of the palace towering before them, they begin to head in, Dewey darting excitedly in front as Helene holds Renee's hand to help him bring up the rear. Even Renee feels excitement drum in his stomach like a tiny dancer anticipating tomorrow's exhibition as it comes closer with the falling of night.

ΩΨΩ

On the roof of the Palace, Renee and Dewey watch the stars shine above. The rising pillars of construction loom miles below in preparation for the art contest like the ancient skeleton of a dinosaur. But the boys know the construction is far from ancient; as anything in Lyceum, it is new and will not last long. See, what buildings in Lyceum boast in beauty, they sacrifice in structure. All of them have but the weakest foundations. When a building crumbles, a bridge fails, or a road surrenders, (as often happens in this city,) its citizens happily begin to rebuild immediately. There is always new construction going on, sensors congregating along the work site's edges, taking in all the drilling, the racket, the stirring scene. In Lyceum, the buildings rise as fast as they fall, eager to wear their badges of adornment though their skeletons may starve.

But tonight the boys look to the stars above, shining and constant in contrast to the dance of stone and hammer below.

"There are so many of them," Dewey says, "So beautiful. This view, this air, it is all so perfect from up here!"

"Yes," Renee tries to nod in agreement, but the sea of stars confuse his eyes, so he concentrates intently on one lonely star, glittering in solitude in the corner of the horizon. Dewey continues.

"Wow! Do you see them all? I wonder how, well, wow, it is amazing that they—so many of them—are all floating, dancing, and glittering so far away, but right at this moment!"

"Well," Renee says, "Not at this moment."

"What?" Dewey's smile fades.

"They are not glittering now. What you see is how they were shining a long time ago."

"Hm."

"It takes time, Dewey, for the sight of the stars to travel all the way from them to our eyes."

"Oh," Dewey says. He does not understand and is glad Renee didn't explain.

Renee looks at his feet. Dewey raises his arms high, and says, "Oh, how I wish I could just hug this night so so tight and take it with me wherever I go, and never ever ever let it go! Isn't it exciting? The lights in the sky, the dance they give off, the life, the *motion.*"

"Do not stand too close to the edge of the roof."

"Huh?"

"Do not stand there. It is dangerous. You can fall off."

"Oh," Dewey looks down, "Okay." A moment passes. Dewey looks back up sharply at his brother, "Why do you always have to do that?"

"What?" Renee says.

"You always…everytime I'm enjoying something…oh, forget it. Never mind."

"Okay."

"I'm cold. Let's go inside."

The boys return to their room and get into bed. An hour passes, but Renee's thoughts keep him awake. He supposes that Joachim has been called forth by the people of Lyceum, the Grandee at their head, to be the judge at the annual art contest event. The people see hope in Joachim's wisdom, and in his experience they feel strength.

Renee wonders if father ever gets nervous. He remembers the times Joachim had advised Dewey of the responsibility inherent in decision-making. 'Allow everything you have ever experienced, all the knowledge you have collected over the years,' he would say, 'to enter your mind, and guide your decision upon the very object under examination.' Dewey would nod in agreement and Joachim would often beam back, meeting his oldest son's eyes, holding his chin between his thumb and forefinger. Renee often watched this and would eventually grow accustomed to the cold webbing of abandonment forming itself upon his small heart.

But Renee could never understand the advice. *What do my past experiences have to do with the parties standing before me now? How can such past experiences guide my present intellect?* Renee wonders awake in bed, eyes to the ceiling hovering above. *Aren't they different? During my past experiences, well, I was in a different mood back then, stuck in a moment, swimming in sentiment, drowning in emotion…And now I am told to apply that to these people's troubles? My personal experiences forced to shake off their imperfections, subjectivity, and emotions that skew, to stand up straight, marching into the courtroom evoking a façade of confidence, as if they had been that way all along?*

Renee finally closes his eyes to the ceiling above his face. By now, he has explored every nook on the ceiling and has ventured down every stain. He has fallen through every crack and has climbed every knob of dried paint so much so that the ceiling is still there, still in his view after his eyelids attempt to close them off. As he closes his eyes, the ceiling remains open, glaring down, studying him from above. They each know their position well, white ceiling to white face, and as the large silver dollar moon slowly turns full, floating, suspended in the sky, the small boy finally rolls over, curls into a ball bathed in the diminutive moonlight sneaking into his chambers, promising a better day to come, imposing a restful night to surround.

ΩΨΩ

Helene has already been awake for hours as she strolls the royal hallways towards the children's quarters. She is used to rising early to serve Joachim his rich breakfast before he goes to work. By now the chamber's halls have filled with a cool white light thinly covering the yellow stoned passageways, bathing all who pass through, turning gray into white and men into ghosts.

Dewey wakes to the touch of Helene's hand though her footsteps have already stirred Renee from dreams.

"Up, up, up we go," Helene begins. Dewey squints, looking up into her face to smile briefly before turning over and closing his eyes.

"No you don't," Helene persists, "It's time to get up. Say, how do you feel?"

"I feel like I need a few more minutes. Go get Renee," Dewey pleas.

"And your brother will say the same thing."

"Well that's fine, I need my sleep more."

"*Well that's fine, I need my sleep more,*" Helene teases. Though the kids love Helene, they often test her patience, requiring her to nudge and tease. "C'mon, baby, up you go—"

Suddenly, Dewey lets out a loud, menacing laugh and jumps out of his bed. He runs towards Renee's room to jump on his younger twin brother. Helene sticks out her hands to stop him, but he is too fast. He charges into Renee's room like a soldier as he has so many times before, but this time Renee stands ready for him. When Dewey enters his room, he is already standing on the bed, pillow in hand, ready to strike. Dewey charges with a shout *charge!* and Renee leaps into the air, bringing down his pillow with the most force a young boy can muster but completely missing his target, he lands atop his older brother. They both fall to the floor full of laughter.

They each take in a breakfast of eggs, fruit, and wine. Dewey stuffs an entire grapefruit in his mouth and his cheeks puff out as far as they can go.

"Now, now, my boy," Joachim tries not to laugh, "You are going to hurt yourself. Get that out of your mouth."

Dewey looks up like a naughty squirrel caught in the act. He allows a big grin, pink juice dribbling down his chin. The food begins to leak out as Helene tries to catch it in her hand, but Dewey reaches up and puts it back in his mouth. He giggles, begins to choke, and finally regains control of himself. He chews his food and swallows it as quickly as he can.

"See what I can do?" he says, "I just ate that whole grapefruit."

"I know you're hungry," Helene says, "But you should be more careful—"

"It's not that I'm hungry. I just want to go to the art contest already!"

"Renee," Joachim says, "You have not eaten anything. C'mon. Eat something."

Renee does not move.

"C'mon. Do you know what the most important meal of the day is?"

"Every meal!" Dewey nearly jumps out of his seat.

Renee does not raise his eyes as he speaks. "I just want a piece of bread."

"Bread?" Joachim lets a moment pass. "Bread with butter? Bread covered with cheeses, fresh kiwi, oranges, cinnamon and raspberries? Or just bread?"

Renee is silent. Joachim slams a hand down on the table, sending drops of orange juice from his fingertips flying across the table.

"Could you believe it? The boy wants bread? Fruit is the staple of Lyceum, the lifeblood of Posteriorians for generations. We enjoy its colorful sensations, wet taste, and variety of forms. But Renee wants bread."

Finally, Joachim shakes his head and continues to eat. Renee eats half an apple as the rest of the table eats quickly, talking and laughing with food in their mouth.

It does not take Helene long to dress the boys up as the judge's children and lead them into the carriage. The three walk upright, their chins in the air, marching straight as an arrow with three sensors scuttling close behind. They enter the carriage where Joachim waits. Joachim turns his head briefly, forcing a kind smile to acknowledge their presence, and turns once again to look straight ahead. The carriage doors close as the carriage begins to move forward down the road into a day that has already been kindled with light filling the grass with warm air to rise through the trees, whispering promises of hope and offers of guidance through the billowing carriage walls as they make their way down the road, towards the plazas that house the great art display to come.

The ride begins quietly, roaming slowly across the large plains on the outskirts of Lyceum. The farms are large and plentiful; since the Posteriorians truly excel at the sciences, the dry weather is hardly an obstacle to the success of their crops. Posteriorian farmers enjoy fame throughout the world for their corn, their beets, their luscious orange groves that stretch for miles and miles. The sensors in the back of the wagon write softly on their scrolls, their hands moving slowly with little effort, for they have seen this many times before and they realize that they have little to record and much time to record it in.

A multi-colored dragonfly flutters close to the carriage. It flies at Renee's side. Renee tries to follow it with his eyes, but it makes him dizzy. He wishes it would go away. He reaches to swat it, but Dewey reaches around him and catches the dragonfly into a glass jar, slamming the lid down just in time.

"Where did you get that?" Renee asks in annoyance.

"Why, I just caught it from outside, dummy. You saw me."

"No. The jar."

"Oh, this?" Dewey holds up the jar. He can see the dragonfly showing off its rainbow wings proudly. Dewey smiles in awe. "I always have one with me. In case there is anything to collect."

"To collect," Renee shakes his head, "And you are going to carry it around with you all day now?"

"It's worth it. It will sure look good next to the other ones in my room."

After some time, the carriage reaches the end of the plains and enters the building-lined streets in the city of the masses. The speed of the sensors' writing hands increase with the buzz of the carriage's surroundings.

The city is a circus. A never-ending, always-flowing maze alive with the chitter-chatter of men, the hustling of dogs, little children at play. Men exchange gifts as the few women present observe; jewelry is bought, produce negotiated, and ice cream savored, all to the pigeons' amusement as they hover in circle above. Through all this glides sunlight illuminated by the bright tree leaves blocking its way, yet urging it on, luring it into every nook and cranny. The trees guide the sunlight, breaking it up into rays and whispering to them where to go. The sunlight ignores the teeming life around it; it has seen it all before, it is not disturbed. It reminds man that among all the shopping, talking, barking, bartering, and laughing people and animals, it is surprisingly quiet.

Tall buildings of yellow, orange, red, and blue emerge from the streets like pillars of rainbow cotton candy raised upon a tray, each displaying its affluent wealth of sensations to any prospective passerby. All boast elaborate ornamentation, a useless jumble of winged birds, flowers and scrolls, moons and stars, fruits hanging, swinging from a vine. Terra-cotta moldings do not limit themselves to the crevices beneath the roof from which they sprout but rather climb from head to toe of each building, swimming, dancing throughout the entire building's exterior, leaving a trail of bold colors that contrast with the pale yellow frame beneath their fervent song.

Each structure boasts the most immense skylights and eye-opening windows that crouch to fit between the many balconies hanging off their sides. The balconies reach out like hands trying to grab every bird that may float near, every smell that happens to careen past. People can be seen upon these balconies for hours, eyes open, breathing in the morning breeze. Each building is equipped for its inhabitants to experience the outside world as much as possible, through its open glass eyes, upon its outstretched granite limbs.

The children pass a school, a small open-air structure cropped between two overreaching buildings that visibly dwarf the school's size. One will never find large schools in a Posteriorian city since this people believe that *real* education takes place outside the classroom's walls, where life is happening at its fullest. While education is certainly a priority (especially in order to excel in the sciences), school buildings are usually neglected since long school days in a classroom are generally frowned upon as an enclosure to the world outside, as if one reading a book is actually missing the show.

The carriage pushes its way through the loud crowds of people collecting in the streets. It is now at the outskirts of the plaza, in the midst of the hustle and bustle of the marketplace and dwelling place of the citizenry. The streets are filled with people squeezing through the narrow passageways towards the plaza. Dewey peeks out and the people look back. He sees them wearing the normal Posteriorian dress, namely, robes of the most vivacious and effervescent colors, mostly blue, yellow, and orange. The robes hang over their large bodies in surplus; for generations Posteriorians have been fat from gorging themselves with culinary experiences, and since this custom has not faded with time, they have grown accustomed to making extra large clothing that they can fit over their big bellies.

The people bear large jewelry. Tremendous stones rest around their necks, upon their chests, their wrists, their foreheads. Most of the women wear nose rings while many wear a ring between their eyes with a large colorful stone at its peak. These rings are customary wedding gifts, to be given to the bride to wear between her eyes for the remaining years of her life. The stone serves as a symbol that such visual beauty should be the closest thing to one's eyes, as if all sense data must pass by the stone before entering one's eyes thus staining itself with beauty making it worthy of entering the bride's eyes.

Dewey sticks his head out of the carriage towards a group of big women. They can see his red cheeks rise with a smile under his two blue gem eyes, and they smile back. Then Renee sticks out his white head and the women look at him for a moment and turn away. Renee wonders why they didn't smile for him like they did for Dewey.

The carriage finally arrives at the scene and people begin to notice its arrival. *Hail Joachim, all hail Joachim, lord of the High Court!* People begin to cheer as they make way for the judge's arrival, scurrying as fast as the obesity of their large bodies will allow them. The Grandee is already there and he smiles at Joachim's arrival. As the carriage pulls in, the people's chatters begin to settle back to their normal mode of talk, though that is also far from quiet since all Posteriorians in general do not hold back with words; they speak extremely quickly, using many words to say very little. Joachim takes his place, Dewey and Renee on his left, Helene on his right. They all smile, and the people smile back. The sensors take their places and the show finally begins.

2

The one considers man chiefly as born for action as influenced by his measures of taste and sentiment, pursuing one object and avoiding another according to the light in which they present themselves. And though these researches may appear painful and fatiguing...obscurity, indeed, is painful to the mind as well as to the eye; but to bring light from obscurity, by whatever labour, must needs be delighting and rejoicing.

This species of philosophers paint her in the most amiable colours; borrowing all help from poetry and eloquence, to please the imagination and engage the affections. Man is reasonable, but man is also an active being. Be a philosopher; but, amidst all your philosophy, be still a man.

David Hume

The golden June sun bears all its strength, weighing down on the scene in the plaza, bleeding the colors, smells, and sounds into one homogenous mass alive. It hovers over the crowd, a yellow yolk most content where it remains, burning such heat it knows its people can stand. The heat descends like a large warm blanket bearing down on the shoulders of the mothers dragging children, the children dragging mothers, everyone rushing to get good seats in the stands. Hundreds of people finally find their seats, gladly settling under their large flowery hats and umbrellas impenetrable by the daylight's glare.

The crowd resembles a large, living mob of life, a Pollack painting at its best, always changing colors, always in motion. Each Posteriorian is a tiny dot in an impossible three dimensional hidden picture, a smorgasbord of color, rainbow pieces swirling around an ovular milky universe, swirling, bleeding into one another, leaving a trail in their wake, a signature narrating their safe passage that precedes.

They are hungry for entertainment, now twiddling and fiddling in their seats. They seek food from the vendors running up and down the aisles of the arena, sensors walking briskly behind them, sometimes even sneaking a piece of fish or meat that had fallen behind in the vendor's haste.

The crowd emits a soft hum of chatters and laughs while excited cries of children come together and fall apart like dancers gliding, skating on ice, never even considering the passage of time.

Many artists are present today, many the greatest in the world. They are already sitting in their assigned places in the center of the plaza beneath everyone's gaze. Their helpers scramble back and forth carrying sculptures, tools, curtains, ladders, canvases, wooden blocks, and jars of paint. Some carry completed pieces of art while others carry unfinished pieces. One carries a full portrait while another carries a sculptured foot. One carries the carving of a raven while another carries untouched blocks of stone. Still another wheels a podium across the floor space. As the area begins to look ready, they continue to scramble this way and that, little white mice in a new glass cage scurrying back and forth to make their new home, feeling out the interior, taking a little away here, adding a little bit there.

A small group of people has already gathered towards the side of the arena to hear the various musical artists who have already begun to play, simply fiddling on their instruments, bringing each to a fine tune. The sea of bobbing heads almost correlates with the musical emphasis towards the beginning of each measure. The entire scene is most interesting since the Posteriorians have increased the music experience to its fullest height, supplying a full 12 notes within each octave, with each of the additional five holding its own sharps and flats. Further, each artist is placed in elaborate settings most probably designed by the artists themselves. Bela Fleck begins on his eight-stringed banjo with the flight of a cosmic hippo circling above. Ween is there too, performing symphonic arrangements in a harmony submerged within an ocean full of teeming marine wildlife; purple mollusks crawl on the ocean floor while jellyfish float above like a gang of pink marshmallows taking a stroll across a high wire. The Flaming Lips hit the ground running with their dancing balls, glitter and glam, with bunnies, ducks, and bears dancing on stage, *such a spectacle!* like Willy Wonka's factory drunk on chocolate. The Posteriorian dancers hardly fit in their bunny suits, bellies flopping up and down with their laughter, often ripping through their bunny skin entirely, only bringing more laughter from the entranced audience still forming below. Smoke is rising and flames are dancing; all is happening and the laughter does not stop.

Finally, the most recent and well respected musical artist in the land, the old weathered man Mr. Sufjan Stevens begins to play his oboe to the now suddenly hushed crowd gathered beneath Sufjan's floating feet, a wooden stick compensating for a leg he lost many years ago. His black worn fingers play methodically yet naturally, his forehead creased like leather, furrowed in concentration under long white hair of snow. He seems to float above the crowd and they gaze up to see the ghost blow a melody from his broken lips about his love that left him, and asking others not to pass him by in his misery:

From the Shoreline of My Heart,
I Never Thought She'd Depart
Leaving Traces of Paper Behind Her.

I Watch Her Swim Through Her Saltwater Tears;
She Ran Away From our Years
As I Scream to People Sailing By On This Ocean:

Don't Put Your Head Into The Ground

So Goodbye Realm of Absolute
And Hello Temperance and Change
I Never Thought That I Would Come Back Here

In This Dark Vulnerable and Cold
Another Wavering Light
To This Other, Don't Pass Me,

Don't Put Your Head Into The Ground.

Sufjan came to Lyceum some time ago and people are just starting to hear about him now. He is the most mysterious of the artists here today, but has become the most anticipated, the most awed artist of all. It is said he has traveled to every province, every state on this here planet, upon just one foot with only the clothes on his back (and the few blankets, pots, and pans carried on the back of his goat Winston), and has written songs dedicated to every people while he was in their province. Now he roams the Lyceumean grounds, sometimes disappearing for extended periods of time to return as if he had never left, hobbling around on his wooden leg, a real Kerouac figure, a Billy goat pounding out elaborate Mozartian sonatas as he hops from mountain to mountain behind the falling sun.

Of course, no one notices the other special visitor here today. The evil one. The one who shall not be named now. Even I have trouble seeing him at times, as he slips from shadow to shadow like a poisonous snake. It was easier to follow him even just a few hundred years ago, when his strength and cunning were not yet fully realized. Yet even these days he will occasionally make carefully selected appearances, his thin long fingers venturing out of the dark corners where no one wants to look.

Posteriorian helpers scramble through the tunnels of the arena like hundreds of working ants hustling to and fro. One of them runs down a tunnel towards the center of the arena, a large bundle of colored confetti wrapped in his arms like a present. He does not notice the hand reaching from the shadows until it grabs him by the throat, jerking him off his feet and into the darkness, leaving nothing but a curious cloud of floating confetti in his place.

ΩΨΩ

Joachim laughs to the crowd before him and the crowd laughs back.

"How do you feel?" Joachim begins. Some cheers are heard from the front, but most of the crowd is engaged in their own fantastical dreams.

"I said," Joachim raises his voice, "*How do you feel?*"

The crowd erupts in a cheer forcing the nearby trees to shake off their leaves.

"Good," Joachim smiles. He takes a deep breath, and raises his hands to the sky.

"Ahhh....what do I see here before me? As I look into your faces, my good friends, faces of young and old, of man and woman, of dreamer and poet, I see a beautiful garden before me. Yes, El Totsira, son of Rekha, Blessed is He, once said that every Posteriorian, each and every one of us, is a small seedling that grows as time goes on, with every new experience that the seedling has. Each of us, He said, is born empty, but as a small seedling that sprouts into a beautiful flower. We are all flowers. And as I look out across this sea of heads, today, my friends, I see the most lovely and vivacious garden the eye has ever seen!"

The crowd cheers once again. Renee stands to clap with his brother, but his mind is awhirl. *I am a flower??* he thinks, *What source is that based on? What does that even mean?*

"Gather," Joachim continues, "that's it, gather Posteriorian nation. Gather we must, for we are here today to witness a dueling of the masters, a fighting of the creators, a war of canvas versus stone, of brush versus blade, and most importantly, a marriage of a nation always together." Joachim pauses briefly, just long enough for people to take in the scene and the commencement of the proceedings. By now everyone has settled into their respective places and the artists' workers have abandoned the inner plaza now completed and vacant so the artists to enter and exhibit their work. Sensors settle into their new places ready to record any words that may be spoken. Joachim clears his throat and looks at Helene. She smiles at him and he smiles back while turning to the crowd, the smile remaining on his lips. He raises his hands to regain attention.

"How have we all been *feeling?*" Joachim laughs at the crowd's applause at that honorable word, "Ha ha! We are all to be proud of the purpose we are here today, belonging to such a nation that I see here in front of my own two eyes. As a Posteriorian myself, I must say that all of us have come here for an experience. We have come here for what we have learned in our Posteriorian past, to make a

Posteriorian present, to create precedent for our Posteriorian future, and for that, I must say I am proud."

The people offer a small cheer that dies quickly, overcome with the desire to hear more words of praise.

"We belong to a nation, a most colorful, active nation, a nation who constantly tithes, farms, and builds. We work to dig through experience with smiles on our faces, finding the jewels in the rough. We are a nation who continuously seeks, filters, and modifies, separating the good from the bad, a nation not scared of crawling through obscurity, crashing heads with the uncertain or the fallible, and wrestling with the unknown in hope of discovering but a small wreath of truth onto which we can grasp. We are a nation that does not let anything pass us by, a nation brave enough to consider every thing in front of it, all evidence in any form, all scientific phenomena from which it can induce constant conjunctions of similar happenings, all architectural speculations though half of them may fail, crumbling beneath our mortal feet. We are a nation not scared to admit that its past efforts may have been for naught, not allowing that to deter us from regaining its ground to try once again. We belong to a nation not scared of brushing shoulders with the mysterious, dirtying its hands in the sea of doubt, always set upon the most worthy task of distinguishing the credible from the lesser, the winner from the loser. We are a nation crawling through tunnels of the darkest degree, with smiles upon our faces and the small light at the end upon our focus. We are a nation who understands that the joy of any journey is not what may come from its completion, but rather from the journey itself. We are a nation," Joachim pauses for effect, "fumbling towards ecstasy, an ecstasy that we reach today in the presence of ourselves."

Cheers rise from the people, and Joachim raises his hands to quiet the crowd.

"But that is not all. Make no mistake, our mission does not stop outside the walls of this theatre; our mission is still with us, always with us, no matter where we may go. Indeed, this nation that I speak of is here today with yet another mission upon its table. Our artists have come from the five corners of Lyceum and beyond, to bring us their strongest efforts, their most interesting sentiments made tangible, carved through stone, signed upon canvas, placed upon a silver platter and given to you to enjoy. So settle down, settle down in your seat and open your ears, your eyes, yourselves to the wealth of experience that will be put forth before you today. I hope everyone slept well last night, because we have much to sift through today; I have been told myself that our artists have brought all our Posteriorian bellies can handle."

Some giggles could be heard from the crowd present as they shuffle to get comfortable in their seats, to finally quiet down for the show.

ΩΨΩ

A Posteriorian helper feels the cold, dead fingers of his worst nightmare wrapped around his throat. He tries not to think of this thing that pulled him into the shadows so quickly. He forces his eyes shut, but he can imagine the ghost behind them.

"Open them," it says. The Posteriorian tries to breath, but gags on the demon's grip. The demon loosens his grip, and the Posteriorian inhales. He coughs on the foul stench of death. He tries to pull away, but the demon also has a tight grip on his wrist. Finally, he catches his breath and looks up, into the face of his captor.

To his surprise, he sees the friendly colored face of a fellow Posteriorian, his eyes a crystal blue, his cheeks as rosy red as his robes. *But he did not look that way before. Did he?* The helper realizes he never saw the other. He relaxes at the stranger's smile. But the man seems hunched over, almost awkward, as if he is going to great trouble to act in this way. The man pulls his colored robes tightly around him, as if he is not used to them. Still, the warmth in his eyes is overwhelmingly persuasive, and the Posteriorian prisoner feels more like a friend than ever. He forgets his troubles at once.

"Haha, you didn't have to grab me," he says, "If you want a friend—"

"A friend! Of course! Excuse me for grabbing you. I…I am just trying to find my way around…" the man seems to speak without moving his immense grin, his red cheeks twirling like a raspberry swirl.

"A—around?" the Posteriorian's fear returns to his stomach, "I can tell you how to go."

"Thank you," the stranger loosens his grip on the Posteriorian's wrist. But he does not let go. "I knew I could count on you."

"Haha," the Posteriorian forces a nervous laugh, "Of course."

"Good. Now. I am looking for the storage room."

"The storage room?"

"Where the art is kept. The art that will be shown today in the contest."

"The art room?"

"Tell me where it is."

"But that…that is not where the spectators go. I can show you…"

"No!" the man tightens his grip on the helper's wrist once again, "I want to go to the art room. I am looking for something there. Something special."

"Okay, but that room is…is not allowed...I mean, the King told me…."

"Tell me now!" A soft red fire simmers behind the warm blue of the man's eyes. The helper stares in fascination. But he does not want that fire to come any closer.

"It…the room is over there, under the center of the arena. The piece you are looking for will be there. Just take this tunnel down further under the arena. Now, if you will please let go of me—"

But in one lightning stroke, the man whips his colored robes off, revealing the blackest cape underneath. Now the helper can see the demon's white hands, five long claws protruding like crude needles infecting everything they touch. The helper glances down in horror, but sees the demon's grip on his wrist spread a pale deathly white upon his skin. It is his worst fear, what every Posteriorian dreads, the lack of color, of pure white, vacancy, death upon his skin. The whiteness spreads towards his elbow as the demon squeezes his arm, the burning of cold fire paralyzing his entire being. But it is the demon's face *that face* that pushes his horror into an explosion of sheer insanity, impeding the helper's speech for the rest of his short life.

Without realizing how or why, the helper sees his hand open before the demon, the shiny golden key lying in his palm.

"The key," he hears himself say.

"Why, thank you," the demon smiles, "You shouldn't have," and he snatches the key for himself.

The red fire simmering in the stranger's eyes before is completely aflame now, two writhing torches blazing like hot embers. Deathly white skin is stretched over his face like wet paper almost showing the bone beneath it. But it is the scar on his face that remains in the helper's memory far after the demon disappears, darting down into the tunnels like a rabid bat, feeding on the dumb rainbow of those around him as the cheers welcoming the artists to the stage thunder up in the arena above.

ΩΨΩ

The great Betzalel goes first, delivering an enormous transparent splash, an explosion of colored glass held in suspense above a pale green triangle base that seems to support the work, bringing out its rapid motion through the contrast of its stillness. The sensual orange and purple splash takes it for granted, riding atop its raw subordination, enjoying its own lavish celebration. The people cheer satisfyingly. Second, Mr. Sufjan performs a final piece and it is as beautiful as expected. Third, Drewgon Medusa raises his arm and opens his fingers wide as streaks of flame dart out of their tips, igniting a flurry of painted sheep's wool lying next to the naked sheep the wool had come from, frozen in mid-run, icicles dripping off its bare pink body.

Finally, Mr. Mojo Risin arrives on the scene all dressed in orange. He is carried into the arena encased inside of a large pile of wax through which he breaks, celebrating his freedom from the plain looking wax locking him in. He celebrates his freedom by dancing violently with long ribbons of yellow and green wrapped around his wrists, flowing from his ankles as he romps around, occasionally turning to the wax and kicking it in anger before continuing his joyful, random dance of rapid motion. This brings great laughs from the people, a relief after the intense displays of the past hour.

One by one, other artists bring forth their best efforts, their works of paint and their works of glass. Oranges, blues, violets dominate the scene. Bright yellows dance around their source: shining harps, tables, oblong spherical entities that never stay the same for more than a transient moment. Always moving, changing, each piece has a dance of its own, a swaying, drifting, a slow transformation taking in the presence of the large crowd, reacting to their sentiments, bending to their moods like a ballerina, a lone figurine gracefully dodging the bullets of light sprinting to illuminate her slim figure. The artistic works reach out to the audience, and they reach back collectively, fully feeding back their fervent enthusiasm line for line, note for note.

ΩΨΩ

As the show proceeds, Renee and Dewey watch continually enthralled by the artist's tactics of presentation adorned with obvious talent. Dewey is especially enjoying himself, gorging on the sensual feast of experience set before him. The artists' dances are mirrored in his little-boy Posteriorian eyes held wide open beneath a blonde mop of hair, never missing a scene. Joachim's attention matches that of the boys', passively absorbing every motion, sound, and smell as fast as the sensors' hands continue to move, their feather pens dabbling this way and that.

But as the day goes on and the sun begins to reach the top of its arch, Renee's eyes begin to wander. He begins to observe the crowd, Posteriorian after Posteriorian in seat after seat, row after row, each a mask equally exhibiting a façade of passive intoxication. He overhears the men's drunken voices, their hairy chests hanging out like their boastful tongues, now volleying a game of words.

"How do you feel?" Renee hears one man say to another.

"How do I feel?"

"How do you feel?"

"I've been feeling pretty excited recently. My ability to feel's pretty good. And today, I feel extremely—"

"Ha ha! Isn't this great?"

Renee studies the thousands of gaping mouths, the rows of yellow teeth, the pattern of lolling tongues, and aisle after aisle filled to the brim with the cotton candy, hot dogs, and ice creams of experience. Suddenly, he realizes what has been bothering him all along, what had been itching him since he had woken up that morning, *that itch,* the spot that can never be scratched.

Everyone looks empty.

Everyone has displayed open mouths, open ears, and hanging jaws, but all the while, everyone looked dead. The masks become thinner and thinner until completely diluting to transparent form, revealing no life underneath. Suddenly, the people *behind* the masks are gone, so that all that is left are masks. Masks are all they are. *How could people experiencing so much life be so dead at the very same time?* Renee secretly wonders. *So...empty?*

ΩΨΩ

Artist after artist, each continues taking their turn, arriving on the scene in the most intriguing of manners and often leaving without a trace. Finally, the time arrives for Olegna Lechim to perform. Olegna is one of the greatest sculptures of the time, a young man who came here from far far away running from the life he held and the beatings he was forced to endure.

Olegna was raised on a small farm by his mother Francesca and his father Lodovico di Simoni, who had always owned a marble quarry. Olegna grew up carving stone from the very beginning, from the moment he left his mother's womb. Indeed, he has been said to have sucked in chisels and hammers with his mother's milk. Lodovico did not approve of this; he wanted a better life for his only son.

In his frustration towards his child's stubborn desire to sculpt, Lodovico beat his son relentlessly, once almost slashing off the poor child's hands entirely after he was caught cleaning a fresh sliver of marble just carved into a brilliant stallion. Lodovico shouted angrily, kicking the child's hands into the marble. 'You wanna create?' he would shout, 'You wanna create and *be somethin?* Then this isn't for you. There's a whole world out there,' he would shout, his face red, pointing in any direction he could find, as if the whole world emerged at the tip of his finger, 'there's a whole world out there just waiting, and *this* is what you gotta do...' He usually quieted down after a bit of soothing from Francesca to turn quickly and march away, muttering a trail of obscenities after every rapid step.

Francesca would always tend to the child's wounds, rapidly but lovingly like a mother bird tending to her young. Quickly and carefully, she would take her son's small fingers in her own, rubbing cool ointment upon his red cracked knuckles, crumbling fresh leaves upon his heated skin. She would stay with him as long as it took, only implicitly encouraging him to follow his dreams even if that meant leaving the farm.

But Olegna was just a boy and he did not want to leave his belongings behind, the vast garden of marble masterpieces he himself had created with his own two hands. At night he would sit for hours and hours watching the moonlight leak in through the rotting wooden rafters, washing over his cool marble creations, slowly bringing them to life. As the moon traveled overhead, an owl's marble eye would blink at him, a young fawn would raise its small granite head, ceasing mid-drink to gaze his way, all with the change of the light. The moon's orbit was the engine and the marble the exhibit. He would sit back night after night and enjoy his show, a show he himself had created so his works could please him, sing for him, worship him in the stone cold solitude from which they were forged.

He became possessive, almost *obsessed* with his title over them, feeling they are all he ever had, the only things that were truly *his* that no one, not even Lodovico, could ever take away from him.

One night, after a terrible beating that his mother was not permitted to remedy, Olegna had fled from the farm. Leaving the only life he knew, he vowed to return again and reclaim his possessions of marble, his creations of stone. Still a young child, he left his farm and found his way to Lyceum where he was taken under the wing of the great Posteriorian sculptor Lorenzo De Medici. As the boy grew older and his confidence grew with the strength in his arms, Lorenzo was always there. Yes, it was Lorenzo who taught him how to shape life with more passion, how to sculpt beings with more motion, how to make his creations *live* without the need for light. It was only with Lorenzo's guidance that Olegna had been able to enter the art contest we now observe.

Olegna's story is an interesting one, a story in its own right, one that may be told on its own. His story is one we will return to, as it is worth telling. However, we are at an art contest now, and our crowd is waiting.

ΩΨΩ

Olegna Lechim enters the scene of the arena, his helpers pulling a cart behind him. The burden is obviously heavy and the helpers truly strained; they stroll out stiffly with slow, well-balanced steps, sweating profusely as they wheel the large cart forward under the hot sun. The people clap and quickly settle down so that by the time Olegna has circled the inner plaza to arrive at its center, everyone is silent.

"Ladies and gentleman," Olegna shouts loudly, albeit sounding as if he has rehearsed this many times before. Before him stands his work of art, almost ten feet tall, covered in a shroud. Olegna grasps a corner of the shroud. "I bring you no mortal today. No," he continues smiling as if in possession of a secret knowable to only him, "No, I will not waste your time with carvings of mere animals who roam the dirt of the earth driven by blind instinct. Further, I bring no ordinary man who has just enough knowledge to understand how much of an animal he really is. Rather, I bring you wisdom, justice, and piety. Rather I bring you knowledge, kindness, and godliness. Ladies and gentlemen, I bring you my own rendition of...*Elllll Totsira!*" and with that, Olegna pulls at the veil. It slips off easily like a blue knit slipper from a baby's foot. Before him stands a large slab of marble Olegna intended to be his creation. It stands tall, naked in horror at its under-developed body so unexpectedly exposed at the pull of a veil.

The stone is completely blank, never touched by human hands.

The entire crowd gasps in horror as Olegna's face radically twists from proud contentment to heated confusion.

"Wha—" Olegna chokes on his own voice, struggling, grasping at verbal straws, "This, this is not right. Something is wrong. El Tots—El Tots—El Totsira is *gone*. All those hours, all those nights, gone to what?" he begins to stammer, reeling to his knees, completely losing control of himself in his forced dance before the crowd. Tears streak down his cheeks and he falls to the ground whimpering beneath the observers' heavy gaze.

After a few minutes pass, Olegna regains his footing as anger begins to enter his heart. "This was *mine!*" he exclaims like a child after a lollipop is seized from his groping hands, "No one can take this from me—it is mine, mine, *MINE!*" The crowd falls silent. Olegna pauses. He looks down at his feet and clears his throat, "I had sculpted the most beautiful, the most exquisite rendition of the great Posteriorian prophet," he looks up, inspecting the crowd with now tear-stained eyes, "the greatest king mankind has ever known, and now he is gone. He has been taken, yes, taken away from me when my eyes were closed!"

The crowd stares back dumbly, as if in a monotonous lecture. A soft buzz begins to rise. Olegna looks back, hurt. *Doesn't anybody hear me? Doesn't anybody CARE?* He begins to feel a cry coming on when he notices an onlooker turning his back to the passionate scene.

Indeed, a tall man turns sharply from the stands and begins to march confidently to the exit. As his robe blows in the wind, Olegna spots the corner of a black garment underneath. Olegna tries to see who he is, but his face hides behind his upturned collar. Before the onlooker can leave, Olegna shouts in his direction. "You there! You don't turn your back on me! Not like this, not when my creation has been taken from me!" But the onlooker walks on, ignoring Olegna's cries of anger. Finally, the artist raises his arm, and, pointing at the fading onlooker, he shouts, "You! It was you, wasn't it? It was you that stole my creation. It was you that took it out from under my eyes! You secretly replaced it with this, this, this raw slab of concrete you would have me call my work! You—you *stole* it from me!"

Finally, the figure stops in his tracks. He slowly lowers his hood and wipes off his colored robes, revealing the black underneath. The people gasp. He turns around to reveal his fire-scarred face. The face looks familiar. It is a face of sorrow, a face of longing for a past too long forgotten. It is a face that hides years of tumultuous wandering and pain behind its thin white veil. A face the whole crowd recognizes at once, and they gasp in unison at the sight of such a thing.

A face everyone here knows all too well.

ΩΨΩ

It is Disegno, the fastest tongue in all of Lyceum. All the people know who he is and they all fear his snide tongue that hides behind his purple hood; they know him as the unofficial jokester of the Grandee, the wandering poet of the nation, the blathering fool of the region. All scorn him behind his back though their mockeries stop when he passes in the street. All make fun and ridicule while his eyes are turned but shrink back in fear when he looks their way. They do so because they know that he could make a toad seem a horse, a boil seem a pie, all with his power of words. He can spit out semantics that convince in probity and rip through rhymes that shock in gravity. Indeed, if he wanted, he could insult as to make people go mad, completely turning on themselves in self-disgust, scratching at their chest and face, trying to make themselves disappear.

While Disegno's origin is in much dispute, many say that over a hundred years ago, he was the official jester for the Grandee of Lyceum. His life was good and the Grandee favored him in his green and yellow suits, his jingly bell hats, the funny walk he would exhibit about the palace. His face was always painted many colors so that no one ever really saw what he looked like, but they didn't care for he was what he was to them, a clown and nothing more. And this was enough for everyone, since he was a good clown *a true wizard of Oz* and he made the people laugh. And unfortunately, that which makes people laugh, that which makes people *comfortable,* is rarely ever probed for its reality.

However, one day in between the songs he would regularly perform for his Majesty, Disegno was juggling while standing upon one foot, blowing fire this way and that. The Grandee's concubines were lying around the Majesty's throne as they often would, striding back and forth with their fruit, their bathing oils, and their fans. They would alternate positions, some strolling over to fan or feed his Highness while others posed in the shade nearby.

However, one precious morning, Disegno had allowed himself a Posteriorian breakfast of fruit, wheat crumplings, oranges, and crème. In less than seven minutes he had eaten over three platefuls. He did not know why he awoke so specially hungry, nor do I. While everyone can agree that this eerie hunger had changed the history of the kingdom, whether it was chance or fate, coincidence or destiny, well, that too must be left for you to decide.

The fact is that while he was juggling fire in front of the great throne, he held one flame behind his back as he stretched to catch a fiery rod he had thrown high up into the air. As he stood up on one foot to catch it, he had flatulated so loud, a passing of air in such great quantity that the Grandee himself was stunned. He grasped the arms on each side of his throne. As the smell of rancid fruit filled the corridor, Disegno screamed as the fiery rod landed, striking him in the side of the face. Furthermore, his flatulence had ignited a great flame from the torch held behind his back that had lit the hair of a mistress who had been passing by at that very moment. This was the favorite mistress of the Grandee. The mistress ran away screaming, all red flames behind her, where she ran into a column blunting her beautiful face forever.

Disegno did not need to be exiled, for he fled as fast as his long chicken legs would take him even before the Grandee could recover from shock. However, he had unexpectedly returned to the Posteriorian kingdom sometime afterward, arriving with a hood that covered his burnt-scarred face and a tongue that had to compensate for his loss in looks, a tongue much sharper than the likes this nation had ever seen. Yes, he had returned, at least most people thought this was really him. He had returned approximately one hundred and twenty years later, though he looked as if he had aged a mere twenty years. No one knew where he went nor what happened to him, but he was different. His face was not painted as before but rather was a pale blanket of white with a smooth pink scar alongside its side. The scar would sometimes bubble up as it had when it was first burnt into his face; it would bubble up when he would get mad, turning different shades of maroon, salmon, and pink as if correlating with the rhymes he spoke. While his face had paled, his walk had stiffened, and his tongue had grown snider, there was something in him that would never change.

He would never touch fruit again.

ΩΨΩ

The heads of the crowd shift to the stands like millions of multi-colored seashells turning with the tide of the sea. The ocean of Posteriorian faces all point in the same direction towards the lone figure in the stands. After being caught abandoning the artist in his worst woes, the figure had stopped mid-way up the aisle, and has begun to turn his head. As Disegno slowly turns his head, all the people in the arena shrink back, waiting to hear him speak. Olegna, however, hardly gives him the chance.

"I beseech you, do not turn your back on me while I—"

"You beseech *what?*" Disegno does not need to raise his voice to cut the young artist off. His words come out in a violent whisper, like the sounds of an angry snake. "You beseech what, you young coward, you stand there quivering, yet you know not what you lost."

"What?!" Olegna seems to look past the figure, as if scared to look right in Disegno's eyes. "I know *exactly* what I lost. I spent many a night leaned over that block of stone, carving, smoothing, perfecting—," Olegna tries to hide the emotion in his voice, "for hours, I—my God, you have no idea, I carved a beautiful rendition of the great El Totsira, from this stone I brought out life, all with my own bare hands. I brought it out myself, when you, old man, well, you could hardly hold onto a fiery staff if it hit you in the face."

The crowd gasps at such a remark, but Disegno remains calm and his green eyes focus on the quivering lips of the young artist. He actually smiles.

"You just said it yourself."

Olegna stays still, nervous that he may have said too much. What is it? *What did I say? A fiery staff? Hit you in the face? That did happen, didn't it? I've heard that it—"*

"You brought it out," Disegno does not let Olegna finish his thoughts.

"Excuse me?" the young artist becomes curious.

"You brought it out, out of the stone. You said that yourself," Disegno explains, "You brought life out of the marble, but that is all you did."

"That is all, you say? What else would you have me do? You, you probably couldn't even—"

"Shut that mouth, child. You miss the point completely, so listen and learn. You did not create anything *new*," he smiles mockingly, "You did not create as Rekha once did; no, my son, you are no such artist. In fact, you did not create anything at all. Rather you took what was already created, already lying within the stone, and you merely set it free. With the turn of a scalpel, you merely unlocked the life inside. And now, you come to display another's work as your own. And now, you stand here today, crying 'mine, mine, mine,' when nothing is really even yours. You call yourself an artist when you are merely a messenger. And worst of all, you bring us all here today to witness a creation that is not really a new creation at all, but rather something that has always been."

Disegno pauses for a moment as the young Olegna hides his face, his deep sobs apparent through his shuddering shoulders, rising and falling upon the slow crumbling of his knees. By now, he is almost at a full crouch, as if bowing down to the weight of the crowd, to the words of the poet. But Disegno goes on.

"Just like the souls in our bodies, El Totsira's form lies in the stone. And like the souls in our bodies, the shape you claim to have so carefully crafted lies inside that marble. The stone seems raw right now, but it is no different than how it was right after you finished toying with it; see, your 'art' still lies within it; nothing has been taken away, you fool, and nothing has been given back. Now it is trying to teach you that itself. It may change faces, altering its appearance temporarily, but one must not be fooled. You, however, are fooled. Well, let me tell you now, you are no artist, Olegna Lechim, you are no artist at all, so unless you can tell us how such a carving can ever be a creation of *yours*, you can just turn around and go home."

Everyone remains silent as Olegna rises to his feet and slowly gathers his belongings now strewn around the dirty plaza. His helpers have abandoned him just as Disegno began to speak. Now, they slowly walk towards their master from the wall against which they cringed during the debate. Olegna tries to swat them away but he is too weak, too defeated to raise his voice. The best he can do is to push their helping hands away as they reach towards him in a feeble attempt to aid. Olegna begins to walk away from the plaza leaving half his belongings behind, as a small voice emerges from the other side of the immense crowd.

"From his labor," the voice seems to say. Olegna stops in his tracks, though no one else seems to pay heed.

"From his labor," the voice repeats. The Posteriorian crowd turns to acknowledge the voice, seeing it inviting as an oasis of confidence in a vast desert of doubt. Their gaze joins that of Olegna's, full of curiosity and of hope, though more of the former than the latter. The small voice continues to speak.

"It is from his carving, kind sir, his hard work and his labor, that he holds ownership in the piece."

It is at these words, *kind sir,* that Disegno is forced to look the voice's way. After being ridiculed as a joke for years, those words *kind sir* makes his head turn in pleasurable servitude to the voice.

Everybody's gaze turns to a boy hardly seven years of age. *That boy.* The boy pales in the shadow of his tall father, *to be born again*, but stands upon his small two feet and speaks of labor, *first you have to die. That boy!* The boy slowly rises, crawling up onto his chair. He stands at full stature, his soft chin raised proudly in the warm afternoon air. To Disegno's amusement and eventual fury, the boy begins to explain himself in a less than humble manner.

"You listen here mister Egno, this Olegna has earned title to his creation, so you mustn't turn his troubles away." The boy's father, a well-known country lawyer, begins to stand up to stop his son from speaking, but then thinks the better of it. Seeing the attention of Disegno now caught on his son, he realizes unless he wants to join the show, he is already too late to stop his son's mouth from saying what it will.

"Every man has a property in his own person, and nobody has a right to this but himself. Of this law everyone is aware, for we have all lived by it even before mere human conventions were formed, though many of you may have not noticed. However, I must say I am surprised that you, Disegno," the small boy says, turning to the shocked clown, "of all people, would overlook such an obvious matter."

Some in the crowd dare to laugh at the jester. But before letting another moment pass, Disegno struggles to hold his ground.

"So here we have another child, another child too young to have experienced the years that build knowledge—"

"Your words offer hardly more than atmospherics, my elder, and if you do not know the dangers of judging words only by the age of their speaker, this is a true shame. Do not judge me by my size, or I can assure you, you will be sadly disappointed. And none of this changes the facts: Olegna has taken months of effort and strain to combine the labor of his living hands with something as foreign to them as cold, lifeless stone."

"Yes, but he had—"

"—and it may be that he had merely removed a creation from the state that nature has provided for it, but that is of no matter," the boy does not allow Disegno any ground, "for as long as he has mixed his labor with, and joined to it something that is not his own, it thereby becomes his property."

The boy makes sense, and the crowd seems to enjoy his clever reasoning. Disegno attempts to lash back, but the boy matches him word for word, fire for fire, until much of the crowd are up out of their seats, straining to hear every word spoken, not letting any sound escape their open ears. Disegno has never seen such steadfast enthusiasm, reasoning so logical and delivered with so much ease, tinged with a flavorful pinch of youthful simplicity.

As the debate ensues, Dewey sees a smile form on Renee's lips as he sits back listening to the oral dialogue that had just become so heated. It pains Dewey to see such senseless fighting, such fierce debate striving to capture such permanent truths of property. Dewey tries to follow the characters' reasoning but his thoughts hurt like rocks rolling around his head.

Dewey studies his brother's enjoyment, bothered that he cannot enjoy it himself. The fierce dialogue continues to disturb him, and he does not understand why everyone has to be so *sure* of things. *Why does everyone have to be so certain? Instead of arguing if the water is safe, just dive into it, experience, and you will learn from your mistakes. If you err, just pick up and go from there!* He studied Disegno's seriousness, the debating child's furrowed brow. *Do they really care that much? Must everyone strive for such...perfection?*

Renee, on the other hand, is celebrating the oral debate. He absorbs every word, swimming in the verbal ping-pong game, following the erratic tide of words, of sentences, jerking back and forth and back and forth, slowly chipping away at the colorful atmospherics of experiential chatter, striving to ultimately reveal a sturdy foundation underneath, permanent principals of reason, a mere beginning from which man can perhaps begin know what real property is, what it really means to *own* something.

But the crowd begins to lose patience, and they begin to shift this way and that. Joachim realizes that the show must continue, so he orders Disegno temporarily seized for suspicion of thievery of Olegna's missing art. Since Posteriorians like to act at the present moment and think about their actions later, Disegno is grabbed and held until the end of the show until a time when they can meet and discuss as they often do, and finally, hopefully, decide what to do with the poor captured clown.

ΩΨΩ

The show continues until there is nothing left to see. The crowd sits back, apparently satisfied from their experiential feast, exhaustion in their eyes, some hands resting behind their heads, others on their round Posteriorian bellies. Joachim begins to balance the odds, weighing the merits of all that he has seen, though his sensors' hands seem to move faster than his mind. He rules with a confidence, a façade surely not seen often in any Posteriorian land, and this brings the people great comfort.

The erratic dance of Mr. Mojo Risin wins first place. It has brought roars of laughter from the people and made Joachim smile himself. Sufjan and Betzalel follow in second, though Drewgon does not come in until fourth. The credits roll on, though this is not much of our concern. Rather, I direct you to focus on a conversation that is taking place toward the exit of the arena, a conversation that will bind a continual friendship, a companionship that will last throughout its character's lives and change the events of this story forever.

ΩΨΩ

After the show ends, Joachim keeps thinking about the debate that has taken place. He is much impressed with the players involved *that boy* and is hoping he can make something of it or at least understand what it was all about. While everyone makes their hasty exit in search of more excitement, Joachim catches up with the boy that has so bravely protected the artist Olegna. When the boy first sees the old judge's tall figure approaching, his instinct is to run away, but he gains control of himself, takes a step back, and grasps his father's hand. But he is still surprised at what he sees, for *what does royalty want with a small child like myself?* he thinks. *So, I had a few good comments. So would anyone after a twelve hour sleep and a few—"*

"What is your name, child?" Joachim begins.

"Rasaa, sir. Le Jocke Rasaa," the boy seems a bit confused, a big difference from the confidence he had shown earlier, "but, uh, most people just call me Jon."

"You sounded pretty impressive out there, today, Mr. Rasaa, wouldn't you say?"

"Thank you very much," the boy is blushing. From a few feet away, it looks almost humorous the way Joachim's seven foot figure towers over the little boy like an old street lamp watching a dwarf stroll by below.

"I'd like to borrow you for a few minutes," Joachim looks up towards the boy's father, "Of course, only with the permission of your old man here."

The lawyer nods his head, releasing his boy's hand in the direction of Joachim the Great. He assures them he will be waiting outside the plaza gate, and they may take their time as they please.

Jon explains what he was trying to say in the inner plaza. As Joachim listens patiently, his warm smile puts Jon at ease. The two speak for what seems like hours, but I do not hear what they are saying. No, I am focused on someone else entirely, namely, Dewey. Dewey's eyes never leave the two figures huddled so close, one looming so closely over the other as if the shorter one is not surrendering, but rather supporting the old man's frame. Dewey always thought of *himself* as his father's supporter, and his heart begins to beat against the ribs protecting his chest. He watches in both jealousy and amazement as the strange boy's words take his father by a storm, almost awakening him to the laws of property, a subject that has never entered Joachim's mind in the past. For this Dewey hates Jon.

Dewey knows he hates this Jon, but on a much deeper level, he feels something else entirely. He sees the boy's enthusiasm, how he is able to twist and wind his thesis to refute all other points Disegno had made, but all the while, keeping his main idea firm, never letting it go. He thinks of how useful the boy could be if allowed into his kingdom, into his home. He imagines how great of a friend, how powerful an enemy this boy could become if given the chance.

3

I have but one lamp by which my feet are guided, and that is the lamp of experience. I know no way of judging of the future but by the past.
Edward Gibbon

Experience is simply the name we give our mistakes.
Oscar Wilde.

It is has long been said that sleep is one-sixtieth of death, no more, no less. Does this mean that while sleeping, a man only needs to live partially? Must his breaths pronounce shorter, his lungs filling less than half their capacity? Does his body get lighter as a piece of his soul departs? How much does a soul weigh? Or does it hang around, waiting to join its other half in life? Which half leaves? Which half stays? Which portion flees, and which portion dreams?

And what if he only lives half as much as he can even when he is awake? I mean, does *any* man ever really *live?*

Tonight, Dewey feels very much alive as he jumps into bed with Renee. *I guess we are sharing a room tonight,* Renee does not acknowledge his presence. Helene flounders not far behind. Dewey is still absorbing the events of the day, the songs of Sufjan, the fires of Drewgon, the venomous words of Disegno, and that boy, *that boy*, and the debate that had ensued. His thoughts keep returning to Jon, to what kind of child he was, to what kind of man he will be.

Dewey's thoughts begin to settle and the boys embrace Helene's presence as she sits on the bed beside them. It has become customary for her to read the boys to sleep, telling them stories, myths, and legends to heighten their spirits and lower their eyelids. She does this each night now, slowly swaying them off to the inviting tumbles of sleep as the moonlight swims across the room and the seasons roll on by.

She tells them stories of great and mighty warriors, of bloody battles once strewn across foreign lands. She tells of great leaders, of evil men, of loyal women. She recaptures the myths of the dwarves, the lives of the elves, the battle of the trolls. She relives spells never unbroken, prophecies that never rang true. Her hands rapidly move back and forth as she speaks, throwing rampant shadows across the walls. The shadows make images, joining the boys in their adventures. A chained beast leaps across the ceiling while hundreds of carriages stroll across the walls; an old man sits by the river near the window, while a lovely princess waits upon the door.

As any Posteriorian room, the walls here are filled with swirls of colors, dashing, sprinting, falling across the scene. The boys' toys are strewn across the colored stone floor, a maze of colored train tracks, building blocks, rainbows, and warriors. As the moon begins to show itself from behind a cloud curtain, Helene prepares to entertain the children in the moving circus already provided by the surrounding room.

Tonight Helene holds Renee's hands in her own, slowly rubbing his white palms back and forth as she steals glimpses at Dewey smiling at the other end of the bed. Joachim must be already sleeping far away in the castle, Helene guesses, his sensors standing guard upon his bed post ready for any twitch that may occur, already recording the old man's long, slow breaths echoing against the stone walls. But perhaps he is still awake, sitting at a meeting, or trying to decide what to do with Disegno's capture. But while troubles swim their way through his head, there is serenity here in the other part of the palace. There is serenity in the children's minds, and Helene is its source.

Renee Don Cartez, she calls them by their full name before putting them to sleep, *Dewey Hume*, before she tucks them in with blankets and kisses. She holds them dearly, her long golden hair tumbling over their heads, a golden river smoothly rolling over soft round boulders, encasing them from shadows, emitting a cool white spray that comforts and protects, lulling them to sleep.

She does not need to entice Dewey with her golden smooth hands or her green comforting eyes. No, she knows her tales regardless will intrigue him. Rather it is Renee she is concerned about, Renee that needs coaxing or else his mind will wander off into darker chambers and mysteries that neither Helene or Dewey would ever care to go.

She knows she could let him wander, saving her energy for Dewey, the boy who actually wants to hear what she has to say.

But that is not what a mother does.

Though Helene is not Renee's natural mother, she valiantly strives to be his mother in every other way. She loves Renee dearly, and feels sympathy towards his apparent unrest. She does not understand his discontent with her joyful entertainment, her active tales alive, as transparent as they may sometimes seem. She sees the way his mind wanders off, his head cocked to one side, his eyes closed in a solitary effort, sometimes showing strain, and deep pleasure in that strain. She sees the boy's love of his own thoughts. *Why can't he love me like that?* she wonders to herself.

ΩΨΩ

"A long long time ago, from the days forgotten by even the greatest of our nation's calendars, El Totsira The Great was conceived. However, he was born without a father. Unlike you two boys, he had no man to look up to, no father from which he could gain example. However, he was not without love, not without example completely. The boy's mother, Rekha, was a patient, compassionate woman, a woman of silent valor. Her husband Ariston left her, unaware of the life she would have inside her, a life he so badly wanted. He tried to plant life inside her time and time again, but it did not sprout. *If at first you fail,* he used to say to himself after sleeping with his wife, *try, try again. If after that you fail, give up. No use being a damn fool about it.* And he was no damn fool. But sometimes, in the end, it is only the fools that get what they want.

"So where did the child come from? But perhaps El Totsira was a child from God, since Rekha's stomach had swelled long after Ariston had left, and certainly well after her years of child bearing had passed, no less. *After fifty years of infertility, here we go!* She had spent years, crying, praying for a child, *fifty years of marriage, of prayer,* but Ariston left her, she fled from her village, and all she had was her walk down the river, *and now this.*

"Even though Ariston left her, Rekha was not without a companion, a male who could help her bring seed into the world. Of course, she could never create one as great as El Totsira all by herself. It was only through the aid of Nicomachus that she could bear such life. It was through the concerted action, the joint effort of both Rekha as a woman and Nicomachus as a man that El Totsira could come into this world.

"But enough about Rekha, since her life had destructed to be born again, at a different time, at another place." Helene glances at Dewey, "She may reappear when you need her most, when you are falling through the deep holes of philosophy, or drowning in quicksands of vanity. But one can never know when, or even if, she will be born again, so we must not waste our time engaging in fanciful speculations—"

"El Totsira, momma," Dewey interrupts, "tell us about El Totsira already." Renee can almost hear the pen strokes of the sensors crouched in the corner, quietly trying to catch all that is said.

"Oh, okay darling, I was just getting to that. Excuse me for straying." Helene is pleased at Dewey's interest, but wishes Renee would at least pretend to show more. But Renee stares at the ceiling and Helene feels her heart drop for just a moment. But she smiles at the children and continues to speak.

"El Totsira, huh? The important stuff. Okay, well, after Rekha's death, he was cared for by Nicomachus who no doubt would have raised him his entire life, but he passed on in the boy's tenth year. El Totsira was left an orphan and placed under the guardianship of his uncle, Proxenus of Atarneus. It was from Proxenus that the boy learned language, rhetoric, and poetry; it is said his mere mumblings would make Disegno's best rhymes look like utter rubbish, wherever the clown is now."

Dewey bursts into laughter and even Renee smiles, turning towards Helene in mild anticipation.

"Even before his interest in the arts emerged, the boy was a prodigy in anatomy, medicine, and biology. While he probably got these abilities from his father, it is said his scientific abilities were like none the world had ever seen. As he grew up under his uncle, he became a great scientist and doctor."

"Was he smart?" Dewey asked, more for a reaction than an answer. This time he will be more than satisfied.

"I'll tell you one thing, my son, El Totsira's mind was so great that when he sat down to study, no bird would ever dare fly over him."

"That is silly," Renee says, "Why not?"

"Well, birds would see what had happened to their little bird friends when *they* tried to do so. See, it is said that birds that flew over him while he was deep in thought or in the midst of profound scientific observation, well, they would suddenly burst into flame!"

At this, both boys' eyes open in wide fascination.

"It's true, their wings would burst into flame and plummet to the ground, sending flaming feathers flying all over the study. Most of the time, they would completely disintegrate before even reaching the ground!"

"Wow!"

Renee asks, "But...where did the fire come from? How could mental energy ignite...is this really true?"

"Yes," Dewey raises his voice, "It is true! It is awesome! Does it matter so much if it really happened? Just enjoy it. Listen."

Helene smiles, "It's all true, but let me get on with the story. Let me tell you what El Totsira had done for us. Besides starting our nation, giving us ethics, knowledge, and virtues by which to live, let me tell you what he left us.

"His birth was the beginning, the cause, of all that will be to come. It's kind of funny actually, that El Totsira was the beginning, the cause of all that is good in this nation, and it was he who taught us that all causes of things are beginnings, that we only have scientific knowledge of things when we know their cause."

"Well, what do you mean by *cause*?" Dewey asks with a touch of frustration upon his face, "You mean, of course, merely what it *just so happened* to come from."

"Precisely, but we need not talk about that now, child. But very good, I am proud of you. El Totsira taught us that causes exist by mere chance, spontaneity, or even coincidence, if you will. Simply, El Totsira's birth didn't *have to* cause this beautiful nation just as my sitting here now never *had to* cause the crease in this bed; rather, these things merely happen by chance, and continue to do so every night I sit in this here spot." Helene senses Renee's confusion and moves on in fear that his attention will soon be lost completely.

"Anyway, El Totsira not only made us live, but he told us *how* to live, how to be virtuous and ultimately attain happiness. He wrote a book called the *Nicomachean Ethics* that still teaches us how to be virtuous."

"Is that all he wrote?" Renee asks.

"No, he also wrote a divinely inspired work from the God Li, well, at least some claim it to be, but we don't read that today because it is vague and practically indecipherable. Besides, he had claimed it to be divinely inspired, and we have no strong certainty there is any such God. We don't know if there is a Creator. At least not the one El Totsira had claimed to have spoken to in the later, less...tame years of his life. Moving on—"

"Wait!" Renee protests, "but you just said that everything has a cause, and all causes are beginnings. It would follow that this world needs a cause. So why can't God be a cause, and—"

"On the contrary, my child, you must have misunderstood." A fire burns in Helene's eyes. "On the contrary, there *need* not ever be a cause, though one may come about just by chance. That is all causes are, I said, chance and spontaneity. But if we never *experience* such a cause, we cannot know it to be there." Renee does not understand, though he wishes he could. *Why would some things have causes and others not?* His mind begins to whirl. *Why must we base things off experience if experience is so...limited; we may miss some things that are here, and invent others that aren't.*

"Moving on," Helene pauses in case anyone has any objection. There is none. "So, El Totsira wrote *Nicomachean Ethics*, still studied today by many great Posteriorian scholars, and it tells us how to live virtuous lives, how to become good. This is not done by studying. It is done by *doing*. As your father said today, we are an *active* nation. So act we must, of course in the best context and with the ultimate goal in mind, so we can reach that goal and attain the Highest Good.

"El Totsira really taught us the power of observation, like we all practiced today at the art fair." Helene turns to her bag sitting on the floor by her feet. The children wait, listening to her shuffling through the bag's contents like two kids apprehensively watching Santa sift through his sack for a gift. She turns back holding two mysterious cards in her hands. She turns the larger one forward so the boys can see.

The card reads *E-X-P-E-R-I-M-E-N-T*.

"Can you read that?"

They both know how to read several words at this age, but they are delighted to see a word both of them know. Of course, they do not know that this is one of the first words taught in any Posteriorian home.

"Experiment!" the boys speak in unison.

"Good. Now do you know what it means?"

Dewey is the first to speak. "Uhm, to do things in science like, well, it means an... artificial occurrence, a reaction caused by human-made conditions."

"Well, sort of. You're getting somewhere. Watch this." Helene turns the other card over and it reads *E-N-C-E*. Finally, she places this card over the last four letters of *EXPERIMENT*, and the boys are delighted to see new word form before their eyes.

"Experience!" the boys exclaim.

"Yes, experience. That is all an experiment is, my lads, a controlled experience. In fact, it even comes from the same word! Now, experiment is derived from the word experience because that is all an experiment is: a controlled experience that can be repeated over and over again. When the experiment yields the same results each time, when the proposed cause repeatedly brings about the same effect, we can induce certain truths from the uniformity we have just experienced. For example, if we experiment with ice and experience that it is cold, we may induce that ice is cold. That is the power of induction. And this is how science works."

"El Totsira," Dewey asks Helene, "so where does the prophet come in all of this?"

"I'm glad you asked. El Totsira was the one who showed us how to arrive at these truths; he taught us this power of experience, of observation. And this power, he taught us, is not limited to science, my children. Rather, he extended it to history, psychology, language, ethics, and politics. And us? We use it every single moment, in everything we do. That is what your father does in the courtroom, as his jurors do in the courtrooms of their own minds. In fact," Helene pauses and nods her head at the two sensors hiding in the corner and scribbling away, "that is exactly what those two buggars are doing right at this moment. See, all experience in our nation is recorded so that we can learn truths from their study, and principles from their considerations. We have buildings and buildings just filled with cataloged observations from which the sensors can induce truths. If all the swans they ever see are white ones, they may induce that all swans are white. If every fire they feel is hot, then we can know that fire is hot. If all they experience following a wound is pain in its subject, they may induce that a wound *causes* pain. This is the only way to obtain knowledge.

"And the more experience we get, the stronger our truths become. That is why the sensors are here, and why they must be spread throughout the nation to collect any experience no matter how small, from the pleasure caused by a bite of cake to the pain of a woman who just lost her lover. And it is from the recordings of all this experience that our nation can reach truth. See, our nation could never function without them; we can never know of anything without our experiences of the world. The sensors bring us their experiences, and El Totsira has brought us the idea of sensors."

"But—" Renee's brow is furrowed in frustration.

"Renee?" Helene says.

"But—what happens when an experiment yields a different result?"

"What?"

"What happens when, say, someone sees a black swan? What happens the day someone experiences a cold fire?"

"Well that has never happened yet, so—"

"I know, I know. But what happens when it does? Do all of our past experiences just turn to nothing?"

Dewey laughs, "You can be so dramatic, Renee—"

"No, really. If this is it, if everything we know to be true is just based off of...some repeated instances of the same experiments over and over, then what happens when it changes? I mean, we discover new things all the time, right?"

"Yes, Renee," Helene says. The boys cannot see the repressed fire behind her cool gaze of love. "And this is why we cannot know of any absolute laws. Science can only produce theories, which change over time. It is the same with our laws, our designs, our hearts! We are constantly changing our notes, constantly learning, improving, exploring. This is no burden, it is a celebration of life! And this is what makes our people so special!"

Renee opens his mouth to speak, "But—" but his thoughts crowd his head. *But there has to be a better way, an underlying principle that does not change. There must be an unchanging anchor upon which these truths can be based, a permanent foundation beyond our confused experience. There must be—*

"What is it, Renee?" Helene asks.

There must be something more.

"Nothing," Renee hears himself say.

Helene continues to describe the events of the prophet's life, how El fought terrible hardships, conquered vicious foes, and wooed attractive women. As many other mothers in the city at that moment, she recounts how he formed the Posteriorian nation hundreds of years ago. She relates how he celebrated shortly after becoming king by partying in his kingdom for six years straight, how his face glowed so great with light that after the second year he was forced to don a mask since all who saw him went crazy with pleasure or died wriggling on the stone floor beneath his feet.

She continues speaking for hours, until the moon is fully risen and the boys begin to fall asleep. Finally, she pulls in close to kiss Renee to sleep.

Renee looks up the Helene's face just as she kisses him on the nose. Something catches his interest, something he has never noticed before. Renee finds that if he relaxes his eyes as he looks at Helene's face from so close, he sees that her eyes overlap, one on top of the other, and it looks as if Helene has only one large, gaping eye. But Renee knows she is not really this way; it is his sight deceiving him. He begins to wonders why it tricks him, but tries not to think about it.

"Thank you," Renee says, waiting for Helene to back away. When she does, Renee finds that her eyes return to the way they were: two separate eyes on either side of her head.

"Go to sleep," Helene whispers so she does not awaken Dewey.

Dewey will never forget what Helene told him that night. No, he will never forget his mother's two cards, his mother's lesson, and neither will Renee. Indeed, Renee Don Cartez will remember Helene's lesson about experience for as long as he will live, no matter how hard he will try to forget.

But oh how he will try.

4

It is a maxim among these lawyers, that whatever hath been done before may legally be done again: and therefore they take special care to record all decisions formerly made against common justice and the reason of mankind.
Jonathan Swift

We believe that Roe should be overruled. The majority opinion are of the view that the precedential force must be accorded to its holding. Roe continues to exist, but only in the way a storefront on a western movie set exists; a mere façade to give the illusion of reality. There is no requirement, in considering whether to depart from stare decisis in a constitutional case, that a decision be more wrong now than it was at the time it was rendered.
Chief Justice Rehnquist
Planned Parenthood v. Casey, dissent.

Let us leave Dewey and Renee for the moment, temporarily venturing over to another story without completely abandoning our two princes as they grow into their young teens. For now, we dare venture into the colorful courtrooms at the foot of the needle, the seventy-foot tower where our court jester is now being held. Though the presence of Disegno is not the sort of thing anyone would invite, it is only proper we pay him a visit. Though Disegno is an evil man *thing* who may very well be proven guilty of the theft of a work of art (surely a high crime in any Posteriorian province), we must pay him our last respects, for I love him as any character of mine and I am hardly ashamed of such love.

After Disegno was seized, his wild tongue had wagged nonstop, calling *you don't understand, you dumbass fools, you don't understand this world, that everything already has a divine essence, that the art Olegna claims does not come from him, but rather it is divine and as divine, it was already there. I took nothing from him that was his. Yes, you fools that is right, it was already there in the stone. He merely brought it out! He merely BROUGHT IT OUT!*

Disegno struggled against the guards holding his arms from each side, squirming violently by jerking his body this way and that. As a young man he could have easily toppled the guards now holding him; he could have demolished them plus a dozen more. But after returning to Lyceum after two lifetimes of any ordinary man, Disegno had aged considerably. And though he had magically aged only twenty years in the last two hundred years, twenty years of aging can certainly make a difference in times such as these.

But Disegno was no fool. He knew his limits. After just a few minutes his tongue had stopped wagging, and he just put his hooded head down, his red eyes now pale and spent. As the three men (or two men and their prisoner, not a man at all) ascended the spiral staircase, they felt the air grow colder. With every step, fear had left Disegno and seeped into the hearts of the guards. As Disegno's steps became stronger, the guards' steps became rushed and awkward. But the guards did not realize Disegno's power over them until Disegno opened his lips.

Until Disegno laughed.

First the demon's steps began to slow, jerking the younger guard off balance.

"C'mon, now," the older guard struggled to say, his hand moving toward his baton, "Come along peacefully now. We've dealt with your kind before, and we've seen all—" but upon meeting Disegno's eyes his mouth kept moving, but he could make no sound.

"Ahem," he raised his hand to his throat, moving his lips up and down like a fish out of water, lying against a wooden table, wondering where his air just went. It did not take long until his eyes looked down, his lips closed and quivering.

"Now, now" Disegno spoke, his white teeth glaring out of a large grin, "this can't be so bad. It was *Tom* I was *really* worried about," he said, cocking his head towards the younger guard.

"Hey! How did you know—" was all Tom managed to speak before Disegno's grin widened from ear to ear, sending an eerie chill down his throat.

And that was when Disegno laughed.

He threw his head back rapidly, his hood sliding back just an inch, but it was a hellish inch, and more than enough. Tom covered his ears as the sounds of the laugh began: a soft scratching sound deep from within the devil's throat, steadily growing deeper like the motor of a city, louder and louder, rising up up up to a screech like fingernails running down a chalkboard, louder and louder. At that moment, a baby bird in a nearby nest died, its mother standing over it, her head cocked, left with her child's food still dangling from her beak. In a nearby home, a baby began to cry. A group of nearby flowers began to wilt, their last petals barely hanging on.

"Stop! *Stop!*" Tom cried, his hands pressed hard on the sides of his head. He spun around in time to see the older guard double over, vomiting onto the stone stairs. Tom's eyes filled with fear. Struggling to stand straight, he closed his eyes and wrapped his fingers around his baton. But looking down, Tom saw that his hand was covered in blood.

As Disegno's laugh grew louder, Tom felt the hot liquid dripping from his nose.

"I'm, I'm bleeding!" he said.

But no one could hear him over Disegno's roaring laughter.

"Help, help! My god."

But suddenly, all was silent. Disegno stood still as a statute, his back to the guards, his eyes gazing ahead. He stood as if nothing had occurred at all.

Brushing off his pants, the larger, older guard picked himself up, hesitated for just a moment, and seized Disegno by the arm. His eyes narrowed as they met Tom's as if to say "C'mon, let's do this." Tom willed himself to Disegno's other side, and the three figures resumed their march upstairs. Eventually, Tom's bleeding stopped.

No one spoke again.

The cell at the top of the needle was originally built to be over three hundred feet tall, but the Posteriorians soon realized that such a height would not do since the nature of their legal system required the prisoners to walk up and down the stairs repeatedly for their new trials. So after the first needle had collapsed (which had taken no time at all since its foundations were as weak as a pile of twigs), it was reconstructed to a new height of a mere seventy feet, low enough so the escorting guards need not strain themselves on the job, but just high enough to break anyone's neck who tried to escape through the large open window at the top. This was the twelfth needle of the nation, but it was still seventy feet.

So up, up they went, two guards on each side with Disegno squashed in the middle, his tall frame towering over them as if he was guiding them up, not the other way around. They made their way to the room in which Disegno would spend much time, where he would dream, sing, dance, and think. This was the room he would witness many more art shows from his ledge, where one day he'll watch Dewey be anointed king. This was the room from which he would see many a moon's cycle, suffer many a harsh winter's bite, many a sweltering summer's weight. This was the room in which he would live and this was the room in which he might die.

Like a wedding bride walking the aisle with a parent on each arm, Disegno ascended the stairs in a sandwich of men, his head down, a small smile upon his face as he listened to the roars of the crowd in the plaza not far away, the waves of people applauding and laughing, drunk at the art show behind his feet. He felt they were applauding for him, giving him one last gift as he ascended those stairs, a parting souvenir for the ride. When he got the top and was thrown to the ground in the middle of the cell, he never turned around or looked back. No, he would not even give the guards the satisfaction of a look, a smile, a wince. Rather, he focused on the crowd's applause, and was glad they were rooting for him as they continued to roar with applause, supporting him even as he entered the room that was to be his new home.

ΩΨΩ

Just the next week, Disegno is summoned to descend the stairs of the needle to stand trial before a jury just formed by hundreds of glad citizens of the Posteriorian nation. Half of them were witnesses to the events at the art show, (and thus will be biased against Disegno after seeing the pain upon Olegna's stricken face,) though that is no matter here. To Posteriorians, all observed experience has its worth in the pursuit of justice, and no evidence can be turned away no matter how many heartstrings it may pull.

Even Disegno stares in fascination at the courtroom he enters. The room is a tremendous oval shape surrounded by multi-colored pillars, each boasting its own carnival of flower bouquets of yellow and red, adorning trinkets, terra-cotta moldings, statues, and ornamentations celebrating the worthy tasks of the living law. The room enjoys the aroma of flower petals, spices, cinnamon, and myrrh. In the center of the room, under the scattered flower petals and leaves (no doubt left behind by prior trials), there is a large open stage where the witnesses will perform. Upon the stage floor lies the most tremendous mosaic. Fragments of red, yellow, blue, and green float around a stone milky universe, but all gravitate towards the orange center.

Joachim instructs the attorneys of the order of events to follow.

"Each attorney," he announces, "is to make their opening statement for no more than three minutes, with the first one to have a thirty second rebuttal. After that, the witnesses are to be called to the stage to give their performances."

"The best part!" one of the spectators exclaims, his remarks greeted by cheers of joy.

"Yes, Yes," Joachim says smiling, his hands out to calm down the spectators, "I know, we all love the performances. In accordance with the Posteriorian tradition, the witnesses will act out the events they have experienced to the jury so that the jury may actually experience the events themselves, as if they personally witnessed the scene. This is because we are a nation of action, not of words." Joachim pauses, taking in the moment before continuing the instructions.

"These performances, my beloved jury, will be observed by you. During each performance, you may shout out questions to the witness, and they must alter their performance on the spot so as to answer your questions, improvising as the questions come. And after the performances of the witnesses, you, my beloved jury will have a feeling as to the defendant's guilt or not guilt, and you must rule accordingly, through the customs as I will set forth..."

Joachim finishes his instructions, and the performances begin. The massive jury observes from the cluttered stands, their fat fingers digging through cups of buttered popcorn, tossing food into their mouths while they watch each witness's dynamical display of experience.

The witnesses perform one after the next. In the defendant's chair, Disegno observes his own story right before his very eyes. He sees the performers act out his past crimes, the way he reacted to each artist's presentation, how he walked away from Olegna's cries, how he mocked Olegna, and was mocked by the young Jon Rasaa. His history is induced, his propensity inquired. And all the while, he sits there, a smirk upon his face and denial upon his lips.

After the performance of the witnesses, each juror is given two beans, one white and one black.

"Take your beans," Joachim instructs. "You are to discuss your observations, and deposit only one of your beans into glass jar as it circles around: white for innocent, black for guilty. A designated counter will then count the beans, white against black, for the final verdict. If there are more white beans than black, then the defendant will be ruled innocent. If not, well, he will be detained as guilty."

Detained, of course, because any sort of real punishment (certainly the death penalty) seemed all too conclusive and final.

But today, the jurors know from experience that their beans will not be counted. This is because most jurors throw their beans at the performing witnesses as they fail to entertain, egging them on for more. Many of the jurors pop their beans in their mouth, eating them in boredom at the fantastical display, crunching down on their verdicts in jest. Knowing this, the counter will lose interest, counting the first few beans and forgetting the rest.

Disegno denies his charges, but the contents of his mind are very different from that of which he speaks. He keeps thinking of the lesson he was trying to teach. *I was trying to help these people, that artist, I was trying to teach them. Olegna may be a fine artist, but he is no creator. And if he wouldn't have started his obsessive "mine, mine, mine" parade so many years ago, I surely would have left him alone. But it is people like him, people who forget that everything is connected and everything has the same divine essence, that nothing is new under the sun because everything has already been created, and we can do no more than change what is already there, like El Totsira in the stone.*

After the witnesses perform, Disegno is questioned, and the closing statements are given. They are interrupted by impatient jurors, and cut short by Joachim, smiling and shaking his head at the impatience of Posteriorian spectators.

The jury begins to deliberate.

"I liked Rahim's performance," one juror begins, "the way he wore Disegno's black cape, they way he did Disegno's sneer made me—"

"Piss your pants?" another juror interrupts, earning the howls and hooting laughter of his comrades.

"Now, now," another begins, "let us discuss—"

"Discuss what?" another says, "discuss how we just sat here n' watched—ouch! Who threw that bean at me? Who hit me?"

"Calm down, everybody," a tall, older Posteriorian juror said, "Now we all know that the performances really showed us that Disegno took pride in Olegna's loss. He seemed to be smiling at his pain, as if, as if he had wanted it to happen that way all along."

The others seem to fall silent, nodding their heads in unison.

"And you heard, well, you heard the demon speak of his beliefs that Olegna's sculpture did not really belong to him, since it did not come from him. He did not create it himself, Disegno claimed. Rather, it was lying in the stone. Olegna merely found it. Disegno thinks he merely brought it out!

"Now, we know that this cannot be true, my fellows, for stone is just stone just as water is just water, paint is paint, and canvas is canvas. We know that we alter the natural ingredients of the outer world to our likings, and this is how we create art. This is how we've always seen it happen! For if it was otherwise, my friends, then there would be nothing new under the sun!"

A silence fills the courtroom.

"Nothing new!" someone says, "What a boring world that would be!"

"Yes, I don't like what Disegno is saying. I don't like his face, either…"

After a moment, one juror whispers in his neighbor's ears, and the other follow. As the hum rises, one can hear a comment here and there.

"This sounds pretty clear," one says.

"Yah, I think that feels right."

"He's got something there, though I don't know what it is."

"Whatever he says, I think it's good. If it brings us to a conclusion, it is good. I am ready to go home and eat dinner!"

A few laughs erupt.

"Alright! Looks like it's time to leave soon…my wives are waiting!"

But one voice is heard louder than the rest.

"Wait! Fools! You forgot the most important thing!"

The sea of voices hushes, then simmers to a cool static hum.

They look to this juror who moves out of the way as a sensor pushes a large wheelbarrow of documents behind him. The sensor screeches to a halt, sending documents flying into the air.

"You forgot what Posteriorians stand for. You began to jump to conclusions based on your feelings, and that is honorable, but we, you forgot to look to our past experiences with this sort of case. We have hundreds of thousands of precedent cases, stored away in the libraries of the sensors, and you have not looked at a single one!"

"He's right," another voice bellows, "and, and I have brought with me more precedent for us to examine and analyze. My sensors have sifted through the libraries, and have snatched the most relevant cases for our review."

The man then tosses a tremendous heap of papers, drawings, maps, and tiny sculptures and the foot of the jury.

"This is our precedent," he explains, "and sculptures of the greatest witness performances of our time, our drawings of what the courtroom had looked like at the time of similar cases of old, some old beans from which we can get a sense of the mood, and of course, a few documents, a few past opinions from which we can direct our present thoughts."

The jurors' eyes remain on the pile of case law. Their eyes follow the trail of papers to the man who brought them, settling on him for just a moment, then returning to the pile on the floor, where they remain locked. The pile is tremendous. It would take months for any diligent person to sift through so many past cases, disposing of the irrelevant ones, and putting the more significant ones aside for further review.

This Posteriorian jury drools in anticipation of such a task.

They begin at once. Hours pass. Days pass. Disegno sits calmly, as if his verdict has already been established. He watches the jurors' fat yellow hands grabbing at the precedent, papers floating through the air like leaves. The jurors grab wildly at the precedent, as if its very devouring was their purpose, rather than any insight they may gleam from such excursion. Fists fly and tempers flare. All the while, Disegno's expressionless face watches from above like a master looking down upon his servants at work.

"I got it! I got it!" shouts one juror, holding up a small piece of paper, "I found the case most similar to this one! A thief! Just two months ago! He stole, he took a work of—"

"Give me that, you hog!" said another juror, grabbing the paper out of his hands.

"Hey, you. That was my case. I found it!"

"Stop it!" an older juror orders. The jurors hush for just a moment, before rambling once again.

"Now hold it," he tries again, "Let us examine what we have found." He seizes the papers from the other juror's hands, and the jurors huddle around to read.

"One such citizen has been brought here today on charges of larceny..."

"...for the seizing of property by one Benjamin Gibbard of Northern Lyceum..."

"...plaintiff has come to us complaining of such actions as we are here to determine...the court has renounced his actions...Larceny is the act of taking possession of the property of another...with the intent to permanently deprive...without his consent..."

"...said object being a woodprint upon canvas of the winged figure El Totsira, son of Rekha..."

"...the court must determine whether the plaintiff has produced sufficient evidence for a finding of the defendant's evil intent and actions...the court cannot make such evaluations until...the plaintiff has not met its burden of production...the court must rule the defendant not guilty because..."

"...the jury has deposited their beans...the color here is white..."

"...white...white...WHITE!"

The jurors look up from the case law, several rubbing their aching necks.

"But Disegno seems pretty guilty to me," someone says.

"You fool! Did you not just read our past case? The defendant was found not guilty! We must stick to our past decisions! If we violate stare decises, if we go changing the law, we may as well—"

"—ignore our feelings? Ignore our present instincts of justice today because of our mistakes of the past?" The jury has never heard anything like this before. They do not like it.

"Fool!" the other retorts, "The citizens of Lyceum hold their faith and confidence in this court. They take comfort in our consistent rulings, in the fact that we don't follow our mere whims of the day, based upon the weather, what we had for breakfast that morning, or, or—"

The first bean thrown finds its mark right in the juror's eye. His howl of pain only invites more and more beans, an army of black and white pellets flying through the air.

"Stop!" the juror shouts, his face red, "Stop! We were going to count those beans. We were..." he throws up his hands in defeat, "Alright, alright, whether you listen to me or not, we need to reach a conclusion," he almost manages to smile, realizing that it is always best to give in to the Posteriorian way, "Alright, let's just see how we all feel. Shall we?"

The jurors clap their hands and begin to chant, the spectator's feet stomping to the rhythm in the stands.

"Bring out the jar! Bring out the jar!" the crowd drums their feet on the stands, and so does Joachim, *"Bring-out-the-jar! BRING-OUT-THE-JAR!"*

At last the empty glass jar is brought to the table. One of the jurors, the biggest man no doubt, knocks out the fellow next to him, stealing his beans. Popping them into his mouth, the large man stands up on the table, bean curd dribbling down his drunken lips. *It's hot in here!* The man shouts, his hands slapping his large chest, a real Tarzan God ofaman, *I need to get outta here, the demon looks like he did it, didn't he? Well, he probably did! Justice be done! Justice be done! What you say? WHAT YOU SAY?*

The large man is met by an uneven hum from below. The other jurors seem to have lost interest in the case. Walking out of the deliberation room, the jurors comment to one another, *Later tonight, at your place* their bare feet, and large neglected bodies under carefully made garments *wine and liquor and women's delight* large men of color chasing *a feast* leaving a pool of beans under their feet. The previously designated bean-counter sighs in humor for this is the thousandth time he has seen such a display. He counts the first few beans, rolls his eyes, and kicks the jar into the air. Turning towards the courtroom *ladies and gentlemen* he raises his hands in the air *now now we have come to a decision* and the verdict is announced. He raises a fist in the air in celebration, screaming the verdict quite clearly, "It seems he is probably guilty, my friends!" as the sensors make sure to write down the final verdict.

Probably guilty.

So up, up, up Disegno returns, escorted up the rainbow stone stairs of the needle. Disegno knows this is not the last time he will be walking these steps, for he has many more trials to go. If you guessed this too, then you are beginning to understand the Posteriorian way.

Justice be done.

5

It is true that two men can lift a bigger stone than one man. A group can build automobiles quicker and better...and bread from a huge factory is cheaper and more uniform. When our food and clothing and housing all are born in the complication of mass production, mass method is bound to get into our thinking and to eliminate all other thinking. This is the danger. The free, exploring mind of the individual human is the most valuable thing in the world. Nothing was ever created by two men. There are no good collaborations, whether in music, in art, in poetry, in mathematics, in philosophy. Once the miracle of creation takes place, the group can build and extend it, but the group never invents anything. The preciousness lies in the lonely mind of a man.
John Steinbeck

Man is a sociable being. Though a philosopher may live remote from business, the genius of philosophy must gradually diffuse itself throughout the whole society.
David Hume

It is told that the Jews were slaves to Egypt for 210 years. The Egyptians enslaved them because the Children of Israel had grown fruitful, increasingly strong and successful by their own merit. So the Jews were forced to build pyramids. Like the Posteriorians, the Egyptians required large storage houses, and made the Jews build two large ones, Pithom and Raamses. The Egyptians enslaved the Children of Israel with crushing harshness. They embittered their lives with hard work, with mortar and with bricks, and with every labor of the field.

But as much as they would inflict upon the Children of Israel, the Egyptians found that the Children of Israel only increased. Jewish mothers gave birth to six babies at one time. And the more the Egyptians tried to stunt their growth, the more the Children of Israel multiplied. They were everywhere. Like the stars in the sky.

Moses came before the king of Egypt, and asked that they be set free. Pharaoh said no. So Moses told his brother Aaron to stretch out his hand with his staff over the rivers, over the canals, and over the reservoirs, and to raise up the frogs over the land of Egypt. And rise they did.

But many say that it was only one frog, a tremendous frog that had emerged from the river that morning. It was only when the Egyptians hit the frog, that it multiplied into two frogs, then two into four, then four into eight, until there were frogs swarming all over the land of Egypt, out of control. And the more they were beaten, the more they multiplied. Until they were very fruitful and numerous.

Like the stars in the sky.

And so, this became the fear of the Egyptians, the fear most all of us has felt one time or another. The fear of multiplicity. The fear of your worst nightmare multiplying itself as you try to extinguish it, like flames spreading as you try to blow them out, popping up wherever you turn, blocking your exit. The fear of having such control over a child, a people, a technology, a creature, and feeling that control starting to slip. The fear that one's invention or creation becomes unpredictable, uncontrollable, and more powerful than its creator.

This was the fear of multiplicity.

This is the only way to explain how Renee feels by what he sees upon entering his brother's room this evening. Helene had merely asked Renee to pay his brother a visit.

"I see you're lost," Helene had begun.

Renee did not answer. His eyes seemed somewhere else.

"Renee," Helene tried again, "Come here. Why are you poised against the wall like that? Why do you stand alone over there? Come over here. Renee?"

"Huh?" Renee blinked, "Lost? Oh no, I was just thinking about, well, I was just in my mind."

"Right. Listen to me. I'm going to lie down. I'm not really feeling up to par, and it looks like you could use some company." Helene had said, "Why don't you go check on your brother, if you're bored."

But when Renee walks down the hall to Dewey's room, he feels a slight tickling on his right foot. Picking up his foot to brush it off, he sees a tiny orange ant settling itself onto his white skin. He is about to brush it off in haste as he feels another one crawling up the back of his leg. He brushes off the ants in annoyance, sighing at the usual state of the palace floor. Since the Posteriorians often walk around sloppily eating food from their hands, crumbs cover the floor like snowflakes. This always attracts a few ants.

But as Renee gets closer to Dewey's quarters, he sees more ants. *That's a bit odd* he stops in place for a moment, wondering what large snack could have brought in so many of these orange creatures. Thinking little of it, he approaches his brother's door, and walks inside. He is shocked by what he sees.

Dewey's legs are completely covered in a sea of ants. He revels in the center of the room, his eyes closed, chin up, a large grin on his face.

"Dewey?" Renee tries. His brother's eyes remain closed and his grin widens. Renee speaks again.

"Ew. All these…these horrible ants! Where—where did they all come from? How—"

"Whoa," Dewey smiles in excitement, "Aren't they neat? Someone once told me, y'know, that there are more ants in the world than there are all the other living beings added up together! Oh, they look soooo cool, so many of them…I love how they all work together…"

"How did they get here?"

"Who cares? I, I think they like me. They're so neat—"

"You are mad! Here, let me help you. Let me get them off! Let me—" Renee tries to take a step forward but finds he is paralyzed in place, less by his brother's contentment than by the sheer number of ants covering his brother's legs. Renee looks in horror as Dewey's legs, waist, and belly become completely covered in orange. Dewey's eyes seem orange themselves, full of life, intoxicated, glazed over by some kind of film.

"Haha!" Dewey laughs in glee, "It is their number, their multiplicity that makes them great," he says to Renee, but he seems to be talking to himself, "You see how they work so hard, never resting, never stopping, all of them together, gathering, foraging, and bringing back the outside materials to examine...see, this is why I love ants. They never stop working. And they all work together. Even as their ant farms crumble, as they often do, they do not hesitate to start building again. It falls again, they build again. They gather materials from the outside world...using them to their advantage...and they just keep going and going..."

As Dewey rambles on, Renee tastes vomit in the back of his throat. He feels his face flash with heat, an expression of unplanned emotion completely alien to him. *What is wrong with me?* He tries to look at the confusing sea of ants one last time *I can do this* but there is too much movement, too much transience, too much motion for him to take. The color, the action, the chaos. It is too much. He doubles over as his dinner comes up, his eyes blinded by the confusing sea of movement in the room, by the fear of an Egyptian, the fear of multiplicity; all he sees is orange. And all the while, Dewey's voice continues in the background *so many of them, so beautiful* Renee grasps his stomach, almost falling to his knees *working so hard so beautiful* so many so terrible so hard to stand up.

Renee manages to stand up just partially, dragging himself out of the room. He can still hear Dewey's voice behind him *yes oh yes keep working* speaking as if Renee was never there. The voice chases Renee as he tries to stumble away from it, away from that room *keep working* this place *keep working* this night.

ΩΨΩ

June makes way for July. The nation seems to resolve itself after Disegno's imprisonment. The ecstasy and celebration of the art contest and the excitement of Disegno's trial begin to settle in the belly of the nation. A Posteriorian calmness (if there can be such a thing) fills the air of Lyceum. For the first time in weeks, the songs of birds can be heard in the morning air, the sounds of gurgling brooks wrapping themselves around the buzzing of crickets dancing through the hot summer nights.

The days pass slowly. Renee's head begins to hurt often now, like a great weight inside keeps growing, a silent weight trying to balance all the outside experience coming in. Renee tries to play with Dewey, hoping that it will erase his pain, but Dewey is always off playing with other boys. When Renee tries to visit Dewey in his room, he sees the ants are still there even days later; they seem to levitate to Dewey, who is overjoyed at their company.

Renee begins to dream, his head emptying its contents while he sleeps. When he wakes up, his head feels lighter, until he gets caught up in the activities of the day.

One night, Renee dreams a most vivid dream: he is walking down the palace hall towards his brother's room, just as he had weeks before. When he enters, he sees Dewey covered in orange ants, smiling contently just as he had before. But this time, as Renee turns to leave, he feels a large hand grasping his ankle, pulling him back into the room. Looking back, Renee sees the hand is not his brother's at all. It is the hand of El Totsira, his rainbow robes gleaming brightly, his head thrown back in a laugh, his hand grasping Renee's ankle tight. Renee tries to break free, but it is no use, and he hears the voice of El Totsira *haha* behind him *you can't run away, my boy,* hot breath on his neck *you can't run away forever* and El Totsira pulls him back, grasping his ankle as O'Talp grasped El Totsira's when he was born from Rekha. Renee feels his body slipping backward, into the hot colorful ghost of El Totsira, into the room. Renee gets pulled back and the orange surrounds him. He wakes up with a gasp.

The dreams get worse with each night. Renee wishes he could confide in Dewey or Helene, but he knows what they will say. '*You fool!*' they will chide, '*We must love El Totsira for what he taught us! He was the greatest man-angel-demiGod whathaveyou that ever lived; your dreams make no sense, my boy. They're just silly dreams. Don't take them so seriously. They're not real.*'

But Renee is not so sure.

But one night, he dreams a dream that gives him hope. He is walking through the narrow streets of an enormous city that looks much like Lyceum; the golden sun showers its light upon hundreds of the most splendid temples Renee has ever seen, courts of justice, shops, a concert hall, and even a large gymnastics building. The citizens swarming the streets seem to mind their own business. Renee sees a prostitute pick up two men. To his right, a vendor gives alcohol out to children. No one looks twice. Renee walks past an old woman. He stops her and asks her why. She answers by shouting to the crowd, "Nothing as it stands is wrong or right. Man is the measure of all things."

Suddenly, Renee feels a sharp pang of heat behind him. He turns around to see a glowing rainbow, no—it is El Totsira himself—running towards him, his hands outreached. Renee ducks under his grasp and runs into the streets. He can hardly hear El Totsira's voice over the beating of his own heart, but he can feel the angel*demon?*'s hot breath against his neck.

"Get back here!" El Totsira roars, "You will learn to serve me just as all the others. You will learn to let me in."

Just as Renee begins to fade, he comes to a clearing in the intersection before a massive temple. He sees a bent over, potbellied man talking to a group of citizens who have stopped to listen. As Renee gets closer, he can see that the old man is extremely ugly. His belly droops over his clothes like his bulging eyes over his snub nose. But Renee sees that the people find him perfectly delightful.

"Who are you?" Renee says.

The man stops talking at once. He turns to Renee.

"I am Setarcos," he says, "Some of the people in the streets stop to hear me speak. But the others do not like what I say. They say that man is the measure of all things, but I give myself to a higher moral code. So I speak to those who will listen until the others come and try to catch me, and then I must run. They will try to execute me, but I will keep running. But now is not my time to run, lad. It is yours."

Renee looks at the man, but cannot find the words to speak.

The man continues, "You must run now. He is coming."

"Who?"

"Can you not feel his colors flowing behind you?"

"El Totsira."

Setarcos turns back to his crowd to speak. But Renee does not want to leave. He sees that in fact, Setarcos is speaking to a small boy, and all the people are watching. Setarcos has an arm around the boy, and the two begin to walk away. As they turn, Renee sees the boy's white face.

Renee sees the boy is just like him.

Before Renee can shout *'wait!'* the boy turns to Renee as if he read Renee's thoughts.

Renee says, "Who are you?" but the boy's eyes look sad. Renee can see that the boy wishes he could speak to Renee, but for some reason he is unable to.

Setorcas says to the boy, "No, not yet. Let's go now. He is not ready for you and he must run now. Renee will find you when the time is right, but you cannot help him now. He must go."

The boy looks at Renee with tears in his eyes. Then, the boy holds out his hand to Renee. Renee can see a white oval object in the boy's hands. He reaches out to accept it, but it is too late. El Totsira is behind them now. Renee feels the prophet's colorful talons dig into his shoulders, the hot orange colors overtake his sight, the intoxicating scents lull him away from the dream.

Renee wakes from the dream. He is in a cold sweat. But as he lifts his hands from under his pillow, he feels something cool and oval. Studying the small object in his hand, Renee sees that it is the white object that the young boy tried to give him in his dream. *I guess he succeeded after all,* Renee smiles.

Renee sees that it is a ball of wax, just big enough to fill his whole hand. *But why wax? What does this mean?*

Looking closer into the wax, Renee can see faint etchings of lettering in the wax. He has to squint to read all of it.

Dear Renee,

Did Rekha die in giving birth, only to give birth to El Totsira? If man gains knowledge through experience, then why is experience so confusing? Is there nothing better?

One day, your head will be clear, your heart steadfast on a road towards real knowledge. But until then, perhaps a walk through the woods behind the needle would help find some answers.

With you always,

A friend

Renee reads the wax tablet three times, turning it over in his hand. Who could this be from? Renee thinks of all the people he ever knew, but that wasn't much. He never really had any friends. Who would want to bother him with such questions, coming in the middle of the night to slip this under his pillow? Renee looks at his sensors standing before him, then he looks away. *Perhaps a walk...would bring some answers.*

Sighing in exhaustion, he tosses the wax aside, unaware of the questions it would leave festering inside his head. *Answers would be nice...for another day.*

ΩΨΩ

Renee waits for the summer to end. He waits for the days to grow cold, for the darkness to come and chase the Posteriorian activity away. He waits for the snow to fall, the calming white blanket to wrap everyone up in their homes. Since everyone smiles during these summer days, Renee makes himself smile too. But he does not smile as they do. They smile in pleasure at the warmth, and he smiles in anticipation of the cold. Of course, the others do not know this. Renee does not tell them. This is because Renee fears being singled out. As anyone, he wants to belong. If that means slapping a smile on his face, so be it. For now.

6

Believe nothing, no matter where you read it, or *who said it, no matter if I said it, unless it agrees with your own reason and your own common sense.*
Buddha

Renee Don Cartez walks alone, between the azaleas on his left, the meadow saffrons on his right. His gaze is cold, his eyes locked firmly on the space before him like two gray stones. He could not find the energy to venture out into the woods today. No, today he is in his father's private gardens, emerged in a sea of swaying velloritas.

Now, any other child in this special place would not be able to help but dance with the hydrangea, laugh at the wonder bulbs set between the Hills-of-Snow. Yes, any *other* child's legs would jump for joy, his voice singing with the fleur-de-lis, his face full of wonder as it faces the asthma weed, his heart pounding with joy at the scent of the bladderpod lobelia with the tulips at their base. But Renee does not see such wonders.

Renee searches through his mind.

And as the sun begins to set and the windows in Lyceum begin to darken one by one, Renee slows his walk, paying no heed to the plants' playful prodding. As little Posteriorian children crawl into bed and birds begin to land on their perches, Renee passes the surrounding plants as they try to reach out to him in defeat. They look at him plainly, chiding him with brief looks of disapproval before lying back into the breeze, closing their yellow pedal eyes, and drifting off to sleep.

Renee continues on, his mind weighed down by the heavy thoughts rolling around inside. He knows Dewey must be going to sleep in his room this very moment, and Helene must be wondering where he is. But Renee cannot worry about that right now, for he has feet that need walking, a head that needs clearing, and a mind that needs healing.

This is not the first time Renee has wandered off. As he has grown older, he has started to spend more and more time alone. It all started when he would remain in the garden after playing with Dewey, sitting in silence for hours after Dewey had turned in.

Sometimes Dewey would call out, "C'mon, Don," after a game had been completed, "C'mon, l'il brother, let's go back inside. What're you doing?" Renee would insist on remaining there, that he will be in in just a few moments. Dewey would stare at him in confusion for just a moment, often shrugging his shoulders, turning around, and quietly walking in himself.

One week ago, the boys went to the garden together. The center of the garden boasted the most tremendous honeycomb that day, oozing with fresh honey and teeming with humongous bees. The boys hid nearby, their hands full of rocks.

"Go, on, throw one," Dewey started, "let's see how close you dare get."

"I can get closer than you ever can!"

"Oh? You couldn't hit the side of—" and Renee threw it in his awkward way, his thin white arm jerking forward, setting the stone straight towards the honeycomb. The two boys braced themselves, ready to run in the event of a wasp attack. They remained frozen as stone, watching the rock land not ten feet from the massive hive. A few moments passed, and Renee was the first to speak.

"Ha. Did you see how close I got?"

"Well, yeah," Dewey obliged, his face turning red with envy, "but I am still braver than you are. For I am going to be king!! Dewey the bravehearted! Dewey the—"

"—the boy who was too scared to throw his stone at the hive," Renee retorted.

"Oh, you think you're so brave?"

"Well, you are the one with the rock still in your hand."

"Ok then, I will throw it." Dewey looked up at the honeycomb, slowly mustering up his Posteriorian strength.

Taking a deep breath, he raised his short stubby arm and lurched it forward, releasing the stone as his arm came down. He watched the stone fly through the air, land directly under the honeycomb, and rest right in its shadow.

"Wha—Wow!! Did you see that? Renee? *Renee?*" Dewey shouts in joy, but he does not hear an answer.

"Renee? Where are you brother? Did you see that?" He would persist, but it was no use, for Renee is already gone, venturing off alone into the nooks and crannies of the garden, into the intricacies of his mind.

In the following weeks came the early departures from family meals. Renee would give a mere "scuse me" before sliding off his chair at dinner, pushing it in politely while looking down at his own two feet, to turn and slowly walk away from his plate still filled with food, away from the six wondering eyes behind him, to return to his room. Helene and Joachim would just look at each other without saying a word, nodding their heads, their eyes filled with a taint of sympathy for the boy and a pinch of worry over his situation. Dewey would usually pretend not to notice. But sometimes, if one would look at Dewey closely, they might be able to see a smile form at the edge of his lips.

The more troubled Renee seems, the more people will love Dewey. Dewey knows this well.

"Should I go get him?" Dewey offers quietly on one such occasion, "I can bring him back to the table."

"Yes, that would be nice," Joachim said, "But completely unnecessary. You don't have to go."

"Oh, I will. It is okay," Dewey stands, wiping turkey juice from his face. "He is my brother. I'll go look after him."

And with that, Dewey gives a very subtle look across the table. He looks for it and he sees it: a small smile of admiration on his parent's lips. Even the guests shake their heads in awe and Dewey can hear their thoughts *such a shame that he has such a brother* as they turn in their heads *his brother pulls him down, but he is glad to help. He is an incredible boy. He will make a wonderful king.* Their thoughts warm his heart.

For just a moment, Dewey's eyes twinkle back at them.

I will be a wonderful king.

Dewey walks outside and goes to the latrine. He examines himself in the mirror, admiring his golden locks, blue eyes, his colorful necklace. He waits a few more minutes before returning to the table.

"I could not find him," he tells everyone, "He could be anywhere." He tries not to smile as they shake their heads.

"You tried," Helene offers, "Thank you, Dewey."

"I did." A small part of Dewey wishes this were true, but he easily forgets this. "Oh, please pass the fruit salad. Yum! Where did we get these mint leaves?"

"Damn Renee," one of the guests mutters.

"What?" Helene says, "What did you say?"

The guest puts down his food. "I've had enough. I'm sorry, but I can't stay silent anymore. Renee is what killed his mother."

"What?" Joachim is almost angry. "How dare you! Everyone knows Katherine died of tuberculosis when the boys were just one. It was a horrible disease! The medical evidence is unmistakable, the symptoms still catalogued in the extensive recordings of the sensors."

But Joachim knows that many people have said this before.

"Sure," the guest continues, "The records. But people will believe what they want to believe. And this is what many Posteriorians are saying. Katherine died sometime after her childbirth of Renee, but he was the one who prolonged her childbirth in the first place, seizing any energy left in her loins. Renee wastes his time taking walks in the garden, he so confidently walks as if above us, as if our society is not good enough for him, our parties, our shows, our food, and our games. Katherine died for giving birth to but a second son, and for what? What do we get from it? A blundering fool too good to even love his own family and share with his own people!"

"Now, now! Enough!" Helene cries. But as she looks around the table, she finds that her anger is not shared as much as she would like it to be.

Suddenly, she sees Renee peeking through a nearby window. *Did he hear?* Renee sneezes and everyone turns. Quickly, he turns and runs away.

"Joachim! Do something," Helene tries, but Joachim looks down. "Do something! Please!" A moment passes before Joachim scoops up some peas and stuffs them into his mouth. Helene looks down. She knows better than to object further, so she hesitatingly continues her meal.

ΩΨΩ

Renee ventures through his father's garden long after the sun sets and the last crow falls asleep. He recalls Disegno's capture, and wonders what El Totsira was really like. He ponders what man can really know, and doubts the experiences and the trivialities that seem to fill up his Lyceumean life. His thoughts begin to come together, slowly building a coherent order, a foundation. However, before his thoughts begin to make sense, they are disrupted by a sudden burst of color, like little explosions in his head.

His mind stops for a moment. Hit by a wall. A burst of color. Flashes.

Holding the sides of his head, Renee closes his eyes, but instead of darkness, he sees spots of orange, thousands of them, crawling this way and that. Thousands of orange ants making their way across his vision, piercing themselves into his mind. First they are orange, but no, ants of all colors abound, glaring, flashing, confusing his thoughts. Dizziness descends upon him like a great weight.

His knees buckle.

As the world spins around him like a rainbow, Renee is forced to sit down and grab hold of something fast. His eyes straining and his vision blurred, he reaches out towards the marble bench next to the orange vines but he is too late. He falls to the ground, trampling a school of daises under his shivering white torso, his black pants crumbling the wet flower pedals below. Renee remains on the ground shivering, his eyes closed and his hands on his temples, trying to understand what is going on in his large troubled head. *What does this mean?*

His mind finally clears some moments later, but he is scared at the power of his own mind, surprised at the great weight of his own thoughts. He picks himself up off the dirt ground and strolls the corner of the garden just to regain his façade of normality, his hands hardly shaking, his walk still straightening. And finally, Renee turns to return to his quarters, quietly entering so as not to disturb his brother loudly breathing in his messy bed beside him.

Renee does not know that Dewey has watched him from the window as he often has whenever Renee was on his strolls. Yes, Dewey would often sit there for hours, spying on his brother with hate, jealousy, and a secret admiration unknown to him at that time. What could he be jealous of, you ask? What could he see in his brother that there is to admire, you inquire? Independence, I say. The proud independence of a true thinker earned by someone so close to him, but in some ways, so far.

See, I told you that Dewey has won the people's love, his father's eye, and Helene's ear. But often the more one has, the more one notices that which he does *not* have, and the more he wants. This is especially true of any Posteriorian; while they are good people at heart, they have an attitude of more more more. Dewey has everything, you see, but for some reason, it is not enough. He does not know what Renee has.

But he wants it.

While observing his brother from the bedroom window that night, Dewey feels a sense of wonder. His brother's solitary walks fill him with a fascination he has never felt before. But when Dewey sees Renee turn to direct his walk towards the palace gates, Dewey jumps into bed just in time to look asleep. Renee feels glad Dewey does not hear him walk in, but of course he is mistaken, for Dewey has seen it all. Dewey has seen his brother's content face twist in pain, his hands shaking and knees buckling under the weight of his uncontrolled thoughts. Dewey has finally seen a flaw, an imperfection. Dewey saw that his brother, too, is human. Standing in a pile of ants at his feet, Dewey saw that Renee too, needs others just like anyone else.

He saw and he is pleased.

ΩΨΩ

On a warm night a few weeks later, Helene tells the boys more stories about El Totsira, but this time Renee does not reserve himself as he has in the past. Helene tells the boys of how El Totsira saved countless lives by stopping the danger of the great thunderstorms of the past.

"See," she begins as the night breeze enters the room, carrying her golden hair like a crown around her, "Before the Posteriorians had lightning rods, thunderstorms actually put the people in grave danger. Since there was nothing to catch the lightning, many citizens were stricken with lightning, often to their death. Though this hardly happened to sensors as they only stand three feet from the ground, many great Posteriorian architects and scientists had been lost over the years. This forced our people to build underground lairs, lightning lairs they called them, in which they hid when it began to rain.

"After some time, the people began to ring the city bell at the top of a tower in order to scare the storm away. They had come to believe that the storm was a bad omen, a negative effect of nature caused by the wrongdoings of their sinners, of those Posteriorians who are not as active as they can be, of those that do not *do*. A bell ringer would be appointed by the Vice Ruler of the nation, a ringer who would run towards the bell tower through the pelting rain while all others scrambled in the opposite direction to hide in their lightning lairs safe beneath the ground. However, whenever the storm had dissipated and the whip-cracks from the sky had all but gone away, the people would come out of their holes to find the bell ringer a dead man, a corpse lying at the foot of the tower, his gray eyes wide open in shock, his hair standing straight up like the tower he would by lying beneath.

"The people believed that the bell ringer took the punishment of death from the storm for the people's sins. This was divine providence, a lawful punishment from the spirit of the storm itself.

"The people believed that the storm would never hurt them as long as they offered the storm a sacrifice, a ringer, an old fool that could be their scapegoat, a martyr that could incur the wrath of mother nature upon himself, concentrating its hate and its harm upon his upheld white sacrificial chest. If there was no ringer, they believed, the storm would seek out and kill each and every one of them in turn."

"Oh, no," Dewey's face shows a most innocent terror. Helene can only smile.

"It was supposed to be an honor to be the ringer and save the people, though most tried to avoid their nomination for such a job. Often the oldest men were picked for they were near death anyway, and sometimes handicapped children, or infertile women with one or no legs. The ringer would head towards the tower at any sign of rain, a lone stumbling figure making its way through the cold wet dark, an old man's last walk, his long white hair blowing in his face as he made his way closer to the tower, his thin but brawny arms clenching the metal rusty chain, pulling it up and down as the glassy shards of rain bit into his face.

"'*Come and get me,*' he was obliged to scream, '*Come and get me with all that you have, or I will keep ringing this bell, ringing and ringing this bell that scares you so much, to scare you away...*' His words were often cut short by the cracks of the sky, though it has been said that they have been heard to continue past one, two, or sometimes even three, hits.

"This would have continued for hundreds, perhaps thousands of years if it were not for El Totsira The Great. El Totsira saw what the storm was doing to his beloved people, how the storms were killing ringer after beloved ringer—"

"So what did he do?" the boys ask.

"See, Old Tots had a real love for his people, the people he had nurtured, the people he had created and had grown to love. El Totsira never really taught us from his words, rather, he would teach us from his actions."

"So what—"

"The next time it began to rain and people scrambled to find a lightning lair to hide in, the ringer was running the other way as he looked up to see a most amazing sight: El Totsira was flying over him at so high a speed. It is said that El Totsira had grown a beautiful pair of wings, each emerging slowly from beneath his rising shoulder blades, flexible but sturdy cartilage ripping though his skin, feathers fluttering about a new pair of wings nearly fifteen feet in span, each individual feather a unique color of its own. Red, yellow, green, and blue, his rainbow wings fluttered, lifting him high into the air like a flying prophet, a soaring spirit, a loving God who saves. He flew through the rain with his feet together, his arms stretched forward in a flying V. As a circling high diver so fast but so calm, El flew to the top of the bell tower and stood there like the master of the world, his arms outstretched on his sides with palms up, his face turned up towards the heavens, his mouth wide open beneath his softly closed eyes so quietly facing the pelting rain above.

"That was when the lightning came."

Helene lets a moment pass. The room is silent. She sees Dewey's face in the moonlight. His mouth wide open in anticipation, he is afraid to speak for fear of interrupting her. Renee is behind him in the dark but Helene cannot see his face. She can only hope his silence comes from a similar anticipation.

"Boom! The first crack was so deafening, its roar could be heard for seconds afterward in the shaking ground. Most say that it hit El Totsira right between the eyes. But the prophet stood his ground, wincing for a brief moment before regaining his footing and quickly returning his hardened gaze to the heavens above.

"Then came another bolt of lightning, and another, and one more. One by one, the crack of mother nature's whip inflicted itself upon the hero's body three more times. By now, the bravest Posteriorians peeked their heads out of the ground to gaze at their savior's demise, and a handful dared to emerge and stand at the base of the bell tower before El The Great, their arms raised to protect their squinting eyes and frost-bitten face from the cold rain's teeth. They saw the first bolt rip through El's left upturned palm, and in it, the vague image of an orange ball; most say it seemed to be a stiff spherical orange mass while others claim a brief glow of orange light, a flicker emanating from his electrified palm. The second bolt of lightning scarred his right palm, briefly emitting a pale white light that seemed to alter its shape.

Finally, the third bolt had passed through the feet of the Posteriorian prophet, his toes stretching out in surprise, his white heels trembling to support their perforated flesh, a smoking hole burning through his feet, a hole almost matching the two holes above it, one in each palm, a trinity of piercings, a triad of hurt that could be felt by the handful of people watching from below, shocked by the sound of the blasts, the stench of burning flesh, their eyes filled with hot tears, their nose filled with the smell of rain stained smoke now curling its way into their poor trodden lungs."

Helene herself is carried away by the story. She is surprised at her own eloquence.

"After the last bolt of lightning landed through the angel's feet, he stood stunned for just a moment, withering slowly as everything seemed to freeze around him in a state of suspension, waiting for him, giving him a moment before the final fall, before finally falling to his side, his feet slipping off the cold wet stone precipice, descending slowly, a small white body slumped beneath two largely disheveled rainbow wings now enflamed at their tips, a firefly injured, a broken butterfly rolling, spinning acrobatics down a shoot of rainbow feathers in fire, a splintered ballerina exuding a most valiant last effort, a diminutive flame falling slowly through the cold electric black."

ΩΨΩ

The two princes listen intently as Helene continues her story. Like so many other storytellers in the region, she illustrates the well-known story and what it had inspired. She sings them songs of their prophet, and she reenacts his deeds. She reads them a poem inspired by the tale, a poem about El Totsira standing tall, a winged creature standing erect upon the highest tower.

As a rock on the seashore he standeth firm,
and the dashing of the waves disturbeth him not.
He raiseth his head like a tower on a hill,
and the arrows of fortune drop at his feet.
In the instant of danger,

the courage of his heart sustaineth him,
and the steadiness of his mind beareth him out.

Helene continues to explain what happened after El Totsira took four blows of lightning, his final fall to the ground, and how his brave actions have inspired the Posteriorians over the generations.

"Did he die?" The boys don't let her finish.

"Well, no, his name lives on everyday through the teachings he exemplified. His words live on to inspire our sentiments and his lessons remain to—"

"No, you know what we mean, momma. Did he die?"

"Haha, you two don't give up, do you? Well, after his fall, he just lay there real still, in a large crater his fall created. El lay there next to the dead ringer in the soil at the base of the tower. He lay still for days and no one would dare go near him. But one day weeks later, just as the people were preparing to mourn the prophet's death, a little girl had been rummaging, playing through the rubble at the base of the bell tower, poking through the mess at the lip of the crater. Realizing their little girl had run off, her parents ran to find her, and find her they did. They found their little girl standing before the large crater now completely empty, save the body imprint of the great prophet and a few orange feathers still smoldering at their edges.

"El Totsira, you see my childs, was gone.

"It is said that, well, based on the depth of the imprint and the condition of the remnants, he must have laid there for exactly three days before disappearing—"

"Just like that?" Renee asks skeptically.

"Well, my love, you must understand—"

"So he didn't save the ringer? The ringer died? And how many ringers had died through the years before El Totsira finally arrived? And he arrived too late to save this one, too!? And then El Totsira just laid there sleeping while his own people mourned and then just got up and ran away?"

"Well, this ringer died, but El Totsira saved all future ringers and the entire future of the Posteriorian people."

"Okay, well how did he do that?"

"If you allow me to speak, my child," Helene speaks firmly, though love can be seen in her eyes, "then you will see how this all comes together."

"Okay," Renee blushes, mildly embarrassed by his premature questions. Dewey is upset by his brother's arrogant questioning and stubborn skepticism, but is scared to open his mouth, feeling the debate beyond his limited grasp. Helene continues to speak.

"Weeks after the crater was found empty, and the people prepared to mourn the loss of the greatest martyr ever known, El Totsira returned. He returned as a scientist, the greatest Lyceum has ever known. After experiencing the power of the lightning, *electricity* he had called it, he learned how it could pass through metal, how it had passed through the bell so many times before, down the metal chain to the hands, the arms, and ultimately to the heart of the ringers below. He taught us all of this."

"How could he have known this?" Renee asks.

"Well, only because he experienced it himself. You see, when he was stricken with that first bolt of lightning, he had felt it rush through his body like vibrations through a metal cord, passing through his forehead, down his spine, through his legs to the iron bell below his trembling feet. Then, when he realized the ringer dead, he had induced that the lightning, the electricity must have passed through his body down to the bell, down the metal chain to the ringer, killing him instantly. This scientific truth was discovered through an experiment, a controlled experience of a cause and its effect, an electrifying cause and a fatal effect from which it can be induced that lightning passes through substances."

"Well, okay, that makes sense I guess," Renee gives his acquiescence, "But, what does that do for us?" Helene's patient eyes hide her disappointment. "I mean, how did that save our future?"

"It was up until these scientific teachings that our people were wound up in their own fanciful speculations of a storm actually having a *spirit*, of a ringer acting as a martyr who incurs the lightning's wrath, removing it from the rest of the nation. It was up until then that our people were fooled into believing in the supernatural, of that which they had never directly *experienced*.

"El Totsira showed them, showed us, that this was all a myth."

Dewey is overwhelmed with joy, nodding in continuity with Helene's verbal song. Though his brain often races faster than his mouth, he cannot help but express himself, finishing Helene's thoughts as if his own.

"So, so wait—after that, we knew the ringer-savior concept meant nothing; the ringer was dying for a cause that never existed, for a, a myth spun from the reason of our intellect, a myth created to try to, uhm, to make sense of the world. But really, the ringer died because of science, because of electricity, because of a force we had never known since we had never *experienced* it!"

Dewey feels the boulders rolling around in his small Posteriorian head, but his words pleasantly surprise him, and he smiles proudly. Helene approves of the boy's trying words, and sees he understands El's teachings as well as his young brain is now able to.

Renee considers objecting to Dewey's quick dismissal of a mind's 'dark chambers,' *What is so great about all this colorful...noise? What is so wrong about closing one's eyes and taking a minute to just...think* but then thinks the better of it, smiling softly, closing his eyes as Helene's words begin to brew up other stories, her tongue telling other tales that shock, teach, and glide, lasting deep into the night.

7

Isn't it true that you start your life a sweet child, believing in everything under your father's roof? Then comes the day of the Laodiceans, when you know you are wretched and miserable and poor and blind and naked, and with the visage of a gruesome, grieving ghost you go shuddering through nightmare life.
Jack Kerouac

Night after night, Helene continues to speak to the two princes, her soft stream of words tumbling down the mountainous blanket hills and over the small rocky boulders of the children's' heads. Tonight she has spoken for quite some time, and both boys now lie still; with both of their eyes closed, she thinks them both asleep. But Renee's mind is hardly at rest.

Is this all? Renee's head begins to reel. *Rekha tried so hard, expended so much effort, even died to give birth to, to El Totsira? This archangel ego that could not even save his people without practically dying himself?! This El, this God, this archangel of colorful illusions, this rainbow of confusion that everyone is raving so much about, that's got everyone so…hooked? Sure, my mommy, dear Katherine, died shortly after giving birth to Dewey and I, because, well, because it was not one, but two creations she was forced to bear in her womb, two loads to deliver, two gems she would never see grow. But Rekha, Rekha had to die for, for giving birth to only this one?*

Helene has always wondered why her stories are not enough for Renee, but her patience has always kept her afloat.

In the past, Helene had patiently tried to explain her words, the creed of Lyceum citizens, the faith of the Posteriorian nation, to this closed little boy. She struggled to see him not as an arrogant boy, but rather just as someone who cared enough to question, to make sure he got it all straight. As a female caregiver, (though officially considered inferior in El Totsira's teachings as a woman who could never hold political office) she has the gift of patience. But she also has the weakness of inconsistent emotion, of rash decision making, of letting her great love for her youngest child repress her anger until it builds up and up and up. You see, many people are good at sealing their anger and poisonous feelings in a tight wooden box and throwing it down the well of their minds. Helene's box had sunk, and had settled deep at the bottom of her well piled upon the many boxes that were thrown in previously. Helene's boxes were locked tight and sunk, and she felt only love towards her son. But when there are too many thoughts unexpressed, too many boxes unopened, the boxes of impatience can begin to poison the waters. Once the waters of one's mind are poisoned, this can affect them in ways that are better left unknown.

ΩΨΩ

Renee cannot understand why it took Rekha so much effort, so much strain to create just one transient life, so much toil that she practically died after its conception. He wonders how someone as light, transient, and feathery as El Totsira could bring such a burden to such a benevolent and pious woman of such inner strength. It just does not make sense.

The question keeps coming back to him: the question he read in the wax tablet that he found under his pillow.

Did Rekha die in giving birth, only to give birth to El Totsira?

Though Helene thinks the boys are asleep, she sits at their bedside watching them as she often does. She smiles, enjoying an inner peace she gets in times like this. Perhaps this is why she jumps in surprise at the sound of Renee's voice.

"But where did El Totsira come from?" Renee says calmly, as if he was in the middle of a conversation. Helene is ashamed of her shock. She hates when Renee does this to her, and is glad that Renee continues to speak. "I mean, what was his birth like?"

"El Totsira's roots, you say? Well, the word 'El' comes from the Hebrew word 'Elohim,' meaning 'God,' though we are not sure he was a God, for the very idea of God, well, we can never be sure there is such a thing. And the word Totsira—"

"All that is fine and good," Renee says, "But what I meant was, is he all that Rekha had to bear?"

"What is it you mean, my child?"

"I am wondering why it took her so much effort to produce just one life."

"Effort?"

"Well, it killed her."

"Ah. See, she had fallen on the path before she was brought to safety. She had lost a lot of blood, and was crawling through the brush pregnant, ready to give birth, when she—"

"Aw, momma, wasn't there anyone there to save her?"

"No. I mean, well, yes, Nicomachus, the doctor from Macedon. He helped her. Yes, he took her into his tent and delivered the babies—uhm, the baby. Excuse me. He delivered El Totsira."

As Renee looks at her doubtfully, Helene feels her heart drop. Has Renee heard the break in her words? The boy's eyes *that boy* seems to pierce her serene façade, exposing her thoughts, revealing her weakness. She hates him for that, but she tries hard not to. She takes a deep breath.

"You mustn't worry my child, Rekha did not suffer too badly. Nicomachus was the best doctor in the world. He was the top physician in his kingdom, working right under King Amyntas—"

"Wait, mommy, I am sorry, what did you say before?"

"Huh?"

"Did you say that Rekha gave birth to, to *babies*?"

"What?"

"You said babies, did you not? In the plural. Was there another—"

"Oh? Oh, no. Well, yes. I mean, I don't—"

"Mommy."

Renee looks at her squarely, just as she had gazed at him so many times before. *The boy is smarter now.* Helene could see the growth and maturity Renee had exhibited over the past few months as he kept growing into his younger teens. *The boy is smarter now; he is more experienced.* Helene pauses and takes a deep breath before beginning to speak again. She continues in a hurried whisper.

"Okay, okay, yes I said Rekha had babies, in the plural. You heard me right. Yes, El Totsira had a twin, just like you. He had a twin brother—" Helene stops to see Renee's reaction. Though he feels hurt inside, he just looks at her plainly, waiting for her to continue. *Go on,* his eyes seem to say. Sensing the fragility of the moment, she obeys.

"Yes, he had another half. A twin, just like you. His name was O'Talp. He was a broad shouldered child, grew up to be a brute, did he. But we aren't supposed to speak of him. You look very tired—"

"I am *very* awake, thank you." Renee says. Helene looks up at the ceiling and tries to decide whether this is a fight she will choose, "I am very awake."

"Ok then," Helene gets up and walks across the room to close the door, looking this way and that down the hall before closing it behind her, finally confident that Renee's ears are the only ones around. The two sensors in the corner are squatting wallflowers well accustomed to their lack of acknowledgement. Helene sits next to the young child, and taking his hands in her own, she begins to speak.

"O'Talp was a broad shouldered man, a warrior, a fighter who was greatly loved by his wrestling coach, who named him O'Talp after the robust figure he had exhibited. O'Talp wrestled at the Isthmian games, and had won many a trophy at an extremely young age.

"He grew to be a smart man, like his twin El Totsira, a smart man, but a little bit...well, different. Anyways, when he spoke, his words were like honey from a bee and his lips parted for only the sweetest of songs, his—"

"Wait, how was he different?"

"Well, while El Totsira was loved by many, his other half, this...O' Talp, needed to be restrained, and El Totsira told him so, but he didn't listen. O'Talp started to—" Helene pauses at the sound of footsteps in the corridor outside. The beating of her heart increases with the rate of Dewey's breaths as she realizes that she may have gone too far, that she may have told the curious boy just a bit too much.

"How was he different?" Renee persists.

"Y'know what, Don?" Helene turns to the boy sharply. "He was a twin just like you, but it really isn't so important." She could feel the poison of frustration rising in her waters, "No one really talks about it, and most of his story, if there even is one, has mostly been forgotten. El Totsira had a brother, a mother, even, well, even a father. The boy had many things, and to delve too deeply into any one would be a shame to the light of El Totsira's legend, a perversion of the prophet's life, and a disgrace to all the lessons and truth that can be reaped from an examination of his story."

"Okay. But momma, why can't—"

"I'm sorry, but now it is my time to interrupt. The life of the other half is just not our concern. I love you so so much," she leans into give him a kiss on his forehead as Renee tries to speak, but submits after some hesitation, "so so much, and I will see you tomorrow, and perhaps we can continue this discussion at another time."

Renee finally closes his eyes, returning to the thoughts of his inner intellect, the place where he has always felt most comfortable. He does not see Helene leave the room; by the time Helene rises from the bed, Renee is already at peace in another place.

Helene rushes out of the children's quarters a bit shaken from Renee's questions *The boy is smarter now* but more from her fear *am I actually scared of the boy? No, of course not. I can do this.*

She knows she made it out clean this time, but fears Renee's curiosity about O'Talp will grow with his years. She may not get away so easy next time. But such fears seem premature and she quickly shoves them away, locking them up tight at the bottom of her well.

ΩΨΩ

The smells of the kingdom rise with the sun as Joachim wakes to the scent of eggs, fresh butter, oranges, and lemonade. He heads to the dining hall to find Helene and

Dewey fully dressed in the regular Posteriorian garb of color, smiling at the presence of their beloved judge. The immensely carved marble table wears the most beautiful tablecloth of multi-colored fabrics craft-fully sewn together, a cloth of suede, cotton, flax, beads, and adornments, a cloth completely covered with the most lavish, colorful foods: waffles covered in sliced fruit, crepes, fresh butter, fresh garlic, eggs and beef of every type, all spiced to the greatest degree, cakes, pastries, fresh milk, and of course, a huge basket of freshly picked oranges.

"The same thing as yesterday," Joachim complains jokingly, as if it is not enough, "and the day before, and the day before that."

The sunlight glides through the immense window hovering over them, filling the room with the golden glow of the teeming wildlife outside, the chirping of birds, the hum of bustling crowds so far away. As the warmth of another Lyceumean day rains down upon them, Joachim moves forward to join Helene and Dewey. Without a moment's hesitation, the three begin to eat.

Helene watches Dewey as he shoves the food in his mouth. She wonders how he fits more food in his mouth when it is already stuffed. She waits for his mouth to explode, food squirting out of his overloaded cheeks like rain. But it never does.

Dewey is using the same purple fork he has always used. Everyone knows it is his; even Dewey himself refers to the fork as 'Dewey's fork.'

Before much time has passed, Joachim picks up his head. With food still in his mouth, he looks around the room, and begins to speak.

"Where's Renee?"

Dewey and Helene look at each other briefly, and Helene opens her mouth to speak.

"He, he wasn't in bed when I went to wake him."

"Well, where *is* he?"

"I, I don't really know."

Joachim shakes his head in frustration and lifts his large spoon to take another bite of a large melon before him. The spoon hesitates in front of his mouth, as if he is deciding whether to continue eating or to look for his younger son. His hand shakes in mad indecision. Finally, the melon goes into his mouth, almost missing and falling onto his lap. Before even beginning to chew, his chair screeches on the wooden floor as he stands up to his full seven foot height. His cheeks are red in anger but his mouth is full. For both reasons he is speechless.

"Oh, I heard him get up early," Dewey offers.

"Aaahhtt?" Joachim realizes he cannot speak, he tries to take his time to chew the food in his mouth, "What?"

"I heard Renee get up early," Dewey lies, "I couldn't hear much because I was sleeping, but I'm pretty sure I heard him get up and out of bed some time before wake-up was called. But don't worry," the boy could see the concern in his father's eyes, "Don has been wandering a lot lately, and I'm sure he is okay."

"Well, what could the boy be doing? I mean what does he—"

"Father, it's fine! He hasn't been showing up for many meals now, he usually just wanders the garden alone, but now he often brings along a book. Can we just eat? Renee is *always* reading, his eyes turned down, his face in a book, his—"

"Oh, El Totsira! Tell me what to do with this child!" Joachim looks up to the ceiling, his hands moving upwards as if praying to a God. Finally, he turns to Dewey and to his lover, Helene. It is times like this when he thinks briefly of Katherine and remembers how comforting she had been. What would Katherine have done if she were here today? Helene has tried her best here in the kingdom, and she has been wonderful indeed, but Katherine, oh Katherine, how her words had meant so much more, how her touch had calmed so much softer like aloe upon a wound, calming, cooling, meaning so much more. Joachim sighs, reminding himself of the goodness of his days, that there will always be troubles and he must concentrate on what he has. He turns to sit down, joining his family for breakfast just as Renee stumbles into the room.

"Sorry if I'm late," Renee says quietly as he walks softly into the center of the room, pulls out a chair from the table and sits down as if nothing has happened. Joachim eyes the boy up and down.

"Where were you? Where—y'know Renee, I don't even know what to ask first. Why don't you tell us all what it is that you are wearing?"

"Excuse me?"

"What are you wearing?"

Renee looks down at himself. Today, he is all covered in black, wearing his white pillowcase wrapped around his waist, supporting the baggy black fabric covering him from underneath.

"Well, it is my pillowcase, that is the only way I could get this on, to support—"

"No," Joachim seems to force a cracked chuckle, "Why are you wearing that? Why are you wearing black? My God, if anyone sees you, the son of Posteriorian royalty, what they would think!"

"I do not care what others think—"

"This isn't just about you! It is about your family. Your nation. We would be ruined!" Joachim swallows his food and takes a deep breath, "You always just think of yourself. I—I just don't understand it. We have given you all these beautiful garments, why would you ever choose to, to wear this, this garbage?"

"I, I just don't see what the big deal is. I am wearing this because it is comfortable and practical. It is baggy, so its room allows me to move comfortably, and its black color is simple, reliable, and keeps me warm." Joachim is at a loss of words, so Renee continues, "Really, what is the big deal? I have always been a bit...overwhelmed at everything being so colorful, so...complex. Why does everything have to be so confusing? Sometimes, well, sometimes I feel as if with all our color, we forget function, and with all our experiences, we forget reason. For me, the colors are just too overwhelming. I'm sorry father, I just needed...a rest."

"*What?*" Joachim slams his fist on the table, sending an olive flying into the air. Dewey considers catching it with his mouth, but he thinks the better of it. "Did you say you need a *rest?* No, my boy, we do not rest. Do you ever see me rest in court? Do you ever see me close my eyes and go to any private chambers to think in peace? What would Lyceum say? What would El Totsira say? No, I face all the evidence, I experience all the parties in front of me, facing all shades and colors of experience I possibly can; I do not run anywhere to be by myself, for what could one ever accomplish without seeing the world in which he lives? We are an active nation," Joachim yells, banging his fists on the table, "a nation who does not dismiss anything when we want to 'rest'. We do not turn from any experience that comes our way and we never get tired. Our lives are full of experience and color, and our clothes must show who we are. You especially, as a child of royal descent, need to show an example to the people that see you, so that the way you present yourself shows the mission you undertake as a Posteriorian, with at least, at least *some* color, let alone the absence of all color, this black empty, this dark—where, where did you get that piece of shit, anyway?"

"Honey!" Helene tries to calm Joachim, but to no avail.

"Where did you get that piece of shit, you, you...I will find who made that for you, and I will deal with him myself. Do you hear me?" Joachim leans in close so that Renee could feel the man's garlic breath on his pale dry skin, he could almost see his own reflection in the many beads of sweat rolling down the brow of the impatient old man.

Renee thinks of arguing back. He thinks of telling his father off, of telling him that clothes don't matter, that it is what is inside that counts, that there is no knowledge to reap from these foolish clothes they wear, the yellow beer that they drink, the loud women with whom they sleep and dream. All of those transient experiences are confusing, *experience is deceitful,* and though the workings of the inner mind may not give much, they are the only things worth looking towards. That is where peace and clarity lie.

But Renee sits quietly with his face turned towards the floor, hot tears silently streaming down his tender white cheeks like soft rain pattering down a glass pane, washing the color from his face. Helene tells Joachim to calm down, but Renee does not hear. Helene puts her arm around the boy's shoulders, but Renee does not feel. Renee does not care. He looks down at his meal. No longer hungry, he manages to choke down most of what is in front of him. He does love garlic, and luckily, that has been put on his plate. But tears fall down, lending his food their salty taste, stinging his tongue, biting his palate as it goes down.

The butler goes to fetch Renee some water. Renee has only drunken water most his entire life, and the butlers know his preference well. But this time, as the butler turns to the barrels of drinks, Joachim gives him a new order.

"The boy will have punch today, Galveston. Thank you, the colorful fruit punch is all he will drink, the kiwi punch, and maybe put some mango and cherry in there" he looks straight at Renee, "That is all he will drink today."

Renee hates punch, and this is something Galveston always knew. But Galveston wastes no time. At once, he pulls the ladle out of the water barrel and pushes it into the punch, which he brings before Renee's frowning face.

Suddenly, Renee feels an unexplainable urge for something he never even thought of using before. When the butler begins to walk away, Renee quickly calls his name and he halts in midstep.

"Sir, I would like a straw immediately."

"At once, young sire."

Renee does not know why he asked for a straw; he never did so in the past. Perhaps it is so he won't have to gulp in as much drink as quickly, but he could just sip it from the straw. Perhaps it is just dumb luck. But when Galveston returns to insert the straw in the boy's glass, the reason no longer matters. For when Renee notices how the straw looks through the glass, he sees a sight that gives him strength, that assures him of his sanity, that tells him he is not too crazy after all.

You see, as Renee looks through the glass, the straw looks bent, crooked, jerking to the side at the water line. He sees how the straw goes into the glass completely straight, but upon hitting the water line, (where the punch begins), it seems to continue downwards from a different point; it offers the illusion that the straw is bent. Quickly, Renee grabs the top of his straw and takes it out of his glass. He observes the straw and the straw looks back at him, in one straight line.

The straw looks completely straight; it was never bent!

Experience is deceitful. Renee feels strength rising inside of him, confirmation of the straw telling him he is right *experience is deceitful* and he remembers how Helene's eyes looked from up close, how one fell on top of the other until they merged into one big eye. He remembers examining a pebble by closing one eye at a time, and how it looked different from each eye. He looks around the room, at the deep maroon lush curtains, the colorful cakes and pastries surrounding, the ornamentation dancing across the interior of the sunlit room, and he realizes that they are all the same thing. They cannot be trusted.

It is all an illusion.

Dewey and Joachim are preoccupied, stuffing their faces as Renee observes them in disgust, but soon it is not them he sees, but the dumbly hung faces of ghosts filling the stands at the art fair, gorging themselves, stuffing themselves with the experiential buffet, and the masks look so dreamful, so empty, *experience is deceitful* he thinks of the Plado, the wax once held in Rekha's grasping right hand, changing shape and color, losing its honey fragrance as its shape alters this way like the multicolored ants dancing across Dewey's feet and that *experience cannot be trusted* he realizes that it is all the same, it is all one big joke, a massive rainbow hoax, a colorful maze of vertigo too full, too heavy, lulling, deceiving, seducing anyone that does not turn away. Renee smiles *that's right* at the fresh knowledge, the great confirmation his drink had supplied. Without wasting any more time, he drinks the pink liquid punch through that straw, sipping up every last drop.

It is the best drink he has ever had.

ΩΨΩ

For most of that day, Renee Don Cartez manages to mostly keep to himself. This is not difficult for him since his solitude is no longer much surprise to the others; it is almost expected. And as the sun begins to set, Renee feels drawn to the inner corridors of the palace, the area where his father would often like to work late at night. Renee makes his way towards the inner offices, a tiny silhouette teeter-tottering through the lamp-lit core of the living kingdom like a tumor sliding its way forward, slipping through the heart of a breathing, living organism, just rolling along slowly, his steps sure but slow as if they know they are probably somewhere they should not be.

Just when his steps begin to grow weary and his stomach begins to warn of trouble, Renee sees a strange light at the end of the hallway. It is a pale light, but full of motion, sending shadows dancing across the inner stone walls. Inching forward, Renee notices that the door to his father's office has been left open and the pale light has been leaking out. *That's strange.* Renee's mind seems to speak to him directly. *That door is always shut.* But Renee sees scratches near the lock, as if someone had been meddling with it. *I think I have seen enough. It is time to go.*

But someone must have left it open. Someone must have left it open for me, just as someone left a wax tablet under my pillow.

But who?

Renee enters the room, almost against his will. His father's thinking lamp is alight in the upper corner of the room. It consists of a dithering flame that wavers both in intensity and in color; the flame changes from yellow to blue or purple, then to orange and green, and often back to yellow to start again. The flame is surrounded by a smokey ball of glass, clouded in most of its exterior except for certain spots that are shaped like horses, birds, cherubs, and stars. The glass ball spins around the flame it encompasses such that the flame shoots blue, yellow, and orange creations gliding across the walls, flickering in intensity, iridescent in warmth. Renee has never before actually seen such a lamp, but had only heard about it from Helene or from Galveston's children that he used to play with during the summer days. The lamp has been said to have been passed along for many generations, perhaps from all the way back to the days of El Totsira. It is claimed that the function of the lamp is to keep the mind of the great judge of the High Court from caving in and drawing knowledge from nothing but itself. The lamp has always been there for every great judge ever appointed, to give him sensory experience of light darting around his room, reminding him that even in the quiet privacy of his own office, he must not venture too deep into his own mind, but rather must consider the outside world, the experience he has absorbed over his life and through the events of the present case considered in front of him. The light distracts him just enough to keep his mind from straying too deep inside itself where he would eventually find himself lost with nothing to grasp, no experience from which to compare, no perspective from which to base all thought.

Renee is drawn to the center of the room. He finally arrives at his father's large oak desk, a monster of a block covered in documents, affidavits, stipulations, old photographs, aged drawings, and small sculptures and dusty trinkets long overdue, sculptures that Joachim was never able to give away. *Turn around* a tiny voice inside of him says *it is not too late.* But then, that other voice speaks out *but the door was open. It is never open. Maybe I am here for a reason, like the wax under my pillow. Someone is watching over me. I am here for a reason. Someone wants me to be.*

No. I must leave.

But as Renee turns to leave, the illuminated creatures on the wall seem to circulate towards him, coaxing him to stay. In his confusion he trips over a pile of Joachim's secret documents. He falls to the floor. As he sees the papers flying out around him, his curiosity is finally hooked.

Renee sees news articles and old drawings of O'Talp staring back up at him.

O'Talp!

He sees scrolls written of the sage's life of the legend known by many as El Totsira's 'other side.' The parchment smells as old as it looks dark, but Renee's face is illuminated by the ancient text. To him, the story is golden.

But there is something else. The documents of O'Talp's story have a smell unlike anything Renee has smelled before. Closing his eyes, Renee inhales the scent with pleasure. It is an old, empty smell and it seems to put his mind at rest, allowing him to think. After a lifetime in a nation where everything smells like flowers, fruits, and juices, this new smell is calming to Renee's nerves.

The documents smell like Nothing.

Crouched on the floor, submerged in a pile of documents and scrolls, Renee Don Cartez does not feel the hours pass by as he makes his way through the chronological life of the neglected twin prophet, O'Talp. No sound from the outside hallway interrupts and no one's presence intervenes (and this too, is a good thing, for even if a loud noise had marched pass, Renee was so engrossed in the documents of his father that he never would have noticed; surely he would have been caught). Of course, Renee's private sensor is there, but both subjects know that sensors may never intervene in any way, disrupting the natural course of events.

Completely absorbed in the papers at hand, Renee reads how O'Talp had emerged from Rekha's womb, his small right hand locked tightly onto his older twin's heel, baby fingernails digging, bleeding, giving way, piercing through skin, leaving their signature on El Totsira's ankle. O'Talp grasped El Totsira's heel without relent, pulling him back into the womb from whence they both came, fighting for his firstborn rights. Renee discovers how O'Talp was always jealous of his older brother's firstborn rights, how he was always bigger, broader, *grew up to be a brute, did he* but never sacrificing brute strength for intelligent speech *his words were like honey from a bee.* Renee learns how O'Talp originally had no name, but was eventually called O'Talp by his wrestling instructor for his broad stature later in life. Renee sees how O'Talp was raised with his twin brother by Nicomachus, but how O'Talp had not been able to fit into the family too well at all, how he had always stood separate, how he had always wanted something more.

As Renee's deep interest intensifies with the rising of the moon, he discovers that O'Talp began to stray away from his unforgiving family at still a young age, how he had these thoughts, these *innate ideas* he would call them, these truths that would speak to him from inside his head, slowly growing, blossoming inside him over the years, seizing his full attention away from the world outside, away from his family and the world that they had so badly wanted him to love. The outside world we experience from our bodies had suddenly seemed so fleeting, so *deceptive*, that it was difficult to learn anything from them.

O'Talp thought there was something better. Something more. *You're dreaming* the others would taunt him *perhaps we are all dreaming* he answered. But as much as they tried to pull him out into their world, O'Talp held fast to his intellect. But the others would not leave him alone. So he set out on his own, and for that, he was held to be a disgrace in every Lyceumean home.

Reading on through the still of night, Renee's mind is excited asleep. Asleep, yes, because he feels a dream coming on too good to be true. Excited, yes, as he feels the surge of self-fulfillment exploding inside of him, an identity he has been searching for for what seems like his entire life, a missing piece in the puzzle he has always struggled to call himself. As Renee reads further about O'Talp's life, he feels a connection, that he can relate to the lonely character. He identifies with O'Talp, something he has never felt before. It is as if he was there with O'Talp the entire time. He feels the loneliness that O'Talp felt, the search for peace, the despair. But now he feels the wind of O'Talp's horse rides pass through his hair. He feels the blows O'Talp received in battle, the great woes the legend suffered through childhood, the warmth the myth had felt as he eventually died under the executioner's axe. As the smoky-cold glass ball begins its hundredth orbit around Joachim's thinking-lamp, Renee feels the reunion of his soul with its counterpoint.

O'Talp was just like him.

Feverishly plying through the catalogues at hand, Renee is now eager to discover more about his forefather O, the one that was always kept secret from him. So Renee reads on.

O'Talp broke away from his family, from his brother who never needed him, from Nicomachus who had tried to love. He ventured off into the caves miles away from home, the cave where mother Rekha had been buried. O'Talp lived here for many years, watching the shadows move across the cavernous walls under Mount Korab. After some time, just as the shadows began to be all that he knew,

O'Talp met a few mountain men with their sled-pulling dogs, a hungry group passing his cave on a voyage to a distant land. The men were hungry but did not want to stop or disrupt their flow of travel, the rhythm their steps had finally attained to get them to their final destination. But when they witnessed the inner strength of O'Talp's mind, when they drank the sweet honey of the prophetic caveman's words, their hunger had waned, their appetites subsided, and as many men would do in the future, in O'Talp they found solace and in his words comfort. From that day on, they never desired anything more.

So, they decided to stay.

O'Talp became their leader, attracting more and more men as they passed his cave on their way through those winter months. He performed miracles, though most would go wrong or succeed more than they were meant to. Once, he turned a dead man into a horned toad as he tried to bring him back to life. Another time he brought back a mutilated arm, but as the man looked down upon his new arm, he saw two hands sprout from his one wrist. But these incidents were rare if ever occurring, so they did little to mitigate the spread of his favorable name. After some time, the men he had influenced became so numerous that the caves could no longer hold his followers and their shelter had been rendered inadequate. So O'Talp moved out to establish his own nation.

But El Totsira found out about this, and he sent soldiers out to seize the alleged prophet. He saw O'Talp as a nuisance and a threat to his power, and he wanted his men to rid the world of all, distractions, as he would put it. El Totsira was not yet a king, but as a young man, he had gained much title in the ranks, and had achieved much power through his boyish looks, his colorful clothes, his smiles and laughs that seduced weak men to walk behind him, following his every whim.

It did not take long to find him. The Posteriorian soldiers spilled over O'Talp's band of men like a tidal wave splashing a great blanket of blood over the few hundred men so horribly murdered that night. O'Talp was captured and brought to El Totsira in chains, a prisoner of his own blood, a wretched mess lying before him, an array of chains, blood, metal, and flesh. O'Talp lay before his own brother's feet. El towered over him, looking straight down in the eyes of his baby brother.

El Totsira, usually a man of so many transient words, could not even bring himself to speak at this moment. He just stood there looking down at his younger twin, his 'other side,' his brother of solitude, of dark abstinence and inner reason. El shook his head and walked away without ever turning back. As he was dragged away, O'Talp had vowed that he would avenge his cause; he prophesized that a true descendant of his would one day reclaim his glory and accomplish what he had not. El Totsira heard these words drowning away behind him, but he kept walking on as if eager to get away from his own brother's fate. This was the last time he ever saw his brother, for just the next day, O'Talp was killed under the executioner's axe.

Sure, it was decades later *to be born* that people began to speak of sightings of O'Talp *first you have to die*. They said he had appeared to them under different identities, first as old Phaedo, then as different preachers over the years, as the young Heracleitus who came to tell a ruler to let things be, since "all things flow like streams," or the wise Protagoras who taught that "man is the measure of all things," and lastly of Theaetetus who came to question the true definition of knowledge before the first Posteriorians burned him at the stake.

But the Posteriorians denied it. They could not believe it was O'Talp. His spirit was dead to them, and so was his mode of thought.

Renee puts down the execution documents, feeling the pain in his forearm for the first time. He waves his fingers in and out, grimacing with pain. He has been clenching the document tightly for some time. As he puts the parchment upon the granite floor, he spots a drawing of O'Talp being dragged to his brother's castle, the chains dragging on the floor behind him, weighing down his large shoulders, breaking his burly back, the blood wetting a path of red footprints following each painful step. Renee's fingers move to pick up the old drawing. He realizes that he has been biting his lower lip for a while as a drop of blood rolls down his chin, a black ruby on a white pillow, falling fast, landing onto the drawing. Renee sees *feels* his own blood mixing with that of O'Talp's.

Renee looks through the surrounding documents, thinking his search almost complete. But underneath, yes, underneath the drawing of O'Talp, Renee finds something he had never expected to see.

Renee finds a picture of himself.

Rolled in a scroll of pictures bound with a red ribbon, Renee finds pictures of himself, pictures of his birth, pictures of his infancy, and drawings of what many believe O'Talp would have looked like as a child. Crumbled in between the photos is a note with messy scribblings on it, and though the scribblings are rushed and messy (as they would be coming from the hand of any Posteriorian,) Renee recognizes the writing at once. It is his father's. Joachim had written this. *What is this?* Renee's mind begins to whirl with emotion, but his intellect is sharp, and he begins to piece things together. *My father's worried handwriting…but why? What is it that worries him so?* Suddenly, Renee recalls the last words from O'Talp's mouth. *One day, a descendent will follow in my footsteps. But that is impossible. No, it cannot be me. I must tell Joachim not to worry; it cannot be me. I must comfort him. I am just a little boy…*Renee could not yet feels the tears now streaming down his cold numb cheeks *a little boy who doesn't know any better. This is too big, too big for me…I don't want this…You don't have to worry father. I'll try harder. I'll try harder.*

Now it all comes back to him: his father's worried looks, Helene's infinite patience masking the troubled worries surfacing in her eyes *we don't talk about that* the way they all jump when Renee goes off missing *where were you* or try to express himself *what are you wearing* or even when Renee just feels a bit tired from their colorful confusions *we never rest.* Now he understands his father's troubled looks, the stressed man he becomes every night as he leaves his courtroom's chambers.

For the first time, Renee understands why his family has trouble loving him for who he is, and for this he hates O'Talp. He hates O'Talp's foolish endeavors and what they have done to his life. He hates O'Talp for turning his family against him, for giving them a reason not to understand, not giving him a chance to be himself.

Feeling a wet warmth spread between his legs, Renee looks down to see he has wet himself in shame. When he entered this room, discovering the forbidden story of O'Talp, Renee felt glad. But now, now the boy is only shocked and scared. He sits as the urine rolls down his thin white legs, darkening his dull gray robes, staining his pride. He looks over to the sensor staring back plainly at him with two blank eyes.

"What? What do you want?" he shouts at the sensor, a mere statue writing down all that is said, "*What do you want?*" he continues, "What? You gonna write this down?" he screams, pointing down at the fresh pool of urine on the floor, "*YOU GONNA WRITE THIS DOWN?*"

The sensor just looks back plainly, a motionless mask staring straight ahead, two glossy eyes free of any emotion looking through Renee as if he didn't exist *I am right here* as if he is a ghost *right here* like the eyes of a dead man desperately telling their evening grave digger a last goodbye, but missing him, see nothing but the wide dark sky.

Suddenly, Renee feels like he is being watched. "Who are you?" Renee looks up towards the ceiling, "Why did you place questions under my pillow? Why did you send me here? I don't want anymore of it! You hear? No more! Who are you?" But there is no answer.

Renee closes his eyes and tries to steady his breathing. Finally, he manages to pick himself up on his own two feet, slowly walking out of the room in despair. Anyone dwelling in the kingdom would know that the maidservant will come in the morning to clean up the mess before Joachim's arrival, but Renee does not think of this; his mind just longs for sleep. Renee walks down the hall to his quarters, a small child trailing drops of urine behind, where the sensor darts this way and that, never tiring, following his subject consistently, with diligence, wherever he may go.

8

We must follow reason despite the caresses, the threats and the insults of the body to which we are conjoined, despite the action of the objects that surround us.

Nicolas Malebranche

"Psst! Hey, over here!"

It sounds as if one of the pines has spoken, a tree whose leaves have remained silent for too long. Renee dismisses the voice at once, assuring himself that it is coming from his mind. He continues his walk along the edge of the woods behind the palace, southward, into the shadow of the needle. He has walked this way many times, though it is usually in the late summer afternoons rather than as it is now, welcoming the coming dawn. See, after he had discovered O'Talp's story (thus wetting himself in Joachim's thinking room), Renee had returned to his quarters as the moon had fully risen. He had managed to clean himself without awakening Helene or Dewey, knowing most Posteriorians were deeply absorbed in their sleep.

Renee lay in bed for some time, sincerely trying to submit to sleep, but sleep never came. He tried to clear his head *one day, your head will be clear*, but all he could see is those words etched into the wax tablet found under his pillow weeks ago *but until then, perhaps a walk through the woods behind the needle would help find some answers.*

Who wrote it? It was signed anonymously *a friend*, Renee recalls. A friend. Renee did feel the need to clear his head. Just before the July sun started stretching its rays over the distant Apuan Hills, Renee put on a fresh set of gray robes. Closing the door softly behind him, he strolled slowly out of the palace and into the cool dawn air.

Now, Renee makes his way south through the forest behind the needle. Looking up at the tower, Renee thinks of Disegno, remembering the terrible scar on the man's face, running down his jawline like the tall needle in which he is now imprisoned.

But Renee wishes for such a prison. Renee envies Disegno for the peace he must enjoy, the silence of cold stone locking off any sensation *distraction* from outside, the comfort of an excuse to be free with his mind. Unlike Renee, Disegno does not have to go outside or smile or be around idiots.

Passing the needle, Renee intends to sit in the eastern farmlands of the kingdom, the place where he had sat many times before when he was younger. This is where he would watch the children's agriculture lessons from a distance. He would often remain there for hours afterwards, wondering where the crops could have come from and the mathematics of how tall they could stand without falling over.

Renee had been forced to attend private agriculture lessons with his brother during the growing seasons. Though Posteriorian scientists had previously found ways to extend the growing season even past the first frost (often into early December), the crops were prime during the original growing season from May to October, and agriculture was thus easiest to teach during that time. However, after just two years of the lessons, Renee had refused to continue. To his family's surprise, he would insist on remaining inside the stone walls of the palace on those afternoons. Helene had nudged him at first, but after Renee's family saw how beautiful Dewey's crops had turned out, they forgot about Renee completely.

For years, Renee continued to be invisible behind Dewey's green thumb. He began to venture out in the later years to watch his brother from a distance. Renee saw the luscious broccoli, the plentiful leaves of spinach, monstrous melons and grapes his brother had produced. But even more he saw the growth of smiles on his parents' faces, Helene's golden cheeks shining like apples. At first he pretended the smiles, the laughs—they were all for him. He smiled back proudly, cold tears on his face. But as the years passed his heart became empty, and he embraced the emptiness. His head filled with numbers, a blank stare upon his face. He felt nothing. It was so much easier that way.

Tonight Renee knows that no one will be there, as the nation is asleep in dreams. Upon approaching the northern tip of Brittany, Renee expects the sun to begin to rise, but the dawn maintains its dark glow over the sparse woods in which Renee travels. However, some light begins to fill the sky equally, emitting a great fog as if someone had raised a dusty flame behind a large plastic screen sky. The light seeps its way into the cracks between the trees, showering Renee in the musty tannish gray of an old barn. As he closes his eyes, breathing in the cool, sterile nothingness, Renee can hear the voice call out once again.

"Hey, prince! Psst! Over here!"

This time, Renee knows the voice has not come from his mind, but he cannot imagine where it came from, other than from this large pine beside him. He knows that no one ever goes into these quiet woods behind the needle, let alone this early in the dawn. He is also surprised at being called a prince for he has not been called that by anyone for so long as he can remember *I am a prince* so he almost passes the voice by, as if it could not be speaking to him *a prince*.

"Over *here!*"

Renee turns but sees nothing but trees. But suddenly, a small dark figure begins to emerge from behind one of the pine trees. It stands there silently, allowing Renee to examine its uncharacteristic figure.

The figure is small, like that of a boy. His face looks young, but his body is bent over, torn by years of strain. Though he is just a boy, just one year younger than Renee himself, he looks twice the prince's age. He stands hunched over, his back bent, hair hanging over his concentrated brow. His beady eyes seem to squint from the musty light, but Renee can tell they are not squinting; they are always that small, two dark rubies shining above a large protruding nose. He wears a musty brown robe, similar to that of Renee's, though it does not fit him properly, hanging off his hunched back like the ripped canvas of a broken kite hanging from its rods. But it is not these characteristics that shock Renee, for the strangest thing about him is that as he walks out from behind the trees, no sensors follow behind him.

He stands completely alone.

Now, Renee has never in his entire life seen any man completely alone, and such a sight of complete freedom and independence causes an incredible feeling of possibility in Renee. From the first day he opened his eyes, Renee has seen people only playing, shouting, drinking, loving, all in the company of others. And, in the rarest of moments when a Posteriorian wished to be left alone, his sensors were there at all times, sensing all that their subject would sense, recording every last detail, so that nothing *Nothing* passed without being shared, recorded, stored, and analyzed for future knowledge.

Renee feels a bit embarrassed at the presence of his own sensors and a slight flush fills his face. But watching this lone character, Renee feels a frighteningly comforting reaction to this boy's solitude, that he may do whatever he likes and *really* not be seen. Oh, to be completely alone! Renee struggles to look the boy in the face. Though the boy's face remains cast downward covered under his dark hair, his eyes look back, straight into those of Renee's.

"I know that I am not such a sight to behold," the boy says gently, "but if you will let me, I think we can help each other."

Renee steps back in surprise. "What, what happened to—"

"Oh, I was born with a crooked spine. It has grown irritated over the years, frustrating my posture. I may look a little…shocking to people at first," the boy smiles, "but after just a short amount of time, you will see, it will be nothing. It may frustrate my posture," the boy takes a step towards Renee, "but it does not alter my step."

"I, I don't know—" Renee struggles to steady his beating heart.

"You do not know. Speak precisely."

"What?"

"You slur your words. Instead of saying I don't know, you should say I do not know. But I am getting ahead of myself, for one day you will speak clearer than any man on the land. And your sight will not shock you, for you will not trust it. But now you are still a boy; your time has not yet come."

Renee takes a deep breath. He cannot tell why this mysterious stranger frightens him. Renee hides his shaking hands behind his back. He is glad when his own voice comes out steady.

"Are—are you the one who...What do you want?"

"Well," the stranger smiles as if he had been waiting for such a question, "for starters, we can start with your name."

"It seems you know who I am already."

"Yes. But do you?"

Renee remains silent, wondering if such a question desires an answer.

"Maybe I shall begin," the stranger takes another step forward, now standing where Renee just stood a moment ago. He extends his hand.

"I am Nicolas," he says.

Renee turns to run back to where he came from, but stops in his tracks as he realizes he has little to go back to. When he turns back to Nicolas, the cripple is standing in front of him, ready to snatch his hand. Renee tries to speak.

"I...I am—"

"Renee Don Cartez!" Nicolas exclaims loudly, as if a great tension has just been broken, a great joke cracked on the young prince, "Yes. Sorry if I scared you there," Nicolas says, patting Renee on the back, "Ha ha! It is a pleasure to finally meet you! You're a lucky one, that you avoided the quicksand around these parts—no one has ever gotten out of *that* alive. Why the long face?"

Renee feels laughter build inside of his stomach, but his face shows confusion. It is strange for him to see so much joy in so...ugly a person. Renee tries to speak.

"I am okay, I just—"

"Cannot sleep, I can guess. Yes, me neither. Ever since this damned nation's colors, sounds, smells, and sensations had overcome the barriers of my mind, leaking into my head, taunting me in my dreams, I have been unable to sleep. It is almost like a hamster's wheel in my head, spinning and spinning and spinning...you are not the only one, dear prince."

"How do you know about me?" Renee does not conceal his surprise.

"Oh, I have been watching you, prince, for when a strange boy like myself leaves his home, entering a hard life caused by his differences from those around him, do not think for one moment that he is to ignore the sight of someone just like him. We are few in number, people like you and I, and it's, ahem, it is best we stick together, if you know what I—"

"How could you know anything about me? You don't know me—"

"Oh, settle down, would you, prince? I have seen you, Renee, and just like me, you seem to be troubled by the…exterior of passion everyone seems to require of you, to interact with the world, to gain the experience you would rather not touch. I am your friend, Renee."

"What? Yes. That could be true, in…so few words. I am just like O'Talp! Do you know of him?"

"O'Talp, hm? I see you found your way through that door already. You move pretty fast for a little guy."

"You were the one who broke the lock?"

"O' what? What have they done to you, boy? They've got you speaking gibberish already? Ha ha! Look at that!" Nicolas throws his head back, turning to his side and pointing at Renee, as if speaking to an invisible audience observing them both, "Will you look at this! Ha! The quiet prince speaks his mind, the apple that fell far from the tree, the prince of peace, quiet, solitude, and silence, finally—"

"Who are *you*?" Renee tries to sound demanding, but his eyes show exhaustion, exhaustion from the life he has lived, from the loss of the peaceful walk he was supposed to take.

"Okay," Nicolas lowers his gaze, "Okay, I apologize. Yes. I am the one who put the wax under your pillow. I am the one who opened the door to your father's office. But that is not all; I have opened the door for many people's lives and I have been watching over you since you were a little boy. Well, let me give you some…perspective here. May I begin again?"

Renee crosses his arms over his chest, waiting for Nicolas to speak. He does not have to wait long.

"My real name is Nicolas Malebranche. I was born into a Posteriorian home near the great arena in the center of Lyceum. My father, also Nicolas Malebranche, used to be one of the many secretaries for the Grandee, and my mother, Catherine de Lauzon, loved him very much. When I came from her womb as the youngest of many children, both my parents loved me very much. But when I was three, they discovered that I was suffering from a malformed spine, and my father had insisted that I remain home, that I could not be seen. I was my parent's shame. An embarrassment. My father feared the children at school would tease me, calling me names such as Crooky Nooky or Ridiculous Nicolas, so he boarded up our windows, and though my parents and siblings were able to come and go as they pleased, I was to stay home, and I was not to go anywhere near the doorway, though I would sneak close to it on summer days such as this to listen to the sound of birds as they would pass, sometimes splashing as they stopped to bathe in our bird bath, the sounds of my siblings playing ball in the yard with the children from their school, their laughs, their joy. It killed me, every time they would laugh, every single time they…well, anyway, so I stayed in the house of my parents, receiving my elementary education from a private tutor. But my Posteriorian education taught me of the beauty of the outer world, the beauty of the sciences, of agriculture, art, architecture, our ecosystem. They made me look at the pictures, and they made me smell the smells. I was forced to learn of a beautiful world that I was prohibited to see. I was forced to appreciate a garden of life just beyond my walls, an entire universe I was not allowed to taste.

"Anyway, it just seemed hypocritical and all, teaching me that knowledge must be sought by experiencing the world, yet not allowing me to do so. So I tried my best to swallow my sufferings, and I began to study the small world in my attic, relishing the few beams of sunlight that managed to pry through the wooden boards lining my walls. I began to study the color of my floor, the shadows on the walls, the dye in the sheets of my bed. I did the best I could, and in time, I became an expert on the nature of light and color. Unlike other Posteriorians who had been given more experience than they could chew, I was able to focus on the few simple things placed under my visage, the way the colors in my room resulted out of different frequencies in the pressure vibrations of subtle matter as it changed through the day. By the time I turned eight, I was able to form a theory. I discovered that different colors result out of different frequencies in the pressure vibrations of subtle matter in the same exact way that different musical tones derive from different frequencies in the vibrations of air.

"But when I presented the theory to my parents, well, they thought I was insane. They asked me if I actually tested my theory and found results. I told them I did not need to; it made perfect sense. They laughed. 'Sense?' they laughed, 'What good is sense without an experiment?' They thought that if their other children cannot conceive of such theories after experiencing the world outside, well, what could I possibly do locked up in a dark attic? And who could blame them? That seems to make sense to anyone who fails to take a closer look. Maybe I *was* insane. But my theories still make perfect sense."

"I would like for you to show them to me one day."

"Really?" Nicolas's face lights up.

"Sure," Renee is intrigued, "I, I have never thought of such a concept, though I have done enough thinking to last me a lifetime."

"Really. Well I, too, would like to hear what you have come up with. I trust we will share many great ideas in the future."

"Perhaps." Renee blinks, bringing himself back to his strange present situation.

"Well, I would like that," Nicolas says, "if, of course, you ever wish to return here."

"Well," Renee's eyes remain stern, showing Nicolas his heart is not yet won, "How did you end up here?"

"Oh, yes, how did we get off track? So anyway, my parents chose to ignore my speculations, as they called them, as they grew more and more rapidly over the following months. But it was when I presented them with my vision of God, that, well, that they disowned me from the house. They kicked me out. Exiled. Banished from the only home I knew. Oh, why," Nicolas buries his face in his hands, "Why oh why did I have to share that with them? Shouldn't I have learned that they weren't going to listen? But it was too clear, too groundbreaking to just keep it to myself…but…but maybe I should have known better, maybe, well…no matter," Nicolas wipes away his tears, smiling in relief, "It is best that it happened this way. For now I am here, on my own, and it is only by this occasion that I have come to meet, well, to meet you."

"Yes," Renee says, "yes, perhaps. But why are you alone?"

"Excuse me?" Nicolas asks incredulously.

"Why are you alone? Where are your sensors?"

"Why are you *not* alone?" Nicolas answers, "Who are these…eavesdroppers," Nicholas looks directly at Renee's sensors, something a Posteriorian must never do, "that are tagging you around? Who are these little nuisances, distractions that will not allow you to think on your own?"

"Oh, no. They are not—"

"Yes, you know exactly how distracting they really are. Nuisances, they are, nothing but small distractions following your every step. Aren't you?" Nicolas looks at the dumbfounded sensors, addressing them directly, though their trained stare never loses its glazed blankness, "*Aren't you?*"

"Stop it!" Renee demands. His hands are shaking, and he hides them in his pockets.

"Why should I?"

"You know these are my sensors. You know why I have them. The law requires—"

"The law requires that which you *let* it require!"

"But, but if anyone finds out what you have done, if they tell the authorities," Renee pauses, disgusted at the Posteriorian words coming out of his own mouth, "that you are all alone, if anyone knew, you would be seen as a great threat to all of Lyceum, a great walking truth, a living example of everything they claim to be impossible. If anyone found out about you, if anyone knew, why, they, they could—"

"Spoken like a true Posteriorian," Nicolas smiles. "I let you speak because I know that you do not believe your words. I can hear it in your voice; they are like poison upon your tongue. It is your upbringing that is speaking, but I know it is not you, not Renee Don Cartez. However, it is the gravity of the truth, the changes it would cause you to make, that cause such hesitation."

"Not true!" Renee is ashamed of his words as soon as they leave his mouth.

"Then why are your hands shaking?"

Renee remains silent.

Nicolas says, "It was only after my family banished me from the household that I was able to explore my options and eventually shed my Posteriorian parts. It was only after I obtained a strong rope, bound my sensors by their hands and feet, leaving them in a place that will not be named, and fled into these woods to set to work, it was only then that I enjoyed real solitude, the kind any other Posteriorian can only dream of. It was only then that I realized just how lucky I really was. To have the freedom of myself. The power of I. It is everything.

"People out there can think what they want. They can never find me. For in their colorful buildings, flavorful orange groves, ecstatic drunkenness, who would ever venture out into these woods? Who, besides you, my prince, would ever have the insight, the type of mind that would desire such a quiet place? No true Posteriorian would ever venture here. And I am happy here. I see no alternative for myself anyways. I would never consider going back. Never. Yes. It was only after my exile, only then that I could enter my mind, building the foundations for unshakable truths, and sharpening the ones I had previously conceived—"

"What is this vision of God you spoke of?"

"Yes, thank you for reminding me. Wow. You see, I have not seen or spoken to another human being in what, say…a few years now...oh to hell with it, who is counting? Ha ha! My vision of God theory. Yes. I simply discovered that nothing can do what it does without God. I discovered that, in reason, just as all human action, or the action of any creature for that matter, is entirely dependent on God, so too is all human cognition. Both the motion of our bodies and our knowledge, or cognition, are completely dependent on the divine understanding. We cannot do anything without God. All of our actions, and our cognition, are completely dependent upon him."

"So you're saying, we can only know of ideas—"

"If those ideas are in God. And so too, no effect can occur without being caused by God himself."

"That is silly. Why does it seem that the cause is formed by something we do ourselves? Why does it seem that stubbing my toe is the cause of the following pain? And why has it *always* occurred that way, in that order?" Renee asks.

"Ah, you are speaking of the illusion of efficient causation between mundane events. Yes, you must realize that this arises out of a constant conjunction that God himself has instituted, such that stubbing your toe will always be followed by pain, or the kindling of a fire will always be followed by warmth. Thus, a person's mind cannot be the true cause of his hand's movement, nor can a physical wound be the true cause of pain. The cause is not *really* the wound, the toe stubbing, or the fire kindling, but rather those are just *expressions* of the real cause, namely God. "

"But," Renee says, "You have not considered that it is I who decides when to move my hand. It is I who decides, through my free will, exactly when I will kindle a fire, or stub my toe. And I only choose to do so at certain times. I only choose to do so—"

"Occasionally."

"What?"

"You choose to do so occasionally," Nicolas says. "See, when you choose to do such a thing, you create an occasion in which God's will is expressed. It is true, as you said, that in this limited world of experience, it seems that you are the cause of the things you affect. And, in a very limited sense, you are. You are the one who chooses, as you put it, to put such an event into effect. And you choose to do so on occasion. But you must realize that those occasions are moments when the previously-determined divine will is expressed. This is how it works. God said what. You decide when. God instituted a constant conjunction between fire and warmth, and you set occasions throughout your life when that constant conjunction is triggered and expressed."

"Right. That sounds nice. But you never told me how you know this. Well. Give me the argument. How did you reach these conclusions?"

"That is too much. Another time."

"I am not troubled by the fact that you suggest God's existence, for I see the way you think and so I trust you have begun at the very beginning, not assuming anything, building up a foundation of truths, one atop the other, never laying another brick until the one beneath it was completely flawless, firming and lasting."

"I have," Nicolas answers, showing no surprise at the rarity of the prince's words in Lyceum. Though one would never hear such words within the borders of Lyceum, Nicolas listens to Renee as if those words were they way all words should be, and have been, as if *of course* they were assumed.

"And I myself," Renee continues, "have reached my own conclusions about the existence of God, based on mathematical logic, on the stone-cold reason of my mind. But your vision of God, well, it belittles my free will, my every movement as merely opening the door for *another's* expression."

"And that, my prince, is exactly what my parents hated the most. They were able to bear me in their attic when I was merely calculating the way light frequencies bounced off different densities of the wooden boards in my room, when I was merely dissecting small insects that had crawled under the eaves, but it was when I belittled their experience of the world, when I told them they were meaningless, that experience did not belong to them, that they were not the agents of change, of movement, of life, it was then that they had decided to disown me, their crippled embarrassment, throwing me out of the house with only the clothes on my back." Nicolas looks up at the prince, "but it is through that, I must believe, that I have come to meet you. And I think we are very much alike."

"How so?" Renee asks, though he secretly agrees.

"From my observations of you, I have seen—"

"You have been watching me, you say?"

"Quite closely."

"How? The walls of the palace—"

"You will know everything in time," Nicolas looks at one of Renee's sensors, and for a second, it seems to Renee that the sensor actually looks back at Nicolas in acknowledgement, like a soldier to his captain *but that is impossible*— "But time is something we have not much of," Nicolas turns to look towards the Apuan Hills, "so I must tell you that I know what you have been going through. You must come with me quickly, for the sun is to rise soon, and we cannot be seen together. I live in my cabin, a small place that I built myself after being thrown into the wild. This is where I have been hiding." Nicolas points in an eastern direction, and Renee's gaze follows that of Nicolas's hand, but he sees nothing.

"I only see trees."

"No. Posteriorian color has blinded you to the subtle. Look closer," Nicolas says.

But still, Renee sees only trees.

"For the first time," Nicolas says, "Look. Really look."

Finally, Renee sees the cabin in the distant wood, a small hidden brown shack, a simple dwelling indeed.

Experiencing the scent coming from the cabin, Renee realizes for the first time that this is what Nicolas smells like too: Nothing. Renee remembers first encountering the smell on O'Talp's documents in Joachim's thinking room. The alluring smell of space, of vacancy, of peace, of nothing. That smell.

Nicolas stands before Renee, his hand pointed towards the cabin, but Renee makes no movement. He is not yet ready to throw away everything he has ever been, everything he will ever be.

"I can help you," Nicolas says, sensing the prince's doubt, "I know what you have been going through, the burdens that you have carried, fitting in, shall we say, with your fam—"

"What could you possibly know about me?" Renee demands, "Tell me! Tell me why I should listen to you! And I do not even know you!"

"Please. I am trying. I know that you have had trouble turning your Posteriorian experiences into knowledge, as everyone else here seems so able to do. I know that you have had trouble…trusting what your eyes tell you, trusting your sensations to be reliable enough to reap knowledge from. I know that you feel that there must be something deeper than experience, something deep inside of you, something that will not change when the emotional climate changes, when the lights go out, when immersed in liquid, or placed near a flame. Unlike your brother, your father, your nation, you are not satisfied with the grand, the colorful, the seducing theories that fall as fast as they rise. The flowery skyscrapers of Lyceum, the lively passions of our 'knowledge,' the fanciful theories of our scientists, all crumbling to the ground at the touch of time, a tremendous failing of wooden blocks as time slips out one foundation after another. And yet, they keep rising, experiences, experiments, the empirical, all based on an exterior view of the exterior world. How could they demand you put your faith in that, you ask? How can they demand that you be satisfied with such hoaxes, such conclusions with faulty premises, such short-lasting truths that fail you time and time again? Well I ask the same question, Renee Don Cartez.

"Leave that all. Leave that all, and come with me.

"I have learned to reject the world of experience, as you will soon learn to do. I have discovered that knowledge may be reaped from the ideas *inside* of my mind, rather than anything outside of it. For we know, do we not, that anything outside of my mind cannot be trusted. It has let me down before and it will let me down again. And you too, have been let down too many times, Renee, by your family, your experiences, by your love of life. Join me. You deserve better than what you have been forced to receive. It will not be easy to leave what you have known, but I am here to tell you what you already know—that you must. I have come here to give you strength.

"I have come here to remind you that you must follow reason despite the caresses, the threats and the insults of the body to which you are conjoined, despite the action of the objects that surround you. I exhort you, Renee Don Cartez, to recognize the difference there is between knowing and feeling, between our clear ideas, and our sensations always obscure and confused. I believe that, perhaps together, with our minds combined, we might find a better place, a more worthy plane in which we can dwell. There are other people out there, people of O'Talp. And I believe you realize the truth. That knowledge can only be found from ideas in our heads. And this, dear prince, is what holds us very much together."

Renee's notices tears form behind his closed eyes as he shakes his head from side to side as if trying to shut Nicolas out. Renee considered him a threat, a mysterious older danger hidden in these trees. Then, for a moment, he felt a connection. He felt he and Nicolas were friends. He thought Nicolas could help him *please* and he wanted to cry out *please, I am so glad you understand* sobbing into Nicolas's robes, *take me with you, take me away from all of this* but that feeling subsided quickly as Renee's Posteriorian upbringing helped push it away. Renee opens his eyes and steps back.

"Yes," Renee says, "We are connected in that way. But we are also different. I make my own road, and my actions are no doorway for God's expression. Even though we agree that man can only attain knowledge through ideas, you believe that all ideas exist only in God. I do not. One of the first things you said is that all human cognition and understanding is completely dependent upon the divine understanding. That is false. We agree that man can only reap knowledge from ideas, but it is only you who believes that we can only know of ideas if those ideas are in God himself. This cannot be true, for the ideas in my mind come from myself alone. Like you said, the power of I. And I am so much more than God's...occasion. I am 'always,' and will continue to be. We are similar, Nicolas, and I wish you the best of luck. But we are not the same. I am not coming with you, Nicolas."

"Very well."

"Excuse me?"

"If that is the choice you make now," Nicolas says.

"Then why are you smiling?"

"Because I am certain we will meet again."

"You seem very sure of yourself," Renee says, his patience waning.

"Yes, I know that you will go back to the world of experience now, and that you will live on the strength of our brief conversation, on the fact that someone like you exists. But as the weeks pass, and your brother's lavish feast of sensations does not stop, your father's case precedent leaking into your head, your food, your room, your bed, filling your heart with nonsensical hoaxes of your dreams, it will keep you up at night, dear Renee. It will pain me to watch, but your choice is a choice I must respect. For if you are ever to join me, it must be of your own volition. That time will come. I know it is hard to give up the world you have been given, Renee, the world in which you have grown. I know it is difficult because I have done it myself. But I am certain it is the right decision to make, though everyone's time to do it will come through their own free choice, as it always must. I will be watching your progress, watching you bear the burden of a world I decided to give up long ago. Do not look for me in your struggle, for I will not be found. Before you are ready, I will not exist for you, but when you are ready, I will be the easiest man to find. "

"Well," Renee says, "I am glad for you that you have reached such certainty, that you will know what to look forward to during the upcoming months in your cabin. So leave now. Go sit there in your cabin, thinking of me as much as you like. You may look forward to my return, but I will never come back."

Renee looks towards the Apuan Hills and sees the sun begin to peek its head over the farthest of the peaks. *People will come out soon* Renee realizes, *though this nation sleeps until the late morning, it is a long way back to the palace, and I must be there for the morning wake up.* Renee looks to the cabin one last time, but this time, it looks different. Sure, it remains a simple rectangle of brown,. but before it seemed a relief. Now it seems a sin. Renee wants to raise his voice to the poor crippled boy *do I look desperate to you* raising his fists in the air *what do I look like to you* raising his chest in the air *do you think I would just run off and drop everything for you* tears of anger streaming down his cheeks *who do you think you are?* but Renee speaks, his voice gentle but firm.

"I swear I will never return to this place," he says.

"And I will not even say goodbye," Nicolas answers.

Renee turns around and begins to walk north, back behind the needle, towards the palace in the distance. He walks slowly, but increases his pace as he nears the palace. The sky has turned misty, its immense cotton clouds staining a dark orange, sprinkling its tears upon the wet grass. Renee is eager to return to his comfortable quarters, the warmth of his room. After thirty minutes pass the sun's limbs manage to touch Renee's shoulders, offering enough warmth to carry him on his walk home. But as his mind savors the brief connection he felt with this stranger just a moment ago, Renee hesitates at the thought of continuing home. He thinks of the greeting he will be met with *where were you* of the incessant *howdoyoufeel howdoyoufeel* he can no longer stand.

Renee begins to realize that even though he walks towards the palace, the family, *the life* he calls his home, if he really wanted to be at home, he wouldn't really have anywhere to go.

9

Animals as well as men learn things from experience...and gradually from their birth treasure up a knowledge of the nature of fire, earth, stones, heights, depths. The ignorance and inexperience of the young are here plainly distinguishable from the cunning of the old, who have learned by long observation to avoid what hurt them and pursue what gave ease or pleasure. Is it not experience which renders a dog apprehensive of pain when you lift up the whip to beat him? (Or) which makes him infer from a sound that you mean to call him? It is impossible that this inference of the animal can be founded on any reasoning by which he concludes that like events must follow like objects. Animals are not guided by reason, and neither is man.

David Hume

Now I have already told you that fruit has always been a staple in most all Posteriorian homes, loved for its colorful sensations, wet taste, and variety of forms. In any Lyceumean kitchen one finds the most luscious star fruit, the sweet sapodilla, and occasionally, the big and thorny durian. Jackfruit and passion fruit fill the countertops of Lyceum while pomegranates and crescent lemons brighten the area below. In the winter, green apples and pears decorate each home. And in the summer, if one is lucky they can find gooseberries of every type. The palace too, is no exception to this rule. The royal quarters always have fruit available, large bowls on pedestals filled with the largest mangos, guavas, citruses, and coconuts one has ever seen, standing high in every corner of the kingdom like tall soldiers boasting their colorful armor, their golden bowled hands reaching out to offer their luscious bounty to anyone who may pass.

But there are a few fruits that the great Posteriorian farmers have been able to alter. By planting the seeds a certain way, the Posteriorians have been able to create these fruits in even twice, or sometimes triple, their original

Posteriorian size. One of these is the orange. This has been most fitting, since this is the fruit (and color) that represents the teachings of the Posteriorians. These oranges are the size of bowling balls. They taste much stronger than any ordinary orange you would know, but they must be eaten quickly or the great acidity of their juice will burn into one's tongue. But of course, eating quickly is no problem for any Posteriorian.

One early summer afternoon, Dewey leans on the outside of the castle wall peeling one of these very oranges on a balcony. He turns the orange before him and enjoys the freedom of ownership and control of such a precious object in his hands. He relishes the process of peeling its plump body, weighing and examining each piece of peel in the light before it comes off its source. Putting the peels aside in one palm, he is about to eat the first piece of orange when he sees a most unusual sight.

Renee strolls past him and into the palace with a black cat right on his heels. The cat startles Dewey and he jumps, accidentally bringing the orange close to his face. The orange sways inches from his eyes just for a second, but it is enough for the acid to sting them fiercely. Dewey grits his teeth in pain. He watches through hot tears as the black feline peacefully walks behind Renee like a faithful servant. But he does not yet notice Renee's face glowing with the novel feeling of being admired, albeit by a cat.

Dewey remains still for a few seconds, fighting the temptation to follow Renee *for he is the one who follows me*. But he trots after his brother and enters the palace. By now, the cat has jumped onto Helene's lap, and she pets it lovingly with one hand and stroking Renee's head with the other. Dewey cannot believe her soft imposition; Helene has never allowed any animals in the house, let alone a stray cat brought in by little Renee.

In truth, the cat has known Renee for almost a few days now. Renee found it during one of his walks in the royal gardens. It was standing still as if waiting for the young prince to find it. Renee wondered how the cat could have gotten there, for it was especially peculiar for animals to be wandering around the palace unchecked. Kneeling beside the cat, Renee smelled something unlike anything in Lyceum, but vaguely familiar to him: the absence of a scent. The smell of Nothing. *That smell.* And just as before, it felt good in Renee's head.

But it was the cat's collar that really caught Renee's attention. It was a black collar held together by a small piece of wax. The wax was pallor. It was shaped in the likeness of a small spider. The wax spider seemed to simplify the complex Posteriorian world around it. But the spider only had three legs. The image of the white spider, its milky body with two rear legs and one front leg, blazed itself into Renee's memory like the hot stamp of a cattle prod. Renee felt an eerie comfort at the way its small extending legs eventually came to a single, unified body. Somehow, it made sense. *Yes*, Renee thought as he examined the cat, *this cat could not have come from anywhere Posteriorian. This animal could have only come from somewhere far, far away. Somewhere where things made sense.*

A special place.

At first, Helene was surprised at the cat's presence when she saw it playing with Renee in the garden a few days ago. Renee would leave his meals early, sneaking a bowl of milk out with him under his robes. After some time, the cat had actually come to expect Renee's milk at certain times; she would sit there waiting, her black tail wagging its white tip, her little sharp teeth framing a rough tongue dripping with moist anticipation. Her small head would lower to lap up the milk slowly as Renee sat next to her, never touching her, just letting her drink. After she was finished drinking she would stand and lower her head and nuzzle it into Renee's white knuckles like a black forest of fur burying itself over naked slopes of white boney flesh.

Helene saw this from her balcony and she felt an immediate rise of doubt in her gut. *It is not proper for a boy, a prince no less, to be playing with a little kitten. Renee is already so different, but now he has a distraction, a toy, another reason to leave his family and wander outside, alone...* but after Helene saw how the boy looked forward to spending time with his cat, after she saw how the cat's affection made the boy feel glad, actually feel *worth* something, her heart radiated a warmth that washed away the doubt inside her. *Just let the boy be,* she said, *let him be happy, let him have what he always wanted. Let him have a companion. Let him feel...accepted. And perhaps, just perhaps, it will make him normal.*

Now Dewey watches Helene pet the cat with one hand and Renee with the other. Dewey opens his mouth to declare his presence *I'm right here* but his lips hesitate; such words *can I play too?* are foreign to his tongue. He has never had to use them before. Dewey stands awkwardly, feeling like an actor in a play who forgot his lines. He waits for Helene to run towards him *Oh excuse me* with her arms outstretched *what was I thinking* leaving Renee behind. But she does not get up. She does not look his way.

Dewey turns away, sinking his misery into finishing his orange. He chews its fleshy core but it does not taste the same. He closes his eyes, waiting for the potent juice to dig into his taste buds and send the right chemicals to his brain. He chews slowly, waiting for his fix. Finally he swallows, frustratingly dissatisfied with his situation. Throwing the orange peels on the floor, he kicks them and walks away.

But just as he reaches the end of the stone hallway, he hears the words he has been waiting for all along. They echo behind him like distant ghosts.

"Come here," Helene says, "Aw, come here. You want to play?"

Dewey smiles *it is as if she read my thoughts* and he cannot stop smiling. His heart beats like that of a child. Too exhilarated to pretend otherwise, Dewey turns and runs back to his mother as fast as his fat legs could take him.

But when he reaches the doorway, he sees that nothing has changed and he screeches to a halt. Helene is looking at Renee who is actually smiling a smile that no one has ever seen before on the boy's face. Even though Dewey stands in their plain view, Helene continues looking around. She speaks again, louder than before.

"Come here, come back! We just want to play with you!"

Dewey's heart melts with longing and he shouts out in a desperation he has never known.

He takes a deep breath and says, "I'm over here," but his words are drowned out by those of Renee's.

"Is she coming, momma?" Renee says.

She? Dewey's heart drops. Who is *she?*

Helene says, "Aw, we just want to play with her but she ran away. Our little furry friend does not understand. But wait here," she kisses Renee on the forehead and gets up from her chair. Dewey quickly ducks out of view. Helene walks across the room. Helene's slender arms reach to open a drawer in the wall. She reaches inside and makes her way back to Renee. She kneels before him, offering him a small object still nursed in her golden brown hands.

"What is it?" Renee asks.

"It's a gift."

Renee looks up at once, his face turning pink in surprise and gratitude. Then he looks down to see a small wooden piece, a tiny hollowed tube looking something like the big trumpets the musicians of the High Court play, just much, much smaller. Helene laughs.

"Try it out, why don't you."

"Well, I mean, what does it do? What is its purpose? How does it work?"

"Ha! Always questions from you. It is a calling whistle. Here. Put it to your mouth and blow."

Renee is still looking up at Helene. Finally, he lowers his gaze to the wooden piece in his hands. Dewey pretends he is in Renee's place. He is angered at Renee's hesitation and imagines how he would grab the whistle immediately and blow as hard as he could. As Renee studies the object to determine all of its details and operations, Dewey forces himself to grind his teeth to help from shouting out in frustration *just blow the damn thing!* Finally, Renee brings it to his lips and blows.

Nothing is heard.

He tries again, this time lifting it deeper into his mouth. Taking a deep breath, Renee blows again. Hard.

Still, they hear no sound.

But suddenly the cat comes sprinting down the hall, past Dewey and into Renee's arms, toppling him over onto the ground. Helene laughs. From where he stands, Dewey smiles with her but his smile quickly disappears as he remembers this laugh is not for him. *But it has always been for me.* Dewey feels hot tears building up *they were not calling for me* behind his eyes like a river piling up against a dam *they were calling for the cat.*

The cat.

Dewey feels jealousy overcome him once more, but he tries to calm himself. *Renee really needs Helene more.* Dewey grasps for mental straws of comfort. *Renee really needs her because, yes, because he is all messed up. Helene's love is not sincere; her laughter is forced, her happiness invented, her love a medicine so she can make the boy feel loved, so she can fix him. Because he is not like me—he is all messed up and he needs to be fixed. But I am so much better.*

Later Dewey will wonder how the whistle brought the cat running if it had made no sound. He certainly didn't hear it make a sound. But now, jealousy overcomes him. He feels his legs turn to jelly. He manages to make his way to the marble statue standing a few paces away, just inside the entrance from which he just came. He struggles to support his weakened feet, grabbing onto the statue with one hand, holding his stomach with the other. He focuses on a spot on the floor, worrying that if his eyes come off of it he may vomit. He stands catching his breath. He no longer hears Renee and Helene's conversation.

"My sweet Cartez," Helene says, did you see how the cat came at once?"

"Yes! And so happily did she come, ha ha! She must have heard the whistle. The whistle must really make a sound!"

"Well, well, not so fast" Helene responded, stroking the cat's body as its black fur slid from beneath her palm, "See, that is the mistake people make. Assuming things they never experience to fill in the gaps."

"What do you mean?"

"Well, you blew the whistle. And the cat came. That is all. The two are constantly conjoined. Yet you assume more; you assume the existence of a sound. But we did not hear one—"

"But it would only make sense—"

"Sense?" Helene looks like she has said a dirty word, "What is sense, my boy? Sense is only based upon what you experienced in the past, and that you expect it to continue to happen in the future. And you confirm and fortify it to your imagination that just like in the past a whistle *causes* something by making a sound, that there is a necessary connection between the two events, one that you invent, in this case, a sound. But sometimes the future is not like the past. Sometimes there is no sound. Like tonight. And this is why I give you this silent whistle. To teach you…so you always remember that sense, well, reason, is something we must strive to keep away from."

"Then, then why did the cat return?"

"You know that. Because you blew the whistle."

"But maybe, maybe it makes a sound that only the cat could hear! Maybe—"

"Maybe, maybe. But we do not know maybes. That is why we Posteriorians live by our experience rather than our speculations. We follow our eyes, not our maybes. And all we know is that the whistle blowing and the cat running have accommodated each other, and may continue to do so in the future. But we know of no connection between the two."

Dewey is trembling, yet in a sense he stands rigid and still like the statue beside him. As the tears finally begin to make their way out of his eyes and the turmoil in his belly begins to subside, he regains focus on his surroundings. He brings his rainbow sleeves up to his face, wiping his eyes with his wrists, cleaning his cheeks. He looks back down at his feet. He sees he is already starting to look a bit like the great kings of Lyceum's past, a small pasty belly beginning to form, his mop of blond hair beginning to thin. It is almost as if he is shrinking, fattening, and balding faster than he thought he would. But Renee seems to be growing, now about an inch taller than he, Renee is growing and thinning indeed.

ΩΨΩ

The week moves slowly and the days are long. Dewey finds himself doing something he has never done before. He retreats to his room often now, and plays with the orange ants still crawling all over his area. Just as before, they seem to levitate towards him like metals towards a magnet. He revels in their love for him, his eyes glowing like a child's, his grin unreserved across his face. And for a moment, Dewey forgets the cat even arrived.

One day, Dewey comes back from his routine efforts to play outside. He has tried to make conversation with Joachim, but he was busy drawing. He has tried to play with Helene and Renee and the cat, but finds he cannot share Helene's love. Though the others do not intentionally ignore him, he misses the spotlight terribly. He feels worthless and awkward around them, like an outsider, an exile lost in the world he once ruled. He hates this feeling, so he grabs an orange from a nearby pedestal and walks back towards his room to play with the only friends he has left, the ants.

But in the hallway, he already notices something different. It is the ants. They are disappearing. They have always been numerous, with never more than an inch or two between them. He saw less of them yesterday than the day before, but he thought nothing of it. But now, he notices they are rapidly fading. But why?

He frowns in disappointment and confusion. He does not like being in the dark. Nevertheless, he walks through the ever-growing islands of floor space between the ants, his head down. When he approaches his door he hears Renee's voice cry out behind him.

"Where are you?" Renee's voice echoes down the hallway behind Dewey, "I cannot see you, my friend," Dewey closes his eyes. *He is only talking to the cat* Dewey scolds himself *do not be fooled again.* Dewey closes his ears, trying to block the sound of Renee out, "Come here, Come here. How am I supposed to play with you if I cannot see you?"

Dewey takes a deep breath but he still feels weights upon his shoulders. He sighs and opens his door before him, ready for sleep. But what he sees stops him in his tracks. The floor lies empty before him.

All of the ants are gone.

Spotting a slight movement in the corner of the room, Dewey sees the cat herself, lazily lying on her side, her belly swelling with food, her mouth open, emitting the foul stench of her breath throughout the room. Dewey does not need to look closely to see the red stains of crushed ants on her teeth, the red liquid of their bodies dripping down onto her gums. That cat!

Dewey cringes, trying to shut out the images in his head of Renee's cat eating his little friends. But the thought drives into his head like a cold needle. He goes into a rage. Screaming uncontrollably, he lunges on the cat, his fists flying, pummeling the poor animal like a beast himself. The cat whines gently and submits without struggle and this upsets Dewey even more.

Dewey presses his weight on the cat. Finally, he can feel her body jerking and twitching under his fat. She squirms, struggling upwards, trying to resist. He smiles and bears down harder. It does not take long until she is still.

He punches the cat long after it is dead, like a dog ripping apart a stuffed animal lying still as in a sleep. Finally, Dewey crawls to the opposite corner of the room. He kneels to the wall shaking, his hands shaking. He does not feel satisfied. Strangely, it is as if killing the cat merely wetted his appetite for revenge rather than satiated it.

But what else can I do?

It takes him a few minutes to realize his fists are curled tight so he loosens them, realizing the orange peels still inside. The orange peels celebrate their sudden freedom from his wet suffocating palms by expanding slowly, stretching themselves out into the air like the petals of a blossoming flower, reaching out to breath in the surrounding air.

Dewey looks down at the orange peels in his open hands, and he hears Renee call out again from behind him *Where are you? I want to play but I cannot see you* and again *I cannot see you I cannotseeyou* and suddenly, as if whispered to him from the orange peels themselves, a solution comes to him. *Yes,* he thinks of a plan *How can I play with you* and hope washes over him *if I cannot see?* As Dewey's face looks down at the orange peels in his hands, *Renee will learn his lesson* he can see his reflection in the oily acid of the peels. He can see the reflection of a smile forming upon his lips. He slips them in his pocket and walks to his room, feeling lighter with every step.

10

Dream manfully and nobly, and thy dreams shall be prophets.
Edward Bulwer-Lytton

An eye for an eye, makes the whole world blind.
Mohandas Gandhi

The golden September sun fades behind the Apuan Hills, illuminating them like a Chinese lamp. The animals take shelter, shaking off the troubles of their day. They know it will not be long before the growing cold takes over, so they relish the last days of their outside playground. But as the chirping of birds gives way to the night crickets, the sun sinks into the blanket of trees, hiding behind their endless silhouette of black leafy shards clattering together like wild birds over the pink dusk.

Darkness is approaching earlier now, announcing the upcoming fall. The leaves have not changed their color much, but their green coat is slightly framed with hints of red, yellow, and orange.

The changes in the air remind Renee who he really is. Lying in bed, he remembers the past winters of his youth. Oh, how he loved the seclusion it offered! The quiet stillness under a blanket of pure white! He would wrap himself in the stillness, he recalls, and embrace solitude in the cocoon of winter, sitting out in the white fields, breathing in the sterile air.

But now, things have changed. What happened? Renee examines himself for the first time in months. He has not changed; he is still the same he ever was. But he found a friend. He thinks of all that was before the cat came along, the people he watched playing without him.

He remembers Dewey.

Dewey has not spoken to him for months. Renee wonders if why he hadn't noticed. Where has Dewey been this whole time? What has he been doing? Renee feels a strange uneasiness hit him in the pit of his stomach. He tries to understand it, but he cannot explain it. Suddenly, he finds himself getting out of bed. He gathers his pillow, blanket, and robes, and moves downstairs for the night. *For a change of scenery* he tells himself. But he knows that is not the case. He feels the fear of his brother, of not *knowing,* of being in the dark. But he tells himself he merely wants *needs* to sleep peacefully tonight.

The boy is very tired.

This is nothing new. Renee has always looked forward to the cold, dark quarters he occasionally slept in when the solitude his regular room offered just was not enough. It began years ago, when Helene had not found the boy in his bed for morning wake-up. She had searched the entire palace, calling his name, a worried look marking her golden face. She paced back and forth, her sensors scrambling behind her, struggling to jot down the increasing urgency weighing upon her heart. Finally, she came across the boy lying down beneath the cellar, all the way at the bottom of the stairs. She opened her mouth to scold the boy, but the pleasant look on his face filled her heart with love. *If the boy wants to be alone* she could still remember telling herself *perhaps, just this once I can let the boy be.* Through the years that followed, Renee slept there those few nights a year when he needed a change. When the upstairs rooms seemed too *full,* too *experiential,* full of creeping sounds, smells, and noises, he would retreat to his lower quarters, enjoying the plain, sterile nothingness enveloping him in black.

Renee descends the stairs slowly tonight, a lone white leaf fluttering gently to its grass bed below. His blankets trail behind him, a long rainbow tail guiding his sensors down with him. When he gets to the bottom, Renee drifts into unconsciousness as quickly as he hoped.

As Dewey struggles for a taste of fruitful sleep far up the stairs, Renee feeds on a bounty, indulging in his dreams down below. Dewey tries hard to fall asleep but his incessant rage will not let him rest. As the moon hovers its arch outside these thick stone walls, the vividness of Renee's dreams increase with the pace of the seas simultaneously tumbling in poor Dewey's head so much higher, higher on up the stairs. Even in his sleep, Dewey already anticipates when to blind his brother.

ΩΨΩ

Now, the careful reader should never think that angels or Gods have unlimited patience. O'Talp has been watching over the boy for some time *dream manfully and nobly* and has been waiting to help him, *and thy dreams shall be prophets* since he feels the boy is tired. And O'Talp watches Renee now, sleeping soundly in the cellar downstairs, inviting *tugging* him down into the prince's dreams *How much longer can I do this?* but O'Talp is tired, too. *The boy needs my help, and his sleep tugs at my loins, but I am tired, for prophets can tire too. Angels can fall too, tumbling to the ground. Gibreel, Saladin Chamcha tumbled out of the skies...Saladin nosedived while Farishta embraced air...El Totsira fell from the stone tower as lightning struck his immortal hide...and Jacob had brought down an angel with no name, the one Penuel...Jacob had struggled in his mother's womb just as I held my brother's heel in the womb of Rekha. And now just like Penuel, I am brought to my knees.*

But deep down, O'Talp understands the truth; he is afraid of his student, for he is just like him and many people are scared of their own reflection. An archangel quaking before a mortal! A boy no less, now isn't that crazy? As Renee *sleeps* walks *downstairs* up the mountain to meet this angel *this God* O'Talp struggles to prepare himself. He is nervous, like a boy on his first date. For a sage whose words are like honey, O'Talp has a reputation to uphold. He takes a deep breath and runs his middle finger along his lower lip, recalling the feel of the legs of a bee that graced his lips upon his birth so long ago. He remembers the sticky trail of sweetness it left behind its great balancing act. He waited for Rekha to help, but all the tent's inhabitants were frozen, entranced by the bee's walk across the newborn's lips until it fluttered its wings and elevated itself slowly out of the tent.

The boy needs my help O'Talp rouses himself from his dogmatic slumbers *for Dewey is scheming and the orange peels are coming.* As Renee falls deeper and deeper into sleep he reaches higher and higher to pull the archangel down and O'Talp is forced to dive down *tumbling* flailing his arms to increase his speed, folding his wings in *as if gravity is not enough* to plummet down to meet the young prince's soul far into the deepest slumber this angel has seen. Falling fast, O'Talp feels the cold that is Renee's sleep, deep like an endless black hole. He reaches out, stretching his thick arm further than it is able to go, and finally, he feels his fingers brush against the boy's prickly black hair. Finally, he is able to reach out to the boy, and wastes no time setting out his warning as clearly as he can. And so it is.

Renee dreams a dream:

He can feel O'Talp's comforting touch. Oh, it's you again, Renee can say. The touch seems familiar to him, as if it comes from a piece of himself. *As Dewey tosses and turns upstairs*, Renee is swimming through honey-sweet words. He can hear the prophet's words, the advice of a friend, a forecast of a not-so-far future.

"Renee, Renee," O'Talp begins.

"Here I am."

"Yes."

"I can hear you very clearly."

"Yes. You are there. I can feel you."

"Mm."

"Renee?"

"Ye—"

"Renee, your companion, he will be with you."

"But...but she is gone. She—she's missing. She will not respond to the whistle. I fear Dewey has her. I do not even know if she is still—I fear—"

"To be born, dear Renee, first you have to die."

"But—"

"He is in the process now, but your companion will return to you when you need him most. When he is sent back to your world, he will be in another, secret place. What is this place? A special place. A place with no distraction. A place of reason. A place of the mind. A place where ideas are submitted to the harshest critical scrutiny, as they should be, before being accepted. And when accepted, they are accepted permanently, as they would then deserve to be. A place of the most severe logic. A place from which I will send your companion to you, to bring you there."

"Ha ha," Renee laughs, "If only there was such a place…maybe somewhere in the heavens…"

"No, this place is in your world, the world of Renee Don Cartez, if only in your mind. And plans have already gone underway out in the west. But you see, you laugh. You are not ready to go yet, my son. When your guide finds you, do not inquire as to how he came and do not ask as to where he came from. Just be happy he is there, and always let him guide you to this place. He will never leave your side, so long as you invite him."

"Ah," Renee has never been one of many words, but he is hardly at a loss for words when he wants to speak. In front of this prophet, however, this archangel of reason, Renee cannot find the words to speak. *Don't worry*, O'Talp seems to *think* towards the boy, as if the exterior sound of the words would be insufficient.

O'Talp continues to pour comforting thoughts into Renee's head. He tells the boy of the new companion, and he speaks of Dewey's downfall. As the subject of his words turn to the fat experiential boy, *Dewey himself feels the rage amplify in his stomach. How could Renee ignore me? ME? I tried to be patient. To share. I tried so hard…but* Renee struggles to push thoughts of his brother (sleeping so high up the stairs) away and asks more about himself.

"My companion—what, will he help me? Will he keep me happy? Will he keep me ali—"

"My son, everybody has their downfall."

Upstairs, Dewey tosses and turns.

"What, what will be my downfall?"

Dewey stops tossing.

"Your downfall…"

"Yes, my downfall. What will cause my downfall?"

Dewey lies still.

"Your downfall will be the downfall of your brother."

"My brother?"

"Yes. When he dies, you will not live. Well, unless you choose to."

"How will he die?"

"His downfall will be caused by the same thing that caused man's first downfall. The original sin," *Dewey's mind is awhirl with anger, for if Renee has not learned his lesson,* "the clever serpent, the terrible snake, the woman Eve *I must teach him myself* the orange *I must go downstairs* temptation to indulge *right now* the snake that causes all downfall, *I must make him understand* the temptation of man, jealousy, tempted by the fruit *with orange peels in my hand* the fruit of another *I must teach my brother for good!*

"A serpent?" Renee is surprised. "But I haven't seen—"

"My half-brother Glaucon once told me that left unrestrained, human beings will always revert back to their natural greedy, selfish lives. The initiator of the original wrongdoing, man's original downfall, will ultimately cause yours."

"And what is that? What kind of serpent can cause such temptation? What kind of serpent can cause such sin?"

"Oh, it was not a serpent. It was an idea. It was experience, my prince. Experience. This is what the first man chased. See, before he ate the orange from the forbidden tree, man saw the world solely through his mind. This is why when they were both born naked, they were not ashamed. It was I who crafted them, perfect in this way. They were not ashamed because they used all of their organs functionally, so that cohabitation was no different than eating or drinking to stay alive. All physical acts, from the tasting of a fruit to the pleasure of sleep, was only significant as a means towards the end of survival, of fulfilling the role of one's life. It was sought as a function of their nature only insofar as it made sense. All they did, they did it because it made sense in maintaining existence, it made sense for the survival of the species. It made sense *in the mind.* And why did it make sense? Reason declared it as such.

"But it was on the day they ate from the orange tree that their eyes were opened. They saw things, and they began to *feel.* The first thing they saw was themselves. They were scared. Distracted. Even Disgusted. They were unable to think as they had before. And what they felt was naked; they felt wrong in their own skin. Worst of all, they stopped doing things for *reason.* Rather, their guide of reason had turned to a chase for *experience,* for pleasure in itself, for fleeting physical desires of the outside world. All of the sudden, their nakedness, the entire physical world became relevant, and they were able to truly *experience.* Now all physical acts, from the tasting of a fruit to the pleasure of lovemaking, could no longer be used as a tool to accomplish that which reason declared suitable: to construct founding principals from which we can grasp truths. Rather, it became something of *experience*, which necessarily brings about the destruction of man, since the hunger for experience can never be satisfied. See, the little knowledge one may gleam from the long trial and error of experience is hardly worth value: it is too little too late. And oh, how it bends this way and that, trying to accommodate new empirical data as it arrives. Oh, how temporary, how flimsy; it cannot stand on its own two feet; the mildest touch of scrutiny, and the entire building collapses! But the feeler does not care. The lover of sights and sounds is glad to spending precious time delving into the depths of destruction with a smile on his face and food in his mouth. This is the crime that man caused to happen on this very day.

"This was the day reason bowed to experience. This was the original sin. This was the greatest sin, and it is this sin that will bring Dewey's downfall as it brought Adam's so long ago. In the form of a snake."

Renee opens his mouth to speak, but O'Talp begins to fade.

Dewey's eyes open. He grasps the orange peels from his pocket and holds them close to his chest. Taking them with him, he rises from his bed and creeps down the hall.

In Renee's dream, O'Talp has disappeared and a scene of nature takes his place. Renee suddenly finds himself in the midst of the most beautiful trees, the most luscious crops, the brightest flowers, a sensation of feeling. He smells the orange groves, the trees and their aroma. The smell is intoxicating for a boy of that age, and he feels his pale skinny body blossom into a moist, golden plump, rolling, spinning, indulging in the experiential feast. This must be the Garden of Eden! Renee's mind exclaims. How could I have gotten here?

Dewey makes it to Renee's nearby quarters, but the boy is not there! Thinking just a moment, he sees the trail left by the boy's rainbow blankets, the sensors small footprints smattering a bit here and there, and it seems they went down the stairs. It seems Renee had gone down to his lower quarters. Dewey begins to follow his trail, a menacing scowl on his face.

Renee enjoys the hallucinogenic orange trees illuminating his dreams. He feels they are his bounty, the oranges his offspring, and he gazes at them fondly. He stares at them intently until he is forced to look away from the sensory overload. But as he looks back, he notices that the oranges have begun to redden. At first it seems to him they have ripened, but no, they are scarred, they have formed a 'strawberry rash' and have begun to crumple inward, rotting from the outside in. What does it mean? Their skin has been scraped at, as if by a small child's hands, tiny fingernails crawling digging, scratching, until the oranges are completely peeled, their orange insides bleeding, their naked bodies completely reddened, red red red—not a spot of orange is left! *Orange peels in hand, Dewey makes his way towards the bottom of the stairs. Looking down, he hesitates for just a second. He closes his eyes and brings the peels to his nose, he inhales their powerful scent. He smiles, pleased with the amount of acidic juice it must have. He thinks it will be enough. He savors the moment he can make his brother see, he can make his brother see the error of his ways. Taking a deep breath, he clutches the orange peels in his hand, and continues his determined descent.*

The oranges dangle from the tree like a thousand diamonds too bright to see. As they become completely revealed, the sight is so intoxicating and acidic that Renee's eyes begin to tear. With salt stinging his eyes, Renee sees a great hoax of colors bleeding into one another, swirling, tearing his kaleidoscope world upside down. Renee falls to the grassy ground, crawling through the brush on his hands and knees. Crawling through the colors, dizzied by the noise, his hands touch upon shards of red clay, broken pottery lying on a dirt path in the grass. There are footprints in the grass as if someone had spent many long months burdening it. But Renee comes to a pool of blood. He turns, struggling to find another way. *Step by step, Dewey has been descending the stairs for some time now, though there are many more to go. His feet thump down the stairs wildly, cluck, cluck, clunk,* while Renee's hands slam into the dirt path, thumping as he crawls *at an increasing speed* thump *clunk* thump *clunk* as the grass begins to thin and give away under his *foot by foot thumping down the stairs*, he gropes for a stronghold, a branch that can keep him steady *Dewey can already smell revenge, a big smile* turns to shock as Renee's hand falls through the grass floor, down, down, down, bringing his whole body with him, he falls to *the bottom of the stairs, Dewey can see Renee's door open before him, he can hear his brother's breaths rising and falling* through the grass sky, past the green earth and into nothing, soaring, sailing, and finally *entering Renee's room* falling down *standing over his brother, orange peels in hand* falls before his body as Renee feels nothing below him and can't feel the *orange peels held above his face, its cool mottled skin* flying through as his sight begins to fade, by the air around his body, he begins to feel *squeezed peels above his eyes* falling *dripping orange acid droplets like little orange ants running* downwards *entering* slipping under *eyelids* hot *acid* sight is fading *blinding* until *everything* stinging *finally* all goes *complete* black.

ΩΨΩ

Dewey's hands tremble in fear, but his breath steadies with accomplishment. He squeezes the orange peels into Renee's eyes once more, but he knows there is no acid left. The deed is done. He listens as the orange acid seeps its way into the eyes of his brother, killing everything it touches. And before the Lyceum sun can rise over the distant hills, Dewey throws the orange peels in the corner of the room, turns, and leaves. He walks back up the stairs to the regular royal quarters, not knowing that many years from now he will pick up those same orange peels once again.

11

The most loving parents and relatives commit murder with smiles on their faces. They force us to destroy the person we really are; a subtle kind of murder.
Jim Morrison

-TEN YEARS EARLIER-

"Run, Olegna, run!"

"Okay, I'm coming."

"Now! You've got to see this."

"Where are you?"

"Over here!"

"I'm tired, Agostino. Can't this wait? I should go back home..."

"Oh, stop whining. This is great!"

"These woods are so dark. We came all this way, and I don't know why."

"I told you, it's a surprise."

"My daddy's gonna kill me."

"What?"

"I said, my da—"

"What in God's name is taking you so long?"

"I'm coming! Where are you?"

"Can't you hear me?"

"Yes, I hear, but I cannot see you—"

"What are you? *Blind?*"

Young Olegna enters the clearing to see Agostino De Medici in the center, standing tall as if a tree himself, his fellow pines huddling around him, towering over the clearing to look down upon the small boy. The trees keep their distance as if subservient to the small visitor below. Though he stands shorter than the surrounding trees, they seem to be drawn towards him, their stiff bodies inclined before him, bowing down in submission. And for a moment, Agostino looks like a God. Black curls frame his white face like a dark halo and his arms are crossed across his chest. He seems almost transcendent as he stands illuminated by starlight, his breath steaming in the cold mountain air.

The Medicis' house can be seen towards the top of the hill just two hundred feet away, its windows aglow as Agostino's mother prepares dinner by the fire. Olegna's house is further in the distance, a flickering yellow dot set deep between the Apuan hills in the same town of Carrara where the two boys grew up as friends. From where he stands, Olegna's house looks like just another star in the sky. Neither of them has ever left these hills. To them these hills are their home; they do not know anything else.

"I'm here."

Olegna is panting for breath but Agostino does not seem to miss a heartbeat. They have traveled quickly, for Agostino has been eager to show Olegna what he made, what he has been working on all these weeks.

"Ho! ho! ho!" Agostino exclaims, "Here she is!"

Olegna cautiously takes a step forward over a tree that has fallen and watches Agostino walk towards his creation now covered by a white sheet.

"Are you ready?" Agostino asks.

Olegna still tries to catch his breath.

"Are you—"

"I'm ready!"

Agostino smiles with pleasure.

"Now, I know I am no sculptor like you, Olegna, but, well, I hope you will like this. I've worked pretty hard on it. So go easy on me."

"Ok. I'm ready."

Agostino slowly pulls the covering away, and as the linen slides off the marble surface, it seems to not want to let go. The white sheet kisses the stone one last time before crumbling to the ground beneath the boy's small feet.

"Ahh," Agostino lets out a sigh of relief. Then he is silent. He turns to see Olegna's face.

Olegna looks at the stone respectfully. He sees his friend's shaky hands, how they scratched the stone here, and left a nick there. The boy was sloppy, but Olegna can sense the innocent effort his friend's good heart had invested. Olegna brings his fingers to his chin, sincerely trying to make sense of the stone before him. *What is it* he wants to say, but he keeps his lips clamped so no such sound comes out.

It is a block of marble obviously cut from the nearby Carrarian quarries. The marble has been carved into a thick and short tubular shape, though gradually coming to a point towards the bottom of one end. A small stone panel has been left protruding from the top.

"That's his flipper," Agostino exclaims.

"A whale!" Olegna laughs, "Haha! A whale!" Olegna laughs because he never would have known what it is if Agostino would not have spoken.

"Yes, it's a whale. Do, do you like it?" Agostino crosses his arms across his chest.

"Well, yes, it's...interesting. I mean, I like it. Sure I like it." Olegna nods his head, but the nods come out forced. He liked Agostino sincerely, and would never want to hurt his friend's feelings.

"I like it very much," he lies.

"Thanks." Agostino smiles. He sees Olegna look at the stone intently.

"What are you thinking, Olegna?"

"Well—I see, it's a whale."

"Yes."

"A whale."

"A whale." Agostino looks at his friend curiously. "Alright. Come, let's get you home."

But Olegna seems not to hear his friend. Rather, Olegna stands in place, looking at the sculpture intently, his fingers on his chin. A moment passes, and Agostino speaks.

"What's wrong?"

"Wait."

"Olegna! What are you doing?"

Olegna seems lost.

"Olegna!"

"Wha—?" Olegna seems startled, as if awakened from a dream. "Oh. Well, this stone can surely make a good whale, but what if...hmm"

"What is it?"

"What if..." Olegna walks up to the stone and looks down at the cold still granite before him. It looks embarrassing. The stone looks like a gray lifeless lump, a mess that once had life infused into it, a life that left it long ago. It seems a failed experiment, asking *begging* Olegna to take it out of its misery, to either feed it back to life, or kill it off completely.

"Wha—" Agostino opens his mouth to speak, but stops mid-sentence as Olegna kneels down to touch the marble block. Slowly, Olegna grips the base of the stone, and groaning softly, he turns the entire stone upside down. He gets up slowly, brushing his hands on his pants, and takes a step back to join his friend. His fingers return to his chin as both boys look back at the stone.

Instantly, the stone seems to make more sense this way; everything looks in a better place, like it *fits* better. What used to be the tail now brings the front of the marble to a point like a ship's bow, and the flipper now sticks out of the bottom of the back, much like a rudder.

"A battleship!" exclaims Agostino in surprise.

Olegna smiles, "Yes, a battleship."

"Ho! Ho! Ho! It looks *so* much better! That was amazing! I would sail the forty seas with this ship! Captain De Medici! That sounds good, no? Captain Agostino De Medici and his faithful mate Olegna Lechim! Haha! It really looks real! How—how did you know—"

"Well, the tail flipper wasn't too strong, but its base was long and slender, like the bow of a ship."

Agostino does not reply, so Olegna goes on, "and the flipper, well, the flipper was too close to the whale's head, so I figured if the thing was upside down, it would—"

"It would make a great rudder!" exclaims Agostino, "That is beautiful! It's amazing how you see things like that Olegna. I wish I could do such things with sculpture. You really have a knack."

"Well, my friend, it looks like you are the one with a job to finish."

"Right," Agostino laughs, "I guess I have a ship to finish. I'll have to get to work on that."

The boys smile at each other warmly, and holding hands, they laugh one last time, for they know their parents must be waiting for them and it is time to head back home.

"You okay for supper?" Agostino offers, "I'm sure we have some extra—"

"No, I…I should go." Olegna says, looking down the hill. His smile disappears and his face turns cold.

"Are you okay? You have supper at your ho—"

"I need to go."

"Hm. Okay. You sure you could make it home alone?" Agostino looks at this friend and for the first time, he is scared. Olegna pauses, and a friendly light grows back into his eyes.

"I'm—I'm sorry. Yes, I'll be fine. It's still a bit light out. Thanks"

"Well, you have a good night, Olegna. And thank you."

"Sure."

"I'll see you sometime soon."

"Sure."

Then, like two flickering stars floating in different directions, the two boys part ways, venturing off to their respective paths, one ascending uphill at a steady pace, the other falling downward slowly, stopping every now and then for a brief moment of reflection, occasionally looking back to his other star, his other half so quickly floating upwards until finally disappearing into the deep blue night.

ΩΨΩ

Olegna finally arrives at his family's small farm. The moon has fully risen and the hour is late. He does not realize how long it has taken to get home, for his mind has been somewhere else. He took his time, traveling through the blue hills, between the trees that stand tall like great spires in the night. He walks past his family's barn, where he spent so much time growing up, learning the ways of hammer and stone. His father's marble quarry lies southeast; he could see the white granite waiting to be reaped, soft white pillows sprouting out of the wet earth. He closes his eyes so that he could see, and finally he is able to focus on the scent of the Lechim farm. He loves the smell of the fresh marble, the pine air, the peaceful nothing that surrounds.

Olegna clambers up the three steps before his home, and opens the screened white door. Francesca is still up; she has been waiting for him to come home.

"Oh, well, look what the wind blew in."

"Hi, mama."

"Where were you? You're *filthy*."

"I was at Agostino's. He was showing me—"

"Oh, no matter. Let's just get you washed up for supper, well, if you could even call it that at this hour. You, you must be famished."

"I am."

"Good." Francesca smiles at her son. "So quickly," she claps her hands, "wash up! wash up! wash up!"

Olegna runs to his room, undresses, and goes to the washroom where Francesca is waiting for him.

"I could do it myself, mama."

"Okay, so I won't do it for you. I'll just watch."

Olegna washes his face, his hands, his feet, his hair. Francesca watches with great affection, hoping that the boy will find his way, will follow his path and fulfill the great potential she believes rests inside of him. She watches him knowing that her husband is soon to return. She prays he hasn't drunk tonight, that the boy will sleep well, that her husband will rest peacefully, and that everything will be fine.

It rarely is.

After a modest supper of clam chowder and bread, Francesca knits a sweater as Olegna wipes his mouth and prepares for bed.

"Y'know, Olegna," Francesca begins, "Your father—" she stops unexpectedly, and Olegna pretends not to see the pain behind her eyes, "Your father, he was out looking for you."

"Oh, gosh, mama."

"Yes, he wasn't too happy about it either," Francesca ruffles his hair and her eyes moisten.

Olegna looks down at his empty plate. He has never understood his father, Lodovico, the man who owned a marble quarry, yet went to town to work. He was the man who raised a son on a farm, yet demanded he learned a city trade. He was the man who never practiced what he preached, the man who understood the art of sculpture, yet reprimanded his son from falling into it too deeply.

"I don't understand father," Olegna says.

"I never did, either. But, still, we must respect your father, Olegna."

"I know, I know, but he could be so mean—"

"Hush! That's enough from you."

Olegna stops speaking, and turns to go to his room. He hears Francesca behind him.

"Olegna. I'm sorry," she says. Olegna stops but he does not turn around. "I understand your worries, I do." Francesca looks at her son with affection in her eyes. "Y'know, you really should listen to him. He loves you."

"I know, mama."

"Okay, son, okay," she answers approvingly. She walks up behind him and rubs the back of his head. She walks him to his room, tucks him in under the covers, and kisses him goodnight. As she leaves his room and closes the door behind her, she is glad he has arrived home safely, and only hopes her husband Lodovico will do just the same.

Olegna lies in bed and stares at the ceiling. He recalls Agostino's efforts and his mind is in a whirl. *The boy is sloppy,* once his mind starts to spin, *scratched the stone here*, it is always difficult to make it stop *left a nick there*. *I could do so much better,* he thinks, *I could do so much better,* and thinks for hours until his little head can't take it anymore. He rises from his bed, wavering between bed and door, deciding what to do. Finally, his feet take him out of his room, past his mother's room now filled with the soft sound of her breathing, his feet creaking on the wooden floorboards, cold white feet pit-patting their way across the house, sneaking through the back door, and slipping back out into the night.

Almost unwillingly, he makes his way through the yard to the nearby old barn, the place that houses the fragile, aged marble he has carved during his time here on the farm. He sits on the dirt ground in the middle of the marble statues. They circle him like white angelic children. He feels comfort in the stones, a comfort he could not feel back under the covers of his appointed room. He feels among great company as he watches his works spring to life as their engine, the moon, makes its way from one side of the sky to the other.

As the moonlight kisses the sculptures, they come to life. A stone infant next to Olegna begins to chuckle as the marble fairies whisper in his ears. The granite dove birds fly around, shuffling through the wooden rafters over their heads. The marble children echo Olegna's laughs, and as the white frogs jump around the stone drums still playing their beat, the marble creations break into song, marching, dancing, swaying through the barn now alight with glee and joy. That is, until someone's voice brings it all to a halt.

"Olegna? Where are ya boy?"

It is the sound of a drunken man, for the boy can already smell the ale on his elder's breath.

"Olegna Lechim! You come here right now!"

Olegna gives one last look at his marble friends to say goodbye. But now they have all gone to sleep: the little girls have closed their marble eyes, lying softly in the pile of frogs, birds, drums, and stones all resting on the grassy barn floor. Olegna turns around to face the barn door.

As he steps outside, his hands go up to shield his squinting eyes, for in his theatrical escapades in the barn, he had not realized how time has passed. The sun has fully risen, blinding him to the sight of this man standing before him. Walking forward, Olegna gets used to the light of day and his eyes regain focus. He tries to move forward, but the man blocks his way. He rubs his eyes quickly and looks up. He sees his father standing before him.

ΩΨΩ

"Father?" Olegna holds his breath. He waits for it to come.

The man slaps Olegna across the face, once, and once again after seeing the white stone powder covering the boy's face, hands, and body. Slap! Slap! Suddenly, the exhaustion of being up all night hits Olegna like a pile of bricks. Instantly, he begins to cry.

"Where were you, boy?" Lodovico has surely been drinking, for his breath stinks and his voice is slurred. "I'll skin you head to foot if you don't tell me."

"I—I was in—"

"I *know* where you were! You don't think I could see that marble on your hands? You, you think I'm a *fool?*"

"I—I don't. I didn't—"

"You didn't what? What do you have to say for yourself?"

"I...I can hardly stand." Olegna slumps over, dehydrated. He kneels to the ground.

"Stand up before your father, boy!"

"Wh—why?"

"*Because I said so!*"

"What is going on here?" says a voice from the yard. Both heads turn *father and son* to see Francesca shuffling towards them, concern on her face. Lodovico is the first to answer.

"Our boy slept in the barn again. He ran away while *I* was stuck looking for him all night long. But did he care?" Lodovico looks at Olegna, "No, he doesn't care. He just plays his fantasy games with the stone, dwelling in his childish world while his parents are out looking for him, trying to raise him with values..."

Francesca's brow furrows in worry. She looks at Olegna and shakes her head back and forth. Lodovico thinks she shakes her head in disappointment, but Olegna knows she nods *You slept in the barn* in denial of what is about to happen *Oh no, you didn't. Lodovico isn't going to like that. Please say you didn't. Please—*

She takes a deep breath and stiffens her face.

"Olegna. You heard your father. You hear what he's say—"

"He *never listens!*" Lodovico interrupts.

"Now, honey, I think Olegna understands—"

"Just *stay out of it, you hear?*

"I was just—"

"*Stay Out!!*"

Francesca is quickly reminded of her place, of Lodovico's size, drunken state, and what Lodovico could do to both of them with one swift stroke of his arm. And what he has done before. Deep down, she has convinced herself that Lodovico really does love his son. Deep down, she believes he may beat his son, bruising his body with wounds that would take weeks to heal, maybe even turning his son unconscious, but he would never, Francesca had come to believe, she *had to* believe, that he would never go all the way.

It is with this belief that Francesca is able to swallow her pride and turn to return to the house. Olegna looks to see his only hope turn her back from him. He begins to cry out *Ma*— but it is interrupted *Slap!* by another blow, and another, and another.

Lodovico beats him. As he falls to the ground under his father's beatings, Olegna keeps his eyes locked on Francesca's back as she fades away, smaller and smaller, disappearing into the hot dust cloud now suffocating the poor child's face.

While Lodovico is no great man, Francesca is right; he surely loves his son. I will remind you not to judge him, for while I was not there, I will guess that you weren't either. I am not saying that what Lodovico did was not wrong, but we must understand that I have chosen to begin his story here, and we do not know what he had gone through the night before, the year before, or as a child himself. I do believe, however, that Lodovico beat his son out of his own love, for he wanted his son to be something more than a sculptor, something more than what he has become. I do know that Lodovico had worked with marble for too long, and had broken his back trying to work in town to support his son's dreams. Everyone has their story, and Lodovico most certainly has his.

ΩΨΩ

A week passes and Olegna does not leave his room. Lodovico stays out doing whoknowswhat while Francesca works in and out of the house. As another week passes, she pumps water from outside, hanging her linen out in the summer air to dry. She enters Olegna's room occasionally, tending his wounds but never questioning his intentions. She brings him food and collects his dishes promptly. No words are said.

Some nights, when Olegna puts his ear towards the door, he can hear his parents making love, his mother's uneven orgasms unraveling from upon the squeaking bed, his father's moans and grumblings settling in. On other nights he can hear his mother crying, silently weeping while Lodovico enjoys a cigar out in the yard. Other nights Olegna can hear his mother plead his case, asking *begging* Lodovico to apologize to him *or at least to talk to the boy, he's your son!* and he feels pain in his heart.

But it is the nights he hears nothing that frighten him the most.

Two months pass. Lodovico's pride begins to falter, and his excuses begin to submit. After Francesca's begging, Lodovico makes an agreement.

"Alright! If you stop hasslin' me, woman. I will go and see the boy."

"You will?!"

"Well, that's what you wanted me to do, right?"

"Thank you. Oh, thank you."

"Alright then."

Then Francesca has an idea.

"Well, since he put that sign up on his door *don't disturb* no one has entered his room or seen him for the past few days. Perhaps I should check on him first, just to see how he's doing—"

"Honey, you wanted me to do this. Just let me get it over with—"

"Okay, Lodovico, you go ahead. But remember, you are his father; he looks up to you."

Francesca watches as Lodovico walks towards the room and knocks softly on the door. Olegna does not answer. Lodovico begins.

"Olegna, boy—son, I just want to speak to you."

Still, no answer.

Lodovico looks at Francesca standing in the hall with her arms crossed across her chest. He sees her apron, her hair messily curled down the side of her face. She never looked so beautiful in his life. He remembers the day they met, not far from where they stand now. She nods approvingly, asking him to continue his pleas.

"Olegna, it's your...your father. Do you mind if we speak for a bit?"

Olegna still does not answer.

Feeling vulnerable *nobody makes a fool out of me,* Lodovico opens the door and walks into the room, closing the door behind him. Francesca waits outside patiently. Many long minutes pass, so she thinks they must be in conversation, and that means things are going well. She smiles and takes a sigh of relief *everything will be alright* as she imagines what the two *I am your father* are talking about. Her thoughts are interrupted prematurely as Lodovico walks out of the room slowly, with great strain across his face.

"Wha—what happened?" asks Francesca, "How did it go?"

"I looked everywhere," Lodovico's face is white, "I—I didn't see him."

"Well what were you doing in there? What do you mean you didn't *see* him?"

"He—he's left us, Francesca. His window was open. A rope—"

"Oh, my boy!" Francesca wails, "What do you mean he *left* us, honey? *Honey?*" she beings to cry.

Lodovico walks towards his wife and puts a hand upon her trembling shoulders. "I'm sorry, my love," he says, "but Olegna, he's...he's gone."

12

Art is the only way to run away without leaving home.
Twyla Tharp

When Lodovico entered Olegna's room, he searched the closet and under the straw mattress still stamped with his boy's body shape. Right away, he knew Olegna had left. *Run Olegna, run.* But Lodovico walked around the room, relishing its order (and disorder) one last time. He knew it would never be like that again. He smelled his son's bed, savoring his son's scent now rapidly fading into the hungry mountain air.

Standing before his son's empty bed, Lodovico remembered how the boy used to sleep. Lodovico would sing to him and read him stories of old, and just a few years ago, told him legends of El Totsira, how Rekha had given birth to the angel El, and how he had saved millions of lives, flying around like a God for thousands and thousands of years. He explained how no one really knew what the angel looked like, for he would take many forms through the years, arriving in one place as an elderly sage or prophet, and spring up in another as a mystical angel. Thus, Lodovico had explained, it was very difficult for any artist to sufficiently portray what the angel looked like, whether through paint, canvas, or stone. If anyone would be able to do that, Lodovico had said, well, *that is one sculptor I would admire, someone I would surely like to meet.*

Though he knew Francesca was waiting patiently outside, Lodovico took his time. He picked up his son's old hat and closed his eyes. Bringing the worn cloth to his nose, he inhaled it deeply, reflecting on the day Olegna was born. He knew he had to face Francesca soon, but he was in no hurry, for he knew the nature of women. He knew she would start shouting, crying, rearranging his room, fidgeting this, destroying that. No matter what the case, Lodovico understood that this was his one moment to savor, his one moment of private, interrupted, condolence.

He walked to the small window still left open from Olegna's escape. Standing right up to the opening, he felt the cool mountain air rush in his face as he stared out deep into the Apuan hills. *Oh, God, Olegna,* his mind beings to turn, *where have you run to now?* After a few more moments, he collected the rope hanging from the windowsill *something Francesca should never have to see* and closed the window behind him.

After he exited the room he told Francesca *I—I didn't see him* that Olegna *he's left us,* had run away *he, he's gone.* Francesca broke down crying in Lodovico's chest as he wrapped his large arms around her convulsing body until her throat could wail no longer and her eyes could tear no more.

After the crying stopped and the tears died down, Francesca was finally able to speak.

"I want my son. *I want my son.*"

"Now, now, honey, Olegna is going to be just fine." It pained Lodovico to see Francesca this way.

"Well, let me see, let me see his room."

Now the two enter the room together, with Francesca leading the way and Lodovico trailing fast behind.

They examine his room together, looking for something *anything* a clue as to where he has gone or evidence to where he has been. They dig deep, finding blocks, childhood toys, storybooks from so long ago.

"Look at this," Lodovico says, holding up a small porcelain doll.

"Yes, that's David. That doll was the first thing Olegna ever really took interest in," Francesca pleasantly recalls, "He, he would play with his dolls and dollhouse for so many hours. Ha! We were so worried he would turn out too girly, but," she continues with fresh tears staining her eyes, "he seemed to turn out alright."

"He sure did, honey."

"Didn't he?"

"Yes, he sure did."

"Mmm."

As more moments pass and the sun begins to set, Francesca discovers a poster wedged neatly behind Olegna's bed.

"What's this?"

It looks normal enough, an aged document folded neatly as if prepared to be taken along on Olegna's journey.

"It looks like he forgot it," Francesca says.

"Well, what are you waiting for?" Lodovico demands, "Open it up."

Francesca obeys at once, and the poster is opened as quickly as her fumbling hands can handle the fine parchment without ripping it. Finally, she flattens it on Olegna's desk and stands back so that the both of them can see.

"It looks like some kind of public declaration. Some kind of...contest or show," Francesca offers.

"Well, does it say where it is?"

"No, I don't see, well, let me see here..."

"Oh, let me see the damn thing," Lodovico grabs it off the desk and brings it to his eyes. He reads the flyer aloud:

HEAR YE! HEAR YE!

AS JUDGE OF THE HIGH COURT AT BRITTANY, I REQUEST THE PRESENCE OF ALL DREAMERS, SOOTHSAYERS, AND FANTASISTS, YOUNG AND OLD, MAN OR WOMAN, AT THE GREAT ARENA IN THE CITY PLAZA OF THIS LYCEUMEAN EMPIRE AT THREE THOUSAND TWENTY TWO MOON-SIGHTS AND FOURTY EIGHT HOURS HENCE, WHEREAS THERE WILL BE A GREAT

ART CONTEST

IN THE LAND IN ACCORDANCE WITH THE POSTERIORIAN HERITAGE OF COLOR AND EXPERIENCE, TO LIVE LIFE TO THE FULLEST AND NEVER LET ANYTHING PASS US BY. SO SCULPTORS, PAINTERS, DANCERS, AND POETS! JUGGLERS, FREAKS, ACTORS, AND WIZARDS! COME ONE, COME ALL, TO THIS WONDROUS AFFAIR, TO THIS SPECTACULAR EVENT, ONE OF COURAGE AND DARING DISPLAY, INTREPID FEATS, AND BOLD ATTEMPTS AS OUR ARTISTS

FROM AROUND THE EARTH GATHER TOGETHER TO COMPETE AND DISPLAY THEIR WORKS. IT WILL BE ONE OF COLOR, ONE OF LIFE! MORE THAN ANYTHING, IT WILL BE SOMETHING YOU WILL NOT WANT TO MISS!

SIGNED THIS DAY OF 12.455.3Ø6Đ

JOACHIM DON CARTEZ

"You're right," Lodovico begins, "It seems to be some sort of art contest that is happening in about...ten years or so, if I read this correctly. In Lyceum, no less."

"Where is that?"

"Oh, who knows?"

"Well, it sounds familiar..."

"Of course it sounds familiar! It is the great empire of Lyceum! Home to the Posteriorians, a busy people, full of color and full of life. Especially since...since Queen Katherine just had twins nearly two years ago. The nation has been truly happy since her recent pregnancy."

"Twins?"

"Yes, after he was born, he really was the talk of the land. 'What a King he will be' everyone had said—"

"He?" Francesca asks, "I thought you said that there were—"

"Twins, yes. But I am talking about Dewey, of course. He is the older one, the firstborn, the Posteriorian prince."

"Well who is the other one?"

"The other one?" Lodovico's face shows surprise at such a question, as if it did not matter. "The other one? Oh, I don't know," he says, shaking his head, "he is exactly that—the other one. That is who he has always been. I know little about him, but I have heard that he did not come out golden orange, as most Posteriorian babies do. Rather, he came out pale, white, and skinny. People say he is quiet, that there's no...*life* in him. As if a spark is...missing."

Francesca remains silent, her eyes asking for more words.

"I—I am sure he is a fine boy, Francesca, but, well, he is no Dewey, that's for sure. And also, well..." Lodovico trails off.

"Well, what?"

"Well, Katherine died of tuberculosis just one year later. It was announced that her death was just random. Just by...chance. That's what they said, anyway."

"And what do you think the cause of her death was?"

"C'mon, honey."

"*What do you think killed her?*"

"Well, it's not just me, honey, but right after her death people started talking. They, they were saying that it was the boy's fault. The younger one—"

"Why?"

"Well, you see, he was just different. It was as if he sucked the life out of her by being born."

"That's silly. Why would—"

"It just...seemed that way to the people. Just by the way, well, by the way he is."

"Okay then. Well, who are these people?" Francesca asks.

"Led under the Grandee, they believe that man can only attain knowledge through experience, as the great prophet El Totsira, the son of Nicomachus, has taught them."

"Hm. Well, how do they gain knowledge through experience?"

"Well, they are sure to document and record every experience and sensation felt within their borders. If we would go there, they would probably not allows us to cross their borders before assigning sensors to us, to follow us and record any and all of the experiences we feel, which they would be required to deposit every twenty three days with the Secretary—"

"Sensors?"

"Sure, a small people measuring not three feet from the ground. Haven't you read anything about this people? They're a wonder to the modern world."

"I—I haven't really," Francesca begins to get frustrated as she searches for the meaning of all of this discussion.

"But, I, I hope Olegna will be okay in this place. Would these…Posteriorians hurt him?"

"Hurt him? No, honey. They probably won't even notice him."

"I—okay, so when do we get back our son?"

Lodovico looks at her in no rush to answer. She tries again.

"We have to go there. We have to get our son back. Where, where is this place?"

"I told you, I do not know. Honey, I haven't left these hills for as long as I can remember, and you never have. It would take nearly a year just to cross over—"

"*Where is it?*"

"I know it is very, very far away."

"So how do we get back *our son*?"

"We don't."

"Excuse me?"

"We don't. We wait until he comes back. He will come back," Lodovico lies. *He better not come back anytime soon* Lodovico's could hear his mind talking *he better stay away for a while, and learn what he is missing. He needs to suffer a bit so he can learn how good he had it, how he could have done so much more with himself.*

"Lodovico! How can you not act? You don't see the urgency in this!" Francesca storms out of the room. But she hears Lodovico behind her.

"Haha," Lodovico laughs softly to himself and shakes his head, "An art contest? He will never win."

Suddenly, Francesca catches herself smile. She takes a deep breath and closes her eyes as if in prayer. "Yes," she whispers to herself, one last tear streaming down her cheek, "Yes you will, Olegna. I know you can."

Lodovico remains in the boy's room well after Francesca leaves, scrambling around in a diligent search, inspecting this, smelling that. Francesca can hear him behind the door, ruffling papers and slamming drawers. The noise is constant as Lodovico searches without rest. Then, what seems to Francesca as hours later, the noise suddenly comes to a stop, and she hears nothing at all.

Perhaps, he has given up, she thinks, or perhaps he actually found something of note.

"Honey? You okay in there?" she offers.

Lodovico does not answer.

"Hon—"

"I'm *just great!*" Lodovico screams as he storms out of the room in anger, "*Just great!*"

"Wh—where are you going?"

Lodovico does not answer, but he exits the room holding a scrap of paper in his hand. He looks at it in disgust. Upon seeing Francesca, he quickly shoves the paper in his trouser pocket, and it seems to Francesca that he is running towards the tool closet.

"What did you find? What is it? What're you—"

"*If he wants to leave his home,*" Lodovico shouts as he grabs a sledgehammer from the tool closet, "*then his home can leave him too!*"

"Please stop! What are you doing?"

"*What am I doing? I am going to make sure this never happens again!*"

Lodovico storms outside with his large hammer in hand, through the front door, down the three steps, and across the yard to the barn. Francesca runs ahead of him, flattening her body upon the barn doors.

"Olegna's sculptures are in there! You're not—"

"That's the point."

"Oh, no, you don't. Oh, please, honey, stop! Talk to me!"

"Get out of my way."

"I will not."

"Then I will hammer you down."

But Francesca stands her ground. She puts her chin up, but she feels her heart sinking fast. "You will stand down," she says.

"No, it's no good. It's *no good!*" Lodovico shouts as he pulls her body forward, shoving her to the ground. Hard.

She gets up at once, and runs back to the house crying. From the den where she sits, she can hear the crack of hammer meeting stone as her husband destroys everything his son has ever made. She can hear the thunderous blows, the metal crushing marble, the crackling and booming of granite explosion for nearly an hour. She can smell the stone dust of Olegna's creations filling in the air, filling her lungs as her husband swings this way and that in a frenzy, smashing the only things that their only son had ever really treasured.

Lodovico continues until there is nothing left.

ΩΨΩ

In the lonely weeks that follow, Francesca and Lodovico mourn the loss of their son. Their cries unite them, and they become closer than they have ever been before. They cry together, but they cry for different reasons entirely. It would be fair to say that if they knew the reasons for which the other person cried, such cries would not unite them as they do here, but perhaps this was the way it is supposed to be. Again, I leave this up for you to decide.

Francesca cries for her boy's safety. She mourns the loss of her only child, praying and hoping that one day he will safely return. But more than anything, she prays that he will find his way, be happy, and live a full and meaningful life, even if she never sees him again.

Lodovico cries for his failure in controlling his son. He suffers more from his son losing him *I am your father* than from him losing his son. He feels he has failed since his influence was not strong enough to substantially affect his son and keep control over him. He cries, not for his son's safety, but for his son's loss at having abandoned his wise influence.

Weeks turn into months and months turn into years. Francesca and Lodovico grow apart. When it is warm, Lodovico is never home. For Francesca, months of crying and mourning on her bed turn to anger, and anger to regret. Now she spends her hours washing dishes that are already clean and hanging sheets up to dry that never got wet, just so she has something to do. Whatever it takes to keep her hands moving, to keep busy and hide from the nothingness around her and the sudden emptiness in her life.

The winters in Carrara become long and severe. The Apuan Hills become desolate, lifeless, and completely quiet. However, it is in this season that the Lechim household contains some form of life, for the cold often brings Lodovico home. Though he hasn't been home for many long months, when he is home, he becomes a better man. The loss of his son still pains him, but now he has less to get angry about. His life is simple, and it is simplicity that keeps a man in his right mind.

Most winters, Lodovico makes love to his wife in front of the roaring fire after a good meal. He enjoys cutting firewood almost as much as Francesca enjoys watching him, and it is for these reasons that winter has become something to look forward to for both of them. Throughout the rest of the year, Francesca and Lodovico know that soon, as the snow isolates everything in its own place, they will be 'forced' to spend time in their own company. They know that in time, it is going to be alright.

But even years later, Francesca catches herself hoping for Olegna's return. On long nights the wind rattles the old metal ring on their front door and Francesca jumps out of bed excitedly *just in case* running to the door, opening it widely at first *you never know* ready to exclaim *Olegna! Welcome home!* but after seeing nothing but white fields *of course* closing it slowly behind her *I just needed some fresh air* and retreating back to bed. Other times she stops when she sees footprints in the snow. *Don't be silly* she scolds herself, knowing that they could only have come from the nearby foxes *it can't be him.* But she always returns to the same spot hours later to study those prints closely. Just one more time.

But Olegna does not return, nor does any news. Francesca and Lodovico learn how to stop looking. No matter how hard the wind knocks on their door these long snowy nights, Francesca glues herself to the bed *don't you get up* lying still with her eyes to the wall *don't do it.*

But she still wonders about the piece of paper that Lodovico held as he stormed out of Olegna's room that fateful day. She wonders what kind of note caused Lodovico to get so angry, what kind of letter made him run to smash his marble quarry. What did it say? She looks through

Lodovico's pockets occasionally, but Lodovico always keeps the paper in his own pocket all the time so that it is always by his side and Francesca can never get to it.

That is, until Lodovico has a heart attack and dies.

It happens towards the end of winter, one of the longest in Carrara's history. While the falling snow piles high outside, the Lechims eat their fill of fish, meat, cheese, and wine. Lodovico has more than his normal share of wine. The two sit back after a good laugh and Francesca smiles, thinking of the great winter they have just enjoyed, of how she could die and go to heaven this very moment because things will never get any better, and tonight is the best it can ever get. But her thoughts are interrupted as Lodovico stops chewing, his mouth opening wide as the food comes tumbling back out, his big sweaty hands grabbing his chest as he bows over in pain.

"Lodovico!"

"*Hmm…aaah, my chest.*"

"Oh, no! *No! My dear, Lodovico!* Can you hear me? *Can you hear me?*"

But he cannot hear her for he is already dead, just like that. It happens fairly quickly; he hardly suffers at all.

After all that she has been through, Francesca is a very strong woman. Lodovico's death is not hard for her, since she is already well accustomed to spending her time alone. Also, her heart is not left wanting after her husband passes. While she loved Lodovico immensely, most of her love was merely due to a lifetime spent with him, for it is the rule of human nature that a person loves that which he is used to. Even when someone thinks they do not love someone, after many years pass they find it difficult to imagine life without them, and they are surprised at how much they desperately need someone whose company they originally thought they didn't enjoy any day of the week.

Days pass. One dark night, she sits outside enjoying the stillness. The wind is resting tonight, she notices. It has never been this still. The stars look like a thousand diamonds strewn across a black velvet sky. Finally, she takes a deep breath. She remembers the pile of Lodovico's dirty cloths she hasn't had the courage to face. But she knows she can't linger any longer. Without waiting for another reason to delay, she turns and heads back into the house.

She grabs Lodovico's dirty clothes without emotion and heads back towards the washroom. She hums to herself as she rubs a white shirt up and down the washboard like she is playing an instrument to her own rhythm. Fumbling with a pair of black pants, she catches a piece of paper slip out of the pants and fall onto the floor. *Of course,* she remembers, bending down to pick it up, *how could I have forgotten?*

She brushes dust off the paper and unfolds it without hesitation. Of course, it is the note that drove Lodovico out of his mind, that caused him to grab his hammer and smash all the sculptures and marble that Olegna ever made *if he could run away from home* as if to exact revenge on Olegna *his home can run away from him* and keep him from ever coming back. Her hands tremble as she struggles to hold the thin piece of paper steady enough to read.

> *In case someone finds this:*
> *I must go now because I cannot stay here any longer. I ~~promise~~ ~~sware~~ swear that one day, I will return home. There is some place I must go, though I do not know where it is. Moommy, if you ever get to read this, I love you so much. I am sorry I have to run away, but it is like what we talked about that night I came back from the Medici's house:*
> *I don't understand my father.*
> *I must find my way all by myself. I will return home one day to collect my works in the barn, to see them one last time, but for now I must find myself. I must find out who I am and even moreso, who I can become. I am so sorry I can't stay.*
> *Love,*
> *Your Son Olegna.*

"Oh, I'm sorry too, honey," Francesca feels old tears coming back anew, "I'm so sorry. But I'm so happy, so happy that you are going to find your way. You are going to be amazing, Olegna. You are going to win that contest. You are going to win!"

She crumples the paper in her hand. Her legs grow weak, and she lowers herself to the floor. She looks down, squeezing the paper in her fist, her eyes clenched shut. And then she hears it.

A single knock.

She opens her eyes, but she dismisses it as the wind against the window. But then she hears it upon the door. *Don't be silly* she chides herself. *There's nothing out there but the wind. I was just there.*

But there is no wind tonight.

She stops herself and stands frozen in place. She hears another knock, and another.

"Is...someone there?" Francesca begins. Her voice is shaky. *Oh now I am imagining things. I have gone crazy. Who can it be? Did they hear me speaking to myself?* She feels vulnerable, scared that her visitor could have heard the crack in her voice, her tongue caught in her throat—

Knock! Knock! Knock!

Her mind is awhirl, for no one has knocked on that door for years, let alone at this time of night in the dead of winter.

Olegna? It cannot be.

She hears the knock once more, but this time it is followed by a voice.

"Are you going to let me in? Hello?" a kindly voice calls out. It is real. *I think.* Wait. The voice seems almost *too* kind, as if hiding a terrible evil inside. Francesca is very intuitive and she can sense such hidden intentions, but the voice does sound overwhelmingly pleasant after so many hours alone, real or not. Besides, she realizes that out here in the Apuan hills, she really has little choice. After some hesitation, she proceeds to open the door. Before the door is fully opened, however, Francesca cannot help but call out. "My son!" she says, "Is it you?"

A tall and slender man stands in the doorway. He towers over her. Francesca figures he must be eight feet tall. His pale green eyes look down upon her from under his dark hood. His eyes are pale but seem to hold a hidden power, as if they had blazed much brighter in days of old. His face, so white, is brighter than the blanket of snow *so white* now behind him. The side of his face wears a long, jagged scar of pink, a fine interruption in the vacancy of his face. The scar curves as he smiles politely at the woman below him, much as one would smile at a small child.

"Your son?"

Francesca feels a heavy blush fill her face. The man continues.

"Hello, Miss…"

Francesca takes a moment. "Oh! Excuse me. Haha. Lechim. Uhm, it's Miss Lechim. I mean, you can call me whatever you—"

"Miss Lechim, a fine name indeed."

"Uhm…Can I help you? Mister…"

"I didn't want to bother you, Miss Lechim."

"Oh, no. I was just washing—"

"Your husband's clothes. But he will not need them again, will he?"

"No," she puts her head down, "I guess not. Wait. How could you know—"

"I just wanted to drop off this package."

"P—Package?"

"Oh, you know. The kind that comes in a box. Usually brown."

"But—"

Francesca looks to the man *ghost* for further explanation, but he merely waits for her understanding. It is then that she realizes that she has not taken her eyes off his face *so white* since she opened the door. Finally, her eyes adjust, and she sees the monstrous object standing behind this man.

"Oh, haha, yes. A package. Of course," she feels like a fool, but chides herself for feeling so *c'mon Franny* and wondering how this nice man can make her feel like a fool in her own house *you got this.*

"Good," the man says, "Don't mind me." And with that, the man turns away and walks towards the package, a large stone object covered in a white sheet. "I'm just going to put this in there," he says, pointing towards the barn. "You may want to keep this covered."

"Wh—why? What is it?"

"It's, well, let's just say someone worked very hard on it."

"But wh—"

"*You want to keep it covered! Always!*" the man says quickly. He pauses and lowers his face for the first time. "I…I had to bring it back. Where it belongs. I had to teach someone a lesson. The day will come when it will be opened, but that day is not today. You must not go near it."

Francesca opens her mouth to speak, but she suddenly fears this man, this ghost, and she therefore fears the package. *I will never go near the thing* she decides right then *I have no reason to.* She retreats to the house without looking back.

She watches from her window as the man wrestles with his package. Even for a man his height, the package stands over him, dwarfing him in size. From the safety of her window, Francesca finds that this man's mysteriousness intrigues her. It has been a long time since she enjoyed the company of a real person, let alone a man like this. She watches his long arms drag the package into her barn, and she hugs herself, longing for a human's touch. She sees the exhaustion in his muscles and realizes how long it must have taken him to bring that package all the way into these mountains, how hard it must have been. As the man turns to leave, Francesca sticks her head out the front door.

"Mister, before you go, would, well, would you like something to drink?"

The man seems interested but hesitant, as if deciding whether to stay. Francesca decides to try one more time.

"Perhaps some coffee? We have some fruit—"

"*Bah!*" the man roars. "I'll be going now."

And as quickly as he came, he spins around and starts to head back down the hill on foot. Francesca can swear she saw his scar change color, turning a deep red as he muttered to himself in anger from her comments. She wonders if it was something she said *what could be so wrong with fruit?* Seeing the road before him, she cannot imagine how he could have gotten here by foot. It is the most arduous journey to the closest town, one that no man has ever made on foot alive. She watches from the window as the curious man turns and begins to walk back down the snowy hill, filling his past footprints step by step. He slowly fades from sight, a shrinking dark spot on a landscape of powder white until finally disappearing, leaving behind a confused woman now stuck with the solitude of herself and a mysterious package staring at her ominously from her barn across the yard.

13

Surely whatever I had admitted until now as most true I received through the senses. However, I have noticed that the senses are sometimes deceptive; and it is a mark of prudence never to place our trust in those who have deceived us even once. Therefore I suppose that everything I see is false. I believe that none of what my deceitful memory represents ever existed. I have no senses whatever. Body, shape, extension, movement, and place are all chimeras. What then will be true? Perhaps just the single fact that nothing is certain.
Rene Descartes

-THE PRESENT-

Long after the sun rises, Renee finally wakes from his sleep. Feeling the warm sunlight through his eyelids, Renee cannot remember ever sleeping this late into the day. He opens his small dark eyes for the light to enter, but the light refuses to enter; his eyes will not let it in.

His eyes do not work.

Quickly, he sits up in bed, bringing his fingers to his face. He does not need his hands to feel the energy fused from his face. He does not need the power of touch to know the deadness in his eyes, the lively motion, the youthfulness his head once enjoyed. Renee knows he has been blinded and he is prepared to suffer his loss. Almost instantly, his blindness makes him remember the deformed Nicolas, the crooked spine such a mind had to endure. *Now I have my own handicap,* Renee closes his eyes tightly, *and thank God, thank O'Talp that this is this the handicap I have been chosen to bear.*

He sits up in bed, sitting up straight as if to make sure his spine still works. Just then, a part of him decides to go to back to Nicolas's cabin *see what they did to me* that now he is ready to give up this world and submit himself to the labour of his mind *look what they did* then Nicolas will forgive him *I am ready,* yes, he will understand.

Deep inside Renee knew all along that he would be blinded, that this is the way it is supposed to happen. It is only because he had been coming out of his shell *things were going so well* that he began to feel Posteriorian, that he could learn to enjoy the sights and sounds of his people. This foolish part of him had caused him to retreat to the cellar for the night *in case Dewey comes back* as if it would make any difference, as if Dewey would not find him. Renee knew it was inevitable, but he comforted his Posteriorian tendencies by sleeping downstairs. He felt he had to do *something,* just because anyone else would. But really, he knew Dewey would find him and squeeze the orange peels into his eyes. He knew he would be blinded, and it would remind him who he really was. For this he feels grateful to Dewey for doing what he could not have done himself.

Finally, he will be able to see.

Renee feels his cheekbones struggle to breath under a glaze of eye wax and dried orange juice like caterpillars in their cocoon, wriggling, pushing, trying to make sense of their enclosure. He squints. It is not black he sees. It is not darkness as we know it, but rather it is vacancy; all sensory experience is barred from entering his head. His head instantly feels lighter. He finds that he can swirl a thought in the center of his mind and hold it in place like a top that does not stop spinning, focusing on it exclusively while it remains under his mental microscope. His thoughts are no longer disturbed by the prodding of entering visions that formerly nudged his thoughts this way and that. For the first time, Renee thinks under control.

Still, Renee's first instinct is to cry out. But then he remembers his dream. He remembers how O'Talp came to him, how he *thought* towards the boy when he was at a loss for words. *That's okay m'boy* the white prophet assured him, *words are insufficient anyway.* Speech, sight, touch, I have relied on these all my life. *But the senses are often deceptive* like the straw that appeared bent through the punch he was forced to drink *experience is deceitful* and now my eyes have been taken from me *so I have less sensory experience to worry about* as my intellect may be allowed to guide me undistracted to unshakable truths.

Yes, I may even be able to see.

Renee remembers his dream quite clearly, as if it had been real. *And who is to say that it wasn't? For I surely saw more clearly then than I do now!* Renee thinks. *Who is to say we aren't dreaming now? How often does my evening slumber persuade me of such ordinary things as these: that I am here, clothed in my dressing gown, seated up in my own bed—when in fact I am lying undressed in sleep! Since I experience the very same things in dreams and out of sleep, how can I claim to be able to tell the difference? But perhaps I may ground that upon the fact that I am feeling my body now, raising my hands to my deadened eyes, feeling my hand move through the air driven by muscle and nerve. I feel it. Yes, I feel it ever more distinctly than I do when I am asleep. But no, this does not help, since I may say the same thing while I am asleep. Those orange trees, that garden seemed more distinct than anything else at the moment I had experienced it. So too here, who am I to say this is where it all starts and ends, that this is the reality upon which everything else is based, that these are the laws of nature that govern, that this is it where it all happens, here and nowhere else.*

My dear reader may think that Renee's mind is beginning to mature, to conceive of difficult concepts that formally seemed unattainable by such a young driven boy. While the latter may be true, Renee is not growing any wiser. In fact, he is more lost than he has ever been in the past. The only difference now is that he *is aware* of his mental inadequacy, for he realizes how much there is for him to learn. He is becoming skeptical. He decides to *demand more* from propositions before deciding them to be true. This morning he learns something no true Posteriorian can ever learn. He learns that he can never trust anybody, any experience, any thing without just foundations. As his blindness shows him what is there as all is pushed away, Renee can finally see. He can finally see how flawed his past beliefs have been, how oh so shaky the foundations were that they rested upon! As Renee awakes blind, he finally sees just how much he never saw.

ΩΨΩ

As Dewey's body cries for sleep, anticipation keeps his mind awake. He does not sleep throughout the night, but lies with his eyes closed, picturing Renee's face with pleasure as he realizes he is blind. He imagines the pain strike across Renee's face in a hundred different ways, shattering the thin mask of happiness Renee just began to assume. Dewey pictures this repeatedly. Relishing each one, he cannot decide which picture he likes best.

As soon as the sun peeks the top of its head over the small hills surrounding the royal palace, Dewey looks out the window just briefly before making his way to Renee's room. The orchards and farms surrounding the palace begin to stagnate with the feeling of the upcoming winter. No ordinary crops would ever be able to withstand a Lyceum winter. But the Posteriorian farmers are proud that at least a few of their crops always make it through, though most shrivel up with their neighbors, diffusing their Posteriorian superiority into the air.

Dewey brings this superiority with him as he bolts out of his room without bothering to put on his shoes. He descends the stairs towards Renee's quarters. Since the boy is still fast asleep, Dewey returns upstairs to wash up. *Let Helene wake the boy,* Dewey thinks, *I have taken the boy's sight away, I can let him sleep. I should give him that.* He washes his face slowly, for he has been up all night, and begins to get a bit dizzy. He is overtired, yet trembles with energy. After drying his face, Dewey once again turns to the window, waiting for the sounds of Renee's screams as Helene wakes him below. His eyes are big and his vision far as he gazes, a lone golden silhouette against the blue glass of dawn. He sees the last leaves clinging to their trees, looking down upon their fallen brothers now crumpled underneath the broad wooden trunks. Dewey can already smell the approaching winter air in his nostrils, biting him in the back of the throat.

An hour passes as he waits patiently to hear his brother's cries from the cellar. But they do not arrive. Finally, he turns to the door, considering the possibility of going back down there himself, when Helene walks in, a friendly look upon her face.

"Well, well, well, look who's already up and out of bed. It's about time."

"Yes, well—"

"Were you—when did you get up?"

"Not, not long ago," Dewey lies. He smiles at Helene.

"Hmm. Well."

"Where were you, momma? Why didn't you come to wake us up?" Dewey asks, thinking of Renee.

"Well, I'm here now, aren't I?"

"Yes, but it's late. The sun has fully risen—"

"I thought it would be good to let you boys alone. You both need your sleep—"

"Renee, I mean," Dewey tries to conceal his excitement, "Did, did you go to wake him?"

"Why do you ask?"

"Oh, I, I just wanted to know. We were supposed to…play today."

"Well. He's waiting for you. He was also up when I found him downstairs some time ago. Ha! I don't know what to do with you boys, up before the sun even rises."

Dewey does not respond. His face is white. He tries to breath slowly, putting some color back into his cheeks. He forces a smile.

"Did Renee…did he speak to you?"

"Of course he spoke to me, silly. Would you rather he not?"

"But…but that's impossible," Dewey says more to himself than to Helene.

"Impossible? Anything's possible, Dewey," she shakes her head in confusion, "Someone woke up on the wrong side of the bed. Now stop asking strange questions and come get yourself together. Come get something to eat. Renee is on his way too. He said he just wanted to wait a moment. I think he wanted to wait for you. The sweet boy…"

"Okay," Dewey's voice is hardly a whisper, "I'll be there soon."

"Bye now."

And even before the door closes behind Helene, Dewey is already there, catching the door in his hand. He stands behind her tapping his foot *c'mon c'mon* grinding his teeth *c'mon c'mon* just waiting for Helene to leave the adjacent corridor. As soon as he feels she has passed, Dewey throws the door open with a newfound energy, and dashes outside his room, sprints down the hallway, and races down the stairs.

Dewey throws open his brother's door. He sees Renee fully dressed in his black garb. The bed is neatly made and Renee is sitting at the table in the back of the room, his back turned towards the door. Renee does not seem surprised as Dewey enters; he does not even turn his head.

"Dewey," he says.

"You—you're *up??!!?*"

"Well you're the one who could still see. So you tell me."

"*Wha? ah!! No! No! No!*" At seeing his brother's steady confidence, Dewey loses control of himself. "It, it wasn't supposed to happen this way!" Dewey shouts, stomping his feet, "*It wasn't supposed to happen this way at all!!*" Dewey falls to his knees before his blind brother, and he begins to cry. "It, it was supposed to be the, the other way around. You were supposed to break. You were the one—"

"It's okay, Dew—"

"*No! No! NO!*" Dewey kicks his brother's mattress. He throws the table to its side, and smashes things here and there. Renee does not flinch. He sits as calm as a statue, indifferently observing his brother drown in his frustrations like an amused zookeeper observing a wild pet in his cage. Renee can hear his brother throw his cup of pens across the room. Black ink splatters against the windowpane and the clay inkwell shatters against the stone cellar walls. Finally, everything is still. Everything is destroyed except the chair upon which Renee still sits. A morning bird chirps outside, but Dewey's heavy breathing is the loudest sound in the room. Renee waits a moment before speaking. He still does not turn his head.

"It is okay, Dewey."

Dewey kneels down in defeat and softly begins to weep.

"No, n—n—no."

"It is okay Dewey." Renee has prepared for this moment all his life, the moment that he can use his intellect fully, the moment that he can tell his brother *the world* that his senses are gone, but that it is okay.

"B—but, how—"

"It is okay, Dewey, since I never have used my eyes for good anyways. They have distracted me from my thoughts, but now that is all gone."

"Oh—b—but how could y—you forgive, I mean—"

"I did not say I forgive anyone, Dewey. I do not forgive you. But I sympathize for you, for you still must live blinded by sight. Now I will be able to attain great truths with my intellect with no interruptions from the outside world, and you, my fat pathetic brother, you will be haunted by your sights, pleasantly distracted by the transient experiences filling your head forever."

"B—but you, you just lost your sight! Isn't that shocking? I, I mean, how, how could you act so, so—"

"Because I have been told many things, Dewey. I know the chain of events. I know that I will soon have a companion who will replace the one you took from me. I know that this animal will soon cause your downfall, the downfall of this entire nation—"

"This—this is mad! What have you—"

"No, my brother, this is truth. This is vision. This is…O'Talp."

"O'Talp? You mean—"

"That is correct. The brother of your fabled God, El Totsira!"

"*Your* fabled God? You, you say 'your' as if—"

"He is false."

Dewey is speechless.

Renee explains, "He may not be as worthy as you think,"

"Oh, okay, w—well," Dewey struggles for words, "well, what else did this…O'Talp tell you?"

"He told me that my companion will come back for me when I need him most, and that he will lead me to victory. He told me that everything will be okay."

"And—that's, that's it?!"

Renee finally turns his head to face his brother. "He also told me that this animal will cause your downfall, and you will be defeated along with the whole Posteriorian nation."

A moment passes.

"Haha! Right. Well don't come crying to me now, you blind fool. Right. We—we will see. Come on, stop crying, crying to me. Listen to you cry. You deserved it. And now you will know, you will know..." Dewey's voice trails off. Renee does not address him.

Dewey stares at his brother who seems to be staring back, seeing *through* him as if he is not even there, as if he never existed, as if he was completely worthless, a fat yellow ghost treating himself to this world but leaving nothing behind. Feeling fear for the first time in years, Dewey is eager to go back upstairs at once. He throws back his head in a forced, jerky motion and lets out a broken nervous laugh. He turns to leave. Slamming the door behind him, he begins to run up the stairs. Renee turns slowly back to the wall. His face is expressionless as it meets the wall and he folds his hands on his lap. He sits back in his chair, gradually regaining his thoughts.

14

When we look about us towards external objects, and consider the operation of causes, we are never able to discover any power or necessary connexion which binds the effect to the cause, and renders the one an infallible consequence of the other. Experience only teaches us how one event constantly follows another without instructing us in the secret connexion which binds them together, and renders them inseparable.

David Hume

"What happened?" Helene demands from the boys.

The truth is, it has taken Joachim and Helene almost an entire day to notice that something was different about Renee, that he can no longer see. This is because Renee has not acted much different. He has not used his eyes much less than he normally would, nor has he walked, gazed, laughed, or smiled any less cautiously and sparingly than he would on any ordinary day. It is only as he reaches for an orange that they suspect something is wrong.

"Renee?" Helene asks. Dewey's face turns to stone as his stomach drops *here we go* his Adam's-apple bobbing up and down as he swallows. Now Joachim senses something in the air. Even he stops at the sound of her voice and he looks at the boy.

Dewey gathers his robes and tries to leave the room.

"Nope!" Dewey almost jumps at the sound of Helene's voice, "Dewey, you stay right here!"

Dewey stands next to Renee. His mind races with thoughts *what can I say* spinning like a rusty hamster wheel *that I had to do it? Sure. Surely no one will care too much. After all, it is only Renee. They will take my side. Or maybe someone else did it. Yes, perhaps…one of the servants—*

"What happened? One of you will tell me right…now!"

Joachim shakes his head in mild disappointment at the boys, whatever their story. But his indifference a few feet away is outshined by Helene's fiery eyes right before their faces. For the first time, Dewey is scared of her. He can feel her hot breath on his face. He opens his mouth to speak, but his throat is dry.

"Ahem," Dewey clears his throat, "It…it was—"

"It was me," Renee says.

What? Dewey is shocked, but he quickly hides this from his face.

"What?" Helene says.

"It was supposed to happen. I was never supposed to have these eyes."

"What…what do you mean?" Helene's eyes well up with compassion and her face twists in pain, washing away her anger. Joachim still shakes his head.

"I was never supposed to see these….sights I have had to deal with every day. So I was supposed to be blinded. It was supposed to be this way—"

Dewey begins to breath easier again.

Helene asks, "But—but how—"

"It was me," Renee says. "I did it."

Joachim finally walks away, shaking his head in disappointment *not surprised* and Dewey gladly follows his path.

Helene brings her hand to Renee's cheek and Renee faces her tearing eyes with no emotion on his face. Helene says nothing as she strokes Renee's cheek, but her brow furrows in anguish *why why why* as she tries to understand. She fears she never will.

Dewey can no longer hear them behind him. He counts his steps *every one* most gratefully, tip-toeing carefully as if anything he might do may disturb his stellar luck. *The idiot!* his heart jumps with relief *he does not even have the courage to stick up for himself! The coward cannot even muster the courage to tell on me. He is too scared, that is why he did not tell on me: he is too scared! Because he knows that I will be the king soon. He knows that I am better than him He knows what I will do to him if he does tell. That is why! He is too scared, he is too scared, heistooscared, that is why!* but deep inside Dewey wonders if he is telling himself this, or he is merely wishing it to be the case.

In the spirit of being true Posteriorians, it does not take long for Helene and Joachim to move onto other matters, partly because they do not know what to do and partly because this is not much of a change for Renee anyway. Either way, Dewey does not need to worry about this for long.

Winter finally approaches, and the boys keep to themselves. Renee spends more and more time downstairs; after a few weeks of this, he even moves all his belongings down there, rarely coming up for food, drink, or sunlight. Dewey remains upstairs, always engaged in conversation, laughter, and meals in the company of family and servants. Helene encourages Renee to join, but it is not long until she is coaxed into living the Posteriorian life with Dewey at her side. He makes sure of it. Finally, it seems that things are back to the way they always were.

Years pass and the divide between Renee and his family deepens. After just the first year, Dewey begins to forget the sound of Renee's voice, the touch of his skin, the look of his face. He indulges even further in the outside world so that, after time, Dewey almost completely forgets his brother so far down the stairs.

Almost. But not really.

As hard as he tries, Dewey cannot wash away the faint tugging in his stomach, the vague feeling that he has done something criminal. So he indulges himself even more with his dreams of food, sleep, and sex. It helps, for a time. But still, something seems wrong. Why had Renee not cried? Just a little. Dewey's laughs become a little bit cracked, his smiles a little bit strained, his eating a bit erratic. So he stuffs himself with food, eating more than he ever has in his life. But still, something is missing. The food tastes good.

But it does not taste great.

Anyone can tell that Dewey's fire does blaze quite as it always has. The most shocking thing about his new behavior is how he wakes up every morning before Helene comes, and he waits for her, fully dressed like a soldier with a forced smile on his face and bags under his eyes. *Oh I just wasn't tired,* the boy explains *I just don't want to sleep*, rubbing his eyes with the back of his hand as he paces the room nervously between forced bursts of laughter.

After the longest of these winters, a new spring brings Renee from the basement. Renee has come to inherit his father's grand height. Now he towers just over six feet tall. His body has thinned significantly. As the next few years pass he remains tall and white, though his body fills in just a bit. After a while, flesh starts to replace the lanky white, skeletal body dragging its tall frame around. Though Renee remains tall, pale and skinny, flesh covers his bones, and his long face matures, now framed with a full-grown head of straight black hair. As a teenager, he looks almost handsome.

Now Dewey has grown up too, but much more in width than in height. He still has the round, sunshiny boyish face of childhood, the doughnut face he will take to his grave. His thick short legs (which will waddle him around later in life) are strong and powerful, though they often kick much like a chicken's would.

Joachim has grown very old, his body bent over, his pace slowed. He still wears his hair in a bun, cropped at the top of his head. It remains long enough to reach his shoulders, but has gone completely white. He is still the judge of the High Court, and he still shows amazing strength even at this age (no doubt impressing even the criminals who quake before him) though his step has slowed significantly. It has become almost painful for him to walk. Nevertheless, he carries on, sifting through the massive amount of evidence put before him, never even pausing for a rest.

But as Joachim forgets how to walk, he insists on staying home to watch Renee relearn how to walk. Helene is surprised at such a quick change of attitude, but Joachim insists *since I never got to teach him how to walk the first time* for he was never home *I am sure as hell going to be there now.* Joachim gives him a wooden stick to feel out his path. The old man spends much time in his room now, cheering on Renee from down the hall as his boy learns his surroundings and learns to see with his stick and with his mind.

Dewey ignores such cheers for his brother though they do not bother him. He is glad he was not reprimanded for blinding Renee for long. Sure, Helene made faces of disgust at him, but everyone knows how difficult Renee can be and how somehow, it must have been his own fault. Further, as Dewey opened his big blue eyes in innocent regret and confusion, it was not easy to stay angry at him. The people shook their heads and went on to help Renee, forgetting about their future king's actions for the time being. Dewey just goes about his business with a smile on his face, having experiential parties with his friends, fattening himself with delicacies, and preparing himself to become the leader of Lyceum in his own Posteriorian way.

Renee learns quickly. It does not take long for him to walk throughout the palace confidently, his chin held high and his step almost steady. He walks slowly and cautiously, not taking a step until sure it is certain. Sure, there are times he bumps a table, feels embarrassed after knocking down a lamp, his eyes turning this way and that, listening over the sensor's scribbling, listening for another's presence, hoping that no one has seen. But these incidents become less and less frequent, though they always accompany his walk as he discovers new places and unfamiliar terrain.

Renee begins to understand the layouts of rooms in an amazing way. Once he knows what the room is for, he understands what should be in it and where. In time he is able to navigate around obstacles in this way. *Reason tells me that a water bucket belongs in this room; it should be right around here…and that means the dining room table must be, well, it would make sense that it would be here, and that means that logically* but Dewey insists that it is only by the experience of trial and error that Renee familiarizes himself a room. But in Lyceum, everything is always changing. Nothing stays in the same place for long. Not even a small table. Still, Renee now knows his way around. Even as the brothers go to a new tavern or just chase each other through the ever-changing city streets, Renee knows his way around as if he has been there before.

The brothers are older now, well into their mid-teens. As they leave the past stage of life behind them, they feel the strife it created between them fade away. They begin to speak to each other, albeit briefly. Their bitter silence evolves into a mere 'scuse me' as they pass each other in the hall, and eventually to a kinder 'gnite' before bed. Finally, after a year or two, they learn to have the occasional conversation, though in a most casual tone.

One sunny afternoon, Dewey walks in the house to see Renee there all alone, lying on the floor. Renee has tripped over a rope that had been left out, and he is hugging his leg, cringing from the pain of the fall.

Dewey walks right by.

He can hear Renee wince in pain behind him. A sob escapes Renee's mouth before he can bite his lip. Dewey takes a deep breath. It is not like Renee to show pain.

"You," Dewey says. He won't allow himself to say his brother's name. "You're okay, right?" He looks back and sees Renee's ankle twisted at an ugly angle. Finally, Dewey turns around, "Are you alright?"

Trying not to show weakness, Renee quickly lets go of his leg. He feels his older brother's eyes upon him.

"Sure. I am, I am fine. It is nothing."

"Right." Dewey stands in place, ten feet from the place Renee lies.

Renee places his palms on the floor and begins to push himself up. *I can do this.* He grimaces and gets to his knees. Then he hesitates, catching his breath. Counting to three, he jerks himself up but severe pain instantly shoots into his leg like a hundred needles. He begins to fall back towards the floor.

But a hand grasps his arm. Renee recognizes the grasp at once. It can only be Dewey's.

"Come, let's help you up," Dewey says, holding out his other hand for Renee to grasp. "Take my hand."

Renee moves his hand around frantically searching for Dewey's. It sways back and forth like a lost reed blowing in the wind, looking for its other half. Finally, their hands meet and so do their eyes *it has been so long* and for one small second, Dewey feels that Renee can see his face *you look so much older now* with his own eyes *but not really* as Dewey could see his. They pause as their eyes meet for one moment, and with all his strength, Dewey picks his brother up from the dusty stone floor.

"Eh, there you go," Dewey says, brushing the stone dust off his brother's robes. A moment passes. Sensing that the two may have gotten too close, Dewey moves to free his hands from his brother's grasp. But Renee's hands will not let go; his long white fingers remain clasped onto his brother's yellow hands.

"Renee, my hands—"

"Thank you."

"Huh?"

"Thank you for helping me." Dewey could see Renee's eyes moisten, and he can feel his brother's hands tighten around his, *thank you for helping me* a touch of skin that has for so long been forgotten. Dewey realizes that he actually misses his brother almost as much as Renee misses him.

"Thank you," Renee repeats, his gaze intense.

"Well, uhm, You—you're welcome."

"That was, well, that was nice," Renee slowly releases his brother's hands. Dewey smiles.

"Yes brother, it…most certainly was."

ΩΨΩ

The two princes enter their later teens. They begin to spend time together again. At first it is slow, but eventually it is almost as if Dewey had not blinded Renee at all. Indeed, it is almost as if they are children again, playing with hoops, sticks, and balls. But unlike children *playing in corridors like passageways running through the body of a large whale* the games they play now *slipping through the veins*, *hanging from the rib cage ceiling rafters*, are more mind-oriented than *jumping up and down on the large tongue beds* what they played as children. Their minds have grown, and so has their conversation. Now Dewey and Renee often debate philosophy with each other, that is, until Dewey's Posteriorian belly grows impatient and he runs away in frustration, *I, I have to run*, looking for more trifling experiences that do not take so much investment, so much effort, or ones that just do not take so long at all.

That is why Dewey is so glad when he spots the new billiard tables in the center of the palace's recreational room. He has just been engulfed in one of the oh so long philosophical debates with his brother when his heart begins to pain of boredom, his belly grumbling with hunger for quick entertainment of another sort. So he leaves the conversation early, *oh, I should go,* turning, walking down the hall to find this shiny new toy in the center of his favorite room.

"Wow! I want to play! Renee? Renee? Are you still there? Come quick!"

"What is it?" Renee asks, jogging down the hall towards his brother as fast as he can go with his walking stick in lead.

"It's, I think it is a billiard table."

"A billiard table?"

"Yes, y'know, for playing billiards."

Dewey circles the table carefully like an animal circling his prey, his chubby hands rubbing the smooth oak table, his eyes never leaving the green velvet surface illuminated by the multicolor flames in the chandelier above. He notices that there are five billiard tables around him, where other royalty are already involved in their own games. Dewey hears Renee enter behind him.

"Interesting. Show me where it is," Renee says, his hands reaching out for the cool polished wood, "When did it get here? How—"

"Oh, there you go asking questions again! I don't know. But who cares? Ha ha! Interesting, you say? I say, let's play!"

Renee can hear his brother's excited large body fumble around *clumsy like a bull,* putting the balls in order *and I'm the blind one* hearing the click clack click of the balls' placement in the triangle. One of the balls flies out of the triangle towards Renee's head.

"Renee!" Dewey says, "Watch out—" but Renee raises his hand like lightning and catches the ball. "Wow," Dewey sighs in relief, "That was close." Dewey takes the ball from Renee and places it back in its proper place.

Renee looks away. "I am ready," he says, "Where are the billiard sticks?"

But Dewey looks at Renee curiously, both in awe and confusion of his mysterious brother. How did he catch that ball heading towards him?

"Dewey?" Renee says, "Dewey."

"Oh, I'm sorry. Yes?"

"The sticks."

"Oh, right," Dewey looks up at the cue stick rack, but he sighs as he sees only one stick left.

"Take it. I think I will be just fine." Renee says. He walks up to the table without hesitation and lifts his walking stick above his head into his palms. He leans over the edge of the table gracefully, like a natural figure skater performing his bouts. Dewey watches in amazement as Renee's walking stick goes right to the white ball, a powerful hit, sending it right into the center of the triangle of balls *Pow!* for a nice, clean break.

"Wha? Renee, I can't hold it in anymore. I am amazed. I know we haven't spoken for…for a long time. But you've, well, I can't believe how well you've…uhm…adjusted."

"Adjusted?"

"To…y'know…your…new life."

Renee towards at Dewey, but to Dewey it looks as if Renee is looking right over his shoulder. Dewey lets a moment pass before speaking again.

"For starters, how did you learn how to do…that? It was incredible! How—"

"I know the rules of this game. I know where the balls are placed."

"Incredible," Dewey answers, shaking his head, "but," he takes a deep breath to gather his confidence, "You still are my younger brother. So watch what I can do." Dewey grabs a billiard stick off the wall and walks towards the table. Still short and stout, he must lean over in order to reach the white ball. But when he does, it is a nice hit and the first point of the game is won.

"Ha ha! I got one in! Did you *see* that?"

"Yes."

"Oh, I, I didn't mean—"

"I know."

"Well, what did you think?"

"It does not matter what I think."

"Wha—I am just asking. Why do you always have to be so serious? I am trying to have fun. I had an amazing shot!"

"It was almost fine."

"Why do you say *that*?"

"It did not count."

"What? Why not?"

"I cannot be impressed since you cheated. And because you cheated on that shot, it cannot count."

"I—You think I *cheated?!* You can't even—"

"I am sorry, but you have to have both feet on the floor."

"What?"

"You have to have both feet on the floor when you hit the ball. It is one of the rules of the game."

"I'm sorry, but how could you know how many of my feet were on the floor?"

"Based on your height and the location of the ball, you could not have made that shot if both your feet were on the floor. If both of your feet were truly grounded, you would not have had the leverage for your short arms to hit the ball at such an angle required to cause the events you purport to have occurred."

Renee is right Dewey remembers lifting his leg off the floor in order to reach the white ball. *I don't know how, but the boy is right.*

"You're making this up. You don't know all that."

"True. But I heard your breathing. You bent over and lifted a foot up."

"Okay then, fine. I lifted my foot off the floor. So what? I never heard of any rule saying that I couldn't. I don't think anyone follows such a rule."

"It is a rule."

"I, I think you're making this up. Have you ever seen anyone following that rule?"

Renee remains silent.

"Have you? Have you ever heard of anyone breaking it? Have you ever experienced someone breaking it? Anyone losing *a point* because of it?"

"The rule does not require me to."

"Ha! Well, there you go," Dewey retorts, "It is not a rule. You made it up. We are keeping my point."

"Good. You will need it."

Renee walks towards the table for his turn, but after all that confusion, his mind has forgotten where the balls are. Dewey aids Renee in his strokes, pointing out the ball here *the black one is a bit to your left* and the ball there *you wanna try to hit this one, a little to your right* lying occasionally, but helping more often than not. Renee scores two points.

Dewey shoots, missing his target completely. Then, Renee does the same. Finally, Dewey hits his target head-on *ha!* but it rolls and settles at the lip of the hole. By accident, Renee knocks it in, but also gets in two of his own. After a few more turns, Renee only has one ball left. Dewey gets two in his next turn, but misses the third. It is Renee's turn, and by Posteriorian rules, Renee only has to score the orange ball in order to win.

Renee could win this game now. If only he scores the orange ball.

Dewey looks to his brother, who seems to be already deep in thought over his next turn. Renee closes his eyes, and imagining the balls on the table, he determines his next move.

"You see that ball over there?" Renee asks.

"Yes, the yellow one at the end of the table? What about it?"

"Ah, it is yellow. Well, I am going hit it into the orange ball, and it will cause the orange ball to roll against the wall and into the hole. I am certain."

"How can you be certain if it hasn't happened yet?"

"What do you mean?"

"I mean, you can try it, but how do you *know* that the yellow ball will cause the orange ball to do such a thing?"

"It is very simple. That is how billiard balls work."

"And how is that?" Dewey asks, "How do they work?"

"When one ball hits another, it causes the other to move in a certain direction."

"You've seen this before?"

"We both have. That is just how billiards work."

"You, well, you think it will happen now because you have experienced it before."

"No. Again, that is how it works. I know it will happen now because it only makes sense," Renee explains indifferently, as if this much is obvious, "The laws of physics require it."

"The laws of...physics? What? You can't be serious. There are no laws, only theories. All the physics in the world can't ever tell you for certain what will happen in the future. Nothing can. Because we haven't experienced it yet. I mean, you can only hope the yellow ball will cause the orange ball to move as such, but you can't actually *know* it for sure."

"And yet somehow, I do."

Dewey sighs. "I hate to get back into a serious discussion with you. But you force me to. We were trying to have fun. But, what I mean is, the only reason why you think such an effect will follow from such a cause is because you have constantly experienced the two in conjunction in the past. But, but that is all you know. When a ball hits another, you see one ball move to a certain point and stop, and then you see another ball begin to move in its place—so you see two separate things. Motion in the second billiard ball is quite a distinct event from motion in the first; nor is there anything in the one to suggest the smallest hint of the other. Yet you go on to call one a cause and the other its effect, and you act like there is some special connection between the two, as if the yellow ball *necessarily must cause* such a desired effect. Throughout the future and always."

"Well, sure, it has been proven if I hit the yellow ball a certain way, it will cause—"

"*No!*"

"Dewey—"

"*There is no causation here!*"

"Do not shout. You know very well that it will make the orange ball—"

"I...We can't *know* anything! Nothing has been proven! You...you have been persuaded into thinking that such an effect must follow such a cause merely by custom. When scientists observe certain phenomena *all swans I have seen are white*, they make such theories *all swans are white* but they are just that—theories and no more. Theories get proven wrong everyday when *I see a black swan.*"

"Then tell me Dewey, if I hit the yellow ball in that way, what else would the orange ball do besides go into the hole? What else *could* it do?"

"Oh, an infinite number of things! Anytime I see a billiard ball moving in a straight line towards another, may I not conceive, as a result of their contact, that a hundred different events might as well follow from that cause? May not both these balls remain at absolute rest? May not the first ball return in a straight line, or leap off from the second in any direction? All of these effects are consistent and conceivable. The only reason you so foolishly *assume* that the orange ball necessarily must go into the hole, is because you are *used* to seeing that type of effect follow that cause. You assume that that will happen every single time—but really, you have no reason to know so."

"That is just confusing. One would never be able to get anywhere. Without laws to depend on, foundations to rest upon—"

"Laws, laws, laws. You have to put everything in a category, don't you? Can't you see that seeing something for the hundredth time is the same as seeing it for the first time? You cannot see the beauty in that? Even today, thousands of years since the creation of the world, we are all like the first man. We are all like Adam. Though his rational faculties be supposed, at the very first, entirely perfect, he could not have inferred from the fluidity and transparency of water that it would suffocate him, nor from the light and warmth of fire that it would consume him. And we are the same. Though we have seen water drown and fire burn in the past, we cannot know the water of fire before us will do the same. Oh, our sense of wonder!

"Or here, present two smooth pieces of marble, present these two shards of stone to a man who has no tincture of natural philosophy; he will never discover that they will adhere together in such a manner as to require great force to separate them...such events, as bear little analogy to the common course of nature, are also readily confessed to be known only by experience; nor does any man imagine that the explosion of gunpowder, or the attraction of a lodestone, could ever be discovered by reason alone. In like manner, when you suppose the cause of hitting the yellow ball to have such effect upon the orange ball, you must make no difficulty in attributing all of your knowledge of it to experience.

"But experience only tells us what happens in the *past*, and from this we can only *suppose* the future. And this is why you can never know it for sure. If one looks out of their window to see a fresh blanket of snow, they may assume that the snow is cold as it was during earlier years, but perhaps, just perhaps it is different now; one has no right to say they *know* it to be the same. Snow and cold happen to be correlated in the past. But there is no necessary connection between them. For this time, the snow may very well in fact be warm and taste like salt."

"Nicolas." Renee says.

"What?"

"That sounds like what Nicolas said."

"Nicolas?"

"Yes. Nicolas. He was…a boy that came to me many years ago, in the woods, behind the needle."

"Oh my! I have heard about that rascal, that...traitor! He came to you? Why? Why didn't you tell me?"

Renee faces towards his brother.

"Fair enough. But when was this?" Dewey asks, "When, when did you meet him?"

"It was the night that I discovered the truth about O'Talp—"

"No more than a story, no doubt—"

"—in Papa's thinking room," Renee recalls, "and I came to certain realizations, certain thoughts that had plagued me through the night, stealing me from slumber, not letting my mind rest—"

"—as if it ever could—"

"—such that I was unable to sleep at all. Yes, in Joachim's thinking room which he never used, I discovered O'Talp's story, how he had left his family at such a young age, abandoning his loving father Nicomachus, venturing out into the wild all by himself, sleeping in a dark cave near Mount Korab—"

"—O'Talp's cave, they call it—"

"—living there for years and years until his eyes forgot what the light of day looked like, shedding his wisdom to any men that strayed by, feeding their sled dogs, offering them the warmth of his fire and the shelter of his words. Slowly, man by man, O'Talp obtained quite a following, and word spread about his abilities. He performed great miracles for the men, no doubt—"

"—mere tricks, I tell you. His hand moved faster than the eye can—"

"—imagine. But soon, his followers grew too numerous for the caves to contain them. They planned to travel west across the Axios River to establish their own nation there. But the word that O'Talp was still alive reached his brother El Totsira's ears, and El Totsira sent soldiers out to find him. As any true Posteriorian likes to do any thing with great numbers, El Totsira delivered hundreds of thousands soldiers throughout the mountains, to 'flesh out' anything of his brother's name. They poured over those caves in a wave, seizing the alleged prophet, beginning him back to El Totsira, where he was killed as a threat. But before he was executed, O'Talp vowed that someday, a true descendant of his would reclaim his glory and accomplish what he had not.

"Well this story disturbed me greatly, brother, but it was when I found a photograph of myself bound up with the documentary evidence of O'Talp's story that I really became stressed. I mean, why did Papa have my picture there? And why did he have a note with his illegible scribbling on it, forced, jerky scribblings surely coming from a hand full of worry? I was not able to sleep that night, Dewey. I lay down in my quarters tossing and turning, but before the sun began to rise, I rose from my bed to go outside and get...some air." Renee sighs, remembering that night.

"But nothing was going on outside that time of night. Why would you—"

"I was walking south," Renee ignores Dewey and looks into the distance as he remembers that night, "I was behind the needle when I first heard his voice. I was planning on making my way to the middle of the orange groves, where we used to have agricultural lessons as kids."

"I still go there quite often, and you would know that if you ever bothered to—"

"And that was when Nicolas spoke to me. He came out of the trees, speaking to me—"

"—about reason, I'm sure. About how much he sympathizes with your plight, whatever that may be. He must have told you about your pathetic soul, how you are almost as dumb and blind as he—"

"Close. But how could you know? You were—"

"—fast asleep in my Posteriorian dreams way up in the castle, as all Lyceumeans *should* have been." Dewey looks at Renee critically, but his voice softens, "But yes, I know all about Nicolas. Sure, no one speaks about him much anymore, for news gets old fast around here fast, but his last sighting was quite the story."

"His last...sighting?"

"Yes," Dewey looks around, and sees they are alone. He leans over to Renee, and whispers, "Did you tell anyone?"

"What?"

"Did you tell anyone you met him?"

"No. Why? What happened to him?" Renee tries not to show much concern on his face. "Tell me what happened."

"Do you not know? Have you not heard? How long have you kept to yourself? Blind to the world around you!" Dewey says, still pretending that Renee would ever care to pursue current events in the outside world, the world of people, "Okay then," Dewey sighs, "Must I fill you in on everything?"

"Dewey."

"Ha! Alright, well you must know that this creature was an evil, evil child. We are still not sure where he came from, though I believe the rumors that claim he fled from the Lyceumean circus. He was our best freak, that malformed boy. That would explain how he was able to swing through those trees with so much...comfort..." Dewey's voice trails off.

"I see," Renee says. *But Nicolas never told me about that* he thinks to himself. Renee is surprised to feel his love for Nicolas grow every time Dewey calls him a fool, animal, or creature. Renee's love for Nicolas grows with his distaste for his brother.

"Anyways," Dewey says, "word of his existence first came from some ordinary citizens of our kingdom. First, a group of old farmers noticed that their crops were missing from the eastern farmlands. At first, they attributed it to the bunnies, but it did not take them long to realize the scientific impossibility of that," Dewey smiles, "You see, the crops were uprooted by the stem; Nicolas left the bulbs intact for future crops that he could continue to steal. A bunny wouldn't have done this. They would have eaten the bulbs. Further, from the periods of time between the crop seizing, and the moisture and density level of the culprit's footprints, our farmers were able to deduce that the culprit could not be dwelling too far at all. In the following weeks, the farmers looked out, up into the wooded hills behind Brittany, but there was nothing to be seen, though one farmer claimed to have seen a brown creature in the earliest dawn, moving slowly, disappearing into the trees. But from the description alone, it was certainly no more than a sloth or a swaying tree. So no one paid it any mind.

"But little more than a year later, there were certain men, an increasing number of Lyceumeans, who would return home to their wives different from when they left. They would walk in quietly, their heads low, arms folded behind their backs, barely touching their dinner before retreating into their bedroom, too tired to make love. Something was happening to our nation, to these men...thank El it was no more than a few...since they came back with something...different inside of them. They were changing. They no longer held passion in their eyes, youth in their movements. They no longer sought experience in the same way...they no longer were...true in the Posteriorian sense....as if something...somebody...had finally gotten to them, clawed at their core.

"Royal agents investigated the situation. They thought there was some sort of epidemic going around, some sort of…virus. They sorted through the great medical books, their scientific minds searching for past cases of illness in the libraries of the sensors, looking for similar cases in the past from which we could heed example. After much questioning (and forced sensory intake), many of these victims temporarily came out of their spell and mumbled about some horrid creature that dwelled in the dark woods nearby, a sneaky creature that tried to harm them by forcing his poisonous words into their ears—"

"Is this the description they gave of Nicolas?"

"There you go again, asking questions that have—"

"Is it?"

"Why is that important? I am giving you *my* impression of what they said. You see, these poor victims must have been traumatized by what they saw in those woods; one must not give their exact words too much weight because...well...they were brainwashed, you see..."

"I see."

"Anyway, ahem," Dewey says, "getting back to the point, we learned that the creature—"

"Nicolas."

"Yes. Uhm...Nicolas. I, I guess that was his name. He...he was speaking to people that would pass by the nearby trees, telling them that their experiences of the world were tainted with sentiment and bias, that they were not firm and lasting but rather fleeting and often deceiving. He showed them how their sensory experiences can be changed, that the way they perceive the outside world could be altered by smoke and mirrors, you can say."

"Smoke and mirrors."

"Y'know. Alcohol consumption, optical illusions, exhaustion, or by altering the irises of their eyes, the taste buds of their tongue. Sure, us Posteriorians do that stuff all the time. But we do it learn from it and he did it to cause confusion and fear. He told them they would never be able to make sense of experience; that they should not even try! Oh, as if they should not be human, the madness of it! After time, he convinced some of our men to follow the clear ideas of their mind rather than 'clouded sensations,' as he called them. Supposedly, his tricks were quite convincing, since he would often pull the wool over our citizen's eyes by altering the way light frequencies and sound waves move through the atmosphere, showing them to be mere illusions. See, he took that which is most precious to us, and turned it into a weapon against us. He filled our beloved Posteriorian men's hearts with fear, fear of the outside world, fear of filtering through our vast experiences to gain knowledge, fear of the Posteriorian mission we all live for.

"He drained them of their energy. He took the life from them. The hope. He told them that they should stop trying to reap order from the chaos, that they should give up. That it cannot be done. He taught them to abandon their mission, to abandon the world around themselves, their family, their loved ones, their body, and to retreat into the labyrinths of their inner...mind, so that when they got home, they were empty, like ghosts. They were jaded, neither here nor there. They had no life inside of them. In Lyceum, they became the walking dead.

"Well it did not take long, you see, for the Grandee to give orders to swipe the woods clean with men, seizing the monster from his home. Of course, the Grandee's orders were carried out by our soldiers just minutes after they were given, though they did change a few times along the way..." Dewey trails off again.

"What happened to Nicolas?" Renee is surprised at the immediacy of his own words.

"Well, the orders failed. We were too late."

"Too late?"

"Our soldiers went through the woods, back and forth again, but they could not find a trace of the monster. Finally, one of the soldiers spotted a small cabin in an opening in the trees. It was a simple shack. Brown and functional enough. Fading into the trees around it. I can't imagine how we missed it, for it was not even hidden, but it was just there. Something our eyes were not used to seeing, I guess. It was boring. We heard sounds from inside the cabin, a heated debate between the creature Nicolas and what sounded like a gentle but confident voice of a young man nearly seven feet tall, a man which we later found out to be one of Lyceum's best lens-crafters by trade. It seemed Nicolas was trying to convince the lens-crafter of something, but since their voices were calm we could not make out their words. When we stormed the cabin, we saw the creature Nicolas dash away, bringing the young man with him. We tried to get a glimpse of them, but they were too fast. The tall, broad lens-crafter carried the creature on his shoulders, and Nicolas told him where to go. Anyway, they disappeared into the north. We sent out search parties, but they were not successful, and as you should know, it did not take long for the Grandee to move on to other matters."

"But what happened to Nicolas?"

"I told you. He disappeared with our lens-crafter. They were never seen again."

"I see," Renee tries to hide the lump in his throat, "well, I mean, maybe the lens crafter brought Nicolas to another place, a…special place, a place where—"

"Where what?"

"Do you think there could be, well, another place, a, a perfect place, a place with no distractions? A place of reason. A place of the mind."

"Oh, I certainly hope not. No such place should ever exist. Why? Have you heard of any such place?" Dewey's face becomes serious.

"Well, answer my question first. I mean, could it exist? Somewhere in this world?"

Dewey looks at his brother.

"I think that it can be found nowhere on earth."

"How can you know?"

"Our explorers have never found or experienced such a place," Dewey scratches his cheek with one fat hand, "You know that our nation has explored most lands in this world. There is nothing we cannot know about. No land would be able to escape our hungry eyes for long.

"Then where do you think Nicolas went?"

"The man and the creature are lost in the wilderness, I tell you, if they are even alive."

"Do you think they will ever—"

"As I said, the creature does not concern us anymore. Do not worry, you won't see him again, whether you want to or not. If he is alive, as I doubt he is, it is nowhere near here. I don't see how his wretched body could have ever handled such a journey into the wild surrounding Lyceum. Why, it would violate all I've ever experienced in man's nature! His life has likely extinguished by now. You don't have to worry. He will never bother you again. We have ruled him exiled, so he may not return. He would never get past our borders. Serves him right, considering the life he took from so many others..." As Dewey's voice trials off, Renee tries to hide the great loss he feels in his heart. *I cannot go back* Renee feels his stomach drop *I had my chance. It is too late now.* Feeling his eyes moisten, Renee struggles to resume conversation, burrowing his way back to a former subject.

"So," he says, "you seem to agree with...this 'creature'...on what he says about causation."

"Never! I can never agree with that, that—"

"But Nicolas said just what you said about causation, namely, that there is none. That it does not exist. Like you, Nicolas says that since we only *experience* a cause and its effect on certain occasions, but we do not see any necessary connection between the two. Just a—"

"A constant conjunction."

"A constant conjunction. But how do you know that it is only through experience? Maybe our mind tells us—"

"I know this because it is our *senses* that sense one event following from another. The mind feels no sentiment or *inward* impression from this succession of objects. And since causation does not reach the mind, it is no more *logical* than our experience of it. There is not, in any single, particular instance of cause and effect, any thing which can suggest that a cause is necessarily connected to its desired effect."

"What about the laws of physics?"

"Huh?"

"You forget the laws of physics, my brother, the principles of geometry. They are permanent and immovable. They are logical, rational *inward* principles that make sense in the mind, and apply to everything in the world without exception, precisely and flawlessly. I know that when I hit this yellow ball here, into this orange ball," Renee walks forward and points to the billiard table, excited in his new argument, "the orange ball will go in a straight line into this hole. I know this to be the case because of the laws of motion, that the moment of force in this yellow ball will be transferred to its obstacle, sending it off in the proper direction. Then this orange ball will go into the hole. I know this for sure; it is a mathematical certainty."

"Hmm. Yes, you make a good point. But still, the discovery of those laws themselves are owing merely to experience."

"Even the laws of geometry?"

"Even geometry."

"How can that be? Geometry is—"

"Only believable because it has held up in the past. It has only held up because our experiences of things have conformed to it. But the assurance of custom may not hold for long. While Posteriorians rely on experience (for that is all we have), we know that soon our judgments may be overruled, our buildings may crumble, our theories may be proven wrong, whether geometry or otherwise. While experience is informative, it is limited, no doubt, but it is the best we can do."

"But isn't there something better? Why are you so eager to settle?"

"Settle?! Now, wait a minute—"

"What about reason? Doesn't the mind—"

"The mind is blank without experience to fill it. You were born empty, with a blank slate, *a tabula rasa ifyouwill* and it is only through experience that your mind has been filled. And regarding your billiard balls, the mind can never suggest to us the notion of any distinct object, such as their cause and effect; much less, show us the inseparable and inviolable connexion between them.

"Besides, even if you know the physics behind something, you still have to know how to operate. Just because a child understands the physics behind riding a bicycle, does not mean that he will not fall off it the first time he tries. Only through experience and practice can he ride that bicycle. It is for this same reason, my brother, that you cannot know what the yellow billiard ball will do until you hit it. But go ahead."

But Renee knows there has to be something stronger than experience, something he must find. One day. Instead of arguing back *let the walking stick do the talking for you* Renee walks towards the table, raises his walking stick and hits the yellow ball.

The yellow ball travels across the table, a perfectly round lemon tumbling its way across the lime green. It takes its time like a small yellow mouse sniffing here and there, feeling its way through, finding its path until *clink!* it meets up with the orange ball, and freezes in place. The orange ball shoots forward, and just as Renee said, travels to the other side of the table, slowly dropping *plop!* into the corner hole for the winning point.

Dewey's eyes remain fixed on the hole far after the orange ball falls in. He waits *it cannot be* hungry for the sight of the orange ball to emerge, *c'mon* waiting for it to *fly out now, c'mon* but the ball is gone. Dewey realizes that he has lost. Renee, his *blind little* brother has beaten him. But before he can feel defeat, the boys hear a deep moan across the room.

Dewey looks up to see a most curious sight.

An older billiard player stands by a nearby billiard table, ready to take his shot. He bends over, stretching out to reach the yellow ball. He moans again, but his opponent shakes his head and points to one of his feet that is not touching the ground. Dewey sees that the man has an artificial leg. Finally, the man unscrews his prosthetic leg. He leaves his leg on the floor and climbs up onto the table, stretching out upon his belly like a large whale landed on the beach. But he keeps his real foot on the ground next to his prosthetic leg. *Both feet on the floor.* Dewey sees the man stretch his stick forward, just far enough to get a clear shot of the yellow ball. Both feet on the floor.

So it is a rule.

Dewey looks up for his brother, in awe of Renee's victory. His eyes scan the room, the colored stone walls surrounding the flickering green light. Renee is gone. As soon as he realizes Renee has left him, Dewey thinks he sees the last of Renee's gray robes flash and vanish from the corner of his eyes. Dewey closes his eyes and shakes his big head as his younger brother makes his way down the hall to his solitary quarters, already pondering the events just taking place.

15

Religion declined not because it was refuted, but because it became irrelevant, dull, oppressive, insipid. When faith is completely replaced by creed, worship by discipline, love by habit; when the crisis of today is ignored because of the splendor of the past; when faith becomes an heirloom rather than a living fountain; when religion speaks only in the name of authority rather than with the voice of compassion— its message becomes meaningless.
Abraham Joshua Heschel

The alleged short-cut to knowledge, which is faith, is only a short-circuit destroying the mind.
Ayn Rand

All men are born with a nose and ten fingers, but no one was born with a knowledge of God. If God did not exist (man would find) it would be necessary to invent him.
Voltaire

The following months pass quickly enough. The two young princes continue to forget their vindictive past and enjoy their present. They converse more frequently, debating politics, the arts, and philosophy in such ways that will shape their personality and influence the men they will eventually become.

More importantly, they relearn what it means to have fun. They even return to the billiard tables a few more times. Both Dewey and Renee improve dramatically. Getting better and better, they return to the table ever more frequently, even sneaking to the rec room twice in the middle of the night. They stand there leaning on their sticks, two silhouettes under the hazy lantern light. Their sensors watch silently in the corner, their soft scribbling emitting a low hum correlating with the cold, loud clanking of the billiard balls against each other. The smell of chalk dust fills the sterile air, the green lantern drawing black shadows across the dark stone walls.

At night, the boys hear more stories about the great and mighty El, how Ol' Tots was a prophet of many, many words, many of which have been interpreted (and reinterpreted) into emotionally inspiring, colorful lessons by which to live. Now the boys are old enough to hear about his other half, about the foolish and confused O'Talp. They hear how O'Talp shunned experience by shutting out the outside world in order to get a clear look at his inner intellect to see what he could glean from unadulterated reason. The boys' ages do not stop Helene from sharing stories with them (for it has always been a Posteriorian custom to share stories through the hours of the evening, and Dewey's appetite for stories has only increased with his age). So Helene continues to tell stories to the boys, speaking them in bed, until Renee leaves in the middle, venturing downstairs to his lone quarters, leaving an absorbed fat brother and Helene to their fables told deep into the night.

Tonight she tells the young men how to refute the arguments of O'Talp and how to learn only from their experience of the world. But when she accuses O'Talp of shutting out experience of the entire world, Renee begins to question her words.

"Wait just one second," Renee begins, "Did O'Talp ever actually *say* that the outside world is worthless?"

"Well," Helene looks at the younger son, not surprised at his concerns, "O'Talp distinguished the outside world from the world within us. He explained that the world within us consists of ideas or forms that are perfect and unchanging, and are only comprehensible by the use of the intellect or understanding."

"So, he never explicitly canceled the importance of the outside world?"

"Well, I mean, he said that everything we perceive from the outside world really just consists of our inner ideas."

"So, our perception of the outside world does have some value."

"Well, it seems like he shuts out its importance."

"But...he never explicitly says so?"

Helene sighs. "No. But, well, I just know he felt that to be the case."

"But if he never said it, how could you know?"

"I just know."

"And what does that mean? What does it mean to know?"

"Well, now you are asking a good question. I know something because I believe it to be true, my belief is justified, and it is true."

"What?"

"I said, I—"

"I know what you said, but what—"

"I believe it to be true, my belief is justified, and it is true. That is actually how O'Talp defined knowledge. Though most Posteriorians don't go by his definition of knowledge, we don't have many others to choose from."

"Hold on one moment," Renee says, "How do you say O'Talp defines knowledge?"

"Well, O'Talp said that a person can say they *know* something if three requirements are filled: they must believe it to be true, their belief must be justified, and it must actually be true. If all those requirements are fulfilled, then it is fair to say that a person knows something."

"But, in your case, that last requirement may not be fulfilled. O'Talp may have never thought that the outside world is worthless. It may not be actually true."

"Oh, but it is."

"Well, you, you can never really know if it is true. No one can. But that is your third requirement of knowledge. But according to that I guess no one can ever really know if they 'know' something."

"I, I suppose so," Helene says, rolling her eyes. She tries to be impressed with the boy's complex reasoning but these days she is constantly overwhelmed with his incessant pursuit of certainty. She is overwhelmed with the knowledge that the boy can go on and on about this, pursuing a precise definition of knowledge until the moon fully rises and the two reach headaches all the nation's medicine would not be able to cure.

"I guess you're right." Helene obliges.

Renee looks down. Helene fears what the boy will become. She attempts to curb his intellectual endeavors to a place within the Posteriorian framework as she has so many times before.

"Y'know," she begins over Dewey's loud snores, "there is much more wrong with O'Talp than his refusal to learn from experience."

Renee continues to look down, refusing to meet Helene's eyes. He is fidgeting with his fingers as bitter doubts water his eyes.

"Don't be upset," Helene continues, "It's just that O'Talp, well, we must understand that he was not realistic. He just strived for a level of certainty that no human being could ever reach. For example, his ideal government was run by a philosopher king having a completely just soul."

"And you don't think that's possible?" Renee looks up.

"Mm. I'm sorry son, but O'Talp believed that this 'completely just' philosopher king would be able to organize and run a government that was also completely just. To be able to do that, well, that is just implausible."

Renee looks back down at his sleeping brother as he listens to Helene's cynical words. Renee has looked up to O'Talp for a few years now—Dewey knew it all along and Helene suspected it. Now, as Helene tries to loosen Renee's confidence in O'Talp, Renee wants to hold on to it more than ever. It has given him identity, an identity unique from any Posteriorian, one he truly believes in. But Helene is steadfast.

"A completely just king creating a completely just nation? A philosopher king with a perfect soul? I'm sorry Renee, but this, this is madness."

Helene stops to let the words sink in to her younger one's head as the two listen to Dewey's disturbed breaths like white noise in their heads. For a moment, the fat prince actually stops breathing to clear his throat. It is likely he is half asleep, his rich dreams subconsciously including the Renee's questions as they make his way into the fat prince's ears. Finally, Renee answers Helene.

"But why? Why is this madness? Why must you not believe in the reason of man? Why must you not believe that a man can have a perfectly just soul?"

"Because man has never come across such a ruler. Have you ever seen one? I have not. In all my years of experience. Not one."

"I believe it."

"See, no one can be fully just—everyone makes mistakes, and that is how we learn. It is in this way that our mistakes our beautiful; they make us grow. They make us who we are. No one can ever be certain that what they know now won't be refuted later. No one has known of such certainty before. Experience just cannot supply such certainty, and we can only learn from what we have seen—the trial and error of our ways. Even your O'Talp himself made mistakes and saw that his past teachings were wrong! It is foolish to even speak of a perfectly just philosopher king because a perfectly just person cannot be found to exist."

Renee has heard this many times before. *Why* he would wonder *why must we…insist on such low standards? Why can we not just try, just attempt to push all the trivial, temporary experiences away, all the lessons that come and go through time, and try to reach something permanent, something…real?* and as his head would hurt with questions *Why must we limit ourselves to mere theories? Why can we not try to attain…real principles? Why am I the only one who suspects that there is something greater? How could everyone be so…comfortable?* he would draw back further into his solitude, abruptly dismissing himself from Helene's presence. It is during times like these that Renee often rises abruptly in the middle of Helene's words, leaving her in surprise and walking down to his quarters to sort out this mental mess such Posteriorian propaganda had created in his head.

But this time Renee stops at the top of the stairs. He looks down into the darkness, the room that holds his meager belongings. His mind turns to his father's thinking room, the place where he first discovered O'Talp so long ago. Suddenly, the pain of Helene's words, *I'm sorry Renee*, discrediting O'Talp's teachings *but this is madness* begins to wash away. He imagines the room where he discovered O'Talp and he smiles. He closes his eyes and he places himself back in the room. He sees the great thinking lamp, its dithering multi-color flame behind a ball of glass swirling above his father's large oak desk. Then he sees scrolls, documents *of the sage's life* and drawings *chains dragging* strewn across the floor. And next to them, he sees the picture of himself. He remembers all of it, the realization, the discovery *O'Talp was just like him.*

Renee opens his eyes. He turns away from the stairs and heads towards his father's thinking room. He hopes that perhaps there, he can clear his head. Helene's Posteriorian lessons still cloud his mind like heavy stains that won't wash away. *Yes,* Renee feels hope *it is here, in front of the fireplace where I can rest my head. It his here, under my father's thinking lamp, by the blazing fire I may sit and ponder my brain.* Finally, Renee arrives at the door, opens it with his walking stick and goes inside.

The air is musty. Joachim's has not used the room for some time. He had it built long ago, and while most Posteriorians looked the other way, some frowned upon him for building such a thing. *Why do you need to seclude yourself* they would say *what do you have to think about?*

Renee does not need to see the room to know it has been empty for some time. *Perfect*, Renee figures as he smells the musty air. He enters the room, brushing a cobweb out of his way. Before him is a tall red chair by the fire *perfect* oddly clean, as if it has been waiting for him. Still, he feels the old leather, his fingers running across it like a brush. He takes a deep breath and lets the solitude surround him. His memory is strong and he knows the room well. He finds that wood is already in the fireplace. He lights the fire from a nearby lantern and takes a seat in his father's plush leather chair. The fire rises from the logs in cool sheets of red. Finally, Renee prepares to think.

ΩΨΩ

As tall as Renee is, the back of his father's chair still towers over him, its maroon leather reaching nearly ten feet from the ground. The fire in front of Renee throws his shadow up against the chair, flickering from side to side with slow life. But Renee is still. He can feel his father's imprint in the cushion from when Joachim was a young and thoughtful judge. *Those were the days* when Renee would live in his multifarious world with his brother, *parading around the kingdom* as Joachim would bring all his evidence into this very room to sit in this chair for hours, sifting through this, weighing through that. But this room is used no more.

Now those days are gone.

Sitting in the musty, old room, Renee allows his mind to be warmed by the fire blazing before him. He closes his eyes and smiles, taking it all in. *The fire was all ready for me to light. The wood laid out so nicely, the lantern already lit,* he ponders *but no one has been in here for years. No one could have done this* Renee realizes *but it must have been caused by something other than itself. But when man stumbles across this universe, can he not say the same thing? Yes, Aquinas, old Tom of course had formed the idea of a God that way* oh the trail of regression, the long chain of cause and effect back to the original cause, the unchanged changer, the unmoved mover, the uncreated creator, this idea we call God. For everything has its story; there can be no thing without a past—but how far back can we go? Not to infinity. It must stop somewhere: park bench, park, town, city, state, country, earth, world, big bang, darkness, God!

Renee takes pleasure from the fire without regarding its origin—much like most men enjoy their world. But Renee is not satisfied with the fire; he shivers with the flavor Helene's Posteriorian words left in his poor head. Instinctively, he reaches towards the night table and his hand touches an object that feels familiar. It feels like home. In it he feels the cool emptiness, nothingness, *clarity,* and serenity he always wished for. He feels all of this in the smooth surface of this clear, pale spherical object.

It is a wax candle.

Yes, Renee recalls that Joachim's servant recently took a large portion of wax from the garden's large honeycomb in order to make rainbow sculptures. But he forgot to add the dye to this poor piece of wax. Thus, it was left colorless and was made into a plain pallor candle that had no Posteriorian use. As such, it was quickly discarded to the old musty thinking room of Joachim for later removal.

Since it was taken quite recently from the honeycomb, the wax has retained most of its honey flavor. Like the Plado of Rekha's time, the wax gives Renee comfort. It retains just a hint of the scent of the flowers from which it was collected. Its subtle scent reminds Renee of his walks in the garden *azaleas on his left* as his brother watched from overhead *meadow saffrons on his right.* Its color, shape, and size are manifest. It is hard and cold; it is easy to touch. Renee knocks on it with his knuckle and finds it emits a simple, predictable sound. He smiles. *It is nice,* Renee enjoys the feel of the cool, hard wax in his hand, *it is nice for a change, to feel such stability, to hold such permanence, such plain predictability. Great,* Renee decides after becoming acquainted with the wax's qualities, *now it is time to light the wick.*

Renee brings it towards the fire, hoping to ignite the wick.

But as Renee picks up the candle and places it before the fire, to his surprise, it begins to change. He feels the wax's form loosen, its scent quickly fading. He feels its size increasing, its stability failing, its temperature rising, pulsing with life. As the wax goes through various forms, Renee struggles to keep the wax as it once was, the predictable cool stability he had first been accustomed to. He tightens his grip on the candle, but it is no use! The wax seeps its way though his fingers, pulsing with heat and a life of its own, a hot gob of lively temperance: ever-changing, morphing, throwing off one façade in turn of another. Finally, Renee can no longer take the heat. Just as the wax begins to tear *burn* through his white palm, Renee lets out the loudest shriek he ever has in his life. He cannot decide what is worse, the physical pain or the emotional disappointment. Throwing the wax to the floor, our prince sits back in his chair nursing his injured hand, crying from the sudden confusion the wax thrust upon his confident, comforted heart.

After a few moments, Renee opens his hand. His skin is bubbling up now, forming a scar he will carry for life. Now the pain seems distant to him. He feels disconnected, disjointed from his physical body for the first time. Eagerly, he bends over to see if the wax remains. He arises from his chair, strolling around the area where he originally threw it bent over, his hands near the ground. Finally he stumbles upon a hard, cold lump that feels like wax. *A ball of wax* it is indeed—but now it smells charred and has taken on the shape of a mottled saucer as its liquid body bubbles while resting on the cold stone floor. *Is this the same wax I just held?* Renee is sure it is the same wax, but now it is different yet again.

It is completely different from before.

I should have known Renee's mind is a whirl. *I've learned not to trust my senses. But what then can I trust? However the wax came under the senses before: taste, smell, touch, or hearing has all been altered—and yet the wax is still here! Then what can I consider the wax to be? The sweet honey-smelling tubular object which sounded as I rapped on it with my knuckle? The liquid hot and lively mass that wriggling in my fingers? The cold mottled saucer now in my hand? The wax has been so many different things, yet all the while, it has been just one thing: a piece of wax. But which wax is the true wax?*

Since my experience of the wax deceived me, Renee thinks, *it is not by experience that I may know the actual wax. Since the wax takes on even greater variety of dimensions than I can grasp with the senses, it remains for me to concede that I do not grasp what this wax truly is through my senses.*

Rather I perceive it through the mind alone.

I will not, Renee vows, looking at his scar, *I will not ever rely on my senses again, no matter how vivid, how distinct they may show something to be. Fooled me once...Fooled me twice...They can promise me the scent of honey, the sound of rapping, the cool and hard touch to my hand, but I will not trust their word again. I will not be burnt again.* Renee forms his opinion, a resolution of which he feels surer of than he ever has in his life.

And to think, all it took was a ball of wax.

The moon makes its way through a blanket of stars above like a golden yellow ship sailing slowly through flickering buoys. Renee sits before the fire now settling in the embers from whence it came. Its flames lower their arms slowly down, back into the wood. Renee remains still throughout the night, the wax cradled securely in his hands, the coals offering their soft glow, flaming arms reaching out just one more time, clawing at the air above before calming themselves down. Renee's mind calms with the fire. And as the white morning sunlight begins to pour its way through hidden cracks in the wall, Renee finds himself asleep. He sits, his head slumped over, wax hugged tightly in his arms, so asleep, dear reader, that he does not even hear as Dewey enters the room.

ΩΨΩ

Dewey opens the large castle door and sees Renee asleep by the fireplace in his father's chair. His wiry body hardly fills the large chair, *a chair meant for a king* and Dewey shakes his head at the extra space left vacant on the seat cushion. He does not like to see Renee in his father's chair. Renee's head is slumped over in a most unusual way. His soft breaths rise and fall with the glowing of the embers before him, the fire that once was, but is no more. Dewey stands there for one moment, surveying the scene. But it is when Dewey sees the wax saucer *what is that* in his brother's hands that he slams the door behind him, waking Renee from his sleep.

"What are you doing here?" Dewey begins.

Renee senses his older brother standing there, but all he senses is a corpulent ignoramus filling up more of the doorway than anyone that age ever should. Renee smells the odors of the outside world on his brother. Though such smells are no surprise to him, they seem to evoke sympathy in Renee, sympathy for a brother who chose never to think. Rubbing his eyes slowly, Renee stretches the sleep out of his limbs.

"What are you doing here?" Dewey repeats.

"I was just—"

"You were having your doubts again, weren't you?"

Renee's silence is taken as an assent.

"Why do you always have to be such a...skeptic?" Renee smiles at such a name, but Dewey cannot understand why. Dewey continues.

"You were having doubts when Helene was telling us stories last night, when she was refuting the teachings of O'Talp, the…man you…look up to."

"O'Talp is no man."

"Oh, then, what, what was he?"

"O'Talp is a God," Renee says, looking away.

"A...*God?!?* Ha ha!" Dewey roars with forced laughter, his face to the heavens, "The boy has gone mad! My brother is crazy!" His laughs finally subside. "You cannot accept that which you sense directly, yet you believe in this thing called...God?" Dewey's mouth opens slowly, as if struggling to say such a word, "Have you ever seen this...God? Have you ever heard him speak to you?"

"I do not *believe* in him," Renee answers, "Rather I *know* he exists."

"What?"

"I have given it great thought, and I am certain there is some God."

Now Dewey has heard his brother say similar things in the past, but this, well, this was just too much for his Posteriorian belly to take. He laughs so hard, he feels his insides shaking aggressively. He holds his sides, his face beet red, bawling over as Renee just sits there. Dewey continues his nervous heckle, a forced laugh meant more for himself than for Renee. Renee's head moves away from his brother slowly, his still white eyes directing themselves down towards the embers. Now facing the fireplace, Renee waits for his brother to recover before speaking once again.

"I am certain a Supremely Perfect Being exists."

"Oh, really? Well so did Old Benedictus, and look what happened to him!"

"Benedictus?" Renee asks.

"Yes, Benedictus Azonips—do you...not know who he was?"

Renee sighs. He is tired of his brother's world, tired of these games. Why can't he just be left alone? But something in Renee's eyes make silence unbearable for Dewey. They compel him to continue.

"Right," Dewey says, "Okay then. Well, Benedictus was one of our best lens crafters by trade—our tallest one by far—and he helped our astronomers improve upon their telescopes, the great Posteriorian telescopes used to observe and study the heavens above. He was a few years older than you, but it did not take him long to become a religious man and somehow, it got into his head, this mystical invention that you just called God."

Renee is suddenly reminded of Nicolas, the one God-believer he ever met, the one who filled him with a faint glimmer of hope that *there was at least someone like me out there, somewhere,* a faint glimmer that disappeared when he heard of Nicolas's retreat into the wild, a journey *his wretched body never could have handled* as Dewey related *his life has likely extinguished by now*. Feeling newfound hope rising in his heart once again, Renee listens as his brother recounts the story of another believer.

"He was almost as bad as that creature Nicolas," Dewey says as if he could read Renee's thoughts, "but not quite. At least he gave *some* value to the senses, to experience, though he too belittled them as inferior to the...intellect. But even his sensory experiences led him down the wrong road. See, he would go out with his lens, carefully studying the scientific, agricultural world. He really was a model Posteriorian in that way. He studied nature. But when we see nature, we stop there. He took it one step further. Perhaps he looked a bit too close. He saw nature as one, single substance."

"A single substance?"

"Yes. He called this substance God."

Renee is silent.

"See," Dewey explains, "The trouble is he did not just believe in what he saw, as we do. Instead he looked at nature and he reasoned. He reasoned that since a substance can only be caused by something similar to itself (something that shares its attributes) and no two individual substances can possibly share an attribute or else they would be identical, then a substance can never be caused. He also believed that substance is infinite since it cannot be dependent on anything else for its existence. Now, since substance is infinite, and it cannot be caused by anything else, there can only be one substance.

"Yes," Renee smiles faintly, "Since two infinite substances would limit each other—"

"And after too much time with nature, he contended that God and nature were two names for the same reality, something he called the Single Substance or Deus Sive Natura.

"And this one substance..." Renee tries to get Dewey to the point.

"This one substance," Dewey says, "well, he believed it to be the same thing as God."

Renee remains silent.

"No wonder he went off the deep end, huh?" Dewey waits for his brother to laugh, but no laughter comes. "Huh? Well...it was after that that the Grandee ordered him—Benedictus—exiled from Lyceum, as a threat to our nation—"

"Where is he now?"

"Oh, we have no idea. He was exiled. We threw him out at our borders, and he just disappeared. I don't blame the sucker—you should have seen his face as we stormed into his home, so surprised, as if he did nothing wrong, as if it is completely sane to speak of some...single substance one has never ever seen..."

"To have known what it looked like, I presume you were there?"

"Oh, who, me? No! I can only imagine—"

"—because I know you would never assume anything unless you experienced it yourself."

"Oh, yes. Of course. But...but I know what faces criminals make as they are seized by surprise—"

"As Benedictus was."

"Huh? Oh yes, as Benedictus was. I have been around long enough to know—"

"Has he been seen since?"

"Huh?"

"Has Benedictus been seen since?"

"Oh, no. Well...not that it would matter...but some claim to have seen him walking across the White Plains months later, as if...searching for something. He was with...some animal. A wolf, many say it was. A white wolf...or was it a gray wolf..." Dewey's voice trails off and his eyes gaze ahead as if picturing the lone figure making his way across the planes led by a wolf a few feet ahead. Renee could picture him too, a tall, handsome youth, someone he would have very much liked to meet.

As Renee feels the faint glimmer of hope fade in his heart, he wonders why everyone has left him. Nicolas. Benedictus. Then he realizes that he has left them. *Why have I been so...complacent? So...foolish thinking my own solitude was enough? Yes, man must be alone to think. But man must be alone together. Alone undisturbed, but together to bring more truth to the world. And perhaps to be away from this awful place. I have not had the courage to unite with Nicolas, to discover Benedictus. I had my chance. And now it is too late.*

Now they have all gone.

A hole forms in Renee's heart, a hole reminding him that the people he has always cared about, Dewey, Helene, his cat, they never really mattered. It was the people he neglected, the ones he has failed to seek out, that ever mattered. And now...they were all gone. But why? Where had they gone?

Who has seized them? What terrible ends have they suffered? Closing his eyes, Renee imagines a great destroyer, a destroyer hunting for men of reason, devouring every great mind managing to break through the experiential field, snipping it at its roots while it is still early, heaving it into the wild to meet its end. But wiggling his toes, Renee feels his feet move before the warm embers and he realizes that he is still here. He can start now. He takes a deep breath and begins to speak.

"I am certain a Supremely Perfect Being exists," he hears himself say.

"There you go again. But you haven't seen him! You know nothing of him!"

"I have seen him indeed. I have seen him in my father's documents. I have heard him through people's stories, through myths, through books, through history, through the testimony of ones who had witnessed true miracles."

"Miracles? Ha! And, and you believe they actually happened?"

"Yes. Hundreds of people have witnessed them. In the caves, O'Talp brought a dead man back to life."

"Yes, I heard that one. But by mistake he turned the man into a toad."

"Once, O'Talp even brought back someone's mutilated arm."

"And replaced it with two hands."

"Those were still miracles."

"Well, since they were each a, a violation of the laws of nature, I, I guess you are right. But they cannot be believed to have…happened."

"Excuse me?"

"The occurrence of miracles must not be believed unless they are, well, experienced directly."

"Why is that?"

"Because any wise man proportions his beliefs to the evidence presented. Just ask Pa how he weighs the evidence in court. And in the case of miracles, we have more evidence against the occurrence of the miracle than we have for it."

"Well, we have evidence that the miracle happened—direct testimony. What is the evidence against it?" Renee asks.

"Are you serious? Everyone else's testimony. All the experience in the whole wide world! The experience of anyone who ever lived, in any time, in any place! Every time someone sees the sun rise in the morning, a plant grow from a seed, a man die from a cancerous disease, such events add to the infinite pile of evidence against the validity of miracles. Because they reinforce the laws of nature. And the only things all of us have ever experienced since the day we were born are the laws of nature. You've never seen them broken, and neither have I. They are well established, as they have been through time. And one day this man *this Moses* may come to you and, and say that the laws of nature can be broken, that he, that he…split the sea in half. Or even worse, you may only get to…read about it in a reproduced script that others claim to be divinely inspired. Now I ask you, my brother, which of these bodies of evidence should you believe? The one you experience directly at every waking moment of every day since the moment you were born, or one you hear about from mere hearsay written by others years before your time?"

"Well—"

"Think brother," Dewey interrupts, "which side is supported by the greater number of experiments? I mean to *you,* what should hold more weight? Everything you have ever seen, heard, or felt directly since the day you were born which correlates with everyone's experience through the history of the world, or one small man's in one small moment many years ago?"

"Well—"

"Are you going to just throw out everything you have directly experienced, just to take this guy's *word for it?!*"

"Now. Let us be reasonable. One does not need experience to know God exists. It only makes sense if you just think for one second—"

"Why? Why do you keep relying on reason? How can you believe in a God or a prophet that you never even experienced? People pray so…hard every single day for something they only *hear about* from their parents! Something they never even see themselves, and neither have their parents! Yet they change their entire lives trying to find something else when they already have so much of nature to just enjoy!" Dewey begins to raise his voice in frustration. "*How can they do so much for so little?!* How can they give up so much of their lives for a mere rumor? For a hidden mystery they can never really *know* to be true?

"And you may ask, how can you never know it to be true? Because bad things happen to good people and good things happen to bad people. Because at first glance the world seems random, and at a second glance, and a third. Yet people cry out for an answer, for a meaning to it all. They ask 'Why? Why me?' yet they refuse to see the most obvious answer before them: that perhaps there is none.

"So they pray. But they never see direct results. There is no way to know if it works. There is no way to know if prayers are heard by any God, or if he even exists. All there is, dear brother, is a feeling. After time, people have given this 'feeling' a name. Yes, they have called it faith. Faith not only asserts that there is more than what man is able to see, *to experience,* which is ridiculous enough, but faith actually drives man to abandon experience and *chase* after that which he cannot see, that which he has no reason, no *right,* to assume is true."

"You refer to it as a right," Renee says. His face shows no emotion.

"That is because, I surely confess, it would be a privilege to have a relationship with God. Who wouldn't want a relationship with an Almighty being? Who wouldn't want more meaning in their life? If it were true, if God had existed all this time, and you would have had a relationship with him, that would be a great thing, for without God, the reason, the meaning of life becomes much harder for many to grasp. To have a God would be a gift to many. Sometimes, I'd even like one myself.

"But I have no right to create one. I have a responsibility to be human, to act in the way I was created, to learn from experience only. I cannot create this…shortcut to knowledge without earning it myself. Neither may any other human. No one has that right. So how dare one claim a relationship with a God without any reason to do so? By what right? How *dare* one speak of meaning in life to come from some creator he has never seen before? How dare anyone run away from the sometimes discouraging truth that we can never know what is beyond the senses? How dare anyone try to give his life meaning by way of lies, by deceiving himself through distortions and fascinations based on…on…"

"No more than a feeling?" Renee says.

"No more than a feeling," Dewey says, "And I'm sorry, but it is only a fool who alters his entire being for an idea, based on no evidence at all, absolutely no more than a mere feeling. It makes so much more sense to stick to what we know, from which efforts we have seen to reap such results. It makes so much more sense to take what we have been given, to live in the present tense. We have so many better things to do! But no, we leave that in search for some idea, some dream, some God that we can never ever know."

"And what have we been given?"

"That which we experience. Oh, the wealth of nature! It is a feast, I tell you. There is no need to chase anything more. A man knows that after a night of sleep, the sun will rise. If he goes near a fire, he will get burned. After a seed is nurtured, a plant will grow. After food is eaten, a hunger is filled. After a week of work, a payment will come. Factories are built, crops are reaped, and buildings created. We create industry, family, sport, and law. We eat, we sleep, we drink, we sing, we share, we laugh, we cry, we work, we earn, we love, and we live. This is being human. This is all we know. And it is good enough. It is great, and it is all we have. We ought to be happy with our lot. I certainly am.

"Yet some humans...many of us are born with this...disease. A childish selfishness for always something more. As we are given this beautiful life, some of us throw it down on the ground, for it is not good enough for them. And they cry 'more, more, more' and go around looking for...something else. And when they cannot find it, they invent it, drowning in the fables of their parents. Oh, if only we can appreciate and enjoy what we are given. What we know.

"And what do we know?" Dewey's head nods to the side, his eyes filling with vibrant color as his mind wanders in his dreamy Posteriorian world, "This is the world of the E. All we can really know, all we can follow, is the world of the E, the world of experience, of examples, of ecstasy and excitement, the empirical, experiments, explanations, *evidence.* These are essential. We can only act on what we see on the surface: empirical evidence of the exterior world through our experience of experiments. Why do you think saying the letter 'e' opens our mouth wider than saying any other letter? Did you not think that the world of 'e' consists of what we see, feel, and taste as symbolized by our oral fixation? Why do you think that the word 'eye' actually looks like a person's face, with the letter 'e' chosen to represent our eyes, surrounding a long nose in the middle? Did you not think that your eyes are 'e's because they represent the *world* of the 'e,' the world of what you see? Hell, is it no wonder that while the word experience is made up of ten letters, nearly half of them are E's? Why do you think the word 'peel' is filled with E's on the inside? Because the world of the E is in the peels themselves—there is no need to break past the 'peel' to find fruit inside—for there is none of which we can—or have any right to—know. This is what an empire begins and ends with. From the very beginning, the middle, and until death—it is with us all through existence. The E. It is in every color we experience: yellow, red, orange, purple, green, blue...but not in the dull shades of brown, gray, and black that *you* feel the need to wear. This is the world of the E. This is what we know, and it is this to which all our efforts must go, after all, it is only in this that they *can* go with any reasonable expectation of results.

"The only reason that anyone can now know of what is beyond the peel is because they have peeled an orange before, and they have found fruit inside. But this has never happened before. The only reason to think that something will yield results is the fact that it has in the past. I mean, can there be any other reason? Even those with faith will admit it. They have never seen God. God has no E. All they have seen is the natural course of things, which may or may not have been driven by a God, though there is no reason to chase after one. No experience. No evidence. 'But I don't need a reason,' they will say with their chins held high and sparks in their eyes, 'for I just believe.' They don't need a *reason?!* A reason to invest their life to a cause? A reason to leave their own ambitions, to abstain from food, to disfigure their body, to sacrifice their youth?! They don't need a reason to abandon the life they owe to themselves, their family, society at large? They just have…a *feeling!?*

"Surely they enjoy it, wearing this warm blanket of meaning they claim to have 'found.' They look down in sympathy on those who were unable to create and wear the blanket in their stubborn refusal to abandon reason, to abandon their human-ness and freely let go to jump off the abyss of the knowable. And many of them will say 'Isn't this great? Religion can never be proven wrong because, it transcends logic! It is above logic altogether! Thus, it can never be knocked down!' But, oh, how foolish this is, for if they only reflected for a minute, they would realize: sure, it cannot be knocked down, but that is only because it has never stood up! Something can never fall if it never stood up in the first place. It was a fallen mess to begin with, so of course it cannot fall. One cannot disprove God's existence any more than one can disprove the existence of pink unicorns. This belief does not 'transcend' logic. It contradicts it.

"And what makes me most sick is that these people may stick to it their whole lives, imbuing their children with this…fable, this feeling, until their children themselves are unsatisfied and eventually sickened with the physical, scientific world they have been given, and thus driven to go off themselves, leaving their progressive society, their self-fulfillment behind, and on and on and on from generation to generation—though the whole while, not one string of evidence arises, the entire time, generation to generation of people surrendering themselves, and the entire time, no explanation exists! If only they were able to point to something, anything, a miracle they themselves experienced, a direct word of God, but…but no…all they can point to as they walk out on those that need them most is…is the word of their parents and the feelings of their dreams. And this is what makes me most sick. Religion, *God,* has never been proven to exist—or at least proven to be reasonable to exist—yet people still feel the need to leave their families, their lives, their own person, things which have been proven time and time again to yield results, such as family, money, social advancement, art, industrial productivity, and self fulfillment, all abandoned to…to invest their efforts into this…idea. This...mood. Religion is nothing more than unfounded atmospherics. And the worst part is, there is so much experience we *have* been given...so much that *is* founded, yet people leave it to chase this…vibe.

"Say there is a community in which each man lives his life as such. Each man goes to sleep and feels rested the next day. They work hard for their money, plant crops for their food, spend time with their children, and make love to their lovers. They produce coal, energy, factories, clothes, families, an entire economy. But one day, say someone in the community falls ill. Say a famine dries up the land.

Many of the men will change their course of action. They will drop what has been proven to work for generations—their tools of metal and stone, medicine, science, and they'll leave their jobs, their governments, their society, and they will go swing chickens over their heads. To 'pray' for his recovery. To 'pray' for rain. Yes, they will rouse themselves from their lives, quickly withdrawing from the beds of their loved ones, ignoring the hunger of their offspring, the fulfillment of their hobbies, the achievements of their labor. They will take the hard-earned income they raised for their family, and go throw it away it on ceremonial branches, breads, candlesticks, goblets, whoknowswhat. And as the world sits by hungering for their hard-working hands, their love, their productivity that they owe it, these capable men will sit for days in the dark to feast on words, on prayer, on symbolic acts they know nothing of, they know not to whom, slowly drugging themselves with the lie of religion, blindly satisfying their…feelings they cannot even explain, because the society that needs them outside has somehow failed to be good enough for their efforts.

"Sometimes the man is healed, the famine washed away, and the people exclaim 'Look! Our prayers have been answered!' as the poisonous…*feeling* is imbedded more deeply into their hearts. But indeed, just as often, the man's life will pass away suddenly and the famine will wipe out the land. When this happens, the people walk away shaking their heads. 'Everything is for the best,' they will shrug as if blind to the complete lack of correlation between their prayers and any results, 'Well,' they will continue to say 'There must be a great plan that we are not worthy of knowing. Why do I know this? Because it must be. It just must!' Ha! Quite a reason to neglect your real lives, I say. But the real reason why they know this is because they convinced themselves of it so as not to face the alternative: that we can never know beyond our experience. As such, they are traitors to the rest of us, humbly doing *living* the jobs we were given as men. They are traitors to the human race.

But look! The man has passed away. The famine has dried out the land. Sometimes it 'works' and sometimes it does not. Just as if nobody had ever prayed at all. Just... as...if...nobody...had...ever...prayed...at...all! Do they not see?!

"They choose not to look. And when they see nothing, they proceed to invent their own visions that everything is for the best. This is faith, and it cannot be disproved. It sure sounds nice, don't it? I wish I could say it too, but man cannot assume such things. We can never know it to be true or false. No will argue. We can never know. So, I say, why invest in something you can never know? Especially when there is so much we *do* know! But even still, man continues to leave that which he *does* know, to chase a feeling he can never explain—" Dewey pauses at Renee's blank stare, "have...have you nothing to say at all?"

"No."

"But I—have you heard *anything* I have said? You always have something to say, some clever comment. Well, do you? Do you have something to say?"

"No."

"What?"

"No. I do not think so."

"No, you *do* think. Too much. And that is the problem." Dewey forces a laugh, "Well, you've always been a boy of little words. It's all up in here for you," Dewey points to Renee's head, "Isn't it?"

"What can you see?" Renee asks, evading Dewey's question.

"What?"

"You say that man chases after what he cannot see. I want to know what you *can* see. What can you know to be true?"

"Have...have you been listening at all? You wanna know what *I* see?" Dewey walks across to room to his father's desk, opens up a drawer, and takes out a small piece of gold. "This is what I see," he says, holding up the piece of gold. "This is what I see, food is what I taste, and women are what I feel."

"Is that all? You would live like an animal—"

"No, my brother," Dewey slams the gold down on his father's desk, "Much more than an animal, but rather a rational animal, as El Totsira had called it, an animal that is able to sacrifice short-term pleasure for the long term, an animal who is able to see the benefits of kindness. This is a human! An animal rational enough to know not to sacrifice too much of his precious time and energy for an alleged Being that he has never even seen! Especially based on just a ...feeling!"

"Just a feeling," Renee says.

"Just a feeling," Dewey says.

"A feeling that everyone seems to have."

"What? What do you mean?"

"Oh, I don't know," Renee cocks his head to the side and waits silently, letting Dewey's tension build, "Don't you think that it is just a bit odd that everyone has this feeling individually inside them? That every single human is born with this...inhuman...as you call it...presence of God in their minds? I mean, from citizens of big cities to the aborigine tribes in the most isolated deserts, everyone has always had their Gods. Don't you think it a bit curious that if God did not exist, everyone would invent him anyway?"

"Well...the human mind is...capable of many unusual things," Dewey says. "And as I explained before, man has always been born with this, disease. This childish demand for something more. It is part of the human condition. We are...thrust into a world where, where the experiences that our sensations feed upon often do not meet the longings of the heart. Where our feasts, our sex, our pride of self-fulfillment can never satisfy this feeling, this...*need* everyone seems to have for, well, for more."

"But I am asking you where this feeling comes from."

"Oh, it comes from desperation. From a lacking. You will never see a true Posteriorian with this...condition. Man's idea of God comes from the same place where one that is lost in the desert gets the imaginary vision of a waterhole. When man is thrust into this world of earthquakes and death and cancer and greed and unearned fortune he is unable to accept the chaotic beauty of it all. So he seeks an answer to his lover's death or his gangrenous leg. In order to feed this hunger, he creates this idea of meaning, of purpose in his life, of God. Then he gorges on his new invention, leaving his true life behind. Religion is man's drug. It is a crutch made to make man feel better about his life. It is not God who created man, dear Renee, but it is man who has created God."

"Perhaps. But you have yet to answer how that hunger, that desperation, as you call it, even got there before it was satiated. If experience is so great, why is it not enough? Why does each and every man innately thirst for something...more?"

"Hm."

"And why," Renee continues, "does this thirst, this *desperation*, most always result in the same infinite being that we call God? Through all the generations. Can this be a mere coincidence? Perhaps this thirst, this...feeling imbued in each and every one of us is evidence itself that God must exist. Why else could we have this feeling? All of us? Perhaps this feeling is God's fingerprint in his creations, his—"

"Well, again, it could have. But it could have come from anywhere. The human mind is capable of many unusual things."

"Yes, but, you do believe that man only learns from that which he actually experiences, yes?"

"You know that I do."

"Then really, where did he get this clear idea of God? I mean, here you have millions, no, billions of people in the world. Swarms of people in large cities to small clans of Bushmen completely isolated in the desert, yet they all come to the same conclusions. They all have born within them this same feeling, this closeness, this conception of God."

"So? What are you saying?"

"Well let us try this, Dewey. Do you believe my mind and my intellect are useless all by themselves?"

"You know I do. They need experience to learn from."

"And do you believe that every idea in my mind could have gotten there only by way of experience?"

"Sure. You were born without any ideas. A blank slate, if you will. All ideas that are in you are similar to or in conformity with certain things you have encountered outside of you throughout your life. Your mind builds up a library of sensations as you interact with the world around you. The only reason your mind has an idea of fire is because fire is in the outside world, and you have experienced it."

"Good. And how do you know this? How do you know that ideas in my mind can only come from the outside world?"

"Well, for starters, this is proven by the fact that these ideas have come into your mind without your consent, without your control. If they were truly from you, the process would have been more voluntary, or you would have at least been aware of it. Since these ideas do not depend upon your will and you notice them whether you'd like to or not, this shows they do not come from you."

"So again, every idea I have in my head has originally come from the world outside?"

"Precisely."

"Well, you just admitted that God does exist in the world."

"What? Explain yourself."

"Well, don't I have an idea of God in my head?"

"I, uh, maybe—"

"Don't we all have an idea of a supremely perfect being, an idea that enables us to understand a supreme deity, eternal, infinite, omniscient, omnipotent, and creator of all?"

"Yes, we… suppose we do."

"Well then, that idea could only have come from our direct experience of such a being," Renee smiles. "As you just admitted, it could not have just sprung from within our heads. Just like the idea of a dog could only have come from experiencing one. As you just said, each idea in our heads is in conformity to things outside us. Just as our idea of fire, with all its qualities, only could have come from fire itself, so too, our idea of God must have come from him himself."

"But maybe, maybe I could think of a God that does *not* exist."

"You can try, but you will learn that existence can be no more separated from God's essence than the idea of three angles connected to each other can be separated from the essence of a triangle, or than the idea of a valley can be separated from the idea of a mountain. You cannot think of one without the other."

Dewey remains silent.

"See Dewey, from the fact that I cannot think of God except as existing, it follows that existence is inseparable from God in my mind. And you have admitted that whatever is in my mind must have come from the outside world—"

"Enough," Dewey says, his yellow roll cheeks turning a pale shade of red, "no, maybe, maybe it…came from a mixture of things we actually experienced, an exaggeration—"

"We have never experienced something infinite, something eternal and perfect. There is nothing from which we could have based such an idea upon in our minds. Since we have the idea of such a being in our minds, only He could have put it there. Thus, a God really exists!"

Dewey decides to try one more time, "But, but we have thought of unicorns by combining a horse and a horn. But we have never experienced a unicorn itself. We can think of magic, of wizards, of men that live a thousand lives. Perhaps we broadened that to conceive of infiniteness. Perhaps—"

"That is completely impossible. Our idea of God cannot have come from such a combination of lesser things, as unicorns have. This is because there must be at least as much reality in the efficient and total cause as there is in the effect of that same cause. If we have such an idea of God, the cause of that idea must match its effect, or else it would not have been able to cause such an idea in our minds."

"I—I don't understand," Dewey repeats himself, "if we could conceive of a unicorn, or a sea monster that does not exist, then why not—"

"The difference, my brother, between the thought of a unicorn and the thought of God is that only the latter entails existence in our mind. See, all thoughts entail certain things. The thought of a unicorn entails the form of a horse, combined with a horn protruding from between its eyes. The thought of a sea monster entails some sort of large and dangerous creature in the sea. But these thoughts do not entail their existence."

"Hm."

"But when one thinks of God, one cannot help but imagine a Supremely Perfect Being with every perfection, including existence. See, a unicorn, whether it exists or not, must have a horn. But a God, whether it has a horn or not, must exist. Just as having a horn is a necessary part of being a unicorn, having existence is simply a necessary part of being an Almighty God. And we imagine him as such. And since, as you mentioned, anything we can imagine must have come from experiencing it in the outside world, this thought could not have been imagined, without it coming from Him alone."

"But—"

"We have directly experienced a horn, which we may combine with a horse to conceive of a unicorn. But we have never, so you say, directly experienced infiniteness which we may combine with a God to conceive of an Almighty, infinite God as doubtless all men have."

"Right, but—"

"There is no other way, Dewey, to explain having this idea of an infinite substance in our minds, than to say that this idea proceeded from some substance which was truly infinite."

"Are you saying, brother, that you received your idea of God from…"

"Yes. From God Himself," Renee smiles.

Dewey remains silent, so Renee continues. "Well, it certainly wasn't through the senses, for I've never actually seen God in real life. I think this idea is just innate in me, just as the idea of my own existence is innate in me."

Dewey smiles mockingly, shaking his head with his disbelief. His face seems to say *I don't know how, but I know you are wrong, you must be.*

ΩΨΩ

"I am certain there is such a God," Renee interrupts Dewey's thoughts.

"Oh, really now? You just finished telling me so."

"You did not seem so convinced."

"I still can't see how can you be so certain."

"Good. Because I am not finished."

Before Dewey can object, Renee clears his throat and rises from his father's chair as if he has been waiting for this moment all along, waiting for his rotund brother to empty out all his words, so Renee can finally say something meaningful.

"I am certain there is a God, my brother, because a God must exist."

"Huh?" Dewey is not surprised by his own confusion. Quick to dismiss his brother *I don't have time for this* he turns to leave the room but is interrupted by Renee's words.

"It only makes sense that God exists. How is that, you ask? I will tell you. Yes, I will say how it is something that must be." Dewey turns to face his brother. Renee begins.

"Everyone knows that a Supremely Perfect Being has every perfection. Even you, Dewey, must agree that whether or not God actually exists, as a God, he must have every perfection."

"I, I guess so. Well, what do you mean by perfection?"

"We can define a perfection as a great-making property, namely, any property that makes its subject greater than it would be without it. God has all of these."

"I...I would agree with that," Dewey assents.

"Now, existence is a perfection, since it certainly makes its subject greater than it would be without it."

"Sure, I mean, something is surely not as great if it doesn't even exist."

"So you agree that a God must have every perfection?"

"Sure."

"And you agree that existence is a perfection?"

"Yes, I just did."

"Then a God must have existence."

"I—" Dewey begins.

"It is very simple. If a God has every perfection, and existence is perfection, then God has existence, so God exists, so there is a G—"

"I get it, I get it," Dewey interrupts, holding up his hands. "But you, you still have no actual evidence for your claim. You have never exp—"

"Oh, Dewey. I never needed to. Its existence does not require me to. And I do not need experience of something as evidence of its existence. My evidence is based upon reason, Dewey, when will you understand?"

"Yes, you have lived in your world of reason, of logic, of *what must make sense* from the day you were born, since the days of O'Talp, the man of reason. But since then, Renee, we have graduated from that. Yes, we have learned to appreciate that which is given, the comfort of sleep, the taste of an orange. We take pride in our sensors," Dewey points to his sensors standing nearby, "our libraries of experience, the results of our experiments, our sciences, our crops, our feasts, our arts. We have opened our eyes to what we have, and through time our...feeling for this...God that we do not have has lessened, our thirst has disappeared, our conscience has dimmed.

"But you," Dewey continues, "you have not moved on. You remain in desperation, chasing some dream stemming out of your feelings. You have failed to see your surroundings. You have been blind since the day you were born. So I say move on, brother. You have already lost your sight, and now you abandon all else? Come and join the party of experience. Join it because I tell you, it is all you have. It is all anyone has. Abandon your dark world of reason and denial, the cold inner contours of the mind. Abandon your idea of reason because the days of O'Talp have died long ago. Come, abandon your idea of God because, my brother, God is dead."

"God is alive, Dewey, so long as he lives in my mind. He lives there in the form of an idea, and his life in me is sustained by the solid structure of reason. This is not faith. This is more than a feeling. This is reason. You must understand, *the whole idea* of God necessarily entails His existence. When we think of God, as we all do, we necessarily think of Him as one with every perfection, including existence. See, we think of Him as existing. A God must exist. If He did not exist, then we would not have such an idea of Him in our heads."

Dewey feels his head begin to weigh; such a Posteriorian has never heard so much logical nonsense for this long. Since part of him loves his brother, Dewey has wanted, *tried so hard* to at least understand his younger twin, but his patience is reaching its end. As Dewey looks down and struggles to keep an open heart, Renee's blindness hides his brother from him, and he is still in his own world. Pondering casually, Renee brings his hand to his chin, looks up, and begins to speak again.

"You know, it is not surprising that in creating me, God should have endowed me with this idea, so that it would be like the mark of the craftsman impressed upon his work—"

"Bah!" Dewey shouts at his brother, *"Enough!"*

"Brother—"

"Enough! I've heard enough!" Dewey shouts as he storms into the room, grabbing the ink well off of his father's large desk.

"Why, why does it bother you so? Dewey, it is okay. Please."

"No. No. *No!*"

"What, what are you doing?" Renee actually sounds scared as Dewey rushes past him. He pours the ink over his hands in a disorderly way, awkwardly stumbling over to the fireplace.

"It cannot be true," he mutters, "for what someone said long ago."

"Please," Renee pleads, "I don't know what you are saying. Just come home—"

"The days of God are over!"

His body shaking, Dewey lifts his inky finger, and writes with it upon the wall across the top of the fireplace. He writes the words of an old Posteriorian, from his grandfather's reign, the first one to ever publicly denounce any belief in metaphysics. Dewey steps back to see what he has written, and the message is clear.

God is Dead.
-Nietchai

Yes, Nietchai was the first Posteriorian to turn against religion. It was not that the Posteriorians were religious people before him, but apathy towards religion was not celebrated in the same way. See, few would ever practice religion on their own, but they were allowed to, and some did in the privacy of their homes. To protest, Nietchai stayed in his bed for two years, eating, drinking, and spilling his waste into buckets that were carried away by his followers Gustav Krug and Wilhelm Pinder.

Since his childhood, Nietchai had suffered from partial blindness, migraine headaches, and violent stomach attacks. His sister Elizabeth would care for him while his brother Joseph played outside. It took years for his word to spread across Lyceum, but finally, the Grandee, Dewey's grandfather, publicly praised Nietchai for his nihilism. He urged all Posteriorians to take experience for what it is and nothing more, to enjoy the scientific world of sex, food, and pleasure, *for that is all we have been given, and the sooner we can accept it for what it is, the better.*

Dewey stands back and reads his own writing again *God is dead.* Satisfied, Dewey begins to walk out of the room, but stops to look at his brother. Renee sits still, cool, and composed. He seems to be thinking, still pondering where his idea of God could have come from. Finally, Renee bends over to pick up the wax and holds it once again in his hands. He remembers what the wax had taught him *never again* to not trust his senses but *only my mind*. His thoughts are interrupted by Dewey's scolding words.

"You, Benedictus…you are all mad!"

Then Renee hears his brother move towards the door of the room in a haste, and he sympathizes with his brother. Renee wishes Dewey could just understand. He realizes it just may not be his fault. Dewey cannot see. As Dewey attempts to walk through the door, he could here the soft words come from Renee's lips.

"Those who don't hear the music, think the dancers mad."

Dewey stops in his tracks. He never expected his brother to carry on this argument into the late morning; Renee has always allowed Dewey the last word. Dewey is surprised at his brother's persistence and frightened at his sturdy reasoning.

"The music?" Dewey's voice is shaky as he turns back into the room to hear Renee's reply.

"The music of the calling whistle. The music of reason. You just don't have the ears, the mind, to understand—"

"I hear just fine. The calling whistle never made a sound."

"Right. Then why did the cat come running every time?"

"The animal that I killed, you mean? That animal only came running because it saw you looking for it after you put the whistle to your lips, and you gave her a nice treat each time she came. That is why she came—from her experiences of you and nothing else. There was no sound at all. I never heard one."

"Are you sure? Though you never heard one, wouldn't it make sense—"

"I am never sure, my brother, and you know that. No one really can be. But I do know that it is custom alone which engages animals, from every object that strikes their senses to infer its usual attendant. The cat experienced you putting the whistle to your mouth. I cannot believe it made a sound, since I never heard one. But the cat came as you put it to your lips as she often does in a usual day, but this time she found that you had given her a treat. It is in this way she associated the whistle with her approaching her owner. Animals may be taught any course of action by the proper application of rewards and punishments. Is it not experience, which renders a dog apprehensive of pain when you menace him or lift up the whip to beat him?"

"Perhaps."

"Is it not even experience which makes him answer to his name and infer from such an arbitrary sound that you mean him? Renee, any creature expects from the present object the same consequences which it has always found in its observation to result from similar objects. Your cat was no exception to this rule. And neither are men."

"Then how would you explain an animal's instinctive fear of fire?"

"They only know it is dangerous because they experience heat when they get close, even on their first time."

"Okay, but how would you explain a cat's innate ability to always land on their feet? How would you explain how birds always know their way south?"

Dewey remains silent. He had not thought of that.

"You walk around," Renee accuses, "in your rainbow robes, confident that the only way to gain knowledge is through experience, but your beloved El Totsira often drifted into abstract reasoning himself!"

"What? Oh, he did not!"

"He did. How do you think he came up with his idea that objects of different mass fall at different speeds under gravity? That premise was based on mathematical reasoning, having nothing to do with experiencing the outer world."

"Okay, well that was one mistake, and it was refuted anyway by Sunopolihp and Oelilag."

"Okay, but how do you think he came up with his mathematical logic?"

Dewey is silent; he had not thought of that either.

"Not by an experience. You know," Renee continues, "El Totsira was the first one to ever conceive of such logic. You say you learn to only use experience from him, but he was the one who—"

"Stop it."

"Used mathematical formulas to attain truths through logic—"

"I know! I know! I, I've heard enough of this."

"Oh, but have you?" Renee says, his brother now shaking with anger, "Have you heard enough? You have still not considered how the cat came to me the very first time I blew the whistle; she had not experienced it before!"

"Well, no. But—"

"And you realize that the cat came to me every single time after that."

"Yes, but," Dewey tries for words, but none come out. He has grown extremely frustrated with his brother's abstract reasonings, his accusations and false Gods. Dewey leaves the room slowly, but before the door closes behind him, Renee can hear the last words mutter from his mouth.

"Well, the cat didn't come to you the last time you blew that whistle..."

16

I have persuaded myself that there is absolutely nothing in the world: no sky, no earth, no minds, no bodies. Is it then the case that I too do not exist? But doubtless I exist, if I persuaded myself of something. But there is some deceiver...he will never bring it about that I am nothing so long as I shall think that I am something. 'I am, I exist' is necessarily true every time I utter it. But what then am I? I have already denied that I have any senses and any body. I am not that concatenation of members we call the human body...nor a wind, nor a fire, nor a vapor, nor a breath. Thought exists; it alone cannot be separated from me. What then am I? A thing that thinks.

Rene Descartes

In the months that follow, the boys continue to debate their thoughts, play their billiards, and laugh at their jokes. But since the debate about the existence of God, things are not the same. Their debates are not as strong, their billiard shots not as powerful, their laughs lacking a certain color; everything has softened, not containing as much effort, as much *feeling* as it had previously enjoyed. Helene even shortens her bedtime stories as the twins' disinterested eyes wander the room, darting her words, their ears shutting out her sentences until she leaves them to themselves. Then the boys lie awake alone at night until falling asleep in silence. They just feel unexcited. Numb.

In truth, the debate has scared both of them in their own way. Renee is surprised at the logic of his own words; he was not aware of the strength of his mind until that night. He has truly convinced himself that there is a God who can only be known through the mind, as must everything else. For him, the wax confirmed that nothing can be known through the senses, for they are deceiving. But if they can't be trusted, what can be? Such questions haunt Renee long after the joy of his new revelations have faded away.

Nothing seems real anymore. There is nowhere to turn and nothing to believe in anymore.

Still, Renee tries to compartmentalize his revelations. He attempts to regain his ignorance and enjoy the present just for a moment. He struggles to laugh and debate and shoot billiards, to go back to the way things were just for a day, an hour, just to enjoy a moment in time. But it is no use. It will never be the same again. Once ignorance is left behind, bliss leaves with it and it will never come back.

Dewey too, suspects deep down that Renee has hit something, that he is different than the rest. Renee has scared him almost as much as Renee has scared himself, and as much as Dewey tries to forget it, he cannot enjoy himself as before. Dewey is in awe of his brother, concerned about what will happen, what Renee will become and how it will affect him and his future throne. Upon playing billiards now, Dewey cannot play his turn as Renee stands directly behind him. He cannot laugh at any jokes until Renee lets go of himself, deciding to laugh too. He cannot take that chance without knowing what his brother will do. Dewey is scared of what Renee can do. He is scared of what Renee may become. But most of all, he is uncomfortable unconsciously knowing that his brother should not be here *doesn't belong here* at all.

However, the brothers' concerns fade with the snow into the ground. A new year is coming, and the leaves are beginning to sprout. It is spring in Lyceum, and it is in this moment that all of nature comes out to play. Flowers, vines, children, and wine, come out, come one, come all! This is one of the most celebrated times for the Posteriorians, as their nation shrugs off its old coat of white, stretches its botanical limbs for the first time in months and shines its rainbow light like it never has before.

The kingdom is a circus. Moving with such powerful commotion, it seems a wild fire reaching, dancing, screaming, grabbing all it can to join it in its erratic dance. A large creature, it *moves* as if making up for lost time. It stretches the sleep out of its long, multi-colored tentacles, its limbs releasing granite crumbs as they shake off the past winter, sprinkling their love and joy all through the land.

Lemonade is squeezed, jewelry is bartered, fish is negotiated, alcohol consumed. Dewey runs outside in glee with all the teenagers and children of the palace, playing ball, tree-climbing, and sword-fighting. But this time, as he looks over his shoulder, Renee is not there.

No, this time Renee remains in his winter, refusing to come outside to play. He stays bundled up in his cold underground cellar, a pale blind young man pondering his mind as the bare feet of golden children dance and play on the warm green grass above. He sits silently, his black hair grown long almost covering his ears entirely. As the spring days pass and the plants' youth shed their freshness, many of the royalty attempt to bring Renee out of his quarters, into the sunlight. Dewey, Helene, even Joachim himself all come to speak to the prince, but to no avail. He does not even honor them with his words. The blind prince just sits there in his black robes, his head unturning, his blank eyes fixed tightly to the wall.

ΩΨΩ

On one of the warmest mornings in the midst of spring, Dewey comes across a group of boys on the great lawn of the palace as he is walking to the fields to play.

"Hello."

One of the boys looks his way quickly, his eyes darting in Dewey's general direction. But, just as quickly, he looks back into the crowd of boys. The boys seem to huddle together and whisper quietly. They pay Dewey no mind.

"Hello," Dewey says louder, "I am Dewey."

Still, the lads ignore him. Dewey notices that half of them are dressed in their shaggy Posteriorian rainbow garb, but the other half of them are mostly naked, their shirts missing from their bodies, their feet and legs completely revealed. They all seem to circling around something and whispering rushed words into each other's ears.

"Hello? What are you guys—"

"Shh!" the youngest and smallest turns to hush Dewey's words.

"Excuse me? I just wanted—"

"Shh!"

"You can't shush me!" Dewey stands as tall as he can on his short thick stumps of legs, but that is not much. He gathers his courage, raising his chest into the air as much as his Posteriorian ego will let him. He says, "I am—"

"We all know who you are, lad," another one of the naked boys steps forward, "You are Dewey Hume, son of Joachim of the High Court." Dewey sees the boy is built well, standing at an average height under neatly combed brown hair. "We've seen you before, Dewey, sitting at the art contest next to your brother, and we have seen you around these parts before, though we haven't seen your brother since the snow last fell..." his voice seems to trail off as he looks down at his bare feet. Dewey looks past the brown haired boy to the center of the group. He notices a saucer, a flying discus in the middle of the boys. He figures they must have been playing a sport.

"We were just planning our next play," the boy explains, seeing Dewey's gaze. Feeling caught in the act, Dewey blinks abruptly, focusing his gaze back to the boy before him.

"I'm sorry, I, can I—"

"Would you like to play?"

"Uhm, no, I—"

"We've hardly started, and we could use another player on our team," the boy walks towards Dewey, extending his hand.

"My name is Yelekreb."

Dewey feels a drop of sweat fall from his shoulder blade, streaming down his back. He squints and fans himself uncomfortably, too hot from his heavy robes. He suddenly feels overdressed and awkward around these new friends. He thinks of Renee down in the cool cellar, away from all of this. He wonders what brew Renee's mind is cooking up just now. He takes a deep breath. Forcing his hand forward, Dewey feels himself smile as his hand is received Yelekreb, and he finally tries to speak.

"I am Dewey. Well, I guess—I guess you already knew—" Dewey looks to the ground embarrassed.

"No worries," Yelekreb smiles. "I like you already, prince," he says as he pulls Dewey into the crowd of boys waiting not a few feet behind him.

They explain the rules to him, *okay, so here's how it goes* that the saucer is thrown from player to player until it reaches the goal, and that *here's how it will be* no player is allowed to move from the spot where they catch the flying saucer until it leaves their hands and that *this is how we play* one team consists of the naked, and one of the clothed. Of course the youngest of the boys decide that Dewey is to play on Yelekreb's team. Since that is the naked team, Dewey is forced to disrobe in front of them all.

The game is an exciting one, and Dewey learns it well. He enjoys the outdoors, being outside with nature, interacting with the physical world. His bowlegged run is comical but he can move his legs fast and get where he wants to go. He feels good as he runs, his large belly flopping this way and that like a large hot cauldron, its sweaty brew steaming up drips of liquid, sprinkling a trail of river behind him as it tumbles down the field. He is not embarrassed, for such a belly is something to be proud of in this nation, a trophy to display that says *I know how to live* and show that *I am a true Posteriorian; I have been living life;* to the point where *it is attractive, for men and women alike* to be so robust, so *full* of food, of gold, of body, that no one can ever accuse you of taking a rest from enjoyment.

But as he is running out into the field for a play, Dewey sees that the saucer thrower is giving him a most curious look. Dewey sees his eyes staring right out into his. Their eyes lock together and Dewey cannot look away and suddenly everything slows and there is no field, no sun, no trees, it is just him and this boy and this saucer in the boy's hands. The boy's eyes seem to speak to him *run faster! run farther!* as Dewey runs as fast as his short stubby legs can carry him.

The discus is thrown.

"Dewey!" one of the naked boys shout, "Dewey, you have to catch this!" As Dewey's eyes are still locked on the thrower, everything seems to pick up speed again, and as the saucer is thrown *up, up and up* Dewey notices the sun, the trees, the sky, the field, *my God* he is almost in the end zone, the touch down, and he looks up to see where the saucer has gone. *I could score! I am ready, I am here, I am in the goal* Dewey's heart leaps excitedly *come here, saucer, come here, and let me score* as his eyes see the small dot in the sky, the flying saucer soaring higher and higher until his squinting eyes can hardly make out the maroon spot in the large white sky.

But the saucer does not come down. It only rises higher. But Dewey does not stop running. He runs and runs away from the field, chasing the saucer over the surrounding fields, the corn, the beets, the large orange groves, and finally over the large stone wall separating the palace from the fields. He has been running for some time now; the other boys must have gone home. He is no longer near the royal field but he does not care. He is not going to give up now. His eyes lock onto the flying disc and he chases it as it soars over the sculptures in the lawns, over the rooftops of the nearby quarters of the royal sensors, a small speck on the horizon that seems to grow further and further away.

After what seems like forever, the speck seems to grow larger, a growing red particle staining the pure white sky. It seems to be descending. As it heads towards the back of the royal palace, it disappears over a hill. Dewey heads toward the top of the hill, his lungs panting for air, his naked body enveloped in hot sweat. He is walking slowly now, his legs burning like a fire never felt before. When he gets to the top of the hill, he looks for the saucer, his eyes wandering for where it may be.

Finally he spots it, lodged in his father's rosebush.

Actually Joachim had ordered the rosebush for the boys' mother, Katherine. Katherine had always loved roses, praying her children to be like 'the flowers with protective thorns.' She hoped that her offspring would give kindness as the rose would give off its scarlet color, its beautiful strawberry rash. Of course, the Gods would try to give this gift to her grandchild, for in this world, miracles often take a generation or two.

But after Katherine died of tuberculosis, Joachim ordered the rosebush in her memory. Of course, the boys were only one year old at the time, but Dewey still remembered as the bush was planted just a year later. He remembers watering it with Renee at his side, his father smiling behind his two offspring with tears in his eyes. Helene was not there yet to take Katherine's place. But as soon as Helene arrived, the roses had begun to wilt. Water was fetched, food was given, and songs were sung, but no matter how much care was given, a blackness spread over the flowers that now nurse Dewey's flying saucer.

Dewey approaches the bush with caution; he has been pricked by the thorns before. He reaches his hand forward, and as his fingers touch the ceramic disc, he hears a familiar voice just behind him.

"Nice fetch."

Dewey stops, putting the disc back into its place. The roses accept it unwillingly, as if insulted by his sudden lack of interest in their gift. He turns around slowly to see his brother standing atop the steps of the rear palace, his chin high in the air, his blind eyes directed straight at him.

ΩΨΩ

Renee looks like a ghost.

He stands there confidently, a tall white young man on the top of the outdoor steps that lead to the rear entrance of the palace. This was the entrance Dewey used so many years ago when he came upon Renee and his cat for the very first time. Now, many years later, Renee stands just beside the place where Dewey stood that day causally enjoying an orange. Renee closes his eyes and breathes in the warm spring air for the first time that season. Dewey sees a small pack tied around Renee's shoulders, his walking stick in hand. Dewey can hear that his brother sounds different as soon as Renee speaks.

"Mmmm, aah, the smell of a spring garden. Makes one think about where he has been all this time, doesn't it, brother?"

"I, I didn't see you—"

"You *never* see, Dewey."

Dewey remains silent, regaining his confidence, recovering from his surprise.

"What are you doing here?" Dewey asks.

"You seem to be asking that a lot these days."

"Only to you," Dewey snaps back, "since you are never where you should be."

"Well, if you must know, I was just on my way out."

"Excuse me?"

"If I must."

"No, did you say that you were *on your way out?*"

"You have mighty bad hearing for someone who cannot see."

"Stop the crap, Renee," Dewey retorts in frustration, "You're the one that cannot see. And why don't you tell me just where you are going."

"Where am I going? Oh, the mountains sound nice, do they not? Or perhaps to the desert, to the woods, to distant cities...I do not know *where* I am going, Dewey. The point is that I *am* going. Far, far away."

"You're just...*leaving?*"

Renee faces his naked brother in silence. His eyes seem impatient and sad. *Oh, c'mon, don't pretend to be surprised. Didn't you know all along?* they seemed to ask in disappointment, *you could see that I don't belong here, right?* But deep, deep inside, Renee holds his pain in a place Dewey cannot see *Dear brother,* Renee furrows his brow in painful disappointment *Why didn't you stop me from getting to this point? Why didn't you realize that it was only a matter of time, before...before it became too late?* but Renee swallows his doubt, mustering hard confidence onto his face.

"You can't just...leave." Dewey feels the worthlessness of his words as soon as they leave his mouth. He knows he speaks in vain, but he feels he must discourage his brother for leaving; he feels that is what he is *supposed* to do.

"You can't just...walk away," Dewey continues.

"But I already have. My body stands here now, but my body is meaningless, ha, it probably doesn't even exist. My soul, Dewey, or whatever I am, it left this place a long time ago."

"What, what do you mean?"

"You know exactly what I mean, big brother." Dewey knows this is true, but he wants to hear it anyway. He wants to stall. But even more, he feels the need to hear it aloud to justify the serenity he knows he will enjoy after Renee leaves. "You know exactly why I must go," Renee continues, "I do not belong here. It is too distracting."

"Distracting?"

"Yes, distracting. All these colors, these dances, this...art. These crops that grow in luscious bounty, these gardens, those whores. I respect the royalty of Lyceum, Dewey, but only because it is my family. But lulling around with hazed eyes before me and drunken whores behind me, well, it is just not what I want for myself."

"But, but this is life! You must understand that those experiences are not in vain. They are not for our mere pleasure, but they are for us to learn. Do not run away from the world, Renee, but learn to embrace it as we all have. Learn to embrace the only world we have been given through Posteriorian experiences. Our experiences teach us about the world, Renee. They teach us how to plant, how to eat, how to sleep, and how to dream. They teach us how to make music, to make love, to make a life worth living. They teach us truths about the world."

"What did you have for breakfast this morning?"

"Excuse me?"

Renee is silent.

"Why?" Dewey says, "Okay. You want to what I had for breakfast. Well, lemme see...I had eight pancakes...no, that was yesterday...right...today I had three grapefruits, two eggs and one large turkey leg. But, but then the butler brought more eggs and fruit..."

"And what did you do?"

"What did I do—"

"—to accept even more food. Your plate was already full."

"Why, I stuffed the old food in my mouth quickly so I can eat the new food. Of course."

"Did you learn anything from this?"

"Well, yes, of course. I... learned the taste of an orange from the taste of an apple...or was it a grapefruit...I don't know...there were so many foods..."

"Did you learn anything real from this?"

"I…well, it's a working process, you see…"

"Well I cannot do this anymore. You see? I will not do this anymore. Nothing is real to me anymore. Nothing…of this physical world. My decision is too leave."

"But, there is nothing out there! You will only find less of what is here."

"And—I hope—more of something that is not here at all."

"What? Like what? There is nothing else under the sun…"

"I am leaving, Dewey. I already made that decision."

"But I don't understand."

"It does not require you to."

Dewey sighs.

"I want more," Renee says, "I want to lay strong foundations, on a new and clean slate. I want to see what we can *really* know. But to do this, I must forget everything I have learned thus far, and this is why I must go. I must cleanse myself of what my senses have caused me to take for granted. I must raze everything to the ground if I want to establish anything firm and lasting."

"Raze everything from the—!? Wha—" Dewey shakes his head in disbelief, "But, you can't just…erase everything you've ever seen! How are you going to do that?"

"I must withdraw into solitude, away from all distractions. I must close my eyes, my ears, my nose, and I must explore my inner intellect. Hopefully with enough time in thought, my mind will be cleansed of the stains that experience and custom have tarnished me with, and for the first time begin to conceive of clear, unadulterated, and objective truths. At last I will apply myself earnestly and unreservedly to this general demolition of my opinions."

"And this is all you're bringing?"

Renee turns his head and touches the meager pack tied to his back. He picks up his walking stick, spears it into the ground, and takes a deep breath.

"This is all I will need."

"You, you can't go like this. You at least need a pair of eyes. Here. Take my—"

"This is all I need. Please."

"Do, you really have to go? We could talk—"

"We have talked enough, brother, we have talked and laughed and debated for years, and all the while there have been truths out there, truths deep in the caverns of my mind that I have never been able to access since I have been so…stuck on the exterior of things."

"Now, wait a second. Experience may be shallow but there is no other way to learn."

"I repeat. Reason is what teaches us truths. A God exists because he *must.* One plus one equals two because it *must.* Absolutely no experience is needed to conceive of such truths. They come prior to, not post, experience."

"What truths? What else could you just 'know'?"

"This is what I am must learn," Renee says, looking away.

"I, uhm, no," Dewey's loss of words come as no surprise to either brother, "I, I think if you want to…leave, you could at least tell me right now one more thing that a man, well, can know for sure. Let's go. If you can tell me one more thing—"

"I am."

"Okay, I'm listening."

"I am."

"Renee—"

"I am, Dewey, I exist. This is what I am trying to tell you. I know that I am something real. I know that I exist."

"Oh." Dewey's mind had never considered such an idea before. He always assumed that he was real, that he always existed in this nation of me, myself, and I, but after giving it real thought for the first time, he realizes his experiences give him no real basis to think so. They couldn't, for they are all offshoots of him.

"How," Dewey asks, trying not to show too much interest in his voice, "How can I know I exist?"

Renee pauses. Then he says, "I guess I must leave you with something. I have decided to leave you with this. See here. If I can prove to you that you can do something, then would you oblige that you surely exist?"

Dewey has a confused look on his face. Renee sighs and rewords his thoughts.

"A person that does not exist can never do anything, correct? So if I can prove to you that you are doing something, then you must exist, in order to do it. Do you understand?"

"Yes, I get it. But what can you absolutely prove that I do?"

"Well," Renee says, turning to the rosebush, "look over there, at that rosebush. Do you see it?" he asks.

"Sure I do. I am looking at it right now."

"Well, if you see it, then you surely exist."

"Huh?"

"If you did not exist, dear Dewey, then you would not be able to see it. To see something, you must exist."

"Yes, but, maybe, I mean maybe, you would say," Dewey's voice turns to a whisper because he knows such words should never be heard from a Posteriorian mouth, "Maybe the rosebush is not really there. Perhaps it is all in my mind. Perhaps it is all a dream, and I am not really seeing it. Perhaps I am hallucinating. Perhaps neither I nor the bush really exists."

"A good question, indeed," Renee smiles, "You are on the right track. Now look at it again, Dewey, and think hard when I ask you, *whether it is there or not*, do you see the rosebush?"

"Well, sure, it is right there. I see it."

"Are you sure?"

"Well, like I told you before, I may not be actually seeing it. It may be an illusion. Just like I may not actually be smelling pollen right now, or even standing here talking to you. But I certainly think I do. But again, I could be wrong—"

"Ah! Precisely," Renee smiles approvingly, "say that again…"

"I could be wrong—"

"No. The other part."

"I certainly think I do."

"Precisely! You do not know if you see the rosebush, but you *think* you do. And to think, you must exist. It does not matter whether you are actually seeing an actual rosebush or not. As you said yourself, you may not see it; it may only be in your mind. But even if it is in your mind only, you are definitely *thinking* it, and if you think, you are. You must exist in order to think. Yes, you could be dreaming, hallucinating, falling for a trick of the senses. Thus, you may not be seeing, but you are surely *thinking* you are. You may not be seeing the rosebush, but you are surely *thinking* the rosebush. This is certain. It is surely in your mind. There is no way to argue that you are not thinking. And since you think you see a rosebush, you must surely exist!"

"Oh. So you are saying that I may not actually be seeing it, but I know that I *think* I do. Whether by reality or by hallucination or hoax, I have the idea of a rosebush in my head, and for that reason, I must surely exist."

"Precisely."

"But, but what if I am not even *thinking*? Perhaps, perhaps I am wrong there too!"

"That is impossible."

"Why?" Dewey asks, "Just as I may not really see the rosebush, perhaps I may not really *think* I do."

"That is impossible," Renee repeats.

"Why?"

"If you do not see the rosebush, you think you do. If you do not think you do, then you *think* that you think you do. See? This can go on ad infinitum, but eventually you must come to terms with the fact that in the end, you are surely thinking something."

Dewey remains silent, so Renee continues to explain.

"You see, Dewey, thinking cannot be refuted since one need not be correct in order to think. Only sensing requires the existence of a world outside ourselves. In order to see, one's eyes must accept the light rays emanating from an actual external object. In order to hear, one's ears must process sound waves from an actual source. But there may be no object outside of ourselves.

"Thinking, however, requires no such outside world. One may be mistaken but they still think, for all thinking requires is conception. When you look to the rosebush and you think that you see it, you know you are thinking because thinking requires no validity, no external world, no reality, as does seeing. Thinking does not require an outside world, which may or may not exist. Thinking only requires a world inside of ourselves, and that must exist. I know this because I know that I am thinking. When I look at an apple, I know that I am thinking that I see an apple. Thinking is the most basic act. It takes place inside of me, so I know it is there. I did not learn to think through experience, but began to think before I left Katherine's womb. I can know I am thinking. Thus, I can know that I exist."

"But, but still, what if you are wrong? What if you are mistaken for some reason beyond you?"

"So too, to be mistaken is to exist," Renee smiles.

"Hmm."

"I exist either way. It cannot be refuted."

Dewey is impressed for the first time. He is not sure whether he truly grasps the argument, but his interest is captured, and that says a lot for a Posteriorian with a rich history of past experiences. For the first time, Dewey feels a cold, odd comfort in the clear precision of his brother's reasoning, as if this is a last gift, a last souvenir of Renee's presence given to Dewey before Renee leaves. However, Dewey's favor is not fully won.

"Okay, well if you are so sure you exist," Dewey asks, "then, what exactly are you?"

"What do you mean?"

"You say you exist, but as what? What *are* you exactly? Here you must use experience like a Posteriorian, because only through experience can I see my own body, my hands, my legs, my tongue…"

Renee had only thought of this briefly before. He closes his eyes to Dewey's smile and he begins to think.

"Well, over the past time in my life, I had thought I was a man. I had a face, hands, arms, and this entire mechanism of bodily members. It next occurred to me that I took in food, I walked about, and that I sensed certain things. But I have learned that my senses are deceiving, that I cannot assume anything to exist from the mere fact of their experiences and sense data. The exterior is meaningless. I must push it away and disregard it completely. I must not let it cloud my reason as I had before. Since I only know my body through the senses, I cannot know my body actually exists. But my soul—"

"Wait a second," Dewey interrupts, "how can you assume your body and your mind are separate things? Maybe they are one and the same, intertwined—"

"I will tell you how. I know they are separate because to be the same thing, two things must have all and only the same properties. And here, my body has a property that my mind does not."

"And what is that?" Dewey asks.

"It is only my body that can conceivably be something that I mistakenly suppose to exist. Therefore, the two are different."

"Well, I mean, is that really a *property?*"

"Would you like another one? Okay. It is only the body that does not function as properly after a loud sensation. After strong stimulation of a sense, we are less able to exercise it than before. Immediately after a loud noise we have trouble hearing, after a bright color we have trouble seeing, after a powerful scent we have trouble smelling, but this is not so with the mind. The thought of an object that is highly intelligible renders the mind even *more* able to think afterwards. It is in this way that the mind and body do not share all and the same qualities, but rather are different and separable from each other."

"Interesting. But you still have not told me what you are," Dewey says, his patience waning.

"Okay," Renee closes his eyes again, "Well, the only way I know I exist is because I think. I cannot assume my body is real; the only thing I know that is real is my thoughts. Thought exists; it alone cannot be separated from me. So what am I?" Renee opens his eyes, "I am obviously a thing that thinks."

"What? What are you?"

"I have said it already. I am a thinking thing."

"Ha, ha! After all this time, that is all you can say," Dewey laughs. He is not used to such little results after so much time.

"That is all I know now," Renee retorts, "But what I know, I know for sure. The knowledge *you* gain, Dewey, is plenty, but it always falls to the ground as quickly as it was built."

Dewey stops laughing.

"So," he says, trying to regain a serious face, "My brother is a thing that thinks."

"Indeed."

Dewey stifles a laugh, but it is not easy. "And what is that?"

"It is a thing that doubts, understands, affirms, denies, wills, refuses, and that also imagines and senses, whether or not those senses are accurate."

"So, so if you do all those things, what do you look like? Do you have, I mean, a smell? Do you have a *touch*? What...are you exactly?"

"I do not know for sure. I know I am thinking thing, of this I am certain. But it may take time for me to learn more about myself, more about the world, if there is one at all. You see, my brother, this is why I must go."

"Go?" Standing mostly naked in the warm sunlit garden, Dewey finds he forgot what is happening. In this midst of *yet another* philosophical debate with his brother, his emotional heart was quick to get caught up in his brother's newfound presence and his slow mind was quick to forget that his brother is leaving, that serious things were actually going to happen. Remembering his brother's decision, Dewey desperately tries to discourage his brother's departure.

"But you can't, well, you can't even see—"

"All the better, my brother," Renee answers, "It is in this way I will be able to concentrate on my mission."

"But," Dewey can feel his large lips flapping *oh why* but not settling on any words *why does this always happen.* He is desperate to stop his brother but he does not know why. His desperation surprises him, but he still searches for what to say, picking at straws, "But, you are blind. You need to travel—"

"You blinded me, Dewey."

Dewey is silent. He assures himself that it is not guilt that he feels in his stomach.

Renee says, "But I suspect it was supposed to happen. I suspect O'Talp has a plan"

"Right, right, whatever. We both know that you can't travel like this. It's dangerous out there."

"You have never been out there, Dewey. So you cannot know," Renee scratches his head, "And my mind will carry me forward on that, as it has until now. I can sense well enough to avoid imminent physical dangers; my ears are sharp and my smell is keener than ever."

"I, I can't believe—Did you tell anybody you're leaving? Did you tell Joachim? Helene?"

"They will know it in time."

Dewey looks down at the ground before him. He feels his heart beating faster and is surprised at the tears stinging his eyes. Renee walks down the stone palace steps and places a hand on his brother's bare chest.

"It's just something I have to do," he says softly in his brother's ear.

Dewey looks down at their feet and his large yellow head rests upon his double chin. He sees the calling whistle dangling from Renee's neck. His hands ball into fists as he remembers the touch of the cat's fur as he strangled her poor neck. He looks into Renee's dead eyes and remembers how the cat had died quietly, finally looking up at him with its dead eyes in a gaze of confused disappointment. He opens and closes his hands, recalling how rich the oranges were as he squeezed them, flooding Renee's eyes with rivers of acid, killing them like hot orange fire from the outside in. He remembers playing with Helene while Renee stood by and watched until finally retreating to his cellar. He closes his eyes and he sees Renee stumbling through the halls, learning how to use the walking stick for the first time, stumbling, falling to the floor, his robes scattered before him until he gets up, indifferently shaking off the dust, his expressionless face pointed forward as he takes his first step again.

"I, I'm—" Dewey begins.

"Don't."

As these thoughts race through his head, Dewey feels Renee's hand remain on his chest, his cool white fingers pressed lightly like piano keys against his skin. The contact reminds him of the time Renee fell in the hall and for the first time in months Dewey stopped while passing him, helping him off the floor. Dewey remembers how Renee grasped his hands *thank you* and he would not let go *that was nice.* As Dewey feels Renee's fingers begin to leave his chest on this spring day, he realizes that this may be the last contact he will ever have with his brother. This is it *I may never see him again.*

Dewey bows his head and begins to cry.

After a few minutes, he hears the sound of footsteps behind him. Turning around, he sees Yelekreb and the boys running towards him in concern, their legs kicking up clouds of dust behind them, their small lungs panting for breath as they try to speak.

"Wh—wh—where *were* you? We—we were looking all over for you..." Yelekreb begins, his hands resting on his knees, tired from the run. "We thought—"

"No, no, I'm fine," Dewey says. He picks his head up, wiping away his tears before the boys can see them. "I was just—"

At a loss of words, Dewey turns to point in Renee's direction, but Renee is not there. The boys stand looking at him confused. "I, I was just—" Dewey's eyes dart this way and that, looking for his brother, his small, thin brother with whom he had done so much.

Renee is gone.

Smiling politely, Dewey wipes the tears out of his eyes. Looking back at curious Yelekreb, Dewey continues, "I, I was just...getting back to you. The saucer flew this way."

"Well, where did it go?" Yelekreb asks.

"Oh," Dewey smiles proudly, "I chased it all the way into this garden, and it landed...right..." Dewey turns towards the rosebush, "right...here?"

Yelekreb walks towards the rosebush and retrieves the saucer with ease. He looks at Dewey like he is crazy and then turns to the boys, eager to return to the game. They begin to turn back to the playing field. But Yelekreb sees that Dewey has not moved from his place.

"Is something wrong?" Yelekreb asks, but Dewey does not hear him.

"Dewey!"

"Wha? Oh. Me? Why—I, no, haha. Nothing is wrong."

"Are you sure?"

"Yes. Haha," Dewey says, "I'm sure."

"Well then, let's go play!" Yelekreb screams with joy as the other boys applaud. Quickly, Yelekreb turns towards the field and begins to sprint away.

"Last one to the field is a rotten orange!"

As the boys begin their run over the hill, Dewey increases his pace. He feels better already. He runs his fat belly over the green hills, passing the children running to the field and is just behind Yelekreb in the lead. Upon noticing the prince's presence, Yelekreb shouts back without turning his head.

"Hey, prince, I'm glad you decided to join us."

Dewey smiles.

"What happened back there anyway?"

"Oh, nothing," Dewey says, "nothing at all."

17

What man actually needs is not a tensionless state but rather the striving and struggling for some goal worthy of him. What he needs is not the discharge of tension at any cost, but the call of a potential meaning waiting to be fulfilled by him.
Victor Frankl

To be on a quest is nothing more or less than to become an asker of questions.
Sam Keen

From his very first step towards the wild, Renee feels the world open like a great blanket before him. Even before exiting the royal grounds, his steps are lighter than they have ever been. The world makes way for him, its obstacles splitting before him like the Red Sea, protecting his passage with tall walls on each side hugging him like a mother, yet gently prodding him in the right direction with whispers of gentle direction. But as the atmospheric distractions of his life fade behind him, Renee finds his mind awash with thoughts and doubt, questions that had no room to bother him before.

The call of a potential meaning waiting to be fulfilled by him, Renee thinks as he walks out of the west exit of the garden, *whatever could that mean? What am I searching for? What further meaning do I need? Thus far in my life, I have had everything I needed. A family of friends, a maternal figure, a great leader of a father whom many seem to look up to, and a brother, well, a brother with good spirit. I have had everything I needed. All the colorful toys, the gifts, the whistle, the companion, the rainbow world of fantasy that had enveloped me from the moment I came into this world, filling my empty head with all the colorful, delightful experiences others can only dream of. Why couldn't I be happy?* Renee remembers Helene's love, *everything I needed* the kingdom's mazes and stairway adventures, Dewey's friendship *everything I needed,* a royal status, food, shelter, *everything.*

And that was just the problem.

Yes, Renee realizes, *these were all distractions, and that was just the problem all along. For all this time, I have had everything I needed. Everything, that is, except the one thing that would allow me to grow, to allow me to become who I was meant to be. What is this one thing?*

Nothing.

I have never, once, had Nothing.

Nothingness, open space, vacancy, white noise, silence, blackness, peace, the space to grow.

Nothing.

It suddenly dawns on the young prince why he had deserted most everything that was given to him. Since he was given everything, he was compelled to exaggerate the opposite extreme in order to compensate his spoiled condition, and thus, he would take nothing. And that which he was forced to take, he had neglected or lost. In his earliest years, he had already been prepared to lose, as he lost his mother Katherine to tuberculosis during his first year of life, as if a precursor to how the rest of his life would go, instructing him to act so as to accommodate such future losses. Thus, he had never cooperated with the palace rules, and in time he had lost his family's respect. He never returned Helene's love, and that too, was severely tried and had faded in time. He had given up his brother through their oral disputes, his cat, and eventually, his sight. And now, Renee is leaving it all behind, giving up the entire Posteriorian past he never really had. For Nothing.

I lost my sight. That was not enough.

I lost my cat. That was not enough.

My mother.

My family.

My people.

Not enough. Not enough. Not enough.

Yes, Renee realizes, *it was not enough.* Even with his blindness, his solitude, his dark quarters down the stairs, it was never enough of Nothing to reach his inner ideas. It was never enough of Nothing for him to grasp his inner intellect enough for it to flourish, to grow, to offer a small piece of its bounty. Rather, he needed to go back and uproot what he has learned *raze everything to the ground* and once his mind is clear from habits and illusions experience has stained upon it through the years, he can finally *begin again from the original foundations of my inner intellect* and start anew.

As Renee makes his way out of the garden's west exit, he can feel the hot sun rise overhead. His nose smells the orange orchards and farmland to his left and his skin feels the breeze from Lake Prespa far from the north. They guide his feet west, step after blind step. Upon nearing the empire's outermost homes, he senses the children making way for him in the streets, flattening themselves against building walls as he passes. The older ones look away sharply, subtly whispering to their neighbor behind cupped hands. The younger ones simply stare and gawk in his direction, some of them surrendering to tears of disturbance as he passes them by.

Steadily walking down a road and tapping his walking stick before him, Renee hears the street fall silent on his approach. He feels the homes on his right, the dirt path on his left. He feels the people hiding there, the lovers of sights and sounds locking themselves inside, their eyes peering at him in fear and awe and disgust from behind the safety of their windows. A tiny old lady stops pushing her wheelcart and looks up in amazement as Renee passes, not paying her any mind. Her cart falls over, spilling its contents to the ground. But she stands frozen in awe with her mouth wide open, staring at Renee's back as her breads and oranges and colored stones roll around, spilling down the rocky dirt road away from her gaze.

Minutes later, the young steps of a small child who was left outside halt in their tracks. Renee feels the small child open his mouth in horror upon seeing Renee's white emaciated body dressed in black garb *mommy, a ghost* not recognizing the young prince, (for who could after he had abandoned them for so long) *a ghost, who, who is that* walking *floating* towards them towering like that. Renee hears the child's hand pulling upon his mother's *mommy* lush colorful robes, *why does he look like that?* burying his small face in his mother's bosom *who is that* as Renee begins to ask himself the same thing *who am I* as the mother picks up her child and walks away *who am I* stroking the child's head *now now,* don't cry, it was only, only *who…who am I* blindly walking *what do I want* into the endless black *nothingness.*

What am I looking for?

Certainty. To be certain of something, no matter how little.

Suddenly, Renee does not feel the children's strange glances anymore. He does not hear the shuffling of their feet away from his path, but rather his ears focus on the path open before him. He becomes deaf to the tumultuous waters of children upheld on either side, but hears his path open up before him like a red carpet. As the waters quiet around him, Renee feels a weightless freedom carrying him along, the freedom to become one with the distance, with no concern for those around him. He steps forward, his chin held high, passing the last of the Posteriorian homes to his left, walking into the outermost fields of the empire that lead to the border of Lyceum.

He walks forward eagerly now, his steps preceding the shuffling of his sensors behind him. As one hour passes, then another, he feels the sensors' curiosity begin to rise. They grow anxious as they near the sensor checkpoint at the most northeastern corner of the Lyceumean Empire. While the sensors are prohibited from showing any emotion, they struggle with containing their pain and anxiety as it becomes more and more apparent that Renee may actually leave the place they had followed him in since his first steps, the place they have been with him since his birth.

Upon approaching the Lyceumean border, one of Renee's sensors starts to panic. Renee suffers from concern for his beloved sensor, for he knows that if his sensor speaks, the sensor may very well be executed. Renee does not want to be responsible for such a death; he has grown to love his sensors, the only ones who have been with him from his birth. But he knows he must not acknowledge this danger, for citizens of Lyceum, as the careful reader will already know, are prohibited from acknowledging their sensors' very existence. Such an acknowledgement may alter their entire experience of the regular world, which, of course, is the sensors' duty to record through its normal course of events. That this normal course of events must not be disrupted by any sensor-Posteriorian communication is the only Lyceumean rule that has lasted this long, and it is the only one that every Posteriorian knows.

However, there have been several times in the past that Renee has had trouble with this rule. On the eve before his fourth birthday, when he was finally old enough to vaguely notice the sensors' hushed presence but still too young to have become accustomed to it, Renee awakened to the sound of his sensors scuttling about. He can still remember his surprise, jumping out of bed in terror, shouting *burglar! burglar! burglar!* as he turned to Helene's room in horror. He will never forget the sensors' gray eyes looking straight at him in desperation. The sensors froze before him, looking at him eye to eye (since they were hardly an inch taller than he was at the time), staring in fear, *pleading* for him to realize what he was doing, that he could get them killed. His eyes met theirs *dwarf and boy* and the figures stood in silence *two statues* for minutes as Renee felt his heart begin to slow. Finally, after what seemed like hours, Renee wiped his tears upon his sleeve and slowly climbed back into bed, returning to sleep. He was lucky Helene did not heard him shout. He has never made eye contact with his sensors since.

Renee has never seen a sensor checkpoint before, but he knew something of them. In fact, most of what he knew about the Posteriorian culture had come from Helene and her bedtime stories. Renee can still recall what he spoke to Helene about the night after his incident with the sensors.

"But why, why do they follow me, mommy?"

"That is what they were bred to do," Helene had said.

"Why?"

"Because, child, that is the only way they can know all of your experiences—"

"My experiences? But they are mine. Why can't I have them, and do with them what I want?"

"Oh, you don't want to be busy with that, do you? Sensors are great at doing what you shouldn't be bothered with: recording every little thing that goes on in this little head of yours," Helene tapped Renee's temple. He reached up and pulled her hand away.

Renee turned to look at the sensors, "But I…I don't like them. They are always watching me. I want to be left alone."

Helene took a deep breath.

"Renee," she said, gently turning his face towards hers, "Renee, look at me. Do not look over there. You can't look at them. You have been told that for years."

"I'm…I'm so sorry. I'm different than…than the others. Aren't I?"

Helene paused and said, "It's okay, just…try to concentrate on me, on color, on the experiential things around you. The sensors are nothing exciting. They are a pale white and gray so that they stay out of your focus; I am surprised you even noticed them at all, let alone at such a young age. It's funny, but, don't tell your brother this, but I'd be happy if he noticed them by the time he is in his late thirties!"

Renee allowed a chuckle, "Alright, I will try to focus on the vivid. I guess I don't mind the sensors themselves so much, since they are so subtle, and mysteriously simple. They somehow don't seem to change at all; they always stay the same. It's comforting to see something stable. I don't know, it makes them seem more…real. I guess I just tend to look beyond the loud colors before me, as if my mind is drawn to venture beyond what is already there, and reading the white space between the lines—"

"Renee, Renee," Helene interrupted, "They, the sensors, they are nothing to look at. Trust me. They are gray, plain, and little. And they will stay that way forever. If you ask me, they're a pretty boring lot. It should not be hard to miss them." Helene says. But she wonders why it has been so hard for Renee. All the other Posteriorian children have had no problem with this rule. Most other children had not even begun to notice them until their early teens. Why has Renee?

"But mommy, do they have to follow me everywhere I go?"

"Do, do you want them to?"

"No."

"Why not?"

"Because sometimes, sometimes I want to be alone. I just want to be, well, by myself."

"Hush, child! You are far too young to be speaking such words," Helene surprises herself with her shock at the prince's words, "Yes, they will follow you your entire life."

Renee was disturbed by the fact that these small creatures will follow him forever and that he could not study them. He was intrigued by their loyalty, their consistency, their unmoving patience, an oasis of stability in such a colorful and busy nation. He found comfort in the permanent assurance of their presence, but great frustration in the prohibition of their study.

"Why," Renee demanded, "Why must they follow me my entire life?"

"That is the law. In fact," Helene explained, "They must follow every single Posteriorian anywhere he or she goes, including the bathroom."

"What?" Renee had never heard of such an idea before. "They follow everyone??"

"Yes."

"*Everywhere??*"

"Yes, well…" Helene's voice trailed off. She turned her head away.

"Well, what?"

"They follow everyone inside of Lyceum's borders."

"What about outside of Lyceum?"

"You don't need to know about that."

"Tell me. Come on."

"The people of Lyceum cannot control the world beyond its own borders. We are only responsible for our own land. We can only hope that others will learn from our example, and follow in our ways. But we cannot, as much as we may like to, control other nations in the way they live their lives. We can only be responsible for ourselves. So outside Lyceum, there the sensors cannot go. But you don't need to worry about that. You will never leave Lyceum," Helene pats the boy on his head, stroking his spindly black hair, "You have everything you need right here...and you always will."

Everything.

"Okay, but what if someone wanted to leave?"

"Please, dear—"

"No, just what if? What if someone were to leave?"

Helene sighed. "Our borders are lined with sensor checkpoints. Thousands of sensors wait there. Mobile sensors, they are called. Whenever someone enters Lyceum from the outside, they cannot pass into our borders until adequate sensors have been assigned to them. The number of sensors they will require is determined by how sensuous they are, to be determined by expert testing at the sensor checkpoint facilities. And whenever someone wishes to leave our borders, well, their sensors must remain behind with the land, joining the other mobile sensors waiting at the checkpoint, to be eventually picked up again by someone else on their way in."

"So, if anyone...like me, were to cross the border—"

"Your sensors would have to stop right there."

"My sensors would have to stop right there."

They would have to stop there, Renee remembers as he walks by the northeastern checkpoint. He listens for the sound of the mobile sensors, but it is not easy to hear. Though he is about one hundred feet from the checkpoint, he listens for the sounds of the mobs of dwarves, of hundreds, no, thousands of sensors grouped together.

It sounds like a whisper.

Renee's sensors start moving faster behind him, scurrying this way, darting that way. The sensors waiting at the checkpoint make as little noise as possible, though they shuffle in excitement upon seeing Renee in the distance, kicking up dust clouds. It is not often that they see someone leaving Lyceum.

Renee hears *feels* his own sensors' pain in having to leave him. For the first time in Renee's life, his sensors seem puzzled, not knowing what to do. At the border, Renee hears them stop in unison and confusion. They remain at the border looking after him, still scribbling on their parchment. Renee does not need his sight to know that behind his back, one of the sensors opens his mouth to speak.

Master.

Did he really make a sound?

Just one word.

Master.

No, Renee realizes, *no.* Renee actually heard one of the sensors try to speak, but the other sensor reached up quickly to cover his fellow's mouth. But what would he have said if he was able? What could he have said?

Master.

No, they did not say that. *It is my own head speaking. Now, outside of Lyceum, this is where my mind may speak to me. Finally. My mind is able to acknowledge its service to me. Master. Finally it is able to fulfill it.*

As his sensors' steps discontinue behind him and he hears one of their mouths open to be stifled by the other, Renee feels the hint of a tear sting his eyes. But he does not stop; he keeps on walking. He feels one tear roll down his right cheek as his heart weighs upon his legs, begging them to stop. The prince slows his pace, weights of his youth pulling upon both his ankles. But his mind speaks back. *Master* his intellect seems to reach out to him *master, I will carry you* a voice he has never heard before *master.*

He keeps on walking.

He hears *feels* his sensors' dilemma, their heartstrings being stretched from the place they cannot move. They have become a permanent part of him, a body part, an extension of his person. The extraction is painful. They do not want him to leave. *Master.* But Renee crosses the border, his screaming heart caged by the cool steel bars of his mind. He keeps on walking long after his sensors have stopped. He feels their pull behind him like strings on his back, but he continues forward. He does not look back.

As his steps make their way out into The White Plains under the hot sun, they begin to increase their pace. Renee can feel the Lyceumean homes fade to his left, he can smell the breeze from Lake Prespa on his right, and for the first time since the day he was born, he can hear himself.

For the first time, he is completely alone.

It is said that before someone dies, their life flashes before their eyes. This much is true. As Renee leaves his Posteriorian life, it flashes before him in all its color, in all its charm. Renee thinks of father Joachim, his big beautiful hands, the large colored robes of royalty they wore, the large books of case law they held, the extensive, poetic opinions they wrote. Also, he thinks of Helene, her golden hair flowing over his bed like a canopy, the reeds of a weeping willow, the wings of a mother bird, protecting, caressing, lulling her children to sleep. But most of all, Renee thinks of his brother. Renee thinks of Dewey during the good times, and during the bad. He remembers their adventures as childhood kings, the art contest, the stories they shared from Helene, the debates they engaged in, and the games they played in the billiard room. Renee remembers Dewey's jealousy as Dewey found his cat, his friend, towards the end of one long summer. He remembers how Dewey killed his cat, blinded him, and took Helene for himself. He vaguely recalls his time in the cellar, months spent studying the inner contours of his intellect at the bottom of the long dark castle stairs. He remembers the troubled silence between him and his brother upon his climb from the cellar, how he had fallen over a rope that had been left out, how his brother had helped him regain his footing. He remembers debating Dewey about where the beauty of art lies, causation, miracles, the existence of God, the existence of self, what one can really *know*.

He remembers all of this and he smiles. He realizes that this all had to happen to bring him to where he is today.

The vast plains open before Renee like the back of a tremendous whale, his path like the long straight spine protruding from his feet, setting a line off into the distance. The plains feel good to Renee's head. As the buildings of Lyceum precede behind him, he enjoys the silence, open *Nothing* before him. He feels his mind clearing as the filthy weight of sense data trickles out of his ears in all its confusion, a circus of color prancing across the yellow fields, swirling blue to the north, sprinkling red to the east. Feeling the sand under his feet, Renee recalls one last memory before leaving it all behind.

ΩΨΩ

Renee and Dewey once built sandcastles at the beach by the southeast edge of Lake Prespa. It was the first time they had seen such a vast body of water. They spent the entire day building sandcastles, a fierce competition indeed. By the end of the day, Dewey's castle had reached a great height. Renee remembers how it towered over their heads, its ornately decorated shell-covered limbs reaching out like vines from a tree. But when they walked over to what Renee had done, Dewey had laughed. He had laughed so hard because Renee had not yet even finished laying down the foundations for his castle, its short and stubby base barely reaching four inches off the ground.

But when they returned to the beach the following day, Dewey was devastated to see his creation lost, the hungry waves devouring the last remnants of its once-fruitful decorations. But it was the look on Dewey's face when he saw Renee's castle that Renee will never forget. While Dewey's castle nearly disappeared, Renee's castle had only grown, its foundations strengthened by the waters of time. Renee remembers how amazed Dewey was, *look! look!* he shouted pointing, *look, it is still here!* but Renee could not hear him since Renee had gone to sit on a distant ledge over the water, staring out into the distance until Dewey was left to poke around bored, wondering what Renee was up to, until finally leaving his brother in solitude, staring out into the ocean blue.

Renee felt proud, but his mind was greatly puzzled by a gift Helene had given him that day at the beach.

"It's a seashell," she told him, as if it was the simplest thing in the world.

"A seashell? What is it for?"

Helen smiled at his question, but he did not know why.

"Not everything has to have a purpose, Renee. But here, take this shell and bring it your ear like this."

Renee looked doubtfully at the shell, then off towards his brother. Renee saw Dewey far in the distance, running and yelling, kicking up sand as he went. Feeling safe enough, Renee brought the shell to his ear.

"Now," Helene said, "What do you hear?"

Renee closed his eyes and listened. And he heard it!

"It's...the ocean?"

"The ocean! That's right, Renee! And there is a little ocean in each and every sea shell—just so that we can take it home and always have our own ocean with us...wherever we may go!"

But that's impossible.

"What are you two doing?" Dewey's voice thundered behind them.

"Wha—" Helene jumped, startled. "Why do you always do that? Oh, Dewey. How are you?"

Quickly, Renee shoved the seashell into his robes.

"What are you two up to?" Dewey persisted.

Helene smiled, "Oh, we were just...leaving. Are you ready?"

And they went back to the palace. But Renee never forgot about the shell. Whenever Renee was alone, he would listen to the ocean inside the shell. He wondered how it could have gotten inside each and every shell; he could not imagine how there is room. He knew what he was hearing, but it just did not make any *sense.*

One day, Renee could not take it any longer. So he smashed the shell on the floor, but it would not break. Finally, he stomped on it but the shell cut into his foot. Bleeding on the floor in pain, Renee looked to see the shell cracked open into pieces. He examined each and every piece closely, but he could not find anything inside.

ΩΨΩ

Renee feels his head clear and his burden lighten as his mind stretches its limbs for the first time. As his mind diffuses the confusion it has collected over his years of youth, it releases strings of random thoughts like a popped balloon shooting its helium this way and that. *What would happen if someone sneezed with their eyes opened...what would chairs look like if our knees bent the other way...why do men have nipples...a bottle in front of me...a frontal lobotomy...*

His mind is uncontrollable as it exercises its newfound freedom, free to roam like locked up children suddenly released into the greatest playground, or solitary prisoners on a spontaneous trip to the circus. Questions enter his mind without his consent, jumping up and down for the sake of questioning, not really wanting a real answer.

How would 'world' be pronounced if the r and the l were reversed...when I snap my fingers, does the sound come from my middle finger leaving my thumb, or from hitting my palm...and when I hum, does the sound come from my throat or my mouth?

But closes his eyes and puts his mind to rest. He curls his toes into the ground. They see the sand is yellow. Renee looks to the heavens. The sky remains a still blue. They do not change. They don't play tricks, they are what they are. Renee finally smiles *it all makes perfect sense.* The clouds, the sky, the sand. For the first time in his life, he feels connected to his surroundings. For the first time, they seem to be as he knows them. They make sense to him, guiding his feet steadily, consistently, through the vast golden plain.

Eight hours later, Renee still trudges on through the large sandy plains. Though his mind has stopped thinking some time ago, his legs seem to keep moving, step after onerous step. He begins to feel his black robes hanging upon his shoulders and their threads have turned to chains that weigh upon his body, digging into his sunburnt shoulders, pushing his frame into the sand. Even in the late afternoon, the sun bears upon him incessantly, a hanging golden yolk bleeding its egg upon his shoulders, stretching, oozing, slowing, weighing upon him as flies seek out his sweat, resting on his flesh of white, playing in his hair of black. Renee swats the flies away from his face. He knows it will not help, but he does it anyway.

His backpack does not help, but rather, it merges with the sun in its weight. *Pack simple* his simple mind had instructed *for you will not need much, only what your body claims it may need to move.* He had taken most of the food out of his backpack for *this colorful Posteriorian food will only distract me from my goal, this fruitful something weighing me down from attaining*

Nothing. Dewey would often tease Renee in his simple thoughts.

"Silly boy," Dewey would say, "You forget to consider all relevant factors before you."

"I consider what I must," Renee would always answer without hesitation, "and leave out all else."

"But all else may be relevant. Maybe, perhaps..."

"Irrelevancies!" Renee would say, "Anything that is not certain is irrelevant! Mere distractions that may seem to induce comfort, but surely slow one down from building something sturdy and lasting. Distractions are all they are, distractions!"

Now in the sandy plains, Renee wishes for such a distraction, a sip of water, a slice of melon. He had not considered the weather, that the late spring can get very hot in this part of the world. He forgot that many of the outer buildings of Lyceum had crumbled, and were being rebuilt further to the west. The empire was constantly changing such that a traveler may easily get lost on his ways to the plains, but such change had been too much for Renee to consider. He overlooked such considerations, miscalculated, what have you, certain factors he had not been able to see.

The yellow sand is dead, lifeless, arid like paper, as if Lyceum had sucked up all the surrounding juices of life. Renee feels his stomach burn with the desire for food *water* something *water* as his stomach acid struggles to moisten his parched, cracked throat.

Finally, Renee feels his nose fill with a breath of cool air. It is sudden and it is brief, but it is there. The air does not aid him to any large degree, but it holds a vague wetness, like a morning after the rain, or that of an old leather shoe. Renee begins to smile, knowing the breeze to have traveled from Cherava Woods, from the currency of leaves nearby, an exchange he must finally be approaching just about now. His cracked lips hurt, but he smiles anyway, knowing it may be the last taste of rain of pain *of life* he may ever enjoy. He closes his eyes and for a moment, he can see the woods in front of him, the tall green canopy reaching out, its steady limbs of water *of life* trying to catch his fall.

But they are too far away.

They are too far away and the sun is too strong, the heat too heavy, the stomach too hot. And as Renee's legs begin to crumble beneath him, he holds his smile for as long as he can. The image of the trees is still captured in his mind and the caption of foliage jerks briefly in his vision. The shadows of trees remain imprinted in his intellect as his body falls into the sand, suddenly leaving his mind to replace themselves with a vacant, overwhelming black.

ΩΨΩ

Now this was not a bad state Renee was in, for people are surely comfortable with what they are used to, and Renee was used to seeing black *nothing.* Unlike Rekha's blackout many years ago, Renee's mind almost wills it upon his body, screaming for the chance to be free from its experience *the sensors are not here anymore* and finally be allowed to be at peace, immersed in Nothing *for no one will ever know.* And unlike Rekha, Renee's suffering body was just a small price to pay for such a vast black.

This is all the more reason, dear reader, that Renee's awakening is not welcomed by the poor prince's mind. It is enough that Renee is awakened by the discomfort of a large, cold wet tongue violently swiping across his peeling face. It is enough that he has to regain consciousness with a stabbing pain in his leg, sharp claws digging into his calve, mangling his lower right leg under his ripped black robes as he chokes up sand and blood, pressing the sand deeper into his eyes as he tries to wipe it out. Yes, this is enough to make him dread his awakening, but this is not the real discomfort of his awakening. No, rather it is the tragedy of stolen slumber. It is the seizing of his mind's enjoyment of this vast black *Nothing.* The sudden jolt of experience is the real discomfort here. It is like being born again, *to be born,* only this time, *first you have to die,* he is not empty.

Still struggling to grip onto consciousness, Renee feels a cold wet tongue continue to wash over his face. It feels wet at moments, but still gives off a dry, scratchy feeling of friction, enough to turn Renee's head sharply from side to side. It moves slowly and powerfully to and fro like the stroke of a large man streaking out a stain with wet sandpaper.

Renee is about to move when he feels the animal's hot breath flow across his cheeks, the smell of burnt garlic like a thick brush across his face. The sandpaper tongue continues to explore Renee's face, burning like a red sand storm piercing his paper white skin. The creature's claws bear down heavy upon him, pressing his skinny leg deep into the ground. Unable to control himself, Renee shouts out loud from the pain *my leg*, the frustration *I've come so far*, the defeat *and now this.*

The animal jumps back in surprise; he thought the young prince dead. While most people have not had their meals shout back at them as they prepare to eat, one can imagine it to be a most unpleasant experience. Growling angrily, the animal stands before the boy. As it raises itself up onto its two hind legs, Renee lies in its shadow, a large one indeed. *An animal in these plains* Renee's mind hums with the creature's growls *a large one with claws, can only have come from Cherava Woods just nearby* Renee's ponders even in such dire straits *must have smelled me, my blood, my sweat* as Renee thinks of the wood's inhabitants, he realizes just what this creature must be.

It is a Cheravian bear.

Now, Cheravian bears, if you must know, are not all that different from the bears in your world. They started out as large white bears, much like that of a polar bear, but had grown different over time. To tell of their few but important differences, however, one may need to reveal the bears' origins.

It has been said that they have migrated here long ago, crossing the frozen Lake Ohrid in a cold winter long past. They came from the thin strip of woods north of here, just west of Macedon. It was here that they fed on the millions of small water animals and crustaceans dwelling by the Lake Tirreno. That had been their home for many years, that is, until their crustacean prey had traveled south, washed down the Axios River, and they were forced to follow.

Yes, Renee remembers learning as a boy, *these crustaceans originated in Carrara and had given the marble its beauty and strength.*

It was these small creatures who gave their lives for the marble, their calcium carbonate skeletons sinking to the bottom of the Tirreno where mud was able to cover their mineral remains, pressing them into limestone so that water, heat, and pressure would transform the rock into marble. But some of the crustaceans, the ones who were not given this honor, had been flushed down the Axios. After some time, the bears that had fed on them were left with nothing to eat. Thus, they followed their crustacean prey down the river, taking refuge in the neighboring Cherava Woods where they would feed on fish and crustaceans of the river, and any lost sensors that ventured into those woods.

But after time, the crustaceans found ways to avoid their bear predators. They began to adapt. They grew faster. They became harder to catch, harder to hold. As a result, the bears adapted too. Many grew small fins from their upper backs, and their claws became a webbed array of knives, increasing their ability to pursue their prey in water. Their claws began to change color, their hands turning a deep water blue so that the crustaceans would not see them coming to catch them in the river. Where the blue ended, the bears' wrists and ankles had grown green, orange, and yellow, to camouflage with the colorful foliage of the woods and the colorful fish of Lake Ohrid, before blending into the pale gray-white the rest of their body had become. Their claws had grown in serration and their grip grew in power. But most dangerous of all was that their claws held a terrible poison, secreted at their base, to paralyze their clever prey.

Renee had never actually seen a Cheravian Bear before. Now he had heard about them briefly, as he had heard about most everything under the sun from Helene. But now, as he lies in the shadow of this large creature, he is glad his vision is lost. He would not want to see his predator with his eyes, for the vision his mind offers is certainly enough.

The bear is still on top of him, pinning him down. It sniffs Renee's face like a brute smelling his meal before consuming it. It will not be long now, Renee thinks.

Renee searches frantically for his walking stick. His fingers run through the grass and sand like little white snakes weeding through grains of rice. Whether from terror or from pain, his body will not move. His mind urges him to roll over, find his walking stick, and pick himself up, but his body does not cooperate. But suddenly, his fingers come across a pile of scattered wooden shards.

His walking stick.

Yes, Renee recalls, *that explains the taste of wood on the bear's breath, the thorny touch of his claws* as he realizes that while he was unconscious, the bear must have toyed with *destroyed* his walking stick until it was broken to pieces. *Well, better the stick than my leg.*

Better the stick than my body.

Renee imagines the beast before him. He senses an animal, a large white pillow of fur softly bordered by rainbow spots that fade into a deep blue. The animal's mottled wrists and ankles remind him of the Posteriorian experience, a shocking mess of changing color, spots, stripes, without any pattern. But as his mind's vision works its way up the animal's limbs, past the color and into the gray, it reminds him of his journey from there to here, from color to gray, from the ever-shifting Lyceum to these clear open fields, from noise to quiet, from rainbows to light, from the brightness of fruit rinds to the pallor of wax, from transience to permanence, from confusion to peace, from everything to Nothing.

A claw comes down towards Renee's face.

His eyes closed, Renee tries to jerk to the side. He feels the claw graze his skin along the jaw line. He moved just in time. For now. *Dewey would have been dead* Renee cannot help but smile, *gone, zip, dead, the fat, slow prince eaten in no time* but his thoughts are sharply interrupted as he is brought back into reality by a stabbing pain in his legs as the bear regains his hold on the boy. Renee squirms his wiry body under the bear's weight, shouting out in horror, but this time it is no use. The bear has learned from experience. As he tightens his claws around Renee's thin white legs, Renee can feel the paralyzing poison work its way into his wounds. It feels curiously cold, even inviting for a moment after the heat of the day his legs had endured. He feels it weigh his movement, fog his senses, drain him of his vigor.

For a moment, Renee lets it overcome him. The blank white comfort of slumber draws him closer. But he worries that if he sleeps now, he will never awake. For a moment, that does not seem so bad. *Oh, to just end it all here!* Renee sighs *to embrace the Nothing and finally sleep. How easy that would be!*

But the bear's weight shifts violently, jerking Renee from his thoughts. It raises another claw to tear into the young prince's neck. *Here we go* Renee tries to move one last time *this is it, after seventeen years, I've finally done it* thinking of how Rekha must have felt while El Totsira and O'Talp took the lifeblood from her, *after seventeen years, I've finally done it,* Renee finds he is completely unable to move. The bear feels Renee's weakness and his growls rise in excitement in anticipation of his meal, meager as it may be. Finally, the claw comes rushing down toward our prince's face *and now this.*

It is now that many such extraordinary things happen; they happen so quickly that Renee is not able to understand just what occurs. Renee feels the claw coming towards him, the spray of its poison heading viciously towards his exposed white throat. Suddenly, the spray of poison turns to the spray of blood, a river of red rushing down the boy's chest like the closing of a red stage curtain *that's all folks* concluding the night's performance *it's time to go* spurting, flowing down, ending his sorry life to the crowd's applause.

Renee's screams turn to forced chokes as the blood sprinkles generously into his mouth. Rolling to his side, he spits out what he can, choking, moaning in pain *pain?* pain as he stops in mid-choke like an actor who suddenly forgets his lines. *Pain?* Renee realizes he does not feel any pain. The bear loosens its grip, and Renee is able to lift his hand to his throat. He feels his skin.

There is no wound; all is intact.

But the blood, *where did all this blood come from if not from me? And where is the bear? Why did it stop?*

Lying down in confusion, Renee listens carefully for an answer. And he hears it! The bear's growls are joined by another, smaller growl to his rear.

Someone—some*thing* else is here. But what?

Renee actually feels the bear's weight lighten, its limbs rising off his body like a great weight rising, allowing for more freedom of movement. Raising his head, Renee tries to look around, but his senses cannot do much without the aid of his sight. Since Renee is blind, he was not able to see the gray wolf dart out of the brush as the bear's claw came falling down towards his throat. He was not able to see the wolf fly through the air, his fangs clenching onto the rainbow spots on the bear's wrist before it reached the boy's throat, diverting its course, spraying blood from the bear's hand onto Renee's throat and face, and into the surrounding sands.

But Renee's mind has developed its own strengths. It does not take him long to understand what happened, that this other growl came from the wolf, a white and gray wolf that had saved him, and that this blood upon him was the bear's, spraying from the deadly clawed hand that could have *should have* brought about his end.

The wolf saved him. For now. But where did it come from? How?

The bear has turned from Renee, but he shows no plans to leave. Rather, he stands facing the wolf, hugging his injured hand tightly. The bear looks from his wound to the wolf and back to the wound again. He looks in surprise that something so small can penetrate his great hide. Renee tries to move, to get up and run away, but pain shoots up through his mangled leg, making it difficult to breath. So he lies helplessly, watching the bear and the wolf like a helpless spectator, waiting to see if he will be saved or if he will die.

The bear wastes no more time. He regains his position quickly, and his cries of confusion are quickly brought back to growls of anger, of a horrible fury towards anything that dare stand in his way. He stands back on his great hind legs, boasting a large display of his body, his silver-gray chest bellowing forth, his tree trunk legs raising him high and mighty, nearly eight feet off the ground.

But the wolf stands his ground.

The bear looks down at the wolf now crouching low, his green eyes shining, his fangs just barely revealed. The bear rushes forward, butting his large head into the wolf's lean body, but the wolf does not flinch. The bear tries again, this time butting the wolf's side gently with his head. But this time, as the bear gets close, the wolf does not stay still. The wolf jumps up violently, snapping his teeth towards the bear's upper back, clawing at his face. The bear jumps back in surprise. He looks at the wolf squarely, nodding his large head as if trying to decipher the animal's intentions. The wolf offers a small bark *whuf* as if to let the bear know it means business.

Renee remains frozen on the ground. The wolf nonchalantly sniffs the ground before him, as if there is no danger present. Then he circles around, gracefully walking over to Renee, though his eyes remain locked on the bear as the bear stands distracted, snorting the air around him to preoccupy himself from his foe's blatant impudence. The wolf settles itself between Renee and the bear. He turns to face the bear, and slowly crouching to the ground, he regains his former stance.

As the wolf sets itself closer to Renee, Renee can smell the wolf for the first time. Since his nose became stronger ever since he was blinded, he recognizes the scent of the wolf right away. It is the scent of O'Talp, of Nicolas, of Nothing. This association is a pleasant surprise to him, but it is given no time to sink in.

The bear stands again, but this time it emits a horribly low growl that shakes the ground. A school of birds fly away in the distance, troubled by the trembling leaves in a nearby patch of woods. The bear beats his chest, holds his head high, and moves to take a step forward.

But as soon as the bear's foot touches the ground before him, the wolf surprises Renee as much as the bear *both bear and boy* by baring his shiny white fangs in full, fiercely snarling and biting his teeth up and down. The bear stops mid-step, and begins to moves backwards, retracing his attempted step forward.

The wolf crouches lower to the ground and takes a step forward.

The bear's growls grow even louder, trying to match the wolf threat for threat, but his dominance in volume does not make up for the low and steady ferocity of the wolf. The wolf stands still, a marble statue of gray and white, his two dark ears raised high, just below his raised tail, a dark streak of gray stretched between the three peaks of fur. His two front paws move forward, white paws brushing the yellow grass before him. The bear roars back loudly, but the wolf stays in his place. The bear knows better than to try to advance again, so he stays in place.

For what seems like hours, the two creatures stand there, friend and foe, savior and beast, David and Goliath, *wolf and bear.* The bear continues his threats, from roar to growl, from clawing at the air to barricading its body from left to right. But all the while the wolf remains still before Renee, its chest slightly trembling from the low steady growls beneath its two green eyes locked onto the bear, following its every motion, telling it they will not go away.

Then, just as suddenly as the bear became angry, he gets down on all fours and his eyes change to a shade of frustration. He turns around. Like a spectator after a show, the bear begins to walk away quietly *humph* as if nothing really happened. Letting out a small *huff* of defeat, he turns back around one last time, his small black eyes meeting the wolf's in defeat, and suddenly turning away once again as his big hide trots away, finally disappearing into the brush beyond.

The wolf turns his head towards Renee. Renee lies in the brush, his leg cut up pretty badly from the bear's claws, his clothes still stained with the red blood of the bear. The wolf's eyes dim and his growls subside, but they do not stop entirely. Renee manages to roll himself onto his belly and he begins to drag himself upwards by his elbows. But when he faces upwards, he feels the wolf glaring at him, his growls still dangerous and cunning. Fearful for his life once again, Renee's heart beats faster and he remains in his place.

Renee senses the wolf. He waits for something to happen, but nothing does. The wolf crouches low to the ground as Renee finally manages to stand up, awkwardly leaning as he shifts his weight to his good foot. Finally Renee stands tall, and he faces down towards this low growling animal just eight feet away, this ferocious wolf *friend or foe* that he cannot figure out. His mind sees the wolf's jaws *that can tear my throat apart at any second* that bit into the Cheravian bear's arm *like a thousand little knives.* His face feels the wolf's green eyes glaring at him, and his stomach feels the wolf's consistent growls, steady and low.

Renee thinks of running, but he knows it will do no good *for how far would you get on one foot* he laughs in his desperate situation *a blind boy with one good leg* haha *running from a rabid wolf…a rabid wolf* he quickly corrects himself, *a canine friend who just saved my life* as he remembers his lost cat *companion* and he remembers his dream *your companion, he will be with you.* He remembers O'Talp's spoken words *your companion will return when you need him most* as it all comes streaming back *let him guide you* as he looks into the eyes of the wolf *to be born, Dear Renee,* and he sees the eyes of his cat *first you have to die.*

Renee walks towards the animal.

Almost immediately, pain shoots up Renee's bad leg, and he begins to fall forward. Without his walking stick, Renee's legs do him little good. Biting his lower lip, he regains his balance, grimacing as he learns how to walk in his present condition. He continues forward, slowly testing the waters of his body, of this animal *threat?* before him. The wolf's growls increase. Renee knows that the only thing compelling him towards the animal are O'Talp's words *your companion will return*, the smallest chance that they may come true, *let him guide you* that this wolf might somehow be, in some unknown way, his lost companion, that somehow, they share the same soul. Renee looks up hopefully and senses that the wolf is just an arm's length away. *Let him guide you.*

But the growls do not subside.

Mustering up his last reserve of courage, *this is it* Renee raises his hand towards the animal *live or die.* He closes his eyes and takes a deep breath, wiggling his fingers, feeling the soft blood *life* inside them for what may be the last time. But as his hand comes just a few inches from the animal's nose, the animal bows his head and pushes forward to meet Renee's palm. His growls subside with the violent beating of Renee's small heart. Renee smiles at the touch of the wolf's warm fur, the animal's brow nuzzling gently under Renee's white knuckles like the soft body of a flower pressing upwards beneath the legs of a trembling bee.

Renee kneels down and pets the animal. It is then that Renee feels the collar around the wolf's neck. It is a black collar bound together by a small, pale wad of wax. Renee feels the wax, his trembling hands trying to recognize the wax's unique shape. It feels familiar to the prince.

Like the form of a spider.

Renee feels the image of three-legged spider shoot back into his head. *Where does it come from* he remembers that an old feline friend of his had the same collar *but what does it mean?*

Just as the wolf seemed submissive enough, it turns from Renee. Without looking back at the confused prince, the wolf darts from the boy, running like lightning, disappearing into the great beyond.

Having been rejected many times before, Renee is more curious than hurt. *Well...*Renee can feel his lips, almost hearing the whisper they move to make, *well...thank you.* Thank you for saving my life.

But as Renee begins to walk forward, he finds things are harder than before. His walking stick is gone and his leg is badly mangled. His blindness confuses him more than before. It is no longer a black vacancy before him, but a wall, endangering any movement he wishes to make. His companion is gone and his body screams with every movement he makes. After ten minutes of attempted movement, Renee sits down in defeat. He knows he will never make it alone. He needs help. A guide. Something.

Almost instinctively, he feels his hands rise to his chest. He feels the calling whistle around his neck, yes, the thin wooden rod just a pinky's length at most. The wood feels warm in his hands as if it had prepared itself for this very moment. As he grasps his whistle and closes his eyes, Renee hears Helene's words *it's a gift* echo in his head *try it out, why don't you* as if he had heard them yesterday *just put it to your mouth and blow.*

Renee blows.

Almost immediately, he hears the panting of the wolf running towards him. *It had no experience of the whistle* Renee cannot help but note to himself *it needed no experience at all. it must make a sound,* Renee cradles the whistle in his hands *for it would only make sense* as he senses the wolf just yards ahead.

Without thinking, he hears himself call out to his saviour *Christian!*

Christian? Is that what I said? he wonders, his hand over his mouth humorously curious what it may say next if left uncontrolled, *Christian the Wolff? Christos the anointed one? One who left me, but came back? The one who left me through death, through running away, but the one who always came back? The Christos the anointed one? Christian the Wolff. That is who he is* Renee decides *and that will be his name.*

Christian runs into Renee, who allows himself a laugh of relief. But Renee feels something locked in the wolf's jaws, something Christian seems to be pushing into Renee's hands. All of the sudden, Renee realizes why Christian had left in the first place. Renee realizes that Christian had run into Cherava Woods to get something very important, something he now gives to the prince from his locked jaws. It is a stick.

The best walking stick Renee ever felt.

Happily brushing the leaves and twigs off his newfound friend's gray coat, Renee is unable to brush the smile off his face as easily. He feels his heart warm his whole body. His injured leg still hurts terribly, but it is stable enough for the time being. Christian waits, circling Renee as Renee rips off the edge of his robe, sits on the ground, and wraps it around his injured leg to stop the bleeding. Renee pulls himself up on his new stick. He plants it firmly into the ground before him, wiggles his toes, and looks up into the distance like the statue of a great traveler. *I can do this* he realizes *we can do this, we left Lyceum for a reason, and that reason can be realized. That reason can now be realized by us.*

With his stick in hand, Renee moves himself forward, his heart swelling with newfound determination. Christian barks, circling around the prince before running off ahead to lead the way. Man and wolf, boy and cat, both not knowing where they are supposed to go, yet both hopeful they will guide each other to their respected destinies. They move forward in concert under the darkening sky, two silhouettes in the flat plains, the wolf always a few feet in front of the boy as if *he,* Christian, is the boy's new walking stick, sniffing out the way ahead. Slowly, they make their way north, towards Cherava Woods. As the stars above begin to blink their eyes, forming a tremendous chandelier twinkling its light upon the sand below, Renee and Christian come to the head of the woods. The sun is almost set behind the blue Apuan Hills in the distance, its mellow body sticking its head up, peeking above the hills for just one last look before it must surrender to the night. Its head hangs there for one last moment, a dim half circle, like a juicy slice of orange fading fading fading away with the Lyceum life left behind as the trees envelope both wolf and prince before disappearing completely, leaving behind the vast black Renee has come to know.

ΩΨΩ

Though he is blind, Renee can feel the darkness in Cherava Woods. It bears down upon him as the sun once did, but with cool wet fingers he has never felt before. The leaves reach out to him, whispering their taunts, cursing as he passes. But Renee soon realizes they are not cursing at him, but rather speaking to each other in excitement, a chattering audience excited by the show of a blind boy and his pet, a show they have not seen in these parts. They reach their fingers out, trying to touch him as he passes like an audience reaching out to an emerging star, stretching, grabbing for a touch, just a stroke of his shirt, of his skin, slowing down his step. But Renee does not relent. He follows the sound of Christian's tail whipping through the dense brush, his walking stick swaying this way and that, feeling out the ground for rocks and vines.

His new companion and new walking stick give Renee hope. But one must not forget his long journey from Lyceum. His leg is still injured, and he has traveled a great distance already. Every time he tries to rest, no more than a few moments pass before Christian nudges him with his brow *c'mon prince*, yelping wildly, pulling Renee by his robes *it is time to go!* until Renee has no choice but to continue into the night.

As the hours pass, Renee realizes he is lost. He has lost all sense of direction long ago; following Christian is his only hope. He smiles briefly at such a thought, for this is the first time in his life that following another is all he can do. His stick clatters against the trunks of oncoming trees. Three crows fly beneath the yellow moon, flashing its light like a signal. Renee can hear the flapping of a bat's wings above him. Trying to keep up with Christian, Renee moves ahead and tries to ignore the nearby owls' stares. But suddenly, Renee feels the itch of a spider web across his face. Spinning and jerking his body out of it, he trips over his walking stick and falls to the ground.

Fearing he may lose Christian, Renee struggles to get up. His hands brush through the dirt to gain support, and his hand touches briefly upon an antfarm. He stops for a second, feeling the ants *an entire nation* under his palm working as busily as they can, ignoring the pending death many of them must feel. The ants work as rapidly as they can, never slowing, their paths becoming more erratic, their joy as the motor of their actions, doing nothing but collecting and using the materials around them.

But Renee realizes that in all their productivity, the ants utilize nothing of themselves in the process. They bring nothing to the table, nothing in themselves, but rather they go on grabbing as much as they can of the *outside* world as compulsive collectors. They only run around in large groups, collecting and using, collecting and using, to their heart's content. Though Renee just trampled and killed hundreds of them, destroying their home, they keep working even faster, as if nothing happened. As Renee lies there with this world under his palm, it is a world that feels familiar to him. It is his life. It is his family, his nation, the nation of the ant. It is the world into which he was born.

It is the world he wishes to leave.

Instinctively, Renee jerks his hand up from the ground. His hands move to his face, and he tries to brush the cobwebs off. But he freezes in horror as he feels its owner slowly making its way up his arm. Renee feels the spider stop in place just below his elbow. It is a pale gray spider, Renee can sense, still as a statue. It seems to be resting silently, waiting for Renee's next move. Suddenly, Renee sympathizes for the lone spider. Remembering the mass transit antfarm resuming its course beside him, Renee feels for the spider whose home he has just destroyed. But unlike the ants, the spider does not need his home, for wherever he goes, he can make his own. It comes from himself. He *is* his home. While ants only collect from the outside world, spiders create substance out of their own selves, Renee thinks. They do this alone, not in the company of others, and their productivity is carried out in a premeditated, measured, and precise manner. The spider is patient, waiting, planning to rebuild a new home. And it will be perfect. Renee realizes that, unlike the world of the ants he grew up in, it is in the world of the spider that he longs to live.

Picking the spider up with his hands, Renee can feel the spider's heartbeat beneath his warm chest. Renee gathers strength from it; *if the spider can carry on without his home, then so can I.* Renee gently places the spider on a nearby tree when he hears Christian bark up ahead. He takes his walking stick in his hands, takes a deep breath, and continues to follow his four-legged guide.

Now, an accurate account of the remaining nightly hours would be as uneventful as unnecessary to the dear reader, for Renee and Christian do much of the same thing. They walk, walk, and walk in a northerly direction, with few rests in between. With Christian in front and Renee at his tail, the two comrades travel through the night by the light of the distorted moon above. The journey is arduous, and their hunger grows. The two pick berries as they walk, stopping every hour for a quick fruity snack. On occasion, Renee spits out a berry, remembering its poisonous qualities from the few agriculture lessons he bothered to attend. *Damn those lessons,* Renee thinks, *but if only I had my book here,* remembering the book of berries he was given as a child.

But suddenly, as soon as the two pass a large boulder, Christian barks and darts up ahead. Christian seems to be excited about something as he disappears into the brush. Renee cannot imagine any reason Christian would run up ahead now. Reaching for his whistle, Renee steps forward and his legs scream in pain. He blows the whistle repeatedly, but Christian does not return.

Groping through the dark, Renee figures he is well into the Cherava Woods, probably in the eastern region. The trees confuse him. Circling around them, he loses all sense of direction. He tries to maneuver one way, but falls upon his injured leg. A muffled shout of pain escapes before he can bite his lip to stop it. He wonders why he does. That is before he hears the loud rustling in the trees before him.

Suddenly, a dark figure appears out of nowhere, blocking his path.

Not now Renee winces in fright *not without Christian here.*

Renee closes his eyes, praying to himself that it is not another bear. Or something worse. It is getting closer. Finally, it is right before Renee. He can feel its presence shake the ground before him. Still, he waits, ready to accept his fate, whatever it may be.

But the shadowy form stops before Renee. The leaves seem to close behind it as if they were the doorway from which it has emerged. The shadow seems to be in the form of a man. Though Renee's eyes have been blinded, Renee can smell the scent of O'Talp's documents, of Nicolas, of Nothing, the scent he had dreamed of many times before. The smell is strong now, hitting Renee like never before. Using his nose, Renee senses that Christian is standing at the stranger's side. Renee opens his mouth to speak *how—*, but his throat is parched; he cannot make a sound. The man's eyes seem to smile at Renee, like a teacher taking joy in his student's efforts. Renee clears his throat, but the shadow is the first to speak.

"Hello, Renee Don Cartez. We have all been waiting for you. We have been waiting a long, long time."

II

INTO THE GRAY

1

Children preserve the fame of a man after his death.
Aeschylus

Since you have left us, dear reader, in your conquest to accomplish things in what you call your real life, much has happened to our two young princes and the people who love them most. You see, the better part of fifty years have passed. Oh, and do not think for one second that this world stops when you want it to, when you close these pages to chase your fanciful ambitions, dwelling in the people, the streets, the buildings you think you see. Oh no, much occurs between these two covers now in your hands while they lie united by your bedside. You cannot know of something's actions you are not observing.

See, look at an object over there. A lamp. A table. The bowl of muffins you've left out for too long. Now look away. Is it still there? You have no reason to know it to be so. Perhaps it has broken into a silent dance, darting away as you read this text. Or perhaps it disappeared altogether, existing only for the moment when you looked in its direction. Yes, when you look away from this tale, you cannot assume its time to stop, its characters to freeze in space just waiting for the hour of your return, for who do you think you are? Are you some God, some motor of my world that is required for it to continue its ordinary operations through the course of time? Why must my world stop when you choose to leave it?

You must never think that it does.

Nearly fifty years have passed in these lands. And what have you accomplished in this time? No matter. Let me tell you what has occurred here.

Lyceum has grown quite rapidly. Activity has spread in Lyceum, construction and production filling far beyond what its borders should be able to hold. Yet the Posteriorians' colorful activities seem to have risen higher rather than pouring into the White Plains that surround; the Lyceumean borders hold their growing population like a large cauldron, its colorful brew steaming, bubbling, darting this way and that, rising up towards the heavens before finally falling back into itself to start again.

Even Dewey, once the golden boy of the kingdom, has grown. His yellow face has maintained its glow, though his cheeks and chin have become a pasty white. Many Posteriorians noted with pride how Dewey their future leader has grown more horizontally than vertically, like 'real' Posteriorian royalty. His solid limbs have grown into large but stout tree trunks hanging down on either side. His legs seem bowed, which come as no surprise given the weight of his potbelly.

His face has gained the Posteriorian look of aging: worn out from an intake of experience enough for many lifetimes. However, even with the solemnity of Renee's absence all these decades, Dewey's face has maintained a boyish doughboy look of his youth, his rosy red cheeks alive with powdered oils, a smile of joy in his eyes as if always laughing at a private joke.

Joachim died. Well, he didn't really die in the way that you would think of dying. For in your world, dear reader, a person is only dead when they suffer a loss of blood to the brain. But in Lyceum, one is dead when they suffer a loss of experiences to their senses. In Lyceum, a person is dead when they are stuck in bed, unable to partake of even a piece of the feast of experience of the outside world. A man is dead when he loses his sense of taste, of smell, of sight, when he cannot enjoy, food, aromas, or sex. In Lyceum, a man is dead when he can no longer live.

It all started when Joachim began to change. Though he was greatly admired in all the nation, the people began to question their loyalty as the older Joachim began to withdraw from public life. In truth, he had always seemed, well, a bit 'less Posteriorian.' Though no one would ever say so, his tall frame and stern features always reminded the nation of Renee. Indeed, the establishment of his 'thinking room' (where Renee had wet himself) had spawned great controversy *what is he hiding from* through the entire nation *what Posteriorian judge needs to think?*

Whenever one leaves the mentality of their habitat, they begin to die. If a fish decides he wants to be a man, and he jumps out of the water, he will die. If a religious man seeks to live a different life than his surroundings will accommodate, he will get tired after time, and find he cannot live such a life. Joachim's death began when he began to jump out of his Posteriorian water. After a whole Posteriorian life, he changed too much too fast. While most today merely say he went mad, a few still whisper that he secretly sought out the teachings of O'Talp. Some say it was this that caused his death.

Just months after Renee had left Lyceum, Joachim began to spend more and more time alone. His body got weaker, so that he was in bed most of his days. He began to ask for Renee in his sleep...saying things like "You can have water. You can have Nothing!" his words would become shouts, "Nothing! Nothing! to have Nothing!" —when the nurses would come in *hurry* and wake him *Lord, you fell into sleep* from his sleep *it is okay* and once he even cried for O'Talp, *Eros* crying for *eros!* as if he was speaking to him, but news of this was quickly contained, and the rumors that got out were not acknowledged as anything, rarely pondered in the day's current events before abandoned for something else.

Dead! Dead, I say! The newsboys on the street began to shout, *Joachim is dead in his bed!* after seven days passed and Joachim still had not risen to his feet. A traditional funeral was planned, with Joachim preparing the lineup of speeches, including his own. The other royalty spent many hours huddled around Joachim's bed, discussing funeral plans with him *and this is where the flowers will be* bickering about what color everything should be *no, the food should go over there!* what music shall play, what food shall be served. In the midst of their arguing they became annoyed at Joachim's refusal to carry on the arguments. It was almost as if he did not care. As Joachim's eyes glazed over with boredom and indifference, they looked over him and continued their debates. But they did not notice Joachim closing his eyes tightly, thinking about his past life, wondering if there could have been more, as the present Posteriorians' words passed over him like paper bullets with nowhere to go.

It was during that year that Disegno was brought to the foot of the needle once again. Joachim demanded to settle his case once and for all. No one had ever heard of such a thing *nonsense! once and for all?* First the people tried to laugh it off *haha no such truth can be found* but then the laughs turned to scared glances *Once and for all?* saying a thousand words *but that is so...final. What if you are wrong? It must be more complicated than that. After all, this is a man's life! There are many factors to consider. Say, you weren't even there, you can't really know if he, he...what is he being tried for again?*

Dewey tried to speak to Joachim, urging him to rest, to not go to the trial with such a mindset.

"You can't go to the trial like this," Dewey said to his father.

"Why not?"

"Because...because you're already dead."

"Well, well," Joachim said with love in his eyes, "I never thought I would hear those words from my own son."

"I love you, father, and I don't want you to leave this world," Dewey's eyes began to moisten. His words were true. "But even if you are dead, well, I want you here as long as possible. You must rest. Please don't go."

"I must judge. This is what I do. And if someone else does it, Disegno well be sent up and down that tower for the rest of his life, which could be a thousand more years, considering how long he has already lived."

"But that is the way it has always been done."

"Something does not need to be more wrong now than it was then in order to change."

"Wrong? But, but I thought that this is the beauty of the Lyceumean Court!" Dewey shrieked, "I, I thought, and you, *you* taught us that nothing is final, that the more the steps of the needle are walked upon, the more the High Court is struggling with a man's case, and, and it is exactly this struggle, this beautiful struggle, that we live for. This honorable labor, this is what makes our nation great."

"Yes. That is what we have lived our lives saying, haven't we?"

"Rightly so. Father, your whole life stood for experience, not finality. And now—"

"That is enough, son."

"Are you going to the trial?"

"Yes."

"Are you—"

"Yes. And I will render a final decision."

"But no one has ever—"

"Will that be all, son?"

"But, but what if you're wrong?"

"I will not be wrong."

"But...but what if you are?"

"Then at least I will be something."

"But that's too scary. No man has the strength to make such a decision for real. Who are you to make such a final decision?" Dewey banged his fist next to Joachim's bed, "Who do you think you are, that you can determine a man's guilt with such certainty?"

"I have been appointed to judge, haven't I? Perhaps before I go...before I go from this world completely, I can do, just once, what I have been chosen for. Perhaps just once, I can really judge."

"But father, you can't know a man's final verdict. You can't be perfect."

"I will be whatever I can be. For the first time."

"You have no right to be rash with a man's life!"

"I will not be rash."

"You will not go to that trial."

"Is that all, son?"

"You must not."

"*Is that all, son?*"

Dewey stormed out of the room that night with tears of frustration in his eyes. Joachim closed his eyes, putting a hand over his face. He grimaced in pain as he turned on his side to fall asleep.

Disegno's trial began a few days later. The large crowd squeezed into the great courtroom at the foot of the needle. The palace stood west to their left like a mild flux of color, while the Libraries of the Sensors stood beyond the homes of Brittany to their right.

Before the trial was about to start, a murmuring was heard at the entrance of the court. Dewey and Helene looked up to see Joachim being wheeled in on his bed, his sensors scampering behind. Dewey felt anger rise in his stomach, but it quickly turned to pain and sympathy towards his father for compromising the principles of his life. He felt a deep sadness *he should know better* watching his father being wheeled down that aisle on his bed *but if this makes him happy.* As the future leader of the people, Dewey managed to put a smile on his face such that when Joachim entered, Helene and Dewey had both smiled. There was a pain in each of their hearts, but it was a different kind of pain.

The charges were brought. Grand theft of art. After the witnesses completed the performances of what they had seen, the colossal jury began to deliberate. No one noticed as Joachim unexpectedly got up from his bed and slowly made his way through the sea of jurors. He seemed invisible making his way through the hundreds of jurors entranced *intoxicated* at the job before them, sifting through the evidence as a means in itself.

No one will ever be allowed to know that it was Dewey's neighbor who noticed Joachim's absence first.

"Dewey," the neighbor turned to Dewey during the deliberations, "Where did your father just go?"

"What? Sh! Can't you see I am enjoying this? The jurors—"

"I know. I am sorry. I just was wondering something."

"Well I don't want to hear it right now."

"You may want to know."

"Uch!" Dewey finally turned away from the scene before him. Looking at the stranger, he asks "Whatever could be so important?"

"Joachim."

"What *about* him? Oh, my father!" Dewey's eyes darted around the room, "My father, where is he?" Dewey saw the empty bed. Turning towards the man, Dewey became angry.

"Why didn't you *say* something?"

Dewey got up *hold on* shouting at the jurors *stop stop where is Joachim* but they seemed entranced by the evidence *where is my father* like pirates digging through gold. They did not hear him. He ran to Joachim's thinking room and found a guard standing by the door.

"He is thinking," the guard said, "and he will decide. You must not disturb."

"How can he decide?" Dewey asked, "He has not seen the witness's—"

"He has seen it many times."

"But the precedent—"

"The precedent happened yesterday, and this is today."

"Let me in that door."

"You must not disturb."

"Says who?" Dewey stood to face the guard, but his height comically lined up his red face with the guard's lower chest.

"Says Joachim, ruler of the High Court."

"Haha," Dewey laughed, "That order does not hold force now, for we all know that Joachim died weeks ago."

The guard seemed at a loss for words.

"Yes," the guard tried, "But he just told me—"

"I know what he *told* you," Dewey seemed to get taller, almost whispering in the guard's ear, "But I am the ruler now," the words felt good on Dewey's tongue, "And you will open that door right now if you want to keep those pretty teeth of yours."

Pushing the guard aside, Dewey began to bang on the door, but no sound was heard. After a few moments, he ordered the guard to help break down the door. The guard reluctantly came back with a few men, and they kicked the door open.

"You can go now," Dewey said to the guard and his men. They looked around in confusion at each other before scampering off down the hall.

Dewey entered the room and what he saw terrified him. Joachim was dead *not alive* at his desk. His eyes lay wide open, his thinking lamp broken on the floor beside him, his sensors trembling in the corner of the small dark room.

And this is what happened in the better part of fifty years. If only you had picked up your book sooner.

ΩΨΩ

Autumn has always been a favorite season in Lyceum. The massive trees of the nation boast the most beautiful array of leaves changing color by the minute *oh what a feast for the eyes!* Indeed, if you have never been to Lyceum, and I assume you have not traveled that far, you have not seen anything like this. The leaves in Lyceum change color on the trees every few seconds, such that one leaf may be red for just a few seconds before turning blue, then orange, yellow, and back to red just a moment later. Each and every leaf is like this, creating a dazzling ever-changing rainbow of color across the landscape, a pixilated painting at its best.

The air has grown colder, as is almost appropriate after Joachim's death. Since Dewey, as the oldest son, assumes the role of his father, and the Grandee's role has become more and more irrelevant over the years, Dewey's power of authority over the nation grows.

Indeed, after seeing the breath of life leave his father, Dewey seems to take the position of authority quite naturally. While one may argue that The Grandee ought to be the ruler of Lyceum, the line between the Grandee and other royalty has blurred through the years. The Posteriorians forgot who their real king is long ago. Some time after that, it always seemed to be whatever man from royalty who spoke the loudest and dressed in the most color. Though he never intended it, Joachim won much of this claim by his tall stature, long hair, and confident step. Dewey pushes himself into this role most easily, his golden presence a delight the nation has been waiting for. He gives orders with no problem at all, and no one, even the Grandee, seems to mind. Posteriorians like orders. It frees them from the responsibility of decision, the burden of consequence. It makes life easy, simple enough to leave time to other things.

But at times Dewey feels himself weighed down by responsibility, usually late into the darkest nights. He drowns his sorrows in wine. His love for wine and alcohol will grow with time. As a ruler, he will become dumb and merciful, worse than Joachim ever was. The thrashing whip will become stained with the blood of criminals, a scent so strong that Disegno will be able to smell it from his cell. The palace *the nation* will grow increasingly strong. They will multiply to great numbers, all under the thumb of one fat and jolly Posteriorian *boy* man. Their king.

ΩΨΩ

It is the first of October. Joachim's final funeral begins. Yelekreb enters the great hall. He can see the fog of his own breath leave his mouth. He cradles his throwing disk under his arm and for a moment, his eyes meet that of Helene's. He feels for her, an inferior woman in a land of men. He wonders what thoughts she may have, what passions, what fears, *so much going on inside* and what it is like not being allowed to express them *not allowed to come out.* Yelekreb's eyes continue across the room to settle on Dewey's face. *His face looked so different then,* Yelekreb remembers the day he met Dewey out in the fields of the palace, at the great lawn, *so much older now.* Yelekreb remembers how he liked Dewey instantly *I like you already, prince* as he admired the prince's golden face, and yellow hair, his chubby hands taking control of the discus. As Yelekreb played more in the following years, he realized that measuring distance is done through trial and error such that a blind man would never be able to tell the distance of objects from him, even if he was given sight at a later age.

Through extensive practice and experience with the discus, Yelekreb learned how to measure the exact distance to throw the saucer. He always knew exactly where it would land. Yelekreb's talent always impressed Dewey, and Dewey often went out to play and learn from Yelekreb through the years. As they grew older, the boys *men* formed an unbreakable bond of trust. Yelekreb became Dewey's unofficial advisor, consistently gaining a place in Dewey's heart in the absence of Renee. It is almost appropriate that Dewey met Yelekreb the day Renee left.

Yelekreb is the brother Dewey never had.

Taking a deep breath, Yelekreb's eyes move away from Dewey's face to the chair beside him. This is the chair where Renee used to sit. The chair is empty. *Such a tragedy,* Yelekreb feels surprised at his thoughts *to lose a father and a brother.* Quickly, he walks across the room and sets himself down in the chair next to Dewey *sorry I'm late* just as the funeral procession begins.

Posteriorian funerals are much like trials, and, well, most everything else in Lyceum: a great performance. The sensors of the deceased (who no doubt know his entire life precisely) perform their master's life, looking at their records lying before them like sheet music. They look down at the records intensely, following every word. But a wind blows and some of the documents fly through the air. The sensors try chasing them, but they are too short, and the breeze too strong. As the winds take the records in an upwards spiral, the sensors begin to improvise like little fools dancing down below.

Finally, the show is over. The sensors leave to return to their checkpoint at Lyceum's borders. It is here they will wait to be assigned to a new Posteriorian, whether born from a Lyceumean house or immigrating inwards from the north. Some may wait for hours, others for years. Yet they stand the same, ready to be called into action at any moment in time.

After Joachim's sensors are gone from the funeral, actors, jesters, and witnesses line up one by one, performing, crying, acting out scenes from the deceased's life. A few elders too frail to move tell stories with words, but most know actions speak louder than words. The crowd watches the life of the deceased; his childhood days, the time he fell into the watering hole, the time he got stuck up a tree, the day he made love, the time he became a man, and the day he died.

There is one thing that makes a funeral different from everything else in Lyceum, and that is sadness. See, Posteriorians in their busy lives usually do not have the capacity for sadness. They just don't have the time. With all there is to experience, they spend their lives running from thing to thing, from wine to women, from dream to dream. But not at a funeral. A funeral is their one genuinely sad day, for this is the day that one of their own cannot go on to experience life as they do. This is the day one's senses shut down, and they cannot see, smell, hear, taste or touch. This is the day they may watch actors act with sad smiles on their faces and hot tears down their cheeks. This is the day memories of experiences are recounted, treasured and mourned. This is the last day. The final day. The day of Joachim's deliverance.

"How do you feel?" Yelekreb regrets his words as soon as they leave his lips.

"Mm," Dewey answers, "You ask me the classic Posteriorian question, my friend." Yelekreb can see hot streaks of fresh tears down his friend's face.

"I did, didn't I?" Yelekreb feels relief.

"How do we feel? Always 'feeling,' us Posteriorians." Dewey almost smiles, cocking his head to the side, "I remember the first time I was asked that question and I really understood what it meant. My mother, well, Helene woke me up the morning of the art contest. I was just a little boy. 'How are you feeling?' she asked. Even then, I didn't fully appreciate just how much that question would become the meaning of my life. The meaning of all our lives. And now, here I am today."

"A sad day," Yelekreb says, "for your father was a great man."

"Yes," Dewey's eyes seem to stray somewhere else.

The men watch the actors perform the last performance and take their last bows. Yelekreb stands to clap his hands with crowd's roar of applause. The actors throw down their batons and horns and trinkets, and begin to walk away. Yelekreb sits back down next to Dewey who has not moved, his eyes straight ahead as if in a fog.

"Joachim will truly be remembered a great man," Yelekreb says, "both on the bench and off."

"Yes."

"How he stood for experience, the world of the e, how he undertook the most beloved task a Posteriorian can undertake, to sift through all that evidence, all our past cases, past performances, past experiences, and was able to dig dig dig until his eyes hurt from all the documents, his belly hurt from all the laughter at the performances, all to find that one gem, that one verdict, that carried us to the next trial, so we could do it all over again, and get just a bit closer to the truth."

"Yes."

"How he made his way to that bench for every single trial, even at the end of his life, after his death, at the trial of that evil Disegno. No judge in the history of Lyceum has ever ruled on a trial after his death. But your father did not let death stop him. Oh, how he never relented, never failed to—"

"I warned him."

Yelekreb turns to look at Dewey, "Pardon?"

"I warned him not to go."

Just then, Yelekreb looks at his childhood friend and sees a strange thing happen to his face. Dewey seems distant, his eyes covered in a gold glaze. His face seems to harden itself into the face of a tried man, the face of a king.

Yelekreb feels admiration swell in his heart, but a sudden terror weighs on his stomach. Turning away, he still sees his friend's new face branded into his vision, the face of the ruler Dewey is starting to become.

ΩΨΩ

After the procession, Dewey dons his father's royal garments. The robes seem a bit long at first, dragging on the ground behind him, but Dewey's potbelly keep the robes from dragging too far behind. Through the years, the robes have maintained their bright colors. The sewed-in forms of Gods, animals, angels, moons, and trumpets only seem to bleed into each other over time, reaching for each other's dye.

The funeral crowd begins to dissipate, *well it's getting late,* sensors scrambling to catch up with their departing subjects *we should get going now, let's bundle that coat.* Dewey is sent to the rear of the palace with Yelekreb at his side, so the most prominent citizens may pay their respects with their new ruler in private.

As the hours pass, Dewey manages to maintain a solemn smile at his followers' condolences. The people enter with their heads down in respect, moving in and out quickly, but with a slower pace in their step. Great writers, farmers, artists, and poets come one by one. The best Lyceum has to offer grace their presence. The one Mr. Sufjan Stevens arrives with poetry on his tongue. One person arrives as another one leaves like customers at a fruit stand. Every now and then Dewey's sobs echo loudly through the hall. He wipes the tears from his eyes, bawling like a child. This occurs quite uneventfully, until Dewey looks up to see one of the youngest guards walk up to him. Dewey sees the guard's hands struggle to keep still, his sword already drawn.

"Sir, may I have a word?" the guard says.

"What is it?"

"Well," the guard seems at a loss. He slowly approaches Dewey's side, and speaks softly into his ear.

"How long has he been here?" Dewey replies.

"He arrived just a moment ago, and he's giving us all trouble at the door. He demands to be let in, and we, we've turned him away time and again, but he will not relent. We told him he must wait in line like everyone else, but he refuses. What is it you would have me do? I can turn him away by force—"

"He did not grant you his name?" Dewey looks at Yelekreb, then back at the guard.

"No, he did not…but, well—"

"Out with it, son."

"He…I know it's stupid, but he says he met you when you were just a boy, at, at the art contest. He said that he had to pay his condolences, not for you, but for Joachim."

"What connection would this man have to Joachim? From what would he wish to pay his respects for my father's life?" Dewey says.

The guard remains silent.

"From what connection with Joachim does this man come?" Dewey persists.

"We do not know this man," Yelekreb interjects, looking at Dewey and then at the guard, "Dewey does not need this right now. If this man can not give us his name—"

"From his labor," the guard says, looking down at his feet.

"Excuse me?" Dewey says.

"From his labor," the guard looks up, "The man told me to tell you that he admires your father for his labor, his love, his toil, for the type of Judge he was."

Dewey is surprised at the effect of those words *from his labor* on his mind, bringing back memories of the past *that boy,* recollections, déjà vu youmaysay. Dewey tries to think where he has heard those words before, but he cannot remember, that is, until he hears his own lips speak.

"Jon."

"Well, Le Jocke Rasaa, to be exact," a voice says from the doorway of the room.

Dewey, Yelekreb, and the guard jerk around to look for the voice's source. They see the man himself, Le Jocke Rasaa, casually leaning against the wall. The grin on his mouth almost looks odd, given the small size of his mouth compared with his large nose and eyes. Dewey notices that Jon's hair has turned a bright white, flowing down over his ears. He looks to be about fifty years of age, though his blue eyes retain a warm intelligence and the joy of youth.

"But of course, Jon will do just fine," he says.

The guard lifts his sword immediately, and even Yelekreb seems startled, grasping the arms of his chair.

"Stop!" Dewey says, lifting his hands in the air.

"But sir," the guard stops, "He has no permission—"

"That will be all," Dewey says.

"Dewey?" Yelekreb starts, "You don't need to do this. Not now. You can—"

"No. I can see this man," Dewey says, ignoring Yelekreb. His eyes remain locked on the guard.

"I—I don't know how he got through—" the guard says.

"And you never will," Dewey says, "for this man *that boy* has quite a head on his shoulders."

"But—"

"That will be all," Dewey says.

Without waiting for the guard to leave, Jon walks confidently up to Dewey and kneels before him. Dewey moves his mouth to speak *you may rise* but decides against it. A moment of silence passes as Jon's eyes moisten with tears.

"It has been a very long time," Jon rises to meet Dewey's eyes with his own, "and I regret that such a tragedy has to occur to bring us together again."

Dewey nods his head in assent.

"Well," Jon continues, "You may remember how your father sought me out after I stood up for Olegna Lechim at the art contest. He really took the time and patience to listen to what I had to say. Even as a judge, he was always a…patient man. I felt close to him. I'm sorry for your loss."

"Thank you, Jon."

"It's a shame that this sadness made its way onto your tabula—it's not too rasa anymore, is it?"

"Excuse me?" Dewey asks.

"Oh, it's okay. It happens to the best of us," Jon ignores Dewey's confusion. Silence fills the room. Yelekreb clears his throat quite noticeably.

Dewey looks down, "I…I just don't know how long this will last. This…weight."

Jon puts a hand on Dewey's shoulder. Yelekreb starts to take a step forward, but thinks the better of it. Jon leans in to Dewey and says, "It will lift soon."

"I know, but it is just hard to imagine. I will miss him forever."

"But your sadness will pass soon. It has to."

"How can you be so sure?" Dewey looks up into his friend's eyes.

"Why, sadness is only a secondary quality."

"What do you mean?"

Jon smiles, "Well, what I mean to say is that this sadness is only felt now because of where you are coming from, but you must know that it only exists for so long as you feel it, and soon, you will not feel it anymore. Since sadness is only a secondary quality—"

"What is a secondary quality?"

"Oh," Jon takes a deep breath, "Excuse me. Getting ahead of myself, was I?" Jon's eyes turn for just a moment on Yelekreb, whose patience is visibly waning, and then turns back to Dewey, "I find that all sensible qualities of objects, their color, smell, touch, size, and so on, well, all of these can be distinguished into two types of qualities: primary and secondary. Primary qualities of an object, like its shape or extension, exist in the object *itself*, while secondary qualities, like color, smell, or taste, only exist in the *mind*. Secondary qualities, like your feeling of sadness from your loss, does not exist outside of your mind. Thus, when it fades from your mind, it will not exist anymore."

"But my father is dead!" Dewey's voice rises just a bit, more from curiosity rather than impatience, "Isn't there sadness in *that*? Forget what is in my mind. Isn't there sadness in *death*?"

Jon takes another breath.

"Dewey. Imagine if you would put one of your hands into a bucket of freezing cold water, and the other hand into a bucket of warm water. And then imagine you took both of those hands out of their buckets, and stuck them both into a bucket of water that was room temperature."

"Okay," Dewey says, his interest undisturbed by Yelekreb's growing impatience.

"Now, your hands will tell you different things," Jon explains, "One hand will tell you that the water is hot, and the other will tell you it is very cold, even though both your hands would be in the same bucket!"

"Okay," Dewey nods.

"Well, tell me. What is the water's real temperature?"

"Ha!" Dewey says.

"That's silly," Yelekreb cuts in, "The water's real temperature is still room temperature, just as you said it is."

"Perhaps," Jon says, "But you would not say so if just one of your hands, in our scenario, was in that bucket. I could tell you over and over what you just told me, namely, that the water is room temperature, but you would not believe me. You would assure me with complete confidence that it is freezing cold or very hot. You would insist!"

"True," Dewey says, "but that is only because that hand would be coming from a hot or cold bucket. But if I just stuck my hand in the room temperature bucket from, say, my pocket, or from the usual place it incidentally was—"

"What is usual?" Jon says, "What makes your pocket, or any other place for that matter, any more 'usual' or 'normal,' or *reliable,* than another bucket of water?"

"Hm."

"So I ask you again, if one of my hands tell me the water is hot, and the other tells me it is cold, what is the water really?"

"Hm."

"The answer is that the water is whatever you feel it is at that moment. The water's temperature is in your mind, not in the water. The sadness you feel is in your mind, not in your father's death, no matter how tragic it may have been. Things only exist as you experience them. For these secondary qualities, perception is reality. See, temperature is a secondary quality because it is not in the water—it is in your *mind*. We know it must be in your mind, and not in the water, since your hands are telling you different things. So it must be in your mind, for if it was in the water, your hands would tell you the same thing. Sadness, too, is only in your mind, Dewey. It is not inherent in the loss of a father. It just feels that way because you are coming from a warmer bucket of water. I tell you this to comfort you. You will be better soon."

"But isn't sadness inherent in *any* loss?"

"Not at all. Indeed if one hates their father, they may not be so sad at his loss. Rather, your sadness is only in your *mind*—the only place it could exist.

"But it gets better. Listen to this. If you did not experience these things in your mind, they would never exist at all. So you are, in essence, a creator. A creator of feeling.

Of art. By experiencing, we are actually *creating* things, such as the temperature of water, or the sadness of a funeral, things that would not exist if we did not experience them, if we did not allow them to form in our mind. And that is why the Posteriorian lifestyle and El Totsira's teachings are so beautiful."

Jon takes his hand off Dewey's shoulder and stands up straight before him. "So Dewey," he says, "While you sit here mourning the loss of your father, as you well should, you must know that you are also acting as a creator—like Rekha—creating a quality in your mind—sadness—to exist in the only place it can."

The men allow a moment to pass.

"May I interject?" Yelekreb asks Dewey.

Dewey nods in assent.

Yelekreb turns towards Jon, "You call yourself a Posteriorian," he challenges, "Yet you only explain the beauty of experiencing *one* type of sensation, the secondary sensations. You explain primary qualities to lie in the objects *outside* of our minds. Since they exist outside of our minds, according to you, what good is it to experience them? You seem to call them worthless! But are we not creating them too?"

"You seem to be Dewey's advisor. Yet you fail to realize that I am comforting him in his time of mourning. When it comes to sadness, Dewey is acting as a creator—the greatest of all things! I am speaking about sadness, a secondary quality, because that is what our prince—"

"King," Yelekreb says.

"That is what our…King feels right now. Have you no decency—"

"I have the decency to know what Dewey stands for, and to know that he will advance El Totsira's teachings of the need for experience beyond your silly…secondary sensations.

"You say, Mr. Ra—Jon, that Dewey acts as a creator since he is experiencing a secondary quality—sadness. But what about primary qualities? Would you limit the beauty of the Posteriorian experience to only one type of quality? As a 'true' Posteriorian who understands what experience is all about, I would not impose such limitations. Rather, I would go so far as to say that the same is true even for what you call 'primary qualities.'"

"You can do as you like if you explain yourself, Yelekreb."

"Well, you claim temperature to be a secondary quality, to be *in the mind,* because in your example, the hands tell you two different things."

"Indeed."

"But you claim shape, size and extension to be a primary quality, to be in the object itself."

"I do."

"Well, what if one person, or one eye of a person, spends many years in a land of midgets...say...people no bigger than the smallest Lyceumean sensor, a land where ropes, tools, foods, and buildings were tiny for the people using them. And what if another person, or the other eye of a person, spends those years in the land of giants. Now if both those persons focus upon the same 'regular' sized object, would they not say two different things about the size of the object? And if they would, then size also, must be in your mind.

"See, I understand distance," Yelekreb explains, "During the many years of throwing discus, I have discovered that a flying object gets bigger and bigger as it comes towards me, and smaller and smaller as it drifts away. I have experienced the workings of distance, and these I have mastered. I know the exact distance of a discus just by its size. I know the exact distance of a target just by its size. Depending on where you are in relation to it, its size changes. So, I ask you as you asked me about the water: What is the object's true size? It is what you experience it to be. It too is in your mind."

"No," Jon says, "One can say the object's true size to be when it is in your hands, and you examine it closely—"

"Just how closely? Three inches from your eyes? Four? Five?"

"Well, perhaps just from a regular place—"

"Regular? Oh, you mean like 'room temperature' in your water example? There *is* no 'regular,' no 'usual,' no 'room temperature.' You said this yourself.

"See, all things exist only as a result of being perceived. Thus, we create sensations in our mind as we experience them, for they would not exist otherwise. Size, shape, color, and smell, would not exist if we did not experience them, then by experiencing, we are, in essence, creating. By living to experience each day, the Posteriorian nation is a nation of creators."

Though Dewey hears Yelekreb's challenges, his eyes remain on Jon the entire time.

"Indeed," Dewey says, "There is *no* quality except as we experience it ourselves. Everything only exists with the characteristics we experience them. Let any man try to conceive a triangle in general, which is neither Isosceles nor Scalenum, nor has any particular length or proportion of sides; and he will soon perceive the absurdity of all the scholastic notions with regard to abstraction and general ideas."

"Well, well," Jon says, grasping Dewey's hands in his own, "I did not want to let anything get carried away. You should, and will, be comforted. That is all."

Yelekreb opens his mouth to say something, but he looks at the comfort in Dewey's eyes and decides against it.

"I pay my condolences," Jon says to Dewey, releasing his hands, "Your loss will be felt all over the world. And now I will go."

Jon turns around and walks towards the door. Guards that were eavesdropping scuttle away. Dewey looks at the floor before him. His eyes still carry the same sadness, but his face is changed. Before Jon can leave the room, Dewey speaks.

"Wait."

Jon stops.

"Wait," Dewey says, "It has been so long. I would like you to stay."

Jon turns around, taking two steps toward Dewey.

"My King—" Yelekreb puts a hand on Dewey's shoulder.

"No," Dewey ignores his hand, "Let me be."

"Well," Jon smiles, "It has been a long time, hasn't it? But in this time, I have gained many responsibilities beyond my old life in the fields. I have many things to attend to. I cannot stay."

"Oh, but you must, just for a bit! Here, have some coffee with me. Yelekreb, get the guard to fetch coffee, there must be some…"

"We have drunk all the coffee, my lord," Yelekreb says.

"Can we get some wine?"

"We have drunk all the wine, my lord."

"Then we will get more."

"If I stay for a few moments, Dewey," Jon says, "I fear that those moments will turn to hours, those hours to days, to months, to years."

"And what would be the harm in that?" Dewey smiles, "I could use a mind like yours around."

Yelekreb turns away, hiding the surprise on his face.

"Well, you have already drunk all the coffee and wine," Jon smiles, "but perhaps I can wait until you can get a little more."

"It would take no time at all to get some more," Dewey smiles, "Perhaps just a few months…or a few years. But you can stay at my side in the meantime. Do you think that is a good idea?"

"No," Jon says, "I think it is a great one."

Jon walks up to his childhood acquaintance, his brother, his king. He nods, smiles, and bows down at Dewey's feet.

2

Thinking men cannot be ruled.
Ayn Rand

"Dinner is almost ready! Come inside, would you?"

Zinbiel hears his elderly mother's call, but he does not respond. He stands in the yard in front of his newly-acquired parcel of land. He watches how the sunset is able to turn the sky a soft pink even in this cold December month. He had to walk outside his home to see the sunset because the wax ceiling of his new home distorts any light coming inside, and the dirt walls have no windows. Indeed, no windows are allowed anywhere in the Republic of Kallipolis.

Zinbiel moved to Kallipolis with his mother Catherina just one week ago. Ever since father Friedrich died when Zinbiel was only six, he and Catherina moved around sporadically, often living off the wilderness for months at time. Throughout the past thirty years, they had lived everywhere, in every kind of place, from the biggest cities, to the sparsest camps just north of Lake Ohrid. Indeed, by the time the blind man came into their dreams, Zinbiel and Catherina had seen it all.

But there was something about Kallipolis they had never seen before—not in any place they'd ever been. Something that calmed them: a lack of frivolous atmospherics, a lack of superficialities. Even more than out in the stark wilderness, there seemed to be more of a reason for everything here. While the architecture of trees, stones, and rivers had enjoyed a mysterious rhythm of reason, it had been shrouded under a haze of trickling chaos. But here in this republic, there is a cold and logical structure to everything, an immovable principle under each object. In

Kallipolis, Zinbiel sees a reason for every road, boulder, service, and structure, and a certain sureness in the disposition of every Prioritan that lives within its borders.

Just as the blind man had promised him.

"Dinner!" he hears his mother from inside the house, "Come inside."

Hmm Zinbiel closes his eyes in pleasure and takes in the scent of the winter dusk, the new land he is excited to settle in, the scent of his mother's stew cooking inside. He opens his eyes to look at the sunset again, *but wait—*

He hears three children running down the street. Zinbiel quickly lowers his eyes in fear. *Did they see me?* Feeling a panic rise in his stomach, he fidgets with his hands, looking for another reason to be outside. He hopes he was not seen taking in the sunset. *Yes,* he remembers, *this has been an adjustment, learning the customs of the Prioritans. What he is permitted to take in, and what is prohibited.*

And what can happen if you do not obey.

In Kallipolis, there is no money, gold, silver, or any other sort of wealth that may detract from the Prioritans' patriotism to the land. Color is not allowed, so the people wear shades of brown, gray, white, black, and only the darkest maroon. They live mostly on potatoes, water, and bread. Alcohol is forbidden, and spices are too. Everything is built simply here, from dirt, earth, or wax, which is the staple of the nation. Art is not allowed, especially poetry. The written language is strictly prohibited, since Prioritans believe that dialogue is the proper way to learn (though there are some written records in dialogue form). Thus, there is no written law, or any law for that matter. Law is considered useless in this land, where the philosopher kings who rule can decide matters of behavior themselves with their exclusive knowledge of Good. (When He explained it to me, I believe O'Talp's words were: *no law or ordinance is mightier than understanding*). There would be little use for visual art or written language anyway, since the most pious of the Prioritans (numbering around one or two for every ten) gouge their eyes or ears out in their mid-teenage years, so their minds are no longer distracted from confusing, and often alluring, sensory experience.

Suddenly, Zinbiel hears cries from the dirt home of his new neighbor. He has not met him yet, since, like most Prioritans, he has not left his home for the past six weeks. Besides, he dwells hundreds of feet away—not far for this spread-out land. But Zinbiel has heard these cries before. Catherina told him that just before she and Zinbiel moved to Kallipolis, the Prioritan rulers had killed the neighbor's infant child. This was his punishment for having sex outside of the allotted time.

Sex is generally prohibited in Kallipolis. However, heterosexual sex is tolerated for the procreation of the species, but only for certain months of the calendar year set aside for this purpose. It is only during these periods that the Prioritans group together, each seizing a spouse to cohabitate with and have children of the land. One's sexual partner becomes their spouse for the duration of the sexual act such that one Prioritan may have three or four spouses in one night. Months later, children begin to crawl out of the ground close to where the respective cohabitation took place. This type of birth began to occur a few years after the first Prioritans settled in the land. This was the work of their God, O'Talp. This birth ensures the Prioritans' strong patriotism to the land, their only mother. Once born, the children are quickly seized and reared together collectively as brothers and sisters, children of the land, just like the Prioritan men and women who conceived them.

Zinbiel tries to shut out the cry of his neighbor. He rubs the fresh scar on the back of his left hand. Catherina told him that the Prioritans branded the hand of each outsider who wished to dwell in Kallipolis, but the blind man had told him it would be okay. Zinbiel traces the dark "P" branded into his hand with the fingers of his other hand. The wound is still fresh, but the cold dawn eases the pain. It is getting better.

Just as the blind man had promised.

In his dreams, the blind man had promised Zinbiel many things. It was almost funny to call him the blind man, since blindness is quite common here. But the blind man was special in other ways. He gave Zinbiel much hope, telling of a better place, a place of justice, a place where

Zinbiel can become a great man. Zinbiel looks at his parcel of land in the back of his home. He smiles thinking of the children that will come out of that earth. He wonders what type of metal the blind man will find in their soul. He hopes it will be gold or at least silver, but he knows they will probably have the bronze or iron that the blind man found in Zinbiel's soul before ordering his hand to be stamped with a "P."

Zinbiel knows he will never be able to see his own children grow separately from the rest of Kallipolis's children. But he smiles at the thought of the superior education they will receive in mathematics. The Prioritans excel at mathematics. The Prioritans hold this discipline of such high importance that they would even permit the writing of numbers for limited purposes. Well, that was, until one Phaedrus got caught for writing language through a code that used numbers in the place of letters. He was swiftly executed, and the writing of numbers has been strictly supervised in Kallipolis ever since.

Despite the continuous cries of his neighbor, Zinbiel's thoughts give him great comfort. He smiles again.

"Son," Catherina sticks her head out of the small wooden doorway, "I know you hear me. Dinner is ready. Just because you're a grown man now doesn't mean you don't need your dinner. And it's freezing outside. Now, are you coming in or not?"

"Yes," Zinbiel takes in his last breath of the cold night air, "I am coming. Right now."

ΩΨΩ

Closing the dark wooden door behind him, Zinbiel trips over the small bags on the floor.

"Whoa," Catherina says, "Watch your step, son. With the few small belongings lying around this empty house, only you would trip over them."

The house is nearly empty. Catherina and Zinbiel threw most of their belongings away before entering Kallipolis. In this land, they would not need much, they were instructed. In fact, more belongings would only act as distractions in their life here. Less was better, so less was brought. The blind man had told them so.

Zinbiel sits across the small round oak table from his mother, two dark forms *man and woman* sitting with a candle behind them, throwing shadows on the cavernous dirt walls curving above their heads. Zinbiel seems to tower over his mother. He looks down at his body. Putting one hand on his belly, he can already notice that he has started to thin; he has begun to look more like a Prioritan. He looks at Catherina and notices the lack of color in her skin. For the first time, Zinbiel realizes that whether they liked it or not, he and his mother have already become a member of these thin, pale people of the mind.

Zinbiel can tell that Catherina is cold even under her sweater, her small hands warming themselves by curving around both sides of her clay bowl like a squirrel holding an acorn. Catherina looks down at the barley, potatoes, and turnips swimming in her bowl and closes her eyes to let the warm steam kiss her face. Opening her eyes, she sees her son before her. Zinbiel eats slowly, rubbing his nose with his wrist every few moments. Catherina smiles, remembering how even as a boy, hot stew would make Zinbiel's nose run.

"How is it?" she asks.

"It tastes okay," Zinbiel offers, "With just a little salt—"

"Zinbiel," Catherina scolds, "You know—"

"I know, I know."

The stew *does* taste okay, but Zinbiel can already feel the weight of dullness from a week of Prioritan food on his palate. After just a week of water, grains, potatoes, and turnips, Zinbiel waits impatiently for his taste buds to adjust. He fears that he will miss the zing of spices, of wines, of *color* for longer than he would like. *Ah, to have a fresh apple, just one more time. A juicy orange*, he quickly pushes such thoughts out of his head. *This won't be so bad, the blind man even promised.* The stew still tastes okay to him, but that may be because Catherina snuck some brown tomatoes in there *while we're still getting used to this place,* and one small beet. Just this one time.

"So," Catherina picks up her spoon, "Did you hear what happened in the news last week?"

"Mmm."

"Zinbiel?"

Zinbiel quickly eats the last bite of his soup, lifting the bowl to his mouth to get the last drop.

"Yes," Zinbiel puts his bowl back on the table, a bit of brown water dribbling on his chin, "They found another one?"

"They did indeed," Catherina says, "Another poet, banished, exiled, kicked out of the land."

"So? They find these poets quite often now," Zinbiel says, "What do you make of it?"

Catherina finishes chewing. "Well, I know what the blind man told you. I know what our God, O'Talp, commands what we do to poets. But sometimes I wonder. I wonder why we must be so cruel, so strict, so—"

"If you really understand what O'Talp commands, you would not ask such questions, mother."

"Okay, well tell me then, if you know so well."

"Poets must be banished because they are bad for our soul. The entire atmosphere of Kallipolis is meant for its citizens to be able to concentrate their mind on obtaining clear truths, on seeing what is real, on seeing beyond what the...lovers of sights and sounds see, and to see real truths. But poets distract us. They take us away from these truths."

"But doesn't every artist, every 'lover of sights and sounds' do this as well?"

"Not like a poet," Zinbiel says, "Only a poet spits out the most artificial things—things easily excitable, such as colorful unicorns and…experimental emotions no one has ever felt before. Through their poetry, poets make us overwhelmed with tears for no reason at all. They make us laugh at base things, or lust after hallucinations. This is not rational. More than a painter, a musician, or a dancer, a poet frivolously delves into the metaphysical, goading us into feeling these emotions vicariously. This is not rational. This is not for us; it is everything we, as Prioritans, are trying to avoid. This is because we know that knowledge is obtained *prior* to experiencing such colorful, baseless, atmospherics. Never *post.*

"It is for this reason that O'Talp commands us to banish poets from the land. While he regrets having to do this, O'Talp commands us not to hesitate; we must send them out with the clothes on their backs, for the slightest hesitation may allow the poet to seduce a Prioritan or two away from their mission. If we let the poet say just one word, he has already won."

"I understand all that," Catherina says, "but it's just a shame that we are put into a position that we have to do that. That we have to inflict such suffering."

"Suffering? No, mother. The poet never suffers. He is alive in his dreams of poetic verbiage; it does not matter where he is."

"Still. We are put in a position to exile men into the wilderness, where they can surely be killed. Or worse."

"We are not in that position ourselves; the poet puts us there."

"Well, one can say, perhaps, that O'Talp put it there, by commanding such cruelty. I mean, if O'Talp our God, is omnibenevolent, omnipotent, and...perfectly good, how would we account for such suffering? I mean, what type of world do we live in where men can do such cruel acts to other men? Where such acts are...needed? Even if it is justified, there is so much suffering here. What type of world is this?"

"The best possible world."

"The...what?"

"The best possible world."

"The best—"

"The best world of all possible worlds. Yes." Zinbiel says, "See, I thought about this when we arrived here. I believe that O'Talp, in his perfection, must have been able to see all the different ways this world could be. He saw some men as kings, some as fishmongers, some as rich and some as poor. The world could have been set up in many different ways. This, I think, is obvious. And if our God O'Talp is perfect, as I believe He is, then He must have been able to see all of these possibilities. And since He is all good, he must have picked the best one. The best possible world."

"Well," Catherina scoops up a large turnip, "those other worlds must have been pretty crappy."

"That may sound funny," Zinbiel says, "but you must realize that this world may not be so bad at all. Perhaps what we see as evil is really good. See, evil challenges us, and often brings out the best of us. Say, do you think we ever would have moved here, if we hadn't suffered and lost our way in the wilderness?"

"Well, aren't you the optimist."

"Maybe so," Zinbiel smiles, "But yesterday, we would have called that suffering unjust. And that wilderness, evil."

Catherina eats her stew, so Zinbiel continues. "Evil brings courage. And the evil and suffering that we have gone through these past years have given us the courage to live the way we are now, to accept such high goals of mental health and concentration."

"Uh, huh," Catherina slurps the last remains of her soup, "Would you like some more?"

"What?"

"Some more soup. Would you like—"

"No," Zinbiel says. He pushes the table away, stands up slowly, and blows the candle out so that the only light in the room is the soft glow of the sunset spreading itself across the wax ceiling like a great fog. "We must go to sleep now."

"Are you going to the prayer service at the House of Wax tomorrow morning?" Catherina asks.

"I wouldn't miss it...for the best possible world."

ΩΨΩ

Like the other Prioritans, Catherina and Zinbiel already began to rise hours before each dawn just days after moving to Kallipolis. The nights have become too beautiful to miss. A thick blanket of darkness hangs in the wet air, a black velvet sheet of space in which one's mind can slowly walk, explore, and meditate. The night is a break from the rare chirping of birds still left in Kallipolis, a break from the sound of crunching leaves, of a passing horse, of a baby's cry. At night, all is silent. And silence allows one to think.

Now, you may ask what makes the night so special if Kallipolis is quiet most all the time. Yes, even the days are quiet here. The dawn is always greeted by a bleak gray sky, a great expanse of beckoning black clouds often pouring their rain against the desolate earth before the day's break. On the cloudiest days, the sky resembles a large herd of great bears, their fluffy gray bellies soaring across the dreary plane in slow motion as their fat legs extend, trying to push them along. On other days, the sky is one great bear, her great lonely body smothering any sound of morning, creating a horrible silence lasting throughout the day. But, dear reader, you must realize that it is only in such silence that noise can be so well heard.

Zinbiel noticed the changed right away. At first, Kallipolis seemed anxiously still. A great vacancy, he first called it, a great lack of color, of noise, of smells, of tastes. But it was only after a few hours that Zinbiel began to listen. And just as the blind man had promised, Zinbiel began to hear.

The crunch of leaves under the men's feet began to sound so sweet, the taste of cool moisture in the air like honey in his mouth. Such mild sensations were never appreciated in any other land because they were drowned out by frivolous song and clamor like a piece of fish drenched in heavy sauces and spice. In Kallipolis, each and every sensation was isolated and appreciated. But even these were distractions from the mind. The night *oh the night* was a break from all of this.

So early early early Prioritans rise each morning, to think, to meditate, to just *be* in the privacy of their mud homes, before the small sounds of nature would tap softly on their doors.

But this very night, Catherina awakens Zinbiel even earlier than usual. This has never happened before; Zinbiel is always the first to rise.

"Zinbiel! *Zinbiel!*" Catherina cries, running into his room. Zinbiel opens his eyes to look at his mother. Even in the dark, he can see the blood is gone from her face.

"What—what is it?" Zinbiel says.

"There—there's something outside. Come quick!"

"Now, just a minute," Zinbiel wipes his eyes, "It is in the middle of the night. Close the door. The cold air is getting in—"

"Zinbiel! Get—" Catherina bends over, coughing with her hand on her throat.

"It's *freezing*." Zinbiel says.

"Get out here *now!*"

Zinbiel jumps out of bed, and runs to his closet. He grabs one of his robes, a light gray one, and follows his mother towards the front of the house.

"There's something," Catherina says without turning back, "something outside, something you should see."

"What is it?" Zinbiel asks. He winces, trying to ignore the cold creeping up his bare legs as he walks across the dirt and wooden floor.

"We've got another growth," Catherina says, slowing down, "On the front patio of our house. I don't know when it came, where it came from…"

"What?! Where?" Zinbiel passes his mother. He throws open the house door and runs into the night.

"No," he hears Catherina behind him, "It is over there, by the side. Look!"

Zinbiel turns around and sees Catherina pointing to the side corner of the home. His eyes follow her finger, and then suddenly, he sees it. He freezes in horror.

It is a small orange flower, growing out between two rocks.

"You didn't tell me it was orange," Zinbiel says, his eyes locked onto the colorful sapling.

"I, I tried, I don't know. Well, does it matter what color it is?" Catherina is frantic, "No color must grow here. We must get rid of it immediately! Before anyone sees it. We, we must…" Catherina's words continue, but Zinbiel does not hear. Rather, he stares at the young flower, remembering days of past. He remembers the red flowers bordering the coast of Lake Ohrid, the soft breeze gently caressing their petals into a soft dance. He closes his eyes and tries to smell the flower *just one sniff* from where he stands *just one last time* he takes a step forward *just one*—

"Zinbiel!" Catherina's voice cuts through his thoughts like a knife.

Zinbiel opens his eyes and takes a deep breath. Thoughts of the blind man come into his head.

"Alright," he says, "Did anyone see this plant? Did anyone see this on our land?"

"I—I don't think so," Catherina says. She tries not to cry, "But I…I can't be sure. I just noticed in for the first time. I woke up early to clear my head. I went outside to meditate—"

"Get me the shovel."

"What?"

"Get me the shovel," Zinbiel says, "We must bury it deep in the ground before it gets light out. And tell no one of this, *no one*, you hear me? We must bury it deep, and we must bury it now."

And bury it they did. Catherina and Zinbiel *mother and son* stand in the dark with their shovels in hand, panting out the cold air from their exhausted lungs.

"I'm sorry. I should not cry," Catherina says.

"It will be okay. It will be okay now. You did the right thing by telling me."

Catherine takes a deep breath and nods. "You should come in for some breakfast," she says.

"You know we don't eat before prayer," Zinbiel says "And you know Prioritans don't ever eat breakfast at all. At least before meditating they don't."

"But you just shoveled, and you need—"

"I said," Zinbiel feels his voice rise, and struggles to lower it, whispering fiercely, "I will have none of it. If I am too complacent during prayer, I will not be able to concentrate. I must be empty. I must be pure."

Without a word, Catherina throws down her shovel and makes her way back into the house. Zinbiel hears the door slam behind her. He walks towards the spot where they finished burying the flower just minutes ago. He rubs his foot into the spot to pack the dirt like it a blemish he wants to wash away. Looking at the stain, he sits on the ground nearby. He closes his eyes and slips deep into thought, a lone figure in gray, waiting for the dawn to come.

3

Your vision will become clear only when you look into your heart. Who looks outside, dreams. Who looks inside, awakens.
Carl Jung

"How are you thinking?"

While the dawn's dark sky makes it hard to see the man's face, Zinbiel can hear his voice quite clearly. Zinbiel smiles at his question, recognizing it as the archetype question of the Prioritans. He remembers the first time he heard the question. In fact, it was the first time he heard any words in Kallipolis. Upon entering the land, Zinbiel was greeted by nobody. The few Prioritans that he saw even seemed to shrink away; he had not known they were only giving him space. However, after a few days of silence, Zinbiel heard one Prioritan say to another, "How are you thinking?" The man answered by nodding his head in assent. Then the two men nodded their heads and parted ways.

Zinbiel sees the man's bare feet are stained and callused by years of exposure to the earth. The land here is unlike any other place. It is dry and dead, seeping up into men's feet, caking them with calluses of white. Looking up, Zinbiel sees the man's loose white pants beneath the dark robes hanging over his legs. Zinbiel sees the man's thin arms, his bold brown beard, his face—the man's face is hidden; it is covered by a thin gray cloth. It is thin enough to see through so he can find his way, but thick enough to shut out extra light and sights of birds, trees, and other distractions. Zinbiel has occasionally seen this type of covering before in Kallipolis, but it still comes as a surprise.

Zinbiel didn't think he would run into anyone on his way to pray at The House of Wax. Indeed, spoken words are rare in Kallipolis; nothing is said without good reason. The streets seemed like a ghost town as Zinbiel left his home this morning. Brushing the dirt from his robes, Zinbiel had to put his brown shoes on, since his feet were not yet used to the cold earth. He liked the shape of the footprints they made behind him. He would look back every few steps to see if they were still there, and wondered if his future footprints would look the same way.

The walk is long because Zinbiel's hut is not close to much of anything. Everything here is few and far apart. Though the Kallipolis nation is nearly fifty years old and hundreds of men and women have come to settle here (no doubt most of them by way of the blind man's guidance), only twelve homes have actually been completed.

But they are perfect. Made from heavy stone and hardy earth, these twelve small structures were designed and built over the course of these fifty years. They stand small and humble, but contain everything one might ever need. The walls have air shafts running through them, chutes and mirrors set in such a way that light may enter the home, but one cannot see outside. These ducts may be closed by inserting a panel of dry earth into the interior wall, which completes the interior wall that surrounds the inside with a thick wet mud. This interior wall of thick mud keeps the Prioritan inhabitants cool in the summer and warm in the winter, while stifling any disturbing sounds from the outside.

Each home has a small stone fireplace that cooks food most efficiently. The stone walls of the fireplace are shaped in such a way that the food is cooked from all sides at once, heating quickly and retaining heat in the best way possible.

While to your eyes, dear reader, these homes may look like a group of monotonous *nothingatalls*, these tiny dwellings were built by Prioritans, the greatest mathematicians their world has ever seen. These homes, mathematically, can never fall. They are built to stand through earthquakes, hurricanes, and other, you may say, actsofGod. They will stand, unchanging, for hundreds, if not thousands, of years.

Zinbiel feels lucky that at least his home is in the process of being built, and he has more to look forward to than the temporary wax hut that most all the other Prioritans are forced to live in. However, the construction of his small home began just fifteen years ago, so its bare foundations are just coming together now. Zinbiel used to wonder why the blind man gave him a house, but soon his anticipation dissolved his questions.

As he left to pray at the House of Wax, Zinbiel was happy to have some time alone. His eyes relaxed looking between the empty ground and empty sky *gray on gray* before him. Moving forward, he felt like a small lone figure sliding between two great sheets *earth and sky* moving forward into *ah this immense* nothing.

But as his path neared the southern border of Kallipolis, he saw mounds of dirt piled high upon the land. Yes, he remembered, a group of angry Posteriorians came from Lyceum a few days ago to rally against the Prioritans' exile of a poet. The 'lovers of sights and sounds' (as they were called here) were stopped at the borders, where they chanted melodies, throwing their color-painted stones, rainbow cupcakes, and fresh smelling flowers into Kallipolis. Luckily, the Prioritan warriors killed and injured many of the invaders before they fled. Before the gray soil became stained with the protestors' red blood, the Prioritans covered the stains with piles of dirt.

This was not the first time such a protest occurred. Under their short-tempered ruler Dewey Hume, the Posteriorians hate the Prioritans' way of life, and the way they treat their citizens. So occasionally, a mob of Posteriorians travels north (with or without their ruler's consent) to throw colored stones and flowers into Kallipolis, holding their big signs displaying blotches of colored paint.

But this hasn't happened often, for each time the Posteriorians try to invade, they lose most of their men to the Axios River. The Posteriorians come with their big bellies, color-dyed hair, and rainbow armor. They bring many men and many boats because they know that most of their boats will drown crossing the Axios. The Axios is not a violent river, but the Posteriorians' beautiful boats are far too adorned and heavy to make it across.

Upon arriving in Kallipolis, the Prioritans began plans to build a three-mile bridge across the Axios. They began to plan *the wonder of the world!*, and the world laughed *it can never work.* The Posteriorians laughed the loudest, claiming that no bridge could ever stand, but the Prioritans silently continued their work. But when a Posteriorian invasion failed and the bodies of fifty Posteriorian invaders were found floating in the Axios, the Prioritans withdrew their plans for the bridge. And the Posteriorians secretly wished they hadn't.

They weren't laughing anymore.

Leaving the mounds of dirt behind him, Zinbiel gets closer to the House of Wax. Drifting forward in between two sheets of gray *earth and sky* he begins to see others with him, coming to pray. He first sees a black dot in the distance, then another gray dot moving at his left, and a few moving on his right. The hooded people are all walking slowly with their heads down, their tall, skinny bodies drifting through the snow like trees bending in concert to the breeze. Many of them, Zinbiel sees, make their way with walking sticks; some to aid their balance, and others to act as their eyes. It takes Zinbiel a while to notice these fellow ghosts, but as he gets closer, he sees hundreds of them huddling in the shadow of the great House of Wax.

Zinbiel looks to his right. A child walking with his father trips over a stone and falls on his palms. He brings his hands up to look and sees small droplets of red blood coming from his right thumb.

"Ow!" Zinbiel hears the boy cry, "It is cut—"

"Do not look upon it!" his father smacks him across the face. Hard.

"But—"

"Do not look upon it! It is colored. It is colored!"

The boy instinctively looks at it again, inviting another blow from his father *you must not see the red*, drawing yet more blood, inviting another look, followed by another blow *mustnotseethered*, and so on. Zinbiel looks away.

"How are you thinking?" the man asks him again. But Zinbiel's gaze is taken by a most peculiar sight. He sees a few enormous balls scattered in the distance. Some roll towards him slowly across the field, while others sit still. Some of them must be at least ten feet tall. Squinting, he can see a person inside each of them, some walking slowly inside of their own bubble, others sitting cross-legged, the mellow sunlight shimmering off the bubbles' tops.

"That is a new contraption some Prioritans are using," the man sees Zinbiel's gaze, "It helps protect them from the outside world, shutting it out. I have heard they work rather well."

Zinbiel looks back at the path before him. Though he is now still a few hundred feet away, he sees many of his brothers and sisters, children of the land. He sees producers, warriors, and guardians only, for the rulers, he supposes, are already inside. He quickens his step, eager to get closer, but the man steps before him. And the man asks this one question. This one, Prioritan question.

"How are you thinking?"

"Just fine," Zinbiel says, "And how are you thinking today, sir?"

"Benedictus."

"What's that?" Zinbiel asks.

"My name is Benedictus Azonips," the man says.

"Ah. How are you thinking, Benedictus?" Zinbiel tries not to smile. He remembers he is in Kallipolis, where smiling is not permitted without reason.

"I am thinking well, thank you. You can call me Ben." Benedictus extends his hand to Zinbiel and Zinbiel can see the dark "W" burnt into it.

"Ah, I see you are a warrior," Zinbiel says.

"Oh," Ben looks at his hand, "Yes," they branded me with the "W" when I came here to Kallipolis," Ben looks at the scar on Zinbiel's hand, "and I see you are a producer."

"Yes. I guess I just did not have the gold in my soul that you do."

"Hm. I guess the blind man will see what he sees, hm? I was surprised, too, since I was always a lens crafter by trade, one of the finest indeed, so I thought only iron would be in my blood. I was sure the blind man would see iron in my blood, so he would brand me a producer, but no. He saw gold, and branded me a warrior. So here I am."

Zinbiel can see Ben's eyes behind the cloth. They look neither blue nor gray, but like a stormy sea in the deepest night.

"Well, maybe if things were different—"

"Oh, things are not so different. I may no longer be a lens crafter, but I still help people see things differently," Ben puts his head down, "Just…in a different way."

"Perhaps. But still. You could have been a producer. If things could have happened differently—"

"Nonsense," Ben says, "Things are always the way they should be, and this is all predetermined. It could have happened no other way. I am a warrior. You are a producer. This was in our blood before we were born."

"So, are we not free to change our future?"

"No."

"Have we no free will?"

"We are free," Ben says, "to accept our fate or not."

Zinbiel looks down.

Three teenagers walk in front of them. Zinbiel can see one of the teenagers is a girl, and one of the boys begins to stand right next to her. Ben calls out to them.

"My brothers," he says "I trust you are thinking well today. But I see you have been walking together for some time."

Instantly, they seem to separate. They look down.

Ben says, "Watch your proximity, you two," looking at the girl and boy.

They nod and turn, continuing their walk a few paces apart. Ben turns back to Zinbiel.

"Yes, young man," Ben says, "Your children will probably be producers, too. It is in their blood. But this is a good thing because it can be no other way. This is the only way, the—"

"The best possible world."

"Yes," Ben's smile transforms his whole face from that of a stranger to that of a friend, "The best possible world. I like that. An optimist, you are."

"A producer-optimist, I guess you can say."

"Well," Ben asks, "What do you produce? Are you a…farmer? A…"

"I have always been a mathematician. But I moved here just one week ago…so I have not been given a job yet. But since the blind man only saw bronze in my blood, he branded me to be a producer."

"You have no position yet. How have you been passing the time?"

"I have been preparing my mind for the type of clear thought I hope to engage in here in this land. I would never 'pass the time' because with every lost hour, a part of life perishes."

"What is it that you mean?" asks Ben.

"Man is not happy, not alive, unless his mind is exercised. Deep, undisturbed thoughts are the way to a healthy and happy mind. I maintain that men could be incomparably happier than they are, and that they could, in a short time, make great progress in increasing their happiness, if they are willing to set about it as they should."

"Very good. And you are new here."

"I am."

"Ah," Ben looks past Zinbiel, "So the blind man must still be fresh in your mind. It was long ago, but I still remember him from my dreams before I came here. I would dream of a harsh wilderness surrounding me, confusing trees taunting me with their colors, smells, their long arms pushing me this way and that. And then, I would finally manage to break free of their grasp. I would land in a great field of white. It felt so clean and...pure, but I was all alone. And then I would look up and see a small cave, a stone enclosure in the distance. It looked like it had just been built. It was perfect. Impenetrable. And he was there, standing on the roof. Stone powder was on his hands, as if he had just built it himself. He let a sledgehammer fall from his hands and smiled at me. Then he jumped to the ground, and trotted away. He showed me the way, this blind man. Even though he couldn't see, he knew exactly where to go. I think maybe it was *the reason* he knew...as if—" Ben looks up, "as if—"

Zinbiel follows the man's gaze and sees a tall woman dressed in all white, her straight dark hair covering her face. She does not look in the men's direction, but she is close enough to hear their words. Ben stops speaking immediately and puts his face down in shame.

"What is wrong?" Zinbiel asks.

"I just do not want to disturb her. I do not want to bother anybody. We have spoken long enough. We should part ways now."

Zinbiel sees that the woman is a producer just like him; a large "P" is burnt into her hand. He sees that her ears have been mutilated; brown stains of altered flesh and blood now lie where her ears once were. She must have severed her ears at a young age, like the most religious Prioritans do. But she still has eyes, Zinbiel notices, as little as she wishes to use them.

"But she cannot hear us," Zinbiel says.

Benedictus ignores Zinbiel and resumes his ghostly walk to prayer, his face down in a most humble fashion, as if concentrating on landing one foot directly in front of the other.

"Sir," Zinbiel says. Ben stops, but Zinbiel could hear Ben's voice mutter to himself.

Ben says, "You should know what they think of talking."

Zinbiel knows that Prioritans frowned against idle chatter. They choose their words carefully and sparingly. They are simple and direct and usually speak only indoors insofar as it is necessary to reach simple truths. Zinbiel's biggest problem is getting used to the speed of their words. They speak very, very slowly. In the streets of Kallipolis, words are almost as rare as people. Chatter is always taboo.

Ben sighs at Zinbiel.

"You will learn," he says, "You will learn like a child learns, you need not speak all the time. You will learn that less is more," he looks at Zinbiel with sympathy in his eyes, "Okay. Just stay by my side. We must remain silent."

"But, well, I am just a bit nervous. I just never—"

"—really left your home since moving here, let alone been to a large gathering like this?"

"Yes," Zinbiel says, feeling his heart steady.

"Okay," Ben sighs, "I can tell you what to expect. But we must talk softly. We must not disturb the others. And we must part ways before reaching the shadow of the House of Wax."

"Understood."

"Good. The reason that you have not been to a gathering yet is that Prioritans most always pray to O'Talp in the privacy of their homes, or in solitude with the elements. Prioritans only gather on rare occasions to pray so that we may all hear the blind man speak. We need this because, though we take precautions against being fooled by our senses, perhaps into thinking that they exist, we have a habit of forgetting this. As we are humans raised in a world of senses, long-standing opinions keep on returning, and we may forget O'Talp's ways. So we occasionally need the blind man to remind us.

"You have prayed in private this whole time. But you must realize, my friend, that this is no different. Though this may seem like a gathering of many people, we are not coming together; it is not a sum of its parts. When you enter the House of Wax, you will be given your own private booth just like everyone else. You will be alone. And like everyone else, you will disrobe completely in that booth, and pray naked just like you do at home so that there are no material distractions or separations between you and God, just you and O'Talp, your bare, unadulterated body and his bare and pure spirit.

"Of course, it will not be hard to concentrate. There will be no art anywhere in there. The walls will be completely barren. Though, many people take time to get used to all the…silence. Well, there will be a large sculpture in the middle of the room, but, well, you will see that when you enter. The booths are divided into three sections for the three classes of our people. The producers are in the back, the warriors are in the middle and front, and the rulers flank the blind man, our King, on either side. Producers, warriors, and rulers: each have their place. What are you looking at?"

"What?" Zinbiel says.

"You just looked back at our path. Why would do you such a thing? I am speaking to you."

"Oh. Oh, that? I was just playing this game. Sometimes I look behind me when I walk…" Zinbiel remembers that the Prioritans frown upon any game made just to pass time, except for mind games involving strenuous mental exercises made to strengthen the mind, "Well, it is not really a game."

"What is it then?"

"Well, I see many footprints behind me, but only a blank sheet of snow before me. I was trying to predict what my footprints will look like on the snow before me, by looking at the ones behind me."

"I know you are new here," Benedictus takes Zinbiel chin in his hand and points his head forward, "but you must not look back."

"But can't you predict future footprints from past footprints?"

"No. That is a trap many other nations fall into—concluding the future by past experiences, rather than by what the future *should* be based on reason. You must not look back because there is no reason to think the pattern will continue. You cannot look forward by looking back. The blind man never looks back. He doesn't need to because, ever since he ran away from his Posteriorian home as a child to start this nation, he has spent his entire adulthood refuting the teachings of his homeland of Lyceum. He has abandoned the teachings of El Totsira, and has spread the light of those of our God, O'Talp. He has determined immovable truths, such as the existence of God, or the existence of Himself. He has never looked back, and neither should you. Look to reason, my friend, not your footprints of the past."

"I will, Benedictus. I will try."

"Ben."

"Ben."

"You will learn."

"I am eager to meet the blind man," Zinbiel sighs, "We must hurry down our paths, to the House of Wax!"

"Lower your voice," Ben says, "and slow your pace. We are approaching the shadow now, and we must part ways."

"I will walk slow, and I thank you for your time. I am just nervous and excited."

"Take deep breaths and bring peace to your mind."

"I will try."

"You will do."

"I will try to do."

"Why have you such trouble?"

"I have dreamed of this, Ben. I have dreamed of the blind man for years before coming here, and I have never seen such greatness before. I am excited to hear the words of the blind man, our leader, once and for all. I am eager to see our philosopher-king, the blind man, the great and honorable Renee Don Cartez."

4

The other species of philosophers consider man in the light of a reasonable rather than an active being. They think it a reproach that philosophy should ever talk of truth and falsehood without being able to determine the source of these distinctions. They still push on and rest not satisfied till they arrive at those original principles, by which, in every science, all human curiosity must be bounded. They think themselves compensated for the labour of their whole lives, if they can discover some hidden truths. (But) this philosophy, being founded on the turn of a mind, vanishes when the philosopher leaves the shade and comes into open day; nor can its principles easily retain any influence over our conduct and behavior. The feelings of our heart, the agitation of our passions, dissipate all its conclusions, and reduce the profound philosopher to a mere plebian.

David Hume

In Lyceum, winter is not really winter. A certain chill hangs in the air, but it floats about unnoticed like a thin ring of tumbleweed drifting across a field of roses. It does not stop the Posteriorians from coming outside. If anything, they look at it as a chance to wear more rainbow cloths, smoke more herbs and plants, and laugh, dance, and live a little harder. To keep warm, of course.

There have been some changes in Lyceum, which isn't a change at all. Joachim is buried, and Dewey rises to the throne with the help of his aides, Jon *that boy* and the discus thrower, Yelekreb *master of distance*. With Jon and Yelekreb at his side, Dewey ages into a model Posteriorian ruler. Under his reign, the nation begins to grow dramatically, nearly doubling in size in just a few years.

However, Lyceum does suffer the death of one of their most influential citizens, Nietchai. Not long after Joachim's death, Nietchai begins to exhibit signs of mental illness. This is a real blow to the Posteriorians because Nietchai has spread his message of nihilism and true, glad apathy towards life, and for this, the people love him. One day, he leaves his large house in Brittany. He runs through the streets shouting obscenities, rushing west towards the plaza. No one really knows what happens next, but the often-repeated tale will say that he somehow knows of the whipping of a horse near the plaza. He runs to the horse, throwing his arms around the horse's neck to protect it, and dies right then and there.

This ultimately saves the horse's life *one life erects itself* but took Nietchai's *but one destructs* and with it, a little from every Posteriorian. Of course, in that moment, only I could have known that in saving the horse's life, Nietchai erased his future influence on Lyceumean society forever. When you learn my identity, when and if I choose to inform you of it, you may understand how I can know such things. But if Nietchai knew the future actions of that very horse, he would not have saved that horse's life, and he still would be alive today.

But Lyceum enjoys good fortune, too. Unlike Joachim was, Dewey is able to open new channels of trade with foreign nations (though he refuses to trade with any nation whose way of life strongly violates El Totsira's teachings). Through trial and error, Dewey finds that by increasing the money supply, the rate of production will also rise. Posteriorians work like herds of busy ants, and soon Lyceum is producing more than it can ever possibly use. No nation works as hard as they do. Seeing the potential, Dewey opens channels of trade to the world. This stimulates the nation's economic growth while making Lyceum the beacon of the productive world.

But Dewey is like his father in most other ways. He starts to sound like the young Joachim in his words. Like Joachim, Dewey begins to make long speeches at the Plaza in the center of town, though he fails to complete them more often than not. His body usually slumps over in the middle as he dozes off, alcohol and stale meat coming from his breath. Or sometimes, to the people's delight, he vomits, throws his head back in laughter, and runs into the crowd to lead another toast. While the crowd interacts with every speech he makes, each speech is different. They range from stories and poems about devils and ghosts as Dewey smears fake blood on his face and sing songs about heroes, to times he stands tall on his stubby feet and point his finger in the air, shouting about the beauty of experience, and loudly cursing those who shun it, those who turn away from the senses they are given.

But lately each speech has a new commonality that only Dewey notices, a commonality that, until now, Dewey has been able to ignore.

Looking into the crowds of the arena, through the clouds of smoke and rainbow color, Dewey begins to see a face of stillness in the clutter. The brown face of an old woman stares at him like a stone. For some reason unknown, this face stands out from all the others. Dewey begins to recognize the raisin face at every speech. He begins to look out for the woman, the same woman staring at him at each one of his speeches. But he does not know who this woman is.

This scares him terribly. He does not know why.

At first he thinks it is the ghost of Rekha. *Yes* he fears *she has come back, she has come to take me away, to tell me that I have not done well enough, that I have let my brother go* and he tries to look away, to laugh it off. After a few minutes, he often looks back to try to find her face among the crowd, her stone cold brown eyes, her thin pursed lips upon her white-haired chin. Sometimes she smiles peacefully at him, but other times she frowns in disapproval, or just looks straight ahead. But each time, just as Dewey works up the courage to address her directly or try to capture her attention, he looks for her, but he is never able to find her.

It is always as if she knows just when to disappear.

ΩΨΩ

"The beginning," Dewey starts such a speech this late winter morning in the Plaza, "It is best to begin at the beginning, yes?"

A large group of Posteriorians in the front cheer their approval, but the majority of the great mass of dreamers carries on with their eating, drinking, smoking, teasing, and sexual activities under a large cloud of purple smoke.

"Even at the beginning, the very birth of this world, experience was needed to learn anything. Just as a man begins his life with no knowledge, born without anything—"

"A blank slate," Jon says at Dewey's side. Dewey ignores him and continues.

"—so too, the world was created with a need for experience. How this world came to be, we cannot know, and it is only a fool who will tell you that he knows, that he knows of a spirit, a being, a God *something* that created our world. One can never know of this thing. But, however this world came to be, it was born without anything, until there was man to experience it. The world was nothing without man. Fire was not hot until someone felt it to be. A falling tree did not make a sound until that sound was heard. Yes, even at the beginning, the first man that ever lived, Adam understood the importance of experience. Born into this empty world, he was the first one to experience, and thus the first one to create the sensations we experience today, all by using his senses."

A roar of laughter explodes from the rear of the crowd around one of the fattest Posteriorians as he runs around on all fours, making the sounds of a donkey. His sensors scramble around behind him, feather and parchment in hand. Dewey focuses on the few hundred Posteriorians attentive at his feet.

"Adam, though his rational faculties be supposed, at the very first, entirely perfect, could not have inferred from the fluidity and transparency of water that it would suffocate him. He could not have known from the light and warmth of fire that it would consume him. Not until he actually experienced this, could he know it. Even if he spent lifetimes studying the components of water or the workings of a fire, he would not know their effect on him. Not until he experienced them himself. This is what we learn from Adam, and this is how we choose to live, as creators living through the world we were given.

"Now, some other thinkers would have us believe otherwise. They would have us believe that we *can* learn by closing our eyes and climbing into a deep, dark hole to, to… think. They would tell us that we don't need the world we were given. 'It is too confusing,' they complain, 'it is too difficult—the job of reaping knowledge from our senses is too much for us!' so they deny it is even there! This is why this species of thinkers takes years to learn anything; they don't even try. They shy away from the task at hand, denying the beautiful gifts of experience they were given by science itself. Instead of sifting through catalogues of past evidence, cases, experiences...instead of *living*, they stand like lonely ostriches with their head in the ground, denying the world teeming around them. And they refuse to speak to us and consider our ways because they are scared of the way we live. They are scared of the world we are brave enough to face every day, of the loads of sweet experience we take responsibility to analyze—"

The group of Posteriorians in the back roar in delight as they beat the fat Posteriorian with wooden sticks. One of them releases a loud fart, and they all drop their sticks, grabbing their sides in laughter. A tall man scolds them for making so much noise, and a young girl ignites some firecrackers in response. Dewey can see that her hair is dyed green, orange, and blue. He looks away.

"They are scared of our courage, of our sheer...ability to live life. They awe at our decision to accept and face this world rather than turn away from it. They secretly wonder at the possibilities of living, of trading with other nations, of being open, one with the outside world. And you may ask the question: Why? Why are they so scared? Why can they not enjoy the world they were given, the five senses they were born with? Why can they not accept it as is?

"Because they don't believe it. They are scared of the error that comes with it. The uncertainty. The doubt. So instead of merely questioning, they deny completely. Yes, there is a species of skepticism, *prior* to all study and philosophy, which is much inculcated by Renee Don Cartez and his...Prioritans in Kallipolis, as a sovereign preservative against error and precipitate judgment. I don't know much about it, but I do know that it recommends a universal doubt, not only of all our former opinions and principles, but also of our very faculties, of our sight, our hearing, our senses of smell, touch, and taste. They would deny we even have a body, or that the outside world even exists!"

As the closest Posteriorians laugh in mockery, Dewey can smell the wine on their breaths.

"How do they seek knowledge? You may ask, without experience, how do they learn anything? What *do* they believe? They believe only those truths obtained by a chain of reasoning, deduced from some original principle, which cannot possibly be fallacious or deceitful. But we all know that this is impossible!"

"Yes," the crowd chants in unison, "Impossible! Impossible!"

"There is no original principle! Or if there were, we could not advance a step beyond it, without our senses, which of course, they fail to trust in. What right do they have, I say, to do as they do? By what right do they claim to begin with clear and self-evident principles, to advance by timorous and sure steps? By what right? What they do, or claim to do, is not brave, my friends. Oh no, it is the cheap way out, and it will lead to nowhere. It is easy for them to commit a mistake in their subtle reasoning; and one mistake allows them to completely start over again from the beginning like it never happened at all. They will just...trash everything they've done because of one small doubt in someone's mind. And they push on and are not deterred from embracing any conclusion by its contradiction to popular opinion.

"But us Posteriorians, who purposes only to represent the common sense of mankind in more beautiful and more engaging colours, if by accident falls into error, works around it, adapting ourselves to return to the right path. See, my friends. To step away from the world and reach into the nothing, is cowardice. To dive in, is divine!"

The crowd roars in applause. Dewey grins like Joachim once did, and lifts his hands to silent the crowd.

"Now...thank you, thank you...now...ahem,"

Dewey clears his throat. He opens his mouth to speak but chokes on his words. He tries again, but for the moment, he finds that he has trouble finding the right words. He holds his chest and feels his heart start to beat faster. A deep chill comes over him, and he tries to take a deep breath, but cannot find the sweet taste of air. As his eyes begin to water, he looks into the crowd, and this is when he sees the cause of his discomfort.

This is when he sees *her.*

He sees the face of the old woman he has seen at his speeches so many times before. Sometimes the face is that of a younger woman, a small girl, or sometimes an old, old woman near her death, but Dewey knows it is always the same person, the same big brown eyes that one could fall into if they just let go. It is the same person each time; of this, Dewey is sure. Though the silent brown face stands still among the swirls of colors, confetti, and rainbow facepaint that surround it, Dewey finds that he cannot take his eyes off of it. Now an old woman, she looks at him disapprovingly *that boy* like a teacher to her student.

"Okay, ahem…haha," Dewey says, but he feels the red blush heat up his face. He looks away from the woman's face. Though he still feels her eyes pressing into him, he clears his throat and finds that he is able to speak again.

"Ahem…now…let's move on. I was saying…how divine it is to have the courage to face our physical, external world. But still, these thinkers are scared that our senses may deceive us. They often preach of such evidence; such as those which are derived from the imperfection and fallaciousness of our sensory organs, on numberless occasions; the crooked appearance of an oar in water; phantom limbs; the various aspects of objects according to their different distances in different lightings; the double images which arise from the pressing of one eye, the creeping similarity between our days and our dreams…all of these make some people question their senses…all of these phenomena make the weak suffer from doubt of an external world…and they therefore suppose that all they sense must come from inside of them. When they find that a table seems to diminish in size as they move farther from it, they ask, 'but what is the real table?' and when they find a hard piece of wax can change when brought near a warm fire, they ask 'but what is the real wax?' and they get scared of their senses, and run away into a dark deep hole. My brother ran away because he saw the wax change in his hand. He saw the crooked appearance of an otherwise straight straw in his glass of punch. He saw, and he got scared. And just like Renee, many people get scared. Many people feel the need to run away from the honorable task before them: sifting through experience to find a gem in the rough.

"There have been stories of some of our own people," the crowd starts to boo in disapproval, and Dewey raises his hands to quiet them, "there have been stories that some of our own dear Posteriorians have suffered such fears, and felt an occasional desire to withdraw…to the north."

Someone shouts, "Not in our land!"

"Get em' outta here!" another shouts.

"Let's have em'!" a few fists shoot into the air.

The booing is very loud now. Dewey waits for it to quiet down before speaking again.

"Yes…but I refuse to believe such stories. Anyone trying to leave this province will be detected at the sensor checkpoints along the border. Anyone spending too much time alone, or in his or her home, will be noticed. Anyone withdrawing will be dealt with. No such people have yet been detected," Dewey lies, "but I just want to reiterate. So I tell you now, as we stand here today:

"Indulge your passion for science, I say, but let your science be human, and such as may have a direct reference to action and society. Abstruse thought and profound researches I prohibit, and will severely punish, by the pensive melancholy which they introduce, by the endless uncertainty in which they involve you, and by the cold reception which your pretended discoveries shall meet with when communicated. Be a philosopher; but, amongst all your philosophy, be still a ma—"

Dewey stops, short of breath.

"…be still a—be still a, a—" *a what? A WHAT?* Dewey sees the woman's face again, peering at him from another place in the crowd. He chokes on his words, puckering his mouth open and closed. He looks like a fish out of water to the crowd, his fins frantically flapping, his moving lips gasping for air.

He has had enough.

"Guards!" Dewey manages to shout, "Guards! Get that woman," he points in the crowd. But everyone is laughing and smoking and dancing and dreaming and no one hears the fat king shouting on the stage. After a few minutes, a small handful of guards that understand what is happening approach the stage.

"Guards," Dewey says, still looking into the crowd, "Stand ready to—"

One of the guards covers his mouth to stifle a burp. The other guards snicker.

"Get a hold of yourself!" Jon says to them. Yelekreb takes Dewey's hand in his, and speaks into his ear.

"It's okay. Just tell me what is wrong."

"That woman. I don't know why, but I can't stand her," Yelekreb could feel Dewey's hands trembling in his, "Her eyes…her eyes…get her away from me."

"What woman?" Yelekreb looks into the crowd. Jon and the guards listen curiously. "What woman do you speak of?"

"In the crowd," Dewey says, pointing, "Over, over…there." Dewey looks to the spot where he saw her face, but a cloud of orange smoke now floats where her face once was. Dewey looks back and forth across the crowd.

"Where is she?" Yelekreb says.

Dewey looks, but he cannot answer.

"She, she…I promise, she was just over…over there…a minute ago?" But all he sees a pig burning on a stake, a group of small girls dancing around a fire, a bouquet of flowers, petals floating in the air. But the woman *those eyes* the woman is nowhere to be seen. She is gone.

5

There will be no end to the troubles of states, or of humanity itself, till philosophers become kings in this world, or till those we now call kings and rulers really and truly become philosophers, and political power and philosophy thus come into the same hands.
Plato

Renee Don Cartez sits on his throne in the great House of Wax. It is a simple chair of wood, the only object not made of wax in this place. In accordance with the Prioritan custom, the chair rests no more than six inches from the ground, so as not to be too comfortable. As if the low chair is not enough, Renee's long legs cause his knees to stick even higher in the air. Not yet an old man, Renee seems to have aged more than his older brother. He wears a thick black cloth across his eyes, though acid from an orange put its own blindfold on him long ago. Long black hair hangs down over his ears and face, past his shoulders, just kissing his upper back. His thin beard fails to hide the necklace under it, a thin strap of leather worn around his neck tied to an old wooden whistle resting at his heart. While the Prioritans are not sure what the whistle is for, some say the blind man was born with it around his neck. They have never seen him without it.

Renee holds a staff in his right hand. A wolf sits on his left. Both the staff and the wolf look old but strong, standing firm on either side of their king. On Renee's right sits a crippled man in a wheelchair. Though he is one year younger than Renee, his head hunches over, falling down towards his lap so that the back of his wheelchair can be seen behind him. His body is limp, but his small dark eyes glisten with life on either side of his large protruding nose. His scraggly white hair falls over his face, down towards his dark maroon robe now opened at the bottom to expose his bony white feet.

Flanked by Christian on his left and Nicolas on his right, Renee sits quietly, as if he is all alone.

Oh, how the sunlight makes everything glow in the House of Wax! Just imagine the walls and the great domed ceiling of the massive cathedral as the sunlight touches its skin, running through its core like mild white cream clouding itself through water. The wax absorbs the sunlight outside, distributes it equally within its transparent body, releasing it inside in controlled amounts, muting it into a soft blanket of comfort for the thinkers inside. As Zinbiel enters the House, he is amazed how the wax uses the sunlight to make *itself* glow, as if the light's source is within the walls themselves. Zinbiel feels the soft light haze towards his arms and face, but stopping just an inch from their source so it is still gloomy and mild in the cavernous hall.

In the middle of the House stands the only piece of art in all of Kallipolis, a massive wax sculpture of the nation's sign, the three-legged spider. It has one leg in its center front, and one on each side in the rear. Engraved upon its front leg is the word "Rulers," while its two rear legs read different words, with "Warriors" engraved in one, and "Producers" engraved in the other. Each of the three class's booths is located in a section at the foot of their respective spider's leg.

Upon entering the House, Zinbiel is escorted to a booth in the producers' section before he even notices the eerie quiet that surrounds. While the wax walls do well to keep the citizens' sounds inside their booths, Zinbiel can hear muffled sounds from neighboring booths. From some booths come screams of joy or pain, or mere moans of pleasure or longing. But from most of booths come nothing at all.

Looking through the wax walls of his booth, Zinbiel can see the hazy outline of the human flesh of his neighbors. Their naked bodies are bent over, their faces in their hands as if they are in a womb. To Zinbiel, they look like frozen embryos. But they are hard to see, like bodies behind a fogged pane of glass on a rainy day. They are all men around him, since the booths are divided by gender within each class. Zinbiel looks down.

Suddenly, he realizes how cold it is in here. He shivers.

"Disrobe," the usher says, leaving Zinbiel to his booth. Zinbiel does as he is told. Naked, he kneels down and puts his face in his hands. He closes his eyes and takes a deep breath. A cool comfort runs through him. Suddenly, the cold feels good on his skin, yet he cannot imagine how. In the calmness of solitude, he feels his mind slowly cleansed of the trivialities of the day. He begins to pray.

Fully naked and pure in the perfect temperature of this silent House, it is easy for him to forget his surroundings, and drift his thoughts away from his body, his feet, his skin, the cool floor upon which he stands. His world gets hazy and distant, and he lets it drift further away. His stomach growls in hunger, but he swallows and shuts it out of his mind. Once he has shaken superficialities away, he begins to look through the big empty. He turns his mind towards O'Talp's firm principals, His agent the blind man, and the creation of the best possible world. He meditates for mental prosperity, for a meaningful being in this new land, for success in the endeavors of Catherina and he, and for his mother's happiness. But most of all, he waits. But he knows not for what.

ΩΨΩ

"Reason," Renee begins, "is the starting point for man, the ladder, the rope by which he may climb to the greatest heights of truth. It is the only tool man can use, and it is the best."

With his mind in another world, Zinbiel does not hear the blind man's voice. Zinbiel feels distant from his body *floating* and the body of material things around *flying* and he feels a special closeness to O'Talp, a bond he enjoys for hours before Renee's voice catches him by the ankle, gently pulling him down, back to this world. Then, Zinbiel feels his consciousness slip back into his body, Renee's voice lulling him awake. Zinbiel opens his eyes and looks at his hands. They are still there, the same hands he was born with, the same he will die with. He touches his feet, his nose, his eyes, his hair. Nothing has changed. Zinbiel smiles.

Renee has been speaking for some time now, Zinbiel decides, for those who wish to listen. The wax walls mute the philosopher-king's voice, so it does not disturb the prayer and solitude for those who wish to remain in it. Zinbiel figures that it brought *him* back to this place only because he is not yet a maverick at such meditation, but even so, Renee's soft voice brings amateurs back with a gentle hand. His voice beams off the cavernous dome walls of the wax hall like a huge eardrum itself such that one does not hear the king's words, but feels them vibrating in his entire being, the rhythm of his warmth breath running through the wax floor to their feet, up to their legs, tapping on their naked skin. It is in this way that all who wish to may listen, even if they rid themselves of their ears long ago.

Zinbiel is impressed by the blind man's silent confidence, how his slow, soft voice grabs more attention than any other man's shouts would ever bring. Zinbiel notes how he never repeats a word, nor hesitates, his syllables slow and clear. There is no applause, no greeting, not the slightest change in the Prioritans as their king starts to speak. They remain statues in solitude, their eyes closed, their bellies empty from fasting, their lips pursed shut, their mind somewhere else. Those close enough to hear him begin to listen.

"Empty your mind. As we withdraw into solitude, freeing our mind of all cares, we find a leisurely tranquility greet us. The cool comfort that we do not need the confusing circus of things waiting to bother us outside these walls. That, even as we go outside, we are not dependent on them.

"How can we know this, some outside Kallipolis may ask. We know the answer, so we need not entertain such questions for long. But they would liken us to the insane. This would be all well and good, were I not a man who is accustomed to sleeping at night, and to experiencing in my dreams the very same things, and even less plausible ones, as these insane people do when they are awake. Why is it, we may ask, that in one's alleged dreams and alleged days, that the very same areas of the brain are stimulated? Why is it the case that if a person looks at a chair while awake, and if he dreams of a chair while asleep, the very same areas of the brain are stimulated? No difference can be seen! What can we learn from this? How can we distinguish one experience from the other? What gives us the right to attach more validity to one over the other?

"As I consider these matters more carefully, I see plainly that there are no definitive signs by which to distinguish being awake from being asleep. As a result, I am becoming quite dizzy, and this dizziness nearly convinces me that I am asleep."

Renee cocks his head to the side. He adjusts his blindfold, scratches his chin, and sighs.

"This is why we must not fall into the trap of assuming, without reason, that the things that we sense actually exist outside of us, as we sense them. Indeed, we sense them in different ways on different days. We are unfamiliar with them. We cannot define what 'green' means, just as we cannot find a universal idea of warm. We must not be fooled into the habit of relying on the existence of such things. We must not be deceived. We must question. We must be critical always. And this is why we do not teach such things to our youth. Science is the study of these things, of the empirical world of nature, through the method of experimenting what we sense happens. The study of science requires observing, playing, altering, and recording instances that happen in the alleged physical world of these…things. Thus, it is a waste of time. But mathematics require none of these.

"Thus it is not improper to conclude from this that physics, astronomy, medicine, and all other disciplines that are dependent upon the consideration of composite things are doubtful, and that, on the other hand, arithmetic, geometry, and such other disciplines, which treat of nothing but the simplest and most general things and which are indifferent as to whether these things do or do not exist, contain something certain and indubitable.

"Yes, mathematics comes from reason. One does not need to experience anything to know that one plus one equals two, or that two plus two equals four. One can know that merely by closing one's eyes, ears, and mouth, withdrawing into solitude, and thinking. And more importantly, those truths that are obtained through reason will never change; one plus one will always be two. They will never change because they are not built upon, nor dependant upon, anything that changes. But science changes as new things are discovered, as the outside world it is so dependant on evolves, changes, deceives, confuses, revealing all its imperfections and illusions. Those alleged truths obtained through experience change all the time, until new theories are built upon the old, and they too, only stand for so long. All swans are only white until a new color swan is experienced, and the theory must be changed to include that too. Man thought the world flat because that is how they experienced it. But if they only closed their eyes and thought about *what makes sense*, they would have known differently. Reason teaches us things *prior* to experiencing them, *prior* to the world of the 'e,' to experience, evidence, experiments. Reason requires none of these. Only our minds. Reason, my friends, not experience. But again, we already know this. We need not entertain such questions for long.

"But it is not enough simply to have realized these things; we must take steps to keep mindful of them. For we were all raised in a world of chirping birds, sweet smells, and other sensations I need not mention. From the beginning, many of us not born from Kallipolis were thrown into a world of sensations, drinking milk from mother's breast, sucking our thumbs, sitting warm and comfortable in our own waste. And now, long-standing opinions keep returning, as is their nature. So we must remain steadfast, regarding ourselves as not having hands, or eyes, or flesh, or blood. We must remain consistent and resolute in this meditation to withhold our assent to what has deceived us, to what we cannot take as true."

Renee draws a long, deep breath. Christian shakes his big wolf head, yawns, and looks at his master.

"But what *can* we know? Well, we can look to our four principles. We know them well by now. But before we do that, we shall prepare ourselves by reviewing the Constitution our founding rulers worked hard to establish as they began our nation, myself included. A review of our constitution always comes first, because it is only a society that lives according to its principles that may achieve the mental tranquility required to achieve truths through reason. It is principles that stand firm like rocks on the shore as the waters of experience come crashing into them. Our constitution is our set of principles, the will of O'Talp our God, divinely inspired by myself, and it lays out the most efficient way to deal with trivial matters that any society falls slave to: how to produce food, shelter, clothes, and progress, so that we can finally look beyond that, and enjoy peace and solitude of one big Nothing, in which we may find real truth."

Renee clears his throat and rubs his chin.

"Since there is to be no written word, it is important for us to hear this frequently, so that we can know it in our memory. I will begin with the first clause, the preamble to our Constitution."

Renee places his hand on Christian's head. In a low voice, he begins to speak the constitution, word by word.

Preamble

We the Founding Rulers of Kallipolis, in Order to form a more perfect Republic that can first and foremost establish Justice, and through our three-tiered caste system, provide specialization for each citizen into a class according to the type of metal placed in his or her blood by the Almighty O'Talp, such that as a nation we may secure the Blessings of Productivity to ourselves and our Posterity, provide for the common defence, and train and create true Philosopher Kings whose judgment may take the place of law, do ordain and establish this Constitution for the Republic of Kallipolis.

One's class is to be determined by the Philosopher King when one is borne into this Republic either by way of entry over the border and branding by hand, or by birth through the ground, according to their natural talents, as evidenced by the type of metal found in his or her soul at time of such birth, so

> everything in the Republic is done at the highest possible level, as the following three sections reflect:
>
> **Producers**, representing the appetitive element of the soul, shall be composed of Members borne into Kallipolis with iron or bronze in their soul, to be craftsman, farmers, or builders, producing objects for the people's consumption and use.
>
> **Warriors** or auxiliaries, representing the spirited part of the soul, shall be composed of Members borne into Kallipolis with silver in their soul, to act both as protectors of the People and to enforce order and peace. However, no legislative powers shall be granted to anyone now or any time henceforth, and there shall be no laws, except few guardians will be selected from the group of warriors to become philosopher kings and rulers who may decide each case or controversy on a case-by-case basis with full discretion, as specified hereafter.
>
> **Rulers,** representing the rational part of the soul, shall be composed of Members borne into Kallipolis with gold in their soul...

As Renee's monotonous voice fills the cavernous hall, Zinbiel closes his eyes and starts to drift once again. Renee passes through the introductory sections and arrives at the principles, and Zinbiel invites the rhythmic vibrations of the blind man's voice upon his skin such that it permeates his entire being.

> No form of currency, money, gold, or any other pecuniary interest shall exist within this Republic, to ensure the absence of poverty, wealth, jealousy, or distraction...

Zinbiel can feel the blind man's voice fully now...

> ...no color shall enter...no art shall be created nor dwell nor exist here...

As Renee concludes with the last clause...

> This Constitution supersedes all previous and future understandings and principles expected in Kallipolis, whether oral or written. Its followers hereby acknowledge and represent, by setting foot in Kallipolis, that said followers will not follow any opinion, belief, statute, principle, rule, or moral obligation contrary to those set out in this Constitution. This Constitution may not be amended, save for the gravest circumstances and the clear and open divine intervention of the Almighty O'Talp as decided by the discretion of the philosopher king. This constitution may not be amended.

Besides a hint of shuffling in the back of the House, nothing is heard. Minutes later, four people slowly make their way through the exit. Two enter. Renee continues to speak.

"We have reviewed our constitution, the setting in which all our goals must be reached for."

A middle-aged woman walks up to Renee and begins conversing with him. The Prioritans continue to meditate in their booths. Since Renee's words were more of a softly spoken commentary or backdrop to which any Prioritan may meditate than anything resembling a speech, the woman's actions are hardly a disturbance, and Renee's pause is hardly noticed. After a few moments, the woman turns away and walks back to her booth, her head down.

"Yes," Renee continues, "Ahem. I was just getting to that. O'Talp himself conceived the constitution, but he also placed in each of us certain innate ideas that we are born with, like logical and mathematical truths. See, we are not born empty, like a blank slate upon which we draw principles as we grow, but rather we are all born with reason in our mind such that we need not live in the world to learn. We are born with everything we need. The potential for truth is already in our heads. There are four innate ideas I have reaped from my mind. All my life I have spent examining, then rejecting the outside world, and in my time away, have exercised my mind to conceive of these four things. Yes, of these four things I am sure. We are all born with these four truths in our minds. Everything else is left to doubt.

"One. That all events have a cause. Reason tells us that something cannot come out of nothing.

"Two. That God exists. Reason tells us that for a cause to create an effect, there must be at least as much reality in the cause as there is in its effect. A stone cannot exist unless it is produced by something in which there is, either formally or eminently, everything that is in the stone, just as the *idea* of stone would not be in my mind, unless it was placed their by some cause that has at least as much reality as I conceive to be in the stone. In my mind, in the mind of every man, lies the idea of an infinite substance, independent, supremely intelligent and powerful. How did it get there? It must have had a cause. A cause in which there is as much reality as we conceive in the infinite substance. And we conceive it to have every perfection, including existence. Existence is inseparable from it in our mind, just as three corners are inseparable from our idea of a triangle. Explain our having the idea of an infinite substance, since we are finite, unless this idea proceeded from some substance which was really infinite. It is not astonishing that in creating us, O'Talp should have endowed us with this idea, so that it would be like the mark of the craftsman upon His work.

"Three. That I exist. While my belief that I see a chair, or smell a flower, may be doubted, the fact that I *think* I do, may not. This is because the act of thinking does not require the existence of an outside world. Even if I doubt everything, I cannot doubt that I am doubting. I know that I can doubt, hope, believe, and think. And to think, I must exist. I think. Therefore, I am.

"Four. Of my nature; that I am a thinking thing. I have established that the only act I can be sure of is thinking. Since I know I think, I am a thinking thing. What is that? A thing that doubts, understands, affirms, denies, wills, refuses, and that also imagines and senses. If I am anything else additionally, I cannot be sure."

"Yes, you can," Zinbiel thinks to himself.

The blind man stops speaking. Moments pass until he speaks again.

"Would you like to comment?"

As another moments passes, Zinbiel looks up in curiosity. Renee seems to be looking right at him. But of course, that is impossible. But with each passing second, Zinbiel's stomach drops further.

Me? No, that is impossible. It cannot be. I didn't say anything—

"Anyone?"

Zinbiel stands frozen *who me?* A deer in head lights, his heart stopped. *Is he talking to me?*

"Yes, you," Renee says, as if reading Zinbiel's thoughts, "Come closer."

Taking a deep breath, Zinbiel questions himself. *I didn't say anything out loud* Zinbiel wonders *or did I? Did I? Okay. I might have muttered it under my breath. Did I? I must have. But still—*

"That's right. Come."

Zinbiel clothes himself in his robe, exits his booth, and begins to walk towards the blind man.

"Your honor," Zinbiel says, standing before Renee's feet. Zinbiel feels the weight in his chest, but after all his anticipation, is surprised he is even standing. Christian looks up into Zinbiel's eyes. This is a rare thing for Christian to do. Zinbiel is pleasantly amazed at the comfort the blind man exudes, keeping the weight in Zinbiel's chest from rising, and enabling his lips to speak.

"I have drifted into deep reflection, and have begun to conceive beyond your idea of one's nature—"

"Yes," Renee says, "Please state your name."

"Oh. Zinbiel, sir. Zinbiel Cirdeirf."

Nicolas looks up for just a moment, moves his hand from his wheelchair's armrest to his lap, and returns his gaze downward.

"Yes, Zinbiel," Renee says, "Then, son of Catherina. Now, son of Kallipolis. How do you think?"

"Well, sir. And you?"

"It is good to meet you again."

"We have met before?"

"Many times. You remember."

"Oh…I have dreamed of you. But that—"

"Was no different than now," Renee says, "Now. Share with me your thoughts."

"Well. You said, in principle four, one may know that he is a thinking thing, but of what else his nature may be is uncertain."

"Yes."

"I think that by understanding a principle of my own, one may reveal the nature of himself to a larger degree."

"Go on. Begin."

"For anything X, for anything Y, if X equals Y, then X and Y have all and only the same properties."

Renee lifts his fingers to his chin. "Yes," he says, "If two things equal each other, then they must have all the same properties, and only the same properties. One must not have any that the other lacks. And if it did…then the two would not be identical at all."

Renee looks to Nicolas, whose eyes remain on the floor. Zinbiel speaks.

"Yes. And this principle can be used to show that two things are identical, because they have all and only the same properties, or are wholly different, because they do not. In this case, well, we can show that you do not equal your body. And then, we will know more about your nature, beyond the fact that you are a thinking thing."

The blind man remains silent, and as a minute passes, Zinbiel hopes that the blind man did not forget he is there, standing before him, starting to feel his heart beat in his chest. Just as Zinbiel is about to lose hope and explain his principle to the Renee, Renee smiles.

"Yes! We must find a property that I have but that my body does not have, and then we can know that the two are not identical. And I have thought of such a property."

Zinbiel tries to hide the excitement inside him *Oh* with a straight face *to have my principle not only be accepted by the blind man,* but he lets a small smile through *but to be used by the blind man,* as he stands and waits.

"It is only my body that has the following property, not myself. This is the property of being something that could conceivably be something that I mistakenly suppose to exist."

Nicolas looks up again. He must have awakened from a meditation.

"Yes," Renee says, "the third principal establishes that I exist. This cannot be doubted. But it is only my body that I can mistakenly suppose to exist. Since I was born, I had a face, hands, arms, and this entire mechanism of bodily members. I took in food. I walked about. As to these things, I had no doubt. But they are doubtful and deceitful, and it is only these things that I can mistakenly suppose to exist. Not myself, because that I know exists. This establishes the following principle. I do not equal my body."

Zinbiel is glad to see the blind man smile.

"Yes," Zinbiel says, "I—I have conceived of other—"

"I do not equal my body," Renee says.

"Yes, I have conceived of other innate ideas, too."

"Go on."

"Well, we know of simple truths, such as mathematical truisms like one plus one is two, or necessary truths like 'what is, is,' through the innate ideas placed in us by O'Talp before birth."

"Granted."

"And there are more complex ones."

Renee nods.

"One," Zinbiel says, "It is impossible for the same thing to be and not to be. If a proposition is true, its negation is false. There can be no contradictions. Reason tells us this.

"Two. There must be a sufficient reason for anything to exist, for any event to occur, for any truth to obtain. This reason is known only to O'Talp.

"Three. Natura non saltum facit—"

"Enough, Renee says, "I know not where you are from, only because you do not know it either. But these ideas must undergo further rigorous inspection. I know that you are new in this land. How can you have conceived of such truths in such little time? And with such little peace?"

"I have spent years in the wilderness, conceiving the law of noncontradictions while wandering on my own—"

"—with Catherina."

"And I—we slept in foxholes—"

"—as I visited you in dreams."

"I was lost; we didn't know where to go—"

"—but I pulled you closer. I guided you here for a reason."

"I can teach my principles to your people. I can amend the constitution. I can change—"

"We do not *like* to change!" Renee slams his fist down, "unless such change is justified. It rarely is." His voice is a hoarse whisper, but it roars in Zinbiel's head.

"But, hear me out. I've been working on a binary number system. I am almost there and I can already see that it can reall—"

"Zinbiel. This constitution," Renee says back in his monotone, as if reading off a page, "may not be amended save for the gravest circumstances and the clear and open divine intervention of the Almighty O'Talp as decided by the discretion of the philosopher king," Renee looks up, "This is what it states. And since this can never happen because our truths are immovable, it closes, 'This constitution may not be amended.'"

"But I—"

"Do not mince words in this place! You are moving too fast. Take three steps back, and three steps forward. Then take a deep breath and speak your thoughts."

Zinbiel does as the blind man commanded.

"Your honor, I have not come to my conclusions by way of shortcut, speculation, nor falling trap to the ideas of lovers of sights and sounds. I have conceived of them only through the most meticulous and tested chain of reasoning, only progressing another step beyond what has been tried and true."

"Yes. We do not amend our constitution. We do not amend our principles. Just like any completed building that stands within this Republic, any principle, command, judgment, verdict, holiday, ordinance, or article that has been established, is perfectly valid, and will not fall. This may be why our Prioritan courts must accept one to be proven guilty 'beyond a possible doubt.' Trials may take decades, but sometimes, this is what the truth requires. Here in Kallipolis, it takes time for a building to be built, or a verdict to be rendered. But once it is built, the building will not fall. No party may appeal their judgment; the judicial process will not allow it! Things may not be changed. Anything that has been taken through a chain of reasoning, pure and unadulterated by any sights or sounds, conceived *prior* to experience, need not be changed.

"Of course, if the reasoning upon which a principle or judgment stood was in fact found to be erroneous, and we were absolutely certain of such error, then such a principle or judgment would crumble to the ground, and we would be forced to start all over again. But this has never happened. And it will never happen, so long as we continue to only establish and build that which is firm and long lasting."

Zinbiel hesitates, takes a step back, and turns away. He hears the blind man's voice behind him.

"I have been in your mind."

Zinbiel stops walking. Standing in place, he hears Renee's voice behind him.

"And you have a great one. There was a reason I brought you here. I have been harsh with you. But I understand you are an expert at calculus and mathematics. You are a producer, but you have not been given a job to do. We do need solid homes to be built. Come and speak with me after services. I wish to show you something."

"Where do you want to take me?"

"You will see."

"Yes," Zinbiel says, returning to his booth to pray.

6

If a nation loses its storytellers, it loses its childhood.
Peter Handke

The thinking room is the only tradition that Renee ever took from his father. This is not a surprise, for this room is the reason Renee became the man *king* prophet he is today. It is also this room that separated Joachim from all the other Posteriorians. This room brought about the growth of Renee and ultimately, the birth of the Prioritans; it is only natural that Renee would bring it along to dwell in Kallipolis. Yes, back in Lyceum, it was in this room, Renee will always remember, that he first encountered O'Talp. Yes, after years of feeling that he never belonged, it was here that Renee first discovered *O'Talp was just like him* himself, where he uncovered the holy God's story, how O'Talp's innate ideas would not leave him alone, so he had to run away from his family. It was here that Renee learned how O'Talp was captured by his brother El Totsira. It was here that Renee discovered O'Talp's principles and teachings, the first concepts that ever made sense to him *so natural* in his short life.

To Renee, the room was a mirror. It was the first time he was able to see himself. When he was reading O'Talp's documents, it was as if he was reading about himself. O'Talp's teachings followed the way Renee had always thought.

O'Talp was just like him.

And buried under those documents, Renee found a photograph of himself. The documents, the photo, the drawings, the stories, the smell *that smell* of Nothing, all of this told a story of a new kind of God and a new kind of nation. It told the story of a reasonable nation. And if a nation leaves behind its storytellers, it loses his childhood, and is no more able than a man with amnesia.

So the first thing Renee did upon arriving in Kallipolis was to build a similar thinking room to that of his father's. However, this room would be better. Yes, there would be no thinking lamp to distract one's thoughts. This one would be underground with nothing but a small wooden stool, a stone fireplace, and a few wax candles.

Renee spent the better part of the last forty years in that room. Beads of sweat would drop down his face, absorbing themselves in his blindfold before they could reach his lips, quivering gently from his mental concentration. Often when his thoughts would hit a wall, and he felt his mind falter, Renee would feel the cool side of a wax candle in his hand. He would bring it towards the fire, and feel it warp into a thousand different forms. Only then he would feel at peace once again, reassured that the senses are deceitful, and eager to use the mind as a refuge. Sometimes he would be so immersed in his thoughts that he would forget where he is completely. One time his robe had caught fire, but he was so deep in thought that did not realize this until the flames had completely engulfed his legs, made their way up to his torso, the highest flames just touching his beard, over the course of a few minutes. But O'Talp had saved him *it is time to go back now* pushing him away, back to the world of sights and sounds *it is time to leave, Renee, go put out the fire. You've gone too far.* Yes, God had healed Renee's burns. But the whistle worn around Renee's neck had become charred.

ΩΨΩ

The House of Wax has nearly emptied by now, the sun making its way west. Its white translucent light seems to be sucked out of the wax pallor walls of the hall, like God himself is extracting the light just in time for night. Many of the wicks sticking out of the ground along the aisles have been lit so that the few thinkers left may find their way out.

Renee escorts out Zinbiel and a small group of thinkers, with Christian circling the group closely, his belly sounding a low growl. Renee tells them to stay close, since *there may be*

Posteriorians about, and we don't need to give them a reason to jump us. While the Axios River and Prioritan guards usually keep them at bay, one can never be too careful this time of night. Especially a Prioritan. They hear Renee but do not respond. Walking silently together in white, the group floats through the dark like a cluster of spirits moving through a black hell, parting ways one by one as they make their way back home. It is not long until Zinbiel is the only one left.

"Come with me," Renee says. In the dark, Zinbiel cannot see that Renee is blind. Zinbiel looks, but he cannot tell if Renee is looking right at him. But he does not want to. He thanks God for the darkness.

Renee turns and walks to a distant patch of shrubbery. He walks around courtly, tapping the ground with his stick. Finally, he stops. He kneels down and begins to brush away reeds and fallen debris. With a brief shimmer of the moon, Zinbiel can see an old wooden trap door on the ground with a round metal handle.

Renee bends to brush away a fresh spider web from the handle. He opens the door in the ground, but it seems to open itself. Christian looks both ways and waits for the two men to enter. But Zinbiel stands in place, looking at the dark wooden steps descending into the ground.

"Come on," Renee says, "They are already here."

"Who?" Zinbiel asks.

But Renee sinks down the stone steps, leaving Zinbiel alone in the black cold. Christian looks at him *go!* cocks his head to the side, and waits. Zinbiel takes a deep breath, and follows the blind man *king* Renee down the long dark steps. The door closes behind him, but he does not know how. Christian stands guard outside.

Upon reaching the bottom of the steps, Zinbiel sees Renee's white robes through the dark. Renee lights a small candle, but the flame is weak. Renee takes a seat on his stool. As the light slowly makes its way throughout the dirt walls, Zinbiel can see for the first time the form of another man. This man sits on the ground in the corner of the room. Zinbiel can barely recognize his face, his features dancing in the flickering candlelight.

"Did I give an accurate account of the House of Wax?," the man says.

"Benedictus!" Zinbiel now recognizes him as the man who walked with him to the prayer services. He gives a sigh of relief at a familiar face.

"Call me Ben."

"I never knew the house would be so meditative, so pure—"

"That, you had to see for yourself."

"Good," Renee smiles, "I am glad you two have been acquainted."

"Yes," Zinbiel says, "We met along the way—"

"I know," Renee says, "That was not an accident, Zinbiel."

"Nothing is an accident," Zinbiel hears another voice say. He looks around and sees the crippled man sitting in his wheelchair and smiling at him.

"I am Nicolas," the cripple says.

Renee says, "Very nice. Now, can we begin?"

"Begin?" Zinbiel says.

"I have a story to tell."

"A story?"

"One you must hear if you want to stay. If you want to remain at my side."

"At your side? Oh," Zinbiel feels an uneasy sense of pleasure wash over him, "A story? Of what—" Zinbiel feels his mouth close as the blind man's face jerks up to face him. Zinbiel could feel Renee's eyes glisten impatiently at him under his blindfold. Renee has a way of saying things with his face. Zinbiel takes a seat on the ground beside Ben, and the two fold their hands on their knees, and look up at their king, his beard shadowing his lips as they open to speak.

ΩΨΩ

Renee begins:

"When I was born, I was empty. Or so they thought. I grew up in the kingdom of Lyceum."

Renee stops, as if trying to detect any surprise or concern from Zinbiel. Ben and Nicolas look at each other while Zinbiel waits patiently for the king to continue.

"Yes, just as Moses came out of the Egyptians to stand against the ones that raised him, I come from Lyceum, the land of the Posteriorians, to stand against them. Of course, some of the people here—the weaker ones—must not know where I came from, for their heart may grow weak and it may overcome them. They may lose the faith and confidence in me that keeps our nation at peace. They may leave, their confidence broken. Or they may stand up against me, or worse."

A moment of silence passes, and Renee clears his throat.

"Ahem. Lyceum. At the beginning, it was almost right, playing with my brother Dewey around the palace, seemingly ignorant of the seeds in my mind. We would drink the nation's wine, dance the nation's dances, laugh the nation's jokes. But as the years passed, I found that this was not enough for me, and I began to wonder. I began to look more closely at the objects around me whom I had relied upon so automatically my whole life. With the help of Nicolas watching over me, I began to question. I began to find that by withdrawing myself for short periods of time, I was able to achieve an inner peace. A bit of tranquility that could carry through the rest of the day.

"But in time, this too, was not enough. I would come back from my father's gardens with only the beginnings of an idea spinning in my head, eager to be pursued. I was eager to discover just what happens, what my mind can conceive in a room of my own. So I retreated to my quarters, refusing any color from my life as my brother ran around in the green grass above my head like the other children of the nation.

"This was all fine, that is, until people began to ask questions. Sure, no one dared say anything out loud, but I could see it in their eyes when they would look at me with frozen smiles, look away, then look at me again. My stepmother was the last to reach out to me," Renee brings his hand up and holds the whistle in his fingers, "But this was too much for my brother. So he killed my only friend. A cat. And he took my sight. But now it is clear that this was part of O'Talp's plan, for my brother was merely an actor in a plan that brought the Prioritans where they are today.

"I knew I had to leave. So I packed up the few things I thought I would need, and I set out to find myself."

"Yes," Nicolas says proudly, "I remember it succinctly; that was a special day indeed."

"I managed to make it beyond the Lyceumean border, across the hot White Plains, and north, into the midst of Cherava Woods. But I did not have the means to make it on my own. A Cheravian bear had attacked me, bringing its colorful claw upon my neck. But Christian saved me from the bear's claws, standing his ground until the bear shuffled away in frustration. Then Christian guided me here. He licked my wounds when I needed to heal and stood over me as I camped, just as he is watching over us right now.

"But one day Christian ran ahead into the forest. I did not know where he went. I was lost. But when I tried to run after him, I saw the shadow of a man block my passage. At once, I recognized the smell of O'Talp's documents, the scent of Nothing. I saw Christian at the shadow's side, his tail wagging. Before I could speak, the shadow said:

'Hello, Renee Don Cartez. We have all been waiting for you. We have been waiting a long, long time.'

"I was shocked to hear such slow talk. Such precise, full sentences I have never heard before...and with no stammering. It was Benedictus. The shadow, I mean. Of course, I did not know that then. I answered him at once, and we conversed:

'Who are you?' I asked the shadow.

'How do you think?' he asked.

'What?'

'How do you think, today?'

'I think with great difficulty,' I said at once, 'but I hope that this will change.'

'Yes,' said the shadow, 'I am Benedictus Azonips. But you can call me—'

'Oh, Benedictus!' I laughed and tears of excitement came to my eyes, 'Benedictus, you...I heard all about you...you were the man who ran away with Nicolas.'

'Yes.'

'You really are as tall as they say…' And he was.

'Especially for Posteriorian standards,' Ben smiled.

'My brother told me one day during a game of billiards that you…you were almost caught by the Posteriorian soldiers…my brother's men almost caught you…they found you in Nicolas's cabin in the woods…but you and Nicolas ran away just in time…'

'Yes, Nicolas brought me from my studio. I was studying wildlife in the nearby woods through a new lens I had just designed. I saw something shimmer, something that could only be seen from these special lens. Nicolas must have known of my inventions. Anyway, after chasing sign after sign through the woods, I came upon his cabin. He tried to convince me to join him in his voyage to the north, to establish a new place, a…special place. We argued intensely for hours, and I was persuaded to leave my home and go with him. Then he spoke of this place…this republic…when we heard the rustling of your brother's Posteriorian soldiers in the nearby trees. Quickly, I took his broken body upon my shoulders, and he gave me simple and quick instructions where to go. Nicolas knew those woods better than anyone, let alone you brother Dewey. So I ran.'

"So I said to him, 'But…but Dewey said you are dead. Yes, the Posteriorians are sure you are dead, wandering out into the wild, and after some time, they forgot about you and tended to other matters…you know how they are.'

'Do I.'

'Yes,' I said, 'Dewey says they exiled you—'

'Ha!' laughed the shadow, 'Exiled me! Is that what they are saying over there? But I already left!'

'And you are alive!' I said.

'Oh, not only am I alive, young Renee, but I—Nicolas and I have been watching over you, my boy. Ever since you stumbled upon his cabin, and turned him away. He knew you weren't ready yet. But we were watching you, waiting. We watched you when you slept at night, when you went to the bathroom, and in the privacy of your own room.'

'How—'

'We planted a 'sensor,' well, not a real one of course, but one that was assigned to you, and in that way we gained access to all your sensor's recordings. There is much you do not know, but you will in time. You do not know that I was the one walking with Christian by the northwest corner of Cherava Woods when we heard a Cheravian bear's growl. It was I who sent Christian to go and save you.'

'But how did you know it was me?'

'Oh, He told us. We knew you were coming because He said your time had come.'

'Who?' I paused before the answer came to me. 'O'Talp,' I whispered.

"Ben looked amused, 'You are not the only one with dreams, young prince.'

"So I, just a teenager at the time, looked at this shadow, this Benedictus, this new friend. Christian trotted towards me, pushing his head under my hand.

'We were expecting you,' Ben said, 'as O'Talp had informed us. But you came earlier than we had anticipated. Indeed, we were on our way to come get you. You, however, came to us first.'

"Oh, Zinbiel, you must know how happy I was to be accepted, wanted, *waited for*! How happy I was to finally have a home of my own. Even though I was exhausted from weeks out in the wilderness, and my body was screaming for nourishment, I could not stop myself from laughing in sheer joy, refreshed at what I had been waiting to hear my whole life, and hearing it so…simply.

"Well. Back to the story. After Ben's words, I pulled my hand away from Christian and stood up straight.

'What will be my role here?' I asked.

"Ben smiled, and said 'There is someone I would like you to meet. He will tell you everything.'

'Who?'

'An old friend.'

"And even though I was blind, I sensed who he was right when I heard his entrance, his old face coming out of the shadows, the wheels of his wheelchair rolling out from behind the trees, the familiar scent of an old friend I abandoned in the woods years earlier. A friend I thought was dead.

'Nicolas!'

'Yes, my boy.'

"I ran up to the young man and threw my arms around him. Though he was one year younger than I, his bones felt frail under my arms. He backed away, laughing.

'Okay, okay,' he said, 'Go easy on me,' and I felt soft tears of joy wet my eyes. Then I remembered our last parting and I felt deep regret weigh on my chest.

'I am sorry,' I said to Nicolas, 'I am sorry I doubted you. I am sorry I turned you away. You were right; there *is* a special place, after all.'

'Well,' he said, 'Not yet. But you are going to help us build one.'

"And Nicolas patted my shoulder and told me that I am here now and that is all that matters. O'Talp had his plan for me, and that was just not my time. And Nicolas was just getting me ready. Then Nicolas said:

'Your role here. You were born a prince, and your father is not here. You are the only true prince of your family. You must lead us to build this republic—'

'Me?' I did not understand. 'But—but I just got here. You know so much more—'

'Not for long,' Nicolas said, 'and O'Talp has already declared it. It is written in the stars!'

'But—you, you—'

'We will remain by your side, my boy, so you need not worry. We will be there as long you need us.'

"And so it was. That was fifty years ago today," Renee says to Zinbiel. The faces of Nicolas and Benedictus remain still behind him, the candlelight throwing shadows across the walls of the thinking room. The men could see (and Renee could feel) their breath steaming from their mouths. Renee continues his story.

"And so it was. Nicolas, Ben and Christian led me to a small clutter of wax shelters just north of the Axios River along which Rekha delivered her water, but west of the Apuan Hills. There were just thirty-six people living in the cluster of wax shelters on that day. There were men, women, and children alike. They all came out to greet me. For the first time in months, they walked out into the light of day squinting, groping, with a calm but anxious pleasure to meet the blind man. With my three friends by my side, they walked up to me one by one, their heads down, their hoods over their heads, taking my hands in theirs. Some called me 'the one,' and others 'the blind man,' and I was their king. I was the one they had been waiting for."

Zinbiel says, "Was that strange for you? I can not imagine the feeling—"

"At this point, I had begun *thinking*, my friend. Yet it was quite odd finding an entire nation waiting for you to be their philosopher-king."

"Yes. But it was...natural, for you, to walk into such a position?"

"Well, Zinbiel. I guess you can say that it took some...adjusting, to this brave new world. There were a few things that I found surprising. In...where I came from, women are viewed as being inferior to men, like incomplete men. They have to ask permission to enter a room that a man is in, since they may interrupt his...experience.

"It was just surprising to me when Ben showed me to my quarters and a woman entered the room. A modest brown hut, I was just getting settled quite easily when an old woman walked into the room. Her head was down and she wore the Prioritan hood so that I could not see her face. But she seemed bent over. I could tell she was very old. She swung a broom gently in her hands. And Ben was quick to ignore her.

"But to me, there was something mysterious about her. Something familiar. I asked Ben who she was and he said, 'Oh, her?' Right?" Renee looks at Ben, "You said to me 'Oh, do not mind her. She is here to clean your quarters my Lord,' as if I need them clean—"

"Yes," Ben says quickly, "Let us move on. There is so much to tell. Zinbiel asked if it was natural for you to go from a wanderer to becoming king."

"Uhm...yes," Renee is merely amused at Ben's urgency to change the subject. But if Renee could see, he would be curious about the sudden blush of uneasiness on Ben's cheeks. Zinbiel wonders why Ben wants to avoid the subject of this woman; *had he jumped in a bit too fast?* But he thinks nothing of it, pushing away his thoughts as mere paranoia.

"Well. It is funny you ask this," Renee turns to Zinbiel, "because it was just as I was getting accommodated to the Prioritans' customs, upon which I have added many more since, that I found in front of me, well, a piece of my childhood that came back to haunt me."

"What do you mean?"

"Well. I was already five months in this republic when I was walking through our fields and I came upon something I had completely washed from my mind: my very own sensor! Yes, it was one of them; he was just standing there, looking down on the dusty ground, tangled in his own thoughts.

"I gasped, as you can imagine, and he looked up, his tiny eyes looking at me for the very first time.

"Nicolas was there and he asked me, 'What is wrong, Renee?' but I shook in horror at the impact *have they come back to get me?* until Nicolas grabbed my hands in his and said to me, 'Renee. This was never your sensor. His name is Custos. We, I sent him to Lyceum when you were just a toddler to act as your sensor and, well, to watch over you.'

"I did not like this at all. 'To…*spy* on me?' I said.

'Well, to guide you. To open doors for you, such as the one to your father's thinking room where you found documents of O'Talp. To leave notes for you, such as the one left engraved in a wax tablet under your pillow. To—'

'But…he is so small.'

'Yes,' Nicolas said, 'he is a dwarf.'

"By now Custos spoke his mind. 'I have a name, you know.'

'A dwarf?,' I said, 'What is that?'

'I said I have name,' the dwarf said.

"Nicolas explained, 'A dwarf is a little person. Kind of like a sensor, but, well...natural."

'Hello? Can you not hear me?' the dwarf said.

"I was confused, not to mention getting quite annoyed by this…dwarf's attitude. I asked Nicolas, 'What could be natural about a little person?'

'I'm not happy!' the dwarf said, throwing his little dwarf-fists into the air.

'Then which one are you?' Nicolas answered.

"And with that, the dwarf stormed away, his hands balled into angry little fists. Nicolas smiled at me as if he had said something clever, but I did not know why. Seeing my confusion, he said to me, 'Treasure your wonder while you have it, young king, because these days will pass. You will learn to be king, my Renee. You will learn the ways of these people, and in time, you will learn to make them learn from *you.*'

"And I did. I learned the incredible ways of these people. They were people from the four corners of the world. Many came from far away lands, many of them rangers from the Apuan Hills, others were citizens of Lyceum that Nicolas had picked up in his cabin as they were walking through the woods. They were people who never felt they belonged. People who knew the truth. They were people who did not fall fool to the sights and sounds that others do. They were carefully selected, and they were all told of this place, a special place, and they accepted to come here. I was the only one that ever rejected Nicolas's offer. So we brought these people to the place they belonged, to this place. And with the help of Ben, Nicolas, and Christian, we began to bring in more. With O'Talp's help, I was able to bring in more. Hundreds more.

"O'Talp has guided me since, becoming closer to me, and granting me the power to guide others in their dreams. I guided you here, Zinbiel, in your dreams, just as I have hundreds of others.

"I made a place where hundreds and hundreds can come to live in peace. Where people who appreciate the power of their mind can have the room and the silence to watch it grow. After a few hundred people arrived, our women began to have six babies at a time, with no pain—yes, they were popping up from the ground in rows, like fields of corn, a miracle, I tell you! We found that the harder we worked to reach our innate ideas, the faster we multiplied. Soon we became many. So, with O'Talp's direction, I established a government, created a legal system, made a three-tiered caste system, all according to His will. I called this place Kallipolis.

"We have the world's greatest mathematicians here. But the rest of the world will never hear of their equations. We have the greatest thinkers man has ever seen, but only we will enjoy their truths. While the buildings of all others fall, ours will stand forever. When their judgments become flawed, their foundations crumble, their principals contradict themselves repeatedly until they run out of themselves, and chaos ensues, in Kallipolis, there will be peace. And only then, the world will look to us as their beacon of hope, of certainty, of confidence. And then the world will see."

Renee lowers his brow, as if deep in thought. Zinbiel can see that he is remembering. Though the blind man's face is now hidden under his hood and blindfold, Zinbiel can see the age in his face, the scratches on his neck from the Cheravian bear, the crow's feet at his temples formed from engaging in the deepest levels of thought, the fullness of his beard from the years in this land.

"What is it?" Renee looks at Zinbiel.

"Oh, I was just curious...well...we have been fasting all day—"

"Yes. You are hungry. I do not usually keep food in here, but I may have something..." Renee opens the empty drawers in his simple wooden desk, "Yes, here it is. A potato. This should be enough for all of us."

Renee takes out a sharp knife, and cutting the potato into four even pieces, he hands a piece to each man. The men eat in silence, slowly enjoying their fill.

The men hear Christian bark faintly outside in the cold. It begins to snow heavily now, a quilt of white crystals burying the men in the silence of the thinking room. Christian barks again, then yawns. He sniffs the clean fresh snow and brushes some away with his paws. He lies down and lets the snow pile on top of him as he dozes off to sleep.

The men stay in the room throughout the night, meditating on their own, waiting out the impending storm. The last breeze of cold air manages to push itself through the crack in the door before it is closed off by the heavy snow. It drifts across the room and settles itself into the bones of these men. Two of the candles blow out. Zinbiel feels a shiver shake him. He looks at his newfound friends sitting around the candlelight: Renee, Benedictus, and Nicolas, the great minds of Kallipolis. He thinks of Catherina and hopes she is safe and asleep in bed.

"We are glad to have you, Zinbiel," Nicolas says, "Not all those that wander are lost."

And so it was.

7

We were all delighted, we all realized we were leaving confusion and nonsense behind and performing our one noble function of the time, move. Our battered suitcases were piled on the sidewalk again; we had longer ways to go. But no matter, the road is life.
Jack Kerouac

Happy, happy birthday! The sun is out; the winter has gone. Oh, the celebration of a birthday in Lyceum is something to see! The smells, the sounds, the sights. Celebrations are always happening in this land, but when there is a real excuse for one, all the better! Erupting fountains of bubbly wine rain their intoxicating purple formula down the pink and green slopes of their volcanic sides, flowing, dripping, pouring into the mouths of the eager Posteriorians waiting below. Since most of the parties are held on the great Posteriorian farmland, many farm animals roam about. Pigs, chickens, cows, squirrels, and rabbits run freely around the chaotic outdoor festivals, often causing accidents in their wake.

In fact, in a birthday party last year, Mr. Sufjan had spent the better part of his day scampering after a squealing pig, screaming obscenities *get him! get him! get the thief, the stealing swine* throughout the event *this here pig took my corn!* Indeed, a cob of corn was seen in the pig's mouth, but no one dared to intervene. A large group of Posteriorians enjoyed the circus before them, laughing wildly, cheering for the poor pig *hoot hoot* with their fists in the air. But it so happened that the pig ran right into the largest cow in the lot just while Farmer Slim was giving him a milking. The cow fell over onto Slim, killing him and his two sensors. The cheering quickly ceased, and the group of Posteriorians turned their heads away, wincing at the thought of being crushed by such a cow. They dispersed like dogs with their tails between their legs, looking for the next big thing.

Sufjan never did get his corn.

Today is such a day in Lyceum. Though it is just the end of March, the sun shines over this birthday celebration any hot summer day. It is only in Lyceum that such wonderful cotton candy, crepes, and bubbly concoctions of every color are made. And the largest, most exotic fruits, nuts, and plants circulate the mob of party-goers. Hashish is smoked, incense burned, alcohol flowing throughout the rainbow-robed Posteriorians as kisses, laughs, cries, and dances pass between them like chemical adhesives keeping them together.

"Ha ha!" a young woman says to one of the men, sitting on the grass next to his hookah, "Come here, my man."

"Ha! And what would your husband feel?" he says.

"Which one?"

The man stands up as the woman approaches, but the hot coal falls off the top of his hookah and into the woman's shoe. She screams, kicking off her shoe. It flies through the air, hitting a performing clown on stilts in the head. He falls over, into a tub of fruit punch, splashing a nearby group of children. They jump in delight at the refreshing shower.

"Yea!" one of the young girls exclaims, "This is more punch than my momma ever lets me have!"

"Ha!" one of the older boys says, "I get all the punch I want. If one of my momma's don't let, I just go and ask another one!"

"Well anyways, I hope more people have birthdays more often. To the person who made this party…happy birthday! I want to wish him…her…who's birthday is this anyway?"

"Uhm…Does it matter?"

"No," says the young girl, "But someone must know, right?"

She tugs on the robes of a nearby man, but his hairy chest pours out of his robe. She turns away in disgust, but it is too late. He notices her, his fat belly shaking right above her head. The man takes one last swig of his ale, and bends down to speak.

"What is it, my girl?"

"Oh, I…I was just wondering—"

"Out with it."

"Whose party is this, sir?"

"Oh, what a party this is!" the strange man smiles, "Isn't it?"

"Yes, yes it is. But whose birthday are we celebrating?"

"Ha! Does it matter? Did you get any cake, my girl?"

The girl frowns.

"Don't trouble me with your questions," the man says. Then he cocks his head to the side, looks at the clouds, and mutters, "Could you believe he is sixty-five already?"

"Who is it?" the girl asks.

"Oh, uh…uhm…I think it is Olegna, my girl. The artist, Olegna Lechim."

"But where is he? A birthday boy should not miss his own party."

"A boy, he is not. Well, not any more."

"Posteriorians always stay young. But a man should not miss his own party, neither."

"No, a man should not. Say, you're a smart girl."

"But Olegna is not here. I haven't seen him out for a week."

"Well…but it could be anyone's birthday. Does it really matter?"

"No," the girl looks down, "I guess it does not."

"Pshhh…" the strange man walks away nodding his head, "Come and bother me about age. Sixty-five already…or was it Seventy-five? Oh, to hell with it! Let's get me some more beer, ha ha!"

Another splash comes out of the nearby tub of punch and drenches the young girl. She can hear the popping of nearby firecrackers and she smells the fresh white smoke. She smiles, forgetting her curiosities as quickly as they came.

ΩΨΩ

The man was right. Olegna turns sixty-five today, but there is no celebrating for him. Not today. Today, Olegna does not show. Behind the sweet smells of celebration, the dancing and laughing of unearned joy, there is a closed wooden door, and behind that door, Olegna sits at home. He sits before his battered suitcases in his small home just south of the farms. He can hear the sounds of celebration coming through his large thin windows, but he does not listen. His body is in Lyceum, but his mind longs for the north, for the Carrarian quarries of his home.

He packed most all his things, and is ready to travel home. Ah, to be home again, to breath the clear air of the Apuan Hills! A smile comes to Olegna's face as he recalls running through the hills with Agostino, *run Olegna run* and seeing his poor sculpture *it's a whale.* He thinks of his small farm, his parent's faces, but his smile disappears when he imagines his father. He smells the alcohol on his father's breath, Lodovico's words *stand up, boy* echoing in his head *he just plays his fantasy games with stone.* But Olegna pushes that out of his mind. He remembers the day he discovered hope, redemption through one piece of parchment *Hear ye Hear ye* he remembers the big, colorful lettering, *there will be an art contest,* and he remembers with great delight, the day he ran away *run Olegna run.*

But that was yesterday, and yesterday has passed. Today is a new day. Olegna has lost the art contest, and his dignity with it. His sculpture, his life-long dream, has been stolen by a monster and he does not know where it is. He looks out his window, at the needle towering above him in ridicule, like his father long ago. Olegna pictures the clown Disegno now, sitting there in is cell so high in the clouds. *Maybe he is looking down at me right now*. Looking at the tiny window at the top, Olegna wishes he could climb all those stairs now. He wishes he could run up the needle right now, heavy stones gripped tightly in his fists, ready to beat the truth out of the clown. Yes, he could have done that years ago. But he was scared of facing those eyes, those teeth. He was scared of facing his past.

Such fears have hounded him in his time here. He has hoped that just maybe, if he stays long enough, justice will be done. But Disegno had been in and out of the courts like a revolving door. In frustration, Olegna has finally realized that such Posteriorian courts can never reach a final conclusion. They will never punish Disegno. And Olegna cannot stay here, so close to this monster. Everywhere he looks, the needle is there, towering over him in ridicule, reminding him of his failure, and the criminal inside. His time in this place, this Lyceum, has been a complete failure.

It is time to return home.

So Olegna sits by his suitcases in thought, while his birthday party goes on outside without him. He will find his home, he determines, or what is left of it. He doubts anything worth carving is left in the barn, but he takes comfort in the fact that his creations are still there. He imagines them waiting there, just as he left them. He closes his eyes and he sees the little girl looking up from her blocks, the owl with his stone head cocked to the side. He is eager to see their lively stone faces peering at him once again, the unity of creation and creator. He is eager to touch their cold faces, closing their cool marble fingers in his own.

ΩΨΩ

Walking through the palace gates, Olegna is surprised at the ease of his entrance. It is around noon, and most of the guards are asleep on their watch. They sit on the ground of the palace's outer stone walkways, their bare hairy legs sticking out of their armor above their golden leather boots. Their bellies stick out of their armor, pulsing up and down with the loud breaths of slumber coming from their open mouths, bringing mists of hot ale and strings of meat dribbling down their chins. The conscious ones nod as Olegna passes, some of them inquiring about his wishes *Why are you here, who do you wish to see* but before he can even finish his answer *I am going to Dewey the King* they seem to nod, dismissing him with a wave of the hand.

"What a poor excuse for security," Olegna shakes his head as he walks on into the palace.

Olegna finally finds Dewey running around his chambers, grabbing this *I need my papers* rummaging frantically *where are my buttons? And my hat was right here* and Olegna must call his attention *Sir, may I have a word* five times *my King* until Dewey stops and replies back to the artist.

"David. Right?"

"Olegna."

"Olegna. It has been a long time."

"A long time indeed," Olegna says.

"What can I do you for?"

"Well, it is an honor to stand before you—"

"Oh, you are the great artist. The honor is all my mine."

"You are very kind."

"Is this about Disegno, my boy? Because I can assure we are doing all we can…say, where *is* that hat of mine?"

"No."

"No, what?"

"No, my king, it is not about Disegno," Olegna lies, though he has convinced himself he is telling the truth.

"Oh, Disegno, ha! What a clown! Who would've thought?"

"Yes," Olegna takes a deep breath, mustering his patience. "Who would've thought."

"I do apologize. My hat was right here…I came in…and now I have to go…I have to go make a speech tomorrow for people already gathering at the arena…but when I came in, I turned and placed my hat right here…I am sure of it…" Dewey runs around the room. He almost stumbles over Olegna's toe and turns to face the artist.

"You," he says, "What are you doing here?"

"You were just talking to me…"

"What?"

"What?" Olegna clears his throat, "I have come with a request, my good King."

"Is this about—"

"No, this is not about Disegno."

"What is then? You are one of Lyceum's finest Posteriorians. Just let me know—"

"I wish to go home."

"Ha! And I thought you wanted to talk. Okay, then, farewell. I will see you around…"

"No. I am going home. To my real home. I wish to leave Lyceum. To return to my birthplace. To the Apuan Hills."

"To the Apuan—" the glaze over Dewey's eyes washes away for just a moment. Olegna can see the confusion and hurt on his face. Dewey speaks.

"You want to leave…Lyceum?! But…why? You are one of our greatest artists! Your home is here."

"No. I am the son of Lodovico Di Simoni and Francesca Lechim. I was born on a small farm in the most northern hills of the Apuan Hills, just east of Lake Tirreno from which the Axios flows. Sculpting marble into life was all my hands knew how to do; I was born with chisel in hand. But my father would not allow this, so I ran away. I discovered the art contest and from that moment on devoted my full self to winning that contest. I was trained by a great Posteriorian sculptor Lorenzo, and worked hard under his guidance. I created the greatest rendition of El Totsira on horseback and made my way here, to Lyceum, to compete. I don't know why I needed to win that contest. Perhaps it was to prove to my father that I can do it. Perhaps it was to prove that to myself.

"All I know is that I did. Without winning, all would be for naught, my entire childhood wasted. But I failed, my King. I lost the El Totsira, and I lost the contest. Perhaps my father was right," Olegna looks at the floor, "but I hope he is alive so I can tell him. I must go back to the land of my father. I must return home."

"Ah, such a story," Dewey nods, tears from his eyes. He burps softly, and this makes him snicker. "I love stories," he says.

Just then, a servant sticks his head in the room.

"Your Honor?"

"Wha—Oh! Yes?"

"A small group of people have begun to form in the plaza," he says, "but the group is growing. They may have enough wine to last them through the night, but they will be waiting for you soon enough."

"My speech! Yes, I must go make that speech, though it is tomorrow, I must leave for the plaza right now, and sleep on the way, if hopping from bar to bar could be called sleeping…haha" Dewey says, oblivious to all else. "Now,"

Dewey begins to run around the room again, "My hat...where is that hat?"

"You mean this one?" Olegna says. He holds up a large maroon hat, an orange and purple feather sticking out of it.

"Yes!" Dewey grabs the hat and twirls it on his head most ungracefully, with a smile on his face. Two servants enter, place colored ribbons around his shoulders, and begin to escort him out.

"My king," Olegna says.

"Yes, thank you for your story. Ha! What a great—"

"You have not answered my request."

"Your request?"

"May I have your permission to return home?"

"Oh...oh yes! Home! How can I have forgotten? Yes, yes, sure, whatever. We will miss you, but go as you please!"

And then, with one fell swoop of his hat, Dewey exits, his servants running after him, and all the men's sensors scampering after them. Olegna looks after them for a moment, almost smiling at the frivolous joy in their stride, their merry faces grinning at the life they do not know, floating through time, scampering out the palace gates like a badly trained circus parade, their feet stumbling over themselves, sprinkling flurries of musical notes in their wake.

ΩΨΩ

The warm air feels odd to Olegna. It would be most fitting, he thinks, for the birds to stop their song, for the bees to stop their dance, for the sun to hold back its warmth, for don't they know he lost his war? He walks back to his house, his head down, while Disegno lives on from high above. Yet, the sun continues to shine, the birds continue to sing. Olegna cannot understand how.

Olegna arrives back at his Lyceum house. His suitcases stand before him like small servants themselves, their thick leather bodies trying to stand erect before their master, but clumsily stuffed with frivolous trinkets Olegna had grown accustomed to having in his time in Lyceum. They stand just as he left them, a group of actors so awkwardly cast, lining up, waiting their turn, just waiting *daring* Olegna to grab them and run out the door.

As if in response to their call, Olegna walks up to his suitcases. He tries not to look around his house, for fear he will find a distraction, a reason to stay. *No* he takes a deep breath and gathers his strength, *I must go now.* Standing in the midst of his suitcases, he grabs their leather strap handles and pulls them up. But they are too heavy. It is a funny sight: a man wrestling with his own possessions, cursing, sweating, balancing, lifting, all while his two small sensors stand by, calmly recording his struggles, never lending a hand to help.

It takes him a few minutes, but soon Olegna manages to carry all of them at once. He starts towards the door of his home, hurrying to leave. But in his haste, a small paintbrush falls from his suitcases and settles right under his heel. He trips, his foot sliding across the floor, paintbrush handle spinning under him, sending him sprawling up in the air with all his suitcases, flying through the air. He lands on his back. Hard.

His suitcases split open upon hitting the floor, spilling his belongings all over the ground. Biting his lip and clenching his teeth, he begins to gather his belongings. But his hand comes upon the chisel that he used to form El Totsira's sculpture so long ago. He sees some stone powder left on the metal blade. He brushes off the powder with his fingers and brings it towards his face, rubbing it on his skin, smelling, *tasting* the memories of his past. El Totsira! Yes, he thinks, memories are all they are now.

He begins to cry.

He cries for all these years he remained silent. He cries for all this time he has waited for justice to be dealt to him, as if the sculpture would just be delivered *I just wanted to drop off this package* by the clown himself. He cries for every trial he sat by and waited, for every change of season he had prayed for a real verdict. Sobs come from him uncontrollably, pouring out in waves built up by the dam of years. And, after a few minutes, our artist feels great release.

He opens his eyes. From where he is sitting, he can see the needle is still there, looking back at him from outside his window. He can see Disegno's sheet white face glaring back at him, scar and all. For a moment, Olegna is sure he can hear the clown's laughter, and cold fingers of terror touch his heart. The laughter is loud but far away, like the crack of hammer blows muffled by a blanket, or the screams of a maniac behind a thick sheet of glass. But soon, the terror in Olegna's heart turns to fear, fear to anger, and anger to revenge.

Olegna looks at the door he was going to walk out. But this time he sees only defeat to greet him. *To leave is to admit defeat* he remembers Francesca's words, *but defeat is impossible if you never give up.* Yes, Olegna's mind is turning as he looks to the needle, the ugly comfort of anger growing in his belly, and from that anger, hope.

Olegna stands up, brushes himself off, and walks across the room. The chisel is still in his hand. He examines the chisel closely, carefully wraps it in a velvet green cloth, and places it in a drawer. And as the smells and sounds of his birthday celebration carry on outside his door, he begins to make his own. Going from suitcase to suitcase, Olegna begins to unpack.

Lying in bed with his eyes open, Olegna stares at the ceiling. He sees the terra-cotta ornamentation running across the Posteriorian stucco, but his mind sees a great map of the land, with Brittany at its center, the High Court at the front, and standing before that, the needle. Olegna sees the stones upon which it stands as a flurry of cards, colorful but thin. They may boast strength, but, Olegna realizes, only through fraud. A hoax. He sees how easily they can crumble to the ground. Yes, with just a blow from the lips, the thin foundation of the needle can be sent in a flurry like a million sheets of paper drifting away, bringing all that is evil down with it. The needle must fall.

Olegna is surprised at the size of his grin and the cold in his heart. He has never felt this before, but for now, he likes it, and it lulls him to sleep. He does not know what the future holds, but only that there is much of it, and every dog has its day. But tonight, Olegna closes his eyes and sleeps like a baby, waiting for the sun to rise once again.

8

Love has reasons which reason cannot understand.
Blaise Pascal

A soft gladness fills the air of Kallipolis this time of year, a kind mist that kisses the Prioritans' faces as they walk through it, whispering nature's preparations for the coming spring. But this is not the weather we are talking about. It is not the spring of the plants, but the spring of the population. It is not the leaves and grass that will sprout for the first time (for that won't happen for a few more months in this barren land) but it is the newborn Prioritans that will blossom. It is this time of year when the Prioritans grow their society, when they group together to obtain a spouse so they can conceive and create new citizens of their land.

When Renee arrived in Kallipolis, there were thirty-six people residing in the land, Nicolas and Benedictus included. And now, there are hundreds of Prioritans. But still, the nation is in its infancy, and great satisfaction is taken in the opportunity to make the nation grow.

This evening, Renee walks to the procreation event on the western border of Kallipolis. Now, this is hardly an 'orgy,' since such a term connotes a gorging of more than is needed. But Prioritans never take more than needed. Nothing is superfluous. All sex, all everything, is for something. While the Prioritans arrive at this event with honor and delight in their hearts, their delight is only in the prospect of their mission to create new lives for the state, not for any physical pleasure of their own. Their faces remain downward and their words remain soft.

The event is held in a designated area on the outskirts of the land because the sexual activity taking place must be separated from the citizens' personal lives. The reader must understand that even though the creation of the nation is celebrated, the sex required to do it is merely tolerated. It must take place by the shore hidden behind the House of Wax, concealed from their homes and streets, where the moments and places of their personal lives cannot reach.

To prepare, the Prioritans bathe in the purification pools on the western shore. They have been fasting all day, so by the time they finally arrive at the pools, the cool waters help to sooth and awaken their exhausted bodies. The fasting and the bathing help to clear their minds and help them concentrate on fulfilling the mission O'Talp gave them, to build a mighty nation where justice and understanding may be shown to the world.

Renee dunks his head seven times, as is customary Prioritan practice. Christian sits by patiently, his ears perked up in wonder, his head nodding up and down with Renee's bobbing head.

Zinbiel and Benedictus are bathing in nearby pools, while Nicolas watches them from his wheelchair. After bathing, Ben fetches one of the buckets stored nearby, used to pour water over infants' heads for purification. He fills it with water, and silently pours it over Nicolas's face. Nicolas closes his eyes, and his head nods in mutual understanding. Zinbiel looks out to the east, wondering if Catherina ever made it to the pools.

As the hour comes to a close, Renee climbs out of his pool. The wind helps dry his body. Through his blindness, he can almost sense the whiteness of his skin against the dark night. Christian circles around him impatiently as he puts on his robes. He feels reborn, cleansed, pure, and empty. He hears footsteps approach him, and he recognizes the voice as Zinbiel's.

"My wise King."

"Ah," Renee nods his head in solemn acknowledgment, "Now is not the time for chatter."

"Good. And how are *you* thinking today?"

Renee tries and offers a smile.

Zinbiel says, "Are you ready for the festival?"

"The moon and sun seem to be so," Renee faces the sky and closes his eyes.

"More than I am, it seems," Zinbiel frowns.

Renee sighs, "I know that this is new to you. Many of the women often show great interest in newcomers, but you must remember the reason for the festivals, and why they are put aside for a special designated time and place—"

"For the procreation of our people."

The truth is, Zinbiel will have many spouses over the next few years, contributing many new lives to the Prioritan people. Indeed, Zinbiel will take many spouses, including the Electress Sophia (of Hanover), her daughter, and the Queen of Prussia. Renee turns away and kneels, feeling for Christian. His fingers find the wolf's fur coat, move to the top of his head, and come to rest on the wax spider on Christian's collar. His hand remains there for a long moment, his eyes closed. Finally, he gets to his feet.

He says, "Who is taking care of Nicolas?"

"Oh," Zinbiel says, "Ben is helping purify him. He is taken care of." *Why does he always worry about Nicolas?*

"Nicolas, you know, is the reason any of us our here today," Renee says.

Zinbiel steps back in fear. *Did he just read my thoughts?*

Zinbiel says, "Yes. But it was Ben who carried Nicolas on his back from Lyceum to this place."

"And it was Nicolas who told him where to go."

A moment of silence passes. The men look into each other's eyes as Christian moans and sniffs his master's feet. Zinbiel is the first to look to the ground.

"Ben is with Nicolas now," he says, "He is taken care of."

"Good. Then I will go into the festival now. Alone."

"Yes."

"Zinbiel, you are one of my closest advisors now. I would love to see it stay that way."

"Yes."

"We will see each other soon, my friend."

Zinbiel gives a small smile, and turns to see where Ben and Nicolas are holding. He decides to wait for them. He turns again and looks at the ground where Renee's feet just stood a moment ago.

ΩΨΩ

With Christian's paws pattering before him, Renee can hear the path he has to walk. With his walking stick in hand, our beloved philosopher king departs from the bathing pools and heads east to the field. Many Prioritans are already there; the mingling has begun. Renee hears the sound of breathing from the group of Prioritans as he draws closer, feeling their presence by the change of wind on his skin.

But before they draw closer, Christian runs off, leaving Renee alone.

"Christian," Renee begins in a calm voice, "Christian?" There is no answer.

The walking stick will have to do.

Repositioning the staff in his hand, Renee walks forward. His walking stick guides him, but without Christian at his lead, it takes him twice as long. He remembers traveling out in the wilderness, through the Cherava Woods away from his youth. Twenty minutes pass. As he gets closer to the event, Renee senses Christian may be close. He reaches for the small wooden whistle around his neck. But before he brings it to his lips, he is stopped more by the scent of the young woman than by her voice.

"Now, now, there is no need for that," the voice says, "Christian is right here."

He cannot see her smile, but he can hear it in her words. At once, Renee is reminded of Helene's cheerful voice getting him up *Up, up, up we go* on the warm Lyceumean mornings *It's time to get up. Say, how do you feel?* The fresh youthfulness of this woman's voice reminds Renee of how many years have passed and how much he has aged.

"Hello."

"Ha ha!" the woman has a child's laugh. She is kneeling before Christian, his wet tongue lapping the garlic from her outreached hand. Her voice has a sweetness rarely found in these lands. "My name is Elizabeth Palatine."

"Elizabeth."

"Yes. I thought the wolf could use some food. I took some out for myself, but oh, how he came running up to me like I was his mother. So I gave him half."

"That was very kind."

"Oh, no, it is not a problem at all. He is a pleasure," she looks at Christian, petting his head, "Aren't you?" After a few moments, she looks up to Renee. "Besides, I could be eating less, my King. We could all be eating less, for the sustenance of our bodies never require much at all."

"Yes."

"Now," Elizabeth stands up from her knees and walks toward Renee. She places her hand on top of his and lowers it from the whistle around his neck. Renee did not realize his hand was still there.

"Are you sure you may touch me?" Renee says. He feels intimidated by her, but refuses to acknowledge as much.

"Yes," Elizabeth says right away, "We are now within the borders of the event, and it is within the permissible months."

"Yes," Renee says, as if he was merely testing her.

There are the soft sounds of people moving around them, acquiring spouses for the evening. Small torches are lit, offering just enough light to enable the attending Prioritans to cohabitate, but not so much as to allow one to see the others' naked bodies any more than necessary.

"And not only may I touch you," Elizabeth says, "But I may be your first spouse for the evening's affairs."

"You may be my *only* spouse for the evening's affairs."

"Ha! I find that mighty unlikely, my King!"

"Why?"

"We all know what you have done to help this nation grow…how many spouses you have taken…how many Prioritan lives you have conceived…"

As Elizabeth's continues, Renee allows her sweet voice to penetrate. He feels a warm comfort overcome his heart. A hot iron on his lungs finally cools with the sting of menthol, sending drops of cool sweat squeezing through his palms. He draws deep breaths but it only becomes more difficult to breath.

Is this what they call love?

Renee has never felt this before. Such a feeling has never been felt within these borders. It was not prohibited; it did not need to be; there was just never any need for it. Love, or most any feeling for that matter, was needed in Kallipolis like a book is to the illiterate.

But, oh, this feeling! How it makes Renee's mind spin! *Is this what they call love? I have heard of erotic love, or Eros, as O'Talp once called it, but that was a love for studying, for obtaining knowledge. But this…love? A word never used in this land. Nothing I have ever felt. But just four letters, that is all this is. How can four letters create so much weight? What happens if I surrender? No, I cannot allow any feeling to guide my actions. I can control this. I must do this for the good of my nation, for the good of the Republic of Kallipolis. I can control this. The whole time, I must look at the ground, at the ground, attheground…"*

"And I shall call you Princess Palatine."

"What?" Elizabeth says.

Christian sneezes and looks at Renee in wonder, as if he, too, is puzzled by the King's words.

"I shall call you Princess Palatine," Renee says, surprised at his own words, "For tonight only. If you will allow it. If you will be my spouse."

Elizabeth smiles and walks over to Renee, taking his hand in hers.

"We will make this nation great, you and I. *I* will be your walking stick now," she says, "Follow me."

And she takes him.

The two disrobe with great meditation. Their honorable goal is imprinted on their solemn faces, on their minds. They stand naked in the silence of the night, studying each other from a distance. Elizabeth can see Renee's white body, his torso tall and thin like stretched pottery *what a beautiful thing to my eyes*. His smooth skin like porcelain, a reason for each and every muscle, each and every fiber. Nothing is superfluous; she realizes in awe, this body has all and only what it needs to survive—nothing more. It is perfect. In the flickering torch light, Elizabeth can barely see the faint outline of six stomach muscles, a mild stretch of small hills making their way down to a tall stone statue, a penis waiting for its role to be fulfilled, a creator waiting to create, made so perfect for this very purpose.

She proceeds to caress his stomach, but he slaps her hands away. She runs her fingers through his hair, but he pulls her arm behind her back. Hard.

"That...hurts," she says.

"Let us just do what we need to do," he says. But his mind thinks *what are you so afraid of?* He lets go of her arm.

Elizabeth makes an angry face at him. But she remembers who he is and stops.

But he cannot see Elizabeth remembers. *So I will open his eyes.* She comes to him. She runs her fingers over his face. He flinches but this time he submits. He brings his fingers over hers. A frown comes to her lips as she presses her thumbs over Renee's eyes because she sees the scars from the sting of orange acid around Renee's eyes, running down his cheeks. *There is only one such species of orange that can do such a thing* Elizabeth realizes *the Lyceumean orange...breeded and grown by Posteriorian scientist farmers...but he would never have gone to Lyceum...unless...is that where he is from? It cannot be!*

Elizabeth withdraws her fingers from his face. Renee smiles: he cannot see the fear in her eyes. No, he cannot see the fear turn to sadness and disappointment, the sadness turn to anger, fury, and plotting. *He brings us here to follow him through his life of abstinence, when all the while, he is from the land of lovers of sights and smells! And who knows what he is doing these days! Perhaps he returns there, yes, he returns to Lyceum when we all think he is hiding in seclusion here* but as the pieces of her shattered confidence in Renee settle in her stomach, Elizabeth begins to feel the cool comfort of revenge wrap itself around her heart. Forcing a shaky smile, she brings her fingers back to the King's face.

Renee feels Elizabeth's fingers reading his mind as they read his face. But he focuses on what his fingers see: a body so young, so sweet, like nothing a Prioritan has ever felt, *should* ever feel. For the first time, Renee can see her, using the eyes his fingers have become. Elizabeth is a short young lady, but thin and warm and inviting. Her face boasts deep brown-green eyes, circle cheeks giving her face a round shape, and a tiny nose. Though she is naked, she still wears a brown necklace made of cloth, with a thin white stone at its center. Her hair is neither brown nor blond, but the color of a rich nectar honey.

But this is a new thing to Renee: enjoying sensory experience to such an extent. Change is something that Renee (nor any Prioritan) deals with easily, and this feeling *just four letters* is no exception. The life he has lived, everything he has stood for, can be surrendered right now, *but no!* He feels Elizabeth's hands move quickly towards his belly, and down to his erection. Startled, Renee pulls her hands away as quickly as they came.

"What is the matter?" Elizabeth asks.

"We are here to make children of the land, of the Republic. Not to favor ourselves."

"Yes. But I am still your Princess. Princess Palatine. Remember?" She kisses his cheek, waiting for his response.

"And, and our creation will be great...because of it."

Elizabeth smiles.

Yes, that is right, Renee promises himself, *the feeling I felt for this...Elizabeth...how can I allow such a feeling to overcome me after all that I am, after all I have done? I can do this now, submit this one time, as I am forced to for the good of the nation. But my child must never be forced to suffer this. He must be better than this; he or she will have peace from the beginning, from the day it is born. Any such feeling must never taint the blood of this child...this child will be the ultimate Philosopher King.*

"Renee?"

"I am here, my Princess. We must touch as little as possible, but we must do all that is necessary to preserve the species, to create Prioritans according to O'Talp's will."

"Of course, my king," Elizabeth says. She lies upon the cool dirt earth, opens her legs, and invites him in. He closes his eyes. Furrowing his brow with intense concentration, he submits. And she takes him.

Yes, Elizabeth Palatine takes the first spouse she has ever taken, and Renee takes the last he will ever take (to the dismay and protests of his people). Yes, something happens this night, something Renee can never admit even to himself. Renee feels something beautiful, something fragile and lovely *just four letters* but something scary and unanticipated. And lying under his spouse, in the deepest throes of sex, Renee promises himself that his child will never be tainted by such alluring and deceiving sensory experiences, so he can become better than his father, the ultimate and just philosopher-king.

But how will I find my child in this large field? If children emerge from the earth upon which love is made, how can I mark this spot? No! I must not seek to find my child, for that is precisely the point—it is not my child, but a child of the land. Yes, but this is different, for if this child comes from Elizabeth, who weakens my mind, who causes me to…feel, then this child may have the same weaknesses. I must protect it. I must mark this spot. But she must not know. No one can know.

Between the slow, concentrated thrusts of Renee's body on top of her, Elizabeth can see the red sun begin to rise. It stretches its rich arms of light into the black sky like a golden yolk bleeding its runny body over a dark pan. Watching the sunrise, Elizabeth does not notice Renee untying her necklace, and burying half of it in the dirt beneath them. *Mark this spot.* If she did notice, she would have stopped it, because her necklace was her family's heirloom *this has been passed through the generations* given to her by her mother *wear it always* and given to her mother's mother *and never let it leave your sight.*

But her mother had overlooked the power of sex. Now, with her necklace lying in the dirt, Elizabeth is distracted by the rays of light filling the sky as Renee fills her, reaching, stretching, grabbing every inch of space for itself, and finally settling *ah* its warm body upon the landscape.

The two bodies lie still for a moment, enjoying their mere existence, naked and pure in the silent dusk. Then they part ways without a word, each gathering their clothes and belongings, making their way back to the east, not knowing of the seed left behind in the dirt whereupon they just laid. And as the sun makes its way higher in the sky, morning comes to wash away all signs of night.

But something is planted, in this very spot, something that is not washed away by the coming day. They say that all men and women come from the earth. The sons and daughters of Kallipolis certainly know this to be true. But often it is overlooked. With the many spouses taken throughout the festival, most Prioritans lose track of where they have been, and are almost surprised at the new anonymous citizens of Kallipolis, sons and daughters of the land, sisters and brothers to each other.

As the sun rises and hundreds of Prioritans retreat to the shelter of their homes to meditate, dozens of bumps begin to form in the procreation field by the shore. Eager to leave the confusing and deceitful experience of sex, Renee is quick to return to his quarters. As Renee and Elizabeth part ways for now, Elizabeth does not see the ground upon which they laid begin to swell.

ΩΨΩ

This was not the first time Renee had taken a spouse for himself. But this time, after parting with her, Renee cannot get Elizabeth *Princess* out of his head. Tossing and turning in his sleep the following night *Princess Palatine,* he feels a cold sweat break *my Princess, give me a child!*

Finally, he manages to get some sleep. He does not dream. His sleep is thin, but it is there. When he wakes up, it is late afternoon. Renee knows that most Prioritans stay in during the day to meditate, coming out to move their bodies or get fresh air at night, if ever. This is especially true after one of the festivals, when Prioritans remain alone indoors long enough to wash away the recent sensory experiences felt at the festival. They must mentally rejuvenate themselves, build walls around their minds, and extinguish any potential for damage the experiences at the festival may have caused.

Perhaps this is why Renee leaves his home this afternoon, so no one will see him. Or maybe his eagerness to see the plot of ground *a child?* draws him near, regardless of being seen. While I am there now watching over our King, I choose not to enter his mind. I will leave that to you.

Renee heads west with Christian lumbering behind. If Christian could mutter, he would *what now?* since he does not like be awakened from sleep. They avoid the southern border where there may be Posteriorians rallying. Posteriorians do not heed the schedule of the Prioritans, and they often choose to protest when Prioritans are in their homes. Perhaps this is to catch them off guard. (There have been stories of Prioritans emerging from weeks of silent meditation to find piles of colored, scented rocks sitting on their land. It took hours for the warriors to don their blindfolds and push the rocks away with their long shovels.)

The land is silent; the birds have ceased their songs long ago. Many in your world may not know, but birds only sing their songs to be heard. But if no one listens, they will stop coming out after some time. It is always fairly quiet here, the land a great desolate field with scattered dirt shelters far apart from each other—one would never guess civilization is here. But Renee takes no time to enjoy the silent expanse. He makes haste, which is not regular for him. He wears his haste uncomfortably, shaking his walking stick this way and that.

It is not long before they approach the large field where the procreation event took place just days ago. Christian gives a soft bark *yes* and sits down to rest. Renee finally smiles and takes in the breeze. He smells the ocean is near, and he knows he has finally arrived.

The field is covered in bumps. Using his pristine sense of direction, Renee makes his way through the field. He tries not to step on any bumps, though his walking stick shows him there are many; the swelling in the ground has begun. In just a few months, babies will come from the ground. Very soon now, there will be many new Prioritans to welcome into the nation.

But Renee moves on. He knows what he is looking for *mark the spot* and he finds it! For as his stick touches one of the bumps, he feels something lying on top. It is a hard object. He brushes away the dirt and lifts it up in his hands. He feels the leathery strap connected to a soft white body, cool and thin as a shell. And then, his fingers see it. It is Elizabeth's necklace!

Wasting no time, Renee throws the necklace aside and gets to his knees to feel the ground. The earth meets his fingers, and now Renee can plainly see the earth here is swollen with life.

"Ha ha!" Renee swells with pride, "You see, Christian? I am a father!" He has brought many Prioritans into Kallipolis before, but not with anyone like Princess Palatine. In his excitement, he finds a small stick, and spears it into the ground next to the swelling. His hands press a mound of dirt at the base of the stick, so it remains there tomorrow to mark the spot.

ΩΨΩ

Day after day, Renee sneaks out to the field. He goes to the spot of his offspring and he begins his work. He begins to leave his speeches a bit early, coming home later at night (dirty and exhausted no doubt), and leaves in the morning at the first daybreak. No one asks questions, for it is customary for Prioritans to mind their own business here in Kallipolis, as I hope you have realized by this time. *He is just going to meditate* the few who see him pass their homes think. Even his closest advisors, Ben, Nicolas, and Zinbiel do not take heed to their philosopher-king's actions; they have their own mental mission to wrestle with in the private dark silence of their own rooms. Of course, it will be Ben who begins to notice something is peculiar, but we must not get to that before he does, must we?

In the procreation field, Renee grunts under the weight of the large rock he is carrying. Christian runs excitedly before him, giving small yelps of curiosity.

"Hush!" Renee says, "No one must know we are here."

This is not only true because Renee's actions are a secret, but also because no Prioritan is allowed in the procreation fields until all new life has been formed and harvested, lest one may feel tempted to find his or her own child. This is because all children are children *of the land*; no one must think otherwise. So no one is allowed to be in the fields at this time. This way, no one will bond with what they think to be their child. It is the time of the pregnancy of the land, and anyone approaching these grounds shall surely be put to death.

Renee manages to set the large stone on top of the other stones he has carried here these last few weeks. The small stones tumble under the weight of this large one, but Renee runs off to get more. Hours pass, and the pile of stones continues to grow.

"Yes," Renee says to Christian, "Yes, these stones will be the materials we will need. And we must bring water and a hammer to crush some of these smaller stones, so we can make cement. Then we can bind the stones together, and cover this bump with the strongest fortification so that no experience from the world can ever get through!"

Christian cocks his head in confusion, and turns away in indifference. He stretches his canine body, yawning. But Renee does not see, and he continues to speak, as if to someone else.

"Yes," he whispers, looking down at the plot of ground, the life he has created staring up at him, "A future philosopher-king you will be, my child, so you will never have to bear the weight of confusing experience on your clean mind."

Suddenly, Renee hears a rustling behind a nearby rock. He looks up, but of course, he cannot see. His body freezes and his heart stops. *Did anyone see?* He realizes he has stopped breathing, and he takes a deep breath. Slowly, he makes his way towards the noise and he hears it again, the rustling of leaves, the flapping of wind.

"Hello?"

His words are met only by their echo. Just then, he hears the sounds again, the flapping of winds. Two birds take off from a nearby rock. They fly above his head and he feels their shadows pass over him. Christian looks up at the birds and looks at Renee curiously.

"Okay," Renee says to Christian, "That was nothing. But let us not get over confident. We shall take that as a warning. But no matter, it is time to work. We must get cement and stone, and with those materials in hand, yes, I will, I will protect my child from the outside world, to make sure that he never has to face it. Yes, he will be born empty as I was, but empty he will remain, until he will be ready to rule! Let us build an enclosure, a cave, a place where he will never leave, where his mind will never be confused, where it can grow without the muzzle of experience, for he will be the first pure man to ever live…completely pure—" Renee stops, his eyes open, surprised by the emotion so uncharacteristic of him. Christian moans. Worried about his master, he comes to him and buries his head in Renee's white hands.

"Yes," Renee smiles once again as if Christian can understand him, "Yes, an enclosure we must build, to make sure experience cannot reach my child. It will take time to build. It must be perfect. It must be impenetrable! He must never escape."

ΩΨΩ

As Elizabeth left the festival behind her, thoughts of Renee stayed with her, scampering behind her all the way home. Now, she sits cross-legged in her underground shelter, meditating, reaching, struggling to get closer to O'Talp. But images of the blind man disrupt her thoughts. She makes a fist, pumping her delicate fingers in and out. She recalls the touch of Renee's worn skin, the scars over his eyes, the yellow stains of acid, the mark of what can only be one thing: Lyceumean oranges.

She remembers the blind man from her earliest dreams. Oh, how it had felt so hopeful, so pleasing! She smiles, remembering the first time he came into her dreams, how she was so scared in the harsh biting wilderness, shivering, until she looked up and he was there. He was not facing her, but she knew he was looking at her anyway. Yes, he could see her not with his eyes, but with his mind. And before him, stood a small cottage—no, not a cottage—but a stone enclosure. It was simple but beautiful. He turned around to face her. He smiled briefly and his eyes spoke *come with me* and she followed him away, out of the wilderness.

As the smile remains on her face, Elizabeth lingers on these thoughts like cold hands near a warm fire. But she shivers as she feels the blind man's face on her hands. Burning sensations of acid tingle her fingers, shooting up into her arms and chest. She moans as she tries to get up to fetch a blanket. Her body fights against her, and she falls over, lying on the cold dirt ground. Her shivers disrupt her exhausted mind, jolting her body into erratic tremors during its desperate passage to sleep.

Elizabeth gasps *Uhh* as she wakes hours later. She stands up, brushing the dirt from her robes, and it is then she realizes that it has been days since the festival, and she has not changed her clothes. She looks to her washing bathe, and sighs at the thought of fetching water in this state. Nonetheless, she must find the energy to wash and pray to O'Talp for guidance. Walking towards her clothes bin, her hands rise to remove her necklace. They grasp at her neckline without thinking as they have done hundreds of times before. Only this time, she finds that her necklace is not there.

Oh! Her hands feel for it again, around her neck *unbelievable!* down her chest *but where could it be?* her tired eyes dart around the room *under the bed?* this is impossible *behind the thinking desk* I have had it my whole life *in the clothes pile.* Faces of her mother *always wear this* and grandmother *never take this off* flash through her mind. She digs into her pile of clothes, throwing clothing this way and that. Finally, she stops and stands still. Her arms cross against her chest, her head bows down, and she shudders. As she holds herself, she realizes she is shivering. But then, as her eyes look down towards the floor, she sees that her robes are covered with dirt, as if she had been lying *rolling* in the ground itself.

The festival! Of course, it has been days, but she has not changed her clothes. The festival is the only place she has been outside of her home for the last few months. Of course, that is where it must be! Though it is just before daybreak, Elizabeth gets ready to set out for the fields. Wasting no time at all, she refastens her robes around her. Taking a deep breath, she walks out of her home, with her hopes behind her and a long road before her.

9

Vanity is the quicksand of reason.
George Sands

How do you feel?" Dewey begins his speech as his father used to long ago.

"I, I didn't really have time to write my speech," Dewey says to the crowd's amusement, "Yes, I was trying to look for my hat, the one on my head, haha! You like it? And, and this artist...Olegna had pestered me about going somewhere...where, where was it? What did he want from me again? Some people are always bothered. Oh, no matter! Have I not planned what to say? Oh, but what exemplifies our nation more than beautiful improvisation and times of spontaneity? Oh, how the word sounds! Spon-tan-e-it-y!"

The crowd cheers. Dewey smiles in approval.

"Now. Thank you all, to those that came. There should be plenty of food and drink to go around here, so don't think you're missing anything by showing up."

Dewey takes a deep breath and continues.

"Today I want to talk about the world of the 'e.' Yes, the world of the empirical, the only world that knowledge can come from, the world where everything contains an e: experience, experiments, empiricism, the world of red, orange, blue, green, and yellow, the world of Lyceum, of the Posteriorian people. The only world there is."

Dewey takes a deep breath. He looks up to see a bird pass over the significant crowd-goers gathering before him. Many of them camped out here the night before. Dewey can see their tents flapping in the wind, their bonfires relit for the morning speech, some cooking eggs, turkey, and coffee.

"Today I want to talk about what has become a dirty word around here, but something that is beneficial to be reminded of, in case one fall prey to such comical beliefs. Today I want to talk about what many call God. I do not speak of the prophet El Totsira, the son of Rekha, whose human feet walked the same earth we stand upon today, whose holy presence is documented in the recordings of the sensors. I speak of the ghost whose existence is only claimed by fools. These fools claim to 'feel' this…God, through the, the whispers of the wind and the stray wanderings of their hearts.

"One may notice that there is no 'e' in God. From the day you were born, all you have experienced with your five senses are the laws of nature. You have never witnessed a great miracle, a violation of these laws. You have never seen, heard, tasted, or touched anything beyond the physical world. All you know of Godly experience are miracles that are founded merely in the testimony of the apostles who claim to have experienced those miracles on their own. And, and even they will admit that their senses are no greater than yours today! Now I ask you, will you believe their senses over your own? Would you rather live your lives according to what many claim to have experienced long, long ago, or would you live according to that which you yourself have directly experienced all the days of your life? The answer my friends, is an obvious one. Yet few…a few choose the first one. They attach more weight to the claims of experiences from those they never met than they attach to what they themselves experience at every waking moment. But this…this contradicts sense!

"The word miracle, in itself, means something that cannot happen—this is why it is called a miracle! Thus, for each claimed miracle, there must be a uniform experience against it, which allows it to be called a miracle. Simply, any miracle must be an exception to the usual laws of nature; it must occur less than its contradiction, otherwise, it would not merit the name 'miracle.' Again: a miracle must occur less than its contradiction.

"If this is the case, then there is always more evidence against the occurrence of a miracle than for it. And a weaker evidence cannot destroy a stronger. You see, my friends: no testimony is sufficient to establish a miracle, unless the testimony be of such a kind, that its falsehood would be more miraculous than the fact which it endeavors to establish. And we see this is impossible! Thus, to believe in anything beyond what your five senses have experienced in your lifetime is to…to…"

Dewey clears is throat. He opens his mouth to speak but chokes on his words. A deep chill comes over him, *when has this happened before?* when he sees the woman looking at him from the crowd. He stops speaking right before his own tears sting his eyes.

He sees *her.*

This time she appears as a middle-aged woman, but Dewey recognizes the big brown eyes as the same ones he has seen so many times before.

"The word miracle tells you itself…its occurrence must be miraculous indeed…against all experience…all…all…"

Her eyes look at him disapprovingly as before, but this time they do not taunt him. They seem instructive, but not hateful, as if saying *do not worry, my confused boy, my confused king, one day, one day you will learn the way.* He opens his mouth to call the guards, but he sees her nod her head in disapproval *no* but he struggles *you don't want to do that* to call the guards *get her!* but decides against it, firmly closing his mouth. He is surprised at his decision, but tries to push such thoughts away. He looks away, towards the other side of the crowd. Unable to resist, he looks back for the woman's face. He will find her this time, Dewey decides. He will catch her.

But she is gone.

Though a bit shaken by the mysterious woman, Dewey is able to shrug off his confusion to the crowd as his regular erratic self. At the closing of his speech, Dewey feels good. *I finished!* He enjoys his small victory over the woman. For this fat Posteriorian King who is so easily distracted, this mental achievement is notable indeed. He feels so good, in fact, that his voice gets louder at the end of his speech, booming over the immense crowd, laughs billowing out his chest. His eyes dart nervously through the crowd, but she is not there *oh she failed to distract me so* she disappeared *gave up!* And with that,

Dewey closes his speech by taking out his Posteriorian pipe (about as long as his body, and just as adorned, but incomparably thinner) and raising it in the air, shaking it with a great *hoo ha!* as most Posteriorians do before smoking in a group. Everyone in the crowd lifts their own pipes above their heads, answers with their own *hoo ha!* and waits for Dewey to light up. Dewey lights and takes a long, full draw, before releasing a large purple ring of smoke to hover above the mass. The crowd follows him with flames of their own *hoo ha hoo ha.* But in their own intoxication beneath a blanket of rainbow smoke, none of them see Dewey turn to return home.

None except her.

It is not long after Dewey leaves the stage that the sounds and smells of the gathering fade from his experience, and with it, his pride. The only thing that remains is the face of the woman *that woman;* those two dark eyes glaring at him from under that hood, following his every move. He can feel them stabbing into his back as he leaves the stage, the laughs of the crowd growing fainter, his smile fading. He can feel those eyes in his head, following him east to the palace, up to his royal quarters, and into his bed.

ΩΨΩ

The sun makes way for the darkness of night, awakening the moon from its daily slumber. As the luminaries change places, Dewey lies awake in bed. He stares at the ceiling for hours thinking of her *that woman*, his hands folded under his head. *What does she want from me?* He studies the colored specks of paint splattered on his ceiling as his sensors scrutinize his thoughts closely from his bedpost. He hears the scratches of their writing-feathers on parchment correlating with his thoughts, but they are nothing to him; he hears them as he hears the sound of his own breathing: sounds he's heard his entire life.

What does she WANT?

Without thinking, Dewey jumps up from his bed. This does not startle his sensors who continue recording indifferently, but it surely would have startled anyone else there. The Posteriorian king stands still for one moment, eyes looking around the room. He realizes he has not taken off his robes from the speech. He longs for some fresh air. His hands pat his robes as they often do before he is about to leave on a voyage *do I have everything I need?* He grabs a golden flask with glittering stones from a tabletop, shakes it to make sure there is drink inside, and pats his pockets. After a moment, he walks swiftly out of his room, trotting down the stairs, and out the rear exit of the palace into his father's gardens, his sensors stumbling after him.

He turns east, towards the stables.

In his younger days, Joachim had built a stable to the northeast corner of the Royal Gardens so that he could keep horses. Young Katherine had thought it a splendid idea; she enjoyed watching her husband working in the sun, his tall muscular arms nailing in the roof, his smile at the sight of her standing by, a large jug of orangeade waiting for him by her side. It was unusual for a Posteriorian king to be so physically active and to work so diligently on one project, but the people loved Joachim, and the few servants that saw him turned their heads away without question.

As his years caught up with him, Joachim began to ride his favorite horse, Dylan, into the woods east of Brittany. Dylan was a brave horse of brown, a horse of good speed and strength, though the nation's scientists and necromancers were disappointed in the Judge's choice of steed; they had bred horses of greater color and variety, but Joachim had paid them no mind. It was Dylan he loved.

Of course, there were other horses. Yes, there was Duster, Love, Ecstasy, Sun, Lincoln, Luna, and Flower (whose name was changed to Katherine after Katherine's untimely death). Love was white with brown spots. Ecstasy was white with smaller rainbow speckles, created by the necromancers. Luna was the smallest horse, and she was completely white, save for a pink patch between her eyes. Lincoln was the strongest and the biggest of them all, a black horse, selected by Joachim for use in the races out near the border, or for his secret long, mighty runs through the White Plains. Yes, Joachim looked regal and noble on

Lincoln, his tall frame bent over Lincoln's massive body, running as fast as the wind would take them.

By the time Dewey approaches the stables, he is covered in a cold sweat. He can still feel the eyes of the woman on his back. The stable is a simple structure made of wood. It is a long building, one of the only standing structures in all of Lyceum vacant of any ornamentation, color, or decoration. Dewey wonders how it has managed to escape such renovations throughout the years. The inside reveals an aisle down its center with horse pens on either side. It is functional enough.

As Dewey approaches, his eye catches the brown hair of a woman through the small dusty window. Perhaps if Joachim had built the windows bigger (like any other Posteriorian would have), Dewey would be able to see if this really was a woman, and if so, who. But through the window, her hair looks familiar to Dewey. Like he has seen it before. *Could it be...that woman? The woman with the brown eyes?* Dewey rushes to the door and goes inside.

But Dewey finds a servant, the caretaker of the stable, sleeping on his chair. Dewey's eyes dart around the room for the woman, but no one else is there. Suddenly, Dewey thinks he hears a rustling of leaves outside the rear of the stable. Dewey strains to look out the small window, but the servant is startled from his sleep behind him. The servant is sure surprised to see his King out and alone at this hour.

"Oh! My, my good ol' king!"

"Wa...was someone just here?" Dewey asks, "I think they may have just run away."

"What? Who?"

"I am asking you if anyone else has visited you just now."

"Does it look to ya' like—" the servant sees the fire in Dewey's eyes, "Uhm, naw. I was just...sleeping. I was alone. No one comes out in these hare woods."

"Then why are there two mugs of ale in front of you?"

"What?"

"You are but one man."

"Now," the servant collects himself, "With all due respect, when has any Posteriorian been questioned about his amount of drink? Now, if ya like, this other hare cup is for you!"

Dewey smiles. He notices the way the old servant's chin moves to the side. His shriveled lips part slowly to reveal a few rotten teeth. He has no teeth on his bottom gum, so his bottom lip peels back into his mouth like an old worn sheet of flesh stretched over a rail.

"Yes," Dewey sets himself down.

"How, how do ya feel?"

"Are you the horses' caretaker?"

"Yup, I am. Noah's my name. An' always has been. Since I was born here in Lyceum. I didn't really want to be born here, but my momma didn't really give me much of a choice. I wasn't in on the decision-makin-process, y'hear? I swear, I been here so long that I can nearly hear these hare horses talkin to me. I could see it in thar' eyes! I got them horses their food this morn, and I been up all day, combin' thar' hair and shining thar' feet, I can't remember the last time I—well enough about me. Yer lookin' for a woman?"

"I am having…" Dewey takes a deep breath, "trouble. Yes, trouble sleeping at night. I need to get some fresh air. I thought…I thought that maybe a horse ride—"

"A horse ride! Of course! Your papa used to come for the same thing. Lookin' just like you, he would."

"Isn't there a horse my father would ride in times of strife? To get some air and…ease his mind, that is?"

Noah smiles. He puts his hands on his knees, stands up, and walks down the aisle. Dewey's eyes wander. He smells the stale air and notices the rotting wood covering the simple structure. He sees Luna and Duster closest to him, their tangled hair dirty, their eyes tired. Lincoln's large black mane is revealed over the top of his fence on the far north side of the stable. Though his mane seems neglected, Lincoln maintains his grace.

"The wood here is rotting. The horses are unkempt," Dewey says.

"Now, I know ya came here for one thing, peace of mind. An' I can give that to ya—"

"And, and why was this stable made with wood anyway? Why not stone, marble, glass, and sand, like everything else in my kingdom? Unpainted, undecorated, unadorned, this stable stands naked, its simple skeleton rotting in shame."

"Please," the servant seems to hide his emotion, "Please let me fetch ya a horse—"

"But what happened to my father's stables? Why are they rotting?"

"Oh, don't ya mind that—"

"Tell me!"

"Okay," Noah pauses, and his eyes moisten in memory, "With all due respect, yar' father was the one Posteriorian that took pride in his work. He took pride not by laughing hauntingly and drinking, nor by rushing to completing a job in order to smoke and celebrate. Naw. He took pride by being responsible, disciplined, and precise. He built these hare stables himself, out of the woods south of hare. Simple as they were, they have stood all this time, longer than most any other buildin' in Lyceum—"

"Now I see why it is falling apart."

"Well, no Posteriorian, except myself, cared to maintain a simple stable as this. Thar' many hidden things of Joachim's life that the Posteriorians would not have approved, so he kept em' hidden. But since they were hiddn', like this here stable, Joachim's death took them along with him. The death of Joachim was also the death of his *things* so closely and secretly tied to his life."

"And, and as a blasphemy of El Totsira's word, they too, shall rot," Dewey tries to ignore the sudden pit in his stomach just as those words leave his mouth.

Noah looks at the ground before him.

"Ya want a horse," he says in a low voice.

"Yes, a new, exciting horse that I can ride fast," Dewey gets excited again.

"Yes. I mean, most of these horses were around in your father's time, so they are not too young anymore. But they still ride well, for it has not been too long in the life of a Posteriorian horse."

"Whatever. I just look forward to the ride. Ah, that will give me piece of mind. Oh, the wind blowing through my hair, I, I want a horse my father would *never* ride, one beautiful horse that can outrun the speed of light…to outrun this woman, the woman's eyes—" Dewey gains control of himself, embarrassed at himself. "Ahem, yes, that kind of horse."

"Peace of mind, eh?"

Dewey expects Noah to question him *What woman?* but he does not, and Dewey feels relief. Dewey's eyes settle on Ecstasy, but the servant seems to think intensely to himself. Then he rises his eyebrows, as if he has just come to a decision. He quickly grabs for Dylan's reins.

"Here," the servant says, "This is Dylan."

"Oh," Dewey says, his eyes still fixated on Ecstasy's colored mane, "Dylan, huh?"

"He may look simple, but he is exactly what you need at a time like this."

"Uhm…"

"I see you fancy Ecstasy, as did your father," the servant lies.

"My father rode Ecstasy?! But I thought Dylan—"

"You thought what your father wanted you to think. But Ecstasy was his horse of choice. Dylan is a good horse. He will listen to anything you say," the servant says, walking the middle-sized horse to his king. Dewey can see the horse look at him quietly, his hair all brown. But Dewey notices the scars on Dylan's rear. *Was he whipped for something bad?* Noah can see the question in Dewey's eyes, but he does not tell him that Dylan was once beaten and whipped by an angry Posteriorian near the plaza, and Nietchai came and saved Dylan by putting his arms around the horse's neck. Nietchai died with his arms around Dylan, ultimately saving the horse, as if he had come to take his own life in exchange for the life of the horse.

Suddenly, Dewey finds himself overcome by the stable's dark walls. A part of him screams to get out on the road.

"Are you sure—"

"*Take Dylan!*" Noah seems to regret his tone, "Uhm, ahem, Dylan hare is a good one, I tell ya!"

"Alright," he says, jumping atop Dylan's back, "Whatever. Do not wait for me, for I may be gone most of the day."

And with that, he gives Dylan a strong but appropriate kick and Dylan sets forth immediately, into the warm evening air. Dust kicks up from the ground, forming clouds behind the King, such that even if Dewey had looked back at that very moment, he would not have seen the strange smile forming on Noah's lips.

ΩΨΩ

Dewey rides to the east, behind the palace, and into the shadow of the needle. He turns south, traversing the beautiful roads between Brittany and the woods. As the Evergreens begin to multiply, he looks to his left. He wonders what is in these woods. Dark stories have been told of the ugly man in the cottage. He remembers all those stories of Nicolas. He wonders how many details are really true. What was it like for Nicolas to live in these woods? Where did the young lens-crafter (whom Dewey does not know is now Benedictus, a high advisor in Kallipolis) take Nicolas on that day, when Posteriorian soldiers came upon them, and the young lens-crafter carried Nicolas on his shoulders, running into the wild. *Did they survive?* Dewey wonders. Where did they go?

Thoughts of Renee flare up in Dewey's memory. Old thoughts. Good thoughts. He remembers the first day they spoke after their fight, after Dewey killed Renee's cat and blinded him. After that, they hadn't spoken for many months. It was a long winter, Dewey recalls. But they first spoke again when Renee tripped over a rope, and Dewey walked by just at that moment *Come, let's help you up* and they held hands for the first time *that was nice* and Renee did not want to let go *yes brother, it…most certainly was.*

Sitting high on Dylan's back, the wind does its wonders upon the king's heart, and Dewey begins to feel better. The woman's eyes are no longer upon him *they can't chase me here.* There is no weight upon his chest. He smiles, throws his head back in jest, and praises Dylan *that's right boy* patting the horse's head and stroking his mane with one hand *run run run!* while holding the reins with the other. The trees seem to shower them with cool air, and Dewey gazes at the beautiful colored birds present in those woods, their small bodies fluttering like confetti above the fat king's large grin. Dewey's grin does not fade, and Dylan seems glad to run with the king on his back.

That is, until they hit the quicksand.

Now, Dylan knew these roads fairly well. Joachim had skirted these woods a few times before. Yes, Joachim had even met Nicolas briefly, and that had been quite a tale in itself, but I must not reveal to you the details of that encounter. Oh, I was there, alright; I saw them and I heard their words. But who I am must not be revealed, at least until I have nearly completed this tale. It is enough for you to remember that Joachim was never quite fully Posteriorian, and it was towards the end of his life when he met Nicolas and he began to change. He wanted to sit at the last trial of Disegno and give a final verdict. His last breaths of consciousness were met by throes of cries for O'Talp—did you think this was all Renee's doing? No matter.

Most all the Lyceumean horses knew of the horrible quicksand spots around the outskirts of their empire. After two horses (Dorothy and Spice) had died from drowning, the other horses knew *just knew* from experience that once stuck, one can never get out. Thus, the other horses had been careful to identify and avoid the scent of quicksand with their 'sixth sense.' Perhaps Dylan took Dewey here on purpose or even under order. Did Noah plan this? But perhaps not. How smart can a horse really be? Here I leave you to your own suspicions.

I will tell you that Dylan senses the quicksand before Dewey does. The king is looking up at the flocks of rainbow birds and butterflies with a huge grin, when suddenly Dylan screeches to a halt, throwing Dewey off his back. Dewey flies through the air, his fat belly wobbling out of his robes. He lands in the sticky, moist quicksand. Struggling to get up before the sand can grab him, he turns just in time to see Dylan turn around in panic, and run off in the other direction.

Dewey tries to move, but the sand is just above his ankles, and he cannot budge. *Dylan!* he could scream, but he saw the horse's frightened face before it ran away, and he knows it will do no good. The mud slips its thick mucky fingers around his ankles, his shins, his knees, and his thighs. He looks this way and that, but no one is around. It does not take long for the sand to pull him down, until his body is mostly covered. The ground is already up to his belly when he begins to scream.

"Help! Help! Is…is anybody there?"

But no one answers.

"Anybody? *Anybody?*"

His eyes jerk this way and that, taking in all the wonder of the natural world, maybe for the last time. His mind reaches around frantically, searching for an idea, a last strand of hope. He wonders who may hear him. Who may be in these woods? No one comes here. There is no one around. But Dewey is the king and he is dying. There must be someone!

"Anybody? Please! Help!"

But Dewey snuck out in the night; nobody knows he is here. *Who is the only one who can hear me?*

The sand reaches his shoulders, and he manages to free one arm, lifting it high in the air. His eyes close and hot tears run down his cheeks. And then, he whispers.

"Oh…oh, God. Please help."

The air is silent. The sand wraps itself around his neck, weighing him down.

"Please, God. Help me."

"You cry for a God, yet you claim He does not exist!" a voice says.

At first, Dewey does not believe his ears. He dismisses the voice as his conscience, his own mind speaking to him in disapproval. Then it comes to him; is there really someone there? Who is the author of that voice?

"Is…is anyone there?" Dewey cries.

Suddenly, he hears a loud rustling in the nearby wood, a rustling much like that he had heard from the stables just three hours ago. And behold! An old and pious woman walks out from behind the trees, her brown eyes glistening, her warm face familiar. Dewey recognizes her as the woman he's seen at his speeches. It is her. *That woman!*

She walks towards the edge of the quicksand and looks down at him, still flapping about for his life. Dewey sees that *to be born* she looks exactly as he had always imagined Rekha to look *first you have to die.*

Dewey feels himself sinking once again, and he remembers his plight.

"Help me," he says, "Please."

"You were asking for God just a minute ago, and now you want me? I can assure you, we are not one and the same."

"Who…who are you? Your clothes are not from this nation. Why do you come to my speeches? Did you follow me here? Was that you in the stable? What…what did you tell Noah?"

"I see Dylan took you to the quicksand."

"Wha—? Was this a…plan?"

"Everything has a plan, my king."

"You…and Noah? Did…did—who are you?"

"You do not seem to be in the right place to be asking questions. But you may call me Princess, for that I once was."

"Well, Princess," Dewey looks at the woman's stick. He knows she can help him, and he is angered by her indifference to his plight. "I did not mean to call out to any God, for how can I ask someone for help that I never even met? But now I see you, so if you would kindly—"

"Yet, in your desperation, you chose to call Him."

"Oh, how foolish, that was! I did not really say such a thing, now did I?"

She looks at him.

"Haha!" Dewey forces a nervous laugh, "So, maybe I did! Now can, can you help—"

"You did."

"Well, I, I couldn't have meant to do such a thing! Since I had never experienced Him, how can I ever know He exists?"

"And that is what I am here to persuade you. A fool you are—you experience him every day! He has left his intelligent signature on the entire world around us! Have you ever studied the mechanics of the human eyeball? The way birds all know their way south? How bats can see with their ears? How toads bring their eyeballs into their head to help push down the food? How the sun is not too close nor too far? How the stars, the sun and the moon, the planets, how everything is just right? How the world is so comfortable, and there is everything one can ever need?"

"Except a rope."

"Take an orange, of which you have many in Lyceum—"

"I hate to interrupt, but the quicksand is rising fast. Please help me, you must grab a stick or something...save my life!"

"Of course I will help you," the woman says, "But you must do something for me first."

"Of course! Whatever you wish, it will be yours! I, I have the greatest treasure in the world! All the gold you want—take it, if you please. It's, it's yours!"

"No."

"What?"

"No. That is of no interest to me."

"What? Then what do you want?"

"You must declare your devotion to God Almighty. Then I will save your life."

By now, Dewey's desperation has begun to give way to his Posteriorian temper flaming up through his belly, motivating him to teach this woman a thing or two, despite his demise.

He slips further into the quicksand, which moves up, closer to his chin.

"Take an orange," the woman begins again, "Perhaps the one you blinded Renee with. Now, if you look closely, anyone can see that each and every drop inside the orange is specially packaged so as to maintain its freshness and flavor to the highest possible degree. But who packaged every individual drop? It can only be He."

Dewey's anger rises with the sand at his throat.

"You know I am finished," he says, "and my life is at its end, and you come here to preach to me? You...woman. My brother, Renee, tried to persuade me of God's existence when we were just children, and it didn't work. Yet he argued by way of reason and you argue by way of experience, by man's experience of the world. You refuse to aid me in my plight, so I will refute your argument and persuade you otherwise, if it's the last thing I do! What you say is that order and purpose are observed only when they result from an intelligent author. I have but three refutations, if you care to hear them."

"Do you have some other place you need to be?"

"The problem is that order doesn't need to come from an intelligent author—it is observed regularly, resulting from presumably mindless processes, like a snowflake or crystal generation. Also, your argument assumes nature and our world to be of intelligent design, but, but this analogy is incomplete, since you have no other worlds to compare our world to—so you can never know if ours is intelligent. See, 'intelligent' is a relative term. Yes, one may know which *human*-designed structures are intelligent—just compare a pile of stones to a brick wall. But in order to point to a designed universe, we would need an experience of a range of different universes. We have no such experience, so I cannot even briefly hold to such an analogy.

"Finally, even if we conceded that this well-ordered natural world requires a special designer, then God's mind (being so well ordered) *also* requires a special designer, and so on ad infinitum. For once you concede that any special design needs an intelligent author, what right do you have to stop after the first step?"

"And that is how, young King, we know God is infinite. Your refutation does not disturb me, for we can rest content with an inexplicably self-ordered divine mind."

"But then why not rest content with an inexplicably self-ordered natural world?"

The woman shuffles her feet. She did not anticipate such refutations, but they do not disturb her.

"Because you need Him. We all need Him. We are all sinking in quicksand. You will see."

She walks right up to the edge of the quicksand and looks down at the poor king, giving her look of disapproval like a mother glaring down at her little boy, his hand still in the cookie jar. She wonders how quickly his nation will fall once he is gone.

The quicksand rises above Dewey's chin and begins to cover his mouth. But at the last moment, he points up his face to the sky. He tries to raise his free hand to brush away the rising sand, but now both of his arms are stuck. Closing his eyes, he remembers his conversation with Renee, how *elevated* Renee seemed because he had something to believe in.

"Just because we need something, does not mean it exists. I…I think you people believe in God because it gives you a special purpose in your meaningless life, don't you?"

"Are you speaking to me, or to yourself?"

"And if God does not exist, man would invent Him anyway."

"Your insults to God are comparable to an infant's kicks at a parent tucking him in. Your fists are small, and you are about to meet Him, face to face. I give you one last chance. Declare your devotion to God Almighty!"

Dewey does not hear the last two words, for his ears are covered in sand. Licking his lips one last time, he closes his mouth *will this mouth ever open again* and lets the sand take it *will I ever taste food again?* The ground covers his ears completely now, *will I ever hear music again* and he lets the sand take his hearing too. Sticking his nose up through the ground, he takes one last smell of sweet forest air *the smell of myrrh, ever again?* before submitting to the earth. His eyes look up at the fluttering leaves above, a blanket of rainbow shapes looking down at him, dancing freely, ushering him a final farewell. Finally, he closes his eyes and feels the ground rise above his head. He waits patiently for the darkness to take him.

ΩΨΩ

Dewey drowns, but he does not struggle. His eyes are closed, but he can see everything. He sees his mother Katherine in her deathbed, Joachim standing close by. Katherine smiles at Dewey and nods her head. She must know he is dying, and she reaches out her hand to Dewey to invite him into the next world. But Katherine looks so healthy, nursing Renee in her arms. Suddenly, Dewey sees his mother get skinnier, her flesh raveling within itself, then fading entirely. As Katherine fades from view, Dewey can see Helene begin to appear in her place. Joachim stands by, unaffected by the transition, as if it had never happened.

Dewey is then taken to the fields of his youth, the agriculture lessons he celebrated as a child. He sees the giant Posteriorian grapes, and he remembers the first time he saw four men carry a cluster of grapes, a man at each end of the pole *how did they taste so good?* He remembers the first time he saw the massive Venus fly traps of Lyceum *how do they know when to close?* The tremendous guavas, star-fruit, pomegranates, mangoes, coconuts, and of course, the great and thorny durian. Also, he sees the greatest fruit chosen by the Posteriorians, the orange, its sheer size matched only by its taste, its beautiful acid dripping through its peels, it juicy body preserved, cradling and treasuring each and every droplet *each one specially packaged* like a jewel.

At last, his lungs submit to the white fire burning in his chest. Dewey begins to exhale his last breath, and as he does, *who made all these wonderful things?* he thinks of God.

Suddenly, he feels a pair of hands grab his own. They grab his wrists and pull him up with amazing strength. His head breaks the surface and he gasps for air. Sputtering sand out of his nose and mouth, he wipes the dirt away from his eyes just enough to see the woman *that woman* securing the end of a rope to a nearby tree, and throwing him the other end. The rope lands in front of him, but for a moment Dewey pauses, looking from the rope to the woman *who are you* wondering *did you just read my mind?* and his eyes gleam with hope. Pulling his other hand free from the earth, Dewey takes hold of the rope. His strong arms pull his fat body up onto dry land.

"You were far below ground. Almost dead," the woman says, "But you came to God just in time. But it took you some time."

"Sometimes, to be born," Dewey smiles, "first you have to die."

"But why now? Why do you believe in God? Tell me!"

Dewey tries to speak, but sand catches his throat, and he rolls over on the ground coughing.

"Oh my!" the woman says, and Dewey thinks he sees her smile, "You really did it, didn't you? Dylan really did you in."

"We, we…ahem," Dewey says, "We both know it was not Dylan."

"Indeed."

The woman remains silent, but she looks at Dewey lovingly, waiting. He looks at himself and sees, to his amusement, that he is completely covered with golden yellow sand; he looks like a plump yellow fish floundering on land, or an old bronze statue from the days of Rekha. Brushing off some sand, he sits up on the ground, lifts his chin, and begins to speak.

"When, when I was drowning, and I began to feel my lungs give out, and I thought of the life I was leaving, the world we all experience, and I wondered if I would ever experience those things again. I remembered the first time I saw the giant Posteriorian grapes. There were, haha, four men carrying just one cluster, and at the time, I…I thought this was an amazing thing! And oh, the guavas, the starfruit, the beautiful durian! You were right—it is all so perfect! Oh, how the Venus fly traps know just when to close, how bats can see in the dark, how birds always know their way home—and even the Posteriorians, the greatest scientists in…in the world, how even we…we know nothing of these things!

"The Posteriorian orange. How big it is, how beautiful and tasty," Dewey notices he is licking his lips, "And how immense they are, but even in their great size, how they carefully and, and…specifically care for each and every specially-packaged drop! Just as we experience human invention, such as the wheel or the skyscraper, to be of design and contrivance, I am forced to infer the same conclusion to these natural things. And, and this is why I believe in God."

"No."

"Wha—" Dewey's mouth opens in surprise.

"That is not why you believe in God."

"What? But didn't you say—I just said—okay, then, why? Why do I believe in God?"

"Because I told you to. You *will*, however, believe in God, because of everything that I have told you."

"What?"

"You believe in God now because you had to. Because you did not want sand up your nose."

"Huh?"

"We are all driven by necessity, my boy. And necessity can even overcome the reason of the Prioritans or the experiences of the Posteriorians. You believe in God because you *needed* to. I told you, we all need Him. As you said once before: out of desperation."

Dewey is confused at the woman's words *didn't she just say before that it was through experiencing the intelligent world?* and how she changed her mind so quickly. 'It is not necessity that allows me to believe in God,' Dewey thinks, 'since I was ready to die. It was the grapes, the oranges, the Venus fly traps that led me to my belief.'

Of course, Dewey does not realize the woman's reason for changing her position. See, women can use their words to make men think certain things are their own idea. But men only use their words for simple commands and expressions. Women use words as tools to change the world around them, while men use words as expressions. Men are simple, especially a Posteriorian man like Dewey. He has no mind like this woman *Princess;* he does not realize that she now speaks of necessity to make Dewey think that the original argument was his idea in the first place. And he does.

ΩΨΩ

Dewey has much time to think on the long walk home. The pain in his legs is offset by thoughts in his whirring mind. He feels like his whole life has changed, his entire belief system, like all his insides have been sucked out of his body, mixed around, and placed back inside in different places. Even his sensors are a bit startled by his changes, but their faces do not change, their hands keep writing, and their tiny legs carry them swiftly behind their master as they always have.

The king's foot snaps a sharp twig. Dewey winces in pain, but continues his walk. After a while, his feet enjoy the soft blanket of leaves and warm grass laid out before them by the oncoming summer months. But Dewey is unpleasantly surprised that no one has run to his aide. Since Nicolas left these woods, Posteriorian guards are supposed to keep watch in the forest, in order to extinguish any threat to Posteriorian society. But no one is here. Dewey treads on for hours, but only silence surrounds.

It does not take long for his thoughts to settle in his head. They germinate their idea of a God, sprouting a religion based on El Totsira's long-forgotten principals as portrayed in his divinely-inspired book. See, El Totsira wrote a divinely-inspired book with drawings and patterns that were mostly dismissed as indecipherable. Few experts were able to see patterns in the way the colors and shades were aligned, but its interpretation has always been open to dispute. But now, the messages begin to wrap themselves around Dewey's heart: the God of Li, the tenants of experience, the daily feasts, the weekly festivals, the abolition of the idea of causation. And thus, the Posteriorian God of Li begins to form in the first Lyceumean citizen.

By the time Dewey arrives back at the palace, the sun has already risen, reminding Dewey of the early sunrise of summer. He takes a cool bath, washing all the sand from his body (though much of it settled on his floor as he walked in). He begins to feel his eyelids weigh. He sleeps like a baby, late into the day.

ΩΨΩ

Dewey wakes to the late afternoon. When he goes to pee, he sees all the sand on the latrine floor from the night before. Making haste, he dresses and goes to Joachim's old thinking room to sort out his thoughts. When he arrives at the door, he stops himself for just a moment *why am I here* completely shocked at himself *I have always used my belly and heart over my mind* but proceeds to enter, though a bit shaken up.

He is greeted by darkness and dust. He coughs and it hurts his lungs, still worn from the quicksand last night. His eyes scan the room as they grow accustomed to the dark. After a few minutes, he sits down in his father's chair, where Renee first sat with wax in his hand. Looking up at the large wall before him, Dewey can see the faded marks of letters he once wrote in a fit or rage *God is dead* but they have been erased *Nietchai.* But as his eyes get used to the gloom, Dewey can see that someone *something* had written over them. He can read it quite plainly now.

Nietchai is Dead.
-God

A miracle! He shudders. Raising an arm to his forehead, Dewey stands up and begins pacing around the room. He almost runs over his sensors, but they scuttle out of his way just in time. Before a minute passes, he sticks his head out into the main hall and shouts in his most bellowing Posteriorian voice.

"Jon! Yelekreb! Come here at once!"

A few moments pass, and a young servant runs up to answer him.

"My King! What can I—"

"Get Jon and Yelekreb for me. I need to speak to them."

It does not take long for the servant to fetch Dewey's friends. Once they arrive, Dewey wastes no time at all. He orders them to gather the people.

"There will be a great religion established here today," he says, "for this is a grand day indeed! Gather them at once!" and Yelekreb and Jon waste no time sending out dispatchers to tell the people to gather for a final celebration, to listen to their King, to accept the God of Rekha and El Totsira, the God called Li.

The Posteriorians have done this many times before, and they do not hesitate to gather to feast, celebrate and listen to their king. I have described the Posteriorian gathering many times, so it would suffice to say this was just as large, with just as many colors, odors, sounds, and flavors, all covered by floating clouds of rainbow smoke and intoxicating smells. But this time, the people see a light in Dewey's eyes they have never seen before. And in their music, sex, and feasting, most of the crowd actually looks up to listen as their king begins.

"Much has happened to me over the last few hours, events that I will not recount...but I have had many informative experiences...for is that not how a man learns the correct way to live? Once again, we must change the way we live, we must seek the most beautiful life possible, no matter what the cost, no matter how arduous the journey may be.

"The Prioritans and other nations may criticize our constant changes, our inability to stay still, our refusal to stop growing. They hold on to permanence like it is a good thing, never giving a reason for such stubbornness. Their minds remain closed to change, and their chins raised above, their eyes refuse to look down upon us. They see change as a weakness, but, but we know better than that. Walk through the streets of Lyceum on any day, and all one would see would be construction, the mending of the broken, the grooming of the unkempt, the adorning of the naked. We have always been open to change, trying to improve upon the trial and errors of our past. And today shall be no different.

"Today I must announce new realizations that have come to heart. I must tell of the intelligence that our scientific world exhibits: the way the sun and moon revolve around the Earth, of grapes so large they can only be carried by a group of strong men, yet light enough to hang from the vine without falling off, of bats who can 'hear' their way through the dark caves, or oranges....oranges whose drops are specially packaged, each and every one in its own brilliant sac, oranges whose juice is so delicious and acidic, only a great chef could have cooked this up!"

The people cheer, but seem a bit hesitant at the path their king is going.

"Yes, that is right," Dewey continues, "only a master chef, a creative architect, an intelligent designer could have made such wonderful things, that all...seem to work out flawlessly. I can speak about the human eyeball for hours, yet I would only tap the surface of its brilliance."

A moment passes and the people do not cheer. Dewey cannot decide whether the people's unresponsiveness comes from disagreement or from mere indifference. He decides the latter, based on his experience with Posteriorians, but nevertheless he decides to cover his bases.

"Now, some of you may be thinking 'What about the physical world we are given, the world of science, the world of experiments, experience, the world of the e? Is this not enough?' Some of you may ask, 'What about what Posteriorians like Nietchai taught us? What about our loyalty to the empirical world, to our physical experiences, and our indifference to anything beyond that, beyond our five senses?'

"But I tell you today: God is not beyond our five senses. We experience him everyday. He is in the wine you taste, the tree you see grow, the flower you smell, the grass you touch. All of these things, these thing we experience directly every day through our faculties, all of these things, the order, beauty, and wise arrangement of the universe, all of these things are an experience of God. We know from experience that an intelligent design is constantly conjoined by an intelligent author—buildings have builders and painting have painters—why must it be any different here?"

Finally, the people begin to clap. Dewey sees one man fart out a plume of smoke with a grin while his neighbor pushes him away. A woman looks up from her roasted turkey leg and smiles. A large young boy shouts his praise, his arms in the air, crashing cymbals above his head.

Suddenly, Dewey sees her again. He sees the woman *that woman* but she is different this time: a golden aura hangs around her head. She smiles at him in approval. Dewey smiles back. And for a moment, it is only them *woman and man* and all else is static in the background. Her eyes seem glad *my job is done here.* Then, she turns away as quickly as she came, disappearing behind a keg of beer. Dewey's gaze lingers after her, but the white noise of the crowd returns. Suddenly Dewey's eyes drawn away, towards another voice in the crowd.

"Your argument is flawed!"

It is the voice of a young man. Dewey sees the crowd before him split as this young man pushes through, rushing up before his king.

"Your argument is flawed!" he says again, "Flawed! Limited! No good at all!"

Dewey tries to identify the man's face, but it is covered in blue paint. Dewey can see that his long brown hair hangs over his face, his bangs dyed a bright orange and yellow. He looks like most any other Posteriorian here today.

"Who are you?" Dewey asks.

"My name is Surucipe, and you must instruct the people to be careful, to be careful of your argument!"

"Why must I do such a thing? What is wrong here? I demand to know!"

"You have acknowledged that the chief or sole argument for a divine existence is derived from the order of nature; where there appears such marks of intelligence and design that you think it extravagant to assign for its cause either chance or the blind and unguided force of matter."

"Yes."

"Where did you come upon this concept?"

"I…I've felt it myself," Dewey lies to himself, "I perceived this myself as I perceive the world around me. It is what I feel."

"So from the order of the work, you infer a workman."

"In so little words."

"But you also know that if a creator, or a cause, such as the workman, is only known only through his creations, then all we can know about him is in his creations themselves."

"What is it you are proposing?" Dewey can feel his impatience growing.

"That you mark your consequences!"

A small group of people begins to crowd behind Surucipe, listening to his words with an attention not common among Posteriorians.

Surucipe says, "When we infer any particular cause from an effect, we must proportion one to the other and can never be allowed to ascribe to the cause any qualities but what are exactly sufficient to produce the effect. No one, merely from the sight of one of Olegna's sculptures could know that he is also a painter or architect. If you experience, say, a loaf of bread, you may ascribe its cause to an intelligent baker, a baker who knows how to bake bread—but only that! One cannot know if he can bake cookies, or cakes, or croissants, because one has never experienced such an effect. Otherwise, one indulges in fanciful speculation that can never end!"

"Go on, go on."

"Therefore, allowing God, this...Li to be the author of the universe, it follows that He possesses that precise degree of power, intelligence, or benevolence that appears in His workmanship—but nothing more!

"Our world is bound by time, so we must not assume its author to be beyond it either. So do not tell us of an infinite God that can alter the laws of nature and make mothers into muffins, for we have never experienced such attributes at all.

"Let your God, therefore, O King, be suited to the present appearances of nature. Be careful! Warn the people, lest they forget and, instead of regarding the present scene of things as the sole object of their contemplation, they reverse the whole course of nature and render this life merely as a passage to something farther; a porch, which leads to a greater, and vastly different building. Warn the people, lest they believe this world is so intelligent that it is perfect, lest they forget the evil and disorder of the world, the cancers, deaths, pain and suffering, the crippled and the insane, and gladly and blindly go off on tangents about God's infiniteness, justice, and might. God made all of this evil too! And this world as it is, the good and the bad, is all we know of Him!

"Of course, all of this most suitably follows from the Posteriorian tenants of our father El Totsira. We learn of God through experience. There is no doubt about it. Our direct experiences are the only standard by which we regulate our conduct. Nothing else can be appealed to in the field or in the senate. We can know of God through our experiences of His creations, as you, our King, have spoken. But we must caution ourselves against attributing Him more intelligence than his creations would require. Your argument is limited in but one subtle way, my king. There is a God—we may shout it from the rooftops! But of calling out to Him in prayer and awe, we must not speak a word!"

The twenty Posteriorians crowding Surucipe have turned to the better part of fifty. They all look to Dewey, awaiting his response.

"You have spoken well," Dewey says, "But you forget one thing. The power of induction. If I have an experience of bakers who know how to make all kinds of things, and I see the single loaf of bread, I may induce, from the specific loaf of bread, to the general nature of bakers, that if a baker exists that can make bread like this, he can probably make all kinds of things!

"It is most common on the streets of Lyceum to see an unfinished building surrounded with heaps of brick and mortar, and all the instruments of masonry; could you not *infer* from the effect, that it was a work of design and contrivance? And could you not return again, from this inferred cause, to, to infer new additions to the effect, and conclude, that, that the building would soon be finished, and receive all the further improvements, oh, the adornments at its top, the large stained-glass windows that most every Lyceumean building proudly wears?

"If you saw upon the seashore the print of one human foot, you would conclude that a man had passed that way, and that he had also left the trace of another foot that must have been erased by the rolling of the sands. Why then do you refuse to admit the same method of reasoning with regard to the order of nature? This world is just one footprint, perhaps from which we may infer another.

"Consider the world and the present life only as an imperfect building, or a single footprint, from which you can infer a superior intelligence that is perfect too! Why stop at our present experiences of the world—experience leads to inference too! Why may you not infer a more finished scheme or plan, which is partially revealed from us, or unfinished, arriving at its completion in some distant point of space or time?"

The people cheer in delight. By now, most of the crowd is more attentive than it has ever been during any of Dewey's speeches. The people are surprisingly excited at the debate at hand, and they raise their fists in the air, rooting for the different parties at different times. Of course they are more concerned with the rhythm and volume of their cheers than of the content of the debate. But they cheer nonetheless.

"Yes," Surucipe replies, "I concede that from the sight of one human foot, I would infer another. But that is only because I know that a man has two legs. And yes, from the taste of a loaf of bread, I would infer baker who can bake many things. But that is only because I know the nature of bakers. But we do not know the nature of Gods.

"Yes, man is a being whom we know by experience, whose motives and designs we are acquainted with, so that, by experiencing parts of his works, we can draw many inferences concerning what may be expected of him, what he is really capable of. But did we know man only from the single work or production which we examine, it would be impossible to make any such inference. This is how we know of God.

"As your argument effectively but solely knows of God through his works before us, He is known to us only by those productions. As such, it is impossible for us to argue from the cause, or infer any alteration in the effect, beyond what has immediately fallen under our observation."

"But," Dewey replies, "One may say that new effects may proceed from a continuation of the same energy which is already known from the first effects. A creation is a creation, no matter who the author. Can we not infer, from its beauty but sorry incompletion, that a greater plan was in hand?"

"You see, my king, your mistake is that you are still thinking in human terms—for how would you define 'complete'? The great source of our mistake is that we tacitly consider ourselves as in the place of the Supreme

Being, and conclude, that he will, on every occasion, observe the same conduct that we ourselves, in his situation, would have embraced as reasonable and eligible. But this is so foolish—it cannot be the case for a Being so different, so foreign, and so superior to anything we can know. We cannot analogize our intent of creationism to those of a Being so remote and incomprehensible, who discovers himself only by some faint traces or outlines, beyond which we have no authority to ascribe to Him any attribute or perfection."

"Ah, yes! But there is still one circumstance which you seem to have overlooked yet again," Dewey smiles. "After all that you have said, I much doubt whether it is possible for a cause to be known only through its effect or to be of so singular and particular a nature as to have no parallel and no similarity with any other cause or object that has ever fallen under our observation. If experience and observation and analogy are all we have, we must use them to the greatest degree possible! All that is required is that both the effect and cause bear a similarity to other effects and causes which we know, and which we have found to be conjoined to each other."

Dewey smiles once again. He looks up from Surucipe and raises his hands to the crowd.

"I leave it to your own reflection to pursue the consequences of these…principles. And now I must go rest."

And rest he does.

ΩΨΩ

The Posteriorians gather at future celebrations and festivals. But now they pass around pages of colorful drawings and pictures drawn from the hand of El Totsira and divinely inspired by the God of Li (whom I have never met). The drawings seem indecipherable, though experts have gleamed scientific lessons from the puzzles hidden in those drawings. The festivals become more religious and the holidays consist of dressing up in costumes, giving gifts, feasting, and drinking until one does not know his head from his feet—all activities Posteriorians are quite accustomed to.

Dewey spent the first few days in a drunken stupor, celebrating the approval of the woman *that woman Princess* who was she? But now he visits Noah and the horses often, and this gives him peace of mind. Of course, he does not know of the anger building in Olegna's mind as he sits in his home near his unpacked suitcases thinking of Disegno *thief!* nor of the evil plans growing in the artist's mind *the needle must fall.*

Dewey also does not know that he is an uncle. He does not know that far, far away, Renee is spending these same days laboring in secret to build a cave, a shelter to keep his own blood—his nephew, a growing boy—locked deep down away from the outside world from the day he was born to a day far from now.

But of course, we must enjoy the present, for those events are far in the future. The brothers are still active men, each a ruler of a nation his own. Dewey sits on his throne in the Posteriorian palace of Lyceum, while Renee sits on his throne in the Prioritan House of Wax in the Republic of Kallipolis. While Dewey celebrates his new peace of mind, Olegna plots his revenge on Disegno. Elizabeth Palatine travels to the fields in search for her necklace while Renee is in those fields building a fortress in secret as he rules his nation in public.

While Dewey builds a new religion, Renee builds a new shelter. Just like Rekha, a creator of worlds, the two brothers create their own, each following a different twin, El Totsira or O'Talp. How can two angels so different have come from the same womb *Rekha?* How can two kings so opposite have come from the same womb *Katherine?* How can it be?

Thus we have it, two nations spawned from the same womb, Kallipolis and Lyceum: one of reason and one of experience, one in the way of O'Talp and one worshipping El Totsira, one of intellect and one of emotion, one of mind and one of heart, one of solitude and one of company, one of mathematics and one of science, one of discipline and one of celebration, one of strict moderation and one of color, one of permanence and one of transience, one of introspection and one of exploration, one of abstinence and one of indulgence, one of fact and one of flavor, one of wax and one of orange peels.

And these nations are led by two brothers, Renee and Dewey, the lone thinker spinning thoughts from within and the busy gatherer of things outside, the spider and the ant.

III

THE EMERGENCE OF KAHN

1

Marriage. A legal or religious ceremony by which two persons of the opposite sex solemnly agree to harass and spy on each other... until death do them join.
Elbert Hubbard (1856 - 1915)

The flowers and brooks of spring awaken on the first of April, stretching their sleepy limbs across the land. Long-empty branches paint themselves with color, exchanging their green currency over the rebirth of life below. By now, the warm sun has melted the ice at the edges of Lake Prespa and Ohrid, and now it works on their centers like a sculptor chipping away at his last mistakes. The Axios River fills with salmon once again, flowing south towards the lake at Mount Korab.

But if you were in Kallipolis, you would not know any of this. No, the flowers and wildlife of this land have not shown their faces for years. Many like to say it is because it is too far north for nature to prosper, hiding in the cold shadow of the Apuan Hills, isolated from the life of Macedon or Cherava. But some remember days when life would flow freely through a richly textured Kallipolis. Days before the blind man came. Some know in their hearts that there was once life here, and that plants and animals do not avoid the land because they can't live here, but rather because they are not invited here any longer.

After the procreation festival, Elizabeth Palatine returned home to realize that her necklace was missing from around her neck. Seeing dirt on her clothes, she remembered the festival. She remembered making love to Renee Don Cartez.

Now Elizabeth travels west to the site of the festival in search for her necklace. Her light brown hair trails behind her small translucent face, her white feather cheeks moving swiftly forward against the eastern breeze like two white kites. Finally, she reaches the border of the field. She stops, considering the consequences if she steps foot on this field at this time. *The penalty is death.* She can see the place where she made love to Renee, and she sees a white glimmering stone protruding from the dirt like a small white sail on a sea of black.

The necklace!

Elizabeth considers her options *it will only take a minute* and thinks of her ancestors that gave her the necklace *if they were here now* worth any risk to retrieve *perhaps they are. No one must see me. No one will.*

She runs forward, but suddenly, she hears a loud crack fill the air. She almost screams in surprise, but covers her mouth with one hand. She stands still, frozen in terror, her hand still over her mouth. She hears the sound of a man. Again, the soft blow of hammer and stone fill the air. Quickly, she dives behind a large stone for cover. The blows repeat themselves like the strange rhythm of a lonely drummer, but she cannot see what is going on. Panting for breath, Elizabeth works up the courage to peek back at her necklace. She turns her gaze back across the field, and behold! she can see it lying in the eyeshot of the man. Looking carefully, she can see that it is him.

Renee is here. But why?

She can see that he is building something, an odd looking structure indeed. Renee has dug a deep trench in the shape of a circle around his *their* child. He is nearing completion of the foundations of solid stone walls. Some sort of enclosure. To Elizabeth, it looks much like a small fortress. Some type of hut. *But that is for the producers to build.* She squints again, wondering what could drive Renee to violate the prohibition of his very land and set foot in this field *what is he hiding?* What could drive him to risk his own life?

What is he building?

She considers tip-toeing forward *he won't hear me* with the blows of his hammer *and he certainly won't see me* but she has heard that the blind man can see better than most other people. Besides, she is more intrigued with his project than her necklace. For the time being, she decides to return tomorrow to decipher just what Renee is doing. Her necklace won't go anywhere, she decides, so long as she keeps close watch.

Elizabeth returns day after day to the very same rock. She watches the same show each day; a spectator kneeling in her hiding place in her brown and white shawls, never getting bored of the same episode: a poor man working so fervently, so secretly, so carefully, and she cannot imagine at what. She sees the calling whistle hanging down from his neck as he works, its thin wooden body catching drops of sweat from his chin on their way to the ground like a branch in the rain. The enclosure begins to look to Elizabeth like some kind of tiny fortress *what could he be hiding?* Elizabeth wonders what in the ground Renee is trying to hide from the world. She does not realize that it is the other way around.

Oh Renee, Elizabeth feels her heart against her chest, *Oh lover, oh evil trickster, traitor from Lyceum,* but she does not know if it is love or hate she feels *why are you always hiding something?* she wonders what his childhood was like, *you build a fortress upon the dirt, but you do not know* how he came to this land *the real fortress you build is around your heart.*

One day, Elizabeth sees Renee drop his shovel from his work. He wipes his brow and faces the sun. He walks over to his walking stick, picks it up, and begins to circle his unfinished structure. Elizabeth thinks she can hear him whistling to himself. Then, Renee stops. He taps his stick onto the ground. The sound of wood on marble. He bends over, and to Elizabeth's amazement, he picks up her necklace in his hands. He brushes off the dirt and kisses the necklace softly. Closing his eyes, he inhales, taking in the scent of the necklace.

But suddenly, he throws the necklace to the ground, shouting *no!* and Elizabeth's heart jumps. She can see his hands trembling. She can hear him muttering to himself as his face reddens.

"No! Just four letters…I can keep them out! I can control them. I will. I must. Yes, Elizabeth," Elizabeth's breath stops at the sound of her name, "You made me feel…yes, feel things I have never…felt before. It is enough you made me feel anything at all. Yes. But our offspring, our…child, will never have to bear such feelings. No, he will never have to carry the heavy weight of experience. He will never have to be seduced by the transient beauty of color and smells, never have to be tricked or filled with doubt and uncertainty. No, in this enclosure, his mind will do what no man's mind has ever been able to do. His environment will afford him the most mental freedom any man has ever enjoyed. Yes, as the prince and future philosopher king of Kallipolis, Kahn will have it all!"

Kahn? Elizabeth moves her jaw back and forth and rubs her ears, hoping she did not hear what she thought she did. *Kahn? Who is that? A child? MY child?* She touches her belly. *A prince? It cannot be!* She feels her body collapse, and she falls back behind the stone. *I must go.* She feels this sudden danger, this extreme feeling that she must not be here one second longer. *I must go now. Right now.*

She gets up clumsily, bringing herself to her feet. But her legs feel like jelly, and they cannot hold her. She tries to regain her footing as Renee turns to pick up his hammer. Taking a step forward, her foot lands on a twig *snap!* and the sound fills the air.

Renee stops at once, and turns around. He looks in her direction, his eyes fraught with concern.

"Hello?" his voice echoes through the field, sounding stronger as it travels. His face quickly changes from one of embarrassment to one of anger. Elizabeth is frightened; but she dare not breathe. She does not seeking a hiding place because she knows he is blind. Realizing that his ears are more dangerous to her than his eyes, she stands still out in the open, fearing that any movement will cause him to hear her.

"*HELLO?*" In all his memory, Renee has never amplified his voice like this.

Can he smell me? Elizabeth bites her lower lip so hard that it is bleeding. She can hear her heart beating against her ribs like a bird violently tapping on its cage, trying to get out.

Can he hear me?

"Hello," Renee is facing her directly now, and his cold gray eyes send a chill to her heart. They wait in silence *man and woman* two statues, each waiting for the other to speak first. *How long can I hold my breath?* Nearby, a flock of birds fly away.

Christian looks up. The wolf looks from Elizabeth to his master, and back. He recognizes Elizabeth at once *this woman is my friend, the human that gave me food at the festival* and he wags his tail happily.

"No," Elizabeth mouths silently to the wolf. "No, no, stay..."

"Is someone there?" Renee says.

Christian hesitates a moment, and Elizabeth shakes her head to the wolf *no no!* sticking her hands out as if to push him away. *I have no food now. I am hiding, don't you see?* Christian cocks his head to the side, a curious look on his face. He tries to make sense of this woman's frantic movements as she waves her hands towards him *stay, stay!*

"Do not think I cannot see. Speak at once."

Christian runs towards Elizabeth. He scampers away from Renee, running into the trees where Elizabeth hides. She tries to push him away gently, but to her surprise, she sees Renee turn around and pick up his hammer once again.

"Christian and his squirrels," he says, "Can't ever just let one go, can he?" Elizabeth lets out a deep sigh of relief. Renee resumes his work. She settles herself behind a tree and catches her breath. She tries not to laugh as Christian licks her face.

ΩΨΩ

The Kallipolis sun lowers itself into the sea, closing the curtains of the first of April upon Renee's weary back. As he travels home, Renee's body cries from exhaustion, but his mind does not listen. No, he is already thinking about tomorrow, the next day of work. He is already planning how to implement the next step of his building plans. *It must be perfect,* he walks home in the classically slow Prioritan pace, his hands behind him, eyes to the ground, his jaw set in confidence, his eyes set in soft determination for the future.

But as he nears the southernmost corner of the republic, he hears a loud group of people near the Axios River. Christian barks, a great excitement! But Renee is skeptical; he knows that people do not unite in Kallipolis.

Indeed, besides for prayer and meditation in The House of Wax (in which each person is enclosed in their own booth), and for the procreation festival (in which it is dark and everyone's eyes are to the ground), never have more than three or four Prioritans spent time together, laughing, talking, or at all. Outside of the familial homes that the new Prioritan immigrants share (for all land-born Prioritans have no family besides the entire nation, all sisters and brothers, and all live alone), there is no conversing besides the occasional passerby's greeting, or the polite nod-of-the-head.

But this does not stop Christian. He runs towards the crowd, a boisterous bunch, no doubt, and Renee has little choice but to follow. His walking stick in hand, he ventures after the wolf, *come on now,* picking up his pace *it is time to return for the night.*

As he gets closer, he begins to smell the scent of spice. Now, Renee has grown into a fearless man and a leader whose confidence knows no equal. But every man has his Kryptonite, and sensory experience is his. As Renee hears the sound of (dare I say it) experimental music, as he smells the scent of myrrh and cinnamon, a terrible fear and repulsion grips his heart. He remembers the thousands of orange ants crawling up his brother's legs *so many of them* covering his whole body *like the stars in the sky* and he blesses his loss of sight. He remembers the colors and smells of Lyceum, the art contests, the frivolous festivals and transient celebration of flavors, dreams, drunkenness, and hallucinations, and he blesses his peace of mind and his quiet nation. But the shields he has created are not enough right now. The scent of myrrh and cinnamon fill his head like a thousand little ants.

"Christian," Renee senses danger, "Come back now. We must go."

Renee stumbles forward into the impending dark, when suddenly, he hears the chanting of the group.

"Ex—per—ri—ence! Ex—pe—ri—ence! Let—it—in! Let—us—in!"

They are Posteriorians. They have come to wreak havoc on Kallipolis as they sometimes do. Renee turns his head both ways, as if he can see. He wonders where his warriors are, and how they let these protesting Posteriorians in. Remembering Christian, Renee reaches to his necklace and brings the calling whistle to his lips. As he inhales to blow, he does not see the bright yellow rock flying through the air. But oh, how he feels the rock hit his skull with a crack. His body hangs in the air for a moment, a ballerina dancer floating in suspended time, and he falls to the ground, not moving.

ΩΨΩ

Warriors of Kallipolis were already there, you see. They struggled to keep the protestors back, close to the Axios and away from the heart of the republic. But it is only when more warriors and auxiliaries come, marching in single file line, their shields on their left, spears in their right hands marked with that unmistakable 'W', it is only then that the protestors begin to spread south, their Posteriorian tails behind them as they run into the Cherava Woods for cover, their sensors scrambling behind them like little dogs.

One may think it odd that none of the Prioritan warriors see their leader, the blind man, lying unconscious in the dirt. This may be because he is hundreds of feet away from where the protest is (for the stone that hit him flew rather far for a Posteriorian slingshot), but I suppose it is because of Renee's overwhelming, well, usualness. True, all Prioritans dress simple and are not noticeable to people unaccustomed to such natural and pale shades of brown and gray. But Renee always has this way of really blending into his natural surroundings, the sky and dry earth behind him. He always has this way of becoming almost…invisible.

It is about five hours later that Benedictus Azonips walks southwest through the dawn fog. Upon entering this land, it did not take him long to start rising early in the Prioritan way, taking long walks across the bleak, empty, and peaceful land. His mind rides upon the subtle breezes, the passing mosquitoes and the soft trembling of the naked shrubs.

Ben looks and behold! he sees his leader, Renee Don Cartez lying face down in the dirt. Ben sees that his robes are drenched in sweat as if he has been physically working very hard (an acceptable, but very unusual thing in this land). At once, Christian rises from where he has been sitting nearby and hovers over Renee. Ben gently pushes the wolf away and brings Renee to his feet.

"Renee! Renee! Wake up."

"Wha—"

"You are going to be alright. What happened?"

Renee opens his eyes. Even though he cannot see, he knows by his touch that this man is his friend Ben. Renee remembers the first time he heard of this man: he was playing billiards with Dewey *one of our best lens-crafters, he was* who didn't know the *young man who carried the creature on his shoulders* was Ben as *they disappeared into the north* search parties fruitlessly trying to find them. Renee remembers the first time he met Ben; Renee nearly died of exhaustion in Cherava Woods as Christian ran up ahead, coming back with this shadow *Hello Renee* this man *we have all been waiting for you.*

"Your head is bleeding," Ben says, "Let me carry you, I can carry you—"

"Where is Nicolas?" Renee's voice regains its tone of authority after the first word.

"What?"

"Nicolas."

"Why do you want to know—"

"Where is he? Is Nicolas okay?"

"Yes. He was not near the protestors. Nicolas is…fine," Ben tries to ignore the jealousy in his heart by regaining his focus, "Why…You are all wet! You are perspired as if you were exerted yourself greatly. What were you doing? Why were you even traveling this way? You do not ever meddle west of the House. What were you doing yesterday?"

"Yesterday? Has that much time passed already?"

"Oh, my king. I want to help you. But please tell me. Remember. What were you doing before you blacked out? Where were you coming from? What were you doing?"

Renee looks up at Ben and he sees in his friend's eyes that he will not give up until he gets his answers. Ben feels the warmth of the rising sun on his back, the smell of spring in the earth. He holds out his hand for his king. But Renee thinks of his future child, how he must be protected from the world at all costs. Even though Renee is blind, Ben is not surprised that Renee grasps his hand and pulls himself up off the ground. Brushing himself off, Renee turns to Ben. He squeezes his friend's shoulder in gratefulness.

"So, you want to know where I was all day, do you?"

"I will not take another breath until you tell me."

Renee smiles, "Come with me."

ΩΨΩ

For Elizabeth, this morning is no different than any other morning of the past few weeks. She rises a bit later than usual, after most Prioritans have finished their morning meditations. While the roads are always empty is Kallipolis, the late morning offers a special silence that provides Elizabeth with the secrecy she needs. Only the birds watch her, her brown hair washing from side to side, her white clothes flying behind her like a cape as she glides from tree to stone like a fairy dancing to her love.

Finally, she arrives at the procreation field where she finds her hiding place. She settles herself behind her boulder. Peering out over the top, she sees the spot her necklace once marked. A few days ago, she retrieved her necklace before Renee had arrived. It is now around her neck. Now she sees the pile of stone, cement, and tools in the middle of field. The unfinished structure seems naked to her, ashamed, as if she has caught it in the midst of an evil act. Then, she realizes that for the first time, she can go investigate just what the structure is. She can finally see what Renee is building. What he is hiding. She can go see because no one is here!

Running out from behind the rock, Elizabeth feels her heart beat faster with anticipation. Renee's solitary rant *our offspring* runs through her head *will never have to carry the heavy weight of experience* like wild animals *it must be perfect.*

Suddenly, she hears men's voices. She runs back to her hiding place and makes it there just in time. The men are still not there, but she can hear their voices getting steadily closer.

"You are taking me all the way out here," one of the men says, "towards the fields of the festival. You know we cannot go there; it is forbidden—"

"You wanted me to take you to where I have been working," Elizabeth can hear Renee's voice, "so I am taking you to where I was working."

"But I never thought—"

"That was your problem."

Elizabeth can see them now. She recognizes them as Renee and Ben, and she kneels farther down behind the stone.

"So this is where you are building the invention you were telling me about," Ben says.

"Yes, I did not want to tell you about it, but you would not go away."

"I did not understand what your invention was."

"I call it a well."

"A...well?"

"Yes."

"And what would be the function of this...well?"

"The well is a tool for retrieving water. For drinking and bathing."

"Yes, I know what water is for," Ben's eyes search Renee's face for something, as if something is missing. "It seems a mighty solid well."

"Yes," Renee says, "As anything built in this land must be. You know that."

A moment of silence passes. Renee can feel Ben watching him and he does not like this. Ben sees a lump in Renee's throat as he swallows.

"Yes," Ben says, "I know that. I just did not know that there was water here, under the procreation fields. This just seems like an odd place—"

"Of course, my pupil," Renee says a bit too quickly, "Water itself symbolizes creation. O'Talp created the world from water. The Israelites were born through the Red Sea. One bathes in a spiritual bath as they once did in their mother's womb: it is rebirth! Baptism comes from this very same tenant."

"Yes, that seems coherent. It just seems odd to build a well here, when the purification pools are so close. We can just drink that—"

"That is holy water! One may not benefit from it in a physical, experiential way."

"Yes. Of course."

Something was off about Renee. Ben does not say that it is still puzzling to him *why build a well here* as confusion fills his face *when the sea is so close by? And why build a well here* but Renee does not see *when it is prohibited to enter this field for most of the year?*

But Ben says, "Of course," for most any man knows when he has rocked the boat enough. "I will leave you to your work...then," he begins to walk away.

Hiding behind her rock, Elizabeth sees Renee wait until Ben leaves. He continues to stand still for almost an hour. Elizabeth's knees hurt from being on the ground. She moves to rub her ankles when Renee suddenly picks up his hammer and begins to work under the yellow sun. Elizabeth watches Renee's aged masculine body lift the hammer high in the air. She sees his chest through his white robes now stained with dirt and sweat, his mouth tightly set in a grimace, his lips shaking with strain, his brow set in concentration.

For four more years she watches him work. She sees his wolf companion sitting patiently at his side, his walking stick in mouth. And finally, in the fourth year, as Renee is installing the ceiling of the enclosure, Elizabeth begins to understand. She begins to study the structure of the fortress's foundations. She begins to see how it will be completed. She begins to see how it can be destroyed.

ΩΨΩ

One day towards the end of a cold April, Elizabeth approaches her hiding place to find Renee at his construction site with a friend. She suspects this man to be Nicolas, the one rumored to be Renee's closest companion. She sees that he is in a wheelchair, his head hunched forward over his crooked back. His dark hair is parted, revealing an unusually large nose between two gaunt cheeks, a face whose horror fades behind the strength and wisdom in the man's crystal white-blue eyes. She can hear his words quiet clearly.

"Renee," Nicolas says, "You have confessed in me great things today. You have told me that you have broken the law of the republic; you have come to the procreation fields, and you have told me of your work here. Now there is something I must tell you."

"I am listening."

"I was the one."

"What?"

"Renee forgive me, but I was the one who got rid of the ants."

"What?"

"It was I who exterminated the ants from Dewey's room. It was I that made Dewey angry, angry enough to kill your cat, to—"

"To have him *blind me?*" Even Renee is surprised at the crack in his voice.

"It was the only way."

"The only way to what?! The only way to play God? The only way to kill the only friend I ever had—my cat?! The only way to make me suffer enough to hate myself and leave my home?! The only way to, to, to—oohhh," Renee kneels down on one knee and covers his face with his hands.

Nicolas sits in his wheelchair. He remains calm as he speaks.

"It was the only way to make you who you are today. Without that, your mind would have been blinded by the cheap sensations flung at you everyday from your

Posteriorian life. It was the only way to protect you, to…shield you from the lovers of sights and sounds, so you can grow and blossom into the great mind you are today."

Renee says nothing.

"My King, you were lost in Lyceum. But there were days when you tried to fit in. When you wanted to fit in. To come and find us, to begin to find your real self, you had to hit rock bottom.

"I know. I know," Renee rubs his eyes and stands up.

"I did it because I had to. *He* told me to. So I knew that one day, it would be worth it. That one day, you would be a great man, that you would become who you are today. And you did! But I never knew if you would understand," Nicolas looks down.

"I understand," Renee says as Nicolas looks up, "I understand. In a way, without you, I would never be here today. I would be confined to my quarters somewhere in Lyceum, or even worse: free to venture into the crowds of blinding smells and colors. If it was not for you. My best friend."

From her hiding place, Elizabeth can see the love in Renee's eyes. But her focus quickly changes to Nicolas.

Nicolas is carrying bags of something (Elizabeth cannot tell what) on his lap as he rolls his wheelchair clumsily through the field. Suddenly, one of the wheels hits a rock. The chair jerks to the right, Nicolas's body with it. His hood falls down to his shoulders and one of the bags from his lap falls to the ground, spilling white liquid into the earth.

Milk? Thoughts begin to race through Elizabeth's mind, *why would he bring milk here?*

Before she has time to think another thought, Renee turns around, his nose in the air.

"Is that *milk* that I smell?" Renee says in a voice Elizabeth has never heard him speak before. The anger in his voice scares her.

"My lord," Nicolas says.

"*MILK?*" Renee says. He waits a moment, takes a deep breath, and speaks in a measured tone few have ever heard.

"Water. I told you my son must only have water. I trusted you over Ben, over everyone. I told you about this, and I specifically instructed you that my son must never, ever, ever experience anything! Why do you think I am building this fortress that he will be born into and never leave until he is ready to be king? Why do you think I am going to all this trouble to guard him from the overwhelmingly confusing experience we must live with every single day? You think I am doing this so you can bring him *milk*? You think—"

"Wait! Did you hear that?"

"You think—"

"My king, wait!"

"You—"

But suddenly, Renee hears it. Nicolas hears it again, and Elizabeth hears it too. In the bleak silence of the fields, the cry of a baby boy fills the air.

A baby!

The sound is coming from within the ground.

"He must have smelled the milk," Renee says, "Get it out of here. Now!"

But Elizabeth cannot hear him now. All she hears is the sound of a child. Her child. Oh, how Elizabeth's heart soars! Her eyes close so that she cannot see Nicolas's jaw drop at the sound of the boy. She wishes she can run up to the spot and put her ear to the ground. She is overcome with the sudden urge to dash towards her child *I'm coming, baby* digging up the earth with her bare hands *mother is coming* but she quickly arrests such a thought. She knows better. *Patience.* But then she hears Renee speak.

"That is my son. My Immanuel Kahn."

Nicolas looks at him, "Where is he? Is that him, in the well?"

"I told you, this is not a well. That is just what I told Ben. Do not look surprised. I've already told you. You know what this is. It is a structure, a protective fortress meant to keep my son in peace, away from all the distractions and sensations we have to shut out everyday."

"Of course."

"Yes, one day he will be the greatest philosopher King the republic has ever known, the star-child of O'Talp, the model Prioritan, the—"

Elizabeth covers her mouth with her hand, but she is too late: a whimper has already escaped her lips.

"What, what was that?" Renee says.

"Why, that is your son, my King. Your Kahn. You were saying—"

"No. In the trees. I heard something in the trees," Renee faces east, his eyes scanning the land as if they could still see.

"I did not hear anything."

"A whimper. Just one soft whimper. But I know I heard it. And I know that voice. I think." Renee's eyes lock onto the stone that Elizabeth hides behind. She realizes she has been squeezing her ankles for a minute now, trying to douse the burning in her lungs from holding her breath.

Nicolas says, "King, you have been working very hard. You have gone through a lot these past few weeks—"

"Helene?" Renee says into the trees, ignoring Nicolas. "Have you come for me?" Elizabeth does not know who Helene is, but she does not care right now. She feels the need to run.

"Helene," Renee says, a strange glare over his eyes is it, "Helene, is it really you?" but Elizabeth cannot hear him anymore. She is already running fiercely through the brush.

2

Never apologize for showing feeling. When you do so, you apologize for the truth.
Benjamin Disraeli

Oh, have you ever run scared for your life, dear reader, never believing just how fast your feet are taking you? I have never done so because I have no legs, but I can just imagine! That one word running through your head: run run run, spiraling faster in your brain like a spinning hamster wheel, washing down the chute of your spine and into your blurring feet. What a marvel necessity is! Oh, the places it will take you!

Running through the brush, Elizabeth can hear the cries of a baby—her baby—crying in her head. Yes, it is her baby *Kahn* buried in the ground just behind her. It takes her a few moments to realize that the cries are not coming from behind her, but are knocking her around from within.

Still, she runs further in the brush. She finds that it is getting darker, but she cannot decide if it is the sun that is setting or if it is her eyes. Finally, she realizes that she has run quite a distance; there is no way anyone could have tracked her, let alone a blind man like Renee or a cripple like Nicolas.

She stops in a clearing. She leans over, panting for breath. She sits on a rock to rest. Her eyes close and her breathing steadies. Her hands reach for her necklace. She grasps its white stone with both hands *I came to find my necklace*, but it gives her little comfort *but I found my child…in that prison…thing Renee is building.* When she opens her eyes, she sees Renee standing before her.

"Oh!" she squeals like a child and covers her mouth. Without hesitation, she jumps up and tries to run past the blind man.

Renee moves stealthily, blocking her way with his staff.

"Wha—?" Elizabeth tries, her hands shaking with fear.

"You need not fear me," Renee's voice is calm, but Elizabeth cannot decide if it is from love or anger.

"Why?" she starts, "Why did you chase me? What are you doing? You, you let me go."

"You know I cannot do that. After all you have seen."

"Let me *go!"* Elizabeth can feel her fear turn to anger. She looks around for a weapon or a way out, but she is surrounded by dense foliage. Her only way is a narrow path, blocked by Renee before her. Renee senses her eyes wandering. He speaks.

"I will not hurt you. I just want to speak. And for you to listen."

"Oh, I've listened enough! First you can tell me, well, how, how did you know where I was? And how—how were you able to—"

"Show up here?"

Elizabeth looks at him.

Renee continues, "I was going to ask you the same question."

"I—I—"

"You wanted to see a child, the child that you conceived."

"Yes. I mean, at first I came back for my necklace. But now, once I saw what is really here, I kept coming back to be with my child. I want *need* to see my child."

"But you must understand, dear Elizabeth, daughter of Kallipolis, that this child is not your child anymore than anyone else in Kallipolis is. This is a child of the land. We are all children of the Republic—"

"Shut up!" Elizabeth can feel herself lose control, but she does not care, "Don't you stand there all calm and lecture me. You live your life feeding off other people while you take what is theirs from them, and no one ever questions you, because, because you have the badge of O'Talp upon you. But they think you are crazy! Yes, you sit high on your throne looking up to the heavens, until daylight when you sneak out like a small white rat, building this...this prison for my baby...this...this—"

"I like to call it O'Talp's cave."

"Well...whatever you want to call it...you can't take my baby away from me! I won't allow it! You can't—what? What did you call it?"

"O'Talp's cave. That is what I have been building. O'Talp told me to build it. He told me how. Just think! A place of peace, where Kahn will never be exposed to the confusing sights and sounds most of us must suffer with, or even worse, which some of us have grown accustomed to. Yes, Elizabeth, Kahn will be chained to the wall, his head away from the door, so even the slightest trace of light will not taint his eyes. He will grow to be empty and pure, his gain of knowledge to be only reaped from his inner reason, his innate ideas. He will never assume, as we do, that the trees around us are as we see them, nor the air in our hair as we feel it. But he will know with all certainty that four plus four equals eight. Yes, and one day, when he is ready, I will let him out. He will have the most beautiful mind the world has ever seen. His thought will be clear and pristine, untainted, unadulterated. Perfect. He will be the greatest philosopher king the world has ever known."

"Oh, what?" It takes a moment for Elizabeth to find her voice again, "Did you say 'he'?"

"I did."

"You know that it is a boy? A boy! What have you done with him?"

"It is no matter to you."

"Please." Elizabeth can feel confidence begin to pour into her heart.

"Your requests fall on deaf ears."

She takes a step towards him and puts her arms on his shoulders.

"Stay away, Elizabeth."

Elizabeth is now enjoying the sound of Renee's voice. She knows having him on the defensive will not last long. So she removes one of her hands from his shoulders and takes the blade from her robes. Renee cannot see the shiny blade wielding in front of his face, moving over his shoulder and to the back of his neck.

"You will take your hands off me. You will leave me alone."

Quickly and gently, in the way that only women can do, Elizabeth cuts a piece of Renee's kingly garment and puts it in her robe just before Renee pushes her away.

"Away with you!"

Elizabeth backs away. But she says, "I will tell the Prioritans you were here."

"They will never believe you, and you will be punished for blasphemy."

"I will take them here. They will see what you have built."

"They will not know how it got here. But they will know where Kahn is. I do not know what they will do with him. He is safer this way."

"There must be someone, one man, who will listen to me."

"There is no such man in all of Kallipolis."

Elizabeth says nothing, but her courage fades.

"You have nothing here, woman. Any life you think you have created is no matter to you."

"My child is no matter to me? My child—"

"You will never know the child. He has no name to you."

Renee cannot see the pain set in Elizabeth's face, but he is surprised at the cruelty of his words as they come out. But he thinks of O'Talp's laws and of the Republic, and he takes a deep breath and regains his strength.

Tears of anger and pain have been building up behind Elizabeth's eyes for some time now, two dams trying to resist the flood, their walls bulging like two bellies after a meal, their chains stretching, belts pressing as cracks in their walls begin to appear. And before the gates come crashing down, tears streaming down her cheeks, Elizabeth whimpers and runs away.

Renee stands in place, listening to her footsteps fade in the brush. He closes his eyes, a faint look of disappointment across his face. After a moment, he turns, and walks slowly back to the fields.

The night passes slower than most. Renee spends his day finishing O'Talp's cave for baby Kahn. Nicolas sits by to offer words of strength. He brings water, feeding the baby by pouring water into the ground, but just enough to carry on. Every now and then Nicolas sees Renee look up into the woods as if he could see, but Nicolas says nothing; he never asks Renee what happened in the brush that day.

Sure, Nicolas wonders what Renee found in the brush that day *Helene?* but understands that sometimes, it is best not to ask. A friend will tell when he is ready. It is in this way that Nicolas is very wise.

One day of work passes, and then another. And another. Renee strikes the final hammer blows and wipes the beads of sweat from his forehead. Christian looks at Nicolas, his little wolf eyebrows concerned.

Renee says, "Have you seen anyone?"

"What?"

"Have you seen anyone, Nicolas? In the brush. Hiding, perhaps."

"No. Who could it be?"

"No one. Just a woman."

"A woman?" Nicolas answers, "Well, what does she look like?"

Renee opens his mouth to speak, but cannot find the words. *What does she look like? Whatdoesshelooklike?* Renee places the sledgehammer down gently and sits on a nearby rock. He remembers meeting Elizabeth for the first time. He was looking for Christian. Yes, he was about to bring the calling whistle to his lips when *Now, now, there is no need for that* she spoke *Christian is right here.* He remembers touching her for the first time, seeing her with his fingers, the unfamiliar feeling weighing on his chest *Is this what they call love?*

"She is short," Renee answers, "but not too much so. And her eyes are set deep like two dark stones lodged deep into a wall, above round circle cheeks. She—"

"Okay," Nicolas can see Renee is tired, "That is very good."

"I just—" Renee looks uncomfortable in a way Nicolas has never seen, "I was not patient with her. I did not speak kindly. I did not practice patience in the way of the Prioritans. My words were hasty, quick, almost, almost…"

"Posteriorian?"

"Yes. I did not want to say it. She ran off, hurt. But she must be close by. We have to—"

"My King, if I may say once: you have taken many spouses over the years, and perhaps you were not perfect at times, but time has moved on. You are the king of this republic, the founder of the nation. There is no need to—"

"She was my Princess. Princess Palatine."

Nicolas looks at Renee.

Renee says, "Christian ran to her at once. He left my side for her. That has never happened before for someone else."

"But—"

"She was special, Nicolas. I must find her."

"You want to…apologize?"

"Perhaps one can call it that. In so few words."

"But you told her of O'Talp's laws. You had to tell her that Kahn was born from the land. You only told her the truth."

"There is always more than one way to say the truth, my friend."

Nicolas remembers telling Renee that he was the one who killed the ants, who enraged his brother Dewey, who caused him to be blinded. And Nicolas remembers choosing his words carefully, at the right time, in the right way.

As he had done so many times before, Nicolas takes Renee's hand *watch your proximity* releases it, and guides Renee to his side. They move south together, Christian flanking their left. The sun sets behind the House of Wax in front of them, stretching its last gasps of light into the air to guide their path, three friends *one king, one friend, one wolf* in search of their lost princess.

ΩΨΩ

Renee, Nicolas, and Christian approach the homes of Lyceum to search for Elizabeth. As the hours pass, the company can see the tiny dirt and wax homes before them. They glow and flicker faintly from their inner candlelight like tiny little stars scattered in the distance, shimmering crystals on a black veil. They remind Renee of old times, gazing at the stars from rooftops with Dewey as little children. He remembers Dewey's fascination while all Renee could think of was not getting too close to the edge. Now, one by one they extinguish, their inhabitants turning in for sleep or for quiet meditation in the dark. A few keep their lamps on throughout the night, growing dim at times, mirroring the musings humming inside.

No sign of Elizabeth is found. As the sun begins to rise, Nicolas's eyes meet those of Renee's, but Renee cannot see the painful sympathy in his friend's eyes. But he can feel it.

"It is okay," Renee says.

"No it is not. How will you find her in this desolate, silent place, as blessed as it is? I can stay with you longer, I can be your eyes on the road—"

"No. You must go home. You have not slept for too long. You have not had your peace with yourself."

"But you have no sight—"

"I have O'Talp, that is more than I shall ever need."

"But—"

"Go home, good friend. I should have done this alone from the beginning."

At this point, Nicolas knows Renee well enough.

"Very well, my King," Nicolas bows, "I trust you know not to venture too far nor look for too long, for even a philosopher-king like you needs his rest. May O'Talp be with you, as well as your common sense."

Renee looks at him.

"Okay," Nicolas says, "Let me just…turn… this…around," Nicolas tries to turn his wheelchair around and a blush fills his face, "They do not make these like they used to…" and Renee cannot help but smile just for a moment.

Renee's smile fades as quickly as Nicolas from the scene. Christian sits and cries softly.

"I know," Renee says, "We will go home soon."

Christian cries again.

"Come. Up we go," Renee says, yanking his collar. He feels the wax spider on Christian's collar and remembers the first time he touched it, after Christian saved him from the Cheravian Bear. He felt he was given another chance, another life, reborn *Christened* to start anew. And in Kallipolis, he did.

Finally, Christian rises up on all fours and continues south.

"That is a good boy."

Renee starts forward. The two friends walk for another hour and Renee feels pain in his feet. Exhaustion washes over the two companions and Renee starts to turn around.

"Okay, my boy. We may return now. We can continue our search this late afternoon. Let us return to rest and gather our thoughts."

But Christian remains in place.

"Let us go," Renee tries pulling his collar, "You were the one who wanted to go home. Now take me there."

But Christian does not budge. His nose lowered to the ground, he seems to be sniffing a trail.

"You have smelled something?"

Christian moves further south, ignoring his master now trampling behind him. Christian picks up the pace as Renee's voice rises behind him.

"That is it! That is it! Good boy."

Even Renee is surprised by his own words; it is the first time he has smiled or felt any kind of delight in weeks. He runs after Christian, his walking stick before him. Even with his keen sense of hearing, Renee struggles to keep up with Christian for fear of losing the guiding sound of his paws.

Before much more than an hour has passed, Renee finds that Christian has halted before him. *It is the Axios River* Renee can hear the water flowing west, a sound he has not heard for a long, long time. *We are at the riverbanks.*

After a few moments at the riverside, Christian runs back to Renee with something in his mouth. He places it in Renee's hands, and Renee can feel that it is wet: a solid string tied in a loop with a large cool stone at the end. It feels familiar to Renee, like some sort of...necklace.

Elizabeth!

Renee runs forward, almost falling into the Axios's torrent arms. That would have been the end of him! He doubts if even Christian could have saved him then.

He bends forward *a king* kneeling *at the bottom of his nation,* his hands sifting through the random stones and roots sticking up. Christian cocks his head to the side and looks at Renee like he is a fool. And Renee feels like a fool indeed *is this what I have come to* an enemy of feelings, searching for a woman he has feelings for *a philosopher* king dirtying myself in the search for giving an apology.

But suddenly, his hand touches something hard. He finds that it is a woman's shoe. And close by, he finds another one. With Christian's help, it does not take Renee more than a few minutes to find Elizabeth's hood, outer robes, and anything else that would weigh her down if she chose to jump into the Axios.

If she chose to...swim across? But to where?

Renee kneels down in the mud, bringing Elizabeth's necklace to his chest. Suddenly, he feels a cool wind come from the south and he looks up, towards...it could not be Cherava, for nothing is there. But Lyceum?

Oh, Elizabeth!

She must have gone south, Renee realizes, to Lyceum. But why? If she believes she is the mother of my child, then that would make Dewey the uncle! She is going to speak to Dewey. But why didn't Elizabeth speak with me? *She did.* She did? *But I did not listen. Oh but but* Renee feels anger rise in his heart *but why must she seek help from my brother, my brother mybrother!*

My brother, who took the respect of my father away from me. My brother, who took my sight, the love from Helene, my cat, and now...my lover!

Must he take EVERYTHING from me?

Renee cannot feel the strained muscles in his arms as his hands ball into tight angry fists. Slowly, he brings his mud-caked hands towards his face. He smells the mud on them, the sweat and blood of months of labor, the powder of crushed stone and hammered earth. And then he remembers Kahn.

"*Kahn!*" Renee roars such that even Christian takes a few steps back, his tail between his legs.

"*Kahn! As my brother and my lover conspire against me, you are all I have left, but you are all I need.*"

Renee feels a drop of rain on his ear, and another on his hand.

"*No one can take you from me! Let them try! They will fail and you will stay here. You will grow to lead this nation. And together, we will show them. We will show Elizabeth. We will show Dewey. Everyone will see!*"

Thunder claps its hands across the sky. Renee can feel a blanket of raindrops on his shoulders now. He does not see Christian walking away.

"*Yes, Kahn. You will grow up to lead this nation, and then you will wipe Lyceum out!*"

3

When it comes to determining child custody, however, sexism is the rule.
Phyllis Schlafly

The thrill of running away from home does not leave a person's stomach as they grow older. If anything, it grows with them. Under dead marriages, years of labor in the same workplace, waking up in the same bed, the imagination does not stop growing under the blanket of static life. It moves and stirs, a monster often reaching out its tentacles for a small peek, a hint, a quick breath of a life it has not known for too long until one day it may throw off its blanket completely, stretching itself away from its harbor and into the open, becoming one with the wild ride of life.

Even though Elizabeth has traveled through the wild many times before, she still feels that youthful thrill of both fear and excitement she felt as a little girl. Of course, she never told Renee that her father was a stargazer before she came to Kallipolis. In this republic, it was not proper to speak of one's 'past life,' the life one had before coming to this land, let alone to their philosopher-king. Because of course, that life never existed. It was just a lie.

It was only a dream.

But the truth is that Elizabeth was taught how to follow the stars from an early age. She knows how to travel and how to navigate through unknown lands.

But that alone was not enough for her to cross the Axios, venture through the dense Cherava Woods, over the vast White Plains, and across the border into Lyceum. Even with talents like hers, she surely could have died. No, Elizabeth would not have been able to do all of that alone.

I was helping her.

The strangest part of her journey must have been upon approaching the Lyceumean border. She had been trudging through the desert sands of the White Plains for what seemed like weeks when she began to fade. She could not stand any longer. She fell to the ground, her cheek smacking against the warm sand. But her eyes remained open. Just before passing out, she thought she saw little heads popping out of the sand all around her.

Like groundhogs, they bobbed their heads up and down and up and down looking at her like some strange exhibit in a museum. They were difficult to notice: gray-brown tiny people blending into the earth around them. Indeed, it was only from her years in Kallipolis that she was able notice such plain and subtle things.

For a moment, Elizabeth caught sight of one and saw that the size of his ears was tremendous. The tiny people began to move towards her from all directions. She noticed that they might not have come from the ground at all; it just seemed that way from their short stature and her exhausted state. *Had they really come from the ground? Only in Kallipolis do children come from the ground.*

Yet these were no children.

"Who…" Elizabeth begins, but the weight of her journey bears upon her, and she falls to the ground.

ΩΨΩ

A sudden jolt of cold water. Sputtering for breath. Elizabeth is forced to wake up. She finds she is sitting in a flimsy wooden chair in some sort of station of glass and brick. She squints at once, blinded by the bright light streaming through, bouncing off colored hanging fragments of glass. But the lights feel warm and a strange joy washes over her heart. She opens her eyes slowly and is amazed by the color around her: red spheres of glass hanging from the ceiling, a yellow chair in the corner, blue and orange flowers growing under her seat. Of course, for Lyceum this is nothing unusual. But for her it is everything: so many colors so bright. She realizes, to her surprise, that she had almost forgotten what colors look like.

She has not seen a flower for years.

"Hello?" she tries, "Where am I?" and she sees the little people she had seen before passing out. They ignore her. She continues to cry out, but to her surprise, Elizabeth can see the little people looking down at long sheaves of papers they hold in their hands.

"Hello? Can you not hear me?"

Elizabeth notices them scribbling on the parchment with their feathers. She wonders why in this place of colorful sights and smells, these little people are so dull. They stop their writing for a moment, and look back up at her. She speaks again.

"There you are."

Instantly, the little people begin to write again.

"No! Look at me when I am speaking to you!"

Elizabeth notices that their writing seems to increase with her anger. She gets so angry that the sensors' feather-pens are moving quite fiercely now; they may rip through the parchment.

"Stop with your writing!"

But they write even faster.

"You may have your own customs, but if this is how you treat a lady—"

"They won't answer you," a voice says from behind her. She can smell fresh whiskey and fish on his breath. "But I can tell you that while we don't treat inferior women as well as we do men, well, haha, and we may not answer a woman every time she speaks, we surely don't ignore her, or write down everything she says for later. It's not a horrible idea though…"

"Who are you?" Elizabeth does not understand why this man uses so many words to say so little.

"Oh, I'm a regular Posteriorian here. I have a few names—"

"Where am I?"

"Whoa, woman. Watch yourself, with all your questions, I don't know how—"

"I do not appreciate having water splashed in my face," Elizabeth stands up and turns to face the man. But his fat belly bulges out of his wine and meat-stained robes. She turns away in disgust.

"And I surely do not appreciate being called 'woman,'" she manages, "Now answer my question."

"Ahem. S'cuse me! Right. You are on the border of Lyceum," the man shakes his head in wonder, "and these little people—hic! S'cuse me ma'am I got them hiccups—these little people are sensors. You should try not to look at them. We're not really even supposed to talk about them—"

Once Elizabeth confirms where she is, she does not hesitate.

"Take me to your king."

The man stands up straight and brushes himself off. Then, he throws his head back with laughter. His mouth opens so wide, Elizabeth can see two golden teeth and one tooth made from a glistening ruby of deep red.

Elizabeth has never heard such a laugh before; the freedom of it both scares and intrigues her. She crosses her hands across her chest and waits. Finally, the man speaks.

"Lord Dewey does not see women at their request, let alone hear their words."

"Well then maybe he will hear this!"

And with that, Elizabeth reaches into her robe and pulls out a piece of Renee's gray robes.

"Look at this!" Elizabeth says.

"I…I don't see anything in your hand."

"Look closer."

"There is nothing—oh! Well, what is that? It looks like nothing! Such a lack of color, such simplicity, it could not have been made in this land."

The man looks closely at the cloth in her hand, and his eyes see the white sign of the three-legged spider upon the dull gray cloth.

"Why, that can only be from…from Kalli—"

"From your Lord Dewey's brother himself," Elizabeth says.

"Why do you have that? Is Renee still alive? Wait don't tell me anything! I don't want to know! We never met…Oh, the trouble I can be in…I must leave now…"

"I am sure," Elizabeth says, "that if anyone finds out that I had important information for your king, and you ignored me, that they would not be too happy with your performance on this border."

"But, but, Lord Dewey does not like to be bothered. He is often busy with his ale, his, his stories—besides, I didn't see nothing!"

"But you did. Let me into the land and I shall wash the memory of your face from my mind. It shall be as if we never met."

The man begins to think, rubbing his thumb under his chin like a fat child staring out the window. It looks odd for such a burlesque and large, dirty man to ponder in this way; it does not fit. Elizabeth tries not to smile at the man, but he looks almost awkward as he thinks, like a monkey in a suit.

Elizabeth can see the man sweating under the weight of thought. After a moment, he says, "Oh, forget it. Get out of here. Go on!"

He raises his left hand and immediately, two sensors move swiftly behind her. Elizabeth turns around, jumping in surprise. She underestimates their abilities, she sees *how do they move so fast?*

"Oh," he says, "don't—hic—don't mind them. They'll stay out of your way, so you won't...even..." but the man sees Elizabeth has already turned south, walking away, and into the streets of Lyceum, "...notice," he shakes his head, sighs, and rolls over to his nap, fearing who will disturb him next.

ΩΨΩ

Yelekreb remembers the days when Dewey confided in him like a childhood friend. He remembers the day they first met as two little boys in the kingdom of Joachim: how he was throwing around the discus with the boys of the field, and Dewey *hello* would not leave them alone *hello* until he shushed him *sh!* But Dewey would not give up *You can't shush me! Do you know who I am?* as Dewey pushed himself into the game, Renee left Lyceum that day, and Dewey pushed even harder to make Yelekreb the brother Renee was never able to be.

And into adulthood, Yelekreb remembers the good times with Dewey and Jon, the drunk Dewey calling him in for advice about the woman *that woman* at his speeches, confessing his deepest fears, his darkest desires.

But since his last speech, Dewey has not been the same. He has changed in ways Yelekreb cannot understand. Yelekreb saw how troubled he was at the woman's presence at his speech. He remained awake that night, gazing out his window. He saw Dewey ride out on an oddly plain brown horse into the fields and beyond. Yelekreb's eyes began to feel heavy, and he succumbed to sleep before Dewey could return.

Whatever happened out there that night, Yelekreb will never know. But Dewey came back a changed man. Sure, his speeches are different now: he preaches a new religion, a New God. But something changed in the man too. While no Posteriorian has been sober or clear-headed enough to notice or care, Yelekreb notices the new Dewey, the distant-Dewey, and he does not like it at all.

Yelekreb prays for the days when he had to shush Dewey and even that would not get him away *You can't shush me! Let's play!* But now, Dewey spends much of his time behind closed doors. Through the doors Yelekreb can hear the bone crackling steak ribs, smacking of lips, chomping of luscious fruits and fishes, the gargling flow of wine, the moans of sexual pleasure, the giggling women Dewey entertains. But Yelekreb knows he is not invited anymore. None of Dewey's old friends are. Yelekreb stands against the door, listening to the sounds of pleasure for another moment, then he turns and walks away for another restless night.

But today another woman comes to Dewey. But she has come from outside Lyceum. She is different than the others. Yelekreb is almost glad this woman has come. He sees a light in her eyes, and a mission on her heart. He does not care where she is from nor why she is here. But the gray cloth she hands him with her words *take me to your king* so earnest and strong, ignites something in Yelekreb, a faint glimmer of hope that today will be different, that this time Dewey will invite him in, that he will bring Dewey something that will change him again, perhaps that they could be the friends they once were.

"My lord," Yelekreb knocks on the large orange oak door to one of Dewey's many "pleasure" rooms. (They were officially known as "experiential rooms" but Yelekreb knew their true purpose, as did every Posteriorian.) Yelekreb sighs and lets a minute pass.

"My lord?"

Another minute slips by. Yelekreb takes a breath and starts to turn away, but remembers the weight of Dewey's drunkenness and decides to try one last time.

"May I—"

"What is it?" Dewey sticks his head out of the door, his robes open revealing strawberry blonde curls of chest hair. A pipe sits in his mouth, bobbing up and down like a flimsy diving board as he speaks. Yelekreb can smell that the tobacco is flavored of cinnamon, black pepper, and orange rind.

"Uhm…"

"At a loss of words, my friend?"

My friend. The words hit Yelekreb's stomach like an iron weight.

"You, you have a visitor."

"I always have a visitor."

"This one brings news from far away. You may want to—"

"Who is he?"

"He is a woman, your honor."

"He is a woman?!"

"*It* is a woman, your honor."

"Ha! You had me there for a second." The pipe bounces up and down. Dewey reaches up and grabs it out of his mouth with a loud puckering sound. He holds it like a fine pen, breathing smoke up into the hallway, "though that would not be such an odd thing in Lyceum."

"No, I guess it wouldn't."

"Well," Dewey says, "You know that I don't see women when they want to see me. I see them when I want to—"

"She says she has traveled a long way—"

"She says a lot of things, I'm sure. What woman doesn't? Now. What does she look like?"

"I—I couldn't see, my lord. Her face was hidden—"

"Hidden?"

"Hidden by her cloak—"

"Alright, alright. Haha! I'm being difficult aren't I? Sure I will see her, but when I want to. When the time is right."

Yelekreb can see the naked back of a blonde woman through the door, smells of thyme and other incense. Laughter.

Dewey says, "Who is she?"

"I told you, she has traveled here from some other land. She was—"

"Her name."

"Oh, something Pala—Palortime? She would know. I asked her to wait outside the palace—"

"It is Palatine," a voice says from behind the two men. Both jump back in surprise. Elizabeth speaks past Yelekreb, directly to the king.

"Elizabeth Palatine. I am pleased to make your acquaintance, my king. I know you must have much to do, but while we are standing here chatting, time is passing us by. Please. We can meet when the time is right, but is there really a better time than now?"

Both men are dumbstruck. Yelekreb blushes and looks at Dewey.

"How did you—" Dewey starts.

"Yelekreb took me right here," Elizabeth says. "It was easy. Like a good little servant."

Dewey looks at Yelekreb.

Yelekreb says, "I, I left her outside with two guards. I don't know how she—"

"That's fine," Dewey smiles. His eyes remain on Elizabeth the entire time. He feels both anger and strange admiration towards this woman, but he tries to suppress the latter. He is embarrassed of his wonder.

"Well, this was quite unexpected," he takes a deep breath and sticks his chin up, "I will not just see anybody when they please, you know. Let alone a woman such as yourself." Dewey can feel his confidence leave with every word, "It is for me to decide—"

"You are an uncle."

"Excuse me?"

"I must apologize for the interruption, my lord. But I have come to tell you that you are an uncle, and I am the mother of your nephew."

"Nephew?" Dewey's shock turns to anger, "How dare you—" but his words stop as Elizabeth holds up what would look like a simple gray cloth to most, but not to Dewey's eyes. Dewey grew up seeing such robes.

"Renee." Dewey can hardly finish the word as his throat becomes dry.

Yelekreb feels a Posteriorian joy in rise in his chest. He smiles, "My Lord, is this cause for…celebration?"

Dewey does not acknowledge him; his eyes remain on Elizabeth.

He says, "Is this true?"

"Yes, I made love to Renee and we had a son. A son whom Renee has named Kahn. But, well, he took Kahn from me, and that is why I am here."

"Wait. He…took Kahn from you?"

"He…he has locked your nephew up in a terrible place. He is doing…horrible things…" Elizabeth looks down. "You must help me get him back."

Yelekreb says, "That sounds good, but first, we have a nephew! That in itself calls for some sort of party? There can be horses and wine fountains and confetti and—"

"Yelekreb," Dewey says, "Thank you. Please leave us now." Turning to Elizabeth, Dewey says, "It seems we have much to talk about. Please. Step into my office."

ΩΨΩ

The 'office' looks more like an overgrown forest, enchanted nonetheless. Elizabeth cannot help but stare in wonder at the vines of luscious grapes running in from the outside, up the walls and across the ceiling like veins from the inside of some tremendous botanical monster. She sees stalks of sugar cane, blossoming hydrangea, wonder bulbs fleur-de-lis, bladderpod lobelia, and all other plants from around the world. Blobs of colored paint (or is it food?) are splattered across the walls in a great mirage of shapes and textures fit for a king.

And towards the center of the room is one of the greatest windows Elizabeth has ever seen: a perfect collage of immense broken fragments of glass—each a different color—somehow blending into each other in a wondrous but coherent way: shades of purple, pink, blue, green, and orange, blending in and out of each other across the glass. It seems random, as if someone had accidentally dropped an immense ball of glass from the heavens, shattering it upon the concrete nation until it is frozen in its chaos, yet somehow perfect, as if it could possibly be no other way.

Looking through the tremendous window, Elizabeth can see the entire nation before her: hundreds of children playing games outside, and beyond them, gardens for as far as the eye can see. With bustling city streets and marketplaces on either side, it reminds her of what the Red Sea must have looked like as it split. And in the distance, the tall structure of the arena stands above the nation like a parent looking down upon its children. And somehow, with it all, every smell, sight, and taste seems to permeate through the window and into the room in just the right amount. Elizabeth's mind is so overwhelmed that she cannot hear the rapid strokes of her sensors' feathers scribbling furiously behind her.

"Ha," Dewey sees her surprise, "It gets me too, every time, even after all these years."

Elizabeth's eyes focus on the room before her. Four women lie upon a golden flowered divan, and two servants stand by with trays of food and a bottle of wine in their hands.

Yelekreb remains in the doorway to listen. Inside, Elizabeth takes a deep breath and collects herself. She speaks to Dewey for a few minutes, describing her child's enclosure. She continues.

"I did not come here to drink your wine, nor to feast on your meat. I just wanted you to know—"

"I am an uncle. But you do not want me to know anything. You want me to act. If I act, if I bring him here, you must know that I am doing it for myself. Do not think I don't know that it is in your interest, too. I am not a fool, Ms. Palatine."

Elizabeth says nothing. Then, "His name is Kahn."

"Is he healthy?"

"I, I sure think so."

"What do you man you think so?"

"Well, I never actually saw him. I just—"

"Never actually…saw him?" Dewey's voice rises, "If you—"

"I am telling you the truth. In the republic—"

"Republic?"

"Republic of Kallipolis," Elizabeth can see Dewey's eyes spark with interest at the word Kallipolis, "It is different there. Babies do not come from their mother's wombs as they do here. They come from the ground upon which they were conceived, as O'Talp would have them be brothers and sisters of the land—"

"*Impossible!* You come here speaking nonsense, woman," Dewey says, "And there is no O'Talp! El Totsira is the only true prophet under the God of Li, there is no other!"

"Of course," Elizabeth remembers the reason why she came, "Yet you have a nephew, and Renee is keeping him from you—"

"A nephew?" one of the Posteriorian servants exclaim with growing excitement.

"We shall make a party!" another says.

"No!" Dewey shouts. All is silent as Dewey looks down and sees his hands are trembling. Even he is surprised at the tone of his voice.

"No??" one of the servants says, a look of utter shock on his face, "A reason to…celebrate? To drink and be merry, my Lord. This is what you always—"

"Why are there always these…people around me? So many! Get *out!* Can't I ever get some peace and…" Dewey catches himself, "Not that I ever need…Oh, forget it! Get out! Leave!" Dewey raises his hand in the air and points to the door. His eyes remain on the wall before him. Elizabeth brings her hand to her face to hide a smile.

Dewey leads his servants to the door. Yelekreb is standing there.

"My lord?" he says.

"Get them out of here. The baby came from Kallipolis soil—well, that can't be true, ahem, but, but in any case, he is still in that damned prison, that damned...Republic, as they call it. Devoid of all feeling, of any joy, celebration, sorrow, and thus, of any learning. They think they are better than emotions, experience, the empirical, the world of the e. But Renee knows I am his brother. He could have named...my nephew something with just, just one e. Perhaps not something like Yelekreb or Renee or Helene, or, or even Dewey, for that matter, but perhaps, perhaps, he could have told me about the boy, he could have sent me a letter, something...And he keeps the boy, my kin, locked in this dark, empty cell, this place of Nothing, and worst of all, I have to find this all out from some...some...*woman.*

"No, my friend. There will be no party. This time, there will be no...celebration."

"Dewey, you have always—"

"I don't care what I have always done. I don't care what I have always preached. I have never had so much taken from me in my life, in such a secret way, such an...insult."

Yelekreb can hear Dewey's words making less and less sense as they go on, and Dewey can too. Dewey takes a deep breath.

"I must speak to this woman, and I must learn about the boy. I must see what can be done. You must leave me now. Go get some rest." Dewey closes the door.

But Yelekreb remains behind the door. Trying to breath quietly, *my friend* he puts his ear on the large oak door *go get some rest.* As his two sensors stand by awkwardly, writing down all he hears and thinks, Yelekreb can hear the low, muffled voices of Dewey and Elizabeth clearly enough.

"My lord," Elizabeth begins, "Kahn—"

"Hup!" Dewey stops her at the sound of the boy's name.

"He…the boy, has been locked in a cell of stone and mortar, where no sight, sound, or smell can ever enter. He may be more than a few months old, yet his mouth has never tasted the taste of milk, his eyes never seen a blade of grass nor a cloud in the sky, his nose never smelled even a breeze of fresh air—"

"Enough! This is sick! The boy is not allowed to live! He is dead every day, killed by my brother with every minute he is down there! Oh, the misery of it all! I can't imagine. Why? Why in El Totsira's name would anyone, let alone my own brother, how can someone be so heartless? So…cruel?"

Elizabeth did not think it would be this easy.

Yelekreb can no longer hear their words through the door; he is already running down the hall. Though he knows that Kahn's existence is a secret, he thinks of how long a Posteriorian can keep a secret. With their wagging tongues, this is not long. And to this rule, he is no exception. This thought makes him smile.

"Renee thinks," Elizabeth says, "that he is doing the boy a favor, you see. Without sensory distractions, Renee feels that the boy's mind can truly blossom into a library of knowledge, by being a fountain of reason rather than a mere vessel of outside experiences, sights and sounds and tastes that blind us, distract us, lull us, into, into…" Elizabeth stops, wondering why Dewey has let her speak for so long. Then she sees his eyes looking out the window. He was not listening, she decides, or perhaps listening all too well.

"Where is he?"

"What? Why do you want to know where he is?" Elizabeth feigns curiosity.

"I will get him. I will bring him back here, where he belongs."

"Back…here?"

"Oh, well, I mean, I can bring him to you, and you will live with him here. Or, or, once we have him, you can take him with you wherever you please."

Elizabeth knows Dewey's lie: no one may leave Lyceum without his permission, an acquiescence rarely given, if at all.

"Yes," Dewey continues, "In fact, I will send you and your son out on golden chariots, if you wish, to any place my stallions' feet may take you, with flowers in your hair, and enough goods and riches to feed you and my neph—your, your…son" Dewey has to swallow at the word, "for as long as you may live. I will reward you for telling me where he is, how to get to him, for rescuing the boy, and will give you…"

Dewey's words continue, but Elizabeth cannot hear them any longer. Her eyes turn towards the enormous window of color. She watches a group of children playing ball outside, the same group, she realizes, that has been there this entire time. One of the taller, 'thinner' kids runs up to the ball for a kick, but his leg misses the ball entirely, sending him flying through the air. Elizabeth can see his immense stomach joggle in the air like a large whale performing a great dive. The child lands on his back and bites his tongue. He lies unconscious, blood streaming from his mouth, a dumb smile across his face, as the boys kick the ball away, and continue to play around him.

"I will send you out…with the finest garments, and all the treasures you can imagine, so you and your…son…can live like Kings…"

Another small group of children are sitting by the side, watching the game. They smoke the largest hookah Elizabeth has ever seen: it stands at seven feet tall, orange and yellow branches blossoming out from every direction. Looking closer, Elizabeth can see intricate carvings around its base: bodies of naked women with large breasts, a deer in flight, large men with snakes wrapping themselves around them.

"If you can only tell me where he is…if you can lead us to him, to his cave in this…Republic…we can take care of the rest…all you have to do is point to this map here…where is it?"

One of the children, a young girl, brings the pipe to her lips. She has begun to gain the Posteriorian weight, swagger, bags already forming under her eyes, but looking deeper, Elizabeth can see the little true blue left in her eyes under the haze, the small true sweetness of sincerity still left in her smile.

Elizabeth can see that she used to be beautiful.

"Oh," Dewey is still speaking, "But I could see no reason why you would want to take your son from here. No reason at all. We have everything you could ever want, you and the boy, you name it…anything you've ever dreamed of, it can all be yours, and all you have to do is tell me…tell me…"

Elizabeth watches as the girl inhales. She can hear bubbles from the hookah water (the Posteriorians actually use fruit juices) popping and cackling like a broken machine. The girl exhales a plume of green smoke. Then, to her horror, Elizabeth watches as the poor girl begins to choke.

"Anything you want…and all you have to do…is just tell me…and Kahn will play with the other children here…we have lots of games…he will never be bored…"

The little girl begins to cough up purple phlegm, running down her chin, as the other children around her laugh. Their laughter grows with her phlegm. The girl tries to wipe the mucus away and catch her breath, her overly-large golden loop earrings swaying violently with her movements from side to side.

"Your son…Kahn, you called him? I will bring him back. I will bring him back here, where he can be happy, where his tongue can taste any food he wants, where his eyes can see the starry sky, where he will be deprived of nothing, where he can become the true Posteriorian he can be…and all you need to do is tell me…" But Elizabeth sees the Posteriorian children outside. She imagines Kahn playing with them, vomit all over his fat belly, a drunken smile on his round yellow face.

And something in Elizabeth begins to change.

"Just tell me…where is he?"

Elizabeth blinks but says nothing.

"Elizabeth? Are you listening? I will get him for you," Dewey puts his hands on her shoulders, and looks into her eyes, "I will bring him home," but he can see her eyes looking beyond him, at something else. As he continues to speak, "Tell me! Do you know, where is the boy?" his words wash over her like a stream of atmospherics. Her head hardens like rocks underneath the river and she knows that if she needs something done right, sometimes she needs to do it herself.

"Tell me now," Dewey tries to maintain his gentle voice, "Where is the boy?

"No" she says, turning to Dewey, fluttering her eyes as if awakening from a dream.

"No?"

"I'm sorry. He could be anywhere now. Anywhere. I wish I knew. And I haven't the faintest idea."

4

Myths which are believed in tend to become true.
George Orwell

Sheets of rain pummel down on the dark field, but they do not stop the cold hammer blows of stone and iron from filling the air *crak crak crak!* Even the howling wind blowing the rain sideways fails to drown out the smack of metal from shaking the ground. But Renee does not notice any of this. No, he does not feel the cold rain nails hammering into his working shoulders. He does not notice the wet dark growing around his steady mind. He is fixed intently upon laying the final completions upon Kahn's cell so that nothing of the outside world can ever find its way in.

Night passes and the rain lets up. Renee lifts his hammer for the final blow and brings it down one last time. It sounds a loud triumphant *crack!* almost as if the hammer itself knows that its job is done. For a moment, Renee wonders if it does.

Renee takes a deep breath and faces to the east. He can sense the tip of the sun reaching its red yellow crest above the Apuan Hills, but not quite clearing their rocky ridges. He feels the cold winter air burn his lungs, and it feels good. *Winter?* He realizes the season has finally come. And just then, he feels the first snowflake of the season kiss his nose. It sits there for a moment like a lost child wondering where to go, tumbling down his nose like a pillow, and finally melting away, disappearing into itself. *Is that what happens,* Renee wonders, *when we don't know where to go?*

He lets his hands fall off the hammer handle and he flexes his fingers for the first time in hours. Finally, he looks down at Kahn one last time, admiring his work. Before he can think about how Kahn will never see snow, breath winter air, nor be able to flex his fingers as he just did, Renee walks south to the House of Wax. He does not look back.

For three days, Renee sits in meditation. It only takes a few hours for his thoughts to clear his mind. He feels them floating out of his head like a flock of helium balloons, a class of children running out of school at the end of the day. With Kahn finally put away, Renee's head feels considerably lighter. Though his body aches from months of labor and his stomach is nearly empty, he does not seek rest nor food. Besides for the occasional sips of muddy water no one had time to clean, the completion of O'Talp's cave is nourishment enough.

Renee leaves the House light on his feet. He puts his head down in the traditional Prioritan way, looking only at the ground before him. But after his accomplishment, he does not want to. He marches towards the house of Nicolas, but finds his friend in the white field in front of his hut, sleeping in his wheelchair, his head slumped forward.

It does not take Renee long to instruct Nicolas to watch after Kahn. Renee pushes Nicolas towards the procreation fields, to O'Talp's cave where Kahn lies.

"You must stay by the cave, my friend," Renee says, "and out there you will have peace. You can meditate, think, have time to yourself. But at all times, make sure Kahn enjoys the same silence you do. Most importantly, let no one near, for you must not allow any sights nor sounds to come inside the cave, just as nothing must ever come out!"

Nicolas says nothing, and Renee is glad.

Nicolas is left sitting in his wheelchair, looking at the cave. It looks a small compact bulge in the ground, a small bump on the skin of a lizard. It rises not as something alien, but as part of the ground itself, a thick layer of mud across its solid iron interior. It is perfectly round, Nicolas notices, such that any piercing or weight upon it will be blunted by support from all of its other sides. It can never crumble, Nicolas thinks, it can never be broken.

Nicolas sits still before O'Talp's cave and enjoys the silent night. A group of elk run by in the distance, offering a soft rumbling to his thoughts. He wonders if Kahn could feel their tremors in the ground. He closes his eyes to take in his solitude, a small dot of brown in an empty field of white. He opens his eyes and sees a passing crow. He wonders if that crow was the last one to stay behind before flying south for the winter.

The bird reminds him of the south, his small brown cabin hidden to the east of the needle in Lyceum. He remembers his early childhood, how he was ridiculed in school for his malformed spine, how his father boarded up his windows and locked him in the attic. He recalls treasuring the few beams of sunlight that would manage to pry through the wooden boards. He remembers putting his ears to the wall, listening for the sound of birds as they would pass, the sounds of his siblings playing ball in the yard with the children from their school, their laughs, their joy. He remembers wishing so badly that he did not have ears so that he could not hear such sounds. *I don't want to hear it I don't want to hear any of those sounds.* He remembers how they killed him inside.

And as the first thick blanket of snow covers the ground around him, he wonders if Kahn can hear anything at all.

ΩΨΩ

Darkness. Black, black all around. Surrounded by filth and dust. And sometimes, between the black and filth and dust, just sometimes, a faint trace of a sound, an echo, a vibration manages to squeeze its way in before the black comes and suffocates it once again.

The dead static in Kahn's mind begins to falter, giving way to faint blips of activity. Nearly one year old, Kahn remembers, or thinks he remembers, a human voice *is that milk I smell?* and though Kahn does not know what the sound was, it sounded somehow familiar to him, as if that is the way it is supposed to sound *milk?!* But soon the voices left to chase something in the woods. But hours afterwards, Kahn thinks he remembers one of the big people had entered, quietly. This person did not cuff him nor feed him, but rather she held him up to her breast and embraced him. He had been scared, and had wailed loudly in his fear. Hot drops of water fell from her face to his. She smelled good. He had not seen her again.

But he held on tight to that memory, and treasured it the short time it lasted.

Kahn's arms and legs are chained to the ground. The iron chains hold him tightly, his head directed away from the door of the cave, locked in place to face the back wall. At first, all had been black, but after a few weeks, he begins to notice small hints of sights and sounds coming from the wall: a gust of wind cradles a small pebble under the crack in the door, sending a shadow of the pebble against the back wall. Kahn begins to see the shadows cast against the back wall by the small hint of daylight under the crack in the door behind his head. Kahn watches the show of shadows before him: the feet of passing men, a passing worm, a rolling pebble, floating dust in the wind. Even the passage of a small bug is magnified in its shadow on the wall. This is the world of shadows, and this is all he knows.

But then something new comes through his door. Sounds. They sneak their way under the door and echo off the back wall where their shadows play. To Kahn, the sounds seem to come from the shadows themselves. A bolt of thunder sends a squeaking mouse past Kahn's door, and the sound echoes off the wall. The clicking march of a beetle, the soft strokes of pebble against pebble, all of these speak to Kahn from their shadows on the wall. The shadows speak for themselves, and to Kahn, they are the most real things in the world.

After many months, Kahn begins to engage in a little game of his own: he names the shadows as they appear. The round ones that roll from left to right he names *milk*, subconsciously attempting to imitate the one human word that ever entered his mind. The tall ones are *morgt*, or sometimes *mort*, and the fast oval ones (that come from passing mice) are *hwee*, or sometimes *squeeh*, depending on the sound they make. This is the game that Kahn plays under his impenetrable blanket of rock, iron, mud, and snow. This is the game that carries him through the long winter months.

J. R. Becker

ΩΨΩ

Throughout his first years in Kallipolis, Benedictus slowly became one of the high warriors of the republic. Ben was one of the first to come to Kallipolis, running with Nicolas on his back. He knew he would no longer be a lens-crafter: he was meant for something more. O'Talp saw silver in Ben's soul, and commanded that his hand be branded with a 'W.' And what a warrior he had become!

He began to appoint warriors himself, from the men that ran into the land soon thereafter. Then, from the best of his warriors he began to select guardian-rulers, leaving the rest to be auxiliaries to aid and obey the guardian-rulers in protecting the nation. It was not hard for them to obey Benedictus; his tall, broad frame made him seem authoritative enough even without his sharp mind and insightful words.

But the auxiliaries became many, and they became difficult to control. Hundreds of them would stroll the republic's borders, from the mountains on the east to the sea on the west. In the empty silence of this land, they would spread out like small black bugs on a white empty sheet, looking for outsiders, Posteriorian protestors, and dangerous wildlife. However, on some days their eyes saw too much, their feet strayed too far, and they heard things they were not supposed to hear. Today, they begin to whisper rumors about a new philosopher-king, a child in the ground.

Ben wonders why he ever thought Renee's absence will go unnoticed. With his warriors fanning out throughout the land, it would be no surprise if someone stumbled upon Renee's "well." It has only been a few days now that Ben can hear the warriors whispering to each other about Renee's plans. But this is more than enough for concern, for in Kallipolis, it takes a lot of bother for a rumor to spread.

Walking towards Renee's hut, Ben appreciates the leader Renee has become. *Why,* Ben thinks, *it must have been over fifty years ago when we brought him here. He was just a boy. There were nearly forty people here waiting for him. Now there are almost a thousand.*

But there have been things he has seen falter in Renee, things Renee may have lost touch with. *Was it love* that tainted him, that weakened him, *what feeling* changed him, made him fixated *obsessed* with building a well? Ben fears Renee is slipping. There are not many times that Ben wishes he is wrong, when he hopes that what he sees is just a ghost that no one else sees, or that things are not as he thinks they are.

But this is one of those times.

Ben raises his fist to the thick mud of Renee's door, but his fist stops in midair: before he can knock on the door, he hears a voice come through it.

"Benedictus Azonips," the voice says. Ben recognizes it as Renee's voice, but it sounds surprisingly distant even for behind the thick mud door. Ben's fist hovers above the door for a moment, before lowering to his side. "Do come in."

Ben opens the door but stands in place, his large frame almost filling the small doorway completely. He says, "How do you do that?"

"Do what?"

"You knew I was at the door—"

"The silence of Kallipolis makes the creaking of my stairs sound like a roar."

"But you—how did you know it was me?"

"It is only reasonable."

"But you would think that maybe it could be Nicolas…"

"No. Nicolas is…busy. Anyway. It is you that should come to see me now."

"But I did not even knock—"

"Are you to stand in my doorway all day?"

Ben walks into the hut, bending his tall frame over so he doesn't knock his head on the clay doorframe. Renee sits barefoot on the ground, a small ceramic cup of gray tea before him. He picks up the cup and cradles it in his hands like a rose. Ben sits next to him, folding his legs under himself.

"So," Ben says "It is I who should come see you now?"

"It would only make sense at a time like this. I have not been straight with you," Renee turns his eyes to the wall. "The last I saw you, you saved my life after I was hit in the head by a Posteriorian's colored rock, but all I could do was ask if Nicolas was okay. And the next day you just wanted to know what I, your king, was doing all day in the fields, so I took you there and told you that I was building a well. I may not have been truthful. And since then, we have not seen each other for some time, so I have been waiting for you" Renee clears his throat. He remembers that once Ben said those very words *we have all been waiting for you* to him long ago *a long, long time*. "Benedictus, I have great respect and admiration for you, for what you have done here, but you must understand, what I have with Nicolas is different. Nicolas—"

"Warriors have been growing suspicious. They might find out—"

"Stop. I see you did not come to speak about Nicolas. But calm yourself. Speak to me like a guardian of the Republic should."

"Yes," Ben takes a short breath, "warriors may have seen what you were building. I have heard them whispering to each other. They are beginning to ask questions."

"Good. Questioning is what us Prioritans are best at, right?"

"They may find out—"

"What?" Renee's impatience shows, "They may find out what? Just what may they discover?"

"Please, my king."

"They may discover that I am building a well? Is that it? Is that what you came here to tell me?" Renee puts down his cup of tea.

"I knew you were lying," Ben says.

Renee looks away.

"I knew you were lying. I knew it was no well."

"I expected as much."

"I have always been your faithful follower, Renee Don Cartez, even before you knew I existed. And it is this I shall always remain. But you must remember, I knew you when you were just a boy. I watched you grow up. I brought you here. The small man you thought was your sensor would report to me every experience you had, every orange you tasted, every dream you dreamed. Through him, I was there with you, Renee, every moment you were awake. Every moment you were asleep. And I learned you, Renee. And this knowledge is something that does not fade easily, as an elder can still know their grown child better than the child knows himself. So, yes. I know you, Renee. And I know what you have been up to. But if you want to call it a well, that is fine with me."

Renee takes a deep breath. "How many know?"

"The warriors? I have heard seven mention your absence, four mention a well, and one mention," Ben pauses, "a child."

Renee closes his eyes.

"You know," Ben says, "that their job is to protect the Republic from outside sources, and that often includes patrolling the border, and going to places where Prioritans usually—"

"I know the principles of my own nation, Benedictus. If you know them so well, then you know that it is prohibited to be in the fields of the procreation festival during the nonseason."

"Yes, but the eyes of the warriors are strong. Though they are Prioritans, they can see far. Further, it is possible that one may not always...obey the laws—"

"Principles! We need no laws in this land. There are only principles which hardly need enforcement, since they enforce themselves. And the people know this: producers, warriors, and leaders alike."

"Yes, principles. Anyway. None of this changes what has occurred."

"Good," Renee nods in understanding, "So the secrecy of Kahn has been compromised. But how?"

"Even in Kallipolis, where the ones that are not yet blind nor deaf only look down at the ground the few times they venture outside their mud huts with no windows where they usually sit in deep solitary meditation...even here, a woman like Elizabeth does not go unnoticed. And when the leader of the entire nation selects such a woman as his spouse, and spends the following months away in secret—"

"Okay. What is done is done." Renee closes his eyes.

Minutes pass, and Ben waits.

"Gather your warriors," Renee says, "Tell them that it is true: there is a child of the land, created by their king and another woman. Do not tell them the woman's name. For it does not matter: it is a child of the land, and Lyceum is its only mother. But the child must remain in the womb of the earth. This is O'Talp's word. He must be contained, you must tell the people, because he is suffering from a most deadly case of scarlet fever. It is horribly contagious, you must tell them, so they must not go near. But it is taken care of; Kahn is, and must always be, completely contained and thus they must not disturb him by their action, word, or thought. They must not speak of him, nor wonder about that which they do not know. They must carry on as warriors of the republic as the silver of their blood is branded upon their right hand. What is done is done."

"What is done is done."

And these are the words that Benedictus tells his warriors on the following day, and these are the words they carry around with them for the next seven years.

ΩΨΩ

In the empty solitude of Kallipolis, it takes many years for even the smallest bit of news to travel from tongue to tongue. But towards the end of the seventh year, the word of Kahn begins to spread. Some say he is the son of O'Talp himself, that Kahn fell from the heavens *on a pillow of white doves, I tell you* from the gray sky into the ground, where Renee locked him in from becoming the next leader of Kallipolis. Others say he is the son of a devil, or an evil genius, supremely powerful and clever, born to deceive them into being lovers of sights and sounds. Still others whisper that the enclosure that Renee has called O'Talp's Cave is really not a cave at all, but a tomb, a grave *Kahn is dead!* a hiding place so that nobody can ever see the corpse of Renee's child for all time.

But most of the warriors believe the words of their ruler. They believe that Kahn is suffering from a terrible scarlet fever and they do not go near. They do not question Benedictus even though Renee began constructing the cave far before he could have known about Kahn's disease. After all the blind man has known, Prioritans do not question his words.

But the word of Kahn spreads like a broken yolk in a black iron pan. It spreads in a way only time can design, spreading from the warriors of Kallipolis to the producers and rulers, and finally beyond the border of the republic, to the mountains of the east, and to the sea on the west. It spreads through the eastern mountains across Lake Ohrid and into the homes of Macedon. It spreads by boat up the Axios River, porting at the Marina De Carrara, and settles onto the dinner-tables of the small towns around Lake Tirreno, moving its way upwards upon the tongues of the stone workers in the marble Carrarian Quarries. Finally, the word of Kahn's *inhuman* confinement flows down into the Cherava Woods upon the tongues of the few wanderers and rangers that dare live there, across the White Plains, eventually approaching the borders of Lyceum. Here, the word spreads like wildfire upon contact, like a swaying flame touching a pool of gasoline *Lord Dewey has a nephew* riding upon the hot wagging tongues of babbling Posteriorians *but Kallipolis locked him underground, locked him away from color, from sounds, from life! Just because he is sick* Posteriorian anger growing in the fat bellies *Kahn is confined! Kahn is confined! Kahnisconfined!*

This is what the people believed. And myths that are believed in, tend to become true.

It hits Kahn just after his eleventh birthday: just a sore throat at first, followed by a terrible fever wrapping the boy in hot sweat. Kahn's tongue becomes bright red with a strawberry appearance. Rough textured rashes of red begin to spread upon the child's back like rust, swelling on his armpits and behind his ears. The area around his mouth becomes pale like white Prioritan mud. By the sixth day, the rash finally begins to fade, but the affected skin begins to peel off the boy like a peeled orange; skin begins to shed from his groin, axilla, and off the tips of his fingers and toes. The skin falls off his small fingers, once youthful and rich, now shaggy like an old, raggedy snake shedding its skin as one last act, one final gasp before it lies completely still, disintegrating back into the aged earth from whence it once came.

5

Behold! human beings living in an underground den, which has a mouth opened towards the light; here they have been from their childhood, and have their legs and necks chained so that they cannot move...and they see only shadows. The prison house is the world of sight. Certain professors must be wrong when they say that they can put a knowledge into the soul which was not there before, like sight into blind eyes. The power and capacity of learning exists in the soul already. Must there not be some art which will effect conversion in the easiest manner; not implanting the faculty of sight, for that exists already, but has been turned in the wrong direction, and is looking away from the truth?

Plato

"*Let Kahn go! Let Kahn go!*"

The shouting and stomping of hundreds of large angry Posteriorians shake the ground on southern border of Kallipolis like never before. The sun has not yet begun to rise, but the dawn offers a stale brown warmth into the night air. Drums pound, bells ring, and shakers clatter loudly; the sound of thrashing, clamoring metal rips through the humid air. Elephants adorned in gold and purple velvet run in every direction, Posteriorians shouting from upon their backs, often falling down under the trampling animals to their death. Droplets of Posteriorian sweat dribbles violently off the protesters' trembling arms, raised fists, and prancing legs, falling, forming hot puddles in the earth, splashing with their dance, soaking their rainbow shoes and baggy pants, robes, and dresses as they drag on the ground before them.

The shouts all but drown out the conversation of two Posteriorian women. They both wear bangles around their thick arms and necks, their black hair hanging down like dark sheets of glass. One of them has dyed highlights of orange and green in her hair. They sit on the sidelines atop a large pile of rocks where they can look down onto the scene. They hold cymbals in their hands. A tremendous sack of colored stones lies by their side.

"Mmmmm," one of the women closes her eyes, taking it all in, "Oh, this is truly music to my ears. Worth the trip!"

"Nearly fifty of our people died during our voyage here, y'know."

"Yes. It is too bad they are missing out on *this*!"

"Do you think that...Kahn—is it—is really...locked away? I mean I heard some pretty horrible things. Can you imagine? Just a baby, chained to the ground in a dark cave, it's, it's just terrible!" She begins to cry and hold onto her chest, "How could this have happened? How can El Totsira let it? How is this allowed...in any part of the world? Is, do you think it's really true?"

"That's what I've heard."

They hear the sound of a Posteriorian flute being played nearby.

"How do you think we found out about this anyway?"

"I, I heard that it came from one of Dewey's closest advisors. Someone who was sick of keeping Dewey's secrets *my friend.* He brought this visitor, this...woman in from some foreign land, and when Dewey saw this mysterious woman, he asked his advisor, the discus thrower, to leave *Go get some rest* but the advisor stayed to eavesdrop by the door and he heard just...amazing things *It is different there; Babies come from the ground* and horrible, horrible things *locked in a cell of stone and mortar* that he could not bear *his mouth has never tasted* to know such terrible things alone *his eyes never seen* and he ran away, knowing this big secret heavy on his chest, and his tongue startin' waggin' and well, y'know how it usually goes from there..."

"Yes, I may have heard that too. But word also may have leaked from Kallipolis itself—" before her words could continue, a sharp colored rock flies through the air and hits her on the head. She falls over, holding her bloody head. Her screams are muffled by the chorus of chants *Let Kahn out! Let Kahn out!* rising around her *Bring Kahn home! BringKahnHome!* as her friend looks down at her, makes a face as if to cry, lets out a giggle, shrugs, and runs off to the center of the protest, dragging the bag of stones behind her.

The rattling of jewels and gold bracelets fill the air as the fat arms of hundreds of Posteriorians toss buckets of colored paint across the border, splashing a rainbow upon Prioritan soil, or upon the Prioritan guardians standing in a perfect, silent line. The guardians do not react. They wait for orders from their superior, Benedictus. Days pass.

But Ben is near the mountain by the northeast border, commanding a close group of warriors to prepare for a bigger war. He has them making the Prioritan sword: a solid piece of iron forged into the shape of a long, thin sword of five feet in length.

"We will make hundreds!" Ben says, "We will not stop until we are safe. We will not negotiate with lovers of sights and sounds. They will not have the honor of hearing our voices speak!"

Additional warriors approach the border. Eight are splashed in green and yellow paint as they approach. They do not react. Others are met by colored stones, heckling, laughing, and spit. They do not react. They continue their march to the border line, steady and slow. Then they align perfectly, settling their shields in the ground.

The Posteriorians back off. They are stricken by the straight rows of the Prioritan warriors, the certainty in their eyes, their stature so flawlessly uniform and strict. While the protestors' smiles do not fade and their heckling only increases, they find they share a secret fear of the Kallipolis warriors that even they never recognized. They question their feet as they move backwards, back into the deadly Cherava Woods.

"Ben," one of the warriors says to his leader, "We have made nearly two hundred swords of perfection. The Posteriorians have left our borders."

"You will continue to make swords."

"But the Posteriorians have—"

"I heard what you said. Did you not hear what I said?"

Immediately, the warrior turns from Benedictus to the flames from which swords are grown. But before he turns away, he thinks he sees a fire burning in Ben's eyes. He does not question, but he can hear Ben behind him, muttering under his breath.

"That was a mere rainfall of fools, if anything. There is more we have not seen," Ben pauses. The warrior can still hear Ben as he begins to walk away. The words are unmistakable.

"A storm is coming," he says.

ΩΨΩ

Dewey was always a dreamer. Since he was a boy falling asleep to the gently rocking breasts of Helene, he dreamt of flowing fountains of wine and candy, of buildings of rainbow cotton, starfruits raining from the sky. Under his big dumb grin, he dreamt of Lyceum becoming one large bubbling pot, spittles of hot wine and beef gravy sputtering and sizzling in every direction. Then it would turn to one large moon-bounce of wild orchids and berries and butterflies that he would share with old wizards in rainbow robes, Sufjan bouncing upon a pogo-stick unicorn, Posteriorians and zoo animals laughing in unison, women flowing with ale and fruit juices until all the world would melt away, floating upwards into Dewey's subconscious as he would begin to wake to the golden Lyceum days of his youth.

But this is not like Dewey's dreams of late. His dreams begin to change. They become more vivid, more real. He does not like these new dreams, but he cannot help having them. He fears they may come true. He wishes they would stop.

Tonight, days after most of his Posteriorian protestors flee from the borders of Kallipolis, Dewey dreams such a dream:

He finds himself walking through the farms before the palace of Lyceum. It is a beautiful day, and Dewey welcomes the pleasantly surprising dream. He feels the sun on him like a blanket. Two blue birds float past him, and he smiles. He closes his eyes and sips in the day. The pollen of flowers is rich. He raises his arms, his fingers spread to catch the air, embracing the currency of life around him.

Suddenly, he hears a faint whistling. The whistling increases into the sound of something roaring through the sky. It is getting louder. His eyes open and he sees it: a fiery yellow ball soars over Lyceum! It comes from the north. His eyes follow its path, and to his horror, it crashes straight into the needle, a huge blast! Black smoke washes across the sky, blocking out the sun. The needle stands for moment as if deciding what to do, orange flames tricking out. Then it crumbles like a deck of cards, raining down boulders upon the panicked city.

Dewey looks into the streets and sees children running and women screaming. An old lady is walking, cane in hand. Her shaking hands are the last thing Dewey sees as she is crushed under a rolling boulder. Small stones pelt his face. He can feel warm blood from his nostrils. He raises a hand to shield his face. But he parts his fingers so he can see through them. He struggles to see the scene, but through all the horrible black and gray, Dewey can see the needle in the distance, now a fiery hot rod blazing onto the landscape. Dewey squints, but it is too bright for him. He looks away, back to the streets. He begins to look for safety.

Then, through the raining stones, he can see the face of Olegna Lechim, the artist. Olegna smiles at him and Dewey screams *help me help me* but Olegna says nothing and Dewey realizes that his smile is not friendly. It is an evil smile, and Dewey tries to turn away, but he can hear Olegna in his head.

"You want to bring Kahn home, do you?"

Dewey looks up and sees Olegna's smile. But a large boulder is coming down upon Olegna, Dewey sees. It is coming down fast.

"Olegna," Dewey tries, "Look out!"

"You think that just as I ran away from home, and Renee ran away from home, Kahn cannot do that too?"

"A, a stone! Above you. Look, look out!" Dewey cries, pointing to the boulder coming down upon Olegna. But Dewey sees that the stone does not hurt Olegna. Rather, it bounces off of him like a pillow. As more stones begin to wash off of the artist, Dewey can see that the stones are not stones at all. They are white feathers. Pillows. Hoaxes, as thin as cards. Olegna begins to laugh.

"Haha! You see, it is true! Do not worry my king, these cannot hurt *me*. These stones are from the needle. From Lyceum. But your nation is not made of solid stone. It may look that way while the wind remains still. But push it with just a pinky, and Lyceum can fall like a house of cards. As thin as paper, you are..."

"Stop!" Dewey feels a rock hit his shoulder. Hard. It does not feel like a feather at all.

"Like a floating feather, a swaying reed, your way of life moves whichever way the wind blows, saying this one day, and that another..."

"Stop this! All of this!" Dewey raises his hands above his head, and they being to bleed from the oncoming onslaught. "They feel like rocks to me!"

"That is because you never felt anything real. It would knock you off your feet."

"Stop this! Stop it all!"

"Can you feel it?" Olegna's voice continues in Dewey's head, "There is a boulder coming, but you must not be afraid. Just know that it cannot hurt you and it won't. Because it is nothing. You are nothing."

Small rocks continue to dig into Dewey's back like nails. He closes his eyes and tries to push the pain away *they are not real they are not real* to convince himself they cannot hurt him *like feathers* but it does not help *theyarenotreal* and the boulder grows closer.

Now Dewey can see its shadow, a dark circle growing around his feet. He looks up and sees it: a huge stone ceiling closing in on him, inch by deadly inch. It is right above his head. He kneels, throwing his arms in the air.

"Stop!"

But it does not stop. It falls upon him like a horrible truth; he cannot live forever. He feels the cold stone marble, the terra-cotta shards digging into his back as the color fades, and he is thrown from his dreams.

Dewey wakes up. He sits up in bed and tries to catch his breath. Without hesitation, he runs to the window of his room to look outside. He expects to see the needle torn down, raining down stone and fire upon the city. But all is still.

The needle stands tall like a spire under the morning sun.

There is a loud knock on the door.

"Who is it?"

"Whoa! Someone woke up on the wrong side of the bed!"

"Just…answer me."

A Posteriorian messenger opens the door, his sensors scuttling behind him. "Haha! You look like you dreamed of a chocolate horse!" Dewey does not recognize him, and wonders if he should. Dewey does not smile.

Dewey starts, "What is it?"

"Well..." the servant seems to consider making another joke, but he sees Dewey's face and thinks the better of it. "Ahem. My lord. It seems you have received a letter—"

"From who?"

"It is from your brother. It came by rider yesterday afternoon…or was it a few days ago?"

"A few days ago?? What took you so long?"

The Posteriorian reaches into his robe and takes out a small pipe the color of jade. "Well," he begins to shine his pipe, rubbing it with his robes, "Y'know how things are. I was going to deliver the message—"

"Yes?"

"…but, well, I came across a party. But I did not want to stay long, oh no, but this one man got sick so we had to help him. He told the best stories…I…But of course I would not stay long because….I knew…this message I had to deliver…that I knew…"

Dewey sighs.

The Posteriorian continues, "It was hard to find you—"

"I was in the palace the entire time."

"Yes, the palace," he begins to stuff the pipe with a hunk of tobacco found left in his beard, "The place of royalty."

"Leave me."

Dewey turns to the wall and opens the letter. He does not hear the door close behind him. Engrossed in his brother's handwriting, Dewey passes through the letter without pause.

Dear Dewey.

How do you think, my brother? It is true. Kahn is here. I can tell you that you need not worry. You need not think of him. He is not of your kin. He is a son of the land and only the land, the republic from which he was born. But I know you will not listen. I have kept him in a place where he will be safe from the sights and sounds that you feed yourself every day. And he will be safe from you.

Why is this necessary, you may ask? I once believed in the things you do: the sights and sounds and tastes running to me from every direction, fighting for my attention from my first breaths of life. There was a time when I would ask such a question you do now: why is this necessary? Even if I may be correct that knowledge comes from reason rather than experience, why must I take such drastic measures?

Because. Because now I realize that there is nothing among the things I once believed to be true which it is not permissible to doubt. Thus I must be no less careful to withhold assent henceforth even from these beliefs than I would from those that are patently false, if I wish to find anything certain. Because it is not enough simply to have realized these things; one must take steps to keep themselves mindful of them. For long-standing opinions keep returning, nor will one ever get out of the habit of assenting to them. So I must protect Kahn from forming these habits in the first place. From the beginning. Before it starts. Even if that means keeping him locked down deep in the ground.

I hope you are well at home, as in days of old.

Sincerely,

R

Dewey pauses for just a moment before crumbling the paper in his palm. He is quick to suppress the unmistakable feeling of longing and love flowing up inside him. He forces anger and hate to take their place like two large stones pressing down upon a fountain of affection, not letting a drop of it reach his consciousness.

Immediately, Dewey storms across the room, looking for a pen and paper. His sensors scramble out of the way, recording every lucid sensation running through his fat head. He grabs at writing-feathers on his desk but they spill over, falling onto the floor. He bends over, grasping for the largest one. As he writes, he keeps his head back, but the rainbow colored feather still hits his face. Even he is surprised by the detailed, loopy script of his lettering, compared to his brother's simple block letters. His pen moves incredibly fast, writing words long before they make sense in his mind.

> *Renee Renee Renee you have never known what it felt like what it feels like to taste something to see something to feel something so special that it makes a mark in your memory which you can go back to for ever and ever and ever and learn from over time and inspire you to create far in the future from something you experienced so far back in the past no no no you will never know the beauty of this the beauty of feeling the splendor of experience you spend your life running like a coward and hiding and shielding yourself and locking yourself alone in a dark dark room away away away from the world in denial of the outside world just because well just because it is easier. It is easier just to sleep. You turn it away, banishing it completely because it just might not exist exactly as it portrays itself to you and and oh what you are missing out on you have no clue oh the madness oh the madness of it all—*

The pen breaks under the weight of his quivering hand. He catches the bottom half of it and begins to write again.

Man is chiefly born for action not inaction not as prisoner not for abstinence not as you demand each man lock himself away from all the beautiful creations given to him in this world as imperfect as they may be but it is not good enough for you no it is not good enough for you to lock yourself up but you will not stop until you rob everyone else of their own lives because philosophers like you are the source of uncertainty and error from the fruitless efforts of human vanity yes you you you people are chased from the open country you robbers fly into the forest and lie in wait to break in upon every unguarded avenue of the mind and overwhelm it with religious fears and prejudices and this is a crime that you cannot run from so know that you cannot run from us Posteriorians and our colors and we will get to you we will get to Kahn we will bring him home even if it—

The sharp edge of the pen rips through the paper this time, and Dewey kicks it to the ground, screaming. He stomps on the parchment, his sensors standing idly by like indifferent spectators from another time. Finally, Dewey picks up the paper and, without looking at it, holds it up to the Posteriorian messenger. Dewey's words come out soft but strong, like the growls of a bear behind a sheet of glass.

"Just...go," he says, "Send a rider out and bring this to my brother."

"My lord," the messenger says, "It will take days for the riders to deliver this, assuming we all make it in one piece—so what you wrote here—are you sure this is what you want—"

"Go!"

And this they do. As soon as his letter leaves the room, Dewey jumps to his feet. An overwhelming feeling of being trapped overtakes him, the feeling of being locked to this game of political debate about things he does not understand. He rubs his eyes. Reading Renee's letter made his eyes hurt *knowledge comes from reason rather than experience* like boulders rolling inside his head. It hurt to read. It hurt to think. It is all too much.

Dewey runs outside, a hot blaze of heavy thoughts streaming out of his head, leaving a trail behind him raining down upon his poor sensor's scribbling hands.

ΩΨΩ

Renee receives the letter in Kallipolis six days later. He clears his throat, holding up the letter like a fine specimen. His fingers trail over the dark orange ink pressed into the parchment like violent scars. His fingers read the first ten words for him, and he nods his head in understanding and returns the paper to the faithful servant at his side.

"Renee." Ben says. He hands the letter back to his King.

Renee says nothing.

"Renee. If you want I can read it to you—"

"No. That will not be necessary."

"I can get my finest lens. Perhaps I can create a magnifying—"

"I have read the first line. It is enough."

Renee thrusts the letter back into Ben's hands and puts his head down in concentration. Ben's eyes survey the letter and he begins to read the letter himself.

Renee walks briskly into an adjacent room, closing the door behind him. He cannot sense Ben's confusion behind him as he circles the room alone. His hands begin to shake just a bit, like the fluttering of a dead moth's wing in the breeze. As the minutes pass, he realizes that he is afraid to read the letter. He realizes his deepest inner fear.

The fear that he might actually feel.

Rubbing his hands together, Renee sees the burnt scar on his palm. He rubs his palm. He remembers hot wax that he trusted burning him, stinging him, digging into his hand. He remembers trusting his sense of smell, sight, and touch, trusting that the wax smelled of honey, looked like a solid spherical object, and felt cool, solid, and inviting upon his hand. But then he feels his scar and he remembers that it was none of those things.

It was none of those things at all.

He promises himself that he will not let experience burn his son as he let it burn himself. He reminds himself why he came here, and what the principles the Republic stands on. He feels rivers of confidence flow through him again, settling into the troughs where they last dwelt.

And it feels very, very good.

ΩΨΩ

Jon Rasaa storms through the halls on the northern end of the palace of Lyceum. Worried thoughts of Dewey rattle in his head like battleships crashing on the sea. He seeks comfort from the only source in the palace it exists: Helene. It has been quite a while since he has seen her. But now that he needs her, it seems like a lifetime. His mouth opens to talk even before he gets to Helene's door.

"I have something…to tell you," Jon takes a deep breath and opens her door, "May I come in?"

Helene sits with her back to him, a lonely old figure bathing in the soft white haze of sunlight streaming through the open French doors. Though Jon can only see the back of her head, she looks to Jon as if she is swimming, floating, almost drifting through a large white pillow of fog, a porcelain doll floating in a pool of milk. Jon sees her two legs under her chair, two thin pencils sticking out of their rainbow box. His eyes rise as Helene turns to face him.

Even after all these years have passed, Jon is still surprised at how Helene has aged. Her hair no longer golden, her curls are white and thin like the shriveled bark coils of an old tree, her skin the remains of a locust's shell, her hands the shed skin of an old snake. But the colors of her youth remain deep in her eyes. She speaks and her voice is a whisper.

"Yes. I am here."

Jon slowly walks inside. Helene turns back to the window. Jon kneels in front of her so that she can see his face.

"Jon!" she smiles.

"I wish I could be so glad," he says. He watches Helene's smile disappear. "Oh, no. I don't mean to upset you." Jon says.

"It's not that. It's not you, honey," Helene places her hands upon his.

"Then what is the matter?"

"Oh, nothing is the matter. I know you came here with troubles of your own. I guess…it is just seeing Dewey like this."

"Dewey?"

"He is just like Joachim used to be."

Jon says nothing, but waits for an explanation.

"I should have not been surprised that Joachim's libido would grow with his age. See, there was a time in our marriage when it was so exciting; our servants had to change the bed sheets at least three times a day. I see Dewey has the same desire; all the women of this nation may not be enough for him—why, look at me, an old woman babbling on while you have troubles of your own. Pray, tell me why you have come."

Jon dismisses her words as the comical rant of an elder whose mind has grown weary. He is just happy to hear her voice. He says in a worried voice, "Oh, Helene! Dewey recently found out what Renee has done, that Renee, that Renee took his son, Dewey's only nephew and—and…locked him in an underground chamber! So that he can never see the light of day! So that he can never smell a flower. Or see a bird. Or taste a fruit. How can anyone do such a thing? Such a vile, nasty…cruel thing? It's inhuman. And…and now Dewey went out to take a walk. Oh, the way he left! How his blood must be boiling! How his heart must be heavy, his eyes just might melt into tears! The misery he must be going through. I don't even know where he went, or when he'll come back…if ever. I just hope he'll be okay," Jon pauses. He feels his eyes moisten, "I care about him an awful lot, y'know?"

Helene turns to Jon. She squeezes both his hands in hers.

"You have been friends for a long time," she says.

"Since the art festival," Jon recalls.

"Well. I don't think you were *friends* just then."

Jon smiles.

Helene says, "Our king will be fine."

"I wish I could say the same thing."

"You could—"

"No!" Jon pulls his hands away, "The cruelty of Renee would drive any man mad. I don't understand it! How someone could...lock their own son up, their own blood, never even telling their own brother...how Dewey must have felt when he found out! His only nephew—"

Helene grabs one of Jon's hands.

"Please!" she says.

"What?"

"Nothing. Just...stop grieving. Dewey will be fine."

"I see doubt beneath your eyes."

Helene says nothing.

"You don't think he will come back alive, do you?"

"Oh, it is not that. He will be fine. I just don't want you to worry—"

"Why? What is it? What are you not telling me?"

"I cannot tell it! Do not ask again."

"But you must. Dewey is going to travel to his brother, all because, because—"

Helene coughs. Jon is puzzled by the tears in her eyes. He waits for her to speak.

She says, "Renee is not Dewey's brother."

"What?"

Silence fills the room. Helene swallows before speaking again.

"I didn't want to tell you. But here: Renee is not Dewey's brother."

"But—but what—how—"

"I've never told anyone this before. But hell, I am old now, and my days are numbered."

"Dewey and Renee—"

"They are not brothers. They never were. Dewey was not born into the royal family. Renee was the only son they had. Katherine and Joachim had Renee as their own, but he came out so white and pale, it shocked everyone in the palace. They named him Renee, hoping he would embrace the world of the 'e', or empiricism, experiments, science, experience. He tried, for a time. But soon he rejected all of that. He was born with his eyes closed, and afterwards he would not open his eyes for weeks, and he refused to touch anything to his lips but the purest of water. Such a stir he caused, refusing his mother's breast. The colorful books and paintings most children adored only shocked him, and made him cry. All he wanted to do was lie quietly and stare up at the ceiling.

"They waited for him to come to life, for the experience to come along and fill him up like a bottle as it had everyone else. They waited for the one experience he would let inside him, one that would trigger him to lust for more. But it never came. He was dead. Empty. And it seemed he was going to stay that way for a long time.

"It was not long until Joachim wanted a true Posteriorian as his son, a brother for Renee to be friends with, to look up to. Someone to influence Renee, as I hoped the cat would."

"The cat?"

"Nevermind that. Anyway, Katherine passed away shortly afterward. Joachim was mad at her for giving him Renee, and he may have cast her away, but she died. Tuberculosis, they called it, though she never looked that sick to me. But I never saw her again. Gone. Leaving Joachim alone with lonely Renee.

"So Joachim began to search for someone to be a brother to Renee. Dewey was recently born in Lyceum, and even though he was an ordinary citizen of Lyceum, he was already the joy player on the street. His golden curls were adored throughout, while his cries for rice pudding would make the people laugh almost as much as his heavy snores and rose red cheeks."

"But," Jon says, "if Katherine was not the mother of Dewey, well, who is? Is she still alive?"

"Yes."

"Okay. But…how can you know this?"

"Because it is I. I am Dewey's mother."

"What?"

"I gave birth to Dewey in the streets of Lyceum. Dewey and I lived in Lyceum as regular, normal Posteriorians. But he became the model Posteriorian. He was very popular with the children on the street. When Joachim heard about us, he brought us in to the palace. He brought Dewey in to be Renee's brother, and he brought me in to be his lover. After losing Katherine, for Joachim, Dewey and I were a perfect fit."

"But all this time…he knew nothing?

"Dewey was too young, and too…busy with life to remember when he and I arrived. The boys were hardly two, and Dewey was already drunk on honey and pudding. And Renee was just…numb, innocent, and blind. He didn't seem to really be paying any attention to his surroundings. Renee did not even notice Dewey nor I for some time after we arrived. When he finally saw us*your new brother and mother* he kind of just shrugged and walked away again."

"But in the nation…weren't there servants and handmaidens in the palace who noticed the new addition? I mean, didn't anyone notice that you and Dewey were not here before—"

"Jon. You know this. Does anyone in this nation notice much of anything? Perhaps one or two raised their eyebrows in passing confusion before going off to a party. As the Posteriorians were busy running from one experience to the other, you think anyone would notice and remember that Dewey and I were not here a year or two earlier? Do you think it would hang around in someone's head long enough to bother them? To…question? No. Joachim and I told everyone that we were his family. We told everyone that Dewey was Renee's brother and that I was Joachim's lover. No one questioned and no one cared. You know the nature of this nation.

"So no one knows…"

"No one knows."

"But, but why? Why didn't you tell anyone? Renee is not even his brother! Kahn is not even his nephew! Why didn't you tell your own son? All these years, he had to deal with Renee! The letter he just got…the pain he is going through…the battles that may be raged! And now, the grief he is going through, thinking Kahn is his nephew! You should have—you should have told somebody—"

"—and compromise his reign?" Helene's voice is firm despite her age. "Make him give up his right to his kingship? How well that would go down. Or get myself killed in the process? Would he not want to silence me? But it is better this way. Deep down, Lyceum does not really care if their king is from royal blood. You think they all know what is going on? All they know is that they like Dewey and they have a king. That is all that matters. And that is not up to me to disrupt." Helene pauses, lowering her voice, "But, no. He is not from royal blood. He has not the blood of a king."

"But now he thinks Kahn is his nephew! He is going to Kallipolis to rescue Kahn for nothing. And he might die!"

"Yes. That may be true. But we cannot be certain."

"Certain?"

"All we can be certain of is that if you tell anyone this thing, death will be upon both of us. But you know this, Jon. You are a smart man. Always was, standing up at that festival. We must let Dewey live the life he has already begun. Besides, if he thinks he is King and everyone else does, then perhaps he really is king! If he thinks Renee his brother, and Kahn his nephew, then so it is! For what is a family anyway? A kingship? Sometimes the truth is what one believes, rather than what actually is. Tell a sick man that to be healed, he should raise his arms, crack an egg over his head, and sing beautiful hymns on one foot. He will do that and he will feel better—and if he feels better, who are you to tell him he is not? Tell a sad man that God will make him happy and his life will have meaning, if only he believes. He will believe, and he will be sure God exists and his life has meaning—and if he believes this, who are you to tell him it is not so? Perhaps the sick man really *is* healed just because he *feels* it is so. Perhaps God *is* the feeling itself, the drug, the placebo effect of meaning, just because it *feels* so. This is what our nation is founded on: taking things as we feel them. Without question. Perhaps brotherhood—as Dewey knows it—is the feeling of a comrade, a companion who shares the same memories you do. Let him have his

Santa clause, his toothfairy whathaveyou. We all have one of our own.

"You see Jon, what one may call the 'truth' is not always so clear. Besides, some boats are best left unrocked. You understand this, don't you Jon?"

"Yes," Jon says, "I understand."

ΩΨΩ

Dewey runs through the yards of the palace as fast as his riders ride north. As his nose is hit by the pollen-sweet smell of plants and his eyes follow a haze of teeming bugs in a cloud kissing his face, it does not take Dewey long to forget the world he left inside. It does not take him long to escape. Dewey smiles at the summer day with all its new smells and sights. Yes, Dewey remembers how each Lyceumean summer day is like a different painting. He cannot wait to see what is next.

But the letter Dewey sent to Renee does not make him feel any better. Dewey is haunted by thoughts *taking a walk* in his head *this is something Renee would do.* He walks even faster. He pushes the thoughts away.

As his sweat soaks its way through his heavy robes, he stops, panting for breath. Drops of sweat sting his eyes. He tries to see through them, but his world looks warped. Twisted. Not the way he is used to seeing it. *But how can I know the real way it is supposed to be?* He moans in frustration and shakes the sweat from his head. His vision clears then blurs again. *What makes one world more accurate than the other?* He wipes his eyes with his hands and wrists. Seeing the horse stables to the north, he realizes he is on the eastern border of the royal gardens. Taking a deep breath, Dewey continues his walk. But this time he walks a bit slower.

Why do I fear my brother? Dewey hears his mind ask. *Is it because he fears nothing at all? Oh, but he must. Is it because he acts as such? Is it because he is so sure, so smart, so...logical, and logic cannot be broken? But it cannot stand. Renee is all alone. He has no one. But that is it. He depends on nothing. He needs no one. He needs nothing outside of him, nothing but himself. His knowledge comes from within, a lone spider spinning its own web out of its own substance.*

His terrifying singularity. While I, a scrambling red ant, must run with thousands around me, changing the world outside me, building, gathering, spreading, changing, but all the while, I am empty, running around with nothing inside of me but the hot air I gather from my friends.

Upon reaching an obstacle, I merely alter my principles to fit the situation, as if they really aren't principles at all. I bend. I lean. I calculate the odds, trim my sails, manipulate, survive. I sway like a leaf riding the breeze, trying to maneuver itself to catch all the slow rain drops wherever they land. I crop what is needed to be cropped, and manipulate what needs to be changed. I add what has been found lacking, and remove that which has been rendered sour. My strokes roll to avoid the punches, just to keep my head above the water even as I am drowning. But even as I drown in uncertainty I keep a smile on my face, as if I am treading lightly and there is earth beneath my feet.

The Nothing of silence surrounds Dewey like a blanket. He does not know where his feet have taken him. Suddenly, the silence is interrupted by the forceful blaze of a fire behind him. Dewey turns to look, but he does not believe his eyes.

It is an orange grove—no—an orange bush still bursting into flame. Like an explosive torch before him, it reaches in every direction, tongues of flames erratic with life. To his amazement, Dewey sees that the oranges do not burn within the fire; they remain plump and whole. The bush's fruit remains orange, its leaves remain whole and green, its wooden branches remain white and alive, all while burning in the heart of the flames. The bush spouts forth more fire, as if this is its purpose, the only way it can live. Dewey steps back. This is when he hears the bush speak to him.

"Dewey Hume. Where are you?"

Dewey cannot speak.

The bush says nothing. For a moment, Dewey wonders if he heard anything at all. But the voice speaks from the bush again.

"Where are you?"

"I am here." Dewey says quickly, as if the words have been building up until now.

"Oh, but are you?" the voice from the bush says.

Dewey says nothing.

"You know who I am," the bush says.

"El—El Totsira—"

"You don't have to be scared, fat king. Haha! Surely you did not think the first person to call you fat would be a…God. Let alone a God who dresses up like an orange bush!"

"A...God?"

"No matter! Yes, it is me. The one. The one Olegna built a statue of, y'know, but Disegno stole it, though he claims otherwise. Y'know, after Olegna was just a boy that ran away from home, Disegno delivered a package to Olegna's parents, or at least to the one still left alive. Do you know what it is? Maybe you think Olegna is there with it now. You granted him permission to return home, dear king, but he did not leave. No, he is still in Lyceum, looking up at the needle. And Disegno…Disegno," even the bush seems to grow a little cold at the mention of the nefarious jester's name, "still sits imprisoned in the needle, looking down at his sorry captors, waiting for his next trial—"

"Why did you come?" Dewey feels proud of his courage, like a dumb child blowing out his birthday candles. The loud orange heat comforts Dewey and makes him feel alive.

"Ah, yes. I am glad you said something, fat boy, for I could go on and on all day. Well. Focus. Okay. You received…your brother's letters. You have been thinking. Having doubts. Your nephew is locked underground, like I once had to lock up my brother—he is chained to the ground, unable to see the light of day."

"I know. It pains me—"

"You must get him! Bring Kahn home! Only you must go to Kallipolis, and you must go alone. You must tell your brother—"

"Alone?! I can't go alone. I don't do well. I need—"

"You need you need you need. Haha! Alright, whatthehell, right? So you can take your closest advisors. So you and Jon and Yelekreb and whathisface can all go together. Ever see a God change his mind so fast?"

Dewey does not know whether to laugh or cry.

"The important thing," El Totsira says, "is that you bring Kahn back. This you must do at all costs."

"But Kahn is trapped! Renee has built a fortress as impenetrable as his ego. I cannot—"

"You can. And you will."

"But—but I can't, I don't know how…"

"I will tell you how. And you will go. And you will get him. And you will bring him home. So this is what you must do. You must go to your brother. And this is what you must tell him…"

And El Totsira tells Dewey what he must do. And Dewey listens.

Darkness descends. A few lightning bugs begin their show early, flickering their lights here and there. In the time El Totsira finds what he wants to say in his shower of words, the dusk overcomes the sky like smoke bellowing out of a distant chimney: yellow, brown, and gold. From where I sit the two look mighty strange, a fat old king and his talking bush, its fire burning brightly in Dewey's eyes. The king leans in close to hear the bush's last words as its flames begin to fade and El returns to my side. But one last flame wavers, as El whispers his last mumblings in the king's fat head. The king will not remember much, but it is not much he needs to remember. And as the king turns to walk back home, the orange bush's flame reaches out its tongue one more time, licking the summer air before it surrenders at last to the oncoming night.

6

A miracle is a violation of the laws of nature…which are entirely uniform and constant; and no instance has ever yet been found of any failure or irregularity in their operation. Fire has always burned, and water suffocated. Let us suppose that the fact which (witnesses) affirm is really miraculous. A wise man…proportions his belief to the evidence. He considers which side is supported by the greater number of experiments…and regards his past experience as full proof of the future existence of that event. No human testimony can have such force as to prove a miracle, and make it a just foundation for any such system of religion.

David Hume

Why must it snow, Nicolas wonders, when I have to sleep outside? He opens his eyes to find his body covered in snow: it covers his wheelchair, rides up to his chest, and blows about, clumping to the beginnings of a beard he did not know he had. *Isn't it summer now*, he wonders for a moment before chiding himself, remembering that there is no such thing in Kallipolis. Sure, it seems to be a bit warmer certain times of the year. But it can snow anytime in this republic. Summer, as one knows it, will always be something of his past.

He coughs, closing his eyes to the steam rising off his cheeks. He squints, letting his eyes get used to the gray morning filling the bleak sky. As he raises his head he moans from the stiffness in his neck. He wonders how long he slept.

For over seven years now *seven years!* Nicolas has sat by, watching over the cave. He likes to think of himself not just as Kahn's guardian, nor the guardian of the peace, but rather the guardian of the Prioritan people, the guardian of their ideals, and of their future king.

He remembers how it all began. It was the day Renee completed his three-day period of solitude in House of Wax. He came to find Nicolas, and Nicolas was sleeping in his front yard. *You must stay by the cave, my friend,* Renee had told him like it was a small matter *You can meditate, think, have time to yourself. But at all times, make sure Kahn enjoys the same silence you do* Renee warned him.

For six years, it was as Renee had spoken; Nicolas was good and quiet to his surroundings, and they were good and quiet to him. Nicolas gave Kahn no disturbance (sometimes briefly forgetting he was even there) and in return he received none. Six years of silence, meditation, and time.

But in the past year, things began to get worse. Nicolas became lonely: a feeling prohibited in this republic. Rashes grew on his legs and arms because they never moved, save to bring bread to his mouth or to scratch his chin. The cold began to seep into his bones, the solitariness to weigh on his heart, the big empty Nothing floating above him like an ominous blimp soaring low, cutting into his mind. He felt trapped, like he was locked in his parent's attic all over again, peering out into the yard to see his siblings playing, splashing, laughing in cool pools of water below his dry prison so far away. Kahn brought all of this upon him.

But nothing was worse than the screams.

The screams began to come from Kahn's cell just two weeks ago. They began as soft moans, mere recognitions of the concept of sound, like a baby trying his throat for the first time as if it is an alien thing, prodding here and there like the faint tiptoeing upon a sheet of ice to see if it will hold. Days later, the screams began to get louder, rattling the chains of Kahn's cell, until they were coupled with loud banging and clashing and idontknowwhat within the cell, as if Kahn has broken free of his chains and was banging on the door. Nicolas knows this could not be true *impossible* but the noises are hard to ignore as they turn to blood-curling screams, penetrating the empty air all around.

Nicolas pays no mind. He looks far into the distance, where he cannot hear Kahn's screams. He also cannot see the scattered clumps of Posteriorian protestors *let Kahn go* left standing by the southern borders. He cannot see how they are finding each other, regrouping, and growing with every passing day.

ΩΨΩ

In a small red tent in the fields before his palace, Dewey clutches a tiny bronze statue of El Totsira in his fist. A circus of words and syllables *Please God Please Li Please El* whispers off his trembling lips *let the people listen*, falling down down down with hot droplets of sweat *give me the confidence*, a waterfall of rainbow nonsense falling, evaporating into a mist below.

The people wait outside, their impatience growing hot under the great Lyceum sun. Six hours have passed, but for them this has been no more than a minute. Indeed, it is only as their ale begins to run out, the effect of their alcohol wanes, their campfires burn low, it is only now that they remember why they have come. It is only now that they remember that they are doing the one thing Posteriorians hate the most.

Waiting.

"My people," Dewey begins. The nation can smell the intensity on their King's breath even before he comes out of his tent. "You may be wondering why I have called you here—"

A loud burp comes from the back of the crowd. Laughter. A large smile of confidence washes across Dewey's face, and the laughter stops. Even Jon and Yelekreb are impressed by Dewey's sudden transformation from the fear he suffered inside the tent to the confidence he now exudes. Ignoring the interruption, Dewey continues in a loud voice.

"I see all the men are here. Just as I asked. The women may stay home," Dewey chuckles, "for they can hear the word of God through their husbands' mouths."

The people laugh for a moment and then the words of Dewey registers *word of God?* And they fall silent. Dewey raises his hands to the sky.

"It is true! The archangel El Totsira has shown himself to me."

Silence takes over. The chirping of a bird is heard in the distance.

"El BlessedBeHisName has appeared to me in the form of a burning orange bush. He told me that He has heard the groan of Kahn, and all the children of Lyceum whom Kallipolis enslaves. Therefore, say to the Children of Lyceum: I shall take Kahn out from under the burdens of Kallipolis; I shall rescue him from their service; I shall redeem him with an outstretched arm and with great judgments."

The men say nothing.

Dewey explains, "But it shall be through us. We must go there. We must go to Kallipolis and bring him back."

"Who? Us? It's so far! And how shall we get there?" The Posteriorian crowd does not wait to ask questions.

"He has commanded us to walk."

"Walk?" This is not a word they are used to hearing.

"He has commanded me to go with ten, or was it...twenty, or..." Dewey trails off.

"Dewey," Jon says at his side.

"Yes, Haha! I must go with many...many of our best men and I must say to Renee Don Cartez—"

"We heard that part already," a child shouts from the left of the crowd.

A hum of panic fills the crowd, but Dewey can make out a few words.

"But we have such beautiful chariots...Why would we ever walk...Haha...A big joke is what this is...Through Cherava Woods...bears...We won't make it through the White Plains...Oh, he's full of lies...Ha! And I'm supposed to just cancel my parties, right?"

"Everything will be asked of us," Dewey repeats to himself under the buzz of the crowd, "And everything will be given."

"Even if we make it through the empty heat of the White Plains, even if we survive through the Cheravian Woods, across the Axios, and through their borders, why would Renee listen to us?"

"He will listen to me," Dewey says, "I am his brother."

Jon closes his eyes in gloomy acceptance that he may have to go, but Dewey does not see him.

"That was never enough for him before," a voice cries, "so why would it be now?"

Jon opens his eyes in relief.

"When…" Dewey's voice becomes shaky, "when the time is right, I am commanded to throw down Renee's staff. I shall throw it down, and it will turn into a snake. Then Renee will listen to the word of El Totsira. Then Kahn shall be set free. This is what our God has spoken."

"What did you say? Do you have any *evidence* of this?" Jon says.

"Is *this* why you called us here?" Yelekreb says.

Dewey is silent. An uproar rises from the crowd like a wave.

"A violation of the laws of nature?! Impossible!" a woman screams.

An old man, skinnier than the other Posteriorians cries, "You ask us to just trust you against everything we have ever experienced in our entire lives—that sticks will remain sticks and snakes will remain snakes—you ask us to throw that all away. For your word."

"Lies!" the surrounding people chant.

The two hundred other Posteriorians that bothered to show up say nothing, their jaws dropped in surprise.

"I said, well," Dewey clears his throat and turns back to the crowd, "The reason why I called you here" Dewey begins to tell them again. He wonders why he thought they would ever believe him. He wonders why he believes himself. But as they stand before him, they begin to notice that he has more color to his face, his eyes shine more blue, his skin pink orange, the youthful vigor in his face radiates like never before. Finally, their lust for adventure begins to wet. Their love for their leader begins to grow. And whether they actually believe him or not, slowly, they begin to listen.

ΩΨΩ

They run home on the adrenaline of Dewey's words. They do not think about whether the prophecy is true or not, if they shall rescue Kahn or merely go on an adventure, if they shall live or if they shall die. They do not predict the future of their nation, nor do they plan. As they run around their living rooms shouting excitedly *oh* to their wives *the places we will go* about the journeys they are going to endure, there is only the excitement of a new adventure in their hearts.

Over half of them are drawn in by the bars, women, feasts, and dances on the way home, forgetting that they ever heard their king speak. Eighty of them make it home to do the dance of excitement to their wives. Once their wives and lovers are done shouting at them *Oh no you don't go leavin me here to go on some goose chase* seducing them to stay *the King said only some must go, you stay here with me so come here yes how does that feel* twenty of them are able to stand up to their wives, some with words and some with sticks. Seven of these men get beaten by their wives, the big women kicking them to the ground, bringing blood from their eyes, broken teeth from their mouth, pleas for mercy from their lips.

Only twelve make it out with their bags packed.

These are the names of the sons of Lyceum that set out to Kallipolis on this day: Alhazen, Avicenna, Ibn Tufail, Robert Grosseteste, William of Ockham, Francis Bacon, Thomas Hobbes, John Mill, Gilles Deleuze, Felix Guattari, Joshua, and Kaleb. They walk forward in three lines of four, each behind one of the men leading in the front: King Dewey leads the center with Jon to his left and Yelekreb to his right. It is in this way they journey north, to Kallipolis.

The men carry large suitcases adorned with glittery gemstones and golden coiling. They carry more than their weight, but their legs are thick and their shoulders are broad. Sacks of beer and meat and cheese pull them down, swooshing around on their backs like some big pillow, an alcoholic cloud swallowing them up. Everyone is excited to pack the most luxurious meals, even if they may break their backs. Everyone, that is, except Jon, who packed one large bag stuffed with white tablecloths—the only solid white fabric in all of Lyceum. Only Dewey notices this, but he feels he should not question Jon. He wonders why.

Upon reaching the border of Lyceum, the travelers shed themselves of their sensors. They will never admit it to one another, but a strange sense of freedom washes over each of them. As they cease to be watched and recorded, their movements and sensations seem to flow more naturally, having less significance, as they will be forgotten forever.

They see this mutual feeling in each other's eyes but they do not speak of it. Jon always seems to be the wiser advisor to Dewey, Yelekreb being the more fun, strong, and agile one. Whether this is true or not, it has always been Jon who comes up with a plan. This sort of thinking is rare in Lyceum, but it is something Dewey has learned to appreciate.

"My lord," Jon begins as the men begin to cross over the White Plains, "When we arrive in Kallipolis, we will be checked, noted, and received most cautiously. We may chide the Prioritans in public, but let us now admit that they are diligent in their actions; they will accept us carefully. So we must be one step ahead of them."

"Yes," Dewey says little, struggling to keep his chin up as if he has a plan. But Jon knows better.

"Renee is your—" Jon begins, "He knows you as your brother, so he will not harm you—"

"He will not harm me," Dewey says, "Only because that is the will of El Totsira."

"Of course. But Yelekreb and I must be at your side, no matter the cost. But the others, the others should stay behind to watch over us. They should hide, fading into the background, so that they can be there if we need them."

"Fading into the background?" Dewey smiles, "Have you *seen* them?"

Jon does not need to look back. He knows what Posteriorians look like.

"So. They are fat, loud, bright, and colorful," Jon says, "But there is something special about our people. We can be quick on our feet at the right time, and luck often follows us, helping us just when we need it most."

"Said like a true Posteriorian," Dewey smiles, "And I admire that," his smile disappears, "But it will never work. El Totsira did not feel the need to tell us to do such a thing. We do not need to hide. And I will not allow it."

"Of course, my Lord. A stupid idea it was—"

"A stupid idea, Jon Rasaa, is to bring a bag stuffed with white tablecloths. But I will not question you, for you are one of the smartest of our nation. But I must go on wondering..."

"In case we have a great meal, my lord. You did not think any right Posteriorian would want to travel without a party? And what Lyceum-born decent Posteriorian would ever feast without a decent tablecloth?"

Hours pass like large rocks rotating slowly beneath their feet. At noon, the sun reaches the center of the sky. It hangs there, laughing down at them, tumbling its hot rays on their weary backs in buckets, before slipping down just a bit, resting, and finally falling like a tired puppet before a curtain of darkening red as the show lights begin to fade, welcoming the dusk.

Dewey squints and sees a cricket hopping on the ground before him. He takes a small glass jar from one of his pockets. His pockets already bulge from tiny specimens he has collected so far, from exotic soil to a pink seashell. He chases the cricket, bending over, ready to catch it with the jar in hand. But when he passes Yelekreb, Yelekreb lets out a great sneeze. The sneeze reminds Dewey of the great horns of Lyceum. As Yelekreb stands bemused at the long trail of golden mucus hanging from his nose, Dewey forgets the cricket and sneaks up to him and snatches the mucus with his hands, collecting it into his jar. He puts the lid on tight and slips it into one of his pockets. He wipes the excess snot off his hands on his robes. It takes him a few minutes to notice the other men's gazes.

"What?"

The men say nothing. They look right at him.

"It is for my collection. Y'know. To remember."

The men shake their heads and continue their journey. An hour passes. Darkness rises from the ground and the travelers welcome it like a cool whisper of strength. But as their vision begins to decrease, they fail to notice the snake slithering by their heels. They don't see it until it is too late.

A scream of pain comes from the back of the line. Felix Guattari falls to the ground, clutching his leg with both hands.

The men spread in a panic. One of the men give a high giggle, but it is cut short by a punch to the face. All eyes turn to Felix, lying on the ground writhing in pain. Only Jon looks into the distance. He is the first to speak.

"A snake bite."

Yelekreb ignores him and says, "With the quickness the snake slid away into the sand, I can bet it is of the poisonous kind. But until I see it, I cannot know for sure."

"How is that?" Dewey asks. Felix's screams turn to quiet, struggled moans.

"If it is black and yellow," Yelekreb does not lower his voice, "it has a poison that is making its way to Felix's heart as we speak. Ah! Let me catch this snake so we know for sure." Yelekreb darts off the path.

"Unless..." Jon says to Dewey, "there is something I can do about this."

Jon kneels down before Felix, who pushes him away. Jon grabs his wrist, and whispers in his ear. "If you want to live, you will lie still for me," he says. Before another moment can pass, Jon brings the snake wound to his lips.

Avicenna says to Gilles, "What is he doing?"

"He's sucking out the poison," Kaleb says.

Jon sucks the venom into his mouth and spits it onto the ground before him. He puts his mouth back on the snakebite to search for more poison.

Gilles shakes his head. "Of course. But what happens when the next of us gets bitten? Or gets strangled, or dies from thirst? In God's name, I have never seen the likes of this," he sighs, "I feel as if we can cross a thousand plateaus and still not be any closer to this God-forsaken place. The hell with it!"

Dewey pretends not to hear.

Suddenly, a noise comes from the sand behind them. The men jump. Yelekreb darts before them *I'm back*. Their heart continues to race even after they hear his laughter, a big smile on his face. His hands hold a dead snake, stripes of black and yellow running down its back.

"Oh," his smile fades as he remembers what this means.

"Don't worry about it," Jon puts a hand on his shoulder, "I took care if it. Felix will be just fine."

"Sure," Yelekreb helps Felix to his feet. He wonders why he ran out there in the first place, "Just fine."

ΩΨΩ

The men continue to journey north. Felix stumbles forward, his arm around Gilles' shoulders for support. Though Felix was saved from the snakebite, the shock of the reality the men are in weighs upon their hearts as their heavy sacks weigh upon their backs.

Still, it is beautiful to be moving, to be *alive*. Dewey plucks a small blue flower from the ground. He brings it close to his face, inhaling its scent. He looks closely into its narrow, tiny chalice and he sees the varicose veins of purple spreading within its delicate petals like cracks in glass. He wonders if Renee saw such beauty on his first walk to Kallipolis. *How can one not learn from this* he shakes his head in awe of the flower, wondering at his brother, *how can one willingly shut this out, let alone resist the temptation to bow down and worship such elegance for all that it has to offer?* Dewey folds the flower carefully and puts it into his pocket.

The days pass slowly. As the nights go by, the travelers realize they packed according to their hearts rather than their heads. It becomes difficult to make fire, to find food, to make camp. At first, they suppressed this worry with alcohol, songs, and laughter. But soon the joy turned to silence, the alcohol to vomit, the songs to soft whispers of pleas for comfort, for a bed to sleep on, for the kiss of water upon their parched lips.

Worst of all is the big, bleak, Nothing. In every direction they look, all they can see is white sand under a white sky. After spending so much time in Lyceum, this place looks like death. The space, the quiet, the absolute stillness that would drive any Posteriorian mad digs into their eyes like an animal's claws. They begin to crave any sight, smell, or sound. They cherish the tumbleweed, following its movement with their eyes as it passes. They stop to listen to the distant jittering of a bug, closing their eyes and smiling to the sifting dance of the sand and the wind.

Today their stomachs groan with hunger. They can only begin to think of hunting; they know their slow bodies and impatient appetites can never supply the discipline and patience needed for hunting. Besides, it is rare to find any kind of life in these plains.

Suddenly, they see two large birds in the distance! They try to run to the birds, but they trip over themselves, their fat bellies rolling like waves upon their thick tree-trunk legs. Yelekreb is the first to arrive, with Jon and Dewey coming up on his left. They can see that the birds are vultures: two extraordinarily large black birds, their scrawny white necks protruding from their body like an old frayed rope from between large flapping wings.

"Who cares what they are," Yelekreb says, "so long as they'll fit in my belly!"

But as the men get closer, they see why the birds have come, and they have no appetite any more. And Behold! they see a fresh Posteriorian corpse on the ground, its right leg mangled and mostly eaten away by the vultures. They cannot tell for sure, but they think it is a woman. Her arm rests above her head at an impossible angle. Her cold white fingers grasp a sign. The red and orange paint lettering still reads quite clearly.

Let Kahn Go!

One of the vultures holds one of the corpse's tendons in his beak, pulling on it like it is a toy. Jon moves to scare the bird away. The bird caws towards him and turns to the side, the bloody tendon still in its beak. Dewey feels disgust inside him and he rushes forward with a yell *get away from her you filth* kicking at the bird clumsily. The bird jerks the bloody coil from the woman's leg and flies away, the tendon dangling from its beak like a piece of yarn. One of the men vomits loudly behind them. Felix pushes Gilles away and walks forward on his own two feet. He speaks for the first time in days, since the snake bit him.

"I don't need your support," he says to Gilles. Then he turns to the other men, "I never needed any of this!"

The men say nothing.

"Where was El Totsira when this protestor was on her way north?" he points to the corpse, "Where was El Totsira when the hundreds of protestors stood and shouted and rallied and died by the foot of Kallipolis? For the hundreds that must have died in Cherava Woods or these plains, traveling, fighting, rallying for our beliefs, the beliefs of our God? Where was El Totsira, our watcher and savior, when

Kahn was locked underground for the past five years, the most important part of his childhood experience taken from him completely? And he can never get it back! Where was El Totsira then, huh? Where *was* he?"

Dewey tries to open his mouth, but finds his throat is dry.

"Oh!" Francis sees flies gathering at the corner of the corpse's mouth. "Look at this poor, poor woman. Just look! A shame!" He looks squarely at Dewey and his eyes turn cold, "Did you bring us out here to die as well?"

Thomas says, "I long to be back home with my wives and my fireplace, and all that is rightly mine. If I would have known any of this, I would never have left! What have you brought us to? What have you made of us?"

Yelekreb steps before his king.

"My fellow Posteriorians," he begins, "You did not think El Totsira would make this easy, did you? For nothing in our history ever has been. And this…this is the beauty of our nation, that even in the face of difficulty and strife, we take on that which no other people could ever hope to. We walk forward, with our flames held high, and we do that which we believe, turning terror into hope, turning darkness into light.

"Our king, Lord Dewey…the archangel has come to him—and he has given us a way out—"

"Lies!" Felix says, "The archangel appeared to him like any of his other drunken, ridiculous dreams," his eyes move past Yelekreb, gazing straight at Dewey, "Who do you think you are, bringing us all out here on one of your wild fantasies?"

"I am nothing," Dewey says, "I am only a messenger."

"He sounds like a Prioritan!" Felix says, "We must leave him right—"

"That is enough," a voice says. The voice is not loud, but confident. The men fall silent.

"It is enough," a man repeats. The men see that it is Joshua, the son of Nun. "Yelekreb spoke of the beauty of our people, of facing difficulty, and never giving up the search for knowledge. But he kindly forgot that in spite of ourselves, we have always been tainted by complaints."

"But our lives—" Felix beings.

"Our lives," Joshua corrects, "are more important than the life of one. We are a collective people, and none of us is better than the other. Us twelve—fifteen—men, we travel for one purpose: to free our brother Kahn from a life of death, of Nothing, of something no man shall ever *ever* have to bear in any corner of the world. This is why we go.

"I am sorry for your ankle, for the countless Posteriorians that have suffered, as this dead woman before us has so strikingly brought to our attention. But these are places we must look beyond. We must alter our paths around these…obstructions and continue continue continue on as we always have, as we always will, all in the name of our nation, our king, and our Gods. To live."

"To live!" Kaleb says.

"To live!" the men repeat in unison.

They continue their walk with their heads down. Felix stumbles forward on his bitten leg. Gilles bends to help him, but he pushes him away and helps himself up. Looking down from the hills, I can see the men moving forward, fifteen lone chess pieces advancing square by desert square, altering their positions like droplets of water slithering down a sheet of glass. They see Cherava Woods before them and they draw closer, their steps slow but steady. Felix totters just behind, grumbling under his breath at the sand, the sky, and everything that lies between.

ΩΨΩ

All is quiet is Kallipolis, as it always has been. The few protestors left at the borders are kept far away by the warriors, a faint haze of red and green noise in the distance like tiny droplets of paint inadvertently left behind by an artist's brush. Their colored torches and signs are kept muted, the brief flickers of a candle behind a fogged pane of glass. The Prioritans remain in their mud huts, a hut for each person, far apart from the world and each other, each alone in their own thoughts. A single bird flies overhead. A fluttering of leaves. The crack of a warrior's club over a sorry protestor's head. But the people do not notice. They pay no mind.

But Renee Don Cartez is not content. He closes his eyes, pulling all the silent air of his hut around him like a blanket, embracing the Nothing. But there is unrest in the air; a faint dropping of water, the blows of a hammer, the sound of men's footsteps coming closer, echoing in his head.

His peace of mind is further disturbed by the old woman entering his hut behind him. She was in the other room this whole time, Renee realizes, the sweeps of her broom fading into the background. But now he cannot help but face her. Her face is hidden by a black hood, as it was the first time he had noticed her years ago.

Back then, Renee remembers, he could tell she was very old. Today she is still bent over in the same way. Had she aged at all? Despite her age weighing upon her bent shoulders, Renee notices her deft dance with the broom. She rids the area of all unnatural disturbances: papers, bugs, pens, clothes, blankets, and all that creates clutter. Anything unraveled or unfolded is done away with, so that any of the hut's inhabitants may have room for their minds to breath.

There was always something familiar about her, Renee remembers, and he feels the same way today. But he cannot place it. *I am the philosopher-king of this whole nation,* he thinks to himself, *and it is my job to know all. Yet I cannot tell even the name of my own maid!* Though it is not the habit for a Prioritan to speak without reason, it is a wonder to Renee that he has never spoken to this woman after all these years.

He does not even know her name.

Renee tries to speak to the woman, but he finds it harder to do now than he ever has. He faces her, but her eyes remain on the ground. Renee turns away, and he does not see her eyes turn to him. Instead, he rises from his chair and walks to the door of the hut. He stands still for a moment, leaning to the side like a reed caught in a wind. He wishes for the peace he has always enjoyed and he wonders why it is so hard to attain now. Finally, he floats out the door towards the House of Wax.

The woman's eyes follow Renee out the door. Of course, Renee cannot see any of this behind him. He does not see the tears forming in her eyes.

"He has gotten so tall," she says, staring out into the distant gray.

Nicolas wheels out from behind a bookcase where he was hiding. He sits beside her, but her eyes do not move from Renee's trail. They watch his body, now a white speck in the distance.

"How long will you wait, Kate?" he says.

"The time is not right," Kate says, "Not yet."

7

Despite the Jewish position of weakness, God sent Moses and Aaron to Pharaoh, who was then the world's mightiest ruler, and granted them the power to effect changes in nature. They were not natural phenomena, nor were they the results of stellar activity or mere coincidence.

Kuzari

Four days have passed since Renee entered the soaring walls of The House of Wax. The sun swam across the gray sky four times, illuminating the clear walls around him, sinking down for the night's welcoming of another moon. Four days have passed, but Renee does not know. He exists out of time for the moment: floating, swimming, just being with the clean, mechanic formulas building in his mind. Time is a detail, a nuisance locked behind closed doors; it matters not at all. To him, it could have been a minute or a year; he does not care at all.

He sits cross-legged on the floor in his father's thinking room as he has sat these four days, the cavernous walls of The House of Wax rising around him. A pitcher of water and the white crusts of bread lie beside him, but he has not touched them for two days. He wears a blindfold across his eyes, under his dark hair now falling to his shoulders. His clothes are completely white and his thin arms look like twigs protruding from his baggy white sleeves.

His arm clutches the whistle around his neck. His closed eyes tighten as he remembers his father's last days. Joachim had wanted to tell him something, it seemed. But for some reason, he never could. Renee wonders what it was. What was that pain behind his eyes? What was he trying to say?

Renee clears his throat. His mind looks around the room. It is much like his father's thinking room: the only piece of Lyceum he ever took with him. He smiles. He remembers the bond he had with Joachim at the end of his life, something Dewey never enjoyed. While Renee was not there for Joachim's very last days, he did witness his father's changes in his old age. It was as if Renee was his only son, in a way. Even if it was only for a few months. Yes, to Renee, Joachim was never fully Posteriorian. While he preached it from the bench, he did not act it in the home. He left parties early, retreating to his thinking room, leaving the guests at the mercy of the Grandee's storytelling. Because of Joachim's stature, the Posteriorians turned the other way. But not Renee. Renee retreated to a room of his own, wondering if his father was more the man than he allowed himself to be.

Renee remembers the time he strayed into his parent's room late at night. He had woken from a bad dream and he longed for their comfort. He walked softly on his tiptoes, so as not to make a commotion. To some he would look like an angel floating forward down the hall in his pale white skin, but to most, he would seem a ghost. He wandered towards Joachim and Helene, just to be with them if even for a moment. But when he got to his parent's doorway, he remembers, he found Dewey already there, entering their room before him, his rainbow pajamas and golden hair glowing in the dark. Renee hid behind a corner and watched as Dewey entered with a gift in his hands. Joachim smiled and Helene lit up. Suddenly, Dewey stumbled, falling forward, his clumsy gift shattering on the floor before him. Helene jumped out of bed *aw honey* running to him *are you okay* Renee remembers watching and asking *could she love me like that?* Renee decided he does not have to hide; they would not see him anyway. But then, as Helene comforted Dewey, kissing his fat shaky hands, Renee thought he saw his father looking past all the commotion his brother had caused, right into Renee's eyes. And then, a smile.

Renee's thoughts are disrupted by a vision: he sees his brother coming towards him with ten men, or is it more, Renee cannot tell. They come from Lyceum, he knows. Their footsteps smack the earthy ground like hard gallops, growing louder, coming close. It is his brother, Renee can see, but Dewey's face shows such aging as Renee never would have predicted. *Has it really been that long? Has my face changed so much as well?*

They have entered his republic some time ago, Renee can see. They must have left Lyceum a while ago, Renee thinks, for he knows that while their step is strong and unyielding, they are easily distracted, and their path is never straight.

The guardians must have let them in, seeing that it is Renee's brother and his best men. The guardians knew they would come. Renee knew they would come.

It had all been just a matter of time.

Renee readies himself. He takes a deep breath and recalls his brother's pollen breath, the sound of his voice among his childhood friends. He remembers the false confidence, a thin layer of jovial cotton-candy chatter thinly shielding a sea of doubt beneath. Renee thanks the minutes now separating him and Dewey like blanket, a cushion allowing just a bit more peace.

But it will not be long now.

His eyes open. His mind alerts itself before Dewey even enters the shadow of the House.

He senses Ben to his right, Christian to his left.

"Nicolas—" Renee begins.

"He is fine," Ben says, "Watching over Kahn, just where he should be." This is true now, though Ben does not know that Nicolas left his post for a bit.

"Nobody else knows this?"

"Nobody. I would have posted guardians to assist him—"

"Nicolas needs no help. He must have his peace."

"Of course."

A moment passes.

"He is almost here," Ben begins. Renee says nothing. Ben continues, "When your brother comes…"

"Have no fear. O'Talp has shown me Dewey's journey. He has no more than a few men…if you can call them men. You will be silent. I will speak only when needed. Kahn is safe in an impenetrable cell. I have hundreds of warriors that I do not need above O'Talp's word. Dewey has nothing. Dewey is nothing. This is the situation and the situation will speak itself."

The two men can hear Dewey being led to the thinking room where they now sit. Nothing is said. Christian looks at his master curiously, wagging his tail in anticipation. The wolf senses that something is going to happen, but Ben can see Renee's lips curve into a smile.

"Well, well, well," Dewey begins to speak even before he opens the door. A guardian opens the door and allows Dewey and his men inside. "You have done pretty well for yourself here. I mean, this place. It's, it's pretty nice. Not what I would've done with it, but hey, we were never that much alike, eh?"

It has been a while since Renee heard someone speak like this, but it all comes back. Prioritans do not speak easily, treating each word like a precious thing, speaking slow and long from the throat as if every syllable can be met with harsh consequences. Posteriorians, Renee recalls, know nothing of consequence. Renee can picture his brother's large blue eyes surveying the House like an ignorant teenager in an old museum. Anger and disgust fill his stomach, but he waits for it to pass.

"Ha!" Dewey continues, "You have the right to remain silent, of course, but rights have always been overrated....in my opinion anyways. Now, you, you may not know why I came here, but...but I'm sure, I'm sure that..." Dewey continues to speak, but his voice fades into the background of Renee's mind like a white noise, the unpleasant aftertaste of a bad red wine.

Renee senses his brother and a man standing on either side of him. The large, hot, sweaty masses give themselves away all too easily, though the one on the right seems taller and stronger. Renee guesses this to be Yelekreb, and the other, Jon. These two Posteriorians stand mostly naked. After being stripped of their colors at the border, they look almost more comical than they did dressed, swimming in their rainbow robes. Renee hears chewing, a smacking of lips coming from Yelekreb's side. He can smell the scent of a roasted turkey leg. *Did he bring that all the way with him from Lyceum?* Renee's mind wanders briefly *or from where did he get that here?* Renee pushes such thoughts away. Finally, he speaks.

"Where are the others?"

"...and I've always said, well, you can't take a fox out of his foxhole...excuse me?" Dewey was in the middle of speaking. Renee had not noticed. He tries again.

"Where are the others?"

"Oh! So you do speak after all! Ha ha! Yes, the others. What, what...others?"

"You came with more men. Ten, or more, I believe. Yet only two stand beside you now."

"Ha! Sounds like a magical disappearing trick I tell you!" Dewey grins *it is fifteen men in all brother, have your senses grown weak?* but soon his grin vanishes and his face becomes serious. "But really? No. I did not come with any...others. Just my two friends here. You remember Jon. From the art festival. And this here is Yelekreb. You should really see him throw."

Renee says nothing.

"Perhaps...perhaps your...thoughts, is it, are not as accurate as they used to be. No, my brother, we have come alone. There are no...other men. How do you feel....how do you think...that there are other men?"

Renee says nothing, but this time his silence is a shield rather than a sword *I have never been wrong; where were the other men I had prophesized?*, a shield from the doubt stirring inside him *they must have died on the way.* Renee thinks of the journey these men must have made; he made it once himself. He remembers the Cheravian bear that nearly tore him apart. He pets Christian, who had saved his life. He speaks.

"Say what you will."

Dewey does not hesitate. His voice booms through the caverns of the house more than necessary. "El Totsira, archangel-man-God-spirit of the east, One of the west, Divinity of the world, he has commanded you to let Kahn go. You must let Kahn go, for El Totsira has commanded it! You must let Kahn go at once! You have taken from him life, the daily treasure of experiences owed to any man, that allows him to *be* a man, the basic requirements to live, to interact with the world around him, nature, the world we have been placed in for better or worse: all of this he has been denied, and he must be given! And if it is evil to him, as you believe, then so it shall be! But this is what we, what each and every man was given to deal with on his own, so we must not deny it to others. And if he wishes to ignore it, as you have chosen, then it will have come from his own volition. When he may decide it for himself. But to take…to take an innocent child, our own blood, and deprive him of this choice, of seeing feeling *tasting* the beauty of the world around him, well, this my…brother, this is nothing short of the worst kind of murder there can be in this world."

Dewey tries not to notice how his voice drones on like a broken alarm, the whine of a cracked ram's horn wavering with doubt each time Christian looks at him. Yes, the wolf *cat* glares at him, as if remembering *to be born* times from long ago *first you have to die.* Dewey tries to look away, but he feels the wolf's stare pressing into his chest. Renee speaks.

"You must have missed my letter."

"What? Your…letter? What does that—"

"O'Talp is the one and only God."

Dewey opens his mouth to reply, but this time, Renee beats him to it.

"I have heard what you had to say. But Kahn is safe now, and there is no way he may leave. I will not do as you ask."

"You…you will. Tell me where he is."

"El Totsira appeared to you, you say? This was another one of your…visions? I see. And what proof do you have that El even appeared to you? That he even exists at all? Even by your low experiential standards. Can you give me anything? Any evidence at all?"

Dewey sticks his chin high, "We shall see. Hand me your walking stick, my brother, and I shall throw it on the ground before you, and by the word of the mighty El Totsira, it shall become a snake before our eyes!"

"Impossible," Renee pulls his staff towards him, "For you know better than most, Dewey, that even if you have ever experienced a staff turn to a snake one time before, you have experienced a staff remain a staff thousands of times. And of course, a wise man must accord his expectations to the evidence of the most weight. For while I live in a world of complete certainty, you choose to swim in a world of probability, where the violation of a law of nature does not cause you to stop and start anew, as it would I, but rather, as you once said yourself: an occasional violation of a law does not in itself necessarily overthrow the law itself, nor the conclusion that the law will continue to operate in the future as it has in the past. You may throw my staff before you, but a staff it will remain."

"Haha! You think you know me so well, don't you? You think that…well…I may not have understood everything you said…but the hell with it! I have experienced El Totsira's word that there *is* a God, and this God *will* do as he says, and this is something I hold true, because, well, because I did not want sand in my mouth…"

Ben, Jon, and Yelekreb look confused, but Renee smiles. Dewey shakes his fist in the air.

"Whatever! It does not matter why or how; all that matters is that El Totsira came to me. He came to me because I am special. I am able to experience his glory without becoming insane…"

"But you said so yourself: You are nothing. You are a messenger."

"How did—so you have tricks of your own, don't you?"

Renee says nothing. His face remains plain like a statue.

"Well I have some tricks of my own! So now why don't you hand me over that walking stick of yours?"

Renee loosens his grip on his staff, but Ben puts his hands upon it.

"You do not have to do this," Ben whispers to Renee, "My guardians—"

"Your guardians do their job well, as I must do mine. The situation will speak for itself."

Ben takes his hands off the stick. Dewey takes a step forward and grabs it *oh give it to me already* from Renee's hand. He lifts it high in the air and holds it there for one brief moment, but for Renee, the moment is frozen in time: his brother stands before him in his own house of thought like a fat clown putting on a most ridiculous show. Renee looks away from his brother's rosy red face and turns towards Christian's cold gray eyes. Renee remembers when Christian brought him the walking stick, running towards him with it clenched in his jaws. Renee wants to say thank you, but chides himself for such thoughts. For we all know that wolfs cannot speak. But if only, if only…

Dewey's arm comes swinging down with Renee's staff, a tidal wave de force crashing down, throwing sticks and stones from its belly. Renee listens as his staff thumps down, tumbling across the dirt ground. Finally, it settles into place. It does not move. The men wait. A minute passes. But the staff remains a staff.

It does not change.

"Well…" Yelekreb is the first to speak.

"Shutup!" Dewey says, "It will change into a snake. It must!"

"I don't see it—"

"You're not looking, you fool," Dewey's cheeks turn from red to the color of a dark cherry wine, "All of you! Look!" And the men wait again.

But the staff lies before the men, no more than a stick. All eyes stay transfixed on the staff. All eyes, except Renee's who have been facing the heavens the entire time. Finally, the philosopher-king speaks.

"Leave this place," Renee says, "Your words are no good here. And my men, leave me in peace."

Ben springs back into action, ordering his guardians to seize Dewey and his men, but his words come out slowly as if he has just awakened from a dream. No one dares go near the staff, until Ben says to Christian, "Boy, go fetch Renee his stick."

"No," Renee says sharply, "No. My staff must remain there for all time. It shall be a symbol of the falsity of experience, that El Totsira's word did not come true, that O'Talp is the one, the true God."

As Renee speaks, the Prioritan guards are swept up in his words. But something twitches in the corner of Ben's eye, something he tries to ignore. But it happens again. It seems to be coming from Renee's staff. *Did the end of the stick just move?* Ben's mind whirs *It cannot be.* Ben considers telling someone, but such a report would only be met with the most hostile response. And sensing the consequences of what this could mean for the nation, Ben pushes such thoughts away. He looks back at the staff and it lies there, an ordinary stick. *It must have been a trick of the eyes.* He looks away, dismissing it. But not fast enough.

"Benedictus," Renee says, "How do you think?"

"Me? Oh, yes. It will be a symbol—"

"You seemed quiet. Like you may have seen something."

"Oh, no. I mean, nothing but your staff. It lies before me like it always has, as a stick and nothing more."

"Are you sure? You sound like you may have seen something."

"Perhaps I am a bit…shaken up. By…all that has been happening."

"It is not like you to be shaken up. But I am glad. Of course, you know that you are my pair of eyes in what we call the outside world."

"Of course."

"And if you see anything, anything at all, you must tell me immediately."

"Of course," Ben's heart begins to beat harder.

"Because you know what happens to people who hide what they have seen."

"Of course."

"Good. Now tell me, have you seen anything, anything at all that may taint one into believing that El Totsira's word can possibly come true?"

Benedictus stands still. He can feel his heart ramming against his chest like a large hammer. If he says yes, he shall surely be put to death. But if he says no, that may be a lie. And a lie like that never goes undetected. Not to Renee.

"Well?" Renee says.

Ben opens his mouth to speak, hoping that the right words will come. But suddenly, the doors to the thinking room slam open and two guardians run inside. Panting for breath, they are hardly able to speak.

"My…my King!" one says.

"What is it?" Renee turns away from Ben. The annoyance in his voice shows.

"Kahn," the other guardian says, "It is Kahn. He…he escaped."

"Escaped? What are you talking about? From where?" Renee licks his lips and gathers himself. "That fortress was impenetrable! It was—*is*—impossible to open. Only I can open it, since only I know how it was built. And even if…he is just a boy…locked in rocks and steel…chained down…"

The guards' panting does not cease. They stare at their king in fear, waiting for him to absorb the truth. Finally, Renee speaks.

"Where did he go? How? It cannot be. I do not understand. Explain yourselves!"

"My King, all we know is, well, Kahn is not there. He…he is gone."

ΩΨΩ

Before the men realize what is happening, Renee is out the door. No Prioritan has ever been seen to move so fast, let alone their king. All dressed in white, Renee streaks across the shadow of the House of Wax like a bird, Christian running behind him, picking up the rear.

The Posteriorians try to keep up, but their fat bellies and thick legs weigh them down. Renee turns back for a moment, and says to Ben, "Seize these intruders, they may not come along. Lock them up, and throw away the key!"

Dewey hears this, and he says, "Please! I am your brother. Kahn is my nephew. If he has escaped, if he is lost to both of us, I beg of the chance to see it too. Let me be. And don't send my men to your prison. We…we will die in there."

Renee's eyes stay on the path before him. He does not even acknowledge Dewey's words. A moment passes.

Dewey says, "I am your *brother.*"

Though all he can see is the back of Renee's head, Dewey can hear Renee's next words quite clearly.

"Ben," Renee says, "Make sure you throw the key *away*."

Renee runs north, vanishing into the procreation fields like a ghost.

The Prioritan guardians fall upon them, with Ben at their lead. Dewey struggles the hardest, his face red, *let us go,* urging Yelekreb to fight, then shouting to the heavens *my nephew* his voice cracking *take me but let my nephew go! You will never catch him! Run Kahn Run!*

It does not take the guardians long to take control of Dewey and his men. It would have been a brief moment but for the sheer size, weight, and strength of the Posteriorians. But their clumsiness is no match for the guardians' disciplined agility. An outsider might see a group of trained gymnasts trying to collapse an army of drunken elephants.

Ben turns to one of the other guardians.

"Gather your men," he says, "and lead a search for Kahn. He is just a small boy. He does not know the nature of things, of light and of water and of land. He must be frightened. He cannot be far. Get him, and bring him to me."

Ten guardians run off in a single file line, meeting up with fifty more in the distance, unifying in perfect order, small streams trickling into one collective river of soldiers, an army of ivory white chess pieces running tall in a perfect straight line.

"Secure the border," Ben orders the remaining guardians, "and keep an eye to the Apuan Hills to the east and the Axios River to the south; none shall be crossed this day."

Yelekreb begins to squirm, but two guardians strengthen their hold immediately. One of them spits in his face. Dewey jolts forward in anger, but is met with a slap in the face. He falls to his feet. Two guardians drag him up by his few strands of golden-white hair. They grasp his arms and bring him before Ben.

"Hello, King Dewey," Ben smiles in ridicule.

"Well, I did not think I would see you again."

"What are you talking about?"

"Well, well. Benedictus Azonips," Dewey says, spitting out blood from his mouth. Ben tries to hide the surprise on his face. "Come on, you didn't know. Ha! That's right," Dewey continues, "I know who you are. I knew you when you were just a boy. You don't remember me?" Dewey looks down and shakes his head. "It's really a shame how you turned out. Tsk, Tsk. Yes, you were one of our best lenscrafters. Before reaching manhood, you already helped Posteriorian astronomers improve upon their telescope, widening our area of experience by miles. And there was so, so much more you could have done," Dewey looks up and meets Ben's eyes, "So much more. And look at you now. Holding your *real* king by his arms. And holding a young helpless child of life in a prison of death and horror.

"Look what you have come to!"

"Enough."

"You had so much more going for you. And now—"

"Silence!"

"Haha, you are really one of us; I see it in your eyes. But you've been fooled into living with these…clowns. By that damned cripple. I, I never would have thought—"

"Enough!" Ben raises a fist to Dewey, but holds it in the air, his fellow guardians looking in horror as his Prioritan mind pleads *feel no anger* against all emotion *feel no anger* pleading for reason."

"From a lenscrafter to an enforcer of lies—"

Feel no anger.

Finally, Ben lowers his fist and takes a deep breath. He turns away, but can hear Dewey speak under his breath.

"You were always afraid—"

Ben whirls around and lands a punch in Dewey's gut, spilling coughs and blood from Dewey's mouth onto the dirt ground below.

ΩΨΩ

Renee approaches Kahn's cell and his feet begin to slow. He does not need to hear Christian's whimpering to know that something is wrong. He stumbles around with no walking stick, his hands feeling out the scene. And through his fingers, he sees that O'Talp's cave has been broken, its lock shattered, its impenetrable shell blown out.

It's busted opened! But how?

"Kahn?" Renee says, but he knows it is no use. Somewhere inside himself, Renee feels a slight urge to throw his body across the broken cave and cry to the heavens *Oh why* questioning God *oh O'Talp* beating his fists against the iron door *oh Kahn* now blasted wide open *poor, confused Kahn* but the cool, rational mindset overcomes him as he has trained it to do his entire adult life. Renee wonders how Kahn could have broken out, or did someone break in?

Feeling his way blindly across the scene, Renee's fingers come upon the cold skin of a dead man, lying next to the overturned wreckage of a wheelchair that was once his. Renee recognizes the face immediately.

Nicolas!

Renee feels his neck for a pulse, but there is nothing. Oh, it is all too much! *If I hadn't asked him to guard Kahn, he would still be alive.* Renee's hands begin to tremble. He struggles to steady them as he walks to Kahn's cell. Ducking inside, Renee tries to imagine, to relish the life he tried to give Kahn. *If only I was given such opportunity.* He can feel the broken chains lying upon the dirt ground. *How had he broken them?* He clenches them in his hands, kneels on the ground, and brings them to his face. He buries his face in the dirt where Kahn formerly lay, trying to smell his son. He remembers today was *is* Kahn's thirteenth birthday. And then, something happens to Renee that has never happened before.

Renee begins to cry.

The avalanche breaking his stone facade begins like a salty pebble of a tear bouncing, skimming, tattering down the stone cliffs of Renee's face, leaving a small crack in its wake. His brow softens in pain and his cheeks begin to shift like old boulders crumbling with the movements of the tectonic plates of bone beneath them.

He remembers how the day had started. He awoke in a deep fast, his stomach pure and empty and as focused as his mind. He had dressed in his whitest clothing. His mind soared like the lonely dove then perched above the House of Wax. Kahn was safe inside the earth's womb. His best friend Nicolas was alive. Yes, all was well. That is, until Dewey had shown himself.

Dewey! his lips open, but it is his heart that cries out. His stomach boils with emotion like a hot cauldron, boiling pain into anger, anger into hate. His fists pump *Dewey!* in and out. He is about to scream out, but suddenly he hears the footsteps of men behind him. He waits for his face to return to stone. He does not need to turn to sense who is there.

It is Dewey. The king of Lyceum stands with his two comrades and twelve men behind them, all dressed in white tablecloths. The Posteriorians are holding Ben and the other Prioritan guards that tried to lock them away.

"It was not hard for my men to blend in until they were needed," Dewey begins, "seeing that everything you wear here is so damn…boring. The hardest part was finding clothing in Lyceum bland enough to work. Luckily, Jon here brought these white tablecloths. No one here so much as raised their eyebrows. Not that they would, anyway."

But Renee is not turned towards them. He kneels over Nicolas and looks into his friend's dead eyes by running his fingers across his face. Taking his friend's hands in his own, he struggles to harden his face. He says, "You…did this."

"Who…me? Pretty little me and my colorful men? No, brother. I wish! We could not do this—it was impenetrable, remember? Besides we had not known where it was, or we would have done it long ago."

That is true Renee thinks *but then who did?*

No, brother," Dewey continues, "it was not we. El Totsira told me he would free Kahn if we came to this place. And he did.

"Perhaps it was Kahn himself who opened the cell, perhaps it was an eastern wind. All I know is that someone did, and well, I'm damn well glad of it!"

Dewey lets a moment pass, before continuing, his chin held high. "Now don't blame any of this on me," he says, "for it is all your fault, your stupid…philosophy. You had to live this life, and lock up your son. You had to have this man to guard him. And look! Your son breaks out, kills your best friend, and could be running anywhere just about now. I pray he is far and free, and continues to elude you.

"And do not feel good for one second that your 'visions' as you call them, are in any way accurate. Yes, you saw the twelve men as we traveled to Kallipolis, but you did not see them when they where here—right in front of your face!

You are blind, my brother, and you have been blind since the day you were born."

Renee speaks, but his face remains turned down towards Nicolas, and his words sound like a croak. "It is time for you to go."

Dewey turns to his men. "Ha! Right. I was just getting to that. Release them," he says.

The Posteriorians' fat hands shove Ben and his guardians to the ground towards Renee.

"Ha!" Dewey says, "Yes, we will go. We will find my nephew and we will give him life. You will not find him. You will never see him again. I bet he will find us first. Why, he is probably in Lyceum, smoking his first pipe right now!" Dewey knew this cannot be true, but he wishes to stab Renee with whatever words he can. "Away with us!" Dewey throws his hands in the air and turns his back to Renee. "Let us leave this damned empty place!"

The Prioritans pay the Posteriorians no mind, and as the fat Posteriorians fade away, silence overtakes Renee and his men. Christian is the first to move. He trots over to Nicolas, his tail between his legs. He licks Nicolas's face, his tongue moving from his friend's cold cheeks to Renee's cold hands.

Ben gets up from the ground, brushing himself off. His men follow. He walks over to Renee and places his hand upon his king's shoulder, but Renee pushes him away. Renee takes a deep breath and stands up.

"How did Kahn break out?" he says. But just as he says it, he wonders if someone had broken in. It was built in such a way, Renee remembers, that it was impenetrable from the outside by anyone but him. That is, unless, someone had seen him build it, someone who knew the blueprints. Someone who saw how the foundations were laid. Someone who knew how it all worked.

It could not have been Nicolas, Renee thinks, because Nicolas is dead. He trusted Nicolas. Besides, Nicolas had not seen the foundations of the cave. He had not been there from the beginning, nor had he watched Renee build it hour after hour, day after day.

Suddenly, Renee hears a squirrel scramble behind a distant rock. His head turns to the east. And then, it hits him. He remembers who watched him build O'Talp's cave from behind the few stones bordering these empty fields. Someone who had come to retrieve her necklace, someone who wanted to watch the son she believed was hers. Of course! She had sat and spied on him every day of his work. She had seen every hammer blow, every peg, every stone from the foundation up. And suddenly, he sees her face in his mind, burning like a white candle flame. And then he knows. He knows it was her.

Elizabeth!

8

If you prick us do we not bleed? If you tickle us do we not laugh? If you poison us do we not die? And if you wrong us shall we not revenge?
William Shakespeare

Olegna Lechim sits in the corner of a tavern on a Lyceumean street. After years spent locking himself in his home, he could stay home no longer. The fingers of the cold city night creep in through the broken door of the club only to fuse with the warm glow of the yellow, orange, and purple colored lanterns hanging from the ceiling like countless branches of light. Olegna bathes under the canopy of light, watching the flickering flames reflect in his drink to the beat of the band. On the nearby stage, Howlin' Wolf wails vocals over the crowd, shouting over the swinging horns spilling noise over the crowd. Over the dancing, laughing, vomiting, and drinking of the crowd, Olegna cannot hear the thunder outside. As the pattering of rain begins against the window in his corner of the room, Olegna's mind wanders.

He remembers the defeat he felt after his art was stolen. The monster *Disegno* was sent to the needle until a decision is reached, but Olegna knew what that meant. Olegna knew that Posteriorians never reach any final decision, so an indictment was for life. And life for Disegno is something Olegna cannot bear. So Olegna had to leave. He had to go as far away as possible. Olegna was going home.

But almost symbolically, his suitcases split open upon leaving, their contents spilling on the ground. His hands came across the chisel that he used to form his sculpture, and he vowed to get revenge. He could not leave Lyceum while Disegno was still alive. He knew he had to act. Perhaps he could just explain his loss, but the judges of the

High Court would never listen to him. He had to do something, but what?

The body of a large woman tumbles on the ground before him, disrupting his thoughts. She lies there for a moment, looking at him. Finally, she gets up and pushes her way back into the crowd. A couple makes love against the wall to his right. Men laugh at a joke over a game of cards across the room. Two men and two women explode into laughter over a joke before him. Their voices suddenly lower to hushed whispers, a rarity in Lyceum. This catches Olegna's interest, and it is not hard for him to overhear.

"...and a dumb naked child running through the wilderness is something I would like to see!" one of them says.

"Well, you missed it. The boy escaped months ago, so he must have found clothes by now."

"Haha! Do they know where he went?"

"Sh!" another whispers, "Most say he headed north from Kallipolis, running across the land, until he died from not knowing how to eat, to walk. He did not know how to do anything."

"So sad."

"Did they find his body?"

"I can't imagine how frightening everything must have been for him. The trees must have been like huge monsters with green hair, the sky like a large blue ceiling, how scary—"

"Or beautiful."

"Perhaps."

"Yes, and others say he ran right into the ocean, where he drowned to death. But I think," the man's voice lowers to a whisper, "I think he is still alive. Somewhere out there. There has...been talk that he may have found help. He may be hiding somewhere in the mountains, the lower foothills of the Apuans, gathering men. People are saying that the kings of the world are scared, that Kahn could be a...a threat to all that do not know his whereabouts."

A waitress comes to take Olegna's drinks. He does not offer the acknowledgement of her presence.

"Yes," the gossiper continues, "The world leaders are scared of Kahn. He is angry, of course. Angry and confused, no doubt. He must not know where to place his anger. So the world's readers don't know what to expect. And that is a place they do not feel at peace being in. Of course, no one will tell you this. I wager they cannot even tell this to themselves. But in this world, the world where knowledge means everything, anyone that is out there that is not...under surveillance...can be a threat. The unknown *is* a threat, especially someone with as much anger as Kahn might have."

"But he is just a boy," another says, "Maybe he just is trying to survive. Maybe he is just trying to find a new home.

"Maybe this, maybe that. But I think it is as I told you, and this is all I can say."

"He cannot know anger yet. He is so young."

"Oh, anger is the first thing that comes to us as a baby! Anger of the lack of experience, of milk, light, warmth, and touching—all of which Kahn never had. There is talk," the voice lowers, "there is talk that he will turn an angry eye to Lyceum first."

"What? After being locked up by the Prioritans, shouldn't his anger be with them? With Kallipolis?"

"One may think so at first, but remember that as much as he may not like it, Kallipolis is his parent. It takes a person great trouble to hate where they came from. Besides, some say that Kahn is trying to spread virtue through the world, after the way he was treated. See, El Totsira tells us that we don't need to intend to be virtuous, so long as we *behave* that way. But Kahn may think differently."

"What? You're changing the entire subject—"

"There is also talk...talk that Kahn is making weapons, rockets—"

"Rockets?!"

"Well—"

"Wait one minute now. You are saying that a scared, uneducated thirteen year old boy who never even—"

"Listen! It was heard, not much more than a week ago, the sound of rockets flying over Cherava Woods. They are testing missiles, I tell you. They call them Kahn rockets, or Kassahn rockets or something. Wreckage was found, and the metal scraps have been reconstructed…"

"We know nothing. Where would he get the help? Who would leave their home and side with this…savage?"

"Listen! Do you remember how many Posteriorians sympathized with the boy when he was locked up?"

"Yes, but that was—"

"Thousands! We lost hundreds of men and women protestors, traveling to Kallipolis by the thousands! And now…now, there must have been some that have tried to find the boy. Perhaps he has met them. Perhaps he has gathered forces, people to help him. Smart people. Scientists."

"You are crazy. Enough of this."

"Well, King Dewey has not been able to find him. Neither have the Prioritans, so far as I know. How can a thirteen year old boy hide so well if he were alone, dead or alive? He *must* have help. No one knows where he is! Can *you* tell us where he is hiding?"

Olegna decides he has heard enough. Looking out the window, he sees how different the city looks through the rain droplets hugging the glass. The city pulses through the water-beaded glass like a breathing animal, its industrial skeleton of bone over bone, its streets like veins, a conduit of life flowing this way and that. And through all the construction of this animal city, its cranes and fallen buildings, he can see its heart in the distance: the arena stands tall in the center of the city, pulsing its energy of art, experience, and creation into the surrounding night.

Olegna notices how the rain on the mottled glass distorts his view of the city life beyond. But, he wonders, doesn't the moisture of my eyes act in the same way? Perhaps it too distorts what the city really is. Perhaps my mind distorts my experience just as much. If so, then what does the *real* city look like? What does the real *anything* look like?

He wonders if one can ever know.

But turning his head, he can see one structure that looks the same as it ever did. Yes, the needle stands above him like it had when he was in his house, taunting him from above. He can still see Disegno in his cell at the top, laughing down at him like the devil clown he is, his red eyes gleaming, the scar on his face turning from red to orange—but then Olegna realizes he has an advantage. He knows where Disegno is, but the demon does not know where Olegna is at any time. Olegna is angry. He imagines the needle crumbling before him, Disegno and all *demon and stone* raining down upon those who kept the thief alive. He smiles at such a thought. He is surprised at his sudden lust for terror and destruction. He realizes he may have something in common with Kahn after all.

Yes, this...Kahn may want to destroy Lyceum, and Olegna would like to see just a piece of it fall. Kahn may be collecting recruits now, collecting any help he can get to make sure Lyceum is destroyed, and all that stands within its borders. Even the needle.

For the first time in weeks, Olegna smiles. He rises and heads towards the door. It will not take long to pack this time, for he knows where he is going. It is time to return home, to the Apuan Hills. But not without a little detour on the way.

9

If the prisoner (is) released...when any of them is liberated and compelled suddenly to stand up and turn his neck around, he will suffer sharp pains; the glare will distress him, and he will be unable to see the realities of which in his former state he had seen the shadows. He will require to grow accustomed to the sight of the upper world. First he will see the shadows best, next the reflections of men and other objects in the water, and then the objects themselves; then he will gaze upon the light of the moon and the stars and the spangled heaven, and he will see the sky and the stars better than the sun. Last of all he will see the sun, and not mere reflections of him in the water, but he will see him in his own proper place, and not in another; and he will contemplate him as he is.

Plato

Kahn was sleeping when the woman entered his cave. He felt her hand tugging on his chains. Clusters of golden light streamed into the cave door, but they were too far away to rouse the boy. He was swimming in dreams of varying shades of gray. Dark flat shapes moved around him, and he knew them as other objects beyond himself. Many of them consisted of three round shapes joined together, with six extensions upon which they stood reaching from their bodies down to the ground. These entities made no sound at all. But a few of them, Kahn noticed, were bigger than the rest, and these were not silent at all. These bigger ones would squeak every time Kahn would move. The loud ones were round and blurry, with just four extensions reaching from their bodies to the ground upon which they crawled, and one longer extension dragging on the ground behind them. Finally, Kahn found that one of them had no extensions at all. Rather, it was an extension in itself, its body one long shape itself, slithering across the ground on its belly. After some time, he began to wonder if these shapes sensed him as he sensed them.

He wondered which of these shapes he would look like himself.

Occasionally, he would see one of them open and devour one of the smaller ones. He wondered where the smaller one went, but no matter how hard he looked, he could never find the smaller one again. But sometimes the large ones seemed to brace themselves, as if pushing out the smaller masses from their rear. Kahn would see small shapes come out of the other end of the larger bodies, but these would not move. They had an odd smell, he noticed. They would lie still for weeks until disappearing back into the earth. He wondered why they remain so still, so quiet. He figured they must like to sleep. Just like him.

This is all Kahn saw as he was awake, so this was all he saw as he dreamed. But in one dream he wondered if the sensations he felt from the cold chains upon his body could be felt from the two-dimensional shapes he shared the world with. And he wondered how large the world was. As he felt the ground below him, he wondered if there was a similar ground above him, or at his sides, and if he could ever reach those boundaries.

But the woman's hand on Kahn's ankles began to steal him from his dreams. He recognized her touch briefly, as if he had felt this touch once before. Her hands were steady and concentrated; they did not shake like the nervous gray shapes around Kahn's world. The woman's hands maneuvered around the chains with skill and great ease, as if the hands knew how the chains operated, as if the woman had studied their links and their locks for a long time. It did not take long for her to free Kahn from his bonds.

But to Kahn, this was not freedom. It caused him great pain to feel the weight of the chains of his womb open up. Birth is no fun at all! Even if you are thirteen years old. Do you remember yours? You must understand, dear reader, the paralysis of fear caused by such a sudden freedom. When you shove a pen into a man's hand and tell him to draw a horse anyway he likes, he will proceed. But if you tell him to draw anything in the world he likes, he will hesitate, his hand hovering over the paper, doubtful and fearful of its sudden freedom thrust upon it without request.

Kahn felt the chains pulled off his body, but he lay still, not knowing what to do. Suddenly, the hands of the woman pulled him up onto his side, into a different position. At first he felt dizzy as gravity drove the blood inside of him to rearrange itself to its likings. The world was spinning slowly and it frightened him. He missed his shadows, his wall, his world. Kahn wondered, will I always feel this way? But he began to feel better. Twenty minutes passed before Kahn suspected that this is the way he is supposed to be according the way his body is designed: with his head at the top of his body now vertical from the ground, not at his side as his body lay flat.

Suddenly, Kahn realized he could turn his head this way and that. He looked around the cave and found that none of it was like before. Light streamed in from the open door and it blinded him. He covered his eyes, wincing with pain. But as the moments passed, he began to see stones on the ground that were only shadows before. He realized how the light that seeped in under the door was able to create shadows where these stones lay, and that these stones were more real than the shadows they had created.

As an hour passed, Kahn accepted this light and these stones as the most real things in the world. But just as he was getting accustomed to them, the woman dragged him out towards the light. Squinting his eyes in pain, Kahn tried to resist, but she was too strong for his young undeveloped body. He was dragged across the earth ground and the most horrible sounds he has ever heard came uncontrollably from his throat.

Suddenly, Kahn found himself bathed in light. He could see less than he was able to see even in the darkness of his cave. But as his eyes grew more comfortable, he looked around himself. To his amazement, he could not see the walls of the cave. But he had known they were there, for he had always heard echoes bouncing off of them. Seeing his confusion, the woman turned his head behind him, and at once he could see the cave from which he came, and that he was now *outside* of it.

"Meeehh..." he made a sound of amazement, realizing that there is that which is beyond the cave. Drool streamed out of his weak jaw, and his mind was awhirl. He saw that the drips from his mouth looked like the droplets coming from the woman's face. The woman gently wiped the drips away with her hand. Her face was twisted in emotion as she watched him, but the sides of her lips were curved upward, and this gave Kahn some comfort. He wondered why.

Looking around, Kahn could see trees in the distance, and he could smell the salt of the sea. He could see many caves, but none as strong as his. He could see the earth tilted upwards far in the distance, culminating into great peaks with white tops. Finally, he could see the ceiling of his new cave: a vast blanket of blue gray above him, with white strands of fluff floating here and there, all illuminated by the big, great, yolk, a golden coin high in the sky, shining its light down onto the world so that all can be seen.

Just then, he understood that all of these things are the most real things in the world, and that the sun is their source. He understood that the light coming under his cave door was from the sun; it was the first thing he saw and it was the last.

Suddenly, the woman pulled his head back and opened a cavity in his head. This cavity, he remembered, was where he had taken in the cool liquid of life before. And now, she splashed the water upon his face, down into the cavity, down his throat.

Choking, Kahn stood for the first time. He wiped his mouth and saw the woman watching him. He took a step forward, but tripped into the woman's open arms. She pulled him up to try again.

He closed his eyes and suddenly, he was back in his cave. But he felt the sun beating down on him like never before. It felt like a good force upon him, his soul escaping, leaving his body behind. He felt his rashes disappearing, washing away, disintegrating out of his skin and into the breeze.

He opened his eyes and he was outside again. And before he knew it, he looked down and saw his naked legs walking under him, taking him back to the cave.

He stopped. The woman stood before him, a bright white stone around her neck. Kahn stared at the stone, mesmerized. It looked like nothing he had seen before. He wondered for the story locked in the stone. Where had it come from? He felt as if somehow, the stone led her to him.

Suddenly, he heard the sound of an old man moaning. He blinked and turned towards the noise, and what he saw frightened him greatly. A chair with wheels was overturned as if it had violently been kicked over, spilling out an old man. The old man lay before the woman, and Kahn could see that his head was crushed upon a rock. Blood streamed out of his skull, trickling into the earth. The woman did not seem to pay him any mind. His moans grew louder, then subsided as the red liquid emptied from his head. Kahn could see that some of the red liquid was also on the woman's hands.

The woman raised an arm to let Kahn pass by her. Kahn turned back to the man from the wheelchair and saw that the breath was gone from him. For a moment, Kahn noticed that these other people are just like him; they have two legs upon which they stand, and their faces…their faces…he wondered if they are like his. He saw that they wear covers upon their body and he wondered why he stands naked before them. Where are his covers? He looked to the woman, hoping for some sort of answer.

Again, she raised her arm as if to say "You may go free now, I cannot drag you anymore," but Kahn found that his feet would not move from their place. He stared in awe as a cloud drifted past, and he raised his hand before his face and tried to grab it.

"Go on," a sound from the woman's mouth. Kahn did not know its meaning.

Suddenly, the man on the ground raised his arm and moaned one last time, a great moan, his arm a great tree root reaching up, his ripped sleeve hanging down like old moss, twisted vines and growth swaying in the wind. But the woman stood before him so that Kahn could no longer see. But Kahn could hear his arm slump back to the ground, the breath leaving him, his body finally still.

The woman seemed relieved. Kahn looked at the woman, his eyes pleading *please let me stay please I don't want to go I am so scared so scared soscared* but Elizabeth hardened her heart. To Kahn's surprise, she began to push him violently away from the cave. She made more noises with her mouth, "Go, go now! You are free! Be free from this place! Go on now," and Kahn tried to make the same noise with his throat, but only a gurgling sound came out.

She pushed him again and he fell. He looked up at her in shock and fear, but she lifted him up again and pushed him away. But this time, he did not fall.

Kahn stood.

This time, he found his legs working. By some miracle, Kahn found himself moving away from all the confusion, towards a great gray Nothing he knew not yet as the sea. One step, then two, he began to walk west. He was able to hurry, his left leg pushing him forward, his right leg dragging behind, forcing him into some sort of a trot, like a wounded fawn struggling from her predator. As clouds passed through the sky, lightning bugs blinked and twinkled before him, the feel of earth kissed his feet, and three dimensional shapes of stones, tumbleweed, and brush made their way past him, Kahn saw many things, but he found that he did not know which were real and which were fake.

Rekha's grave stood before him, but he did not know who she was. She stood upon it, her legs halfway into the ground, as if she had come up to speak to him, and perhaps for a breath of air. Dirt covered her face, but Kahn found that she was beautiful. Then she opened her mouth to speak.

Return things to one, she told him, *synthesize and return things to one, as they were before they left my womb*.

But Kahn did not understand, of course, and he ran faster west. He embraced the quiet freedom of the large unmoving gray ocean before him, and he ran even faster to seek its peace. He saw the vast sheet of metallic gray open before him, but found that it was broken up into small circles upon its edge, as it faded into the land. Coming closer, he stopped at one of the pools. He tried to step on it, but found that it could not support the weight of his foot.

He looked down to see what happened to his foot, but to his horror, his foot was gone, swallowed by the watery ground. Worse, he saw another body looking back up at him.

Kahn jumped back in fear. He was horribly frightened and his hands shook. He wondered where this other could have come from. Had he followed him here?

Then he realized that this face was much like the face of the woman and the man lying on the ground. Slowly, he waited for the courage to step up and look down at the other again. Again, he peered over the pool and saw the other. But this time, when he drew back in horror he saw the face below him do the same thing. He blinked, and the other blinked. He gaped, and the other gaped. But it was only when he looked at many of the purification pools and saw how the rocks tore their sheets apart did he realize that the faces in the ground were not real, but mere reflections of him.

Just like the shadows.

Looking into the watery mirror, he touched his face, pulling his cheeks this way and that, learning that which he was never able to see. Then he saw again how the rocks and wind tore the water apart and he remembered it is like the liquid of life he had been drinking all his life. Kneeling down, he cupped his hands and drank the forbidden water until his thirst subsided and his belly filled with comfort.

Now, the night deepens. A chill fills the air. Kahn grows cold and he wishes for the coverings that the woman had on her body. Suddenly, he hears a rustling toward the sea. And he sees before him another body. It looks much like his own but it is completely covered in hair, crawls on all fours, and has three long fingernails on each hand. He notices that its nose is turned upwards into a snout, and its eyes are farther apart than the other people's were.

He wonders how long it has been there, and why he has not noticed it before. Then it turns its head and Kahn can see how slowly it moves. But for him, it moves quickly enough.

Over the past few hours, Kahn has seen many other animals like this one and he wondered where they all got their coat from. Looking at the sloth before him, Kahn grows angry that everyone else has a covering for their body, but they will not share it with him. Then he sees a sharp rock before him and he remembers how these hard objects were able to tear water apart and crush the old man's skull. Could they cut off the animal's coat?

Kahn picks up the stone. He studies the sloth and he decides that the sloth's coat is warm and it is about the same size as he: a perfect fit! He runs toward the sloth, but the sloth is ready. The sloth meets him with raised arms and begins to push him down. Kahn can smell the sloth's breath as the two grapple *boy and beast.* Kahn tries to push back, but his legs have not been tried and his muscles are not yet fully formed. He topples backwards falling onto the ground, the sloth above him, and the stone flies out of his hand, landing a few yards away.

Kahn stretches his arm towards the stone. But the sloth claws his delicate skin by his ribs. He pulls back, writhing in pain. To his horror, he sees the red liquid again, a few drops coming out of his side. In a panic, he lifts his legs and kicks the sloth away.

Again, Kahn reaches out for the stone, but this time the sloth grabs his leg and pulls him away. One more time, Kahn stretches as far as he can and finally grasps the stone but the sloth is on top of him. He can see the sloth's fangs, the animal's sharp teeth about to dig into his shoulder. Almost instinctively, Kahn finds his hand comes down upon the sloth's head in one fell swoop, the stone cracking into the animal's skull. Struggled cries of pain rise from the animal. Then, a muted grunting. Some more movement. Then, stillness.

Kahn lies still on the ground, the sloth moving up and down on top with him as his chest bellows with pants for breath. Kahn finds that he is covered in the red liquid. And like Nicolas had, the sloth lies still once and for all.

Kahn lies underneath the sloth's large body like it is a cave of his own. *I could stay here forever* he thinks, curling on his side like he did in his cave *oh how much easier it would be* but he remembers the woman and what she showed him.

It is time to move.

It does not take long for Kahn to take his coat. The job is messy in the dark, but for Kahn, any coat will do. Wrapping himself in the furs, Kahn finds his body exhausted; it cries for sleep. He has not moved so much in his life, let alone traveled across the land, wrestled a sloth, and taken its coat. He lets his legs fall under him. His mouth opens to yawn, but he is too tried even for that. He is asleep by the time his mouth closes.

ΩΨΩ

"We have made a ring around the borders," Ammonius says, "The boy must be somewhere. Find him!"

Ammonius is the guardian that Ben appointed to lead the search. When Kallipolis was just forming, Ben found him working the docks on the eastern shore. Ben did not like his passion nor his confidence, and wanted him to clear out *we're building a nation here* but he refused. Ben was angry, but Renee saw the burly arms and strong will of Ammonius and he let him stay if he would become one of them. Ammonius had agreed.

"As you say, Ammonius" the guardian replies, "Our men have formed an impenetrable line running vertically just west of The House of Wax. It runs down to the Axios, and across to the Apuan Hills. We are strengthening our line across the Apuan Hills, but there is no chance he has gotten that far east in just a few hours."

"It has been more than just a few hours. And your 'impenetrable' line better be more 'impenetrable' than O'Talp's cave was."

"Yes, Ammonius."

"Wait. Did you say the western line of guardians stretched north and south from the House of Wax?"

"Well, yes, Ammonius. It reaches—"

"What about the land *behind* the House? West of the House."

"Well, that…that is the Procreation Fields, Ammoni—"

"Stop saying my name! I know what lies behind the House of Wax."

"But, well, we may not set foot there. It is prohibited—"

"Does Kahn know of this rule, young guardian?"

"What?"

"Could Kahn have set foot there?"

"I…sure. He does not know it is prohibited. He could be there. He could be anywhere."

"Then we must be everywhere. For the procreation fields, we may not set foot in there when it is not the festival season, but we can still surround it. You must surround it. Especially if he is there…he does not know…why, he could be desecrating one of our purification pools this very moment! If Kahn is there, you can still catch him if you surround it, moving your men near the House just a bit closer, pushing further west down near the Axios. You don't need to line the Axios and Apuan Hills just yet, young guardian. As you said yourself, he could not have gotten that far."

And so it is. The guardians begin to move away from the Axios and Apuan Hills. They move to circle the Procreation Fields and try to push Kahn into the sea.

Hours later, Ben finds Ammonius. He does not look happy.

"Why can we not find him?" Ben demands an explanation.

"We will find him. The men are closing in now."

"Where could he have gone?"

"Patience," Ammonium says, appalled by the foolishness of his guardians, "Patience will treat us well now."

"It just does not make any sense."

Ammonius says nothing, but he can only agree.

ΩΨΩ

Kahn wakes to the caws of a crow flying over him. *They fly, too?* He does not know how long he slept, but it does not matter. He feels a mysterious desire to keep moving, as if danger is afoot. The dawn is a pale yellow; its sun just starting to peek its yellow head over the distant hills, sprinkling its golden brown fairydust upon the west like intoxicating pollen from a dusty old flower.

Kahn's eyes follow the crow's trail. He wonders if he could ever fly like that. His eyes follow it across the sky as it glides in circles above him. But Kahn can also see its shape following its path on the ground beneath it. Kahn understands that this is its shadow, once the only thing he ever knew.

With every hour, Kahn has learned to adapt to the world outside the cave. At first, all he could ever think of was the cave. He longed for it all the time. The confusion of other entities moving around him, making noises, and reacting to his actions produced the terrible fear that grips a farmer his first time in a big city. But it did not take long for the fear to turn into awe, awe into enjoyment, and enjoyment into an appreciation that Kahn thought he would never have.

Still, he must stay away from the other men. They do not look friendly, Kahn fears. They are not like the woman who broke his chains. He walks over to one of the purification pools and studies his reflection once more. He smiles, watching it smile back at him upon the silver glass of the water's surface. He is not like them, he decides. But suddenly, Kahn sees his reflection shake. The water ripples from sounds heard in the distance.

Looking up, Kahn can see the other men. They are still far away, but he knows they are getting closer because he was not able to see them before. He can see them in the fairy dust of the sun: as white dots they move on the gray parchment of land like tiny lice on a tan sheet falling and rising with the breeze of their conscience. He knows they look for him and he does not care why. Somehow, he feels their displeasure at his experiences, and he hopes to experience and learn all he can before they take it all away.

He begins to move away from the sea, but he feels weaker as he parts with the liquid of life. His new coverings are warm, but they are not enough for the cold growing inside of him. He moves south, the sea on his right and the land on his left. As he feels his legs move again, Kahn feels great freedom wash over his heart, the joy of possibility, of motion, and of light. But this is cut off by the voice of a man just yards away.

"Hey!"

The voice penetrates the serene stillness Kahn has enjoyed this whole time. It is close, but Kahn cannot focus his eyes from far to close very quickly. Instinctively, he looks for a place to hide. He looks for a rock, a tree, some brush, but there is nothing in this barren land. He feels something inside his chest banging to get out but he does not know what it is. He falls to the ground in despair. Lying low, he tries to remain as still as possible. He pulls his coverings tightly around him. He thinks that somehow, being still may help.

"Hey! Come here."

Moments pass. Finally, Kahn can hear the rustling of the man getting closer. Kahn can hear his breathing. Why, he must be just a few feet away! Kahn struggles to crawl forward, but in his terror, he finds it difficult to move. But he slithers forward slowly, his face turned downwards, hidden to the ground. He can feel the man's eyes looking down at him as he moves, but he continues to slither forward under the man's gaze.

Kahn waits for the man's hands to grab him. He waits for his warm coat to be torn off his naked body, writhing in resistance as he is dragged back to the world of the cave. But a moment passes, and the man does no such thing. Instead, he speaks, and Kahn cannot understand his words.

"Damn sloths around these parts…move so slow I cannot even tell if they are sleeping."

Another moment passes and Kahn remains still. Silence. Finally, the man spits onto the ground. He shuffles his feet and walks back towards the land.

"Hey," he shouts to the others in the distance, "Did you not hear me calling you? I told you to come here! Come and line this border with me. Move it!"

Still on his belly, Kahn crawls on. He senses that lying low has somehow kept the man away. So he hurries south on all fours, crawling like a newborn baby towards his mother's milk. When he is far enough that the men are but specks on the horizon, he stands up, brushing himself off.

When he arrives at the Axios River, the sun is high in the sky. It begins to weigh on his shoulders. It makes him tired again, but he knows he must go on.

The wild Axios is like nothing he has ever seen. Oh, the gushing river throws itself in every direction like a wild juggler sweating on stage, its body swaying, throwing foam and fire high into the air to shower upon all who care to stop and see. Kahn tries to sooth himself, reminding himself that it is the cool liquid of life. It moves steadily, he tells himself, a stream of moving life like the shadows he grew up with. But in the roar of the river he sees only death. This frightens him. He does not try to cross. He does not get too close. He sees that he is locked away from the south and west by water, so he heads east, in the only direction he can.

The sun beats down upon him, and he begins to overheat. He grows thirsty again, and his stomach begins to growl. He looks to the north and he can see a line of men waiting, the guardians securing the southern border, their back to him. A group of them huddle around what seems to Kahn to be another sun. The sun on the ground burns like the one in the sky, Kahn decides, only it is much smaller.

They are far enough now, Kahn decides, and he strips off his furry coat. The cool air kisses his soaked skin. He sees that the guardians have moved to where he just was, as if they are following him. Kahn slipped out of there just in time. He had just missed them, but he wonders if his luck will last much longer.

The Apuan Hills lie before him in a straight line, like a row of soldiers themselves, pawns standing tall, waiting for the onslaught of battle. Kahn thinks they are close and he raises his leg to step over them just in case. No, in a few steps he sees they stand miles away, their stone faces not making this any easier on him. The mountains seem friendly to Kahn, comforting him to take shelter in their foothills. As the earth beneath his feet begins to turn to rock and stone, Kahn feels the familiar comfort of his cave.

Hours pass. Kahn finds that the sun in the sky is leaving him, falling down into the hills before him. He wonders if it will crush the mountain or if they will be able to bear the big yolk. This is the first time he has seen the sun set, and as he watches the last of it disappear, he wonders if he will ever see it again.

The air grows cold around him and he begins to look for another coat. Animals pass him, but he is too weak to bring the red liquid from their heads. Finally, he sits, his naked body shivering upon a rock he spent an hour trying to pull from the ground. Now the southern Apuan Hills are around him, but they do not keep him warm. Instead, the wind whispers through their narrow passageways, taunting him with their murmurs and rhymes.

He used to like the dark, he remembers, but that dark was not cold like this. It did not move but was still like a blanket. He hugs himself, his skinny arms trying to hide his skeletal body from the wind. As his body begins to shiver without his help, he wishes for the sun that the guardians had. It had seemed to grow out of the ground around them and keep them warm, Kahn figures from the way they were all huddled around it.

How can he grow such a fire from the ground?

Suddenly, a huge streak of light comes from the sky. Kahn jumps to his feet. A moment later, a loud crack of thunder whips down upon the earth, shaking the ground around him. Water begins to pour down upon the ground, washing away any warmth left in the Apuan rocks.

Kahn begins to cry.

Now he understands the drops of water that came from the woman's eyes as the same that come from him now. Oh, how he wishes for his coat, the fire of the sun, the dryness of his cave. He lifts his head and screams to the heavens. He does not know what he says nor why he is driven to make such a loud noise, but only that he must.

Blood-curling shrieks come from his throat. His arms reach up towards the sky. Then he remembers Nicolas. How comfortable the old man looked, lying with the red liquid from his head. How warm. If only he can feel like that! If only he can draw the red liquid from his own body right now.

Kahn walks to find the right stone. And there it is! Before him, a long skinny jab of rock sticks out of the rocky ground like a long banana waiting to be picked. It is perfect!

Kahn runs to the stone and wraps his hands around it. The rain beats down upon his body in torrent showers, but he closes his eyes. And he pulls.

Nothing. He tries again, but his hands fly off the slippery stone. He repositions his feet for leverage, and channeling all the energy of his anger, he tries again.

This time, the stone comes out at once, and he reels backwards, falling onto the ground. Without hesitation, he lifts the stone above his head. He looks at its perfect body, a long slender blade, coming to a point at the end. He takes a deep breath and prepares to strike himself. He looks to the mountains to say goodbye, but another streak of light crashes from the sky and in that brief moment, his eyes see a black hole in the side of mountain.

A cave!

Now Kahn can see that there are many of them: dark holes opening up into the sides of these mountains like gaping mouths waiting to him to enter. He forgets about the old man as quickly as he remembered and he drops the stone from his hand. The rain stops as if on cue.

Kahn stands and gladness fills his heart. He runs towards the caves in the mountains. *This will keep me safe.* He enters one of the caves before another drop of rain can fall. He settles into his cave as if it is his womb, but as the days pass, he works up the courage to venture out into the world once again. He drinks from the small lakes to which the Axios feeds. He finds another coat, and learns how to bring the sun from the ground.

But his stomach still growls. He grasps it, wondering if this is the same creature that tried to break out of his chest before. He remembers how it tried to break out by banging against his chest just like he banged against his cage for most of his life. He feels bad for it and he rubs his stomach soothingly, but it does not satiate his pain. Suddenly, he remembers the liquid of life, how it makes everything better. He drinks the occasional rain, but it is not enough. He feels the need to fill himself. Perhaps with something more substantial. Then he remembers how the grass had absorbed the rain so well. Is this where the liquid of life resides? It must be full of it!

He grabs a handful of grass and puts it in his mouth. It fills him, but it does not last long. But grabbing at the grass one day, he feels a small red object in his hand. He examines its soft plump body and he finds that it is moist. He pinches it open and finds the liquid of life inside! He eats grass and then berries and he relearns to sleep. His body becomes satiated again, and his feet begin to heal. He lives in the caves this way and he is at peace. He hopes the creature inside of him is happy too. He does not hear from it again, so he figures it is.

Weeks pass. Kahn is sitting before his fire, wiping his mouth from his first big meal. He looks down at himself and is surprised how his body has filled itself in just a few short weeks. His ribs no longer stick out as they once did and his arms and legs are curved with flesh. He takes off his hat of fox fur and thinks back on himself.

The fox had not been easy to catch. He had brought the red liquid from the fox by following it into its hole and bringing himself upon it as it slept. He had used the stone he once almost used on himself. But this time he saw the flesh under the coat and he desired it too. He dragged the fox corpse home with him, its coat over his shoulder, his mind searching for an energy to transform the fox's flesh to meat.

He found that by rubbing his stone against other stones (such as on the walls of his cave) he can sharpen it into a deadly and useful weapon. It was also in this way that he found sparks of the sun's light coming from stone against stone, and this he transferred onto the wood of the ground, as he saw the guardians had.

His first fire brought great excitement from him. As the sun grew from the ground before him, he ran forward to embrace it. His left hand reached forward to touch the sun, but he reeled back in terrible pain. Not understanding what had happened, he ran to the liquid of life in the creeks outside and thrust his hand inside. The water cooled his hand but he found that his hand had turned color. He found that his senses deceived him, and he was angry at them for this. The sun had marked his hand permanently, and the scar would stay to always remind him of his err.

It was in this moment that he grew wary of the experience that he previously thought was his savior. But returning to the world of the cave of his mind seemed too empty. Confusion weighed upon him, but he rested and the comfort of indifference set in.

Tonight his eyes move from the burning embers of his fire to the three coats hanging on his wall. For the first time in a long time, he is content. He does not yet know of the anger brewing inside of him. He does not know of the fury rising in his heart towards his past captors, and the outside world in general. He does not know of the lust for revenge that will overtake him, a lust that will be fed and aided by wandering Posteriorians and rangers and exiles that find their way into his cave. They will teach him to read and to write and most importantly, how to make weapons against the ones who use weapons against them.

His eyes begin to close with exhaustion just as they do every night in this cave. But this night is different. Just before closing, his eyes catch a glimpse of something they have never seen before.

A small dot of orange is seen out of the corner of his eyes. He has never seen such a shade of color before; the pale white yellow of the Kallipolis sun was all he had seen like this, and that did not come close.

He gets up and walks to the orange object in the corner of his cave. He kneels down in wonder and examines the object. It is a small orange flower. He brings it to his nose, closes his eyes, and inhales. He has never smelled anything like it. The smell makes him smile, but it frightens him inside. He places the flower back on the stone upon which it was resting.

Then he sees a small ball of colorless wax next to it, resting on the same stone. This he brings to his nose, but there is no odor. The wax reminds him of the nothingness of his cave, of the bleak gray fields of Kallipolis.

Finally, Kahn sees that the stone upon which these objects rest is unlike any other stone he has ever seen. It is a perfect cube, though its corners and edges have crumbled away, weathered by the aging of years. It stands taller than any of the stones around it, perhaps three for four feet from the ground. It is a gravestone. In his very cave!

Kahn remembers seeing a similar stone during his journey here, but he decides that that one was not real. Not like this one. Or did it follow him here?

Kahn notices small engravings on the front of the stone. He brushes away the dirt, but he cannot make sense of the words he sees. His fingers trace the lettering, his pointer moving along the curves of the *R,* and across the woman's name. He cannot read the words *Rekha lies here* but then he can hear her voice once again. *Return things to one* she says to him, *synthesize and return things to one.*

10

Over the years people I've met often ask me what I'm working on, and I've usually replied that the main thing was a book about Dresden. I said that to Harrison Starr, the moviemaker one time, and he raised his eyebrows and inquired 'Is it an anti-war book?' 'Yes,' I said, 'I guess.' He replied, 'You know what I say to people when I hear they're writing anti-war books? Why don't you write an anti-glacier book instead?' What he meant, of course, was that there would always be wars, that they were as easy to stop as glaciers. I believe that, too.

Kurt Vonnegut

The summer sky passes over the west like a sliding veil of glass, its body finally frosting from the incoming cold of autumn, cracking, raining down hard shards of frigid air onto the earth. As the months pass, Kahn stays inside his cave, conjuring up images like the orange flower: an orange universe, with a sky lit by a great yellow sun, with fiery crows soaring through the sky at lightning speeds, raining down whips of thunder upon his enemies as they run back to their mud huts in terror. He remembers the crow he saw soaring across the sky on his travels south, but he dreams that the crow was a fiery orange, like the flower on Rekha's grave. The image of the fiery soaring crow stays with him as he swims through weeks of rest, experience, and thought.

His sense of wonder gives him courage to go for a walk each day. Like Rekha once did, Kahn takes a walk the same time each day. Now that he has settled, Kahn notices that he has become a strictly predictable person. The neighboring animals, one might say, may tell what time of day it is by Kahn's present location.

As he ventures out of the cave on his daily explorations, jumping down rock scrambles, riding down waterfalls, swimming in small pockets of water, looking out at the views, his eyes begin to hurt. The sun digs into his eyes and makes his vision blurred. His eyes take longer to focus and the pain grows.

One morning, he wakes up with a terrible pain in his head. His eyes try to focus on the daylight, but all he can see are flashes of red and orange. The sense data around him becomes almost overwhelming, impossible to sort. A bird flies past and a swarm of honeybees float by, but to him, they are an impossible circus of chaos like clothes strewn across a room. As it becomes almost impossible to see, he closes his eyes and remembers the world of simple shadows, the world of the cave. This is where his mind had begun to conceive of the concept of reason. He was just putting pieces together as Elizabeth broke him from his bonds. But it felt safe in there, Kahn remembers. Simple.

But reason, Kahn remembers, was empty with nothing to apply it to. It was a river channel with no river, or an empty tree brace with no tree to grow through it. He needed a river to guide, a tree to grow *within* the framework of reason. And on the other hand experience was a river, but without reason it had no order, no framework. It was like the fire that burned his hand. Experience can be so beneficial, he decides, if only some sense of order is applied to it through which one can weed out the gems from the rough. But now it is fading.

Suddenly, a rustling comes from one of the other caves below him. This is not the first time Kahn has heard such noises. It is from the others, as Kahn had named them in his mind. They came a few days ago, Kahn decides, and they have been living in these caves with him ever since. Kahn has seen them a few times, when it was light enough to see. At first, he hid scared from them, his sharp rock trembling in his hands, poised and ready to draw the red liquid from their heads. He darted away from them whenever possible, making sure not to meet their eyes.

But one morning he awoke to find a slice of roasted pig by his doorway, prepared and ready for him to eat. It was from the others, Kahn figured. It was not a gift, but a symbol. After that, it did not take Kahn long to sense that they are not here to take Kahn away as the other men had been. These men were different. They did not dress like the other men, but they wore furs and foliage like Kahn himself. They are here to have Kahn embrace them, to take them in as his company, whenever he is ready.

He did not know if he should thank them, so he passed them by casually when he came upon them, looking at them in questionable gratitude. One of their workers traveling with a pile of lumber over his shoulder stopped for a moment to lock eyes with Kahn. He stopped briefly, nodded at Kahn in mutual understanding, and went on his way. Kahn thought this curious but he did not inquire, for he figured this was best left the way it is.

He does not know where they came from, only that they wish to live as he, taking refuge in the caves. He is merely one of them, he realized, and they, one of him. Exiles, runaways, lost souls, dunces ifyouwill, told by their mothers and fathers and kings and lovers to leave and sit in the corner of the world.

He has managed to ignore them until now, merely raising his eyes in curiosity as they pass his cave, meeting for eye contact for a few seconds and then clambering on, hardly acknowledging each other's presence as if they are nothing but a passing wind. He is impressed by their patience, but then he fears that they do not need him, that they come here looking for the same thing he does, and that he is no matter to them.

But this morning he finds that the pain in his head is too great for him to stand alone. His vision burns with red and orange flashes like the sun itself is behind his eyes. It is too much for him, and he needs to find help. He closes his eyes, rubs them, and puts his arm across his face. *Ugh* he moans in pain and frustration. Reaching out his other hand, he touches the wall for guidance and stands up. He walks out of his cave but finds that the men are waiting for him before he can find them.

"We were waiting for your help, but it looks as though you can use our help more than we can use yours."

Kahn struggles to stand tall. He can hear the other man speak, but he cannot understand. He takes a step forward and flashes of red sting his vision. He falls on his face.

"Come here," the man says, "Do you not understand my words? My name is Marcus. Marcus Herz."

"Marrr...cuss," Kahn says. He winces from the pain in his head.

The men behind Marcus fall back, confused. That is, all except Martin Knutzen who smiles at Kahn's weak attempt to speak. Like Kahn, he came from Kallipolis. After years of studying Christian, the wolf at Renee's side, (for he was quite intrigued by the animal's behavior), he left for the mountains when he heard of Kahn's escape. Somehow, he had known Kahn would be here. And he was rarely mistaken.

Martin steps forward and hands Marcus a strange veil. It is partially transparent, tinted, like a novel sort of lens. It is neither white nor orange, but the color of a perfect dawn.

"It is time," he says.

Without hesitation, Marcus skillfully ties the veil across Kahn's face as if he has practiced this many times before. "This is a gift. From us," he says. "Try and walk with it. See what it does for you."

"Marcus, that is all now," Martin says, "Let us give the boy some space."

Marcus takes a step back and Kahn stands upright, brushing himself off. Slowly, he takes a step forward.

Marcus runs to help him, but Martin blocks him with his arm.

"Wait," Martin says, "He must relearn to walk himself."

The men stay still: Marcus, Martin, Reinhold, Beck, and Fichte standing like stone statues before the lone figure of a boy as he walks out across the high-wire of the ground with a new blindfold over his eyes.

Kahn blinks, scared to adjust to the strange new cloth across his face. But he finds that the veil makes it easier to see. It acts as a filter, blocking out the bad sensations, he finds, while letting the good ones in, but only at a pace that his mind can handle. It only allows him to see that which he can properly absorb and translate with his mind. The sunshine that was once overwhelming is softened, and everything is suddenly a bit more acceptable. He feels better already.

Kahn takes a step forward and he finds his vision cooled. His mind clears and he is at peace once again. He will never forget this moment, for as he steps towards the men, these steps are towards more than he can ever know now. And he will never turn back.

The men take him to more men he did not know were there before; there are twenty-two in all. For days and weeks and months the men teach him. They begin with reading and writing and thinking. The boy catches on fast, his mind soaking up that which he never heard of like an empty sponge that was completely dry.

Autumn passes into winter and the men enjoy their time together, accepting the bitter cold as a chance to withdraw from distraction and educate each other. By the end of the winter, Kahn can speak quite well and the men begin to learn from him.

Sitting around the campfires of winter, they speak of their old lives. Each man tells his story. Kahn finds that most of them came from Lyceum under strict orders to find him and bring him back. But as they saw him, they were enraptured by his courage and their hearts were too big and their minds too small and they were unable to drag him from his home. So they forgot their orders and they stayed. Other men came from Macedon, Carrara, Kallipolis, and the small mountains around the great Lake Tirreno, sailing down the Axios to find him. They were not ordered to find him but they left their homes on their own volition. They identified with his story, they tell him, and they wanted to offer any help that they could.

They speak of freedom, of morals, and of truths. At first, Kahn is most interested in the natural world that is so new and exciting for him. The men look at the stars at night, wondering if they will ever walk upon them. Kahn deduces that the world once formed from a large cloud of gas, and that the Milky Way above was once a large disk of stars that also formed from a spinning cloud of gas. He wonders if there are other such nebulae farther than he could see. He does not tell the other men, but he guesses that there are.

The men oppose democracy and they teach Kahn to do the same. Since Kahn was born from the earth of the

Republic rather than in one of the lands under El Totsira's democratic influence, he finds a hate for democracy quite easy to nurture. Pride swells in Martin's heart as he answers Kahn's questions the best he can.

"So," he asks, testing Kahn's beliefs, "Why is democracy an ugly contradiction in itself?"

Kahn answers with little hesitation, "Because it claims to es—es—establish—"

"Establish."

"Because it claims to…estab—lish…an executive power in which 'all' decide for the whole. But it cannot be all because they decide even against one who does not agree; so really it is 'all' who are not quite all, who decide."

With the men's help, Kahn distinguishes three forms of government that he names democracy, aristocracy, and monarchy, and the men argue about which may be the most fit for harmony and productivity. While they differ in their opinions, they all agree that the world is sick and it must be changed.

The men encourage Kahn's fascination with fire and they show him how to channel that energy into small amounts to burst upon impact, making their mark upon the earth. He is fascinated that not only can you experience the world, but you can change it. It can be made and it can be destroyed.

And then Kahn remembers his dreams. He recalls the fiery crow in the sky, smashing into buildings, raining fire upon his enemies, cleansing the world of their ideals. He shudders with excitement of the thought of such destruction, of such power to change the world. After the life of passivity he has always been forced to live, he dreams of the feeling of having control, of changing the world around him, whatever that change may be. And Kahn tells the men about his vision of the fiery bird and he asks them if it is possible, if they can make something like that. And the men begin to tell him of their discoveries, and they speak well into the night.

And between the deep boulders and crevices of the dark Apuan foothills the men converse passionately around a roaring fire. Their passions ignite them, crashing their words through boundaries of reason. They grow mad with possibility, with a mission to change the world. They lose sight of any cause, but lash out at their past mothers and fathers and kings and queens that exiled them, beat them, and told them to leave. They get angry and their anger feels good. And slowly, they find themselves filling with purpose, a reason to cope and rise from the ashes of exile and poverty. The former Posteriorians in the group insist on destroying Lyceum, while the others swear vengeance upon the Prioritans who locked Kahn away to hell. They compromise and agree to change the world *to be born* to give birth to another world, but *first you have to die.*

We must awaken Lyceum from its slumber, they declare, *and bring the end of days to Kahn's captors in Kallipolis.* This will be the end of days for the two world powers, they vow; the Prioritans and Posteriorians must be shaken to the ground.

ΩΨΩ

The change of seasons is hardly noticed in Kallipolis. It is always cold here, so the seasons' effects have not been able to reach past the constant bleakness of the land. Sure, the Prioritans are aware of the passing of the seasons on a mental note, but such currencies of nature have left their blood long ago.

The guardians have resumed their regular posts weeks ago. They pray for Kahn as their brother of the land and they hope that he is safe. They hope that he stays protected from the confusing world of the senses and that he finds the guidance to return to his cave.

Ben walks alone through the mud huts of the republic. He looks to the ground in Prioritan custom, but his brow is creased in worry and his shoulders slumped in defeat. He wonders how Kahn was able to get away so quickly *he must have had help* and why he was unable to catch him.

Suddenly, he sees a sight rare in Kallipolis. Twenty, no, thirty men sit clustered around a fire in the shadow of one of the huts. He knows it is against Prioritan conduct to congregate except on the rarest occasions and for the most important purposes. Approaching the group, Ben can see

Ammonius and many of the other guardians sitting there, their voices rising up with the smoke of their fire.

"Yes," one of them whispers, his hands illustrating his points, "Their buildings are crumbling and they are scared, I tell you."

"Their buildings have always fallen," another says, "So this is nothing new. We know the Posteriorians cannot give a damn about their foundations. As long as their designs hold up for a bit, as long as they are having fun, then they are happy."

"People are dying! Do you not see? They are not having fun. Last week, two taverns in north Lyceum exploded after a flaming man ran into them, shouting horrible things. The northern edge of their royal gardens caught fire, and two horses have gone missing from their stables. I heard just last week, an immense tower by the center of Lyceum came tumbling down onto the plaza, killing at least fifty Posteriorians on the edge of the crowd. And hundreds of small but deadly rockets have landed on Lyceum over the past few days. I fear we can be next."

"Now, now," a third one chimes in, "let us not get ahead of ourselves. Let us not react upon our…feelings. We do not know if any of this true. For once we lose our diligence and slow, methodical concentration, what more do we have? We must think this through. And that will take time."

"They put nails in them."

"What?"

"I heard they put nails in the rockets, nails and glass so that when they explode, they have a deadlier impact to all around them. Women, children, families in their homes—"

"Stop it. That is enough."

"Kassahn rockets, they call them. Homemade by Kahn's people, they are nothing to shrug your shoulders at. By next month, next *month,* they will be able to reach towards the House of Wax—"

"Enough!"

"Will you not listen to him," another says.

"But this does not make sense," Ben says to the men, "Kahn is our brother. He is a child of the land just like you and I. And if," Ben looks down, "if he truly found home in another place, would he not want to build that up? Would he not do what we have taught him, and what we have done upon coming to our land with nothing? Would he not take what was given to him by the world and love his men and the world around him? Would he not want to educate himself, to plant crops, to build, to be one with the world around him? Would he not want to build himself a home?"

"I suppose so," Ammonius says, "But that would take work."

The men look at each other.

Ben says, "Well you may be correct. So we must act. But first, as one of you said, we must think this through. And this may take time."

"We do not have time. Kahn is—"

"We must *take* the time, my brothers," Ben says, "Our actions must be perfect, so we must plan accordingly. And what will be will be."

"What will be will be? Is that all?"

"What would you have me say?"

The men look down. Ben can see their faces lit by the light of their fire, faces of twenty or so guardians of young and old.

Ben says, "Speak your mind."

"If I may," the youngest looks up, "We can not help but notice how you seem…indifferent to our plight. As if we can not change what will happen. As if action is merely a gift we may someday allow ourselves, rather than grasping the situation as it is. We wish you to appreciate the urgency of what we are facing."

"Oh, I appreciate the danger here, young guardian. But I also appreciate that we can not decide which action to take; it is already decided for us. Whatever will happen will happen; it has already begun, and we are merely players in someone else's game. Kahn will do as he will. If he is meant to win, whatever that means, then our actions will set occurrences in motion that will lead to his victory—"

"I do not mean to interrupt," the young soldier says, "But you speak as if we have no free will."

"Free will is a matter of extent, young one. We start as a fetus with no free will, let alone a will of any kind. We are born a crying infant. As we are thrust into this world without a guidebook, we scream for our mother's breast and we sleep when we are satiated, waiting to react to the next random stimulus to our body. Thus, would you say such an infant has free will?"

"Certainly not."

"Well, what about a three year old, kicking and screaming for that toy in the window? Doubtful. What about an eight year old, driven by sibling rivalry and a quest for attention? A twenty year old driven by lust and ego and fame? Or how about the fifty-year-old alcoholic man tied down by addiction and temper tantrums, who is in many ways less mature than the three year old that many would say does not enjoy free will? Does he have free will? Do any of us? This is not so easy to answer, my brother.

"Anyway, we can speak all we want, but it is no matter. For Renee will command our actions, and our fate decides their outcome. So, in the matter of just Prioritans, might I suggest you all disperse from the shadow of this hut and retreat to the solitude of your own huts?"

Ben begins to walk away from the group. His mind has grown heavy and he wishes to meditate alone. As he walks away Ammonius calls out from the group, "Ben?" and he rises to catch up with him. Though Ben is now many feet away from the group, he can hear Ammonius running up behind him. Ammonius calls out, "You are leaving our conversation early? We still have much to discuss. I—" and suddenly his voice is cut off by the most tremendous explosion in the history of this land.

The mud hut behind them explodes into green and purple flame, engulfing the group of men in fire.

Bodies fly into the air, silhouettes of dancers soaring upwards surrounded by the spray of dirt and mud, all falling, breaking into pieces of arms and legs and clumps and rocks, and finally landing as one.

It lifts Ben off his feet. He flies through the air and lands rolling on the ground. He knows that the men behind him are dead. Ammonius lands behind him, his back on fire.

Ben watches in horror as his friend rolls around screaming in pain. Finally, Ben digs his hands into the ground and grabs fistfuls of moist earth. He rubs the mud on Ammonius's back and rolls him against the ground, putting out the fire. Ammonius breathes in relief. He sits up, thankful the flame did not burn much through his robe.

"Kahn," Ammonius says before Ben can speak, "He must have planted a bomb. He is coming for us. And we are not ready for him."

"No," Ben says, shaking his head, "We are not ready at all."

ΩΨΩ

Though Renee buried Nicolas back into the ground months ago, the dirt is still fresh. Renee and Zinbiel stand in silence before the fresh mound of dirt. Behind them, the moon begins to illuminate the House of Wax into the amber glow of a lava lamp one last time before leaving for the rising sun. The House glows softly, a warm ember flickering pink heat from beneath its white shell.

The two men can feel the light on their backs, but it does not warm the cold in their hearts. They can smell the soil before them. They stand in silence, each man a lone statue, their eyes closed, their hands at their sides, their heads down in silent mourning. And they remember.

They remember the young Nicolas. This was the man that lies before them, back in the dirt, the womb of the motherland where all Prioritans return. In his cabin behind the needle at Brittany, he had started it all. His face was ugly, but the beauty of meaning was in his eyes. As a strong-willed vehicle for O'Talp's will, he made Kallipolis what it is today. He guided Benedictus here, and ultimately Renee. Zinbiel wonders if he will ever know such an important man ever again. Renee wonders if he will ever feel such a connection to anyone again. The knowledge and wisdom Nicolas showed only strengthened their friendship, and his guidance let Renee feel safe without feeling inferior. Nicolas was the father-figure that never asked for honor, who merely motivated Renee to reach his own decisions with no more than a twinkle in his eyes and a small smile on his lips. It was in this way that Renee knew that whatever came his way, he was never alone.

But he knows this is no more.

Zinbiel turns to retreat home. Renee's eyes stay transfixed on the mound of dirt before him. But he turns around as he hears Ben running towards them as fast as he can.

"My king!"

Zinbiel is alarmed as he hears Ben panting for breath, but Renee's brow only furrows and he listens intently.

"It is Kahn. He has been attacking Lyceum for weeks, and now he brings his bombs here! He just blew up one of our mud huts during a meeting of our guardians—"

"Meeting?"

"Well, yes, I mean, it was not a scheduled meeting…"

"You know the principles of the land."

"Yes, of course. I do not know why there was a gathering. I think—"

"You think."

"Yes, the attacks on Lyceum had placed such a…worry in the men—"

"Worry. A feeling."

"Well, they were worried that Kahn would attack here."

"Yes?"

And Benedictus proceeds to tell Renee all that had happened. Renee listens to Ben as he would listen to the wind, his face still, his eyes closed. Ben is finished, but Renee remains still, his eyes still closed. He says nothing. Minutes pass and the men wait. Finally, Renee tells the men that which they should do.

"The job required for our producers is twofold. First, we must build a dam," he says, "blocking off the Axios River, Kahn's sole source of water. We will cut off their water source. We will dry them out. It will not take long for our producers to travel just east of the Apuan Hills and clog the river. Yes, we will turn off their water, and we will get ours from the sea.

"Second. We will impose a blockade on our eastern border. I hate to do this, but that is no matter. No one may enter this republic without proper security measures. Further, we must make sure no materials from Kallipolis are exported to the east. We cannot allow them to take any materials with which they can build rockets or weapons."

"But there are no such materials to reap from our land to begin with," Ben says. Renee ignores him.

"Third. We will build a wall. Kahn has gathered few followers, but the hearts of rangers and wandering Posteriorians are weak, and many will sympathize with his influence. This...problem may last for more than a few years, and with Lyceum growing, their protestors demonstrating, and our fragile silence and privacy growing weaker and all the more necessary for our minds to work, it is only fitting that we build a wall. We have spent most of our lifetime striving to build a wall around our minds. Now we must build one around our land."

Renee feels a faint sting in his heart at these words, but he hides it from his face. As he plans to build yet another wall between him and Dewey, he feels his aging hands and wonders if he will ever see his only brother again. He knows his days are numbered, and wonders just what would happen if he broke down all walls, embracing his brother and the world around him. Quickly, he pushes such thoughts away.

He can only say, "I wonder what the state of Lyceum is," but he thinks, "I wonder if my brother is safe."

"We have worried enough," Zinbiel finally speaks, "O'Talp will not let such misfortunes occur upon us. This world will not and can not be one in which Kahn succeeds, but rather, if Kahn's efforts are to put us in danger, they will surely fail!"

"How can you know this?" Ben says. Renee's mind seems to be elsewhere.

"God assuredly always chooses the best world. And one in which Kahn reigns and Prioritans hide under his heels can never be a good world at all. O'Talp would never allow it!"

Renee says, "Still. We must understand the state of affairs around us. Carrara, Macedon, Lyceum, Cherava. We must understand what is going on."

"When have we ever cared about anything outside of our borders?"

"I know our policies. And they do not change. But this is only so we can better decide what to do here. We must send someone to Lyceum. A spy who can tell us what has been destroyed and what is still standing, if anything at all."

The men sigh.

"We have to know what is going on."

The Prioritans do not like to consider events outside the republic, and they never have. Indeed, they have spent many years denying anything exists out of Kallipolis, for if it existed, it was meaningless and not worthy of any type of acknowledgement.

"Yes, King," Ben says, "I can send two guardians out to see—"

Renee says, "No. We cannot afford to lose any more guardians after the explosion. We need to send someone more…dispensable. A producer. He must wear a glove on his hand to cover his scar."

"But a producer knows only to produce. A producer has no idea how to lie nor fight. He will be exposed as soon as they put sensors on him."

"Can I speak?" Zinbiel says, "I know of a certain producer who houses a white dove. This is the bird we see floating around the Kallipolis sky from time to time. I do not know her name, only that she brought the bird here from the trees around Lake Ohrid to be the only animal in this land, and that the bird returns there often, returning to her with tree branches in its mouth.

"We must send the dove to Lyceum. She can tell the dove to bring back that which it sees, a symbol of the state of the nation. If it returns with life in its mouth, then all is still growing in Lyceum, but if it returns with nothing, then death is surely upon us and we must be ready."

And this is what the men agree to do.

ΩΨΩ

Thousands of Posteriorians gather in the arena under the setting Lyceum sun. For the past week, the sounds of rockets and screaming have become white noise in the background. All around the great city, the smell of smoke still fills the air.

But while half the nation dies, half the nation lives. They lie out on their balconies, pints of margaritas in their fat hands, their women massaging their chests, smiling through their intoxications as Kassahn rockets blow up their neighbors. Many of their sensors have been kidnapped or killed but they hardly notice. *Live and be merry* they sing from their rooftops *for tomorrow we die! Or maybe this afternoon!* Never have such words been so relevant, they say. They stuff themselves with food and wine as if each moment could be their last.

But now, they have agreed to gather *one and all* in the arena. Some say it is to be together one last time. Others say it is to clarify what has been going on, and decide what action the Posteriorians must take. Still others say it is for the last show, the greatest show on earth. In a sense, they are all correct.

The show begins as twenty men run into the pit in matching uniforms of pink, blue and orange, ribbons flying from their hair, glitter sparkling on their childish glowing faces. They come out skipping high, their fat bellies jumping up and down with their bodies, swimming in their glittery robes. The crowd goes wild, clapping their hands and stomping their feet to the beat of their dance.

Suddenly, they strip off their robes. The crowd finds that underneath, they are wearing nothing but small animal furs on their crotches. They crowd explodes with laughter at the men's nakedness.

The dancers are mostly naked now, hardly covered by their furs. Sensors run onto the arena, rolling a large model of cave walls around the dancers. The dancers pretend to huddle together, hugging themselves from an imaginary climate of cold. They pretend to be Kahn's men, surviving in a cave. They run back and forth throwing small fiery oranges this way and that, making exploding noises with their mouths as the oranges land. The oranges actually open on the ground *poof* and orange and yellow smoke shoots out of them as they roll, filling the air with the color of fire. The smoke fades and the crowd finds that the dancers have disappeared.

The dancers hide behind the cave walls. When they come out, they are covered in robes of a clean, pure white. Almost immediately, the crowd begins to boo. They shout curses at the men, their thumbs pointed down in disapproval.

But one of the men is still dressed in furs. One of the others grabs a hose and begins to squirt the man with water, and the man opens his mouth to drink. He drinks the water hastily, as if he has not drank anything for a long time. But the other men (still dressed in white) gather around one of the dancers, a blindfold across his eyes, a staff in his hand. The men in white form a line, making a wall with their bodies that blocks the stream of water from the drinker's mouth. The booing grows louder.

Finally, the dancers strip back down to their furs. They huddle together in an imaginary cave. They seem to be conspiring and planning. The crowd's boredom grows. Confusion settles, and the crowd begins to shout for more entertainment. But suddenly, the dancers part to display a most frightening weapon: a tremendous wooden bird wrapped in flame. It wheels across the arena, soaring into the air and exploding into the sky. The actors waits for the crowd's cheers as fireworks rain down upon them.

But the crowd is silent. *Is this what Kahn's men are planning? Could any man build such a thing?* Fear grips the hearts of the thousands of Posteriorians, a fear all too real, all too unexpected. Murmurs rise from the crowd.

And then, as if on cue, a terrible whistling fills the air. The Posteriorians close their ears and eyes, but not before seeing two Kassahn rockets flying into the top of the north end of the plaza. To their horror, one of the supporting towers crumbles before their eyes. A large section of the stands collapses. Bodies fly. Dust and stones fill the air. Screams are heard at every turn. Everyone runs for the door.

"Get me out of here, you fools!" Dewey shouts over the commotion to Jon and Yelekreb.

"Let's go," Yelekreb takes his arm and pulls him forward.

With Jon leading the way, the three men make their way through the windy passageways within the plaza walls. They pass a jolly group of men singing, their fists flying wildly in the air with their last death-song as they sing themselves to death. Dewey can hear them and for the first time in his life, the song makes him sick to his stomach. He looks away. He does not know why he feels this way. The men proceed.

Like three blind mice running through the veins of a dying organism, they dash forward, ignoring the pain in their knees, riding along with the blood-rush of the crowd before the great plaza collapses, its arteries closing in on them completely, pushing them down into the ground to their deaths.

The ceiling above them begins to give way, boulders flying down around them. Yelekreb dodges the stones skillfully, bending his large body over Dewey's to protect him from the rainfall. Jon winces in pain, but he struggles to think, and his mind remembers the way out. He guides the men. And as the ceiling begins to shower down on them for good, Dewey can see the sunlight before them, and finally, the end of the tunnel rushing towards him.

ΩΨΩ

Almost an hour later, they sit together in a nearby abandoned house. For days the western wall of this house has been blown out by rockets and the windows have been smashed. A man and woman lie still in a large bathtub upstairs, now exposed to the outside by the crumbled wall. Upon entering this house, Jon had seen their naked bodies clinging to each other, unmoving. He could not tell if they were dead or alive.

Dewey sits on a sofa in the living room downstairs. Jon and Yelekreb stand before him. They can hardly make out his face in the dark; they wonder at the quickness of the sunset. Piles of documents lie around them. Sensors continue to deliver relevant documents of Lyceum's history from which the men may gleam the proper path to take with Kahn's men.

"Well," Dewey drops the document in his hand. He looks up and slurps on an old banana he had found between the sofa pillows, "It seems much of the plaza has been blown out." His men look at him and say nothing. He continues, "This just means that Kahn is angry. He is hurt. Lost. After what my brother did to him, what could one expect? Hell, the poor kid. We just have to send him some more aid…so he can live. Now that those damn Prioritans have shut down his only water source, we, we have to get him more water. And we have to bring him food."

"We can make sure of it," Yelekreb says, "Hell, I am ready to go out there myself. Bring the boy a coat or something. I feel chiefly born for action! This is what we are all about, right?"

"You seem pretty eager to put yourselves into Kahn's hands," Jon says.

"What do you mean?" Dewey says.

"Well, whatever the causes, Kahn is angry. And he wants us dead—"

"Now, now," Dewey says, "He doesn't want anybody dead. He is just lost and angry, that's all, and after what he's been through, who could blame him? We should send more Posteriorians out to help. Maybe you should go out there yourself, and you will see that maybe they are not as bad as you think. They are only trying to survive."

"Survive? They are only trying to survive? Did you *see* that explosion that almost just killed us? Did Kahn's men build and fire those rockets to our innocent women and children in their struggle to survive? Was this really their intention? Because if it was, then I completely missed it."

"I…I don't think they really want innocent people to die."

"They just sent rockets into a gathering of Posteriorians!" Jon's face begins to redden, "Hundreds of people…*your* people…are dead! And you sit there thinking about what their killer's intentions were? And if you really wonder this, well, they have told you their intentions explicitly with their words. They say they do not acknowledge our right to exist. They say they will not stop until Lyceum is off the map. And you, you sit there making excuses for them more than you would for yourself! So if you can't believe what they tell you with actions, can you not believe what they tell you with their words?"

"Yes," Dewey says, "but you are jumping to conclusions. We did not see where the rockets came from."

"They came from the north! Who else—"

"Listen, my friend! Kahn is only a boy. He has lived his first thirteen years chained to the ground in a cold dark cave. We cannot begin to imagine what that is like, the world he is in. No one can. He knows not what flies in the air nor that water is wet, let alone how to make a rocket. He is like a lonely animal, just beginning the long process to learn by observation to avoid what hurts him and to pursue what gives him ease or pleasure. He is not thinking of you, and he is not worrying about how to kill other innocent people."

"Yes," Yelekreb agrees, "If only the Prioritans could hear such words. It is terrible what they are doing to Kahn and his men. I understand they want to protect themselves, but building a wall and shutting down Kahn's water supply is just piling on more difficulties for Kahn, as if he hasn't had enough already."

"Difficulties?" Jon says, "Yes, they are making it difficult, as you may call it, for Kahn's men to keep terrorizing the innocent world. Perhaps we should all just kill ourselves to make things a little easier for him…so things aren't so *difficult…*"

"Enough! What the Prioritans are doing…you…you don't turn off someone's water supply nor build a wall to shut them out…it's…it's too much! It is a disproportionate response!"

Jon takes a deep breath, but he feels his patience waning. "A disproportionate response…to terror? Is there such a thing? Maybe we should look critically at Kahn's men, since they are the ones at fault here, and they are the only ones who can change this. Instead of mitigating their losses, they deepen them. They may claim that the world has stabbed them, but instead of mending the wound, they twist the blade repeatedly and exclaim 'Look! Look how I suffer!' and they use this as a license to destroy, sucking the world's sympathy forward with one hand while destroying us with the other. We have tried to be patient with them. Some of our men have gone out there with support. And what have they done with it? They could have built irrigation ditches, nurseries, gardens, education. They could have built life...but repeatedly they choose death. And they send us this message everyday, yet we fail to grasp it..."

"But why do you think that is, Jon?" Dewey asks, "I have sent much of our treasury to their aid. You are correct, they could have built themselves. If we are only trying to help them...why do they insist on biting the hand that feeds?"

"Because it is easier to hate than forgive. It is easier to destroy others than to build yourself. And it is easier to blame than to be inspected."

"But still, we must not sink to their level."

"Sink to their level? All that matters is how we have acted throughout our history, and how we will act in the future. The kind of people that we are. But now—"

"Now we need to find it in our hearts to give love and outreach to Kahn's men. He...he is my nephew, and as much as you don't like it..."

"But we have already given so much—"

"Maybe just a little more..."

"Maybe a little more," Jon repeats, shaking his head. He walks out of the house, muttering under his breath, "If the Prioritan's decision to protect themselves is such a disproportionate response, then why hasn't it worked?"

Dewey and Yelekreb look at each other. Yelekreb allows himself a small smile, but Dewey shakes his head. And as the moon slides across a black sky, the men speak of the future. They speak of protecting Lyceum and they tell stories of old, speculating on how to act towards Kahn by learning from their past. They send out more sensors to gather materials from their libraries, and just before the sun begins to rise, they begin to read through long documents and storybooks, re-enacting old Lyceumean wars and fairy tales from the early years.

A nearby rooster crows. The sun begins to rise. Dewey and Yelekreb find themselves sitting in reels of parchment, long after Jon left. The documents are now up to their shoulders. Jon is gone. Sensors are still running into the house like little mice. They almost look funny, pushing wheelbarrows of documents twice as high as their heads. They run into the house, dumping their wheelbarrows of documents onto the two men, and come running out towards the libraries for more just as fast as they ran in, only with their wheelbarrow empty.

"Look at this one here," Yelekreb says as he pulls another document out from under his chin, "Sir Goldmund watched The Battle of The White Plains from atop his horse, high on the dunes near Lake Prespa for two and a half years. During that time, consuming eighteen bags of apples, three hundred bags of oranges, and four bags of starfruit!"

"Ha! Tell me more. We must figure out a way to use this to make a battle plan now, just in case Kahn gets to be trouble."

"Well, let me see," Yelekreb, discards the document in his hand and reaches for another one, but Dewey grabs one first.

"Look here," Dewey says, "Hundreds of years ago, the rainbow child Aisha led an army of Posteriorians north to destroy Macedon. She led them naked, a tremendous cloud of orange butterflies floating over her and over her soldiers like a huge protective shield. El Totsira guided them with a cloud of fire by night and a cloud of sand by day. They fought with fire, but the Macedonian guards were too much for them."

"A woman? Leading?"

"Well, yes....this was years before we understood El Totsira's words about women correctly, as we do today."

"Hm. And they fought with fire? Perhaps we can smoke Kahn's men out of the caves."

"Or here...it says they fought with sticks...I am not sure..."

"Interesting..."

"And best of all, there are pictures of many of the butterflies, look here…most of them are orange, but see how this one shines in green…"

And so the men continue to speak, dwelling over irrelevant details, fancying flavor over fact. They do not notice the passing of time nor the danger at hand. The sun sits high in the sky now and the men return to the palace. As they exit the abandoned house, another wall collapses behind them. They turn around and laugh. They know they are not any closer to any particular plan, but the many ideas in their heads gives them much pleasure, laughter, and peace of mind.

11

Human beings are the only creatures on earth that allow their children to come back home.
Bill Cosby

It is not long after leaving the tavern that Olegna begins to travel home. Alcohol buzzes in his head to slow him down, but the plan in his head moves him forward. Finally, he has a plan! He knows what to do!

Trying to find his way through the Lyceum streets with his head swinging from side to side, his step haggard, ale on his breath, he looks much like anyone else outside at that time. A woman in her fifties (which is quite old, given the Posteriorian life expectancy) looks up at him, her thick legs like tree trunks sticking out from her faded red skirt. Suddenly, her head jerks forward. Her mouth opens and she vomits onto her lap. Olegna can see this is not the first time; there is a pool of vomit to her side. Looking down the street, Olegna can see that she is no exception; hundreds of people sit outside, smoking pipes and smelling flowers and vomiting up their night's pleasures, their eyes staring up at the sky in the dumb wonder of a child.

Olegna continues his march as part of the circus of Lyceum. He walks like all the others, stumbling every few steps, and regaining himself to the next stumble. But unlike the others, his mind is clear. He remembers his home up in the north Apuan Hills: the long, skinny white wooden house with a red roof and blue windows. It was nestled between the step-like roadways and ridges of cut stone, standing on a narrow ridge towards the top of a mountain. He remembers how the white paint was always chipped but never seemed to fade completely, covering the house in a shroud of gray, becoming one with the stony white cliffs of marble around it.

Olegna knows the way. He has walked this way many times in his dreams. He would leave Lyceum behind him and he would feel the warm rainbow glow of the city on his back. He would walk north in a straight line, staying east of Lake Prespa, and resting in Macedon for a night before heading northwest until he was home. This is the route that always made sense. But this time, Olegna has an extra stop to make, so he plans to take a different route.

He approaches the sensor checkpoint without worry; Dewey has given him permission to leave.

"What did you say?" the sensor supervisor doesn't hear Olegna over the wind.

"I said, the king has allowed me to leave," Olegna repeats.

"He...he said you could leave?"

"He has granted me permission."

"Alright. Let me see here..." the guard begins sifting through documents. He wears a pointed hat tied under his chin, making him look like a baby. Necklaces of gold chain hang around his neck, jingling as he walks. Sensors run around him, taking and feeding documents into his hands. "I don't see it here...was this permission ever filed...? Ha! Silly me. Everything is filed. Every word, every thought. On what date was this permission given? Maybe...oh, look at this...this is interesting, did you know that a child ate thirteen lambchops for dinner last night?" the man continues as Olegna's patience wanes. Finally, Olegna slips past the guard (if you can call them that) and is miles away by the time the guard raises his nose from the documents, not remembering why he had studied them in the first place.

The hours pass quickly and Olegna's step does not relent. The plan in his head and determination in his heart pushes him forward. Towards the end of the day, Olegna enters the east end of Cherava Woods. He has not heard of the bears that live in the woods so he is not scared. But when he sees the dark figure of a man following him, fear grips his heart. The man seems like a soldier to him, a bow and arrow in his hands, fresh moccasins protecting his feet.

Olegna begins to walk faster, but so does the man. Finally, the man calls out.

"Hey, you!" he says, "Stop right there."

Olegna's heart stops. The man could be a friend, Olegna knows, but he has few friends that could possibly be in these parts. Olegna wavers, deciding whether to stop or to run. He does not want to get shot now; he wants to live. He has to. He sees the man's thick strong legs, broad shoulders, and his scant but skillfully made garments. Then Olegna's eyes fix on the knife hanging at the man's side. Olegna sees more weapons on his back.

Olegna runs.

He sprints north through the woods. Small branches and leaves slap his face and they slow him down into the hands of the soldier, as if they are on the soldier's team. Olegna hears the whistle of arrows fly by him and images of his home flash through his mind. He sees himself resting in his father's favorite chair, his mother Francesca and father Lodovico sitting with him before a roaring fire. *Are my parents still alive?*

An arrow nicks his ear, landing into a tree before him. Its shaft quivers and he sees the entire point disappear into the tree. He swallows, turns, and keeps running. More arrows fly around him. *How many can one man carry? Or is it one man?* As he tries to run east towards Lake Ohrid, the arrows seem to hit the ground before him, forcing him to turn west, as if the shooter is guiding him *can it be* giving him a way out *but why?*

Suddenly, he comes to a clearing. He can smell the nearby lake water; he knows he is close. But as he tries to continue forward, a soldier drops from a tree before him, blocking his path. He turns, but another soldier drops before him again. There are many of them now, Olegna can see, and they are quicker and stronger than he. They fall upon him, pinning him towards the ground. Before he knows what is going on, Olegna finds that his hands and feet are bound. He is unable to move.

Minutes pass. A soldier runs up behind them, his voice still, "I told the man to stop," Olegna recognizes the man's voice as the original soldier he saw, "I do not know why he is here, in our lands."

"Reinhold," another says, "he has seen our faces. He has heard our voices. You know we cannot let him go."

"I know."

"You know what we have to do."

"I know, Beck. We have to take him in."

"So let's move!"

The men place a black sack over Olegna's head. He does not fight. He does not quarrel. He feared his capture would hurt more than this; he did not think it would be this easy. As the soldiers lift him up on their shoulders and begin to march to their leader, Olegna is glad for the sack upon his face, for he knows the men cannot see his smile.

12

The men of experience are like the ant, they only collect and use; the reasoners resemble spiders, who make cobwebs out of their own substance. But the bee takes the middle course: it gathers its material from the flowers of the garden and field, but transforms and digests it by a power of its own. Therefore, from a closer and purer league between these two faculties, the experiential and the rational, much may be hoped.

Francis Bacon

A large handful of men sit huddled in a cold dark cave. There is over thirty of them there, and most all of the original members are present: Marcus, Martin, Fichte, Schelling, Haigle, Holderlin, Peirce, Schopenhauer, Habermas. The cave is neither large nor small, but just big enough to fit the league of men comfortably. The men wait around a small fire, their shadows flickering against the walls like nervous cutouts of black paper jittering slightly, unsure of where to go.

They stare into the fire and its flames reflect in their eyes, producing many tiny fires in a circle around the cave. They sit and wait as they stare into the fire; some think of their mother's faces, others think of when and how they will die. They each see their own visions in the fire, save a few men near the entrance who dare to look outside. Those men sneak a breath of the cold mountain air. They look out and see the western end of Lake Ohrid's silver lining like the edge of a metal coin cutting into the landscape.

Kahn appears at the doorway of the cave and the men stand. Kahn wears a strange veil across his face. Many of the men have never seen his real face; it is difficult to see through the veil, but they know it helps him to see out of it. For Kahn, it filters out the bright light that partially blinded him as he broke out of O'Talp's cave, organizing the sense data that comes through it so that he can make sense of it.

The men look at Kahn's skin. His rashes have mostly faded now, but one remains on his forehead, sticking up out of the veil.

He enters the cave and sits in his seat. The men gather around him, their ruler-child. They listen to his young tongue as he tries to speak.

"We...have come together over the course of year. But what brings us together is only, ahem, only our common will to do good. I look around me and I see your good faces, come from everywhere all over the world. And I see the good will in all of you, in all of us. I say in all of us because that is where it is—not in some leaf or tree or pebble, and not in some cloud or spirit above, but the good is inside of ourselves.

"And what is this good will? The will to act for the universal mor...moral laws that we know inside of ourselves. Because every man is born with them. He knows. Even I, before I even left my cave to come into the world, before I even knew of the experiences of the world, I saw one shadow engulf the other, and something inside me thought it was wrong. Where did the other shadow go? I wondered. There is an......inherent......is this how you say it, inherent...sense of right and wrong in all of us. And we must have the good will to do the good."

"How do you think that is?" Haigle asks. Haigle is the youngest of the men (besides Kahn). He is small and sickly, but the smartest one of all. The others usually speak over him, not noticing he is there. But Haigle notices all, and he spends much time in great thought, planning how he will improve upon and complete Kahn's teachings later in his life.

"Excuse me. How do I think—"

"How do you think it is that we are all born with moral laws inside of us?" Haigle asks.

"It must come from the one, whoever made us, he must have put it there." Kahn looks up to the cave ceiling.

"And who is that?"

Kahn faces down and closes his eyes. And he whispers, "Summum Bonum."

The men say nothing.

"Uhm," Martin says, "We haven't taught you that word—"

"We are good," Kahn ignores Martin, "In this cave, we are all good men. But the world has not been so good. The Prior—Prior—"

"Prioritans."

"Yes. The Prioritans have not been good. The Prioritans have it wrong because, while we can know things in our minds with certainty, we need experiences to apply them to. Or else they are worthless. And the Posteriorians have it wrong because their world, the world of the senses, the phenomena, is worth nothing unless it is arranged, organized, and…primed by the truths of reason in our minds."

"Truths of reason we have in our minds?" Holderlin says.

"Yes, the concepts of our…understanding. The concepts in our mind through which we interpret experience. And we interpret experience through space, time, cause and effect, substance, unity, plurality, necessity, possibility...but the Prioritans stop at these concepts as if they are enough in themselves, and the Posteriorians don't acknowledge their worth at all.

"Rather, to obtain knowledge, we must take both our inner reason and our outer experiences and we must…synthesize them, by using the former to interpret the latter. Synthesize them, and return them to one. Experience is the river—the liquid of life—and reason is its irrigation ditch. The waters of experience must be guided, sifted, encouraged. It was once this way," Kahn's eyes seem to be somewhere else, "Yes, before it came out of Rekha and split in two. It used to be one.

"But the Posteriorians jump in," Kahn perks up, "and they let the waters wash over them uncontrollably drowning in their sensations. And the Prioritans stay on dry land, dying from dehydration. But it is only by passing through the lens of our rational mind does our sense experience become valuable. Any sense perception that does not pass through the lens of our mind is irrelevant, as we can know nothing of it. And those experiences, I have called noo—noo—"

"Noumena."

"Yes. Noumena. That refers to the sense experiences that may be floating around, but we do not catch them. Therefore, we do not know them. Like the true nature of an object. We can only view it from a certain distance, in a certain temperature, in a certain light. But what is the real object? This we miss completely. It can never be known."

Fichte seems agitated, "But this can be the truth. The way the world really is."

"Indeed."

"But, so you are saying that we can never know the way the world really is? All we can know is how we perceive and experience it, which can be, well, completely false! And not the real world at all."

"Yes."

Fichte throws his hands up in the air, "So why don't we all just become skeptics and let the rest go to hell?"

"Enough," Martin says, "Sit down."

"It is alright," Kahn says, "Fichte is correct, it is a shame. A shame we do not know."

Fichte says, "Just a shame? Is that all it is? I think it is more than that. It says that our consciousness is what is going on in our head—and nothing more. It is not what is happening in the real world—"

"Well, it *can* be—"

"—and it is not grounded in anything but itself."

Haigle shakes his head.

"So what must we do?" Kahn raises his voice, speaking to all the men at once, "We are good. But the world has not been so good. The Prioritans sharpen their tools of reason, but they have no experience to work on, and the Posteriorians gorge themselves with experience that they do not know how to accept. Both have not been good. But perhaps this is not all their fault. Perhaps they just suffer from the human condition, a condition that we have been able to surpass.

"It is hard for a man to be good in the absence of external aid."

"Yes," Haigle says, "Are you going to tell us what we should do?"

"We must be that external aid. We must be a light unto the world. We must rock the ground of Kallipolis, and we must awaken Lyceum from its slumber. Even if it costs us our lives. First we must…we must…"

Kahn's voice stops and he looks up. The others follow his gaze and watch as Reinhold and Beck enter the cave.

"Kahn," Beck says, "I am sorry to interrupt. We…we found a man outside. He was…snooping around."

"Who is he?"

"We…are not sure. We think…we think he may be the artist. From Lyceum."

"Let me see him," Kahn says.

And they bring Olegna in.

ΩΨΩ

Five additional men enter the cave. They carry a bound man on their shoulders, a black bag over his head. He does not struggle. They drop him to their feet. Reinhold and Beck lift the man up and sit him before Kahn.

"We found him in the woods," Beck says, "We don't know what he was doing there, but we were scared to let him go. Who knows what he could have seen? So we took him in."

"I can see that," Kahn says, "Is he alive?"

"Yes," Reinhold says, "I mean, I think so. He has been so still. He did not struggle. It is almost as if…as if he does not mind being captured."

Kahn says nothing, but he nods. He looks down at his hands and clears his throat. Finally, he says, "We can make him one of ours is he is willing and able, or else he shall be killed. But I can bet the latter will be the case."

But when they take the bag off of Olegna's face, Kahn sees the artist's face and he is taken from the moment. He sees a face like he has never seen before; a face carved from the most delicate porcelain itself, a skin of wrinkled glass, a cool white stream flowing down from between the old man's eyes and turning to avoid the rocky cheekbones and falling down on either side of the face's pursed lips. Kahn raises his fingers to the man's face and traces the course of his flowing face down to the mouth with his thumbs. Kahn holds his fingers on either side of the mouth and looks at the artist's old leather lips, two frayed coils, their stitching ripping from the weight of their years. *So…much…pain.*

So this is what men look like in time? Kahn wonders, *Will I ever look like this?* and he touches his own face. But the aging of the artist is lost to Kahn as his blazing blue eyes look at Kahn like flickering stones. Kahn sees the eyes so white but so blue like two granite mountains brushed with a pinch of snow.

"Where are you from?" Kahn asks.

"I come from Lyceum," Olegna says, "But I was just passing through here on my way home to Carrara. I meant no harm—"

"Carrara?"

"A small village in the eastern part of the north mountains in the Apuan Hills."

"Yes, Carrara. I like the sound of that."

"Yes," Olegna takes a deep breath, "I just want to go home," Olegna lies. "If you could let me pass—"

But Kahn does not hear him and Olegna can see by the child's eyes that he is somewhere else entirely.

Kahn says, "I, too, ran away from my home. It seems like yesterday. But so much has been accomplished since then. And it was never really my home. Just the place God placed me into for my beginning. Which makes one wonder, what is a home?"

The men look at their child leader with surprise and deep interest, like men gazing at an incredible animal they've never seen. Kahn feels the men's eyes on him. For the first time, he feels a slight pang of inferiority in his youth. He wonders if this is a normal feeling. What is inherent in age itself that seems to have authority grow with it? He wonders if it is experience. Finally, he pushes these feelings away. He hopes to never feel them again.

"What is a home," Olegna repeats Kahn's question under his breath. But he does not wonder; he only thinks of his own home in the mountains, his parents, his stone statues sitting, waiting for him to arrive at the door.

"You said you came from Lyceum?" Kahn asks.

"Yes," Olegna is glad for Kahn's interest, though he is not surprised, "and it was just about time I left that place."

"What do you mean? What is it like there?"

Olegna smiles. He did not think it would be this easy. "The nation is growing like never before," he looks down as if disinterested, "But that is no matter to you—"

"I want to know everything."

"Yes. For every Posteriorian that has been killed in the…attacks, many more have come to life. The women are giving birth to six babies at a time. The Posteriorians are producing at an uncontrollable rate, like the stars in the sky. King Dewey is unrelenting. He grows mighty in his throne of orange gold and rubies and gems. His greed has taken him and he wants to take over the world," Olegna looks down again and his voice trails off. He wonders if he sounds convincing.

"How do you know this?" Kahn asks, "Why should I believe you?"

"Hey," Olegna shrugs, "Maybe you shouldn't. I don't want to be here," he lies, "I just want to go home. I'm just telling you what I know so you will let me go. Maybe I am lying to you, and maybe not. But if what I am telling you is true, it is something you would not want to ignore, right?"

"There is something missing…"

"What?"

"What is it," Kahn asks, "You have not told me everything. There is something, something you have left out."

"It is nothing."

"It is nothing when I say it is nothing. Tell it to me."

"Yes," Olegna's eyes look into Kahn's, and the face of Disegno blazes inside his head, "Your attacks—*the*…attacks…have turned Dewey's hate towards the north. He has left his throne and has set himself at the top of the needle at the head of Brittany. Here he sits, looking out into the west, and he watches carefully for you, my child Kahn, and hate fills his heart each day like wine used to fill his cup.

Though the needle sways this way and that in the wind, ready to fall off its weak foundations, Dewey sits upon it like a child grinning in satisfaction, studying rats before him, deciphering how he can make them pay for his own amusement. He sits in the needle looking for you. He uses the needle as his eye to the west, and it is one of the buildings the Posteriorians are most proud of."

"Why would you tell me this? Why would you help me?"

"Well, does it look like I have much of a choice?" Olegna nods to his bindings and the guards on either side of him, a blade in each of their hands. "Besides, I left Lyceum for a reason. I would not mind if it fell, for I am just a wanderer, what do I care? I just want to go home. Hell, let Lyceum fall.

"Of course," Olegna adds, trying sound nonchalant, "if the needle fell, the entire nation would fall with it."

Olegna had worried that fear would show in Kahn's eyes and he would shy away. But hate blazes in Kahn's eyes more than Olegna had hoped. It is hard for Olegna not to smile.

"The Posteriorians...well," Kahn seems to hesitate, "What of the Prioritans, the ones who locked me away?"

"Once the Posteriorians have been broken," Olegna smiles, "the Prioritans will fear for their lives, and they will join you. They will see the error of their ways and they will repent. You are a child of Kallipolis, as I understand it, so once the Posteriorians are gone, you will be able to sway the Prioritans to join you. They will remember where you are from and they will see where you have gone, what you have accomplished. And they will change."

Kahn says nothing, but Olegna can hear his thoughts. But Olegna wants to bring them out, for he knows that thoughts do not always lead to action, but what the tongue speaks is always difficult to ignore.

Olegna says, "Dewey has told his nation that he will find you and your men and kill you all. I've heard him say this myself," he lies, "and he vows to have your head for the birds to eat on the top of the needle. He is sitting there now. Waiting for it."

Olegna can hear the fear and anger hiding behind Kahn's voice as he speaks.

"Then the matter is finished. We know what we must do."

"Once the needle crumbles to the ground," Olegna says, "The Posteriorian pride will crumble with it. And the world will fall into your hands."

Kahn closes his eyes. He remembers the soaring crow that followed him for much of his journey from O'Talp's cave. Then he remembers the fire. Finally, he recalls the fiery winged rocket that his men have been preparing. It comes to life in his head, warming his insides in a way he's never felt before.

ΩΨΩ

Kahn thanks Olegna mildly in front of his men but his heart wants to thank him more. Then Kahn turns away and the warm glow of his mission makes his fingers shake. His heart beats with anticipation. He has a way, a goal to show the others how wrong they have been. Oh, the joy of seeing a road before you! Kahn knows exactly what he has to do and how to do it.

The men work hard under the setting sun. Even after the last ray of light has been chased away by the enormous Mt. Korab, the men work, their backs bent in unison as they pass materials forward, shaping the metal with fires and hammers. Kahn sits uphill on the mountain in the entrance of a small cave. He looks on with approval from within the darkness, his veil barely illuminated by the flickering torches of the men far below.

He turns upwards to see flickering stars on a black sky. He looks down to see flickering torches on the black valley. He sits in between and he sees all. Kahn has always liked the dark, where he can see all yet remain unseen. He waits, and days turn into weeks. He thinks of Dewey at the top of the needle *how dare he* looking out *he thinks he can look for me??* and hate grows in his heart. But his eyes always return to the weapon forming below and he feels an intense pleasure of anticipation inside.

It is larger than he had imagined. It is a long, spherical object with the shape of a bird's head at its front, and a wing on each side. On the one hand, it seems incredibly advanced with its exterior of smooth metal sheets. But it also carries a barbaric quality, as wrangled, knotted wooden vines and branches pierce through its metal shell, coming out of the bird's eyes and wrapping themselves back around the metal body.

"It will carry a nice fire," Beck says one day to Kahn as he sees the weapon, "Martin and Marcus have been leading the men's hands. It will make a beautiful blaze in the sky." The excitement in his eyes outshines the exhaustion from lack of sleep just as it does in the other men. All but Haigle work with purpose; the young soldier does what he must to contribute, but spends long hours standing by watching, his head shaking from side to side.

The only one who does not speak the entire time is Olegna. Rather, the artist sits still at a distance. He looks on intently, watching the men in their business as if he has every interest in knowing their job is done. They do not notice he is there, which is strange for these men. Only Kahn remembers Olegna, but he can kill him later, he figures, or make him one of his soldiers if need be. For now all that matters is the weapon, the fiery bird in the sky that will bring them all home.

After just a few months, Olegna can see the weapon come closer to completion. When he is satisfied his revenge on Disegno will finally be carried out to completion, Olegna nods his head in satisfaction. He stands up casually from his perch as if he had been sitting there for just a minute rather than a few months. He looks at the sky and takes a deep breath, turning this way and that. Finally, he sets his feet north. Before Kahn can peel his mind's eyes away from the weapon, Olegna slips out of the mountains to begin his final journey home.

13

The ache for home lives in all of us, the safe place where we can go as we are and not be questioned.
Maya Angelou

How do birds know their way south? Olegna would often wonder as a boy. He would look up at the black birds against the white Carrarian sky, trailing them with his cold blue eyes as they would swirl and tumble like pieces of dark paper trying to find their way home. He would always close his eyes and wish that they would find their way so that they could feel as he felt in his earliest days.

Olegna crosses the Axios River a few miles before it spills off into Lake Ohrid. There he looks for a place to make camp before nightfall. The cold has moved in and tells Olegna he is getting closer. It reminds him of home where it is always cold; he would not know that winter is coming if it were not for the birds flying above. He looks up at them again, trying to find their home. They glide through the air like shadows on a deep blanket sky of ice and glass, sliding, just scratching the surface of exhaustion. But they continue on, guided by their inescapable desire to wrap themselves in the nest of home quickly, before they choke on the loneliness of the wild and go sputtering off their path. It is in this way, Olegna decides, that the birds are just like him.

Olegna finds a good, strong spring just above the small brooks breaking off of the Axios, winding themselves through the trees just north of the river. He makes camp here. Late in the night, he sits by his fire, sucking the bones of a large fish he found in a nearby brook. He watches the Lake Tirreno in the distance, the faraway torches of the Marina de Cararra blinking like yellow eyes. He wonders how his family settled in Cararra long ago, if they had ported at the Marina, and what it was like.

In the morning he sets out again. It is not an easy climb through the mountains and Olegna finds that he is not so young anymore. Nevertheless, Olegna's desire to see his home lives inside of him and it hurries him along. Only two days pass before he can see the northernmost mountains, their homes still standing like little children waiting for him to tell them what to do.

He moves forward and looks upwards. He can see his house now. No, he realizes it is not his house, but merely one of the houses of his childhood. It is the house of his friend, Agostino De Medici. He remembers the day he chased Agostino *run Olegna run* through the woods behind the Medici's house. Agostino was so proud to show Olegna his sculpture *a whale* but it was messy and evidentially the product of unskilled hands. Olegna had turned it over, and Agostino had exclaimed *a battleship* as it transformed into a different object entirely.

Olegna realizes he has been traveling too far west. But his home is close now; he knows the way from here.

Every minute seems like an hour as Olegna trenches closer to home. He wonders how the first month of a walk can feel like a day, and the last day can feel like a month. His feet move faster and faster under him, and it is not much more than an hour before he finally arrives.

From a distance, the front of the house is just how he remembers it. In it, he can see the secret parts of himself, the scars and craters left on the dark side of a broken childhood that imposed their dark chains on his working hands. Everything seems as he left it, for better or worse. But as he draws closer, he sees the windows are broken. The house has not been maintained. All is dark, empty, and silent. Out of the silence comes the one sinking question Olegna has been trying so hard to push away.

Are my parents still alive?

He shivers, the cold wind breathing down his back. He looks through a broken window and sees cobwebs blowing under the wooden stairs like tattered gray flags in the wind.

Of course they are Olegna tries, but he does not sound convincing even to himself. All around, Olegna can smell death. Another cold wind blows. Olegna stops at the doorstep and calls out.

Nothing.

He moves towards the door, taking his hands out of his clothes. He rubs them together and grasps the door handle and pulls. The door is locked. Angrily, he jiggles the door in and out, calling out *is anyone there?* but again he finds no answer.

Olegna inspects the door with his hands. The glass panel is still in place, though the wood of the door is infested with holes. A nearby window is loose, and Olegna tries to open it, but it does not budge. Finally, the glass pane begins to slide, but it falls over into the house, shattering loudly on the floor.

"What is it?" the voice of an old lady cries from deep within the house, "I told you to leave! Please just take what you want and be out with it! Let me be." Her voice lowers into a mutter, more for herself than anyone else. "I don't want to hear you again; I am an old woman," she pauses, "Please let me pass my last days in peace."

Olegna says nothing, but finds it hard to breath. His heart beats against his chest. Finally, Olegna calls out, "Mother?" but it is nothing but a whisper. Quickly, he reaches his arm into the window and opens the door. He rushes inside and the cold air rushes to greet him; it is colder that it is outside.

And in the back of the house he finds her: an old lady lying with her feet up in the corner of a dark green sofa. She is wrapped in a faded tan blanket, and her legs stick out like two white twigs, ending in two old white leather shoes. It is Francesca. Olegna is sure of it.

"Mother!" he cries, rushing forward into her arms.

"Son?" she says, the hint of a smile on her face, "I, I thought it was you." Though her eyes remain glassy and distant, Olegna is glad for the warmth of her old smile.

"No, it did not seem like it."

"No, it didn't, did it?" she smiles, "Oh, oh you're hurting me. I don't need any tight hugs, just that. Yes. I'm okay. I'm okay," but Olegna keeps her in his arms, his eyes closed, thinking only of this moment that has finally come.

ΩΨΩ

In the Lechim house up at the top of the Apuan hills, Olegna and his mother begin to share more than the tea cupped in their cold, aged hands. They share memories as they sit at the round wooden table in the center of the room, their lips moving with the stories of their words pouring into the air with the steam from their breath. A strong fire warms them from the fireplace that Lodovico once built. The windows are fogged and they cannot see outside. For this they are thankful. They have each other and they do not need to look anywhere else.

"Your father died of a heart attack," Francesca tells her son. She can see his questioning eyes, that he did not want to ask.

Olegna says nothing. His face shows no emotion.

"Yes, we were eating fish and wine one day. This was quite a while after you left. And your father, he just…stopped chewing. I, I could tell something was wrong. Lodovico! I called out his name, but nothing. He was still. And then, that was the end. He, your father, was gone."

Olegna looks down and lets his mother speak as if she hasn't been speaking for him, but for herself. Francesca looks to the ceiling, past Olegna. She says, "It was almost as if…you running away was not enough. Lodovico had to die and I was left all alone."

Olegna wishes he had something to say. Suddenly, he remembers what he has been thinking about for the past few weeks. "Oh, mother. How are my darlings doing? Tell me, please."

"Your darlings?" Francesca's eyebrows perk up the way they sometimes used to.

"Yes. My creations. The relics of my childhood. They should be in the shed out back…right? All the stone sculptures I carved when I was young?"

Francesca looks away.

"Mother?"

"They…they are gone."

"Gone?"

"Lodovico…he was angry. He found your letter, Olegna. I found it in his pocket after he died. After he found it, he grabbed his hammer and ran into the shed…and…and…"

"Uhp!" Olegna slams his feet on the floor and stands up. "After all this time, everything I did to get there, I don't believe it! I won't!" He storms a few feet away, then stops, thinking the better of it. "I don't want to hear it," he takes a deep breath and lets a moment pass. "It is okay," Olegna says but his heart burns in his chest. He tries to take another deep breath but finds it hard to breath. Suddenly, he jumps up from his chair and runs to the door.

"Olegna! Wait! There is something, one thing you should know—" Francesca surrenders to fits of coughing. Olegna does not turn around. He runs out the door and across the stony pathways hugging the nearby cliffs. As he jumps over crevices, tears sting his eyes.

Francesca cannot stop the terrible feeling that Olegna is leaving again from weighing on her heart. *Just a few hours* she cannot help from thinking *and then he is off again* but she follows him out the door.

Minutes later, Olegna approaches the door to the shed. He remembers the night he spent in there with his creations. He had smelled his father's drunken breath as he was caught. He touches his stomach, remembering how Lodovico had beaten him *where were you, boy* fists pumping *you don't think I could see that marble on your hands?* blood falling *you think I'm a fool?* but he pushes such thoughts away. He throws the shed doors open and runs inside.

The smell of stone powder still lingers in the air like chalk dust from an old classroom. He stands before his marble studio, strands of faint yellow light leaking through the cracks in the walls. Two bats flutter from under the belfry like clapping hands applauding the artist's entrance.

Everything is broken. Nothing is whole. Olegna can see pieces of his art strewn across the dirt ground: an eagle's head lies in one corner, the once slender arm of a ballerina in another. He can see the axe of a warrior, the marching hooves of a stallion, the perfect lips of a commander calling for battle lies crumbled on the ground by his feet.

Olegna stands still, hoping to become a statue himself. He pretends he is the last remaining sculpture, the only one who will tell future generations what their world used to look like. He is of the most beautiful white marble, but he is dead inside. As the old artist sees his entire childhood smashed into dust before him, he puts one hand over the dead cold in his chest, and holds his breath for the pieces of himself being ripped away.

He hears the shed door open behind him. He does not turn around.

"You have come all this way," his mother sounds old behind him. Dying. "And you have finally come back home. Be with me," Francesca says.

"Is there nothing left?"

"Nothing." Francesca takes a deep breath. "Well," she says, "There is something."

"What?"

"One statue. That is all that's left."

"What? Where? Which one?"

"But you did not carve it here," Francesca ignores his questions, "You created it after you left. But it is here now."

"What? How—"

"Please. Listen. A man, though he did not seem like anything human, he came one day and he dropped something off. His face was so white. But on his face was burnt a strange scar like I have never seen before. He was so…tall. Ominous. Like nothing I've seen before," Francesca shudders at the memory. "And in his eyes was a mysterious…wisdom, but, I could see an evil that he was trying to hide. A strange intensity. A fire was in his eyes like you've never seen. He came all this way, and he would not even come in for some fruit—"

"What did he leave here?"

"Oh, I don't know. I never unwrapped it. I was waiting for you; I thought you should open it if you should ever come back. He wanted you to."

"Where is it?"

"Have you been in Lyceum so long, you've forgotten to see?"

And suddenly, Olegna can see that which he could not before. He can see that the back wall of the shed is not a wall at all, but large gray sheet wrapped around a package by a tight thin rope. Cobwebs have formed around it, but they seem to not get too close to the marble, as if the statue somehow eludes them and they do not want to desecrate its holiness.

Suddenly, Francesca falls to her knees.

"Ooooh," she says, "I am so cold."

"Mother!" Olegna reels around.

"Oh, it is alright. Just hold me, my son. My son. Don't let me go."

Olegna feels his heart about to break. "I am right here. I won't leave you this time. I will stay here…I will stay with you until the end. Just come back to the house. Let me take you, and we can…we can finish—"

"Sh! Listen to me, my child," Francesca brings a hand to Olegna's cheek, "You came back. You came back for me. That is all that matters," she smiles, then looks away, "I have been ill. I am old, Olegna. But I could not die, not yet. I was waiting for you. And God has given me the grace of seeing you alive again. This is all I wanted. That is what I have waited for. And look at you," she holds his hand in hers, squeezing his fingers with surprising strength. "You have become an old man yourself. A good man," she smiles, "But you have to stop running. You must stay here, Olegna, and you can build a garden of creations once again. You can restore this shed to what it once was. And you can live well. And living well, my son, is the greatest revenge one can have. And now, I can rest in peace."

"Revenge? What? Mother! No, stay with me, stay…" but Olegna knows it is over. He feels his mother's body get lighter as her soul leaves *how much does a soul weigh* taking away the little warmth it offered with it.

Softly, he kisses his mother's forehead and lays her body on a bed of hay against the wall of the shed. He pauses just for a moment, looking over the body of his mother. He closes his eyes. But when they open, they settle on the package against the back wall.

Immediately, as if awakening from a dream, Olegna pushes himself up and walks briskly across the shed. He approaches the statue. It stands shrouded, frowning down upon him like a ghost. He tries to look through the thick gray sheet but he looks deep into it and for a moment, the sheet looks like marble itself, its wrinkles handily crafted by the purring strokes of the sculptor's knife like rolling waves on a beach of white. A cool breeze whistles through a crack in the wall and billows the sheet, jolting Olegna from his thoughts. Finally, Olegna unties the knot of the robe. He sees the age spots mottled over his hands. He feels his old age and takes a breath. Grasping the sheet with both hands, he positions his feet. And he pulls.

The sheet comes off quite easily, a thin layer of pastry dough sliding off a white crème dessert. Olegna looks up and sees the only God he has ever known looking down at him.

El Totsira!

It is his statue of the stone archangel demon God, dreamer of dreams, hoaxes of hoaxes, a poet, an artist, a winged rainbow to which all Posteriorians bow. *Welcome back* El Totsira seems to say to Olegna *now did I create you, or did you create me?* Olegna can see the God's eyes are wide open, his eyebrows raised, his lips pursed in a subtle smile as if he sees all. His ears are perked up as if he is listening to the most wonderful music, his nostril flared, his eyes creased with joy. He is in the moment. He is alive. And he feels everything.

El Totsira stands over ten feet tall. He wears a large golden crown on his head. A beaded nose ring hangs from his flaring nostrils. His feet are immense and his thick muscular legs are beautifully sculpted. The antler of a deer and the horn of a bull protrude from his head. His belly swells as if after a good meal, and for a moment, Olegna thinks he can smell a faint scent of peach from his breath. *Was this the way I created him?* Olegna is not sure *but now I have him back. He was stolen from me, my best creation, but now I have him back.*

The old artist turns and looks at his dead mother *Oh Francesca*, her body growing white now. *I lost something but I got something in return.* And suddenly he remembers the one who has caused all of this, the demon who stole the statue from him, embarrassed him at the art festival, and came to his home, terrorizing his mother. But it was this demon, Olegna realizes, that brought back his El Totsira, a package that reminded Francesca of her son, and kept her alive until he came home. Olegna thinks of the demon's ghastly face, his red eyes gleaming behind the rusted black metal bars in his window up in the needle.

He sees his old hammer and chisel lying in the corner of the barn. He reaches out and grasps them tightly with his hands. They feel familiar in his hands, as if they've been there all along. They fill him with purpose, and with purpose comes hope. Suddenly, Olegna finds that a desire within him is strangely satisfied *the best revenge* that he can stop running *is to live well* and that maybe it is time to go home.

His lips tremble and they shout his name.

"Disegno!"

ΩΨΩ

It is at this very moment that Disegno is awakened from his sleep by a distant whistling in the air. *Did someone call my name?* He finds that he is still in his cell at the top of the needle; he was hoping this was all a dream. He rubs his eyes, his fingers cold from the biting rain clouds high above Brittany in which the needle stands *I am too old for this.* He finds that the green paint the guards brought him yesterday had smeared all over his face during his sleep *perhaps by a few hundred years.*

The whistling grows louder. As it gets closer, he can hear noises below the whistling: the twisting of wood and metal, the flapping and whipping of vines, the popping and cracking of burning branches. Still, the whistling of smoke and wind grows louder like a siren piercing the early morning fog.

Disegno looks out his window as he has on every single other morning. But this morning is different. This time he does not see a peaceful Lyceum sky as he has many times before. He does not hear the song of the red and yellow birds, and he does not smell the pollen and meat and honey and fish from below. He does not hear the crowding jury in the High Court below, scrambling like working ants sifting through their evidence. He has lived for hundreds of years and what he sees this morning he has never seen before.

He sees Kahn's weapon flying towards him, a tremendous fiery bird ripping through the sky. It is just as Kahn had imagined. The whistling turns to a scream. Disegno covers his pointed ears, his thin white fingers squeezing together. But the ringing comes from inside his head, and his fingers do no more than contain it. His body wants to fall to the floor but he cannot peel himself from the window. But he does not believe this is the end.

So he stares in horror, a look of disbelief on his face. He sees a young man—one of Kahn's men no doubt—driving the weapon towards him, his arms flailing with victory, nostrils flaring, his mouth calling *die Dewey die* until he grows closer and he can see that this is not where Dewey is at all.

And the two men collide *boy and demon* equally confused, a look of disbelief on both their faces *infant and elder*, the communion of devil and warrior, sin and saint explode in a great blast *the big bang* that started it all *the big bang* that ends it now.

A sound fills the air throughout all of Lyceum, a blast like Lyceum has never heard before. The city shakes with furor. But the needle stands still, its entire head engulfed in flame. It hangs upward from its precipice, unsure what to do next. The streets fill with clouds of dust and stone powder below, people choking and crying and screaming as they run in every direction. For the few who dare look up, they can see guards begin to jump from the needle's windows halfway down, some shouting messages to their loved ones, other singing their last songs to the waiting ground below.

Finally, the needle falls. It crumbles into itself like a deck of cards, disappearing into a cloud of dust that mixes with the tears of the witnesses below. The Posteriorians too scared to run are frozen in disbelief, their eyes fixed to the sky. They do not notice a faint plume of green smoke float upwards from the wreckage below, a green smoke that was once Disegno's body. And for the first time in the city's history, Lyceum is silent.

14

Ours is a world of nuclear giants and ethical infants. We know more about war than we know about peace, more about killing than we know about living.
Omar N. Bradley

On the Posteriorian day of 12.455.3Ø6ð (I believe this is somewhere around the middle of August for you, dear reader), two men run into the southern tip of Lyceum and head towards the Libraries of the Sensors. No one knows who they are, nor where they come from. As they get close, they ignite their bodies on fire. They make clucking noises with their throats and strange noises with their mouths *Khanna, Khanna,* and their shouting puts false courage in their hearts. The few Posteriorian guards at their post jump out of the way as the flaming men break into their libraries, a trail of fire behind them, setting half of the records on fire. Half of one of the libraries burns completely to the ground. Years of diligent recordings lose themselves to a plume of smoke, until a gardener in southern Brittany decides to point his water hose in the right direction.

Ten days later, a man hijacks a horse carriage carrying eight aristocrats from the center of Lyceum for a tour through the Royal Gardens. The man holds a strange blade in his hands. The carriage explodes shortly afterwards, destroying a small part of the garden and scaring the horses out of the nearby stables. The one survivor is a small boy who can no longer use his legs. From his hospital bed, he claims the hijacker was dressed in nothing but a few animal furs.

That night, fifteen Kassahn rockets fly into Lyceum, lighting up the night sky like screaming fireworks soaring across the black curtain firmament, landing wherever they will. One of them explodes before it is launched, killing two of Kahn's men instantly. Seven of them explode in the air before they can reach Lyceum. Four of them land in the farms before the palace, hitting nobody and nothing. One of them crashes through a Posteriorian's ceiling, landing beside his bathtub where he lies playing with himself and dreaming of large women. He stares at the rocket, his eyes wide open with fear. But all he hears is a faint hissing sound; the rocket does not explode. His fear subsides as quickly as it came. He resumes his activity, humming to himself beside the large rocket like it is not even there. The remaining two rockets hit homes in northern Lyceum. The blasts kill two adults and one child, and injure another. When the panic clears, no one notices that thirty sensors have gone missing. They are kidnapped in the dark and held under Mt. Korab as hostages for later use.

Two more rockets fly into Lyceum, killing a roaming dog and his newborn puppy. Three of the rocket shooters die from hunger and malnourishment. Posteriorian funds they had received for food were spent on the rocket. Their superiors pray through the night that the world notices their death and sees their suffering. How much they have given! How low they have fallen!

In Kallipolis, three flaming men come running through the night. They hardly pique the interest of the Prioritan guards watching them from the border. One of the men explodes before he can reach the border, and the guards watch with stone faces as his limbs fly apart. The others break through the border, but once inside, they see nothing but empty field. They scramble around like headless chickens, quickly looking for someone to kill. But no one is outside and no human structure is close. It is desolate; there is nothing here. So they run in circles as the guards watch them like indifferent spectators patiently waiting for the show to end. The two men scream in their wild dance, two flames floating through the night like terrified ballerinas swinging from a string, twirling in fiery circles on a tremendous dark stage. Finally, the two men smash into each other in confusion, exploding with the loudest sound ever heard in the republic. Workers slowly approach to clean up the mess and the guards turn their heads back to the border and resume their watch.

The next day, three rockets fly into Kallipolis. They land in the desolate earth, where two of them explode and one sits still. At the moment they hit, the closest Prioritan is meditating in his mud hut a mile away. The tremor sends a small bird flying from his roof. The sound mildly disturbs him from his thoughts; he opens one eye for a moment and then closes it, drifting back into his world.

ΩΨΩ

Dewey sits on his golden throne in the palace he has spent his entire life. His closest advisors have been wondering about him; he has begun to spend time increasingly alone. The light once shown in his face has dimmed from more than just age. For the last few days, Dewey has been seen strolling through the palace walls alone. He walks with the use of a cane now, and he remembers Renee's cane lying there, waiting to turn into a snake. He wonders where it is now. His old hands tremble with memories as his eyes wander during his walk, gazing at the golden orange cherubs painted on the arced ceilings of the narrow passageways. He once raced through these halls with Renee, he remembers, two young boys playing hide and seek and other nonsensical Posteriorian games. They would make up their own games, spinning themselves in circles to see who will be the first to fall. Dewey can hear their giggles now, spinning themselves around the corridors in a similar fashion as the boys once had. Of course, this was before Renee became different. This was before he became dark. Dewey wonders if Renee had changed or if he was always this way and Dewey had just failed to notice.

Dewey is taken from his thoughts as Jon enters the room.

"My wise and faithful friend," Dewey begins before Jon can speak, "That was great, what you did out there with those bed sheets. Or tablecloths, were they? Blending in with the Prioritans. I like it. What brings you here now?"

"What brings me here now? Really? Have you heard what has been going on? Have you seen our men dying?"

"Well, of course. But have you tasted this caviar?" Dewey points to the dish beside him, "Oh, it looks like I just finished it. I'm sure there is more—"

"I did not come to eat, my king. Seven more sensors have gone missing today. Rockets are still falling on us and they are getting more advanced."

"Yes, yes," Dewey throws up his hands, "You think I want to hear more of this?"

"Well this you must hear. Kahn is on his way. He is coming here with his men. Whether you want to hear it or not. He wants to clean out whatever is left of Lyceum, and he wants to make sure you are dead."

"How can you know this?"

"From our eyes on the border. They predict—"

"They predict nothing! Lyceum has lasted for hundreds of years, and you come to worry me about a gang of hooligans who live in caves? You may leave now."

"The needle has fallen!"

"The needle has fallen six times in my lifetime. We will build it again!"

Jon sighs. "But what if I am right? What if you would just close the border, or put more guards there, and it saves us? How much trouble would that be?"

"Our guardians are enjoying themselves, experiencing their lives as Posteriorians do. I will not disturb such activity—"

"Maybe if you just looked out the window. Just once. You will see buildings in flame, and dead bodies in the streets. Are you going to do *anything* about this? Or are you going to just sit and eat…eat…caviar?"

"Oh, I am already doing something about it."

"And what is that?"

As if on cue, William of Ockham, Gilles Deleuze, and Felix Guattari enter the room with heavy bags in their hands.

"Alright," Dewey claps his hands, "My friends. What have you got for me today?"

Felix is the first to speak. "Show him what you found, Willy."

The men throw their bags before Dewey. Precious stones spill out of them: gems, rubies, pearls, and a few pieces of gold. Another bag, Dewey can see, is filled with beads and fragments of broken colored glass.

"What is this?" Jon asks.

"Oh, this?" Dewey says, "This is what I am doing about Kahn."

"You are collecting beads and pearls?"

"Not just any beads. These are the best in Lyceum, discovered and cloned from deep in the ground. They are for the new wall. See, we are already ahead of you, my friend. We are building a wall to keep Kahn out. Oh, but it will be a beautiful wall—the *most* beautiful wall—for all to see! No one will ever want to destroy it. Even Kahn. We are looking for gems and stones to place in the wall. It will go down in history as—"

"A wall? But Kahn could already be here!"

"I like what you have here, gentleman," Dewey turns to the men, "But let's leave the colored glass out for now. Try to find some more of those pearls…yes, that'd be nice…and a touch of green if you could find it…did you send men out to the seashore? I hear there are some goodies there…"

Jon does not hide his impatience from his voice, "A wall? But…but that is what the Prioritans were building. And you said that it was a disproportionate—"

"What I said, was for then. We change our mind all the time. You knew that, didn't you? Also, their wall was a wall of hate. Ours is a wall of love. It will not just be a barrier, but a beautiful symbol of strength and acceptance that will stop anyone trying to lift a finger to us. It will fill them with awe, and they will come forward in love as their weapons drop from their hands.

"Jon, you have always been the smart one. My helper against me. But now things have changed and, oh…oh! Look at this one!"

Felix fishes a tremendous amethyst from his bag and places it before Dewey. Its deep violet color glitters in front of the king's eyes like rock candy before a child. Dewey can see many reflections of himself in the rock. His heart beats faster.

"I love it!" he exclaims, "This stone will fill with warm sentiment anyone who lays eyes upon it. It's just…irresistible! Jon come here. You see this?"

"Yes. I do."

"Oh, come over here. Would you like to help me look through these?"

Jon crosses his arms over his chest.

"Alright. Listen, Jon. You have to lighten up. Okay, you want me to hear you out. So tell me, you say Kahn is coming right now. He wants to make sure that I am dead. If that is true, then tell me why is Kahn so full of hate."

"Poverty. They do not have the fruit, the women, the experiences we learn from everyday. They have nothing, so they must give themselves something. And hate gives them something. A reason for all their suffering. Hate is a tool they use to turn the blame for their suffering from themselves onto others. They do not have what we have, so instead of building it themselves—which would take work and responsibility—they tell themselves that they don't want it, and that we are wrong for having it. This is precisely why poverty breeds hate."

"Yes, yes, so why don't we give them running water and coffee shops and fancy horse carriages and they will be just like us."

"What? They hate us. We have to be ready for them. We need to smoke them out of their tunnels—"

"Oh, let's see what you have here…" Dewey sees a deep red ruby lying near one of the bags, "Bring me this one. Oh, this will shimmer and glimmer and sparkle from far, far away and everyone will come to see it, and…and…Jon, I am sorry you were saying something? It is difficult for me to speak of worldly affairs with all these gorgeous stones in front of me. Maybe you should come back. But wait. Did you see this one? It must go into the top of the wall. Maybe Kahn and his men will see how beautiful our wall is and they will be in awe and admire us and they won't want to come near us for, lest they spoil it, eh? Eh?" but Jon does not answer. Dewey sifts through more stones, his heart on fire, his mind so entranced he does not even notice as Jon leaves the room.

ΩΨΩ

A lonely boy walks under a fruit stand in the Lyceum market, a veil over his face. He stands just five feet tall. He is skinny and small, so the sellers cannot decide if he is an older man or just a boy. He walks past the starfruits, the mangos and coconuts littering the ground like fallen snow. He stops at a box of plums and peaches and picks up a peach, and his young hands examine the peach's hide. He studies its velvety body like it is a rare jewel that may disappear from his hands at any given moment.

"How much will this be?" he says to the seller.

The seller is one of the larger Posteriorians in the market. He is obese, even for a Posteriorian. He is unable to stand, the customer figures, studying the seller's short bowlegged legs sticking out of his purple robes as he sits on a short wooden stool. The small wooden pegs holding the stool up strain under his weight, creaking with stress and tension at his every move. From under his veil, the customer wonders how the stool can stand even now. He waits for it to break. He imagines it crumbling under the fat Posteriorian, his hairy feet flying up in the air as he shouts angrily at the customer, flailing on the floor like a cockroach, his temper rising with the red in his face.

"Let me see that," the vendor says, grabbing the peach from the young man's hand. He smells it. "Ahh. It is a firm, healthy peach," the stool creaks and croaks and the customer holds his breath, waiting for it to fall, "But it is still young, and has some time before it fully ripens. I can sell it to you for three pieces of silver. Yes…" his voice trails off and the boy can see small droplets of perspiration drip down his face.

The customer smiles under his veil and begins to sift though his purse for silver. A minute passes. Finally, the customer's hands settle on something. But before he can lift them out of his bag, one of the women sitting in the back of the fruit stand screams in horror. The men turn.

"How many times do I have to tell you to shut it? You'll scare away my customers!" the vendor shouts back to her, "You have no right to speak, especially when there is a customer here—"

"Ah! You do not see who this customer is?"

A moment of silence passes as the other male sellers look the boy over. And then the boy speaks.

"Oh, there must be some kind of mistake…"

"There is no mistake," one of the sellers says, "He is Kahn! Our danger of the north! His veil! Get his veil!" Then, they begin to shout their accusations.

"You killed my aunt," one says.

"You killed my three sisters, two of my brothers, and my ma and pa!" another says.

The boy backs away, "You must have the wrong guy. Please—" but he is too late; they grab his arms and pull him back into their shop.

"My veil," he screams, "Please! My veil—" but he can feel the cold silver blade of a knife in his back. His young body wriggles with shock. Just before he lets go of his life, the men pull the veil off his face and he can see them clearly now as he says his last words, "The veil is just a fun mask," and the vendor can see his dead nephew's eyes staring back at him, three pieces of silver glimmering in his open palm.

Miles away, Kahn marches through the northern streets of Lyceum. He is flanked by men on either side. He walks quietly but briskly, his walk confident but comfortable enough that one would not know he is in a rush. Just as the veil hides the young boy's face, the men who surround him hide his body, so one could not tell he is even there. They float towards the Plaza like ghosts, Kahn carrying the men along in his silent way, his eyes just barely open, but his chin straight and upright.

He glides through the marketplace like an acrobat through a circus, mastering the high wire with apparent ease. The flow of currency and produce surround him as he becomes one with it, using it only to quicken his pace when others would be distracted. Few people notice him and still fewer turn and gasp for a second before something else catches their eye and they join their busy colleagues in the alluring circus of sights and smells, relishing them with a deep colorful intensity before they slip away with the end of summer.

The men pass piles of rubble where buildings once stood, their thin walls once weighed down with the intricate terra-cotta ornamentation of the deepest red, exaggerated depictions of gargoyles, flowers, and thorns, heavy enough to tear their walls down into the rubble they have now become. But just as much, the men pass the construction of buildings rising quickly to the heavens like a jumble of vines sprouting upwards, cluttering together over the streets, fighting against each other for air. Kahn is amazed that even in such a time of death and destruction, these men continue to build. They scramble even faster, working and building they know not for what. It is as if, Kahn thinks, it is all they know how to do. Oh, how they build so quickly, with such joy on their faces! It seems to Kahn's men that a building rises in the place of their heels after each step. This only quickens the step of Kahn's men, for fear they will get lost in the construction and find themselves confined, lost in a new building that was not there a moment ago.

Kahn continues, drawing close to the farms just before the palace. One of the last stores he passes has all different kinds of masks on display. Marcus, Martin, and Haigle notice the smorgasbord display: a mottled jade mask glitters in gold while masks of gold-plated porcelain and white clay drip with glittering diamonds and purple paint. Haigle shakes his head, wondering why the Posteriorians put so much trouble into hiding their face behind such intricate things.

Kahn cannot help but look for just a moment; he has never seen such a thing before. Colored faces peer at him, but he finds that they have no bodies. At first, he wonders why they stare at him as such, and he waits for one to blink. But he finds that they have no eyes. They hang from just a string. They have no bodies, no feelings, no souls. But the masks do not seem much different than the people here. Kahn wonders if they are really the same. He looks away.

But before Kahn can look away completely, a row of veils catches his eye. The mask store has them on display too: transparent veils of different fabrics and colors, glittering with fashion. A row of them hangs from a post like a rainbow of yellows and oranges. Kahn can see one of them missing. It has not yet been replaced; it must have been purchased recently, Kahn figures. Some of the veils, Kahn notices, look a bit like his.

Finally, the buildings begin to clear and farmland opens before them. But before they can walk out into the open, someone from a nearby store approaches them. Kahn thought he had heard this person before, and wonders how long she had followed them.

"I know who you are," the woman says, her hands open, her fingers waving like claws, her legs poised in a certain stance, "And I know why you have come."

The men turn around. They are hardly startled as they ready themselves for an attack.

"Please," Kahn says, "Calm yourself. We do not want to trouble you. You must let us pass."

She says nothing, but Kahn can see the incredible anger blazing behind her eyes. He speaks again.

"You have been a victim of a discriminating society—" but the woman shrieks in anger and rushes towards them. She breaks through the men and grabs onto Kahn, who falls to his knees under her weight. Her teeth close onto his ear and he opens his mouth to scream in pain but no pain comes. Her teeth do not tighten. Kahn opens his eyes and he sees Marcus behind the woman, holding a knife to her throat. Kahn can see the slit in the woman's throat like red ink streaked across a fine white parchment, blood pulsing out in rhythm with her fading heart. Marcus lets go and the woman collapses to the floor.

"We must move," Kahn says to the men, "We have let enough time pass."

The men say nothing but they quicken their pace. The farmland lies before them like an open invitation, and after that, the palace, looming over them like a big bully growing larger as they draw closer, their hearts steady with their mission, their hands ready at the waist.

ΩΨΩ

They are not surprised to find the palace unguarded; the guards have run away to better things long ago. They look back over their heads at the dying city. Columns of smoke and flame rise across the city like large trees of fury twisting and turning upwards, raining down leaves of ash and soot upon the haze of flies clouding over the dead bodies that no one ever bothered to pick up. Small explosions emanate from the hot fuss like the sprinkling aftertaste of fireworks moaning their last flashes before disappearing completely. Their light of the destruction shines on the faces of Kahn and his men. But their faces show no emotion. Instead, they turn forward and advance through the palace gates. They enter the gates without hesitation, as if it is their home.

They enter the palace and it is like they are entering a large whale. Some of the men stare in awe and delight. Others turn away in disgust. But Kahn is especially amazed; he has seen nothing this incredible that is man-made. It is like the caves, Kahn thinks, just bigger, smoother, and more comfortable.

The men storm through the outer cardiac chambers of the palace's heart. They move down the beast's long throat hallway, their bare feet soaking in the lush maroon carpet tongue. Kahn drags a little behind, trying not to show too much awe in front of his men. But he cannot peel his eyes from the lush fabrics, the curtains made of ocean blue and gold swaying over each doorway like waves crumbling themselves onto the shore, each revealing yet a new room full of treasures and earthly goods the like of which Kahn never could have imagined.

The men begin to breath easier as their fears of claustrophobia subside. They are used to living outside and the danger of being locked in some foreign building is always carried with them. But to their surprise, they find the palace incredibly open. Large windows fill each wall, rising up to the domed ceilings that are made of glass themselves. Even the elevated crossways that connect each of the three sectors are completely glass, such that one walking through them would seem as if he is flying on air.

One of the curtains blows back in a breeze. Behind it, Kahn can see a fat man sitting on the floor, blood oozing from his severed leg. The end of a rafter has fallen on him from the ceiling. It lies diagonal, touching down upon the man's leg on the ground. Kahn watches as the man's short fingers reach into a tremendous fruit basket. He pulls out a banana and takes a large bite from it, peel and all. For a second, his eyes meet that of Kahn's and he stops chewing. They stare at each other for a moment *man and boy* from the same height. Then the curtain that separates them sways back into its place, bringing the show to a close. Kahn hesitates for a moment, then he runs to keep up with his men.

They venture deeper into the palace. The rooms seem larger now. Of course, they cannot see inside since they are closed behind large oak doors, but the from the height of the ceiling and the tremendous stature of the doors, they can figure just as much. Finally, the long hallway comes to an end, stopping at a pair solid gold doors. The sunlight streaming in seems to point only to the doors, as if it has come through the tremendous windows for the sole purpose of illuminating these golden doors and all who come close. The men squint as the light bathes them. Finally, it is Kahn who reaches his hand up. He palms the domed handle with intense determination and devotion. With incredible strength, he pushes the doors open.

The doors open easily. The gold is surprisingly light. Even more sunlight streams onto the men; it as if they have opened a door to another world. As their eyes adjust, they see Dewey himself, sitting naked on the floor beside his bed, his hands stained with the black blood from a cluster of concord grapes.

"My nephew," Dewey says, looking up like a baby. He grabs a nearby bed sheet of orange and blue and wraps himself with it clumsily.

Kahn stands still, his face motionless. The men's faces around him light up, their eyes opening wide in surprise *he is alive* but Kahn is a statue, his eyes focused on Dewey in cold determination. Kahn's hand moves towards his fur skirt at his waist. He takes out a knife and the blade gleams in his hand.

"You have been sleeping in a sea of experience," Kahn begins, "But you have had it all wrong, uncle." The room is silent, save for a bird chirping outside somewhere in the distance. "And now I must awaken you from your dogmatic slumbers."

"What?" Dewey sits up, "What are you talking about? You are much too serious. Why don't you sit down...have...have a drink," Dewey smiles and Kahn can see two golden teeth shining like coins themselves. Suddenly, the King reaches under the bed, his big butt jiggling from under the gold-trimmed bed skirt too close for Kahn's taste. After what seems like an entire minute, he comes out, holding up pieces of gold. His hands shake from old age, but Kahn mistakens it for fear.

He says, "There is more where this came from. Much more. So let's just sit and talk some business—"

Kahn says nothing. He takes a step forward, grasping the sharp knife tightly.

Dewey rolls over and scrambles backwards on all fours. "Please!" he says, "This is so silly! I can give you whatever you want! Women, wine, meat, money, you name it and it can be yours!" and slowly, Dewey begins to throw the gold pieces *take it take it takeitall* at Kahn. One by one, they land on the floor before him with a clump.

Kahn wonders what these yellow slabs of metal in front of him are for. He wonders what he would want a woman for, what money is, and why anyone would want meat from the fat king when they can go out and catch it fresh for themselves. He sees Dewey's hand shaking with more fervor and he feels confidence consume him like a warm flame. He holds up both his hands now, one to peel back Dewey's head and one to slit his throat with the knife. He can already imagine the red liquid coming from Dewey's head. He squeezes the handle of the knife and takes a deep breath.

Kahn grabs Dewey by the hair and pulls his head back. Dewey screams. The boy's arm struggles with the king's large head like a child with a bowling ball, forcing his dance upon the thrashing fat king below. Kahn brings the knife closer until it gleams before the king's face. Dewey sees the blade and it frightens him. He does not want to die. Not by his throne. Not like this.

But, dear reader, there is something Kahn does not know. But I know. For I was there when Posteriorians built the palace centuries ago, and an old woman came to decorate the royal hall that was now Dewey's room. She was just finished when her rooster ran off through an exposed duct. She followed her rooster and came to a cool area partially underground. Snakes lived there, she saw, in the cold wet stone room that she found. When she showed the room to her superiors, they cleaned out the snakes from the room. Seeing that it would make a wonderful second room for their king, an attachment to his room that he could wander to cool off from the Lyceum heat, they ordered her to clean out the room and make it nice. She did so feverishly, installing a small door with a lock for privacy and bringing in lush carpet and a full bed, hoping to impress her superiors. The room became secret hiding place for every king: a place where they could go the few times their Posteriorian hearts wanted quiet.

She never saw her rooster again.

Kahn tightens his grip on Dewey's hair. He brings the knife closer. Suddenly, and with one fell swoop, Dewey raises his legs and kicks Kahn back. Hard. His men run to catch him. But by the time they recover, they find Dewey has slipped through the small wooden door into the other room, a room they did not notice before. They hear him bar the door behind him. They run to the opening, but it is too late. Kahn stands back, his anger burning inside him, as Marcus begins to kick the door. Martin and Reinhold rush to help him but he pushes them away and begins to attack the door like it is his worst enemy. Kahn closes his eyes *I was so close.* He cannot see the deep red hue wash over Marcus's face but he can hear the terrible thumping sound, the popping of bones and the roughing of skin as Marcus surrenders himself to killing the door and getting to Dewey *after all this time* until the other men manage to hold him back *enough Marcus* pinning him to the floor *enough.* Kahn takes a deep breath and turns around to the wall. He sees Haigle in the other corner of the room.

"Well, we could just wait here," Haigle says, "He has to eat. He can't stay in there forever," his arms across his chest, his head shaking in disappointment.

ΩΨΩ

Dewey hugs his knees and curls into a ball. He turns his head sideways to avoid the low ceiling and he looks out the tiny window between its metal bars. He listens to the banging on the small oak door. He studies the wooden boards as they vibrate with the shock of each blast, dust clouds spitting into his face like tiny needles, the small black metal ring handle rattling with each blow. He feels his heart beat against his chest and wonders if it will break through before Kahn's men do. Finally, he walks to the far side of the room, sits on the floor, faces the wall, and waits.

Dewey learns to tell the passing of time by the rhythm of the blows. After a while, they sound like footsteps to him, each following the next in song like a perfectly expected event. Twenty minutes pass but for Dewey it seems like hours. Dewey shivers. It is cold here, he realizes, much colder than up in the main room. He hugs the bed sheet around his large body, wondering why he does not have any clothes with him. He cannot remember why he was naked when the men broke in.

He cannot remember much these days.

But in this moment Dewey can remember his brother. He remembers the time they climbed up on the roof of the palace to look at the stars. The family was sleeping, but if they were caught Joachim would have beaten them good. Dewey looked up in awe, dreaming he was one of them, just floating around the luminescent sky free of any trouble in the world. But all Renee could say was, "Step away from the edge of the roof, brother. We do not want you to fall." Dewey had admonished Renee in his heart for that. But in the end, Renee could have saved his life.

Are we really that different? Dewey then remembers the woman who saved him from the quicksand. *We are all driven by necessity, my boy* she had spoken to him *and necessity can overcome the reason of the Prioritans or even the experiences of the Posteriorians.* We all are doing the best we can.

There is a tiny window with metal bars next to Dewey. Suddenly, a dove lands on the window ledge. It cocks its head to the side plainly, greeting Dewey with mild curiosity. The dove is so pure and so white, Dewey can see, that it must have come from the north. It must have come from Kallipolis.

The banging on the door continues, but Dewey does not hear it anymore. His eyes scan the room for something, a way out. Suddenly, his eyes fix on a bright object on a dark corner of the room. He squints and sees that they are orange peels, shriveled and hardened from years of age. He reaches towards them and picks them up, studying them intensely. He does not know why. Then, something clicks: this is near the room where it all started. These are the orange peels he blinded Renee with.

Oh, Renee!

Yes, this room must be adjacent to the room that Renee would sometimes climb down into to get away from the world above. It must be just behind this wall! The room he would often sleep in, the one that Dewey snuck into one night to blind his brother. But how did the peels get here? A mouse must have moved them here through a hole in the wall. But was this just by chance? Nevertheless, Dewey holds the orange peels in his hands from so long ago. He is glad to see them, but he does not know why.

Dewey looks back at the dove in the window. It seems to be waiting for something Dewey cannot tell. Dewey looks from the dove back to the orange peels, and back to the dove again. Suddenly, as if El Totsira is sending him a message at that instant, Dewey knows what he is supposed to do. Quickly, he finds an old feather on the ground, left from a scrambling rooster long ago. He holds the feather in one hand and peels back the bed sheet clothing the other. He presses the sharp stem of the feather hard into his skin until blood rises from the wound. He places one of the orange peels before him. Dipping the end of the feather into the bloody wound like a quill, he sets himself to work. He writes his message on the orange peels as the dove watches approvingly from the window above.

15

I am a prince I have it all, and I hear your footsteps on the wall, I wait in silence for your call, and take a shot and watch you fall.
Trey Anastasio

The sound of falling rockets is nothing new to Renee Don Cartez, but this one sounds too close. It begins in the middle of the day, when all Prioritans are alone in their respective huts to seek refuge from the hesitant chatter and little earthquakes of nature that dares disturb their peace. As the tickling fingers of nature stop at their doors, they withdraw deep into meditation, living in the different worlds of concepts and ideas in their minds. Almost half the nation is in the process of fasting at any time, eating only what they need at night for three months out of the year. The others know not to speak to them. This is not difficult since they hardly leave their small mud huts, if ever to relieve themselves in the bushes, or catch a breath of air.

Renee has recently completed a phase of fasting himself. He sits cross-legged on the floor of his hut, eating rice, cabbage, and a special blend of barley water the woman who cleans his house made him. Katie, he heard her being called. But Renee wants her to leave. She is a distraction, he tried to explain to Nicolas, but Nicolas would hear nothing of it.

"Just ignore her," he said, "She is so quiet, you will not even know she is there."

"But what do I need this for? Her presence may disturb me."

"You may sit on the floor like everyone else, my friend. But you are still a king and your floor should be clean. You must have something to remember that, whether you like it or not, you are a king. I am sorry, but you must be treated like one. Besides, she will not make a sound."

Nicolas had been right, Renee sees, the woman is quiet. She is only there when needed, stepping out of the way as Renee asks. But there is something wrong about her, Renee senses. He cannot get it out of his mind. Usually, he has a sense for these things. When Renee is in the world of his mind, even the sound of a loud brass band will not disturb him. But this woman, *that woman,* her presence always seems to weigh on Renee's shoulders, as if she is always there looking over him. Even when she is gone, her noise lingers. It is not clear to Renee. A fog. When he feels her presence most, he looks over his shoulder. But she is never there.

But this rocket is. The droning grows louder as it nears his hut. His clay cup of water begins to tremble, spilling the drink onto the mud floor. But Renee does not want to leave the peace of his mind. He does not want to wake up. He does not want to move. Finally, he opens his eyes. There are no windows, so he would not be able to see the rocket even if he had the gift of sight. But he can hear its scream with his entire body. This rocket is louder than all the others have been. It is about to hit his hut, and his old body does not seem to want to move fast enough.

The Kassahn rocket closes in on his hut, a trail of fire behind it. It whirls around like a released helium balloon gone horribly wrong, looking for a place to strike. It almost pauses like a snake before its strike, deciding when to move in. Then, as if focusing on Renee's hut from all the others, it turns and shoots down from the sky like a fallen star. The walls begin to tremble and clumps of dirt falls from the roof. *It is my time* Renee thinks, closing his eyes and rubbing his aged hands together *I just did not think it would end like this* his old body accepting its fate, unable to escape in time.

Renee hears the blast. The ceiling opens up above him like a great divide. Through the sounds of screaming metal, Renee is thrust outside. He closes his eyes and waits for the pain, but there is none. But the woman's hands are on him, and she is carrying him out the door. Katie had dropped the broom and grabbed Renee, he realizes, at the last second, and pushed him outside, out of harm's way.

Renee falls onto a sharp stone a few feet from his hut. He grimaces and looks up to feel his hut burst into flame. Of course he cannot see, but he hears the popping and crackling of the fire and feels the heat on his face. But the woman's fingers are there, cooling his face with their genuine care.

"You, you saved my life," Renee says his first words to the woman who cleans his house.

"We are not done yet," she says, examining his legs. The sounds of more rockets fill the air.

"Oh, these rockets!" Renee exclaims, "They have not disturbed the peace of Kallipolis. But it has not been easy."

"Nothing has been easy."

"I know I am not supposed to feel. But I fear for my life." And as he says these words, he knows they are true. He cannot believe he is confiding in this stranger what he could never tell anyone else. He wonders why. He tries to stand, but his legs cannot find the strength.

"I need my walking stick," Renee collects himself, "Before I die, if I die, I need to be with it. We must go get it right now."

The woman says nothing.

"I need my walking stick now," Renee says, "Where is it?" Renee asks.

"It could be in Lyceum by now."

"What do you mean?"

"Your walking stick is gone."

"What? What do you mean?"

"It has moved from its place."

"But that is impossible. Ever since Dewey threw it down, I commanded that no one touch it."

The woman says nothing.

"You are not saying…it did not turn into a snake?" And as he says it, he remembers his brother's men in The House Of Wax *El Totsira has commanded you to let my nephew go,* Dewey's arm throwing down his staff *to prove it* with silent fervor *it will change into a snake.*

The woman does not answer.

Renee says, "My God. I need to…someone needs to tell my brother. If he is still alive." As he says these words, he is suddenly overcome by the misery of it all. He feels tears begin to sting his eyes. "Oh, what is the point? What was the point of all this…separation? If only I could tell my brother. If only I could see him one more time…just one last time…" but Renee's voice trails off.

"He is not your brother."

"What?"

"Dewey is not your brother, Renee."

Renee says nothing.

The woman continues, "He is not your brother."

"How can you know that?"

The woman looks at Renee and he can feel the hesitance in her eyes.

Renee struggles to speak, "Tell it—"

"I am your mother."

"What?"

"Oh, Renee, my boy. My baby."

"Katherine?"

"Yes. It is me."

"But, but, no. This is impossible. You passed away years ago. I remember. You died of tuberculosis—"

"No, I died from fear. I was not strong enough, not brave enough. I allowed myself to be exiled from our nation. Lyceum. We were not good enough for Joachim, you and I. We were not…Posteriorian enough. After I brought you from my womb, they banished me. They brought Helene and her son Dewey in to…replace me. To give you a life. To make you…normal. But Nicolas found me and took me in. He brought me here and together, we waited for you. We waited a long time. And you found us!"

"But, I am so old. You must be…how can you still be alive?"

Katherine smiles, "You have made miracles happen yourself, my son."

Renee faces the old woman before him. He cannot believe she lived in his house this entire time, picking up after him, sweeping his floor—his own mother! What a lie! This is no mother, Renee decides. He looks past her at the skeleton of his hut, now a small pile of dirt remnants melting like twigs in a screaming fire. He stands up and says, "I do not need my walking stick to get up. I can go alone now." He turns and storms away.

"Son! Come back."

"Stop calling me that!"

"I do not have much time left," she says.

"Then you should have told me earlier."

"Please. I let you walk away from me once. I could never bear it again."

And where did it get me? I've been running my whole life.

Renee stops. He turns around slowly. The dam of his mind begins to break and a torrent of tears unleashes itself down his cheeks. For the first time in his life, it is all too much; he surrenders to the tidings of his heart.

He falls into his mother's arms.

Her arms close around him like a cocoon. He feels protected. He feels home. He remembers the feelings he had for Elizabeth *is this what they call love* and realizes he has not been so good to reason as he could have been. But has it been so good to him? Oh, if only Dewey could see him now! He remembers Dewey's rosy cheeks and golden curls, how it secretly excited him as a child, how he would steal a glance at his brother's laughter, his eyes resting on Dewey's face just a little longer than the others, just a little longer than necessary.

Renee's face twists with pain, reeling with regret.

"Oh, Renee! What is the matter?" Katherine asks.

"Oh, mother! They said…" Renee tries, "They said it was me. They said that I killed you. I mean, they never said it explicitly. But I could tell. From their eyes. They all thought it was me. That the birth…that I was too much. They said it…they said—"

"Sh! Shhh. I know," Katherine holds Renee tight, "But it was you, Renee, that gave me life."

Oh, how Renee wishes he could see Dewey one more time! If only he could tell him that the staff turned into a snake, that he was not so wrong after all, that they are not bound as brothers, that things can be okay again. Renee wants to tell Dewey all of these things, but Dewey is so far away.

ΩΨΩ

Bang, bang, bang! Marcus begins to kick the door again. His foot crashes against the small oak panels, his leg swinging back and forth like the pendulum of a grandfather clock. The black metal hinges rattle with each blow, and after some time, it seems to Kahn's men that the door just may give way.

Kahn puts a hand on Marcus's shoulder. Kahn does not need to say anything; Marcus stops kicking the door. He steps away, letting Kahn take his place.

"Dewey! We are going to give you one more chance," Kahn says through the door, "Sure. We want to kill you. But do not think of it as dying, my uncle, but rather think of it as living. To be born, first you have to die. You have freed me from the Prioritan way, and you have shown me the value of the sensations. You have awakened me from my dogmatic slumbers, and thus, I must do the same for you. You have it all wrong, trying to experience all you can with no structure, no formula through which you can weed out knowledge from the overwhelming stimuli. Oh, what a burden you must have! Forcing yourself to choke on the vast amount of sensations you experience everyday, scrambling to fix your attention to each fleeting one as it demands your attention and then floats away for another knocking on your door. Oh, to have to live through that; I can never guess what that is like. I only know its opposite. But this is why we must come together, you and I. Perhaps this is why I am here. Oh, how terrible it must be for you to sift through all that living demands! Especially when it is not the way. But I will show you. If you let me, I can take the confusion away. I can free you from your burden. Yes, I can bring the red liquid from your head. And then you will see. And then you will be free. Both with the eyes and with the mind.

"I implore you, good King, let us in!"

Kahn falls silent. Not a sound is heard. Kahn sighs, looking down at the floor. "Marcus," he says, "Resume your...activity."

Kahn steps back, Haigle and Schelling beside him. This time, it does not take long for Marcus to break open the door. On the third kick, the door crumbles inwards like a rotten cardboard box. Powder from the rotten wood floats up and the men cough. Holderlin steps up and scrapes the opening with his foot, clearing the passageway for the rest. He climbs through the opening first, Marcus second, the Kahn and the rest of the men, with Haigle following in the rear.

After the weightless light of the palace showering them freely, this new room thrusts itself upon the men like a horrible surprise. The wet darkness fixes itself upon them like the wet kiss of a black toad. They wait for their eyes to adjust.

If they could not tell from the rotting wooden door that the room was built a long, long time ago and has not been visited frequently, they can tell from the room itself: long, thick strands of ivy and moss grow up the walls, hugging the old stone like two lovers in their silent dance of old age. There is a thickness in the air, a wet smell like a dirty bog.

From behind their veil, Kahn's eyes are the first to adjust. He is the first to gaze upon the room. He notices a white feather on the windowsill lying there like a fresh white flower. And below the window, he sees King Dewey sprawled across the floor on his back.

"Dewey?"

But the king does not answer.

"Lord King? Get up! Face us!"

But he is still. His body is as white as a naked chicken, the color from his face is disappeared. He looks like a different person entirely, nothing remotely Posteriorian.

Haigle kneels before the king, lifting up the king's hand. He drops it, and the king's fat arm lands with a dead thud on the soft ground. The king is dead, the men can see. But it is Kahn who sees the two puncture holes in Dewey's neck. Something must have bit him, Kahn can see, something that could kill in minutes.

Suddenly, the sound of a slithering snake strikes from the corner of the room. Kahn's eyes dart towards it and he can see the snake, its body long, thin, and straight. As if it knows it is being looked at, the snake stops. It turns to the men. It lifts its head and looks at the men, its tongue slipping in and out of its mouth. Its jaw opens and it sneers at Kahn, meeting his gaze eye for an eye. Fear grips the hearts of the men and they step back. But Kahn does not flinch. He opens his own mouth, moving his tongue like the snake's, a subtle smile on his lips.

Finally, the snake allows itself one last sneer and then turns around, slipping under a crack in the wall. It is at that moment that Kahn can see that the snake is not brown nor gray, but exactly the shade of a wooden staff.

The men remain silent, wondering what they have seen. But Kahn says nothing and his silence speaks to the men. The king is dead. This is why they have come to this place; there is nothing more they can do. Kahn does not know the meaning of the snake, nor where it came from, but somehow he feels that things have happened as they were supposed to happen. Somehow, he knows that Dewey has died from his own revelations, that in the end, his own way of life did him in. With slight hesitations in his mind but a strange contentment in his heart, Kahn turns and leaves the palace behind.

"Our time is done here," he whispers, but all the men hear. "We have done that which we have set out to do. We will gather all of our people from the corners of this world. It is time to go home."

He sets himself north, to the Apuan caves, his men following him faithfully into the heart of the setting Lyceum sun.

16

"Why Yes," Narcissus continued, "Natures of your kind, with strong, delicate senses, the soul-oriented, the dreamers, poets, lovers are almost always superior to us creatures of the mind. You live fully; you were endowed with the strength of love, the ability to feel. Whereas we creatures of reason, we don't live fully; we live in an arid land, even though we often seem to guide and rule you. Yours is the plentitude of life, the sap of the fruit, the garden of passion, the beautiful landscape of art. Your home is the earth; ours is the world of ideas. You are in danger of drowning in the world of the senses; ours is the danger of suffocating in an airless void. You are an artist; I am a thinker. Goldmund, let me tell you today how much I love you, how rich you have made my life. It will not mean much to you. You are used to love; it is not rare for you. My life has been poor in love; I have lacked the best in life. If I know nevertheless what love is, it is because of you. It is thanks to you alone that my heart has not dried up, that a place within me has remained open to grace."

Hermann Hesse

I must apologize to you, dear reader, for while I have told you this story I have been focusing on the characters within the narrative and I may have turned my back from you. But perhaps this has been most appropriate, seeing that there is good chance you have forgotten me completely. But do not think because of your forgetfulness that I have ceased to exist. I love you, but it is for this very reason that I must tell you that things are not always in this world as they are in your mind. For example, you think that I am almost finished my story as the back cover of this book seems a lot closer than the first, the pages in the end getting fewer, your false confidence getting louder. You think you are almost at the end. But you forget that I am not finished yet, and thus I can change my story this instant, narrating far into the future such that the next time you pick up this thing you call a book, it may seem a whole lot thicker. I can do mostly anything, for I am omnipotent and powerful. I see everything, and you, well, you do not even know who I am.

Even now, I look down upon my beloved movers from above. I watch Dewey's body lying still in his palace, his golden face motionless for the first time, his rosy cheeks faded into a pure white parchment with nothing on the page. The body of the large king lies still, an ashen stone statue of pure white save for the tiny red arteries still visible on his perfectly round belly like tiny hairs of scarlet on a dome of snow. But his soul retains its color as it rushes up towards me, its jellyfish tendrils laughing as they whip out, draw themselves in, and whip out again like the tentacles of a retreating octopus, splashing winged tears of rainbow sugar on its trail like a thousand butterflies rising to my throne. It is almost here.

I see Olegna, the artist, the seeker, the sculptor, the creator. He stands tall over a block of stone in a dilapidated barn high in the Apuan Hills. His arms shake with old age, but his fingers work skillfully as they carve life from the stone. Olegna becomes like me as he creates a world from nothing. He works intently, with purpose, digging, scraping, cleaning, and studying his works and beginning another anew. He knows these are his last days. He knows he will join me soon. But he continues on, creating new life as his own diminishes, like Rekha always did. Beside him I can see numerous new creations: a little girl dancing in a red dress, a bald eagle perched upon a rock. Standing tallest before him is the great El Totsira, magnificent in white stone.

Olegna turns towards this sculpture, his knife raised in his hand. *Synthesize* his heart says *and return things to one.* His hands sculpt a three-legged spider standing tall upon El Totsira's shoulder, meeting the archangel's eyes in partnership and mutual understanding. Now Olegna cannot see this statue standing in the center of Lyceum years from now. But I do. I can see it quite clearly in the distance, streams of Posteriorians and Prioritans standing in unision around it in the Lyceumean square, laughing, sharing, speaking, throwing flowers and lighting candles at its base. But today it is enough to see the hint of a smile on the artist's lips, rising with his arms as he works. It is the smile of purpose, of utilization, of potential being filled even as the life behind it begins to fade like an old dusty flame.

I look back up in my world and I see the black mark in the distance, the stain in the heavens that used to be Disegno. He is not quite as high as I, though he is not in the lower world either. He is in between—lost—as he has been here a few times before, his tongue snaking in and out of his fangs of his gaped mouth. Now he floats far in the distance, one black spot in the ether floating together with millions of other souls like stars in the sky, some far and wanting, and some close, joyously bathing in my light. He will be wandering for some time, I imagine, perhaps making it up here eventually, or finding another form to infest down below. He has not made it up here before, and even I do not know if he will.

I look down upon the Republic of Kallipolis, so straight and honorable in its simple demands. I see Renee sitting on the floor in a small dark room in the back of the House of Wax. The sun has mostly set behind the Apuan Hills, but it stretches itself heavenward in one last great effort, splashing hairs of light over the horizon, barely kissing the wax walls of his room with light.

I watch as Renee lies down on his back in a room of his own. His eyes stare upwards and even though the life has gone from them long ago, I feel he is looking right at me. Thoughts weigh heavily upon his heart *how I wish I could see Dewey once more* as he feels the cold iron grip of his brother's death take a hold of him *he is the only one who knew how to live*, squeezing the desire to live from his heart *so why must I be the one that is not asked to die?*

Though he is blind, Renee closes his eyes and he sees everything: a rosebush of thorns so sharp, glistening their yellow-green stems over roses of red and orange tumbling through the summer breeze. Dewey's deep blue eyes smile through the roses. His eyes are framed by golden curls as the roses are by their leaves, waving at Renee *come play* chiding him, singing him their songs of life. Oh, how odd it is, Renee thinks, that it is only Dewey who knew how to embrace this world, yet it was Dewey who must be taken from it. Oh, the ugliness of things! The injustice! Yes, Renee knows he still breathes in the air of life. But it feels ugly in him, like a dead man's slippers on his murderer's feet. It is not real. It is a counterfeit life, the mask of a reward he did not earn.

He does not want it anymore.

"Oh, God," Renee whispers to me, though he does not know I listen. "I am ready. I am old and I have erred with my brother. I have no more reason to live. Take me, God. Take me as you will."

I summon my aides and they come to me, El Totsira grinning contently on my left and O'Talp trembling with humility on my right. Their wings flutter in unison, wings of color and wings of transparency flailing wildly to their great dance in the sky. And together, we look down upon our last child, the philosopher-king. Renee lies quietly, closes his eyes and takes a deep breath. His soul begins to flurry upwards with surprising obedience, but his body begins to react, holding onto its soul with a firm grip. The soul begins to apply pressure, squirming this way and that, searching for freedom like a snake caught in an ugly trap. Instinctively, I begin to twitch downward to meet it like a magnet to its match, my arms contracting downwards, descending just slightly before regaining their posture under my command.

But his mother is there, lady Katherine standing over her son with a heart still pumping life through her ancient body from the finger of O'Talp high above. She pleads with her son to live, but he does not bend.

"I am no longer good," says Renee, "It is time for me to go."

"But look at me," Katherine kneels behind him and places his hands in hers. Her gray eyes look to meet his, but the king's dead eyes stare straight up, as colorless as the wax ceiling to which they gaze. "I am still alive," Katherine continues, "and a mother should never have to bury her own child."

"But I died a long time ago, do you not see? This world is all around me, this world of life, but I deny it. I place locks on my senses and I deny it is there. I am not fit for this world you have brought me into, mother. I never was. So please, let me take myself out."

"But your brother lived for you! He lived for all of us."

"He was not my brother."

"He was sent to you, was he not?" she says, "For what is a brother anyway?"

Renee says nothing.

"He was the color of your life. He lived for all of us, Renee. And now you must take over. With your time left, whatever that will be, you must show him what he has taught you, what his life really meant. You must show all of us. And then, and only then, your time will be complete."

Renee breathes deeply and licks his parched lips. He opens and closes them slowly, tasting the taste of life one last time, letting it linger, as if deciding if it is good. The distant sun settles its yellow haze behind the distant hills, retreating itself from the walls of wax. The room falls completely dark. And Renee speaks.

"No. My time has been complete long ago. My time has been complete since I made powerful choices in the right direction, but forgot how to live."

Katherine stands up in defeat. She looks across the room and lets a moment pass before speaking again. The faint rumblings of distant rocket explosions sound in the background like muffled whispers. Silence returns and the room grows colder.

"Very well," she says, "You will go to sleep now. And Kahn will have had his reign over both Lyceum and Kallipolis. Perhaps this is what you wanted. I do not know if I will live forever, but I will do everything in my power to avenge your death. And one day soon, Kahn's reign will end."

"What if you can't? What if he is too strong?"

"Well one day, perhaps far after I have passed from this world, there will be peace. But this can be only when Kahn stops the killing of others and begins the construction of himself. This will only be when Kahn learns to love his children more than he hates ours." Katherine looks at her son one last time. Though it is dark, she can see no emotion on his face. Suddenly, she sees something glisten in the dark near Renee's face like a liquid jewel. Katherine wonders if it is a tear, but it is gone. She turns away.

"One day," Renee says, a tremor in his voice, "I can forgive Kahn for killing my sons. But I can never forgive him for making me kill his."

Renee closes his eyes and listens to his mother leave. He waits, lying still for me to come and take his soul. I give O'Talp the choice to do as he will, for Renee has been his subject, so he must be the one to choose. El Totsira chose death for Dewey because the king had gone too far. But now it is O'Talp's time to choose. Trembling in fear, O'Talp begins to descend. He cannot resist Renee's pull. The words of death are on his lips and he readies himself to destroy the mind he has always nurtured. Renee remains motionless, readiness on his face.

Suddenly, a bird lands on the small window. A dove of the purest white. Renee tries to ignore it, but it disrupts his concentration and stops O'Talp in his tracks. Usually Renee's mind remains steadfast, but there is something different, Renee feels, about this bird.

A feeling.

Renee opens his eyes. He sees the white dove on the windowsill. It holds an orange peel in its mouth. His eyebrows wrinkle with curiosity. It is the bird the Prioritans decided to send out, Renee recalls, to see the state of things in Lyceum. Renee smiles as he feels the orange peel, which tells him that the Posteriorians are still planting.

They will be okay. They will rebuild, which is what they are best at. Only this time, the city will look a little different than before.

But the bird cocks his head this way and that, waiting for Renee. Slowly, and with great curiosity, Renee sticks out his hand. At once, the bird drops the orange peel into his hands. Closing his fingers around it, Renee realizes this is the orange peel that cost him his sight. But rubbing the inside of the peels with his thumbs, Renee can feel that it is different. He can feel the dried blood of his brother. Dewey's blood is written on the peels in faint lettering that does not take Renee long to read.

My entire life, I have
lived to feel. My time is
ending now, but that is

okay. I know you are my
brother, and it is only
love I feel now.

Rubbing his thumbs up and down the crusty lettering, Renee reads it again and again. His fingers press into the orangey leather skin like an old man squeezing his wife's hand. After a few long minutes, Renee puts the peel back onto the windowsill. The bird looks at the peel, then at Renee. Renee feels tears covering his cheeks, something his cheeks have not known for years. The bird turns away as if not to embarrass the old king. It flies away to the fluttering of wings. Renee listens as it bleeds into the blue sky like a small white stain fading into the deep atmosphere of space.

Renee feels sadness overwhelm him. For a moment, he feels as empty as the day he was born. He does not know what to do. He turns his head to the side in defeat and behold! he senses a small orange flower sprout from the ground before him. But it is only partially orange; every other one of its petals is white. It begins to blossom slowly and it reminds Renee *to be born* of the bleak absence of life this past winter *first you have to die.* Then blue ones, green ones, and white ones join the fray and they stand around him like friends.

And in that moment, a joy overcomes him. The thrill of action, of completion, of purpose, of *life.* Renee opens his eyes. Spring is coming now, the emergence of new life. He can almost see the flowers blooming, the birds and bees of his childhood summers, and it is like he is seeing it for the first time. He wonders in awe at the amount of knowledge he can learn by living with the world just enough to reap what he needs. He blesses his time left in this world, and he begins to rise. Renee feels a strange new life inside of him, a life he has never felt before. He thinks that maybe it is time to begin. Maybe it's time to live.

And it is an amazing, amazing feeling.

THE END

ABOUT THE AUTHOR

Joseph R. Becker earned a B.A. in Philosophy with a deep interest in literature and creative writing. With philosophical stories brewing in his head, he earned his J.D. from Emory Law School even though his research papers were more like stories. Joseph currently lives in Manhattan with his wife Leah and their golden retriever Mister Benson, where he practices as an entertainment attorney by day and a drummer by night. *The Spider and the Ant* is his first novel.

visit jrbecker.com

www.ingramcontent.com/pod-product-compliance
Lightning Source LLC
LaVergne TN
LVHW041050080826
845145LV00007B/1525

* 9 7 8 0 6 1 5 4 5 1 1 2 1 *